MAGILL'S
LITERARY ANNUAL

1988

MAGILL'S
LITERARY ANNUAL
1988

Essay-Reviews of 200 Outstanding Books
Published in the United States during 1987

With an Annotated Categories Index

Volume One

A-Maj

Edited by
FRANK N. MAGILL

SALEM PRESS

Pasadena, California   Englewood Cliffs, New Jersey

Library of Congress Catalog Card No. 77-99209
ISBN 0-89356-288-2

FIRST PRINTING

PRINTED IN THE UNITED STATES OF AMERICA

PUBLISHER'S NOTE

Magill's Literary Annual, 1988, is the thirty-third publication in a series that began in 1954. The philosophy behind the annual has been to evaluate critically each year a given number of major examples of serious literature published during the previous year. Our continuous effort is to provide coverage for works that are likely to be of more than passing general interest and that will stand up to the test of time. Individual critical articles for the first twenty-two years were collected and published in *Survey of Contemporary Literature* in 1977.

For the reader new to the Magill reference format, the following brief explanation should serve to facilitate the research process. The two hundred works represented in this year's annual are drawn from the following categories: fiction; poetry; literary criticism and literary history; essays; biography; autobiography, memoirs, diaries, and letters; history; current affairs and social science; science; art; and miscellaneous. The articles are arranged alphabetically by book title in the two-volume set; a complete list of the titles included can be found at the beginning of volume 1. Following a list of titles are the titles arranged by category in an annotated listing. This list provides the reader with the title, author, page number, and a brief one-sentence description of the particular work. The names of all contributing reviewers for the literary annual are listed alphabetically in the front of the book as well as at the end of their reviews. At the end of volume 2, there are two indexes: an index of Biographical Works by Subject and the Cumulative Author Index. The index of biographical works covers the years 1977 to 1988, and it is arranged by subject rather than by author or title. Thus, readers will be able to locate easily a review of any biographical work published in the Magill annuals since 1977 (including memoirs, diaries, and letters—as well as biographies and autobiographies) by looking up the name of the person. Following the index of Biographical Works by Subject is the Cumulative Author Index. Beneath each author's name appear the titles of all of his or her works reviewed in the Magill annuals since 1977. Next to each title, in parentheses, is the year of the annual in which the review appeared, followed by the page number.

Each article begins with a block of top matter that indicates the title, author, publisher, and price of the work. When possible, the year of the author's birth is also provided. The top matter also includes the number of pages of the book, the type of work, and, when appropriate, the time period and locale represented in the text. Next, there is the same capsulized description of the work that appears in the annotated list of titles. When pertinent, a list of principal characters or of personages introduces the review.

The articles themselves are approximately two thousand words in length.

They are original essay-reviews that analyze and present the focus, intent, and relative success of the author, as well as the makeup and point of view of the work under discussion. To assist the reader further, the articles are supplemented by a list of additional reviews for further study in a bibliographic format.

As mentioned above, history-oriented books are once again included in *Magill's Literary Annual*, as they were prior to 1983. Readers who are especially interested in biography, history, and current affairs are invited to consult the twelve-volume *Great Events from History* and the *Great Lives from History*, which covers significant historical figures.

LIST OF TITLES

LIST OF TITLES

LIST OF TITLES

TITLES BY CATEGORY

_____

ANNOTATED

TITLES BY CATEGORY

TITLES BY CATEGORY

TITLES BY CATEGORY

TITLES BY CATEGORY

page

Yellow Raft in Blue Water, A—*Michael Dorris* 1004
Three generations of Indian women tell the story of their oddly configured family in a way that gradually reveals the profound and difficult love that binds them together

You Must Remember This—*Joyce Carol Oates* 1009
A story of a young girl's coming to maturity and its effects on her family

POETRY

Archer in the Marrow: The Applewood Cycles of 1967-1987—
   Peter Viereck.. 46
A complex inquiry into the potential for freedom, this poem sets out in traditional yet innovative form both the quest of the individual and the movement of all human history

Arkansas Testament, The—*Derek Walcott*......................... 52
In a voice capable of both diversity and discipline, the poet presents numerous settings and tries to find comfort in each

Articulation of Sound Forms in Time—*Susan Howe* 63
Articulation of Sound Forms in Time presents a vision quest by sixteenth century minister Hope Atherton and twentieth century American artists

Collected Poems of Octavio Paz: 1957-1987, The—*Octavio Paz* 169
A bilingual collection that brings the achievements of Latin America's foremost poet into sharper focus

Flesh and Blood—*C. K. Williams* 330
C. K. Williams' poems build by refinement and qualification of an observation or idea, capturing in their hesitations and modifications the very process of a subtle mental and emotional instrument struggling to register its experience

Gold Cell, The—*Sharon Olds*.................................... 353
Olds's treatment of female sexuality escapes the traditional stereotypes as well as the contemporary ones; everywhere, there is a sense of health, of sought and deserved satisfactions

Happy Hour—*Alan Shapiro* 368
Twenty poems present various angles on the unsuccessful relationships fostered by desire

Oregon Message, An—*William Stafford*.......................... 636
A collection of poems in the Romantic tradition, on the subjects of nature, intuition, youth, and age

page

LITERARY CRITICISM
LITERARY HISTORY

TITLES BY CATEGORY

page

page

page

Voices and Visions: The Poet in America—*Helen Vendler*, Editor 943
Thirteen essays on American poets from Walt Whitman to Sylvia Plath, by thirteen major critics, with an introductory essay by Vendler on the development of the American poetic voice

ESSAYS

Artificial Wilderness: Essays on Twentieth-Century
Literature, An—*Sven Birkerts* 68
A brilliant array of essays on prominent twentieth century writers from all corners of the globe

Bottom Translation: Marlowe and Shakespeare and the
Carnival Tradition, The—*Jan Kott* 116
Jan Kott's essays collected in this volume explore how certain plays by William Shakespeare and several of his contemporaries are animated by imaginative transformations of sixteenth and seventeenth century literary and festive traditions

Collected Prose—*Robert Lowell*. 173
A posthumous collection of reviews, essays, prefaces, eulogies, interviews, and memoirs by the most celebrated poet of his generation

Congregation: Contemporary Writers Read the Jewish Bible—
David Rosenberg, Editor 189
Reflections by leading contemporary American Jewish writers and critics on the individual books of the Jewish Bible

Essays of Virginia Woolf, Vol. I: 1904-1912—*Virginia Woolf* 288
Most of the pieces included in this first volume of Woolf's complete essays have not previously appeared in book form

Every Force Evolves a Form: Twenty Essays—*Guy Davenport* 298
These essays examine work by particular painters, poets, and other writers to explore questions of form and meaning in art

History of Private Life Vol. I: From Pagan Rome to
Byzantium, A—*Paul Veyne*, ... 386
A series of essays on private life in imperial Rome, medieval Europe, and the Byzantine Empire, this volume considers diverse aspects of personal and family life during the first millennium of the Christian era

I Tell You Now: Autobiographical Essays by Native American Writers—
Brian Swann and Arnold Krupat, and *Arnold Krupat*, Editors 413
An extremely valuable and diverse collection of autobiographical essays, varying in length from five to twenty-four pages

LITERARY BIOGRAPHY

TITLES BY CATEGORY

page

page

AUTOBIOGRAPHY
MEMOIRS
DIARIES
LETTERS

TITLES BY CATEGORY

page

BIOGRAPHY

TITLES BY CATEGORY

page

page

HISTORY

TITLES BY CATEGORY

TITLES BY CATEGORY

page

Joan Didion's analysis of the Cuban exile community in Miami exposes the delusions at the heart of their struggle against Castro and the particular ways these delusions have manifested themselves in American political life

This exposition of the Soviet leader's views on domestic and international concerns is alternately candid and defiant in its discussion of his policies and programs

A sociological and historical analysis of the post-1945 urban poor and the nature and causes of their problems, this book also describes the views of the urban poor held by liberal and conservative social scientists, as well as the author's solutions to urban poverty

A journalist's account of CIA covert operations from 1981 to 1987

A moralistic indictment of the United State government's backing of dictators in the Philippines, particularly of the Marcos regime from 1965 to 1986

SCIENCE

A report on the development of the mathematical study of turbulent systems and the interdisciplinary scientific cooperation that produced a startling reappraisal of the nature of chaos

For centuries astronomers have pondered the riddle of the dark night sky, and the quest for a solution abounds in strange and interesting ideas and personalities

A synthetic analysis and description of the American scientific community in the mid-nineteenth century

A memoir that shows how two vocations—scientist and writer—came together in a single person, with the result that the author is a leading popularizer of science

page

ART

TITLES BY CATEGORY

CONTRIBUTING REVIEWERS FOR 1988 ANNUAL

Michael Adams
Independent Scholar

Thomas P. Adler
Purdue University, West Lafayette

Kerry Ahearn
Oregon State University

Terry L. Andrews
Rutgers University

Andrew J. Angyal
Elon College

Stanley Archer
Texas A&M University

Edwin T. Arnold
Appalachian State University

Anthony Arthur
California State University, Northridge

Jean W. Ashton
The New York Historical Society

Bryan Aubrey
Maharishi International University

David Axeen
Occidental College

Dean Baldwin
*Pennsylvania State University—
Behrend College*

Dan Barnett
Butte College

Robert Bascom
Independent Scholar

Carolyn Wilkerson Bell
Randolph-Macon Woman's College

Richard P. Benton
Trinity College, Connecticut

Gordon N. Bergquist
Creighton University

Dale B. Billingsley
University of Louisville

David Warren Bowen
Livingston University

Harold Branam
University of Pennsylvania

Gerhard Brand
California State University, Los Angeles

Peter A. Brier
California State University, Los Angeles

J. R. Broadus
University of North Carolina at Chapel Hill

Rebecca R. Butler
Dalton Junior College

Rosemary M. Canfield-Reisman
Troy State University

Karen Carmean
Converse College

David A. Carpenter
Eastern Illinois University

John Carpenter
University of Michigan, Ann Arbor

Norman S. Cohen
Occidental College

John Coleman
*Pennsylvania State University—
Behrend College*

Frank Day
Clemson University

Leon V. Driskell
University of Louisville

Robert P. Ellis
Worster State College

Bruce E. Fleming
United States Naval Academy

Robert J. Forman
Saint John's University, New York

Leslie E. Gerber
Appalachian State University

Dana Gerhardt
Independent Scholar

Kenneth Gibbs
Worster State College

xli

Richard Glatzer
Independent Scholar

Lois Gordon
Fairleigh Dickinson University—Teaneck

Sidney Gottlieb
Sacred Heart University

Daniel L. Guillory
Millikin University

Steven L. Hale
Berry College

Terry Heller
Coe College

Jane Hill
Peachtree Publishers

Ronald W. Howard
Mississippi College

Philip K. Jason
United States Naval Academy

Ronald L. Johnson
Northern Michigan University

George Burke Johnston
Virginia Polytechnic Institute and State University

Judith L. Johnston
Rider College

Carola M. Kaplan
California State Polytechnic University, Pomona

Cynthia Lee Katona
Ohlone College

Steven G. Kellman
University of Texas at San Antonio

Paul B. Kern
Indiana University Northwest

Pamela Kay Kett
Moorhead State University

Henderson Kincheloe
North Carolina State University

James B. Lane
Indiana University Northwest

Saul Lerner
Purdue University, Calumet

Leon Lewis
Appalachian State University

Elizabeth Johnston Lipscomb
Randolph-Macon Woman's College

Janet E. Lorenz
Independent Scholar

Steven A. McCarver
Auburn University at Mongomery

Mark McCloskey
Occidental College

Margaret McFadden
Appalachian State University

Arthur E. McGuinness
University of California, Davis

Nora A. McGuinness
University of California, Davis

Charles E. May
California State University, Long Beach

Laurence W. Mazzeno
United States Naval Academy

Sally Mitchell
Temple University

Leslie B. Mittleman
California State University, Long Beach

Robert A. Morace
Daemen College

Gordon R. Mork
Purdue University, West Lafayette

Katharine M. Morsberger
Independent Scholar

John M. Muste
Ohio State University

Stella Nesanovich
McNeese State University

George O'Brien
Georgetown University

Robert M. Otten
Assumption College

Lisa Paddock
Independent Scholar

Robert J. Paradowski
Rochester Institute of Technology

CONTRIBUTING REVIEWERS FOR 1988 ANNUAL

David Peck
California State University, Long Beach

Robert C. Petersen
Middle Tennessee State University

Thomas Rankin
Independent Scholar

David Rigsbee
Saint Andrews Presbyterian College

J. Thomas Rimer
University of Maryland at College Park

Bruce Robbins
Rutgers University

Mary Rohrberger
Oklahoma State University

Carl E. Rollyson
*City University of New York
Bernard M. Baruch College*

Joseph Rosenblum
University of North Carolina at Greensboro

Diane M. Ross
Lake Forest College

Robert Ross
Southern Methodist University

Marc Rothenberg
Smithsonian Institution

Francis Michael Sharp
University of the Pacific

T. A. Shippey
University of Texas at Austin

Anne W. Sienkewicz
Independent Scholar

Thomas J. Sienkewicz
Monmouth College

Jan Sjavik
University of Washington

Harold L. Smith
University of Houston—Victoria

Ira Smolensky
Monmouth College

Katherine Snipes
Eastern Washington University

Leon Stein
Roosevelt University

Jean T. Strandness
North Dakota State University

James Sullivan
California State University, Los Angeles

Patricia E. Sweeney
Independent Scholar

Thom Tammaro
Moorhead State University

Daniel Taylor
Bethel College

Shelley Thrasher
Lamar University—Orange

William Urban
Monmouth College

Ronald G. Walker
Western Illinois University

Craig Werner
University of Wisconsin—Madison

David Allen White
United States Naval Academy

Bruce Wiebe
Independent Scholar

John Wilson
Independent Scholar

James A. Winders
Appalachian State University

Michael Witkoski
South Carolina House of Representatives

AESCHYLUS' *ORESTEIA*
A Literary Commentary

Author: D. J. Conacher (1918-   )
Publisher: University of Toronto Press (Ontario). 229 pp. $35.00
Type of work: Literary analysis

A highly respected classical scholar offers a running commentary and dramatic analysis of Aeschylus' Oresteia

> *Principal characters:*
> AGAMEMNON, the Greek king murdered on his homecoming from the Trojan War
> CLYTEMNESTRA, his wife and slayer
> AEGISTHUS, his cousin, Clytemnestra's lover and coconspirator
> ORESTES, his son and avenger
> APOLLO, the god of prophecy, who sanctions Orestes' matricide
> ATHENA, the goddess of Athens, who oversees Orestes' exoneration
> ERINYES, the Furies, goddesses of vengeance who become the Eumenides (Blessed Ones)

Aeschylus' *Oresteia*, the only surviving complete tragic Greek trilogy, consists of *Agamemnōn (Agamemnon), Choēphoroi (Libation Bearers),* and *Eumenides.* First produced in 458 B.C., this trilogy was an initial and permanent dramatic success. The *Oresteia* was read and imitated throughout antiquity and served as the core for the seven plays surviving in the medieval Aeschylean manuscript tradition. Rediscovered in the West during the Greek revival of the Renaissance, the *Oresteia* has continued to be admired and read in the modern world, but predominately by readers of ancient Greek. In the twentieth century, however, the spread of education among the general population and a remarkable increase in the number of translations of ancient Greek literature have made these three ancient plays readily accessible to the general reader.

With his highly metaphoric and dense language, however, Aeschylus is notoriously difficult to understand, even for a reader fluent in ancient Greek. Readers of the plays in translation, often perplexed by the apparent obscurity of the text, search in frustration for an interpretive aid, literary study, or useful commentary. Conacher's book offers such a commentary, making this trilogy more fully understandable to the general reader and clarifying the complicated, longstanding questions raised about these plays by classical scholars.

While the *Oresteia* has been the focus of heated scholarly attention for centuries, much of this debate, directed primarily toward readers of the Greek text and often written in scholarly French or German, has long been inaccessible to the general English reader. Furthermore, work on the *Oresteia* has tended to focus on the traditional concerns of classical philology: the establishment of the text and meticulous verification of the correct reading, often line by line, word by word, and even letter by letter. Whenever literary criticism in the modern sense has surfaced in such discussions, it has usually been tied to debates on textual readings, the assumption being that those judging the issues can read the Greek text for themselves.

The standard commentary on *Agamemnōn*, the first play of the trilogy, is Eduard Fraenkel's three-volume study (*Agamemnon*, 1950), an impressive product of German classical scholarship. While Fraenkel's work is seminal to criticism of the play, few general readers would manage to undertake more than a cursory study of this commentary, laden heavily with untranslated references to the Greek text. For the other two plays in the trilogy, *Libation Bearers* and *Eumenides*, nothing comparable to Fraenkel's study exists to assist even the reader of the Greek text, let alone the Greekless reader.

Conacher strives admirably to fill the gap. His study is intended to be not only a running commentary and plot summary for the Greekless reader but also an abstract and analysis of the most significant scholarly discussions of all three plays. The book is consciously arranged to satisfy the various needs of a diverse readership. Each play receives a single chapter devoted to commentary, plot summary, staging, and discussion of general issues of the tragedy and the trilogy. Inevitably, discussion of *Agamemnōn*, the longest and best known of the three plays, consumes nearly half of the space devoted to commentary.

These three chapters of commentary account for only half of the total book. In the other half, the reader will find both extensive endnotes, where technical details concerning textual readings and scholarly debate are discussed, and several excellent appendices in which Conacher discusses more complicated issues of interpretation, such as the problem of Agamemnon's guilt and issues of contemporary Athenian politics in *Eumenides*. Words and phrases from the Greek plays, as well as quotes from French and German scholarly works, are generally translated or paraphrased in endnotes. Readers who limit themselves to the main chapters and do not examine the endnotes and commentaries closely will miss much of what Conacher has to offer in the way of a carefully selected survey of classical scholarship on *Oresteia*.

Particularly noteworthy is Conacher's summary of political and social aspects of *Eumenides*, including a history of the Areopagus, the Athenian tribunal that is featured in the last play of Aeschylus' trilogy. Much of the material presented in this appendix, critical to a fuller understanding of *Eumenides*, would be very difficult for the general reader to cull from works directed specifically toward the classical scholar. An excellent bibliography is offered as a source for further reading on various issues raised in Conacher's study.

Despite Conacher's best effort to serve the needs of the general reader, it should be cautioned that his study still contains technical language which will be unfamiliar to those who have never studied Greek tragedy. Such terms as "epirrhematic kommos" and "parabasis" are sprinkled throughout the text without either definition or explanation. While metrical features of the plays are both unavoidable in any discussion of Greek tragedy and impossible to appreciate fully in English translation, the many such references in Conacher's commentary usually appear without any lexical aid for the general reader.

All readers, whether professional classicists or novices, will benefit from Conacher's careful reading and critical judgment of these plays. In particular, emphasis on what he calls "double determination" makes discussion of the complicated questions of causality and guilt in the *Oresteia* much easier to comprehend. Again and again, Conacher wisely illustrates how the trilogy must be analyzed with reference to a complicated web of heredity, personal ambition, social pressure, and divine sanction.

Agamemnon's fate is bound up in the history of his family, including the violation of his mother by his uncle Thyestes and the horrible vengeance extracted upon Thyestes by Agamemnon's father, Atreus. While the murder of Thyestes' children by Atreus and the grotesque pleasure Atreus gains from making his unsuspecting brother dine on the flesh of his own children are not part of the dramatic action of Aeschylus' trilogy, these crimes remain in the dramatic consciousness of an Aeschylean audience which is expected to possess this knowledge already as part of the Greek mythological heritage. Furthermore, as Conacher carefully notes, these events are the subject of powerful dramatic allusion. In the "Cassandra scene" of *Agamemnōn*, for example, the king's pathetic captive mistress prophesies her own and Agamemnon's impending murders by reference to the voices of young children crying out for vengeance.

The death of Agamemnon must be seen not only against this hereditary background, but also in the context of Agamemnon's sacrifice of his own daughter Iphigenia to remove divine impediments to the Greek foray against Troy. The king's decision to slay Iphigenia is dramatically reenacted by Aeschylus in the parodos, or entrance song of the chorus, of *Agamemnōn*. Conacher's analysis of this focal song is a powerful reminder of the complicated causes of the king's actions. On the one hand, Agamemnon's decision to slay his daughter is a consequence of his own personal ambition and the guilt of his father, Atreus. On the other hand, the decision is mandated by the will of the god Zeus that Troy be defeated and by the insistence of the goddess Artemis that Iphigenia be sacrificed. Put in Aeschylean language, a combination of *ananke* (necessity) and *ate* (folly) compel Agamemnon to slay his own daughter.

Yet all these events occur before the dramatic action of the *Oresteia*. In

Agamemnōn, which begins with the victorious return of Agamemnon from Troy, the questions of complex causality continue in Conacher's analysis of the motivations for Clytemnestra's murder of her husband on the very day of his homecoming. As with Agamemnon himself, there is no simple Aeschylean explanation for the actions of this imposing queen. Clytemnestra, who is repeatedly described in masculine terms, has taken as a lover her husband's cousin Aegisthus, the son of Thyestes and determined avenger of the crimes of Atreus. While she clearly resents the relationship between her husband and Cassandra, as well as the loss of her personal power that her husband's return will effect, she still sees herself as the divine avenger of the death of her daughter, Iphigenia.

A similar pattern of human will and divine determination is noted by Conacher in *Libation Bearers*, the second play of the trilogy. In this play of "darkness and horror," Aeschylus carefully develops the complex motivation which drives Orestes to avenge the death of his father and commit matricide. Central here is another dramatic song, called a *kommos* because it is sung together by chorus and actor(s), by which both Orestes and the powerful spirit of the dead Agamemnon are roused to action. Similar to his parents, Orestes exhibits motivations of personal revenge and ambition accompanied by an unambiguous command by the god Apollo to avenge his father's death by slaying his mother.

In *Eumenides*, the final play of the trilogy, this complexity reaches a climax in the question of Orestes' purification from blood guilt. In the opinion of the Erinyes (Furies), traditional Greek goddesses of vengeance, there can be no forgiveness for Orestes; these awesome goddesses demand nothing less than his death. Exoneration for Orestes is supported both by Apollo, who had sanctioned the matricide, and by Athena, who establishes a special tribunal at Athens to judge Orestes. In this trial, which is a startling combination of mythological, religious, and historical material, the Erinyes emphasize the blood relationship between Clytemnestra and Orestes. They care only that Orestes has committed matricide; his reasons are ignored. On the other side, Orestes and Apollo argue for the dominance of the male and the paternal; they introduce a new concept of justice which recognizes motive and circumstances. In the end, Orestes is judged not guilty.

In the midst of this dramatic action, Aeschylus presents an extraordinary and dynamic evolution of the Erinyes from traditional goddesses of fury and vengeance into Eumenides (Blessed Ones), goddesses of order and retribution. Conacher justly notes how this transformation mystically resolves the conflicts of multiple determination which have troubled the trilogy.

Conacher's interpretation of the *Oresteia* surfaces through careful analysis of individual plays and scenes. In particular, the attentive reader will note the reference to imagery, especially of robes, blood, and the number three, which runs throughout the plays. While not a definitive interpretation of the

Oresteia, Conacher's book is what it is meant to be: a thoughtful introduction to a major piece of ancient Greek drama.

Thomas J. Sienkewicz

Source for Further Study

Choice. XXV, November, 1987, p. 466.

THE AGE OF GRIEF

Author: Jane Smiley (1949-   )
Publisher: Alfred A. Knopf (New York). 213 pp. $15.95
Type of work: Short fiction
Time: The 1970's and after
Locale: Mainly the Midwestern United States

> *Five short stories and a novella about the loves and marriages of people who came of age in the 1960's*

In five of these six pieces, Jane Smiley illustrates how the current central problem of a protagonist pervades the whole of his or her life until it is resolved. Her characters wrestle with one crisis internally while apparently handling other difficulties that are visible to observers. The external activities become means of working through the inner problem. For this reason, there are usually two main threads to Smiley's plots in *The Age of Grief*.

In "The Pleasure of Her Company," Florence, a pediatric nurse unlucky in love, finds friends in her new neighbors, Frannie and Philip Howard. Drawn especially to Frannie, Florence becomes virtually a part of their family. She finds their marriage comforting, but also mysterious, for Frannie refuses to confide about her husband. While she is enjoying and wondering, Florence begins to fall in love with Bryan, a new friend, and the Howards announce their separation. Florence tries to understand the separation at the same time that she is trying to decide whether to marry Bryan. Love for Frannie blinds her to Philip's position until she learns that Frannie is moving in with her lesbian lover. Then Philip tells her that he and Frannie used her as a kind of buffer in their conflict. He says that she was the only one of the three who was happy in this relationship, but nevertheless, seeking happiness in marriage is worthwhile.

In this opening story, Smiley develops themes that recur throughout the collection. Intimate relationships, however simple they may appear on the outside, are always intricate and complex from within. When intimates are troubled in their relationships, they can be utterly ruthless on behalf of love, even in their kindness, as they work out their difficulties. The second story, "Lily," develops these themes in a way parallel to the first.

Lily is a successful poet who has never been loved. When Nancy and Kevin, a couple to whom she was close in college, come to visit, she hopes that they will tell her why she is so lonely. Instead, she is drawn into the complications of their troubled marriage. Though they like being married to each other, they are troubled in many ways, each irritated by the other's rough edges. Nancy finds Kevin sexually attractive, but too inept to please her, so she is unfaithful. Kevin, a college football star, now a successful businessman, has been discovering that his athletic grace and strength do not transfer as easily to marriage as to business. He loves Nancy, but her reluctance to have intercourse makes him aware of his inadequacy. The desperate Kevin turns to Lily with a question like her own. He asks if she believes that Nancy loves him. With the coolness and distance that make her a good poet, Lily answers honestly that she thinks not. Nancy then says to Lily, "You hate tension, you hate conflict, so you cut it off, ended it. We could have gone on for years like this, and it wouldn't have been that bad!" In this way, Nancy answers Lily's question. Without this messy tension, there can be no loving. Like Florence, Lily has not yet appreciated the complexity of intimate relationships.

"Jeffrey, Believe Me" is an exception in this collection. Though all the stories have moments of humor, this one is a delightful romp in the form of a letter to Jeffrey, a homosexual or bisexual, whom the female narrator has seduced in order to become pregnant. She explains her overriding motivation in seducing him: her desire to possess his genes for her child. In every important way, he strikes her as the ideal specimen for biological fatherhood. The fun of this story is in the means by which she seduces him and in her doubts and desires during the process. One of the more amusing ironies of her attempt is that she accidentally renders him unconscious. Rather than mate with him in this state, she gives up and goes to sleep. Then she awakens to discover that her being unconscious does not restrain him in the same way.

In "Long Distance," Kirby, a young academic, tries to resolve his guilt over seducing and abandoning Mieko, a Japanese schoolteacher, while he was a guest teacher in Japan. His struggle is shown in the context of a Christmas visit with his two older brothers and their families in Minneapolis. Before he leaves home, Mieko telephones with the news that because her father is dying, she cannot make her planned visit to the United States. When she weeps over this lost possibility, almost certainly her only chance to escape her loneliness, he is witness to a loss that only he could remedy. He is, however, unwilling. He is relieved that she will not come, for he is unprepared to give her what she is bound to expect. During his visit, he watches how his brothers, their wives, and children manage to get along despite many points of tension and conflict, and he broods over how to relieve his guilt. From his sister-in-law, he learns that he is wrong to think that he can get something for nothing. His guilt is a price he must pay for succumbing to the temptation to make love to a Japanese woman, knowing full well how immensely complicated cultural differences would make such a relationship.

In this story and in "Dynamite," Smiley develops another theme. Her protagonists approach thirty, unmarried and with pasts characterized by the kind of freedom sometimes admired by those who came of age in the 1960's. Each finds the range of choices seemingly narrowing, and the desired freedom comes to seem not to be enough.

Alexandra Day is a former radical who, as Sandy Stein, once made bombs for "the movement." At that time she was a Jewish New Yorker, a student at Barnard College with a loving family. Now she is a chemical engineer at a fertilizer plant in Missouri, working with a man whom she loves enough to marry. Wanted by the Federal Bureau of Investigation (FBI), she has become so habituated to her new identity and evasive behavior that she hardly thinks about them. The story shows her being drawn to thoughts of her mother, to the images and memories of her early life. Contented and comfortable as she is in her new place, she finds herself longing to risk everything to return to New York and see her mother again.

The novella, "The Age of Grief," develops fully the major themes of the collection and impressively demonstrates the possibilities of the double-action strategy. Dave and Dana Hurst are successful dentists. Their combined practice enables them to live in material luxury while each works a little more than half-time. They have the kind of family and security most Americans consider ideal: three healthy daughters, a small, friendly community, two cars, two homes—one in the mountains—and no visible end to this comfortable and safe life. Furthermore, they are truly happy, having values and spiritual pursuits that hold them together and fulfill them. They have the difficulties that any solid family would have, but they also have the strength and the resources to handle their problems. Then comes the age of grief.

Dave, at thirty-five, is beset by multiple family problems, all of which might be manageable, except that he has discovered that Dana is in love with someone else. In the face of this loss, other problems begin to seem insurmountable. The age of grief is the moment when one realizes that "the cup of pain must come around, cannot pass from you, and it is the same cup of pain that every mortal drinks from." While many human problems contribute to this realization—deaths of friends and parents, love ending, children leaving or lost—they all add up to the breaking down of those "barriers between the circumstances of oneself and of the rest of the world." The careful attempts to gain control of life and to protect oneself from catastrophe begin to unravel. Youth's illusion of immortality fades.

Dave manages to stave off the disaster of Dana's leaving him by adopting every possible strategy to prevent her telling him that she loves another man. Even when he realizes that the man probably does not return her love, he studiously avoids giving her the opportunity to confess. Only when it seems clear that she has decided to stay with him does he ask her about her decision.

In this tale, Smiley's technique of keeping two stories going simultaneously works especially well. Dana's affair governs Dave's life and narrative, but their daily routine occupies the foreground. Rearing three young daughters fills their lives. Two-year-old Leah decides that only her father can parent her. She proceeds to tyrannize him at almost the same moment that Dana falls in love. As the unacknowledged tension of the parents' secret seeps into every cranny of their lives together, the older girls develop symptoms, both physical and mental, responding just as sensitively as if they knew what was happening. While Dave loves and nurtures his family, he also uses every symptom and problem to bind Dana to the family and to fend off her imminent confession.

When the flu strikes, the Hursts follow the family battle plan that allows their practice to continue and the children to get to their various places despite the siege of incapacitation that lays them out one at a time, but always with some overlapping. Dave seems positively heroic when, just after his recovery, he nurses first Leah, who will accept care only from him, then the rest of his family through days and sleepless nights of illness that culminate with daughter Stephanie's frighteningly high fever. Despite his exhaustion and his deep concern for his daughters, he never forgets his goal of holding on to Dana. He lets this crisis help him.

As in all the stories, Smiley here aptly captures the complexity of motives and moves in intimate relationships. She illustrates well the sometimes overlooked truth that when an issue is serious, even the best person's motives are always a mixture of the noble, the irrational, the disinterested, the selfish, and the loving. Dave seems heroic because, under great stress, he manages himself so well. Yet he is far from perfect. One of his defenses against utter disintegration is to split his personality. When the tension at home mounts too high, he finds himself becoming Slater, a cynical dental patient who fends off confidences with callous disbelief and rough manners. Despite these episodes, Dave still manages to keep his life going while preventing Dana from irreversibly damaging their marriage before her affair with the other man is settled one way or another.

Though imperfect, Dave is admirably strong. His strength comes from caring about Dana, their children, and the quality of the intimacy and love they have created together. He manages never to blame Dana for what she clearly cannot help. Ultimately, he finds an appropriate way to help her. Though their marriage survives this crisis, the age of grief, he knows, is just beginning. He hopes for the rumored "age of resignation," but knows that it will be long in coming.

A professor at Iowa State University, Smiley has also published three well-received novels. *Barn Blind* (1980) presents a woman so absorbed in raising and training horses that she fails to understand her family. *At Paradise Gate* (1981) is a portrait of a family at the nexus of three crises: birth, death, and marriage. *Duplicate Keys* (1984), perhaps the most successful, is a murder mystery set among Midwesterners relocated in New York City. Some of the stories in this collection originally appeared in *The Atlantic*, *Mademoiselle*, and *TriQuarterly*. In all of her books, Smiley captures in accomplished prose, with evocative details and utterly convincing observation, the inner dynamics of intimate relationships.

Terry Heller

Sources for Further Study

Library Journal. CXII, August, 1987, p. 145.
The New York Times. CXXXI, August 26, 1987, p. C21.
The New York Times Book Review. XCII, September 6, 1987, p. 12.
Publishers Weekly. CCXXXI, July 10, 1987, pp. 56-57.
The Wall Street Journal. September 8, 1987, p. 28.

THE ALLURING PROBLEM
An Essay on Irony

Author: D. J. Enright (1920-   )
Publisher: Oxford University Press (New York). 178 pp. $19.95
Type of work: Practical literary criticism

An exploration of the idea of irony as it manifests itself in hundreds of specific examples from both literature and life

No one who has followed D. J. Enright's impressive but somewhat atypical career will expect from his book *The Alluring Problem: An Essay on Irony* a definitive taxonomy of ironic types or a systematic inquiry into the history of irony through the ages. Enright has once again distinguished himself from his scholarly colleagues by eschewing pseudoscientific methodology, focusing rather on the practical sort of criticism for which he has become well-known: a criticism designed almost as much to delight the reader as to inform.

The Alluring Problem is not only an essay in the common understanding of the word (that is, a small work of prose on a particular topic, with an analytic or interpretive goal) but also an essay in the older and narrower sense of the word (that is, an effort to perform or accomplish something that is both difficult and uncertain). *The Alluring Problem* is an effort, first of all, to remain unfettered by fashionable, and usually overly simplistic, literary theories. It is additionally an attempt to avoid the creation of preconceived categorical systems, which are frequently satisfying in their illusion of comprehensiveness but which inevitably suffer rather pathetically when measured against the individual examples of irony which they are presuming to illuminate. Finally, it is a tentative beginning step toward a rich, abundant, and necessarily complex understanding of irony as it actually occurs in literature and life.

Many fellow theorists of irony are gently chided by Enright for being pedantic, humorless, and, most unforgivably, unintelligible. For example, Lilian Furst's *Fictions of Romantic Irony* (1984) is rather ruthlessly, and humorously, quoted as a salient example of the impenetrable prose produced by many literary critics. Søren Kierkegaard's *The Concept of Irony* (1841) also receives special attention for its obscurity and ambiguity, even though it is later credited for recognizing Socrates as one of the first great practitioners of irony. Is it not essentially ironical, Kierkegaard wonders, for Socrates to wander about the town asking provocative questions, appearing to look for answers, while all the time teaching in the guise of trying to learn? Is it not ironical, the reader wonders, for Enright to state quite clearly, in the face of so many critical failures, that he is not even going to attempt to give the reader a formal definition of irony, while at the same time he succeeds in giving a much enhanced, though informal, understanding of it?

Enright's method is one of indirection. He supplies the reader with literally hundreds of examples of irony from a broad range of sources: from Socrates to Umberto Eco, from Great Britain to China, from world literature to his own personal and often-idiosyncratic experience. Inductively, the reader begins to formulate a very specific idea of what irony is, and also what it is not.

In some ways, *The Alluring Problem* is a retrospective of Enright's entire literary career with irony as a focal issue. For example, Enright's early poetry and his four "travel" novels written between 1955 and 1965 were rarely reviewed without specific mention of their intelligence, irony, and wit. It may, in fact, be his special insight as a creative writer with a decidedly ironical tone that has made him so wary of oversimplifying the subject of irony in his role as a critic.

Echoes of Enright's unpretentious book *Shakespeare and the Students* (1970), which gives neophyte readers help with some of Shakespeare's lesser plays as well as with the critical and popular favorites, are clear in the chapter entitled "Shakespearian." Enright returns again to *Love's Labour's Lost* (1594-1595), *Hamlet, Prince of Denmark* (1601), *Julius Caesar* (1599), *Macbeth* (1606), and *The Winter's Tale* (1610), this time seeking out and displaying numerous Shakespearean ironies, both in individual lines and in the plots of the plays themselves. He reminds readers of Antony's famous speech in *Julius Caesar*, "For Brutus is an honourable man"; of the undeserved banishment of good Cordelia in *King Lear* (1605-1606); and of the painful and ironic reconciliation of Leontes and Hermione in *The Winter's Tale*. *Hamlet* is singled out for extensive analysis as Shakespeare's undoubted ironic tour de force. It would seem that the idea of irony, often referred to metaphorically as the salt of discourse, has certainly spiced Enright's enjoyment of what could have been for him old territory and rather bland critical fare.

Enright returned to his own poetry in 1973 with an engaging account of his youth in a working-class family, *The Terrible Shears: Scenes from a Twenties Childhood*. His ironic skill is undiminished as he recounts his childhood days, which were, the reader is told, not that bad by worldwide standards:

> No one was dragged out of bed by
> Armed men. Children weren't speared
> Or their brains dashed out. I don't
> Remember seeing a man starve to death.

It is not surprising that the many personal anecdotes in *The Alluring Problem*, no doubt culled from a lifetime of careful observation and his writing of poetry, represent some of the book's most engaging examples.

In 1979, Enright delivered up an eccentric little work called *A Faust*

Book. It was primarily a satire on the decade of the 1970's, parading around in the clothing of the sixteenth century. It spoke to the follies and vices of mankind as all Faust retellings seem to do. Enright returns to this theme also in *The Alluring Problem* in a chapter entitled "The Fortunes of Faust," in which he surveys Christopher Marlowe's *Doctor Faustus* (1588), as well as Johann Wolfgang von Goethe's *Faust: Eine Tragödie* (1808; *The Tragedy of Faust*, 1823). The Faust myth is clearly an archetypal story replete with ironic material—for example, Faust's continual misjudgment of Mephistopheles' character and power, his egotistical exhortations to Mephistopheles about accepting a fall from grace with virile fortitude, and the triviality of the baubles for which Faust bargains away his immortal soul.

In 1983, Enright collected several of his book reviews in a compendium called *A Mania for Sentences*, and the loose organization of that volume and its ultimate coherence, because of the fundamental principles which underlie all of his prose, presage the form and style of *The Alluring Problem*. Enright the reviewer emerges as a writer who gently satirizes obfuscation, who revels in specific detail, and who constantly returns to reality to check the validity of his theories. He makes the reader think that literary theory just might be in the province of persons of common sense and good will after all.

All of this is not to say, however, that *The Alluring Problem* is entirely recapitulation or that Enright is not almost preternaturally erudite. It is not unusual for him, for example, to interrupt a discussion of Marcel Proust's *À la recherche du temps perdu* (1913-1927; *Remembrance of Things Past*, 1922-1931) with a remembrance of his own, about an irony in a short story by Yukio Mishima; or for him to combine jauntily Kierkegaard, Socrates, and Blaise Pascal in a single short chapter entitled "The Unexamined Life Not Worth Living"; or for him to allude to Evelyn Waugh, Joseph Heller, George Eliot, D. H. Lawrence, Herman Melville, and Nigel Williams in less than the space of a single paragraph. The reader who can easily follow all of Enright's many topical and literary allusions will be a consummate reader indeed. Yet even the reader whose experience is very limited will profit from seeing the great panorama of international literature through Enright's eyes.

Enright's view of irony is truly international. For more than twenty years, he taught English literature in Egypt, Japan, West Germany, Thailand, and Singapore. Both the skills he acquired in teaching such a culturally diverse student population and the experiences he inevitably gained in such faraway places considerably enrich the examples so abundantly proffered in *The Alluring Problem*.

A chapter on the Chinese, for example, is especially winsome. As Enright says of his experience, "Then I broke off to visit China. Irony was mislaid at Heathrow; or else it had no valid passport. In the People's Republic either there was no irony at all, or it had changed into something unrecognizable." Enright's apparently futile search for modern Chinese irony was a useful reminder, however, of those wonderful ancient Oriental ironies of Li Po, Laotzu, and Su Tung-p'o.

Enright's sojourn in China is only one of many evidences of the thoroughness of his quest for all possible types of irony. *The Alluring Problem* calls attention to salient details in the works of Poland's poet Czesław Miłosz, Germany's playwright Bertolt Brecht, France's remarkable Pierre-Augustin de Beaumarchais, England's great novelist Thomas Hardy, and Malaysia's censored writer and later deputy prime minister Mahathir bin Mohamad. Enright's book, like irony itself, accepts no boundaries of time or geography.

The Alluring Problem also fearlessly confronts, head-on, all the really thorny issues which are often avoided by other theorists of irony: Is there a tendency by most people to confuse irony with things which are simply, on the face of it, sad or odd? Is there a kind of irony that is specifically situational, depending entirely on context for its double meaning? Is Romantic Irony a useless term, perpetuated by overzealous literary critics and slavishly applied by gullible graduate students? Can there be real irony without an obvious victim? Can irony ever be sweet? Is irony such a self-evident concept as to make analysis nearly impossible, or perhaps unnecessary? Is irony a major mode of expression in twentieth century literature? Can irony be a harmless, self-protective behavior, affording what Enright calls a "Negative Freedom"?

These perplexing and alluring questions, if not all their answers, can certainly be found in Enright's *The Alluring Problem: An Essay on Irony*.

Cynthia Lee Katona

Sources for Further Study

Library Journal. CXII, March 1, 1987, p. 76.
The Literary Review. February, 1987, p. 41.
The Times Literary Supplement. October 17, 1986, p. 1151.

ALNILAM

Author: James Dickey (1923-   )
Publisher: Doubleday and Company (Garden City, New York). 682 pp. $19.95
Type of work: Novel
Time: 1943
Locale: Atlanta, Georgia, and Peckover, North Carolina

Alnilam *is an epic novel that chronicles the desperate searching of a recently* *blinded man for his lost son, the victim of an air crash on an army air corps base in* *North Carolina*

> *Principal characters:*
> FRANK CAHILL, the owner of an amusement park, a middle-aged man recently blinded by diabetes
> JOEL CAHILL, his son, an aviation cadet presumed to have died after a crash
> STATHIS HARBELIS, an aviation cadet, one of Joel's special group
> HANNAH PELHAM, a young woman in the town of Peckover
> COLONEL HOCCLEVE, a commandant of the base where Joel was in training
> McCLINTOCK McCAIG, a civilian flight instructor
> CAPTAIN LENNOX WHITEHALL, a combat veteran, instructor in navigation

James Dickey offers a quotation from Lucretius as the epigraph to this long and rewarding novel, alerting his readers that *Alnilam* will take them into "the great sea of air" in much the same way as Herman Melville explored the symbolic and literal meanings of the sea in his great classic, *Moby Dick* (1851). For *Alnilam* is, indeed, concerned with the air, both as the surrounding medium in which Frank Cahill gropes and finds his tentative way, and also as the mysterious element that must be understood and conquered by class after class of young army air corps recruits as they make their first solo flight over the hills of Peckover, North Carolina.

Alnilam is really three novels in one. On the first level, it can be read as a good war novel, another well-told yarn about the international enterprise known as World War II. Dickey comes by his lore honestly, since he served in the air corps during World War II and is intimately familiar with the technical aspects of navigation, bombing, and stunt flying. On the second level, *Alnilam* can be read as a novel of existential discovery in which a middle-aged man is suddenly and unexpectedly ravaged by a severe case of diabetes. This tragic disease blinds him and catapults him into an entirely new relationship with his environment, which is transformed into "a whole new country of feels." Finally, on the third level, *Alnilam* is a sort of occult and mystical tale in which Joel Cahill, the victim of the air crash, becomes a kind of airborne guru, a poet and litanist of flying who exerts a powerful and eerie influence over his many followers. In fact, the term Alnilam serves Dickey in numerous ways: It functions as the title of the book, the name of the middle star in the constellation Orion, and (most important) the name of the bizarre cult of the air which Joel Cahill had secretly organized prior to his violent death.

The plot of *Alnilam* can be neatly and briefly summarized, although its significance is far more subtle. Frank Cahill, a strong, self-taught carpenter who has built and operates an amusement park in Atlanta, is suddenly hit by two awesome blows: first, the onset of diabetes, which causes his eyesight to degenerate quickly into total blindness and which also requires daily injections of insulin, and, second, the shocking news of his son's death in the mountains of North Carolina. Accompanied only by Zack, the wolflike dog he has trained as his guide and companion, Cahill boards the bus for North Carolina, and for the next four days he unravels the mystery of Alnilam.

Much of the book, then, is focused on the typical activities of a rural air base in World War II. Dickey brilliantly evokes the military world of raw recruits, starched uniforms, identical barracks, institutional food, and standardized clothing and equipment (sheepskin-lined flying jackets, the E6B navigational tool, and Ray Ban sunglasses). It is a world of colonels, cadets, and classes—endless classes on fuel consumption, internal combustion engines, and the physics of flying. There is much discussion of the Stearman airplane, a slow biplane used as the trainer for the new cadets. They must master figure eights and rolls, but only the truly gifted (Joel Cahill, for example) can perform such difficult maneuvers as inside and outside loops and a special trick known as "the falling leaf."

Not everyone at the Peckover Air Base is a green recruit or a bureaucratic pencil-pusher. A few genuine heroes serve as models and mentors, including Captain Whitehall, the navigator, who tells an extraordinary tale of getting lost near New Guinea while leading a bombing run against the Japanese. In the bad weather that followed the attack, Whitehall had to guide all the planes back to Australia against almost impossible odds. His ultimate success is a triumph of personal heroism and sheer luck—a miraculous break in the weather allowed him to make a crucial triangular fix on the stars. Captain Faulstick, the bombardier, recounts an equally harrowing tale of leading a bombing run over the skies of Germany, a trip that leaves the turret gunner in pieces, a grisly fact that Faulstick discovers when he tries to rescue the man. These narratives represent some of the finest writing in *Alnilam*; the stories are told in a vivid, breathless prose that ranks with the best war fiction of recent decades.

Faulstick and Whitehall are genuine heroes, and for that precise reason they stand out amid the sea of khaki automatons who populate Peckover, notably the pompous and inefficient base commander, Colonel Hoccleve, and the martinet of the base, Lieutenant Foy. Most of the base personnel, however, perform their jobs in predictable, if undistinguished, ways: Major

Iannone, who serves as the camp physician, and McClintock McCaig (known as "Double Mac"), the civilian flight instructor who befriends Frank Cahill and aids him in the search for his missing son.

All these characters are known through the probing contacts of Frank Cahill, a cantankerous old loner whose only true friend is Zack. Cahill possesses an extraordinarily intuitive grasp of the world, a sensitivity that displayed itself long before the onset of his blindness. Throughout his life, Cahill has understood the natural laws of balance; two of his favorite reminiscences involve his effortless skating on the hilly streets of Atlanta, Georgia, and his strange encounter with a young boy who flies a rubberband-powered airplane beyond the horizon. Cahill is a kind of unconscious poet, always sensitive to the slightest nuances of beauty, as suggested in this epiphanous moment at a waterfall of

> lifted and silver water, going past, a split downpour that held him exactly in the dry center of its upper falling. The few ferns on the rock glittered with drops, hardy and delicate, and slowly, as he did nothing but be there, he felt building up an exhilarating sense of new authority. It was like the space beneath him, the nothingness under the rock, the effortless disappearance of himself into bright cloud, into the thunderous and fragile foaming of air, should he move slightly in any direction but back.

Cahill is also an exquisite craftsman who derives supreme satisfaction from his carpentry and blueprints: "There was something about nails and nailing that struck a very deep response in him." Cahill does not merely pass through life; he experiences it to the fullest, as in the opening pages of the book, in which Cahill feels his way down the stairs of a boardinghouse, in the middle of a snowy night, so that he can relieve himself out of doors. Drinking whiskey while soaking in a warm bath becomes a virtual out-of-body experience for the diabetic. Even though his blindness is recent, Cahill's auditory and tactile powers have become hypersensitive, as shown in this scene where he and McCaig are driving across an old bridge:

> He was sure the bridge was swaying. He leaned a little way out of the window to bear down with his hearing into the complex snatching sound of the bridge structure. Long things were in it, he guessed, long and slender, bolted but not rigid; also an alternating edge-noise that was like a successive cutting of grasses; there was nothing to stop it.

Cahill's complete immersion in physical sensations prepares him for his mind-boggling night flight with McCaig, a dangerous venture during which McCaig lets Cahill take control of the plane. For a few transcendent moments, the blind man is metamorphosed into the young boy he once was, skating with wild abandon down the hilly slopes of his native Atlanta. Cahill's blindness endows the narrative with its existential edge; all the characters at Peckover live their lives a little bit more intensely because of this blind man, bumping around the base with his huge dog, always asking questions about his son.

What Frank Cahill discovers about his son is not altogether pleasant or comprehensible. In fact, almost everything about Joel Cahill is shrouded in mystery. Everyone agrees that he was arrogant, talented, bright, and magnetic; other cadets flocked to him naturally and seemed to hang on every word he uttered. Young Cahill impressed his instructors, also, because of his innate flying skills—he was the first cadet to solo, and only McCaig could match his ability to perform aerial tricks. Joel Cahill inexplicably violated all regulations by flying his Stearman over a forest fire, however, and the dangerously turbulent air caused him to crash almost immediately. He was pulled from the airplane by a farmer and briefly comforted by the farmer's wife (who shows McCaig and Frank Cahill the bloody blanket on which Joel briefly lay). Even pain could not stop Joel Cahill, however, because he ran away from the farm house, into a wall of fire and smoke, never to be seen again. The only remnant is a zipper from his flight boots, found by McCaig after careful searching in the ashes.

Joel Cahill apparently believed in a sort of astral projection, an ability to fly without the aid of an airplane. By virtue of his own intelligence and impeccable flying skills, he was able to convince other cadets to join him in a secret society called Alnilam, complete with its own litany and ritual (all devised by Joel). Indeed, Joel Cahill's admiration for the symmetry and beauty inherent in the constellations is almost Blakean, and his playful discovery of mathematical relationships in the universe sounds positively Pythagorean.

Yet there is also a measure of fanaticism and monomania in Alnilam and its leader. Joel is smug, unable to tolerate authority, and given to petty vices (from which he has contracted a painful venereal disease). He spreads rumors, and, worst of all, he masterminds a deliberate sabotage of all the aircraft at the base, a crude climax to much high-sounding but ultimately hollow rhetoric, such as "He who makes the world alive is full of delight."

For readers who are familiar with either the poetry or the prose of James Dickey, *Alnilam* will contain some familiar motifs. As in his earlier novel, *Deliverance* (1970), Dickey is clearly captivated by the colorful idioms and inimitable drawls that typify Southern speech, especially the varieties found in rural North Carolina. Not since Mark Twain or John Steinbeck have we had a major writer with such a keen ear for authentic American dialects, as shown in this sample spoken by Mrs. Bledsoe, the wife of the poor farmer who found Joel at the crash site: "Hit was right over yonder. Hit was right out chere about three hundred yards." *Alnilam* is filled with such archetypal Southerners as Hannah the bobbin-girl, who has worked in mills all of her life, somehow finding time to perfect her skills of cooking greens and playing the mountain dulcimer. There is McCaig, a bona fide good old boy, who speaks eloquently and graphically on the joys of cockfighting. And there is McClendon, who rents Frank a room in Peckover and tries to convince him of the existence of "jackalopes" and "doars" in his smoke house, when in reality only haunches of wild boar and deer are hanging there.

Alnilam contains other Dickey trademarks, such as his tendency in the early poetry to divide the lines into distinct halves (here suggested by the division of the text into columns, one in dark type for Cahill's perceptions, the other for the remarks of the narrator). Finally, there is Dickey's fascination with violence, as shown in the scene in which Zack kills five of Peckover's worst dogs, or when Cahill crushes Lieutenant Foy's hand, or, most dramatically, when the entire airfield self-destructs and faithful Zack is decapitated by an onrushing propeller.

Like Oedipus before him, Frank Cahill is blinded in order to see more truly. He is privileged to make an essentially mythic journey from sight to insight; and, even though *Alnilam* is of epic length patient readers will be similarly enlightened, seeing and experiencing a heretofore undiscovered world.

Daniel L. Guillory

Sources for Further Study

The Atlantic. CCLX, July, 1987, p. 98.
Booklist. LXXXIII, April 1, 1987, p. 1153.
Chicago Tribune. May 24, 1987, section XIV, p. 3.
Kirkus Reviews. LV, April 1, 1987, p. 490.
Library Journal. CXII, June 1, 1987, p. 128.
Los Angeles Times Book Review. June 7, 1987, p. 1.
The New York Times Book Review. XCII, June 21, 1987, p. 7.
Publishers Weekly. CCXXXI, April 17, 1987, p. 65.
Time. CXXIX, June 29, 1987, p. 71.
The Washington Post Book World. XVII, May 24, 1987, p. 1.

THE AMERICAN AMBASSADOR

Author: Ward Just (1935-   )
Publisher: Houghton Mifflin Company (Boston). 326 pp. $17.95
Type of work: Novel
Time: 1986
Locale: Martha's Vineyard, Massachusetts; South Central Africa; Washington, D. C.; and Germany

In this realistic novel of public government service and of private family life, an American ambassador is confronted by his terrorist son with a life-or-death choice

> Principal characters:
> BILL NORTH, a fifty-year-old American ambassador
> ELINOR NORTH, his devoted wife
> BILL NORTH, Jr., their revolutionary son who practices terrorism
> GERT MUELLER, Bill Jr.'s German lover and fellow revolutionary
> KURT KLEUST, a German diplomat, Bill North's friend

Ward Just is one of the few serious American novelists who write well about contemporary public figures, and *The American Ambassador* further establishes his reputation in this field. As a former reporter for *The Washington Post* and *Newsweek*, Just has a familiarity with such public figures—senators, ambassadors, top presidential advisers—which brings authority to his work. With *The Congressman Who Loved Flaubert and Other Washington Stories* (1973), his first collection of short fiction and his most widely known work, Just captured the atmosphere of the city of Washington, D.C., with an artist's touch, presenting his fictional figures with a detached, precise prose that recalled the language of Ernest Hemingway. All these stories appeared in *The Atlantic Monthly*, where Just became a contributing editor. He has been less successful in such recent novels as *In the City of Fear* (1982) and *American Blues* (1984), which contain compelling characters and have some moments of real power, but which finally do not exhibit the sense of form necessary for a first-rate work of fiction. *The American Ambassador*, constructed along sounder lines, is a traditional novel which explores the psychological dimensions of character within the confines of a focused plot. Because of the clandestine terrorist activities, some critics have termed the novel a thriller, but overall it is characterized by slow-moving explorations of morally ambiguous situations and events—a traditional field of the serious novelist.

Although the story is narrated omnisciently, with the events viewed from the perspectives of four different characters—Bill North, his wife Elinor, their son Bill North, Jr., and Bill Jr.'s German lover and fellow revolutionary Gert Mueller—the central focus is on the character of Bill North, the protagonist, on his personality and on his traditional American values. The specific values embodied in his character are his sense of family, an idealism which finds expression in his patriotism, forthright honesty, ingenuity, and loyalty. In his sense of family, the relationship he has with his wife Elinor is one of the central aspects of his life; it is also one of the triumphs of the book. Seldom in contemporary fiction has the bond between a middle-aged man and woman been portrayed with such sensitivity. Their relationship, which holds much compassion as well as passion, is one of mutual support and understanding. It is a traditional American marriage in that Elinor, although an artist in her own right, spends much of her energy and time in support of her husband; she moves largely in an orbit around his sphere of personality and concerns.

That sphere of concerns is a considerable one, for Bill North is a man of exceptional abilities. The youngest man in his foreign service class to reach the rank of ambassador, he has participated numerous times in ceremonial activities at the president's Oval Office. The most noteworthy public event in his life, which is related in a series of flashbacks, occurred in South Central Africa in 1963, when he was a twenty-seven-year-old foreign service officer. The country in which he was stationed was involved in the beginnings of a leftist revolution; in a search for the names of the revolutionaries, Bill North and a young German diplomat friend, Kurt Kleust, travel away from the capital out into the bush country to visit a German missionary. They are successful in learning the names, but on the return trip, they are ambushed by a band of those revolutionaries. Their driver is killed, and although Bill is wounded by grenade fragments, he helps Kleust fight off the attackers, shooting several of them and killing at least one. This physical action is rendered with vivid detail, with the kind of authority which someone who has witnessed combat can provide. (As a war correspondent for *The Washington Post*, Just was wounded by grenade fragments—as Bill North is—during a fierce firefight with North Vietnamese regulars, in which more than half of the American company were either killed or severely wounded. These events in Just's life are related in "Reconnaissance," which is a chapter from his first book, the nonfictional work *To What End: Report from Vietnam*, 1968. Published at the height of the war, Just's "report" was remarkably farsighted.)

Ironically, the State Department officially does not approve of Bill North's actions in going into the bush, but the attorney general and the president although not mentioned specifically by name, they obviously are Robert Kennedy and John F. Kennedy—view his daring with approval. The revolution is aborted, and American interests are preserved.

The present action of the novel opens twenty-three years later, in 1986. An old grenade fragment has worked against Bill North's spine, causing a loss of feeling in his left hand. He must extend his current vacation leave to have the fragment removed in a Washington, D. C., hospital. While undergoing preoperative tests, he is visited by a government official who questions him about the activities of his son; the government has learned that a senator is planning a public hearing into the relationship between Bill North and

Bill Jr., in an attempt to link both of them to terrorism in Western Europe, and this official must learn all he can in order to avoid embarrassment to the present administration. It is within the framework of this intermittent interrogation, which takes several days, that much of the past action is related through flashbacks. Central Africa—the heat, the countryside, the people—is rendered with effective detail which places the reader in the setting.

This setting becomes crucial in another important element of the plot: It was during the Norths' first stay in Africa, when Bill was wounded, that Bill Jr.'s negative attitude toward the American government began to form. Five years old at the time, Bill is brought to his father's bedside at a hospital in the bush; afterward, unknown by his parents or the authorities, he encounters one of the wounded revolutionaries—whom his father shot in the firefight—secretly being treated at the same hospital, and the experience becomes a cornerstone in the development of his life. When his father and mother leave for Washington a short while later so that his father can receive further medical treatment, and so that he can be questioned by government authorities about the revolutionary situation, Bill Jr. is left in the care of the house staff, who are secretly sympathetic to the revolution. Natives of the region, they view the revolution as a movement toward freedom, and against Western imperialism. Instead of seeing his father as a hero, young Bill comes to see him as a representative of the imperialistic forces which hold the country under its influence. The irony of the situation arises out of moral ambiguity: On the one hand, as a representative of the United States, Bill North has behaved in a heroic manner, and he is commended for his actions by the president; on the other hand, his son views him as a man who has worked to destroy the hopes of the common people—including the members of the house staff—for their political self-determination. It is in exploring situations such as these, in which there is no clear right or wrong, that Just achieves stature as a novelist.

The narrative method of relating the larger lives of Bill and Elinor North through the interrogation finds its counterpoint in long scenes between Bill Jr. and Gert in various cities in Europe, in which he tells of his life with his parents. The prologue of the novel is a passage in which Bill Jr. relates to Gert the scene in which he left his parents, while on Thanksgiving vacation in 1979 in Hamburg. The German settings—in particular Berlin at the end of the book—are done with fine attention to detail; that the action should occur during Thanksgiving, that quintessentially American holiday, works to focus attention on the traditional American values of Bill North; later in the novel, in an extended scene which is powerfully rendered, Bill Jr. recalls a Thanksgiving visit by both sets of grandparents to his home in Washington, D. C., when he was a child. He tells Gert that he relates this incident to illustrate the characteristics of the ruling class in capitalism, but the novelistic value of the scene goes far beyond this clichéd reasoning. Bill North's father, a German Jew who came to Boston in the 1930's to avoid prosecution, and who there married Bill's Gentile mother, is confronted by Elinor's father, a Chicago businessman who is being ousted from his company by a Jewish banker with high government connections. The humanity and the values of both men are portrayed brilliantly in this confrontation; it is the kind of scene which recalls Theodore Dreiser, with nuance of behavior subordinated to the direct dramatic force of the characters' presences. Indeed, there is often a directness of character portrayal in Just's work that recalls Dreiser; Just's roots are deep in the Midwest, and his portrait of Harry Ballard, Elinor's father, is another in his gallery of Midwestern characters.

The relationship between Bill North and his son, which is the focus of the interrogation, gradually becomes the central concern of the plot, and it is this relationship which fully challenges Just's powers as a novelist. The father loves his son, although he knows his son despises him for what he is—a representative of the American government. When Bill North learns that his son plans to assassinate an American government official, he follows a series of clues to meet his son in Berlin without disclosing his location—he chooses his son over the state. (Ultimately Bill North learns that he himself is his son's intended target.) This choice between family and country is a classic one, which has been treated from the beginnings of literature, notably in Sophocles' *Antigone* (441 B.C.). Just's treatment of the theme is successful from the viewpoint of the father; the father is confused, angry, and deeply hurt over the choices that his son has made in life, but in spite of his disappointment, he ultimately chooses the son. Although Bill North may be finally a limited man, Just's tone is sympathetic.

Bill Jr. is a much less sympathetic character, although in many ways he resembles his father. When Bill North was seventeen, he rejected the Jewish traditions of his father to embrace an American life-style, adopting as his hero Abraham Lincoln. In turn, at age seventeen Bill Jr. rejects the values of his father to set his own course in life. Both men are idealists. Bill North's idealism is embodied in his patriotism; Bill Jr.'s, in his revolutionary vision of the world. And both men are committed completely to their women. In his own way, Bill Jr. is as devoted to Gert Mueller, his fellow revolutionary, as Bill North is to Elinor. Both men occupy the central role in the relationship; Gert follows Bill Jr.'s lead as much as Elinor follows that of her husband. It should be noted, however, that there is a vast difference between the characters of Gert and Elinor; Gert is an emotionally maimed person, who mistakenly has been identified as mentally retarded by the German authorities, and during the action of the novel, she shoots her own father—an old-guard revolutionary himself—to revenge his actions against her mother. She is a fascinating character—many of Just's young women characters are—without a traditional moral base; she recalls some of the alienated young women characters of Joyce Carol Oates, who have a strangely detached response to violence.

The one crucial difference between Bill Jr. and Bill North is that while Bill North rejected the ways of his father, he retained his love and respect for him, whereas Bill Jr. hates his father. Some reviewers complained that Bill Jr.'s hatred for his father is presented without sufficient personal motivation. It certainly can be argued that, given Just's psychological explorations of the major characters in the novel, to supply simple political motivation in clichéd Marxist terms for the son is a failure of imagination at a critical juncture. Consequently, instead of a tragic figure, Bill North remains a sympathetic character whose death does not so much affirm the basic characteristics of the human condition, as it works to void any achieved meaning at all.

The many fine accomplishments of the novel, however, should not be overshadowed by this flaw. The portrait of Bill North—his decent characteristics, including his mature love for his wife—gives this novel value, for it is men such as Bill North—supported by women such as Elinor—who have represented the establishment in American society during the 1960's, the 1970's, and the 1980's. Whether as career bureaucrats in government offices, as diplomats, or as executive officers of large business corporations, they have played an important role in the national life, and it is to Just's credit that he has brought the powers of the novelist to bear on this area of experience—the public realm all too often neglected in contemporary fiction.

Ronald L. Johnson

Sources for Further Study

Booklist. LXXXIII, March 1, 1987, p. 981.
Chicago Tribune Books. March 15, 1987, XIV, p. 3.
The Christian Science Monitor. May 1, 1987, p. 26.
Kirkus Reviews. LV, January 15, 1987, p. 82.
Library Journal. CXII, March 1, 1987, p. 92.
Los Angeles Times Book Review. May 24, 1987, p. 11.
The New York Times. CXXXVI, March 9, 1987, p. C16.
The New York Times Book Review. XCII, March 15, 1987, p. 1.
The New Yorker. LXIII, May 18, 1987, p. 116.
Publishers Weekly. CCXXXI, January 16, 1987, p. 62.
San Jose Mercury News Arts and Books. March 29, 1987, p. 23.
USA Today. V, March 20, 1987, p. 40.
The Washington Post Book World. XVII, March 22, 1987, p. 3.

AN AMERICAN CHILDHOOD

Author: Annie Dillard (1945-   )
Publisher: Harper & Row, Publishers (New York). 255 pp. $17.95
Type of work: Literary autobiography
Time: 1950-1963
Locale: Pittsburgh, Pennsylvania

An autobiography which traces the origins of Dillard's artistic, mystical, and naturalist preoccupations from her earliest years through high school

> *Principal personages:*
> ANNIE DOAK (DILLARD), the writer as a young girl
> FRANK DOAK, her father
> PAM LAMBERT DOAK, her mother
> AMY, her younger sister
> MOLLY, her youngest sister

Annie Dillard is still best known for her 1974 Pulitzer Prize-winning classic, *Pilgrim at Tinker Creek*. Even though most of her subsequent books have treated spiritual and mystical themes (sometimes to the exclusion of the natural world), the public views her as a "nature writer." Both her visionary probings of nature and her explorations of Christian mysticism shed much light on her latest work, a first autobiographical volume, *An American Childhood*.

The title is ironic. It implies an averageness and typicality which in fact was not Dillard's lot. Born and reared in Pittsburgh, of a white, Protestant, upper-middle-class family, part of the elite of the city, she knew little about ethnic diversity, working-class poverty, or racial tension. She had two younger sisters, a father who was a business executive, and a mother who did not work "outside the home." There was a black maid and a boat, and the children were sent to private schools, weekly dancing classes, and the elite Presbyterian church.

Yet Dillard was not even a typical aristocrat. Her writing and, more important, her perception of childhood, may be unique in American letters. She will take a usual occupation of a ten-year-old—drawing or rock collecting, for example—and delve deeply into herself as that child, so that the occupation is no longer typical but uniquely her own. She writes, "When you pry open the landscape, you find wonders." That sentence could be an epigraph for all Dillard's life and work.

Moreover, the unique intensity of Dillard's experiencing of her own life places her in a position far above the average. The dust jacket says, "Dillard's ecstatic interest in the world begins here in childhood." The word "ecstatic" describes Dillard's work perfectly. The Greek origin of "ecstasy" is "a being put out of its place"; the word also means a trance or "overpowering religious emotion or rapture." "Ecstasy" is one of a series of words with religious overtones that Dillard often uses: "passionate," "exultant," "enthusiastic," "ecstatic"—all these describe the young girl's attitude toward the world and life. The very vocabulary underscores the theme of all Dillard's work—the spiritual pilgrimage, the mystic quest.

Dillard's autobiography is centered on two contradictory processes: coming to conscious awareness and the periodic ecstasies of transcending self and losing consciousness in the glory of experience. The excitement derives not from losing identity but rather from gaining consciousness *after having lost it*. Ironically, if one is awake and conscious all the time, one cannot have the ecstatic experience of coming to consciousness. It is Dillard's thesis that children come to consciousness gradually, and this process is a visionary and passionate one. At ten, says Dillard, "I noticed this process of waking, and predicted with terrifying logic that one of these years not far away I would be awake continuously and never slip back, and never be free of myself again." Thus Dillard's mission is to continue to awaken to consciousness, to capture the sensation of aliveness one has in standing under a waterfall or seeing an amoeba in the microscope. Recalling *Pilgrim at Tinker Creek*, the project is to continue to be open to moments of pure transcendence, as when—while patting a puppy in the gas station—she watches the sun break through the clouds on Mount Rogers. One recalls also her describing "the tree with lights in it" that the newly sighted recount.

In order to live in this way, one must learn to *notice*. All creative conceptual work begins in the same place, with noticing, and Dillard the scientist, the philosopher, the poet, and the artist learns early its craft. As a child, she sketches the same baseball mitt every day for a month, memorizes faces and makes police artist drawings, painstakingly identifies and catalogs 340 rock specimens, memorizes "miles" of Bible verses (whose rhythms sing in her head as she writes poetry), and finds one-celled animals in pond water with her microscope. Her pun on the process is pure Dillard: "One took note; one took notes." She concludes near the end of the book in a sentence-paragraph typical of her style. She gives the general point, then a long series of detailed descriptors, the whole ending with a philosophical, often epigrammatic thought to ponder:

> It all got noticed: the horse's shoulders pumping; sunlight warping the air over a hot field; the way leaves turn color, brightly, cell by cell; and even the splitting, half-resigned and half-astonished feeling you have when you notice you are walking on earth for a while now—set down for a spell—in this particular time for no particular reason, here.

The structure of the book complements the double theme of consciousness and self-consciousness. The prologue has two main sections. The first is a lyrically historical overview of Pittsburgh's topology that ends with the first settlers ("tall men and women lay exhausted in their cabins, sleeping in the sweetness, worn out from planting corn"). The second introduces her father and juxtaposes the many Pittsburgh suicides her father watched from his high office window with his quitting his job to sail down the Ohio River on a small boat. Part 1 of *An American Childhood* encompasses Dillard's early childhood memories; it closes when she is ten, "awake now forever." Part 2 is the center of the book and covers the wonderful preadolescent years of ecstasy—consciousness and self-consciousness together. Dillard describes here her various passions—from baseball to reading to learning to tell jokes to bicycling all over the city.

A crucial thematic anecdote—her attempt to fly—reveals much about Dillard's method. Her desire to fly is, she realizes, quite mad: She is old enough to know better but also old enough to know about faith, belief, and miracles. She is, she says, "exultant." The word "exultant" comes from the Latin, meaning "to leap for joy." What is astonishing about the preadolescent Dillard is that she is sometimes so joyful that she feels like leaping out of her skin; she is always on the verge of levitation. So she tries to fly: running down the main street, arms outstretched, heart pounding, knowing she will not be able to do this and doing it anyway, rapturous, exultant. She passes people who will think her a fool but does not care; she sees a woman who meets her gaze and seems to understand; finally she slows to a walk. "So Teresa of Avila checked her unseemly joy and hung on to the altar rail to hold herself down," writes Dillard, making explicit her own identification with the great mystic. (Perhaps the very young Saint Thérèse of Lisieux would have been a better comparative model for Dillard here.) This anecdote foreshadows the flying image she uses at the end of the book to mark her departure from Pittsburgh in adolescence.

Part 3 of the book covers adolescence, the time when she begins to have a sense of wonder. As she says, "Young children have no sense of wonder. They bewilder well, but few things surprise them." It is always, she asserts, the adult who points out the glory of fall leaf color, or the way ice coats every branch in a storm. Dillard, at thirteen, was beginning to wonder self-consciously, less able to transcend herself in the experience, more likely to retreat and examine it. In the epilogue she reiterates the two contradictory sensations that pull her—the transcendent epiphany, when one loses oneself in the experience, and the "sensation of noticing that you are here."

In their descriptions of the contradictory emotions of a bookish but athletic girl who likes solitude, the sections on adolescence may be some of the most perceptive in recent literature. Dillard fluctuates between boredom and anger, with passing moments of ecstatic wonder. She writes passionate poetry in the style of Arthur Rimbaud, drives wildly all over Pittsburgh, pounds the "Poet and Peasant Overture" on the piano, is maniacally in love, makes obsessive pencil drawings, is suspended from school for smoking, and cannot wait to leave home. "I couldn't remember," she frets, "how to forget myself."

Gender stereotyping and the stultifyingly limited choices for girls growing up in the 1950's are also themes. This is surprising because Dillard's work heretofore has been remarkably unconcerned with current issues of contemporary feminism. Her resentments surface strongly in the sections about her passion for baseball (especially pitching) and her early realization that Little League did not accept girls. At dancing class and at Sunday school, boys were mysterious and clearly better—they were in control and had real choices. "The boys must have shared our view that we were, as girls, in the long run, negligible. . . . We possessed neither self-control nor information, so the world could not be ours." In the 1950's, women spent most of their time alone in their houses, their work and identities invisible: "No page of any book described housework, and no one mentioned it; it didn't exist. There was no such thing." No wonder, then, that Dillard identified so strongly with her father; the book is in a sense a love letter to her father, beginning and ending with his love for travel, adventure, and jazz music. The role models she has as she leaves Pittsburgh are all male—Huck Finn lighting out for the territory, Jack Kerouac in *On the Road* (1957), and her father taking his boat down the Ohio River. In fact, Dillard had planned to use a male pseudonym for *Pilgrim at Tinker Creek*, saying she knew of no female theologians except Simone Weil.

Dillard's style is both compact and elaborately intricate. She can write a periodic sentence full of soaring phrases or the terse four-word "I quit the church." The influence of biblical rhythms and metaphors is very strong; the prologue rings with prophetic power reminiscent of the Book of Isaiah or the Psalms: "I will see the city poured rolling down the mountain valleys like slag, and see the city lights sprinkled and curved around the hills' curves, rows of bonfires winding." Both the repetition of the word "curves" and the ending of the sentence on a present participle ("winding") are characteristic of Hebrew poetry. Dillard loves ironic juxtaposition, wordplay, oxymoron. Still, there is less of this dazzling display here than in her previous works.

Her description and analysis of the epistemological status of memory is vivid and intriguing. Memory, she writes, is fleeting, "like blowing tissue across some hollow interior space." Once one tries to trap such memory fragments by writing them down, they are utterly changed. "The sentences suggested scenes to the imagination, which were no sooner repeated than envisioned, and envisioned just as poorly and just as vividly as actual memories. . . . It was easier to remember a sentence than a sight, and the sentences suggested sights new or skewed." Such epistemological ruminations call to mind others who have wrestled with the concept of memory, from Saint Augustine to Henri Bergson to novelist Lawrence Durrell (*The Alexandria Quartet*, 1957-1960), and in particular, essayist Loren Eiseley, especially in his autobiography, *All the Strange Hours* (1975).

But it is perhaps the young Dillard's emerging perceptions of nature, her tentative growing knowledge and enthusiasm for insects, one-celled animals, birds, rocks, butterflies, and moths that will give this book's readers their greatest pleasure. For Dillard the nature writer—the solitary seer, the solitary stalker—here reveals how she got her start in the natural world, from the weekly trips to the library and the discovery of Ann Haven Morgan's *Field Book of Ponds and Streams* and Gene Stratton Porter's *Moths of the Limberlost* to the gift of the microscope and her friend Judy's weekend place in Paw Paw, West Virginia.

One of Dillard's favorite symbols, found also in *Pilgrim at Tinker Creek*, *Holy the Firm* (1977), and *Teaching a Stone to Talk: Expeditions and Encounters* (1982), recurs in this work, that of the wounded or incandescent moth, its death the occasion for an emanation of the Divine. Here the moth is a huge Polyphemus, clawing its way out of its cocoon in a too-small Mason jar in front of a classroom of horrified school children. Its wings are matted and crumpled from not having room to unfurl them before they dry. The teacher takes the crippled moth outside, too late, and lets it go. It crawls down the driveway, unable to fly, its golden wing clumps, pulsing. Remembers Dillard, "Nevertheless, it was crawling with what seemed wonderful vigor, as if, I thought at the time, it was still excited from being born." The moth becomes a kind of objective correlative for Dillard's view of the world. Her own desire to fly is an obvious connection to this part of the natural world.

An American Childhood is less esoteric than some of Dillard's recent works (*Teaching a Stone to Talk*, for example), and for that reason will probably appeal more to the general reader, but it helps if one can view the book within her literary canon, where it functions as her Genesis, an account of the origin in her own life of her concerns with transcendence and self-consciousness. Dillard is a deeply theological writer, and readers need to interpret *An American Childhood* in the light of the mystical *Holy the Firm*; if Dillard is read as just another autobiographer, her point is lost. That doubleness of losing self and finding self—the transcendent grace of oneness with the All and the ecstatic awakening—these are the essence of life for Dillard: "And still I break up through the skin of awareness a thousand times a day, as dolphins burst through seas, and dive again, and rise, and dive."

Margaret McFadden

Sources for Further Study

Booklist. LXXXIII, August, 1987, p. 1700.
Chicago Tribune. September 13, 1987, VII, p. 1.

Commonweal. CXIV, November 6, 1987, p. 636.
Kirkus Reviews. LV, July 15, 1987, p. 1042.
Library Journal. CXII, September 1, 1987, p. 177.
Los Angeles Times Book Review. September 20, 1987, p. 1.
Ms. XVI, October, 1987, p. 78.
New Leader. LXX, November 2, 1987, p. 17.
The New York Times Book Review. XCII, September 27, 1987, p. 7.
Publishers Weekly. CCXXXII, July 24, 1987, p. 180.

THE AMERICAN HISTORICAL ROMANCE

Author: George Dekker (1934-   )
Publisher: Cambridge University Press (New York). 376 pp. Paperback $34.50
Type of work: Literary criticism

George Dekker examines the American historical romance tradition, particularly as it derives from the romances of Sir Walter Scott, from its beginnings in the nineteenth century to the middle of the twentieth century

The American Historical Romance offers an ambitious approach to a kind of novel that seldom receives sustained, systematic, or comprehensive attention, in spite of its importance and popularity. There is good reason for the neglect. Coherence is difficult to discover in the sprawling category known as the historical romance. Even so, George Dekker has undertaken not only to identify the origins of the American branch of this genre in the works of Sir Walter Scott, but also to explore in interdisciplinary fashion a broad range of cultural issues very much at the heart of the historical romance— prevailing theories of social progress, the scope and limits of history qua fiction, the political implications of regionalism, and gender roles. The text and notes are rich in references to excellent secondary materials.

The first chapter constitutes a preview in which the trifocal nature of the study is explained, with particular emphasis laid on each word of the title— American, historical, and romance. Limiting the discussion to a few major works by authors who could be termed "elite" is justified on the grounds that these works are representative of all, and that these writers possessed insights into historiography that lesser writers lacked. As for the word historical, the intention is to consider both "the history *of* historical romance and the history *in* historical romances," but not the conventional questions about what makes a novel historical (must it contain historical personages, and how far in the past must it be set?). It is the third term, romance, that introduces the spirit of clashing energies so important to the genre, for while "historical" implies reality, "romance" implies exactly the opposite, particularly in literary studies. It is just such a combination of "irreconcilable forms," according to Dekker, quoting Henry James, that produces the "extraordinarily rich, mixed, and even contradictory character" of the historical romance.

The second chapter begins with a discussion of the scope of the influence of Scott's *Waverley: Or, 'Tis Sixty Years Since* (1814), a story of the uprising of the Scottish highland clans, and ends with an analysis of *The Wept of Wish-Ton-Wish: A Tale* (1829), Cooper's story of Indian wars on the Connecticut frontier. Dekker argues persuasively that what made *Waverley* so influential a book, inspiring dozens of writers to chronicle the traumatic transitions of their own national struggles, was not simply that its subject was revolution in the Age of Revolution, but also that the conflict was universalized. It is the principles of progress and reaction that are at war when the Hanoverian Whigs meet the Scottish Jacobite supporters of Prince Charles Edward Stuart at Culloden. Scott's merit, as Samuel Taylor Coleridge saw it, lay in his powerful portrayal of the conflict generated by two interdependent forces: the adherence to the past, the ancient, the permanent versus the passionate drive for progress and "free-agency." Dekker identifies this polarity in Scott's novels more specifically as the "overthrow of a heroic society by the modern post-feudal state," which is the theme of the "*Waverley*-model" and of the thousands of historical romances that follow its pattern. Considerable attention is given to these two features, the bipolar structure and the heroic, indeed, epic dimensions of the historical romance. This Romantic tendency to polarize sometimes took the form of parallel lists, which Dekker introduces in this chapter, and which becomes a unifying method in the ensuing chapters. The following list, drawn up by the respected leader of the Romantic Revival, Edward Young, could serve, according to Dekker, as a description of the imperialistic conflict of the *Waverley*-model:

natural	artificial
spontaneous	labored
natural graces	studied graces
liberty/wildness	order/boundaries
poetry/mystery	prose/reason
individuality	mass
sublimity	correctness

On one side are values often associated with an older culture, declining aristocrats, or primitive folk, and on the other some of the values of the new, progressive conquerors.

In looking, finally, at the test-case of Cooper's *The Wept of Wish-Ton-Wish*, the parallels, while meaningful, seem less than consistent. If the novel tells a story of "a heroic culture overthrown by the post-feudal state," what group represents the heroic culture? Not the vengeful Indians, as they are described by Dekker. If it is the original, patriarchal group of colonists, displaced by the second-generation whites' bourgeois objectives, where do the Indians fit? Some readers will find Dekker's analysis more illuminating in its details than in its broad outlines.

Chapter 3 examines an idea and a pattern as useful and widespread as the *Waverley*-model, one espoused by Scott, Cooper, and, notably, Thomas Jefferson. Stadialism, a theory of the laws of social change, imagines development or change as a trajectory, rather than a cycle, and posits four stages of social growth: a "savage" stage based on hunting and fishing, a "barbarian" stage based on herding, a "civilized" stage based on agriculture, and a stage based on commerce and manufacture (sometimes considered over-civilized).

This simple classification provides material for some of the book's most engrossing speculations. Dekker does well to show how explicitly Jefferson incorporated this formative concept into his visionary assurance of an ever-improving American society: from "savages of the Rocky Mountains" to "the pastoral state" on the frontier, then "our own semi-barbarous citizens, the pioneers," eastward to the "improved state in our seaport towns," the prospect revealing "the gradual shades of improving man" which Jefferson dared to believe would culminate in the eventual disappearance of barbarism from the earth, as he wrote to William Ludlow in 1824. In 1827, Cooper's novel *The Prairie: A Tale* painted just such a landscape, Leatherstocking himself representing the first stage, the Bush family cast as the patriarchal, nomadic second stage, the bee-hunter Paul Hover representing a combination of stages and then elevated by his marriage to the refined Ellen to stage 3 as a yeoman farmer; the overly cultivated stage 4 is represented by the Creole Inez, wife of the army officer Middleton. On the darker side, it should come as no surprise that some used stadialist thought to justify the displacement of the Indian as well as the dismissal of the frontiersman: Were they not predestined victims, unable to partake in the higher stages of social development? Dekker's cross-disciplinary method works well in this chapter.

The next issue, one of perennial interest in American literature, is that of regionalism. The term has come, over time, to carry negative associations of narrowness and limitation. Dekker, however, addresses the social and political dimensions of literary regionalism with an eye to the ambition and loyalty of the writers who, like Maria Edgeworth, Scott, and Washington Irving before them, desired "to bring the Muse into their own country." Some of their aims were to reinforce regional identity and pride, to condemn regional social evils, and to champion cultural diversity; Nathaniel Hawthorne, Cooper, Willa Cather, Allen Tate, and William Faulkner all pursued these goals. One of many valuable points made about regionalism here is the recurring problem of preserving a regional identity against a dominant national culture—whether the culture at risk happened to be Virginia or Dutch New York.

With the big issues of the *Waverley*-model, stadialism, and regionalism addressed, Dekker turns to individual studies of two major figures, Hawthorne and Herman Melville, each in a separate chapter. It is, happily, the strong points of their individual talents that are examined; Hawthorne's irony and Melville's ambiguity are brought into focus through the framework of the *Waverley*-model. For example, Dekker notes a strong kinship between Scott's Puritans and those of Hawthorne. "The Gray Champion" is a direct descendant of *Peveril of the Peak* (1823), national heroes who return from the past, *redidivus*, to save the besieged faithful. Yet Hawthorne's Puritans, while invested with some sinister values, as Scott's always are, are invariably granted a moral force that cannot be discounted. For readers of American literature who may be much less familiar with European literature of the Romantic period, the discussion of Hawthorne's irony placed within the larger context of "Romantic" irony as defined by Friedrich Schlegel will be valuable. It seems eminently sensible to view Dimmesdale, as Dekker does, as a Man of Sensibility. Two enriched readings emerge from his analysis: one of Hawthorne the historian, the other of Hawthorne the Romantic.

Melville, according to Dekker, did not respond to the influences of historical romances that he had read avidly in his youth until late in his career, but when he did, in *Israel Potter: His Fifty Years in Exile* (1855), "Benito Cereno," and *Billy Budd, Foretopman* (1924), he not only demonstrated the bold polarities quintessential to the Romantic mind and examined the imperialistic clash of savagery with civilization, but also "succeeded in forging a new mold for the historic romance," something not even Hawthorne accomplished. One fault with this otherwise engaging close study is that this "new mold" lacks sufficient delineation. Calling "Benito Cereno" a cautionary fable of imperialistic decline, Dekker seems to contend that the sinister avatar Babo, who breaks Cereno's will to live, is a figure of prophecy. At any rate, in Dekker's readings, both "Benito Cereno" and *Billy Budd, Foretopman* end in mystery, and mystery in the form of the detective story is an important departure for the romance in the twentieth century.

Before moving on to particular writers of the twentieth century, Dekker introduces the issue of gender. While men were predominant in the writing of romances in the nineteenth century, women writers of comparable stature appear in the twentieth—Cather and Edith Wharton foremost among them. Especially relevant to his thesis are Dekker's interpretations of Scott's light and dark heroines, and here again is a list of opposed values:

MAN	WOMAN
sentimental	naïve
intellect / learning	intuition / instinct
history	myth
art	nature
modern	primitive
fragmentary	whole

Dekker discovers that Scott and Hawthorne both "upset traditional gender-role expectations," that Cather and Wharton were the first women to write works of international standing, and that Jim Burden of *My Ántonia* (1918) and Newland Archer of *The Age of Innocence* (1920) are Sentimental Heroes. These readings should stimulate questions and further exploration.

In the longest chapter of the book, Dekker raises the provocative idea that fiction influences political reality. He cites Mark Twain's often-quoted charge that Sir Walter Scott was responsible for the Civil War, a facetious statement that has been seen by some to contain a grain of truth. Dekker enlarges upon it, naming other prominent romance writers who could be blamed for keeping sectional differences alive. The parallel lists of opposed cultural values for this chapter on the Southern historical romance was drawn up by Jefferson in 1785. "In the North they are cool" but "in the South they are fiery"; people are "sober" in the North, "voluptuary" in the South, "laborious" in the North," "indolent" in the South, and so on. Dekker's point is that by the end of the eighteenth century—before Scott's novels appeared—a consensus regarding regional traits was already forming.

In any study that attempts so much, there will be something to criticize, but *The American Historical Romance* does its job well. Although the text is dense with facts and with implications, the writing is clear and inviting. In his closing chapter, Dekker reasserts the generic continuity of the novels he has considered, with their emphasis on recurrence ("the historical romance is the Jaffrey Pyncheon of literature"), on variation (the regional resistance to centralization), and on improvisation (Tony's dance steps in *My Ántonia*). He argues convincingly that the American historical romance combines healthy tradition with stimulating experiment.

Rebecca R. Butler

Source for Further Study

Choice. XXV, April, 1988, p. 1242.

AND THE BAND PLAYED ON
Politics, People, and the AIDS Epidemic

Author: Randy Shilts (1952-   )
Publisher: St. Martin's Press (New York). 630 pp. $24.95
Type of work: Current affairs
Time: 1976-1987
Locale: San Francisco; New York; Washington, D.C.; Paris; Africa; and Denmark

Shilts follows the AIDS epidemic from its origins as a mysterious and ignored African disease through its development into a plague that has claimed tens of thousands of lives in the United States and abroad

> Principal personages:
> GAETAN DUGAS, a French Canadian airline steward stricken with AIDS
> DR. ROBERT GALLO, a retrovirologist with the National Cancer Institute in Bethesda, Maryland
> DR. MICHAEL GOTTLIEB, an immunologist with the University of California at Los Angeles
> LARRY KRAMER, a gay novelist and playwright
> BILL KRAUS, a prominent San Francisco gay leader
> GARY WALSH, a gay psychologist and AIDS organizer

Randy Shilts's *And the Band Played On: Politics, People, and the AIDS Epidemic* is the first major history of the Acquired Immune Deficiency Syndrome (AIDS) epidemic. There is no reading this book without feeling intense anxiety about one's health and the health of one's loved ones; furious anger toward the organizations and individuals who have cost thousands of lives through their blindness, prejudice, and egotism; enormous respect for the people who have bravely sought to cure this disease; and a bottom-of-the-well despair for the unfathomable suffering this plague has caused and will continue to cause tens and hundreds of thousands of innocent people.

Shilts is exceptionally, perhaps uniquely, qualified to write this book. Not only is he a health reporter, but he is also self-avowedly gay—a fact of critical importance, since the AIDS epidemic was and largely still is identified as a gay disease in this country. Since 1982, Shilts has worked in San Francisco, the gay mecca that would be so hard hit by this epidemic, for the *San Francisco Chronicle*, perhaps the only newspaper in the United States to recognize the epidemic as a newsworthy topic almost from the first signs of its arrival. Since 1983, Shilts's sole professional topic has been the AIDS epidemic. *And the Band Played On* is filled with information that only someone in Shilts's position could have culled, from doctors and government officials interviewed month by month to early AIDS sufferers now long dead. At more than six hundred pages, the book is a heroic attempt to cover the ramifications of this plague from every possible perspective: political, medical, journalistic, social, and personal. It is also clearly the work of someone who has lived on intimate terms with horror for five very long years.

The book is structured chronologically, beginning in 1976, when Dr. Grete Rask, a Danish surgeon working in Zaire, first fell ill with a mysterious and wasting disease. Shilts concentrates heavily on the period from 1980 through 1985, those critical first years of the American AIDS epidemic, and concludes with a brief update to 1987. Organizing his material under precise date headings, Shilts jumps from topic to topic within his overall subject. In the sections devoted to 1983, Shilts's entries follow each other with only a few days' interval—the year was that critical to the AIDS epidemic. Such an approach has its shortcomings: There is an enormous amount of redundancy—something perhaps excusable in a book that documents the redundant, hapless efforts of scientists, gay activists, and a few politicians to save lives. There is also diffuseness, a blunting of some of Shilts's arguments because of his peripatetic structure. Yet Shilts's method has one supreme merit: It allows the reader to watch the unfolding of this grisly drama linearly, with a scope and understanding one could not possibly have had while actually living through it. *And the Band Played On* is not a historian's book, but a reporter's, raw and undigested but vital.

The disease that would eventually be known as AIDS first came to attention in the United States in 1980, when men in both San Francisco and New York began to fall ill with a form of skin cancer known as Kaposi's sarcoma and a pneumonia called Pneumocystis carinii, both rare and deadly diseases ordinarily found in someone with an immune system damaged by birth defects or chemotherapy. It was in December, 1980, when Dr. Donna Mildvan of Beth Israel Medical Center first noticed that these diseases were attacking homosexual men; April, 1981, when Dr. Michael Gottlieb of the University of California at Los Angeles first identified this as a new epidemic; and June, 1981, when the Center for Disease Control's *Morbidity and Mortality Weekly Report* published the first paper on the disease. As infants, drug users, transfusion recipients, hemophiliacs, Haitians, and Africans fell victim to the disease, scientists in the United States and abroad struggled to define its nature and to identify the means of transmission.

By December, 1981, French doctors Jacques Leibowitch and Willy Rozenbaum had already concluded that a virus was responsible for the disease. It would not be until April, 1984, however, that an American government official would announce that the new virus had been identified. The delay was the result of a number of factors: insufficient funding to finance medical research, the unconscionable lag in publication caused by the endless reviewing procedures of top medical journals; and the egotism and prejudice of a few doctors themselves.

Emerging as a shadowy figure in the medical drama is Dr. Robert Gallo, a retrovirologist with the National Cancer Institute in Bethesda. According to Shilts, Gallo threatened colleagues who left his domain to work for other researchers and relentlessly fought with French doctors pursuing the same line of work. Ultimately, the Pasteur Institute filed a lawsuit against the National Cancer Institute, resolved only in 1987 out of court by Jonas Salk. Four years after French scientists had applied for a patent on the AIDS virus, the American government finally allowed them to share credit for the discovery with Gallo. Yet Gallo's behavior is the exception in Shilts's history; much more often, the medical profession acts with selfless determination and energy, bravely confronting this frighteningly enigmatic disease.

More controversial than Shilts's treatment of the medical profession is his depiction of the gay community. Shilts is anything but soft on this topic. A longtime proponent of health over politics, Shilts describes with a fascinated repugnance the 1970's promiscuity that followed in the wake of gay liberation. He is angry that gays continued to have orgiastic sex in back room bars and bathhouses while doctors such as Selma Dritz warned of possible health hazards, and he is angrier still that gay activists insisted on defending their rights to such orgies long after the AIDS virus had reared its ugly head. Much of Shilts's book focuses on the controversy over closing the bathhouses once it became apparent that AIDS was being transmitted sexually. He has little sympathy for the San Francisco community leaders who worried that locking the bathhouse doors might be the first of many measures denying gays their civil rights and even less for the New York gay leadership, whom he charges with being more concerned with keeping their jobs than with stopping a modern plague.

Although Shilts is very convincing in arguing the need for closing the bathhouses, his voice here is much more strident than when discussing the medical profession. Given the long latency period of the AIDS virus, figures indicate a phenomenally responsible reaction by the gay community as a whole, almost from the time the first facts about the disease came to be known. Yet Shilts prefers to dwell on the relatively few gays who straggled to the baths in the mid-1980's, knowing full well that they were playing a kind of Russian roulette. In particular, he dramatizes at great length the story of Gaetan Dugas, the French Canadian airline steward known to the medical profession as Patient Zero. Flying from city to city across the globe, relishing sex everywhere he went, Dugas was proven before he died to have had a sexual connection with at least forty of the first 248 gay men diagnosed with AIDS. The ugliest part of the story is that the steward continued his behavior even after he became aware that he was infecting his sexual partners with a deadly disease.

Once again, there are positive examples here to counterpoint the negative. Particularly moving are Shilts's portraits of Gary Walsh, a psychologist stricken with AIDS who helped organize victims of the epidemic, and Bill Kraus, a political aide who fought for victims' rights in Congress before himself falling victim to the disease. Yet the positive gay figures are always presented as mavericks in Shilts's book, outsiders fighting self-destructive fools who defend promiscuity with inane political rhetoric. Apparently a firm believer in monogamy, Shilts seems to see the AIDS epidemic as a kind of corrective to the rampant sexual freedom of the 1970's. At times, as when he praises Larry Kramer's play *The Normal Heart* (1985) for advocating gay marriages, Shilts confuses the moral with the medical. One cannot help wishing that *And the Band Played On* were less shrill in dealing with gay issues and more compassionate toward the victims of this horrible disease, no matter how they contracted it.

A member of the journalistic as well as the gay community, Shilts is equally hard on his colleagues for their behavior during the AIDS epidemic. This time his criticism seems warranted: Citing figures for the amount of coverage given the disease, Shilts shows how little interest newspapers across the country had in the epidemic when it was strictly a disease of homosexuals and drug addicts. The repeated cry of editors and reporters was, "Show us an angle for the heterosexual community and then we will be interested." It is only in 1984, with the growing awareness of AIDS transmission through transfusions, that newspapers began to pay the disease serious attention. That and the death of a celebrity, Rock Hudson, finally made a disease that had already killed thousands of people "newsworthy" to journalists.

Shilts is particularly angry about newspaper neglect because, he persuasively argues, newspaper attention might have spurred the government to do something about this devastation. On all levels—federal, state, and city— the government needed spurring. Shilts demonstrates indubitably that only the government of San Francisco recognized the AIDS threat early and cared enough to do something about it. Torn between her hetero- and homosexual constituency, Mayor Diane Feinstein certainly did not have a clear path to follow, but, according to Shilts, she, with assistance from congressmen Phil Burton and Henry Waxman, provided facilities for specialized health care and AIDS education many long years before the rest of the country allocated funds for the disease.

Alongside San Francisco, New York seems particularly remiss. Although New York was the source of the epidemic in the United States, although the number of New York AIDS patients dwarfed those elsewhere, the city, under Mayor Ed Koch's nominally liberal administration, failed to provide adequate funds for an AIDS clinic, long-term services, or education. Finally, in April, 1985, Kramer's play *The Normal Heart* criticized the Koch administration harshly enough to provoke action. Governor Mario Cuomo was equally remiss, threatening in 1983 to veto the Republican-dominated state senate's push to appropriate $5.2 million for AIDS research, education, and prevention. As late as 1985, Massachusetts governor Michael Dukakis submitted a $3.3 billion health and human services budget that failed to allocate one cent for AIDS. As Shilts illustrates, labels such as liberal and conservative, Democrat and Republican became almost irrelevant when dealing with the AIDS epidemic.

Yet it is the Reagan Administration that is the target of Shilts's strongest criticism. Once the disease began to kill drug addicts and gay men, the administration simply chose to ignore it. As Shilts points out, public health threats such as Legionnaires' disease and Toxic Shock Syndrome had been dealt with instantly, with great public fanfare. Yet long after it had claimed many more lives than both of those diseases combined, AIDS was still being shrugged off. The difference, as Waxman pointed out at a budget hearing, was that Legionnaires' disease had hit a group of predominantly white, heterosexual, middle-aged members of the American Legion, whose respectability had brought them a degree of attention and funding. Yet AIDS victims were not typical, Main Street Americans. They were drug addicts and gays.

As Shilts shows, people such as Dr. Edward Brandt, Assistant Secretary for Health of the Department of Health and Human Services, pleaded desperately behind the scenes for more federal AIDS funding. In public, however, they were coerced by the administration to make statements reassuring the country that AIDS research had all the money it needed. Meanwhile, people across the country were catching AIDS through transfusions, because blood banks lacked the resources and encouragement to screen blood. Significantly, the president himself did not speak to the nation about the AIDS epidemic until May 31, 1987—more than six years after Dr. Gottlieb first diagnosed the disease. By that time, 36,058 Americans had fallen ill with AIDS, and 20,849 had died of it.

Understandably, *And the Band Played On* is not a coolheaded book. Its subject is a disease whose toll in this country is rivaling that of the Vietnam War. Its overriding implication is that many of those lives could have been saved had the United States not been awash in a sea of reactionary prejudice. Shilts undertook a herculean endeavor in trying to distill so much of one decade between the covers of one book. There is much that is wrong with *And the Band Played On*. The writing is often slovenly, the structure problematic, and the tone sensational and lurid. Yet it is also a book of great and wide-ranging significance—an informed book, a convincing book, and a heartbreaking book, for those who care to read it.

Richard Glatzer

Sources for Further Study

Chicago Tribune. October 18, 1987, XIV, p. 3.
Kirkus Reviews. LV, September 1, 1987, p. 1303.

Library Journal. CXII, November 15, 1987, p. 71.
Los Angeles Times Book Review. December 6, 1987, p. 6.
The Nation. CCXLV, November 7, 1987, p. 526.
The New York Times Book Review. XCII, November 8, 1987, p. 9.
The New Yorker. LXIII, December 28, 1987, p. 124.
Newsweek. CX, October 19, 1987, p. 91.
Publishers Weekly. CCXXXII, September 11, 1987, p. 72.
Time. CXXX, October 19, 1987, p. 40.

ANYWHERE BUT HERE

Author: Mona Simpson (1957-   )
Publisher: Alfred A. Knopf (New York). 406 pp. $18.95
Type of work: Novel
Time: Primarily the 1950's to the 1970's, including flashbacks to prior years
Locale: Bay City, Wisconsin, and Beverly Hills, California

A compelling portrait of an unusual mother and her soon-to-be-a-child-star daughter, Anywhere but Here *describes the dynamics of dreaming for success and its effect on family relationships*

> Principal characters:
> ADELE AUGUST, a Midwestern working mother whose dream is to "make it big" in California
> ANN, her daughter
> LILLIAN, Adele's mother
> CAROL, Adele's sister

As the novel opens, Adele August is driving across country, headed for Hollywood in a white Lincoln Continental that she can hardly afford, with her second husband's credit card and Ann, her almost-twelve-year-old daughter, in tow, so that Ann can become a child star while she is still a child. Adele's flight, from her small-town, Midwestern roots to the glamour and success she is sure they will find in California, is at the center of the book and explains its title. *Anywhere but Here* is about Adele's restless dissatisfaction with things as they are, about a certain kind of dreamer's perpetual desire to be "anywhere but here"—but perhaps even more important, it is about the often-devastating effect this kind of character can have on those who are close to her, particularly, in this case, on Adele's daughter Ann. The portrayal of this difficult mother-daughter relationship is what most makes this novel (Mona Simpson's first) worth reading.

Four female narrators, representing three generations of the August family, tell the story, in sections of varying length, primarily through flashbacks and reminiscence. Ann, the closest to Adele, narrates most of the work. It is appropriate that the reader see Adele through the hard and clear eyes of her child; if Adele is the type who wishes to be anywhere but here, Ann, stranded in the wake of her mother's dreams, can recount what being "here" is really like.

"We fought," Ann's narrative begins. "The fights came when I thought she broke a promise. She said there'd be an Indian reservation. She said that we'd see buffalo in Texas. My mother said a lot of things. . . . Places she said would be there, weren't." Like most children, Ann cannot stand a broken promise, but she grows up on plenty of them. Adele is the kind of dreamer who in the very dreaming finds her nourishment; it does not matter that the promise goes unfulfilled. Sometimes the dream is a manipulation, as when Adele, longing to create a better bond between Ann and her new husband, Ted, suggests that Ted has the connections to get Ann on a local station (which, as it turns out, he does not). Other times it is simply the sheer will to resist an unpleasant reality, as when, in a Beverly Hills restaurant, Adele turns brightly to her daughter and says she is sure that they are both going to make it big, though they are nearly broke and friendless. The dream is also a cover-up for motives she is less willing to admit. Adele routinely invokes the myth of her self-sacrificing efforts to keep them in Beverly Hills so that Ann can stay in the best school system and make the right sort of connections to become a star eventually; yet it becomes clear that Adele's real dream is that by living in Beverly Hills she will find herself a rich husband. When Ann finally does get an audition, she has to find a way to get there by herself, because her mother would rather go to a meeting with the psychiatrist she imagines is in love with her.

Adele is never without a new hope to carry her forward. Ann comments wryly that her mother is forty-four years old and every night still makes a wish upon a star. Despite a self-protective cynicism, Ann finds herself continually drawn in: She wants to believe her mother because the dreams are so appealing, tapping into her own innermost desires.

This cycle of baiting and disillusionment inevitably leads to another: a fight, then a routine abandonment and reconciliation. Rather than take responsibility for her failed promises, Adele turns her daughter's disappointment into a betrayal that demands punishment. Adele pulls the car over to the side of the road, tells Ann to get out, then drives away, disappearing over the horizon; after enough time has passed so that Ann thinks that she really has been left for good, Adele returns, opens the door, and in a cheery voice suggests that they go for ice cream. One Christmas season Adele leaves their Beverly Hills apartment and calls Ann to say that she is driving her car over a cliff because Ann does not really love her and will be happier with the insurance money anyway; after several frantic hours and calls to hospitals and the police, Ann sees her radiant mom drive up with a huge Christmas tree in the trunk. It is a ritual that for Adele wipes the slate clean and allows her to go on; it is also one which protects her from taking responsibility and growing up.

It is no wonder that Adele often has to remind her daughter that she is the adult and Ann is the child. As is often the case with children of irresponsible parents (Ann's father ran off when she was quite young), Ann develops an overactive sense of responsibility, a desire to keep up the façade that the family looks good. When a committee of neighbors confronts her stepfather about their poorly kept lawn, Ann will not wait until the next day, when a neighbor boy has been hired to do the mowing; she drags the mower across the lawn herself on into the night. Ann is intelligent, level-headed, and often the caretaker. At her audition she puts on a clever and impressive performance and realizes her mother's dream for her—she gets the part and becomes a (minor) television star. Having endured a dizzying array of mixed messages, disappointments, and abandonments while she is growing up, Ann develops the hardiness of a survivor.

The real strength of Simpson's portrait of these two characters—what makes them seem so true—is that they are neither simply good nor simply bad. Adele can be as likable as she is terrible, and, for all of her hatred of Adele's weaknesses, Ann is often very much like her: manipulative, deceitful, overly concerned with superficial appearances. What strikes the finest note of truth is the novel's depiction of the bewildering but unbreakable love Ann feels for her mother. Though it seems to tear with each betrayal and rejection, it always snaps back. "It is always the people like my mother," says Ann, "who start the noise and bang things, who make you feel the worst; they are the ones who get your love."

Recurrent symbols reinforce the characterizations. Adele's inability to create a real home for Ann is symbolized by the absence of furniture in all the houses in which they live. From the house with Ted on Carriage Court to the succession of small apartments in Beverly Hills, all are virtually devoid of furnishings, underscoring Ann's lack of stability, her rootlessness. In contrast are the solid wood furnishings, ornamented with ironed doilies, of her grandmother's home on Lime Kiln Road, where nothing has been moved for years. Her grandmother's home offers the warmth and security that is missing from Ann's childhood, and she returns to it, literally and in reminiscence, often. Appropriately, she is fascinated with the furniture in a schoolmate's dining room, with the permanence of its brown wooden chairs. Staring at the back of a chair she thinks, "It seemed the security of a whole childhood. It stayed there, all day, the wood worn and glossed like a held chestnut."

Food also carries symbolic meaning in the book. Meals—typically a time for family unity—are generally eaten out, or while standing in front of a refrigerator that is nearly bare. Unlike grandmother's kitchen, where it seems a pie is always baking, in Adele's household the sense of family is cold, thin. The two are often on diets, but Adele is always in the mood for ice cream; like her own brand of maternal nurturing, it is a food that is exciting but ultimately devoid of nourishment. Adele's passion for sweets (once she spends her last dollars on pounds of sweet dried dates which the two eat for months) is like her passion for dreams; it is the hunger for instant and easy gratification, with no mature thought of tomorrow.

Also significant is Adele's passion for cars, big and showy ones, emblems of the appeal of superficial impressiveness and of her restless urge toward a more glamorous life. Ann and Adele replace the sense of roots and home life with frequent and generally aimless drives around town. Ann is infected too, perhaps because it is what she knows: She enjoys one of her safest and warmest moments when she locks herself inside her stepfather's new Cadillac with its rich smell of fine leather; she dreams of going to California.

She too is attracted to movement and the illusion of slick surfaces. "We both loved airplanes," she says, ". . . they made us feel rich and clean. We were dressed in our best clothes and new stockings charged at Shreve's. No one seeing us would know anything true."

This fascination with surfaces sometimes infects the work itself; it is rich in detail, sometimes too rich. Simpson's narrators see individual details so clearly that at times the larger meaning of the scene goes out of focus. The poetry of the images is often stunning, but not always necessary.

Simpson's employment of four different narrators also seems unnecessary and hence problematic. Though the sections narrated by Adele's mother, Lillian, and sister, Carol, offer moments of profound insight and beauty, rarely do they contribute anything that is not also delivered by Ann's sections; often they seem to take the reader away from the primary flow of events. The final section, narrated by Adele, though true to her character, is a fairly superficial few pages, and coming as the last chapter in the novel it is disappointing; one expects more revelation, some final insight into her character.

The narrative sections from Bay City—Carol's and Lillian's voices—do serve as a counterpoint to the Beverly Hills sections, however, contrasting the old style of family life with the new. Interestingly, life in Bay City comes across as no more happy or stable than life in California; there are unhappy marriages, alcoholism, premature death, disappointments. *Anywhere but Here* portrays the dark side of the American family; at its best, as in a sharply etched description of one family Christmas, it breaks stereotypes to give the reader something painful, but very true.

Dana Gerhardt

Sources for Further Study

Booklist. LXXXIII, November 1, 1986, p. 370.
Boston Review. XII, February, 1987, p. 26.
Glamour. LXXXV, January, 1987, p. 134.
Kirkus Reviews. LIV, November 1, 1986, p. 1611.
Library Journal. CXII, March 15, 1987, p. 92.
Los Angeles Times Book Review. January 4, 1987, p. 3.
The New York Times Book Review. XCII, January 11, 1987, p. 7.
Newsweek. CIX, February 2, 1987, p. 69.
Publishers Weekly. CCXXX, November 1, 1986, p. 54.
Time. CXXIX, April 13, 1987, p. 76.
Vogue. CLXXVII, January, 1987, p. 98.
The Washington Post Book World. XVII, February 1, 1987, p. 7.

ARCHER IN THE MARROW
The Applewood Cycles of 1967-1987

Author: Peter Viereck (1916-   )
Publisher: W. W. Norton and Co. (New York). 260 pp. $14.95; paperback $6.95
Type of work: Poetry
Time: From the creation of the world to the present
Locale: Various physical and spiritual realms

> *Principal characters:*
> You, the representative of humankind, sometimes male, some-
> times female, sometimes both
> God the Father, who seeks to keep humans docile and obedient
> God the Son, who defends humans against the tyranny of the fa-
> ther but who occasionally discourages "you" from trying to sur-
> pass his limitations
> Dionysus, his half brother, a symbol of fertility

A complex inquiry into the potential for freedom, this poem sets out in traditional yet innovative form both the quest of the individual and the movement of all human history

Peter Viereck's first book of poetry since *New and Selected Poems 1932-1967* (1967), *Archer in the Marrow: The Applewood Cycles of 1967-1987* is the culmination of twenty years of poetic exploration, a lengthy and difficult song cycle celebrating the triumph of human will and creativity over the forces of doubt and repression. Consisting of a poetic prologue, eighteen cycles, two recapitulations and reversals of cycles, a poetic epilogue, an appendix on form in poetry, notes, a glossary, and numerous epigraphs, *Archer in the Marrow* chronicles the evolution—both physical and spiritual—of the drive of humans to "selfsurpass" or transcend their limits.

Viereck, a distinguished professor of European and Russian history as well as a poet, has treated the theme of individual will and repression in his earlier historical works such as *Metapolitics: From the Romantics to Hitler* (1941), an account of the Nazi mentality. In *Archer in the Marrow*, as in his other poetic works, including *The Persimmon Tree: New Pastoral and Lyrical Poems* (1956) and *New and Selected Poems 1932-1967*, Viereck employs both rhyme and meter, but within its traditional form, *Archer in the Marrow* also represents a significant new stage in the poet's development of a supple meter and rhyme scheme.

To some extent the traditional versification of *Archer in the Marrow* resembles the wry, witty forms of W. H. Auden or the energetic rhythms of Theodore Roethke. Such masters of traditional forms are the exception in contemporary poetry, dominated as it is by free verse, yet there are signs of a counterreaction. If this return to traditional forms can be called a movement, Viereck has written its manifesto: "Form in Poetry: Would Jacob Wrestle with a Flabby Angel?" In this vigorously argued appendix to *Archer in the Marrow*, Viereck defends and promotes the use of meter and rhyme; using Ezra Pound as an example, Viereck also argues that the poet's ethical stance cannot be ignored in evaluating poetry. Form in poetry, Viereck maintains, is a biological necessity, stemming from the infant's learning of iambic rhythms from its mother's heartbeat. To ignore such a basic lesson, as modern poets such as Pound, T. S. Eliot, and William Carlos Williams have done, is to ignore the reader's most elemental needs; indeed, poetry attains its most complex meaning not in the denotations of its language but in the frequent tension between meaning and rhythm. Rhyme is perhaps not as basic as meter, but it often serves to punctuate and set off the line. Furthermore, rhyme need not be the stultifying restriction it so often is in English, for the innovative poet may set up internal rhyme and cross rhyme as well as end rhyme; Viereck envisions such an enriching of rhyme by new poets.

This evaluation of modern poetry greatly oversimplifies its accomplishments and subtleties, but even those who find Viereck's aesthetic program overly simple will probably admit that he has successfully carried out his aims in *Archer in the Marrow*. A densely textured drama of freedom and repression, the book avoids the dryness of much academic poetry through its intricately varied rhythms and its playful wit. The poem emerges as a profound meditation on life and death—profound not because of its overt didactic proclamations but through its harmony of form and content.

Viereck's emphasis on the ever-changing organic structure of poetry recalls the variety and unity of the work that most often surfaces in *Archer in the Marrow*, namely Johann Wolfgang von Goethe's *Faust*. As in *Faust*, a hero struggles to transcend his limits and finally does so with the help of a woman (the man and woman in *Archer in the Marrow* being the male and female sides of the character "you"). The antagonist in the modern dramatic poem, however, is not Mephistopheles but God ("father"), who wants human beings, represented by "you," to remain static, faithful puppets. The father is at times aided by the son (Christ), who as a modern messiah counsels "you" to find comfort in materialistic salvation. Yet toward the conclusion of the poem, the son merges with his half-brother, Dionysus, who symbolizes innovation as the son symbolizes restraint. This synthesis simultaneously allows "you" to "selfsurpass" and enables the poem to effect its own resolution. This individual struggle recapitulates the broader struggle of all humans caught up in history to move forward, to avoid stagnation or regression.

Such a struggle falls into three periods: a pre-Christian stage, in which man begins to emerge (physically from the primordial swamp and spiritually from unconsciousness) as an entity independent of his creator; a Christian stage, in which man is lulled into a false sense of comfort by a religion that promotes meekness and self-denial, a religion that allows atrocities such as

Auschwitz to occur; and a post-Christian stage, in which humans reject the dichotomy between self-denial and hedonism in order to attain a true fulfillment. The poem uses a central image—wood—to mark these stages: According to a medieval legend, the tree from which Adam and Eve ate the forbidden apple became the Cross of Christ's crucifixion. The apple represents not sin or pride but the attempts of humans to exceed the stagnating perfection of Eden. The cross, then, becomes a symbol not of liberation but of oppression through its message of self-denial. Viereck envisions a third use for the wood, to be made into arrows for a true progress, a change that comes from the very marrow of mankind (hence the poem's title).

The poem begins with a dramatic struggle between "you" and father: "Showdown on Land's End." "You" loses the showdown and is taken out of time to "Part Zero," where he witnesses the agony of the son ("Cycle One") and the ritual slaying of Dionysus ("Cycle Two"). "Part Zero (Outside Time)" describes, in its third cycle, the chaotic merging of past and present, as characters, situations, and slogans from ancient Tarsus and modern Los Angeles intertwine; in this alternative universe, there is no history, neither as sequence nor as tradition: Christopher Columbus falls off the flat Earth while trying to prove it is round, and Lucrezia Borgia becomes the first woman pope. In "Transition Two," the speaker Dionysus, as a kind of liberator, prepares the character "you" to enter time in "Part One." His questioning of the crucifixion of his half brother Christ explains the poet's concept of the historical role of Christianity: "But why did you staple him to a tree and sic/ Saints on him? Saints made my brother/ The killjoy he wasn't; they changed his wine back to water."

In "Cycle Four: Waltz," the first cycle of "Part One," the son muses on man's difficulty in obtaining consciousness and freedom: "Toys don't know they're toys/ When they do, I ache." The character "you" then argues with the father that "you" is independent and free of his creator, but the tyrannical creator, "Half Ghengiz Khan, half Groucho Marx," mocks these futile attempts. Humans seem doomed to repeat the same three-step waltz throughout history, a pattern ordained by the creator. At the end of the cycle, however, "you" discovers an irregular beat, a fourth step that presages his potential for freedom. This concept of freedom through a random irregularity is developed further in "Cycle Six: Rogue"; here, the poet describes the progress of a lungfish whose rogue gene enables it to leave the comfortable water and struggle for a new life on land.

"Cycle Five: Bread" establishes another key image that, along with wood and dance (waltz), suggests freedom and growth: the image of green. Against black (traditional evil) and white (traditional goodness, but here presented as sterile and frozen, like snow), the poet juxtaposes the color green. As a symbol of organic metamorphosis, green is not black and white—that is, a simplistic philosophical concept—but rather a complex reality existing outside the human tendency to reduce things to a clear-cut dichotomy. In the twentieth century, however, the green that is born through fertility and love (symbolized by the goddess Ceres, a double of Eve) has become the fleshpot of the modern city. A quest for satisfaction through lust is no more productive than the Victorian repression of sexuality.

In "Cycle Nine: Stain," at the close of the first part, the force of repression, here represented as the inexorable law of entropy, seems about to defeat the human's quest for freedom. The prologue to the second part, however, repeats the struggle between father, son, and "you," and here the father's words foreshadow an eventual triumph for "you":

> When lives are green, not white or black,
> And no affirms them more than yes,
> When dots are circles staring back,
> Never till then can heaven crack.

The movement of this second part traces the gradual weakening of the autocractic father's control over mortals. Three cycles—"Eyes," "Book," and "Auschwitz"—form the core of this struggle. "Eyes" and "Book" describe how the father, fearing human liberty, manipulates Christianity to enslave the world through its doctrine of meekness. "Auschwitz" explains, through its characterization of Germanic anti-Semitism, how the sentimentality of the Christmas tree is easily fused with the inhuman cruelty of the concentration camp. Unlike John Milton, who in *Paradise Lost* had sought to account for evil as a necessary part of a benificent God's design, Viereck here questions the moral (or immoral) order that would allow evil to exist in any form; rather than replacing evil with the abstract opposite of goodness, Viereck proposes a living love as antidote to the false black-and-white dichotomy. "Auschwitz" then ends with one of the most beautiful passages in the book, a love song by the son, promising empathy and healing:

> Say yes to the breezes.
> If any dishevels
> One curl of a ringlet,
> I'll know and be with you.
> ....
> For what is a song for
> If not to smooth ringlets
> Of daughters too hurt by
> The prose of the world?

In "Part Three" the poet develops further the role of love in the human quest for freedom. The feminine side of humanity, here personified as Eve, opposes the oppressive sterility of the father with her fertility. The female life force, however, is thwarted by technology and mechanization, as the cycle "Mek" points out; mass production substitutes conceptualized abstract ideals for real human needs, just as the invention of the wheel replaces the individuated cave drawings at Dordogne. Technology without human love leads to the ultimate threat to human "selfsurpassing"—nuclear holocaust.

Eventually, the feminine value of love seems ready to overcome the inexorable death drive established by the father. In "Cycle Seventeen: Toward" the son allies himself with the lovers—male and female sides of "you." The father tries to corrupt the erotic impulse by introducing death, represented as a "snuff film," a pornographic movie in which one of the participants is actually killed. Unfortunately, the male side of "you" is unable to maintain love; seduced by the desire to be God, he kills his love.

The quest for "selfsurpassing" then seems doomed by man's egocentric desire to transform the real into the ideal, to assume the role of the very God that had deprived him of freedom. Yet the son concludes in the "Applewood Ballad" in the last cycle, "Threads," "Seed is for vineyards, not crosses." At this point, the poem "snaps back to Part Zero," outside time, and replays the first three cycles. Whereas earlier the fertility god, Dionysus, had been hacked to pieces and the son had been trapped in an infinitely repeated shuttle between past and present, here the two divinities may attain freedom if humans can avoid the dichotomy that led to the original imprisonment: "the release of both gods from sky depends on man's try at uniting on earth these severed halves."

Discovering this unity is the role of the artist: The fully realized work of art shows that it is possible to surpass human limitations without falling prey to a damning egocentric pride. "Part Zero" concludes with synthesis and surpassing, with the vision of the arrow replacing the cross, "*Pierced hands . . . bending cross into crossbow./ Look: goatfoot Jesus on the village green.*" Nevertheless, Viereck does not suggest that this reconciliation will be permanent; such finality would inhibit the organic growth that the poet seeks. Thus, in its epilogue *Archer in the Marrow* ends on a cyclical note, with "you" boasting of his triumph and father preparing new canvases for the ongoing struggle.

The poem *Archer in the Marrow* itself is not free of human imperfections. Occasionally the colloquial tone of a passage seems trendy or anachronistic rather than satiric, and at times the meter calls more attention to itself than the poet might wish. Additionally, many modern readers might question the male perspective of many of Viereck's assumptions; the emphasis on an eternal feminine typically glosses over the historicity of the repression of women, and Viereck's repeated use of "man" and "mankind" to represent all people further abets this repression. Still, on its own grounds the poem represents a remarkable accomplishment by a uniquely talented poet. The achievement of *Archer in the Marrow* lies not so much in the vast erudition and breathtaking wit of its allusions, nor in the recycling of traditional literary themes, such as the Faustian concepts of the eternal feminine and of the need for continual striving, but in its poetic synthesis of material and form. Through this synthesis, the poem marks a significant stage in the development of modern poetry—not a step back to an archaic past but a step forward to a new exploration of the potential of traditional rhythms and rhymes when handled by a creative master of form.

Steven L. Hale

Sources for Further Study

Choice. XXV, October, 1987, p. 316.
The Christian Science Monitor. May 27, 1987, p. 19.
Library Journal. CXII, February 15, 1987, p. 150.
Los Angeles Times Book Review. June 14, 1987, p. 6.
National Review. XL, February 5, 1988, p. 55.
The New Leader. LXX, August 10, 1987, p. 16.
Publishers Weekly. CCXXXI, January 16, 1987, p. 65.

THE ARKANSAS TESTAMENT

Author: Derek Walcott (1930-   )
Publisher: Farrar, Straus and Giroux (New York). 117 pp. $14.95
Type of work: Poetry

In a voice capable of both diversity and discipline, the poet presents numerous settings and tries to find comfort in each

In exploring their homelands, poets often sacrifice their ability to feel unfettered unity with their native brothers and sisters. For example, because James Wright examines and records in poetry his heavily industrialized Ohio, he gives up a portion of his gemütlichkeit—his sense of hominess. If Wright had been completely at home in Martins Ferry, Ohio, he may never have noted the slow despair of its residents' lives in "Autumn Begins in Martins Ferry, Ohio."

Like Wright, Derek Walcott lovingly offers his homeland to readers. Perhaps more than any other living poet, however, Walcott is preoccupied with a sense of separation from his homeland (St. Lucia, the West Indies), and in *The Arkansas Testament*, he attempts to find his place among his fellow islanders. Short of doing so in the book's first section, entitled "Here," the poet searches other lands, in the "Elsewhere" section, not so much for home, but for goodness and justice. Walcott never finds what he is looking for; in fact, readers would be suspicious if he did.

Walcott's predicament, as he presents it in the first section, is that his demonstration of love for St. Lucia in poetry is useless, for the islanders' language is not a written one. In the first six poems, written in lean quatrains, the poet arrives at this dark understanding and erects pillars, in appearance and function, upon which the rest of the collection is built.

In "The Lighthouse," the first poem, Walcott's speaker walks through Castries, a seaport on St. Lucia and Walcott's birthplace, to the New Jerusalem Bar, where he meets an old friend who has left the island only once in his fifty years. The man is completely comfortable, at home, but the speaker is ill at ease. He sees dots to be connected everywhere, unstated questions to be answered: Stars appear as "those to-be-connected dots/ in a child's book" and "Black hands/ in a corner slap down dominos." The speaker seems to wonder if his love for St. Lucia and for its people must always be bitterly incomplete.

In "Cul de Sac Valley," Walcott sets out to answer this question. Since his demonstration of love is poetry, he attempts to give the written word to the people by using linguistic and poetic terms in his description: A dog is "a black vowel barking"; "Chalk flowers . . . scribble/ the asphalt's black slate"; and a girl "climbs straight/ up the steps of this verse." In "Roseau Valley," however, Walcott questions the use of this gift: "my lines/ led to what? They provided/ no comfort like the French priests' or the Workers Hymn." Later in the same poem, he attempts to legitimize his poetry by marrying it to the land: "my gift . . . still sweats with the trickling resin/ in a hill's hot armpit."

The fourth poem, "A Latin Primer," is a digression in which Walcott recalls his development as a poet, his groping for a voice and for a resolution to his conflict. When he sees a frigate bird, "that slowly levelling V/ made one with my horizon," he understands that the process of finding his place as an islander is as important as the process' result. The image of the frigate bird and its meaning charge the poet with purpose, and in "The Villa Restaurant," he celebrates the commonplace of his environment—the waitress whose breasts are "clay goblets"; "the blue gesso behind her/ head is my Sistine Chapel." In "The Three Musicians," the speaker's voice at times blends with that of Madame Isidor, the poem's main character. In this humorous, ironic retelling of the story of the three wise men, the speaker's slips into the island dialect signal the momentary union he feels with his heritage.

This union, however, is fleeting. Walcott surrounds the pillars of his first six poems with a balanced gathering of what makes up St. Lucia: the history, religion, and superstition; the people and places. Yet he returns several times to the nagging feeling of homelessness which preoccupies his art, and in "The Light of the World," perhaps the collection's most powerful and moving poem, Walcott's speaker is at once united with and isolated from the people around him. The setting is a mini-bus filled with the music of Bob Marley, and at moments the speaker seems unself-conscious, just another person heading somewhere. He enjoys the music and quietly lusts after a young woman who is humming along with it: "I imagined a powerful and sweet/ odour coming from her, as from a still panther,/ and the head was nothing else but heraldic." Soon, however, an old woman trying to catch the transport breaks the speaker's peace. "Don't leave me stranded," she says, and he thinks of abandonment, of how he has abandoned his people, and, hence, of how he is abandoned:

> I got off the van without saying good night.
> Good night would be full of inexpressible love.
> They went on in their transport, they left me on earth.
>
> Then, a few yards ahead, the van stopped. A man
> shouted my name from the transport window.
> I walked up towards him. He held out something.
> A pack of cigarettes had dropped from my pocket.
> He gave it to me. I turned, hiding my tears.
> There was nothing they wanted, nothing I could give them
> but this thing I have called "The Light of the World."

The last lines of the poem are Walcott's lovely, accessible statement of the painful duality of the gift of his art. He is at once giving his people everything and nothing—a warm light to which they are blind.

The last three poems of "Here" serve as the section's denouement, with the last, "To Norline," offering the reason for the author's long-term focus on St. Lucia. Walcott is held by the island, "like when some line on a page/ is loved, and it's hard to turn."

In the "Elsewhere" section of *The Arkansas Testament*, Walcott does turn from his native Caribbean, but he no longer looks to connect himself with the people and the land. Rather, as he suggests in "Eulogy to W. H. Auden," his search is less personal, though of great universal importance. In commending Auden's spirit to the heavens, Walcott asks "that the City may be Just/ and humankind be kind." The prayer is sincere, simple, but as one might suspect, doomed. In this sense, the "Elsewhere" section is predictable, for anyone looking for justice and kindness is likely to find the opposite. Indeed, Walcott mourns in characteristically musical poems many of the world's woes: "a summary rifle butt/ breaks a skull into the idea of a heaven"; a rat doubts a peace resulting from stockpiled weapons; in Wales, "no hymn/ rose from the dark throats of the mines"; for a man whose wife dies, "cancer/ kills everything but Love." Fortunately, glimpses of beauty ("a twinkling of butterflies" and "hair that shines/ blue as a crow's wing") and startling epiphanies (that ideas outlast empires, that to die is to enter "a wisdom, not a silence") prevent the "Elsewhere" section from becoming a dirge.

Ultimately, however, what Walcott sees in the cities and in humankind sends him back to the familiarity of St. Lucia. In "Tomorrow, Tomorrow," Walcott's speaker notes the sorrow of leaving and of staying home: "A world's outside the door, but how upsetting/ to stand by your bags on a cold step." Toward the end of the collection, "Summer Elegies" and "A Propertius Quartet," in a final evocation of the island, not only suggest that life is preferable to art ("The statues themselves would choose life over Art"), but also give the poet an adequate breath of his homeland to sustain him in the last, long poem, after which the collection is named.

In "The Arkansas Testament," a short epic in twenty-four sections, each sixteen lines long, Walcott returns to his search for identity, for a heritage to claim. The speaker's journey is from a motel in Fayetteville, Arkansas, to an all-night cafeteria and back again. From the time he enters the motel, his vague sense of his own identity is apparent: He wants to change his name at the register, but instead he pretends "whoever I was,/ or am, or will be, are the same"; in his room, he sees "a smudge on a wall, the mark/ left by two uncoiling selves"; "a candle repeats the moment/ of being blown out," neither fully lit nor extinguished.

When the speaker's 5:00 A.M. craving for coffee drives him out into the darkness, he feels the entire burden of Black America's oppression, the fear of a siren, the pain associated with the name Lee, the unfair laws ruthlessly upheld. Acknowledging that "What we know of evil/ is that it will never end," the speaker offers in section 23 his Arkansas Testament, the last four lines of which summarize his attitude toward the heritage of the South:

> and afternoon sun will reprint
> the bars of a flag whose cloth—
> over motel, steeple, and precinct—
> must heal the stripes and the scars.

That the oppressed in the United States, particularly in the South, have experienced pain and still do is not so troublesome to Walcott as the notion that they are expected to heal their own wounds without the hope of seeing the nature, the "cloth," of people change. His Arkansas Testament, therefore, promises nothing:

> Bless the increasing bliss
> of truck tires over asphalt,
> and these stains I cannot remove
> from the self-soiled heart. . . .

The climax is anticlimactic, and one cannot help but think that the issue of identity and heritage is not resolved in Walcott's poetry.

It is this sense of anticlimax, or incompleteness, on which *The Arkansas Testament* ends that unites "Here" and "Elsewhere," Castries and Newark, the West Indies and Arkansas. Regardless of his poems' settings, Walcott presents the world in images that echo homelessness. Examples range from the mythological Sphinx, siren, and satyr, none of which is completely at home as human or animal, to the commonplace—a woman "maternal at the pelvis/ yet girlish at the wrist," telephone numbers to unknown people, "the unhinged door of a varnished cupboard." Although such images create a rather melancholy tone throughout the collection, Walcott's poetic vision, his tendency to view the world from different points of view simultaneously, leads to striking and legitimate revelations. When he writes of the moon ("black is the music which her round mouth sings"), he celebrates darkness' claim to beauty and its necessity in giving meaning to light. Further, Walcott's discovery in "The Light of the World" that literature is invaluable, yet worthless to the illiterate, would not be possible save for his seemingly effortless ability to spot each idea's and detail's capacity for incompleteness.

Walcott also uses poetry itself to unify the book's sections, but his efforts are sometimes self-conscious, his results uneven. In "Cul de Sac Valley," for example, when stanzas take their shape from "a panel of sunrise," the joining of land and art results in a gift for the people and in comfort for the poet. Yet in the poem "Elsewhere," an image is fragmented to small effect so that the art can refer to itself: "Through these black bars/ hollowed faces stare. Fingers/ grip the cross bars of these stanzas." The images here almost repeat one another, with the reference to "stanzas" perhaps not earning its place in the poem.

The poet's hand is also occasionally visible in his execution of end rhyme. Although he is usually successful, often astoundingly so considering the poetry's impressive diction, rhymes like "excelsior/emptier" and "ammonia/ only a-" are not up to the high level of Walcott's grace.

Such failures are worth noting, but they are ultimately minor dents in the collection. *The Arkansas Testament* evokes the sadness and joy of searching, the peace and despair of isolation. The poems, without any annoying ring of didacticism, remind the reader of the world's diverse realities and of its necessary, often painful opposites.

John Coleman

Sources for Further Study

The Library Journal. CXII, October 15, 1987, p. 84.
The Los Angeles Times Book Review. September 6, 1987, p. 1.
The New Republic. CXCVII, November 2, 1987, pp. 46-47.

ARMED TRUCE
The Beginnings of the Cold War, 1945-46

Author: Hugh Thomas (1931-   )
Publisher: Atheneum Publishers (New York). Maps. 667 pp. $27.50
Type of work: History
Time: 1945-1946
Locale: Europe, Asia, and North America

An analysis of the events and personalities that shaped the change from the hot war between Allied and Axis powers to the Cold War between the Soviet Union and the United States

> *Principal personages:*
> JOSEPH STALIN, General Secretary of the Soviet Communist Party, 1922-1953; Soviet Premier, 1941-1953
> VYACHESLAV MIKHAILOVICH MOLOTOV, Soviet Minister of Foreign Affairs, 1939-1949 and 1953-1956
> FRANKLIN DELANO ROOSEVELT, the thirty-second president of the United States, 1933-1945
> HARRY S TRUMAN, the thirty-third president of the United States, 1945-1953
> JAMES BYRNES, Secretary of State of the United States, 1945-1947
> GEORGE F. KENNAN, the American ambassador to the Soviet Union, 1952-1953
> SIR WINSTON LEONARD SPENCER CHURCHILL, Prime Minister of Great Britain, 1940-1945
> CLEMENT ATTLEE, Prime Minister of Great Britain, 1945-1951

In *Armed Truce: The Beginnings of the Cold War, 1945-46*, Hugh Thomas explores the men, the political forces, and the events which led to the Cold War between the United States and the Soviet Union after the defeat of the Axis powers, Germany and Japan, in 1945. He focuses on the twelve months between the death of American president Franklin D. Roosevelt and the withdrawal of Soviet troops from Iran. This period marked the collapse of cooperation among the Soviet Union, the United States, and Great Britain, whose collaboration against Nazi dictator Adolf Hitler had given hope for postwar harmony. Thomas recounts the end of the war, the Potsdam Conference, the establishment of new governments in liberated Europe, and the organization of the United Nations among the many events, large and small, which shaped the new political order of the globe. *Armed Truce* is the first volume of a projected series tracing the history of the Cold War.

Thomas is a well-regarded British historian best known for three books about Western democratic nations' clash with revolutionary ideologies: *The Spanish Civil War* (1961), *Suez* (1967), and *Cuba: The Pursuit of Freedom, 1762-1969* (1971). In addition, he is the author of the controversial *A History of the World* (1979). His historical work has been highly praised for its literary style and its unorthodox, nonnarrative structure. Thomas is commended as a historian who does voluminous research (*Cuba*, for example, runs to nearly seventeen hundred pages), though his research has been sometimes faulted for relying on secondary sources in English and for maintaining a European-centered perspective.

Armed Truce possesses the virtues of the previous books but suffers less from their weaknesses. The structure of the book is complex and unusual. It begins with an account of Joseph Stalin's "election" speech of February 9, 1946, and ends with Winston Churchill's speech at Fulton, Missouri, twenty-four days later. The 540 pages in between range backward and forward in time to illuminate the causes, significance, and consequences of those two speeches. Thomas' account is divided into five sections, the subjects of which are Stalin and the Soviet Union; Harry S Truman, his foreign affairs advisers, and the United States; the political situation in liberated lands; the development and deployment of the atomic bomb; and the events of March, 1946. This structure results in some duplication and overlap of analysis which may tire the nonspecialist reader, but it permits Thomas to suggest one of his important themes: The sheer complexity of political events ensured that postwar stability would be more difficult to achieve than wartime victory.

Armed Truce is clearly the product of intensive research. The analysis rests upon a foundation of almost twenty-five hundred footnotes; the majority of citations are to the memoirs, diaries, letters, and official papers of the important participants. The massive annotation is more than simply a sign of energy and diligence. It reflects another theme of the book, which the author explains in the preface: the role of individuals who exercised authority from 1945 to 1946 and who, by possessing the centralized power of modern states, shaped the world for good or evil. Thomas uses these men's own words to assess intelligence, intuit motivation, and draw conclusions about character.

Thomas' sources help him avoid one of the complaints lodged against his previous books, reliance upon secondary material. Thomas has clearly read materials long available as well as materials recently opened to public scrutiny. If there is a lack, it is Soviet source materials, though here the fault is clearly not Thomas'. The Soviet Union has never given to its own citizens, much less to foreign scholars, access to diplomatic files or internal documents.

The conclusions that Thomas explicitly draws mark a new stage in the four-decade debate about which nation deserves blame for beginning the Cold War. For the first twenty years, the consensus among Western historians and political analysts was, predictably, that Soviet aggression and expansionism were the culprits. In the mid-1960's, a revisionist school argued that what seemed Soviet aggression was simply an attempt to protect borders from American bellicosity. The revisionists argued that America's own imperial ambitions, often veiled as economic development in the Third World, forced the Soviet Union into a hostile posture.

Thomas' book will give comfort to neither the Cold Warriors of the Right, who blame the Soviet Union, nor the Cold Warriors of the Left, who blame the United States. The Cold Warriors of the Right emphasize the Soviet Union's naked aggression against Eastern Europe, which placed many nations behind the Iron Curtain. Thomas points out that neither American president, Roosevelt nor Truman, contested Soviet plans for Poland, Hungary, Bulgaria, or Czechoslovakia. Content with the rhetoric of democracy and self-determination, American presidents knew little of these nations and had no political contacts with them. By contrast, Stalin knew these nations and directed their Communist parties. The establishment of Communist governments in these nations was the inevitable victory of a proximate, powerful, suspicious neighbor over a distant, powerful, unconcerned correspondent.

To the Cold Warriors of the Left, anxious to exculpate the Soviet Union, Thomas offers some painful reminders. He shows how Churchill, Roosevelt, and Truman went out of their way—even willfully blinding themselves to certain inconvenient facts—in order to think well of Stalin. Eager to resolve postwar disagreements in the Western tradition of compromise, all three Allied leaders tended to read the same eagerness in Stalin's words or gestures. Stalin was willing to play the game, supporting the Western leaders' benevolent blindness by assuming the avuncular mask of "Old Joe," whose innate desire for peace was undercut by Marxist-Leninist hardliners within the Soviet bureaucracy. Stalin's attempt to keep Soviet troops in Iran after the war was a classic instance of his instinct for taking advantage of American and British camaraderie.

Thomas' account of the origins of the Cold War is more complex than those of his predecessors. He carefully measures the human factors within ideological and international competition, keenly aware of how much ignorance, ambition, fear, and self-delusion intensify the natural animosities created by geography, history, or political philosophy.

The underlying cause of the Cold War, according to Thomas, is the nature of the Soviet Union. Rather than accepting Churchill's clever but despairing appraisal (Russia "is a riddle wrapped in a mystery inside an enigma"), Thomas shows that Soviet policy has been directed by a jigsaw-puzzle ideology wedded to a historical inferiority complex and geographical vulnerability. Prior to 1940, Stalin brutally forced the Soviet Union into industrialization (to eliminate inferiority) and into collectivization (to answer the demands of Marxist-Leninism). Stalin so devastated his own people that to rally them against Nazi invaders he had to appeal to religion and nationalism, not ideology. The Nazi invasion demonstrated that the Soviet Union was as vulnerable to attack in the twentieth century as it had been in the twelfth, seventeenth, or nineteenth centuries. To protect the country's borders, Stalin sought a ring of satellite nations governed by obedient regimes. This natural, self-protective instinct was intensified by Stalin's decision to emphasize ideology over nationalism after the war. The easiest way to do so was to portray the United States and Great Britain as the capitalist enemies which, Karl Marx and Vladimir Ilyich Lenin proclaimed, would ultimately have to be fought to the death.

Western leaders now faced a dual, cruel antagonist: a powerful, unconquerable nation (ruled by a tyrant who might well be insane) and an ideology that demanded an external enemy to justify a harsh internal system. Such a situation was unprecedented in these leaders', and perhaps the world's, experience. Their ability to deal with such antagonists was complicated by several factors. First, Western leaders were crippled by a lack of accurate knowledge about their rival. Neither Churchill nor Roosevelt had studied the Soviet Union, Stalin, or Marxism closely, nor did they encourage subordinates to do so. Truman, unexpectedly elevated to the presidency, received contradictory advice from subordinates about the nature of the Communist leaders and their system. Only George Kennan seemed to have much firsthand knowledge, but his views were not taken seriously until the famous "long telegram" of February, 1946.

Second, Western leaders allowed a gap to develop between wartime rhetoric and postwar planning. The idealism of the Atlantic Charter, promising democracy and guaranteeing the Four Freedoms, was consistently undercut as Churchill and Roosevelt accommodated Stalin's plans for Europe's future (which often clashed with the charter) because they feared the Soviet Union's withdrawal from the war effort. Third, Western leaders had their own grandiose agendas. Churchill, hoping to preserve the tottering British Empire, envisioned the globe divided into spheres of influence. Roosevelt, hoping to prevent future wars, envisioned a world order directed by the United Nations and policed by two or three cooperating superpowers. Fourth, Western leaders had to cope with the simple wish of their constituencies to demobilize quickly after the war. Decreasing military strength hampered their ability to negotiate with Stalin.

The spectacle of uninformed, weakened leaders trying to deal with the Soviet Union was complicated by one additional factor: the huge scope of political transformations in Europe and Asia. World War II had destroyed the colonial empires of many nations and disrupted the territorial boundaries established after World War I. The collapse of this order opened the way for traditional, ethnic, and religious rivalries to resurface during the struggle to define national borders. Most Americans remain ignorant of the fighting and the killing that took place after the end of the war in many countries. Whole nationalities were summarily expelled (for example, the German populations from Poland and Czechoslovakia), slaughtered (the

Croats in Yugoslavia), or forcibly returned to the authority of hostile governments (Cossacks to the Soviet Union). Attempting to keep track of, much less manage, such international upheaval was practically impossible in 1945 and 1946.

A final destabilizing factor was the invention and use of the atomic bomb. The existence of the bomb destroyed all the old formulas for computing a nation's strength and predicting its behavior. Once the technology was discovered, it was inevitable that several countries could manufacture the bomb; no nation could keep a monopoly on this or any other weapon. Did the atomic bomb make war obsolete or more likely? Should it become the staple in every nation's arsenal or the private stock of an international organization? Would the bomb spur the natural aggressiveness of some nations or teach all of them temperance?

In the preface, Thomas refers to the history of the Cold War as the unrolling of a tragedy. He seems to employ the term carefully. His account suggests that Western leaders, like tragic protagonists, faced in 1945—and face in the 1980's—a situation to which there is no correct solution, no satisfactory alternative. A world divided between two competing superpowers is a predicament from which intelligence or goodwill alone cannot extract humanity. Thomas ends his analysis with a reference to George Orwell's essay of 1946 which prophetically argued that the Soviet Union is an unconquerable nation determined to consider itself at permanent cold war with its neighbors. The Soviet Union presents a continuing dilemma to what Thomas calls the "high-minded, experienced and cultivated men and women in Western administrations." Insufficiently trained to understand their opponent, locked into political conceptions foreign to ideological thinking, overwhelmed by the complexity of global politics, they cannot thaw the Cold War.

Too strong to be fought, too strident to be persuaded, the Soviet Union still defies traditional political accommodation.

Robert M. Otten

Sources for Further Study

Book World. XVII, February 1, 1987, p. 5.
Booklist. LXXXIII, February 1, 1987, p. 819.
Business Week. May 4, 1987, p. 19.
Kirkus Reviews. LIV, December 15, 1986, p. 1850.
Library Journal. CXII, March 1, 1987, p. 74.
Los Angeles Times Book Review. March 22, 1987, p. 4.
National Review. XXXIX, May 22, 1987, p. 42.

The New York Review of Books. XXXIV, June 11, 1987, p. 44.
The New York Times Book Review. XCII, March 1, 1987, p. 1.
The New Yorker. LXIII, March 23, 1987, p. 100.
Publishers Weekly. CCXXXI, January 9, 1987, p. 74.
The Spectator. CCLVII, November 15, 1986, p. 30.
The Washington Post Book World. XVII, February 1, 1987, p. 5.

ARTICULATION OF SOUND FORMS IN TIME

Author: Susan Howe (1937-   )
Publisher: Awede (Windsor, Vermont). 52 pp. $8.00
Type of work: Poetry

Articulation of Sound Forms in Time *presents a vision quest by sixteenth century minister Hope Atherton and twentieth century American artists*

During the 1970's, a new group of poets, dubbed "language" or "language-centered," sprang up in New York and San Francisco. These poets, who detach language from its conventional meanings and forms, produce an "unreadable" text. They protest political oppression by rebelling against the restrictions which the traditional structure of language imposes on the reader. Among the leading figures in this group are Ron Silliman, Charles Bernstein, and Susan Howe.

Articulation of Sound Forms in Time resembles a long ski run. With no titles or page numbers, and little terminal punctuation, the poems allow the practiced reader to glide in their synchronic flow. Reading the work is like skiing fresh powder. The brief book contains two major sections: "Hope Atherton's Wanderings" and "Taking the Forest." Immediately preceding these two sections, an extract from a letter dated June 8, 1781, describes how Atherton, a minister ordained in 1670 in Hatfield, Massachusetts, participated in the fight against the Indians at the falls above Deerfield in May, 1676. Atherton, unhorsed and separated from the company, wandered in the woods for several days before he reached Hadley, on the opposite side of the Connecticut River from where he first lost touch with his companions. According to his own story and that of his son, who had talked with the Indians, Atherton offered to surrender to the Indians, who fearfully ran from him.

Section 1 consists of sixteen brief poems, easily identified as separate pieces because of their unique forms and placement on the page, although none has a title. Form ranges from that in poem 10, which consists of two lines jammed together vertically, through poems composed of triple-, double-, and unspaced lines, to the uniqueness of poems 14 and 15. These poems each contain seven lines consisting of exactly the same words. Lines 2 through 5, however, mirror one another, one section beginning with "*is*" and ending with "Mohegan," and the other beginning with "Mohegan" and ending with "*is*." Also, the final two words of the last two lines in these poems are set apart and reversed: "upside/sideup" in poem 14 becoming "sideup/upside" in poem 15.

Skiing through section 1, the novice reader can tumble not only on the variety of forms but on the poems' sparse terminal punctuation, their broken syntax, and their varied spacing. The punctuation scheme of the poems makes the reader stop completely only twice, signaled by the period after "etc" in poem 1 and the colon and dash after "Loving Friends and Kindred" in the final poem of the section. Added to the scarcity of terminal punctuation, broken syntax causes the reader to inch through the majority of poems in section 1, making poems 8, 9, 13, 14, and 15 especially challenging. For example, poem 8 reads in its entirety:

> rest chondriacal lunacy
> velc cello viable toil
> quench conch uncannunc
> drumm amonoosuck ythian

Other devices slow the reader, such as triple spaces between some words and no spaces between others, emphasizing the fractured syntax of many of the poems in section 1.

In contrast to this unconventional punctuation and spacing, the diction in section 2 relies heavily on tradition. Words such as "espied" and "Mylord," coupled with "Prest" and "Stedyness," lend a seventeenth century flavor, as do abbreviations such as "abt" and "ordr." Such diction permeates especially the first seven poems of section 1, as do such proper names as "Capt. Turner" and "Clay Gully" and such food items as "two rotted beans" and "Pease of all sorts."

The diction in poems 12 and 16, however, sounds distinctly twentieth century. "Grail face of bronze or brass" and "Talismanic stepping-stone children" evoke the power of twentieth century figurative English, whereas a line such as "We must not worry/ how few we are and fall from each other" shows the plain, direct style popular during the same period.

Howe also provides, in poems 8 and 9, a clear distinction between two major contributors to both seventeenth and twentieth century English language, the classical and Germanic antecedents. Of the thirteen words in number 8, ten have either Greek or Latin roots or references. Poem 9, which totals fourteen words, includes nine with Germanic origins, such as "scow" and "quagg."

Although section 1 contains primarily concrete diction, in poem 13 abstract words—"perceiving" and "realm"—begin to appear. Poems 14 and 15 contain "spatio-temporal" and "Immanence," adding momentum to the work's glide toward philosophy. By interweaving traditional words in unique patterns, Howe provides the reader with a varied landscape; with each perusal of this section, the reader can discover new trails.

Section 2 of the book offers fresh challenges. Although it contains seventeen poems indicated as separate units by their brevity and placement on the page, poems 1 and 2 are almost indistinguishable, and poem 11 could stand as two poems. This point, coupled with the facts that poems 1, 2, and 11 are much longer than any of the pieces in section 1 and that no terminal punctuation appears, enables the reader to glide without impediment in this section. In addition, Howe abandons her dazzling experiments with form and alternates between only couplets and single lines.

Her diction changes also. All references to the seventeenth century are gone. Instead, philosophical-religious diction and twentieth century language dominate. Figures such as Baruch Spinoza, Puck, and Icarus surface briefly and randomly. Phrases such as "Parabolic scholar" and "World as rigorously related System" help to create the philosophical tone. Such terms as "Corruptible first figure" and "lilies spin glory" incorporate the Christian tradition in this section, whereas "Hares call on Pan," "Celt heaven," and "Mahomet touched a flower" bring to mind other religious traditions.

Howe uses twentieth century language, as in section 1, both in figurative and literal ways, employing such metaphoric language as "pin-eyed children" and "Sharpshooters in history's apple-dark." Literal phrases—"Love leads to edge" and "halves draw into a circle"—occur throughout this section, lending clarity to an otherwise mystifying text.

Whereas section 1 alludes to the historical event of Hope Atherton's wanderings, making the reader move slowly and observe unfamiliar sites, events, and people, section 2, "Taking the Forest," creates this historical setting only occasionally. Such scattered references as "oakleaf wreathe" and "Threadbare evergreen season" focus the reader on a concrete setting. Poem 12 uses forest imagery throughout, and the address in the final poem to "kin" in the "Iron-Woods" helps to coalesce the section's forest references.

Drifting above this setting, Howe or her persona meditates on history and language. She mentions the "Linear theme" which "Vision sweeps away" and asserts that "System [is] impossible in time." Stressing that one must transcend the limits of history in order to find authentic completeness, she says that when "Recollection moves across meaning/ Men shut their doors against setting." In other words, memories of the past prevent people from participating fully in the present. Humankind is fated either to "Collision or collusion with history." Becoming more specific, she talks of the discovery of new worlds: "Caravels bending to windward" whose colonists establish new civilizations which "stray into custom," each one becoming a "kingdom of Possession," the "Pagan worlds moving toward destruction." In a direct reference to the discovery of "Far flung North Atlantic littorals," she describes how "Lif sails off longing for life/ Baldr soars on Alfather's path," setting in motion the patriarchal possession of America.

Howe finds possible solutions for this tendency of civilizations to limit the spiritual development of the individual in three areas: language, the inner journey, and reunion with nature. In answer to the "Wagons pegged to earth/ Tyrannical avatars of consciousness/ emblazoned in tent-stitch," she suggests the "Five senses of syntax" and says, "Dear Unconscious scatter syntax/ Sythe mower surrender hereafter," and scatter syntax she does.

The poet can fragment traditional linear thinking only after an extensive inner journey, which Howe describes throughout her book. By beginning with concrete language, she shows Hope Atherton still tied to the ordinary sense perception of this world. The first seven poems of section 1 describe his consciousness as disoriented yet conventional. In poems 8 and 9, however, he loses touch entirely with conventional modes of perception, reaching to the roots of his existence. Alternately opening and closing himself to his new views, experiencing moments of clarity and experimenting lavishly within his expanded horizons, Hope Atherton melds with the poet or the poet's persona, who speaks clearly and directly in the section's final poem. Addressing her fellow artists as "Loving Friends and Kindred:—," who are "a small remnant/ of signal escapes," she says that "We march from our camp a little/ and come home." Such explorers lose "the beaten track" and experience the "dark," but "We must not worry/ how few we are and fall from each other." She advises: "Hope for the artist in America & etc." Howe concludes section 1 by saying, "This is my birthday/ These are the old home trees."

The birthday to which she refers is the birth of vision, the reunion with the self which can occur only after the inner journey. Section 2 continues the journey on a more meditative plane, circling the notion of "home trees." Phrases in section 2 such as "Coming home through past ages," "Left home to seek Lost," and "Home in a human knowing" bring the reader to the "Last line of blue hills/ Lost fact dim outline/ Little figure of mother." Yet Howe does not end on a soft note of comfort. In her last poem she explains that she will turn again to "dark Fells." Much work remains in this land of "Crumbled masonry windswept hickory."

The book's final word, "hickory," draws attention to a important element in Howe's book. "Hickory," one of approximately one hundred Algonquian words assimilated into English from the most widespread Indian linguistic family in North America, points the reader to the natives of the forests through which Hope Atherton wandered. The forests dominated the life of the Indians in the northeastern tribes, and many tribes used the Youth's Vigil to initiate their young men into manhood. During his time of testing, the young person fasted for many days, remaining alone in the forest to test his fortitude and to learn to feel the supportive yet challenging forces of nature. His fasting provoked dreams and visions of supernatural forces that would guide and protect him throughout his adult life.

Howe enables the reader to experience the vigil of a historical figure, Hope Atherton, paralleling his experience to the psychological journey undertaken by modern artists. The rough ground of the first section illustrates the difficulties involved in undergoing such an experience. Once the vision is clear, as it is at the end of section 1, the poet's language can become more fluid and lyrical, her forms less experimental, because she has achieved her vision and now may synthesize it into the rest of her life in order to learn in what ways nature is supportive. Relying heavily upon alliteration, such lyricism as

> Sigh by see
> Smoke faces separate
> Lore and the like
> Sucked into sleeping

enables readers to dream their own visions. Howe's work provides a challenging yet delightful journey.

Shelley Thrasher

Source for Further Study

London Review of Books. IX, October 15, 1987, p. 6.

AN ARTIFICIAL WILDERNESS
Essays on Twentieth-Century Literature

Author: Sven Birkerts
Publisher: William Morrow and Co. (New York). 431 pp. $20.95
Type of work: Literary reviews and personal essays

A brilliant array of essays on prominent twentieth century writers from all corners of the globe

It was Thorton Wilder who at an important conference in Aspen, Colorado, in 1949 reminded the world that Johann Wolfgang von Goethe was the first great thinker to suggest that the literature of the future would be a world literature, a literature with a "planetary consciousness." That future has arrived. The scholarship of comparative literature and the great histories of Ernst Robert Curtius, René Wellek, and Erich Auerbach, have demonstrated that indeed a common vein of ideas and conventions runs through all of Western literature. The archetypal criticism of Northrop Frye has also made profound contributions to the understanding of the underlying uniformity of literary heritage. Nevertheless, the obstacles of language and skeptical attitudes toward the value of translation have continued to promote parochialism and outdated nationalism in the minds of contemporary readers, particularly in the United States, where knowledge of foreign languages is perhaps even weaker than in previous decades and where the native tradition remains largely insular, feeding on its short history and reclaiming lost writers instead of thrusting forward with a sense of the world as it is.

Enter Sven Birkerts. Presently he teaches expository writing at Harvard University and writes excellent reviews for *The New Republic*. He is in his thirties, hardly the age of a sage. Unlike Goethe, who was a sage and who enjoyed the stimulation of Weimar, Sven Birkerts earned his B.A. at the University of Michigan in 1973 and then worked for many years as a bookseller in Ann Arbor, Michigan, and Cambridge, Massachusetts. The stores were his Xanadu: He was close to books all the time, an intimacy he has treasured since childhood. In one of the most moving essays in this volume, "Notes from a Confession," an essay named one of the best of 1986 by Elizabeth Hardwick, Birkerts tells the reader what books mean to him.

He concedes that he has been suffering from an obsession: "Psychopathia librorum." He surrounds himself with the printed word and muses on the sexual nature of his pleasure. Perhaps, he thinks, the same "pleasure" Roland Barthes connects with writing can also be found in reading. This pleasure does not come from escaping the so-called real world. On the contrary, immersion in a story provides the distancing from self that brings reality closer. Birkerts has read *Madame Bovary* (1857; English translation, 1886) four or five times. Why?

I reread and cherish this book because it allows me, while I'm reading it, and for a period after I have put it aside, to perceive my life not as a random sequence of events, or an accident, but as a destiny.

Birkerts' hunger to intensify his own life through wide reading takes on the urgency of a mission in his reviews and criticism. He has translated the sense of personal growth and direction his reading has given him into a prescription for a new literary cosmopolitanism. He believes that it is absurd to quibble over the accuracy of translations when the real enemy of literary culture, the media and the writers of "Docu-fiction," circumvent both the word and the differences between fact and fiction. Television threatens the very existence of books, and journalism posing as literature undermines the liberating distancing of great fiction. The solution, says Birkerts, is to reach out and partake of the great banquet of world literature which invites the reader to a luxurious feast. Although twentieth century writers have been forced to voice the suffering and alienation of one of the most troubled centuries in history, they have done so in an inspired variety of styles, voices, and visions. At the very moment when the world seems most fragmented, with sublime irony that world is called to account by its writers, who rise above ideological and cultural differences to sound the unified note of their "international perspective." What Birkerts hopes to do is to hasten the day when the literary world will admit its internationalization and readers will be mature enough to be global in their outlook.

This is no simple task, even for a successful and intelligent bookseller-reviewer. There are moments when the reader believes that there is something both quixotic and vainglorious in Birkerts' approach. His collection of essays, some eight years in the writing, has an encyclopedic look about it— as if it belonged in a literary dictionary responsible for postmodernism. Birkerts seems to be his own academy, bolder than Samuel Johnson, who took the same number of years to write his dictionary but who had the help of some clerks. Yet Birkerts had to start somewhere in his single-handed effort to internationalize popular reading habits in the United States. His essays impart a considerable amount of important information on worthy writers who are semiobscure to most American readers; what is even better, Birkerts passes on this information in impassioned explications which often rise to analytical brilliance. He has managed to fuse the talents of reviewer and critic and then go beyond them both to the wise meditation of a Montaigne or a William Hazlitt. In short, he is a sage after all.

In the section on German writers, Birkerts captures the elegiac power of Joseph Roth's *Radetzkymarsch* (1932; *The Radetzky March*, 1933), a great Austrian novel that sounds a dirge for the Habsburg Empire. By carefully comparing the novel to Thomas Mann's *Buddenbrooks* (1901; English translation, 1924), a novel better known than Roth's, Birkerts makes a place for it in the reader's sense of the modern German novel. Later in his book, when he discusses the work of the great German critic Walter Benjamin, the strangeness of Benjamin's wanderings in literature seems less exotic because by sharing in Birkerts' sensibility the reader has been prepared for Benjamin's. In this way, the essays become a living example of the cosmopolitanism Birkerts is urging.

There is no guarantee that immersion in foreign experience will always be enlightening or liberating. It may be disturbing and burden the reader with insights that bring him closer to tragedy or to alienation outside his own sphere. Here is where the appeal to sympathetic imagination, the nurse of cosmopolitan virtue, sounds its most poignant tone. After a sensitive and tactful comparison of two of the Third World's best writers, Birkerts strikes just the right note in celebrating the true benefits of being a reader of world literature:

> Viewing Naipaul and Walcott, their separate natures and modes of response, we get a sense of the complexities—emotional, political, linguistic—facing the writer and, by obvious extension, the citizen of the third world.

A sense of complexities—that echoes the principle Lionel Trilling professed in his famous collection of essays, *The Liberal Imagination* (1950). What Trilling urged on the American reader after World War II is even more vitally needed now than it was then, and whereas Trilling was content, in the main, that Americans should discover that complexity in the Anglo-American tradition, Birkerts is right to insist that Americans no longer have a choice. To see things as they are, one must see internationally.

Peter Brier

Sources for Further Study

Booklist. LXXXIV, October 15, 1987, p. 357.
Chicago Tribune. September 27, 1987, XIV, p. 3.
Kirkus Reviews. LV, August 1, 1987, p. 1121.
Library Journal. CXII, October 15, 1987, p. 81.
Los Angeles Times Book Review. August 30, 1987, p. 4.
The New York Times Book Review. XCII, November 8, 1987, p. 16.
Publishers Weekly. CCXXXII, August 7, 1987, p. 43.
The Washington Post Book World. XVII, September 27, 1987, p. 3.

BANDITS

Author: Elmore Leonard (1925-   )
Publisher: Arbor House (New York). 345 pp. $17.95
Type of work: Novel
Time: 1986
Locale: New Orleans and Carville, Louisiana, and Gulfport and Bay Saint Louis, Mississippi

In this stylish thriller, a former convict and a former nun plot to steal money raised by Nicaraguan Contras in New Orleans

> *Principal characters:*
> JACK DELANEY, a former model, jewel thief, and convict
> LUCY NICHOLS, a former nun in Nicaragua
> COLONEL DAGOBERTO "BERTIE" GODOY, a Contra leader
> CRISPIN REYNA, the colonel's assistant
> FRANKLIN DE DIOS, a Miskito Indian and killer
> ROY HICKS, a former policeman and convict
> TOMMY "CULLY" CULLEN, a former bank robber and convict
> AMELITA SOSA, the colonel's former girlfriend
> WALLY SCALES, an agent of the Central Intelligence Agency
> JERRY BOYLAN, a member of the Irish Republican Army
> DICK NICHOLS, Lucy's father, a Contra supporter
> LEO MULLEN, Jack's brother-in-law, a mortician

Elmore Leonard wrote more than twenty novels over almost thirty years before he was discovered by critics and the mass public, making the transition from pulp entertainer to literary stylist. Leonard wrote Westerns in the 1950's and early 1960's, and when that genre became no longer fashionable or profitable, he switched to the crime novel, a form in which, his proponents claim, he has been unmatched by any other American writer in the 1970's and 1980's.

Leonard does not write about the same kinds of characters, settings, and situations in each book. His protagonists are policemen, criminals, and businessmen in Detroit, Miami Beach, and New Orleans. They are men living on the edge of society who find themselves caught up in situations out of their element. In responding to the pressure of these circumstances, they find that they are not the people they had seem themselves as being. In presenting such characters, Leonard, according to Jonathan Yardley, "raises the hard-boiled suspense novel beyond the limits of genre and into social commentary."

Jack Delaney lives his life by chance. While working in a New Orleans department store, he is led by chance to a brief career modeling men's clothing. While working on a modeling assignment, he encounters a jewel thief who is in the process of robbing the hotel room in which Jack and his employer are sleeping. This meeting leads Jack into a more exciting life as a hotel burglar. Trying to impress his girlfriend, however, he is caught and sent to prison. As *Bandits* opens, he has been paroled and is working for his

brother-in-law, Leo Mullen, a mortician. After three years of handling muti-
lated corpses and smelling embalming fluid, Jack is forty and bored. Chance
leads him into much more excitement than he could ever anticipate when he
becomes involved in a plot to steal the money which a Contra leader has
raised from wealthy American right-wingers.

Lucy Nichols accompanies Jack to a leper hospital in Carville, Louisiana,
to pick up the body of a young Nicaraguan woman, Amelita Sosa, who
Lucy, then a nun, helped to escape from her native country. Lucy reveals
that Amelita is not really dead; she is being pursued by her former lover,
Dagoberto "Bertie" Godoy, a Contra colonel who plans to kill her because
he believes that she deliberately attempted to infect him with her leprosy.
The former nun effortlessly begins to take control of Jack's life, enlisting
him in helping Amelita escape from Bertie.

Lucy has to explain the political situation in Nicaragua to Jack, who
knows almost nothing about the Sandinistas and the Contras and does not
know which side the United States government supports: "It was hard to
keep the borders and the history down there straight." Lucy takes charge of
Jack's moral education while, ironically, getting him involved in illegal activities. One of the themes of *Bandits* is the difficulty of distinguishing good
guys from bad, the impossibility of always knowing right from wrong. Jack
is willing to be instructed by Lucy because he respects her commitment to a
cause and especially because she, who has spent nine years in Nicaragua,
has experienced war: "This lady was not as nice as she appeared; she could
show you a hard edge."

Lucy has chosen the right man to help her. Although ordinary in most
senses, Jack enjoys danger, likes taking risks, and, as can be said of most of
Leonard's heroes, can think quickly. When the thugs working for Bertie
confront Jack and Lucy on their way back to New Orleans with Amelita,
Jack sets off the burglar alarm at a closed service station so that they may
escape.

Lucy's efforts to combat the Contras are complicated, since her father is
one of the rich Americans backing her enemies. Dick Nichols, who sells
helicopters to the oil companies drilling in the Gulf of Mexico, has given
sixty-five thousand dollars to Bertie, but Lucy's plan, once Amelita is safely
on a plane to Los Angeles, is to steal the colonel's blood money. She will
use half to rebuild the leper hospital which Bertie destroyed in Nicaragua,
and Jack can have the other half for helping her. That Dick Nichols previously gave one hundred thousand dollars to the hospital attacked by
Bertie underscores the moral ambiguities which engulf these characters.
The more Lucy explains to Jack, the more confused he becomes. She says
of her father, "he's a nice guy. . . . Except his values are all screwed up."

Jack begins recruiting accomplices, two of his fellow parolees, to help
Lucy. Roy Hicks is a tough-guy bartender who was once a New Orleans

policeman. Tommy "Cully" Cullen is a sixty-five-year-old bank robber who has just been released after twenty-seven years in jail. Jack rescues him from another form of prison, a nursing home. Jack intends to use Roy's police skills and menacing demeanor together with Cully's knowledge of banks to find some way to sting Bertie. They are willing to take part in the scheme because they, like Jack, are bored.

The dangers posed by the operation are obvious—Lucy has told many atrocious stories about Bertie and his troops. Then Roy investigates Bertie's henchmen and discovers that Crispin Reyna, a Cuban-born Nicaraguan, has a criminal record in Florida and has been suspected of gunrunning and drug pushing. Franklin de Dios, a Miskito Indian, has been a suspect in a triple homicide in Miami. Roy also finds that they have connections with Wally Scales, an agent of the Central Intelligence Agency (CIA). Jack breaks into Bertie's hotel room and finds a letter from President Ronald Reagan offering his support for the colonel's fund raising and military activities and expressing his admiration for Bertie's "determination to win a big one for democracy."

Jack is joined in the hotel room by another intruder: Jerry Boylan of the Irish Republican Army. Boylan has just arrived from Nicaragua and also intends to rob Bertie. Jack wants to involve Boylan in his plot, but Wally Scales has tipped off the colonel, who has Franklin assassinate the Irishman.

Franklin, though an uneducated Miskito peasant, is more than a mindless killer. He suspects, correctly, that Bertie and Crispin plan not to return to Central America but to take the $2,164,000 they have raised to Miami and continue to live their cocaine and-champagne existences. After Wally warns them of Franklin's suspicions, they decide to kill the Indian, hide his body, and claim that he stole their money. "It's shameful, isn't it," says Bertie, "that we can't trust anyone?" Wally, tired of the duplicities of espionage, also warns Franklin: " 'Cause no matter what we do or who we use, we're always so . . . right."

When Bertie sends Franklin to kill Jack, the former convict is cool and casual, disarming the Indian with charm. Franklin begins telling his problems to a sympathetic Jack, explaining how he wants only to help the Miskitos, who have been persecuted by the Sandinistas, yet has become a pawn of hoodlums and of rich Americans who want to spend money to feel they are patriotic while looking down upon the people they think they are helping: "One rich man said to me he gave twenty-five thousand dollars and wished he could join me in fighting for freedom, but his wife wouldn't let him go. I said to him to bring his woman. She can work with my woman in the camp."

Meanwhile, Jack still has no plan for robbing Bertie. As with everything in his life, he is leaving it all up to chance, hoping that turning Franklin against the crooked Contras will somehow help him achieve his goal. Franklin obliges him by killing Bertie and Crispin but intends to take all the money. Lucy makes a deal with him: Half the money goes to her leper hospital and the rest to his Miskitos. This agreement leaves Jack "wondering if it all made sense. Still wondering, after all this, who were the good guys and who were the bad guys." Roy is unwilling to abide by her decision: "I'd shoot my mother for a million bucks." Only Lucy can stop Roy from taking his share, and she surprises everyone by doing just that, wounding him with her father's gun and then taking him to a hospital.

Jack and Lucy tell each other that they are not the same people they once were, and Lucy adds that they are also not the people they will become. Lucy has evolved from spoiled rich girl to sentimental liberal nun to hardened realist. She helps Jack change from a selfish, immature, uncaring man into someone willing to take a risk for someone other than himself. The end of *Bandits* makes clear that neither has finished evolving.

Jack first sees Lucy at a shelter for the homeless, touching people he considers bums. She speaks of touching lepers in Nicaragua and of Saint Francis of Assisi, her personal saint, kissing a leper's sores. She tries to convince Jack that touching people is the purpose of life. He begins feeling guilty for his indifference to the world around him, but Leonard is careful to make this change gradual and believable.

Leonard makes clear that Jack, Bertie, Wally, and Roy, although they would not agree, are not that much different, that each has chosen to blind himself to certain aspects of life. People are able to do this because they lie to one another and to themselves; they even distort the language to fit their conception of reality. Bertie points out to Wally that the CIA has instructed the Contras "on the selective use of violence to neutralize people against us. What does that mean, neutralize? Your own President Reagan tells us it means, 'Well, you jus' say to the fellow who sitting there in the office, you not in the office anymore.' Isn't that beautiful, he think is so easy."

Theme and plot are secondary to character in an Elmore Leonard novel. Jack works as a protagonist because he is an everyman, someone with an equal number of vices and virtues who would like to make the world a better place as long as he could have fun doing so. Although Leonard has been criticized for his inability to create believable women characters, he succeeds with Lucy. She became a nun because she fell in love with the idea of Saint Francis of Assisi and is perceptive enough to realize that while her feeling for the saint was a teenage crush, it still has some validity. While she has enough insight to recognize that she no longer fits into the Catholic church, she cannot stop living a life based on its values.

The most compelling character in *Bandits* is Franklin de Dios. Seemingly an automaton, Franklin is revealed to be a compassionate man who has resorted to violence as a refuge from a world he does not understand. Bertie and even Wally have convinced him that he is a warrior on the right side in a war against the forces of evil, but he decides there may be more than two sides, that those who allow themselves to see the world in simplistic black-and-white terms are doomed to be exploited by those with wealth and power.

The most praised aspect of Leonard's art is his dialogue. Unlike Ernest Hemingway, he does not write stylized dialogue that merely gives the impression of realism; he tries to re-create the profane, inarticulate, often illogical way people really speak. Each of the characters in *Bandits* uses the language differently, and some are even aware of their usage. Jack becomes angry when Leo Mullen quotes him as having said "punk," a word he says he has never used. Leonard's style can be seen when Roy says to Lucy, "I'll tell you right now, the time comes I see it's a no-win deal, I'm out. I am *sure* not gonna die for a bunch of lepers I don't even know." Leonard has enough insight into the vernacular to realize that the way real people talk is heavily influenced by how television and film characters speak.

The many pleasures of *Bandits* include the seemingly extraneous stories which help to establish character, as with the bizarre circumstances which send Roy Hicks to jail for a crime he has not committed and Cully's account of his absurd attempt to seduce a seventy-five-year-old woman in his nursing home. Leonard also provides the details essential in popular fiction to convince the reader that the author knows what he is writing about, describing how hotel thieves break into occupied rooms, how corpses are embalmed, how newly arrived prisoners can resist the homosexual advances of other inmates.

Leonard's thrillers have been favorably compared to the works of such writers as Dashiell Hammett, Raymond Chandler, James M. Cain, Ross Macdonald, John D. MacDonald, George V. Higgins, and Graham Greene. One additional predecessor to whom he seems to owe a debt is Charles Dickens. Like the nineteenth century Englishman, Leonard writes moral entertainments filled with colorful characters trying to find their way in a corrupt universe. Yet this is a universe, again like that of Dickens, in which good will always triumph over evil.

Michael Adams

Sources for Further Study

The Christian Science Monitor. LXXIX, January 28, 1987, p. 19.
Macleans. C, January 19, 1987, p. 61.
The New York Times. CXXXVI, January 8, 1987, p. 21.
The New York Times Book Review. XCII, January 4, 1987, p. 7.
The New Yorker. LXII, January 19, 1987, p. 94.

Newsweek. CIX, January 5, 1987, p. 58.
The Observer. April 5, 1987, p. 25.
Publishers Weekly. CCXXX, December 12, 1986, p. 40.
Time. CXXIX, January 12, 1987, p. 72.
The Times Literary Supplement. January 9, 1987, p. 36.
USA Today. V, January 2, 1987, p. 50.
The Village Voice. XXXII, February 24, 1987, p. 41.
The Wall Street Journal. CCIX, January 19, 1987, p. 16.
The Washington Post Book World. XVI, December 28, 1986, p. 5.

BECOMING A DOCTOR
A Journey of Initiation in Medical School

Author: Melvin Konner (1946-   )
Publisher: Viking/Elisabeth Sifton Books (New York). 390 pp. $19.95
Type of work: Memoir
Time: 1980-1985
Locale: A teaching hospital in a large city in the United States

Konner, an anthropologist, relates his experiences and observations during the third year of medical school

Principal personage:
MELVIN KONNER, a successful anthropologist who entered medical school in his mid-thirties

Although Melvin Konner gives passing mention to other phases of medical school—the admissions hurdles, the first two years of intensive book learning, dissecting, and physical examinations, and the fourth year of "consolidation, exploration, and thought"—*Becoming a Doctor: A Journey of Initiation in Medical School* concentrates on the student's third year. Konner's reasons for such a concentration are that "the third year is the first of total clinical immersion" and "the year in which the most important phase of socialization is largely completed, when the adoption of the values of physicians is effected." During the third year, the medical student must begin to apply all of his or her previous learning, under the supervision of attending physicians, and to develop a doctor's lifelong skills. This initiation occurs amid the frequently bloody hurly-burly of the clinical setting in a teaching hospital, with the student often suffering from sleep deprivation, poor food, and the pressure of life-and-death situations. The initiation consists of "rotations," stays of from two to eight weeks in each of the main medical specialties—emergency care, anesthesiology, surgery, neurosurgery and neurology, psychiatry, pediatrics, obstetrics, gynecology, pathology, internal medicine, and so forth—corresponding to the hospital's various wards and taking on some of the aspects of Dante's journey through the circles of Hell, Purgatory, and Heaven.

The opening of Dante's *The Divine Comedy*, with its reference to the midpoint of the path of life, is evoked to help explain Konner's motives in undertaking the study of medicine in his mid-thirties, after he had conducted research among the !Kung San (Bushmen) of Africa's Kalahari Desert, taught at Harvard University, and established himself as an anthropologist. How far Konner means the parallel to Dante to apply is uncertain. Dante was lost in a dark wood and threatened by allegorical beasts; although Konner writes vaguely about "having in some important manner lost one's way," he says he was beset only by "an appetite for experience that exceeds the normal restraints of pride." Yet there might be more beasts around than Konner will admit. The word pride is important here, and important to Konner. A few pages later, he confesses that his study of medicine fulfilled a quaint childhood fantasy induced by the cultural environs of his lower-middle-class Jewish neighborhood in Brooklyn, and his book is dedicated to his parents, Hannah Levin Konner and Irving Konner, both of whom "were handicapped by severe hearing impairment."

Konner's justifiable pride here might be touching if it did not possibly reveal a fearsome dybbuk compelling his life. One can also tolerate his bragging about how many top medical schools interviewed him and how his earlier book, *The Tangled Wing: Biological Constraints on the Human Spirit* (1983, published during his third year of medical school), was nominated for a National Book Award. Less tolerable, however, is Konner's overly critical and holier-than-thou attitude toward many of his fellows—medical students, residents, and other doctors—in *Becoming a Doctor*. Most of the medical students and residents were a decade or so younger than Konner, so he should look upon their struggles somewhat kindly and indulgently (an attitude he clearly had toward the patients). Instead, he could be accused of showing some of the same egotism, immaturity, and even vulgarity that he criticizes in others. For example, he escapes from the hospital in order to "taste just a little bit of more or less mature excitement," but "after a couple of drinks" he tells a friend that he suffers from "a new syndrome"— "R.P.T.A., or Rapidly Progressive Testicular Atrophy" (that is, "destruction of the [male] ego"). Such passages make one wonder whether Konner is as much a representative as a critic of the shallow medical mentality that he documents.

Despite these caveats, *Becoming a Doctor* is an important addition to the growing list of recent books by and about doctors. For some general readers it will perhaps have much the same appeal as the television show "St. Elsewhere," with its cast of flawed and zany characters (Konner's more critical portraits tend toward caricature). For premedical students and medical students in their first two years it can also provide a good introduction to the rigors of the third year of medical school—and a break from all those scientific texts. Most significant, however, is its contribution to the current debate about medical care and medical training in the United States.

Konner comes down strongly on the side of those who believe that the more medicine has advanced, the more impersonal and dehumanized (not to mention expensive) it has grown. In this view, the fascinating new knowledge, techniques, and machines have distanced doctors from their patients, breaking down the traditional relationship and the caring attitude that, to Konner and many others, are the essence of medical practice. Then there are the medical students, faced with the monumental task (generally judged impossible) of committing this ever-growing body of knowledge to memory; thus, the brutal demands of medical school are dehumanizing and alienating in themselves. Finally, students and doctors must face the frustrating realization that, despite all the advances, a yawning gulf of ignorance still confronts the medical profession—about such matters as the brain, psychological disorders, cancer, and Acquired Immune Deficiency Syndrome (AIDS).

From this point of view, the medical profession is in crisis, as its representatives in *Becoming a Doctor* tend to illustrate. Competence and even brilliance are the rule at "world-famous" Flexner School of Medicine (Konner attended Harvard Medical School but has fictionalized the names of places and people) and Galen Memorial Hospital, but both students and doctors nevertheless are frequently working at the limits of their knowledge. The students and residents also suffer from the fatigue and sleeplessness of their long shifts. Of greatest concern, however, are the attitudes and values expressed by many of the doctors and captured in "A Glossary of House Officer Slang" at the end (for example, "crispy critters" means badly burned children). Egotism and arrogance, often combined with ignorance, are much in evidence. Two of the most obnoxious exemplars are Marty Wentworth, the chief surgical resident, who drives, insults, and intimidates the students and other residents under him, and Sally Brass, the resident in internal medicine who keeps Konner from sleeping, criticizes him until he suffers from R.P.T.A., and orders him to perform a dangerous procedure on a patient that she is afraid to do. Other residents are neutral or uncaring toward patients, poking fun at them behind their backs and mocking a doctor who sheds tears over one. Konner sums up doctors by describing them as "eternal adolescents." How did such people ever get into medical school, or how did medical school ever produce such people?

One solution to the problem is a more humanistic medical education, which Konner proposes. At present the typical premedical student is an overachiever drilled in the sciences. Then in current medical training almost all the emphasis is on technical know-how and expertise, little on the human dimension. More room needs to be made in premedical studies for the humanities, and medical schools need to put more stress on the ethical, emotional, and social aspects of medicine. Computers might replace memorization and help provide some of the necessary room for such changes. Meanwhile, until such changes come about, Konner has decided not to pursue a residency; after receiving his M.D. degree in 1985, he returned to teaching anthropology.

Harold Branam

Sources for Further Study

Booklist. LXXXIII, July, 1987, p. 1636.
Chicago Tribune. September 7, 1987, IV, p. 3.

Library Journal. CXII, September 1, 1987, p. 171.
New England Journal of Medicine. CCCXVIII, January 14, 1988, p. 125.
The New York Review of Books. XXXIV, September 24, 1987, p. 6.
The New York Times Book Review. XCII, July 26, 1987, p. 1.
Publishers Weekly. CCXXXI, June 12, 1987, p. 79.
The Washington Post Book World. XVII, October 25, 1987, p. 8.
Wilson Library Bulletin. LXII, November, 1987, p. 83.

BEFORE THE DAWN

Author: Tōson Shimazaki (1872-1943)
First Published: Yo-ake Mae, 1929-1935
Translated from the Japanese by William E. Naff
Publisher: University of Hawaii Press (Honolulu). 798 pp. $30.00
Type of work: Historical novel
Time: 1853-1876
Locale: The village of Magome in the mountains of central Japan, Tokyo, and other
locations

*The novel provides a gripping account, centering on the life and career of Hanzō
Aoyama, of the vast changes that came to Japan, politically, culturally, and spiritually,
through the intrusion of the West into the life of a society that had been secluded since
the 1600's*

> *Principal characters:*
> HANZŌ AOYAMA, the headman of Magome village
> KICHIZAEMON, his father
> OTAMI, Hanzo's wife

Despite a formidable reputation as a premier novelist of prewar Japan,
Tōson Shimazaki has remained largely unknown to Western readers, as his
novels, always lengthy and complex, have daunted the enthusiasm of potential translators. This fine English version of his most significant and longest
work of fiction presents the author's compelling vision of the Westernization
of his country. *Before the Dawn* has long assumed the status of a modern
classic in Japan.

Tōson, as he is usually called in Japan, was a prolific writer, and *Before
the Dawn* took him many years to compose. The work first appeared in a
monthly journal, in segments printed between 1929 and 1935. Tōson revised
it for publication in book form; book 1 appeared in 1932 and book 2 in
1935. Tōson was already a famous writer when he undertook this tremendous effort, and the publication was to cap his long and distinguished
career. He was the son of an important village official who lived on the old
Kiso road, an important mountain artery in the Tokugawa period (1600-
1868) that connected this remote area to the major road networks near what
is now the modern city of Nagoya. Tōson was able to use his family history
as background for the novel, but his career took many twists and turns
before he would return to the subject of his own childhood.

Tōson spent his formative years in Tokyo, where he came in contact with
new movements in Western literature and thought. His first great work of
fiction was published in 1906, the epoch-making novel *Hakai* (1906; *The
Broken Commandment*, 1974). In this story, Tōson's sense of the social and
spiritual tensions in contemporary Japanese society were encapsulated in his
account of a young teacher of the *eta* or outcast class, who faced bravely the
hypocrisy of the world around him. Tōson's next novels, such as *Haru* (1908;

spring) and *Ie* (1911; *The Family*, 1976), began to draw more specifically on his own personal experiences. In 1913, Tōson went to France; after he returned to Japan during World War I, he published one of his most striking works, *Shinsei* (1919; new life), a lightly disguised account of his own spiritual rebirth in a European setting.

Tōson was a lively correspondent with readers in Japan during his time in Paris, writing with insight and vigor of the artistic and intellectual brilliance he found in Europe's "capital of light." At the same time, however, his inevitable and growing sense of isolation and loneliness in an alien culture led him, as his diaries and other writings indicate, to reflect both on his own personal past and on the recent past of his own country, which had changed so remarkably since the coming of the Americans and the Europeans in the 1850's and after. It was without question this extended trip outside his own cultural milieu that led Tōson to contemplate the composition of a narrative to describe the significance of Japan's recent experiences on both a human and a national scale. Once home, Tōson undertook a considerable amount of research in order to reconstruct the kind of life his father had led, an existence that by the late 1920's seemed almost impossibly remote. In a sense, Tōson was attempting to catch and record a last glimpse of the past before it slipped away forever.

In *Before the Dawn*, Tōson combined his ability to express larger social concerns, as he had done in *The Broken Commandment*, with his skills in delineating the personal, interior life of his major characters, an ability the novelist had perfected in his later novels. Tōson chose as the main focus of a complicated story his loving recreation of his father in the character Hanzō, who like his father, had witnessed and been afflicted by the vast changes that had come to Japan in the latter part of the nineteenth century. As the story progresses, Tōson moves relentlessly back and forth from Hanzō's small, personal world to the larger stage of the shifting society, juxtaposing personal and national responses to the coming of the West. In this layering, Tōson is quite skillful, so that one level helps to illustrate and explicate the other. Hanzō's sympathies for the poor farmers in whose midst he lives, and his distaste for the old and decaying feudal system, make him an advocate for what he perceives will be changes for the better. Yet eventually Hanzō is to be betrayed by the new order as well.

In re-creating the mental world that Hanzō inhabits, Tōson sketches in great detail the intellectual debates of the day in order to show how powerful the commitments were on all sides. Hanzō's father, Kichizaemon, is a firm believer in the virtues of the hereditary Tokugawa shogunate, the samurai bureaucracy that has ruled the country in the emperor's name since 1600. Hanzō, on the other side, feels that the whole feudal enterprise has failed. He subscribes to the beliefs developed by the school of National Learning, which emphasizes the importance of the ancient direct rule by the emperor and the simpler, more open virtues of ancient times. When the shogunate collapses under its own weight, is dissolved, and the Emperor takes political power in 1868, not much more than a decade after the American Commodore Matthew Perry and his black ships appeared on the scene to force commercial treaties on the Japanese, Hanzō and those who share his views are filled with profound joy. As the narrative continues, however, Hanzō's hopes are slowly, inexorably destroyed. Rather than restoring ancient Japanese virtues, the new society that springs up around him seems altogether bent on material gain. Hanzō's own idealistic beliefs mean little among a new breed of greedy men who have little understanding of the significance of tradition, personal ties, and self-sacrifice. For Hanzō, the implicit doctrine of the survival of the fittest that he sees acted out all around him brings first a personal sense of pain and then more serious dislocations.

The early scenes of the novel are set in Hanzō's remote village in the mountains. He must thus learn of the various wrenching changes that come to his society through secondhand accounts told to him by friends or travelers. This structure allows Tōson to write at length about the larger issues with which Japan was grappling during that period. Some of these narrative sections, such as the lengthy soliloquies on French classical drama, occasionally seem to suggest that the real excitement is offstage, but the composite picture these incidents provide remains remarkably compelling.

Caught up in these changes, with the fall of one system of government, the outbreak of local rebellions, and the creation of a new kind of bureaucracy aimed at creating a Japan at parity with the West and its perceived values, Hanzō can scarcely keep pace with or understand his own shifting reactions. He clearly does not understand many of the people who surround him, particularly in the latter sections of the novel, when he travels to Tokyo in an attempt to find a place for himself in the new world being created there. The doggedly idealistic Hanzō, faced with so many difficulties, becomes prey to melancholia. He begins to drink to excess and slowly moves from the status of an eccentric to that of a madman. Finally, back in his native village and in disgrace, Hanzō is locked up in a woodshed, like some wounded King Lear, where he dies. The year is 1886.

For all the cumulative power conveyed to the reader by Tōson's account of the trajectory of Hanzō's life, the book has other focuses as well. In particular, some of the set pieces, such as those describing the battles during the last days of the Tokugawa shogunate, provide a wealth of specific detail that will recall to many readers the kind of loving and painstaking research that Leo Tolstoy put into the composition of the historical frescoes that crown *War and Peace*. Too, Tōson's ability to portray the clash of ideas and ideologies in terms of human response allows even the reader who may be a newcomer to the sometimes competing concepts of Buddhism, Confucianism, and the National Learning movement to grasp their significance and their differences, at least in terms of the human dimension.

Perhaps only a novel written with this much care, and this much controlled passion, can make the realities of this complex and crucial period in Japan so alive and so compelling for Western readers, who are unfamiliar with the intricate ideological and cultural issues involved. The roots of contemporary Japanese attitudes toward the West, and toward Japan itself, are beautifully articulated in this novel. As the complex of facts that helped create them have slipped away from the memories of younger Japanese, many readers there, since the publication of *Before the Dawn*, have come to form their own sense of the period and what has happened since through their perusal of this dark and thoughtful account. Tōson's greatest qualities as a writer—his simplicity and sobriety—are well-employed in this final homage to his family and their generation. Long, sprawling, occasionally unfocused, *Before the Dawn* is as real as life itself. Reading the book in William Naff's crisp and eloquent translation can provide a unique glimpse into a moment of time and complex opportunity that is still felt to be central in the minds and hearts of the Japanese. The story is one that should concern Westerners as well, who opened Japan and continue to be intimately involved in that country's story.

J. Thomas Rimer

Sources for Further Study

The New York Times Book Review. XCII, October 18, 1987, p. 44.
The New Yorker. LXIII, August 3, 1987, p. 72.
Publishers Weekly. CCXXXI, June 26, 1987, p. 58.
The Times Literary Supplement. January 1, 1988, p. 14.
The Washington Post Book World. XVII, August 23, 1987, p. 11.

BELOVED

Author: Toni Morrison (1931-   )
Publisher: Alfred A. Knopf (New York). 275 pp. $18.95
Type of work: Novel
Time: 1855-1874
Locale: The outskirts of Cincinnati, Ohio

Two former slaves struggle to come to terms with their past

> Principal characters:
> SETHE, the mother of four, a former slave
> PAUL D, her friend, a former slave
> DENVER, her younger daughter
> BELOVED, her older daughter
> BABY SUGGS, her mother-in-law

A child who has suffered a violent death haunts the house where her grandmother, mother, brothers, and sister live. The grandmother dies; the brothers disappear; the mother takes a lover; the sister grows up. The ghost grows up too, assumes a human form, and seduces and drives away the lover. Then she takes possession of the mother. So might run a plot summary of Toni Morrison's fifth novel, *Beloved*. Yet *Beloved* is no ordinary ghost story. Brilliant, complex, haunted and haunting, it is a remarkable event in American fiction. With the stark, cathartic power of Greek tragedy, *Beloved* compels attention, on an intimate and personal scale, to the "Sixty Million and more" victims of slavery to whom the book is dedicated.

Morrison's principal character is Sethe, a former slave. In 1873, when the novel opens, Sethe is living with her eighteen-year-old daughter Denver on the outskirts of Cincinnati. Sethe works as a cook in a restaurant, but Denver never leaves the house, which, the reader is matter-of-factly informed, is haunted by the ghost of Denver's sister, a baby whose throat was cut when she was not quite two. The dead baby's tombstone reads, simply, "Beloved," one of the two words Sethe remembers from her daughter's funeral sermon; she paid for the inscription by having sex at the grave with the stone-carver. Over the years, Sethe and Denver have uneasily adjusted to the disappearance of Howard and Buglar, Sethe's sons, and to the death of Baby Suggs, her mother-in-law; they have also learned to live with the ghost's spiteful visitations. Then Paul D appears. Also a former slave, Paul D lived at the Kentucky farm called Sweet Home from which he and Sethe both escaped before the beginning of the Civil War. The two have not seen each other since the night the Sweet Home slaves tried to run. Each knows details about the escape of which the other is ignorant, and this knowledge, along with their shared history at Sweet Home, pulls them together. "The kind of man who could walk into a house and make the women cry," Paul D moves into Sethe's life, confronts Denver's jealousy, and, with great dispatch, exorcises the dead baby's ghost.

Since their terrifying escape from Sweet Home and its brutal aftermath, both Sethe and Paul D have "worked hard to remember as close to nothing as was safe," but in each other's presence their stories are slowly and inexorably revealed. Sethe comes to feel that "her story was bearable because it was his as well—to tell, to refine and tell again. The things neither knew about the other—the things neither had word-shapes for—well, it would come in time." By the end of the book, Sethe and Paul D know everything, and so does the reader. Faithful to the complex processes of what Sethe calls "rememory," Morrison's method of unfolding her story bit by bit and her use of multiple points of view produces a relentless tension—in the reader, as well as in Sethe and Paul D—between the hunger to know what has happened to the Sweet Home slaves and an equally urgent desire to avoid that terrible knowledge. Sethe's and Paul D's reluctant yet insistent storytelling makes *Beloved* both excruciating to read and impossible to put down.

If Paul D's dominant trait is his ability to stir women's deepest feelings, Sethe's is a maternal love so tender and fierce that it defies rationality. The context for her maternity is the slaveowners' practice of breeding slaves as though they were animals and separating families so that slave parents were deprived of knowledge of their own children. "Men and women were moved around like checkers," Morrison reminds her readers; "anybody Baby Suggs knew, let alone loved, who hadn't run off or been hanged, got rented out, loaned out, bought up, brought back, stored up, mortgaged, won, stolen or seized." Paul D cannot recall his mother, has never seen his father. Baby Suggs has known only one of her eight children as an adult. Sethe remembers the wet nurse who took her mother's place, remembers too the hanging of her mother, who disposed of all of her children but Sethe because they were fathered by white men. At Sweet Home, Sethe's unusually enlightened owners, the Garners, allow her to marry and to remain with her husband and growing family. When Mr. Garner dies, however, Sweet Home is taken over by a new master, called "schoolteacher," who treats the slaves with cold cruelty. They decide to try to escape. At the appointed time, Sethe loads her sons and unweaned daughter onto a wagon, promising to get to them as soon as she can. Barefoot, pregnant with her fourth child, suffering from a savage beating, separated from her husband and from the other escaping slaves, Sethe gives birth on her way to Ohio and manages to get to her mother-in-law's house in time to resume nursing her older daughter as well as the newborn Denver. Miraculously, she has milk enough for both. For a month she enjoys friends, her mother-in-law, and her children and begins "claiming ownership of [her] freed self." Then schoolteacher appears to take the fugitive Sethe and her children back to Sweet Home, and Sethe, certain that death is better than life in slavery, commits the only act she is sure will keep herself and her children free: "I took and put my babies where they'd be safe."

In the course of the novel's long opening section, Morrison makes Sethe's violence against her children entirely comprehensible. At the end of that section, when Paul D learns what Sethe has done, he moves out of the house, leaving Sethe and Denver with the mysterious young woman who has come to live with them at about the time of Paul D's arrival. The woman calls herself Beloved, and Denver is convinced that she is the grown-up embodiment of her dead sister. Sethe is slower to recognize Beloved, but once her lover is gone, she perceives the truth. Becoming absorbed in this daughter who has come back from the dead, this daughter with whom she need no longer remember anything because Beloved knows it all already, Sethe loses her job and, eventually, her senses. By the end of part 2, which includes a series of luminous interior meditations on possession, the three women have closed their door against the world, "locked in a love that wore everybody out." In the third section, Beloved's insatiable craving for her mother threatens to consume Sethe completely: "Beloved ate up her life, took it, swelled up with it, grew taller on it. And the older woman yielded it up without a murmur." Denver realizes that she must somehow rescue her mother from her ghost-sister, and her courage brings the novel to its moving and satisfying conclusion.

As characters, Paul D, Denver, Beloved, and especially "quiet, queenly" Sethe, her dark eyes so unwilling to see that they have the blank, stylized look of African or Greek sculpture, are completely convincing. Equally vivid are the many characters whom Sethe and Paul D remember, but who are now dead or missing. Each of these also has a story as startling as those of the foreground characters. Among the most memorable of these figures are Sethe's mother-in-law Baby Suggs, the expert cobbler deemed "holy" because once freed, she is called to help other former slaves experience their freedom; Halle, Sethe's husband, who works extra hours and days to buy his mother's freedom from the Garners and who is driven mad by what happens to Sethe during the escape attempt; Sixo, the Sweet Home slave who walks thirty miles to see the woman he loves and whose flame-red tongue, indigo skin, and dying laugh Paul D cannot forget. Even the house where Sethe and Denver live, "peopled by the living activity of the dead," takes on a vigorous human personality that varies with the mood of the ghost who haunts it.

The house belongs to the Bodwins, white abolitionists who allow Baby Suggs and then Sethe and her children to live there rent-free. Although the Bodwins' generosity to freed and escaped slaves is legendary, they keep an open-mouthed pickaninny figurine, labeled "At Yo Service," at their back door. Like the Garners, who "ran a special kind of slavery, treating [the slaves] like paid labor, listening to what they said, teaching what they wanted known," the Bodwins, though relatively admirable, are portrayed with serious reservations. Amy Denver, a white woman with good hands, is less objectionable; she tends Sethe's wounded back and ruined feet and helps her give birth to the daughter who bears her name. Then there is schoolteacher, who runs Sweet Home after Mr. Garner dies and who uses ink Sethe herself has made to record her animal characteristics, and there are schoolteacher's nephews, boys with mossy teeth who hold Sethe down and steal her milk. For a time, Sethe thinks that she can discriminate among whites, but experience teaches her that

> anybody white could take your whole self for anything that came to mind. Not just work, kill, or maim you, but dirty you. Dirty you so bad you couldn't like yourself any more. Dirty you so bad you forgot who you were and couldn't think it up.

Despite the punishing difficulty of its subject matter, *Beloved* leaves an impression less of anger than of profound astonishment—at the stunning cruelty of slavery, at the death-defying endurance of love, at the sharp beauty of the natural world. Morrison's style in this book, as in her other novels, combines the magic of Afro-American idiom, the density of poetry, and the speed of the plainest prose; she has never written better. Over and over, her words "say things that are pictures." Here is her description of a turnip: "A prettier thing God never made. White and purple with a tender tail and a hard head. Feels good when you hold it in your hand and smells like the creek when it floods, bitter but happy." Her figurative language is often extravagant and daring: There are "berries that tasted like church," "winter stars, close enough to lick," "a dress so loud it embarrassed the needlepoint chair seat." Her use of color is sometimes precisely literal, as with Paul D's "peachstone" skin, and sometimes symbolic, as with any occurrence of red, Beloved's color. The tree-shaped scar on Sethe's back, the scar which Paul D caresses and which Sethe has never seen, symbolizes her "sorrow, the roots of it; its wide trunk and intricate branches."

Written with such generosity and intensity that the reader more than willingly suspends disbelief, Morrison's ghost story about Sethe's love and grief stands for the sixty million and more untold—perhaps untellable—stories that Americans black and white must hear. *Beloved* is a rich, intricate, and liberating book that leaves a permanent mark on the mind and heart. One can only be grateful to Toni Morrison for this magnificent gift.

Carolyn Wilkerson Bell

Sources for Further Study

Booklist. LXXXIII, July, 1987, p. 1627.
The Christian Science Monitor. October 5, 1987, p. 20.
Commonweal. CXIV, November 6, 1987, p. 631.

Kirkus Reviews. LV, July 15, 1987, p. 1023.
Library Journal. CXII, September 1, 1987, p. 201.
Los Angeles Times Book Review. August 30, 1987, p. 1.
The Nation. CCXLV, October 17, 1987, p. 418.
The New Republic. CXCVII, October 19, 1987, p. 38.
The New York Times Book Review. XCII, September 13, 1987, p. 1.
The New Yorker. LXIII, November 2, 1987, p. 175.
Time. CXXX, September 21, 1987, p. 75.
The Times Literary Supplement. October 16, 1987, p. 1135.
USA Today. V, September 4, 1987, p. 6D.

BEN-GURION
The Burning Ground, 1886-1948

Author: Shabtai Teveth (1926-   )
Publisher: Houghton Mifflin Co. (Boston). Illustrated. 967 pp. $35.00
Type of work: Biography
Time: 1886-1948
Locale: Europe, the United States, and Palestine

A detailed, carefully crafted, and politically revealing biography of the man who became the first prime minister of Israel

> *Principal personages:*
> DAVID GRUEN, who took the name David Ben-Gurion
> PAULA MUNWEIS BEN-GURION, his wife
> CHAIM WEIZMANN, a moderate Zionist leader and his political rival
> VLADIMIR JABOTINSKI, the radical leader of Revisionist Zionism

David Joseph Gruen was born in the Polish village of Plonsk in 1886. His family lived on the edge of poverty, but they had ambition. His father earned a living as a writer of petitions, who knew how to mediate between the local Jews and the czarist authorities. David liked to think that his father had been a lawyer. As a small boy, David quickly proved that his large head was capable of great intellectual feats. His mother, a pious soul, wanted him to become a rabbi, while his father, who was less devout, hoped that he would be a doctor. David wanted to study law.

First and foremost, however, he saw himself as a Zionist. The Hebrew language was the key to forming a Jewish nation, he believed, and though he developed fluency in a half dozen languages over his eighty-seven years, secular modern Hebrew was his favorite. He joined Poale Zion, a Marxist Zionist party, when he was nineteen, and by the time he was twenty he was in Palestine, combining the life of a laborer with that of a political activist. As a pen name he used Ben-Gurion, a name which recalled a renowned defense minister in Jerusalem during the Jewish struggle against the Roman Empire. In 1948, David Ben-Gurion would be the defense minister of the new Israel which declared its independence of the British Empire.

Ben-Gurion's political development went through many stages, as Shabtai Teveth, a well-respected Israeli journalist and political analyst, shows. Whether Ben-Gurion's policy was pro-Turkish, pro-British, anti-British, pro-American, or anti-German, however, it was always dedicated to the establishment of a free and strong state of Israel. Zionism was for him not an abstract wish, but an urgent necessity. He believed that the ground was "burning" beneath the feet of the Jews of the diaspora and that only the creation of a Jewish homeland would permit their ultimate salvation. Whatever his political conflicts with Jews or Gentiles, and they were many and vigorous, this goal of the foundation of Israel was always foremost in his mind.

The present account, though theoretically covering the period up to the founding of the Israeli state in 1948, actually ends with events of 1944, with the following few years covered only in an impressionistic epilogue. A full treatment of Ben-Gurion and the Israeli state must await a further volume. Here, the complex and carefully documented story of Ben-Gurion as a man and a political leader revolves around his relationships with three men, two of whom were fellow Zionists and one of whom was the dictator of Nazi Germany. These relationships were totally interwoven, at least during the period between 1933 and 1945, but for the purposes of analysis they are best examined one at a time.

Chaim Weizmann, like Ben-Gurion, was born and reared in Russian Poland. Having left the country to pursue his education, he became a leader of the Zionist movement and one of the founding fathers of Israel. Despite these similarities to Ben-Gurion, there were many differences between them, both personal and political. While Ben-Gurion's academic career was never successful, Weizmann became a successful chemist, with a position of modest wealth and social prestige in Great Britain. When they first met, just after World War I, Weizmann was already renowned as the leader of Zionism; he had excellent connections to the British establishment. Because of the Balfour Declaration on a Jewish homeland and the British Mandate in Palestine, such connections to those in power in London were precisely what Zionism needed. Ben-Gurion, on the other hand, was but a private in the Jewish battalion of the British army, a labor leader with a few publications to his credit, and a rough-and-ready agitator for the cause.

Their relationship, which continued through the founding of Israel a generation later, was a productive one, but it was almost always filled with storm and stress. In order to maintain some semblance of unity in the face of common perils, much of the stormy nature of this relationship was kept behind closed doors, papered over by compromises and public professions of mutual respect and good will. Teveth, excellent historian that he is, does not hold back the details of the behind-the-scenes conflicts between these men. Though he clearly is sympathetic to Ben-Gurion's position in the politics of the time, he is scrupulously fair in setting forth the content and the private rhetoric of the struggles. In 1936, for example, when the dreadful nature of Nazism was beginning to become apparent and when the British seemed about to renege on earlier promises to the Zionists in order to appease the Arab population of the Middle East, Ben-Gurion was mightily displeased with the moderate stance of Weizmann. "Weizmann is no statesman," Ben-Gurion stated at a closed political committee meeting. He later complained that "every mistake of Weizmann's has become a destructive force for the Zionist movement." Teveth sums up Ben-Gurion's views in a chapter entitled "Weizmann: A Danger to Zionism." During World War II, Ben-Gurion found it increasingly difficult to work under Weizmann's titular leadership, and in 1946 he had Weizmann removed from the presidency of the Zionist organization. Yet through the many crises, they were able to work together, and they emerged in final triumph as prime minister and as president of the new Israeli state.

If Weizmann was too moderate and too aristocratic for Ben-Gurion, Vladimir Jabotinski was too radical and violent. Taking his cue from Benito Mussolini's Fascist Party, during the 1920's Jabotinski set about creating marching and fighting units which would aggressively defend Jewish interests in Palestine against the Arabs and the British alike. Ben-Gurion's rejection of this approach was based in part on his commitment to the socialist ideas of his Labor Zionism and in part on the moral and practical belief that the Jews had far more to gain by peaceable expansion and settlement than by fighting the Arabs stone for stone. In contrast to his attempts to keep his struggle with Weizmann out of the limelight, Ben-Gurion was public and forthright in his denunciation of Jabotinski and the Revisionist Party. He did his utmost to advocate and enforce a policy of restraint against Arab attackers, even during the major disturbances of the 1930's, while Jabotinski took the more popular road of calling for retaliation. In exasperation, Ben-Gurion eventually went so far as to refer publicly to the Revisionists as "Nazis."

With the coming of World War II and the death of the flamboyant Jabotinski, this phase of the internal struggle among Zionists faded. Still, the subsequent history of Israel and its relationship to Palestinian Arabs shows that the conflict between the advocates of restraint, such as Ben-Gurion, and the advocates of aggressive reprisals, such as Jabotinski, would have continuing significance.

In 1933, shortly after Adolf Hitler took power in Germany, Ben-Gurion bought a copy of *Mein Kampf* (1925-1926) and read it cover to cover. Thereafter, he knew that his concept of a "burning ground" beneath the feet of European Jewry was no mere metaphor. While large numbers of Jews, including the majority of those in German-speaking lands, clung to the ideal of assimilation, Ben-Gurion believed that the possibility of such policies was past. After the brutal violence of Kristallnacht (the riotous night of broken glass in Germany) in 1938, and the weak and uncaring response of the Western Powers to calls that German Jews be allowed a place of safe haven, Ben-Gurion realized that time was very short. If Hitler succeeded in dominating Europe, the destruction of European Jewry was sure to follow.

Yet Ben-Gurion's policies, both long- and short-term, seemed always to be directed toward the goal of the creation of Israel rather than toward the more immediate goal of rescuing the suffering. At times he even spoke as if he welcomed the persecution of his fellow Jews, because it simply proved his case that Israel was a necessity, thus bringing its realization closer. In October, 1941, in a public speech, he said,

This is our Zionist message: to pour the Jewish disaster into the molds of redemption. . . . We have strength. . . . A great disaster means strength. An idea can spark disaster into redemption, can turn the disaster of millions into the redemption of millions.

Teveth devotes a full chapter to an attempt to determine whether such statements were really as opportunistic as they sound on first hearing. The Zionist leader's philosophy of "beneficial disaster," as Teveth calls it, was based on Ben-Gurion's inability to comprehend that the Holocaust was actually in progress. In retrospect, historians and political leaders know that Hitler meant what he said and that he had given orders to carry out his genocidal goals. The firing squads and the gas chambers were at work, even as Ben-Gurion spoke. At the time, however, even so well-informed and patriotic a man as Ben-Gurion could not comprehend that Nazi policies were going well beyond the level of persecution which the Jewish people had been forced to endure in years past. Only in 1944, when the evidence was overwhelming, did Ben-Gurion realize that the slaughter was unlimited and that immediate rescue had to take precedence over the goal of creating a new state.

Throughout his political career, Ben-Gurion was willing to work with opposing forces when it seemed necessary or useful to the realization of his goal. During World War I, he at first thought that the Jews of Palestine should support the Turks, and he even volunteered to join the Turkish army to prove his loyalty and to gain leverage with the Turks, whom he expected to win the war. Luckily for him, perhaps, the Turks arrested him and expelled him to British Egypt. Eventually, his application of the same logic led him to throw in his lot with the British. Similarly, he was always willing to work with political rivals, whether in Palestine, in Great Britain, on the Continent, or in the United States, if it would further his cause.

It would be quite incorrect to see this policy as unprincipled opportunism. Rather, it was a kind of Bismarckian realistic politics. Like the Iron Chancellor who unified Germany in the nineteenth century, Ben-Gurion realized that he had to keep many options open for himself and his political movement. No one could be sure exactly how events would turn. The Jews in Palestine were technically in a position of great weakness, and Ben-Gurion knew that only by manipulating superior forces could he move toward his goal. When the British, at one point during the 1930's, appeared on the verge of partitioning Palestine between Jews and Arabs, Ben-Gurion saw that it might be necessary to support that policy as a first step toward a viable Israeli state. His attitude toward the Arabs was never naïve or pacifist, but he realized that if he were an Arab, he too would look with dismay on the loss of his homeland to another people. He continuously advocated a policy of restraint and understanding toward the Arabs, even while planning for an eventual Jewish majority. When the British produced their 1939 White Paper, which gave in to virtually all Arab demands and would have nearly eliminated future Jewish immigration to the area, he vigorously opposed the new policy, announcing that the Jews would fight it by force if necessary. Yet, as soon as World War II began, he realized that the British were fighting the Nazis and must be supported in that endeavor. He announced the policy of "war against Hitler as though there were no White Paper, and war against the White Paper as though there were no Hitler." The policy was logically inconsistent, yet magnificently Bismarckian in its subtlety. Eventually, it worked.

Though aspects of this book will undoubtedly be controversial for years to come, Teveth has done a great service by producing such a comprehensive, balanced, and moving work on this important leader. Readers will be looking forward to the second volume with anticipation.

Gordon R. Mork

Sources for Further Study

Booklist. LXXXIII, June 1, 1987, p. 1489.
Choice. XXV, November, 1987, p. 535.
The Economist. CCCIV, August 29, 1987, p. 81.
Kirkus Reviews. LV, May 1, 1987, p. 709.
Library Journal. CXII, July, 1987, p. 74.
The New Republic. CXCVI, June 8, 1987, p. 48.
The New York Times Book Review. XCII, June 21, 1987, p. 3.
Publishers Weekly. CCXXXI, April 17, 1987, p. 60.
The Washington Post Book World. XVII, July 5, 1987, p. 8.

BERLIN DIARIES, 1940-1945

Author: Marie Vassiltchikov (1917-1978)
Edited, with a foreword and an epilogue, by George Vassiltchikov
Publisher: Alfred A. Knopf (New York). Illustrated. 324 pp. $19.95
Type of work: Diary
Time: 1940-1945
Locale: Germany

A diary of life in Germany during World War II

> *Principal personages:*
> PRINCESS MARIE "MISSIE" VASSILTCHIKOV, diarist
> PRINCESS TATIANA VASSILTCHIKOV, her sister
> PRINCE PAUL VON METTERNICH-WINNEBURG, her brother-in-law,
> Tatiana Vassiltchikov's husband
> ADAM VON TROTT ZU STOLZ, her friend and an anti-Hitler
> conspirator
> PRINCESS ELEANORE-MARIE "LOREMARIE" VON SCHÖNBURG-
> HARTENSTEIN, her best friend

Marie "Missie" Vassiltchikov was, to use one of Adolf Hitler's favorite epithets, a rootless cosmopolitan. She was born into an aristocratic Russian family just months before the Russian Revolution in 1917. Her family fled the Bolsheviks in 1919 and wandered from Germany to France, where she went to school, and then to Lithuania, where they owned property. In the summer of 1939, Vassiltchikov and her sister Tatiana, visited family friends in Silesia and were still there when the Nazi-Soviet pact of August 23, 1939, suddenly threatened the independence of Lithuania and opened the door to the joint Nazi-Soviet invasion of Poland. Under these circumstances, it was not advisable for White Russians to return to Lithuania, and Missie and Tatiana decided to move to Berlin in search of work. It was at this time that Missie began writing her diary. Her ability to speak Russian, French, English, and German landed her a job, first at the German broadcasting service, and then with the foreign ministry's information service. There she became intimate with some foreign office members of the conspiracy against Hitler which culminated in the attempt to kill him on July 20, 1944. Loyalty to the conspirators held her in Berlin, where she endured some of the worst bombing of the war, until September, 1944. She then moved to Vienna and endured more bombing raids, barely escaping the advancing Soviets at the war's end.

The diary is not complete. Wartime conditions resulted in the loss or destruction of parts, but most of the diary, including the critical year of 1944, survived. As the July 20 plot neared its execution, Vassiltchikov began to keep the diary in a shorthand intelligible only to her. She wrote up this section immediately after the war in 1945 and also retyped the entire diary. Although an occasional hint of a 1945 perspective sneaks into the diary, Missie's brother, George Vassiltchikov, reports that she made a conscious effort both then and in the 1970's, when she was finally persuaded to prepare her diary for publication, to maintain the integrity of the diary as a contemporary account. No one who reads the diary will doubt that she remained faithful to its truth. After her death in 1978, George ably edited the diary and saw it through to publication.

As a refugee in wartime Germany, Missie was doubly an outsider. She was a foreigner in a Germany gone mad on nationalism and an aristocrat in a totalitarian regime bent on leveling German society into a common *Volk*. Vassiltchikov wrote her diary in English, a language she learned as a child in the nursery, thus preserving the vantage point of an outsider even in the language of her personal diary. Although she was an outsider in Germany, her aristocratic birth gave her an entrée into German aristocratic society, and it was this connection which drew this outsider into the inner circle of the conspiracy against Hitler.

The aristocratic world in which Missie Vassiltchikov moved, however, was crumbling. Famous names people her diary. Prince Paul von Metternich-Winneburg married Tatiana Vassiltchikov in 1941. Missie attended a dazzling wedding of a Hohenzollern (the Catholic, Swabian branch of the family) at Sigmaringen Castle in 1942. She became friends with Gottfried von Bismarck. None of these scions of famous families was a powerful person. Indeed, their aristocratic status automatically made them suspect in Nazi Germany. They tried to maintain the urbane life of high society as the bombs rained down, as food was rationed, as water and electricity were cut off. By 1945, there were such severe food shortages that Vassiltchikov literally went hungry, but even then her life was punctuated by an occasional sumptuous meal. Thanks to the conquest of France, champagne supplies remained abundant, and oysters were one of the few unrationed food items. Thus Vassiltchikov was able to attend pleasant soirees at such salons as that maintained by Friedrich "Freddie" Horstmann, an art collector and diplomat who had been forced out of the foreign service because his wife was Jewish. At the Horstmanns', one could escape from that strange Nazi mixture of barbarism and philistinism into a world of high art and good manners. Freddie Horstmann's country house was later bombed, but he managed to preserve some of his art collection until the war ended. Trying to protect what remained, he refused to flee as the Soviets advanced into Germany. He was soon arrested; he starved to death in an East German concentration camp. Many of Vassiltchikov's friends met similar fates.

Although the aristocratic class to which Missie Vassiltchikov belonged may offend some American sensibilities, one can only admire the calm stoicism with which she endured the destruction of her way of life. There is no complaining in her diary, no handwringing lamentation of a passing age. Perhaps she was too young for that. She simply relates with mounting effect the events as they occur, so that by the time the reader has reached the end of the diary, any thought that she might be something of a lightweight has dissipated, and one is instead filled with admiration of her courage and dignity under the most trying circumstances.

The diary reveals a remarkably clearheaded and objective mind. Vassiltchikov had friends and relatives on all sides of the war. Although she could not abide the Nazis and apparently had no close friends who were sympathetic to them, many friends did fight in the German army, including her brother-in-law Paul von Metternich, and several of them died. She especially liked German air ace Prince Heinrich zu Sayn Wittgenstein and took his death very hard. Her cousin, Prince Ivan "Jim" Viazemsky fought in the French army, was captured in the Battle of France in 1940, and spent the rest of the war in a German prisoner-of-war camp. Her older sister, Irena, lived in Rome and spent the war there. Her brother, George, spent most of the war in Paris, where he became involved with the French Resistance. Some close friends were killed when the French Resistance blew up their train. An aunt was killed by German bombs while riding a bus in London. Vassiltchikov, herself, endured some of the worst Allied bombing raids in Berlin and Vienna. Under these circumstances, a broad perspective came naturally.

The diary's account of everyday life under the bombs gives that terrible experience an immediacy that no general account could ever convey. The small details Vassiltchikov provides—a sixteen-year-old girl sitting dazedly on a pile of rubble, driven mad by the death of her entire family; the poignant messages scrawled on walls of shattered houses by people trying to locate loved ones; the smell of the dead that lingered in one's nostrils for days; the difficulty of keeping clean when no water was available; the difficulty of disposing of a body when a city has fallen into chaos; the shortage of coffins, which caused long delays in burials; the tremendous effort required simply to get to work; the valiant efforts of a hotel staff to maintain restaurant service in a bombed-out hotel with no water or electricity; the lack of sleep because of constant night raids—all show what the bombing meant on an individual level as no other account has.

The bombing never broke the spirit of the Germans, and they fought the war to the bitter end. Missie Vassiltchikov's diary, however, shows a more discontented Germany than one usually sees. She tells of bombed-out Hamburgers being openly critical on a train and comments that people were saying virtually what they pleased on trains. The war did not diminish the famous Berlin wit, and Vassiltchikov relates a whole series of jokes that circulated after Rudolf Hess's flight to Great Britain in 1940. (Example: The One Thousand Year Reich has just become a One Hundred Year Reich. One zero is gone.) In Vassiltchikov's circle, it was de rigueur to be anti-Nazi and pessimistic about the war. Her friend Curt-Christoph "C.C." von Pfuel was making pessimistic assessments in June of 1940, when Germany was winning its greatest victory of the war in France. Heinrich Wittgenstein spoke only half-jokingly to Vassiltchikov about how he could have killed Hitler, as he had been allowed to keep his side arm when he received a decoration from Hitler personally. According to Vassiltchikov, in her division of the foreign office, everyone groaned when a new departmental head proved to be too enthusiastic a Nazi. Herbert Blankenhorn, who later played an important role in the Federal Republic, regaled Vassiltchikov for an entire evening in January of 1944 with his plans for postwar Germany, including splitting it up into autonomous states.

Some of Vassiltchikov's friends did not content themselves with anti-Nazi witticisms and postwar plans; they plotted to kill Hitler. Her account of the July 20 conspiracy provides the main dramatic tension of her diary. She was apparently drawn into the conspiracy by Adam von Trott zu Stolz. Trott had been a Rhodes Scholar in England and still had many contacts there. He hoped to use these connections to try to gain better peace terms for the anti-Nazi government the conspirators hoped would seize power upon the death of Hitler. He worked in the German foreign office and was to be an undersecretary of state in the foreign office of the new government. Soon after he and Vassiltchikov met, he arranged to have her transferred to his department at the foreign office. Vassiltchikov never makes clear why he did this. She had no direct role in the conspiracy and seems mainly to have served as a confidante. She and Trott were powerfully attracted to each other. He wrote of Missie Vassiltchikov to his wife: "She has something of a noble animal of legend . . . something free that enables her to soar far above everything and everyone." Vassiltchikov confided to her diary the day that she met Trott that "there is something very special about him." In 1944, after having dinner with Trott, she wrote, "Our friendship is somewhat overwhelming, and I have consciously avoided this so far. He is a man completely out of the ordinary." They had long intimate conversations in English, and on one long walk together shortly before July 20, 1944, he poured out to her the story of his life before the war.

Readers who hope to find insight into the plans and ideas of the July 20 plotters in Vassiltchikov's diary will be disappointed. She knew of the conspiracy far ahead of time, first mentioning it in her diary in August, 1943. She was well enough informed to know the exact date of the assassination attempt ahead of time, but her diary provides almost no details. Trott never told her the exact nature of his role in the plot. She professes that when he spoke German he was too intellectual for her to understand him. She reports listening to him discuss his "lofty thoughts" with a friend one evening but tells nothing of the nature of these lofty thoughts. The diary discusses the conspiracy only from the perspective of her daily comings and goings.

Only one time does Vassiltchikov venture into the strategy of the conspiracy. She was convinced that the Allies would not negotiate with any German government and believed that the plotters should stop futile efforts to gain such assurances and kill Hitler immediately. She and Trott quarreled bitterly over this just ten days before the assassination attempt.

Vassiltchikov's deeply personal account of the grim days after July 20 is perhaps the most compelling part of the diary. The mental anguish was intense as the plotters learned the bitter truth that Hitler had survived the bomb explosion. They knew full well the terrible meaning of that for themselves. Gottfried von Bismarck's wife, Melanie, broke down and moaned pitiably that she and her children would be left widow and orphans. (Gottfried von Bismarck was arrested, tortured, and placed on trial. On Hitler's orders, however, he was acquitted. Hitler did not want it known that a Bismarck had tried to kill him.) The rest awaited the inevitable with stoic dignity and thought only of trying to kill Hitler again.

One of Missie Vassiltchikov's closest friends, the outspoken and headstrong Princess Eleanore-Marie "Loremarie" von Schönburg-Hartenstein, had lost five brothers in the war and never made any secret of her detestation of the Nazis. Before July 20, she had continually alarmed her friends with her outspokenness, and sometimes her indiscretion even threatened the security of the conspirators. She had no fear, however, and now she began visiting Gestapo headquarters almost every day to bring food to Adam von Trott and Gottfried von Bismarck and to try to make connections that could secure their release. Vassiltchikov even seriously considered going directly to Joseph Goebbels on their behalf, but an actress friend who knew Goebbels talked her out of it. Despite their close association with the conspirators and their efforts on their behalf, Schönburg and Vassiltchikov were never arrested.

Adam von Trott was hanged on August 26, 1944. His friends were tormented before and after by conflicting reports on whether he was alive or dead. Only later did the press officially announce his death. Loremarie von Schönburg had caught sight of him being led down a hall at Gestapo headquarters. She told Vassiltchikov that he had looked straight through her and that his face was that of a man in another world. They knew that he was being tortured. All of his friends hoped for an early death to release him from his suffering, except Vassiltchikov. She desperately wanted him to live. Her grief is apparent in these pages, but even in the privacy of her diary she is stoically laconic. Her style is never even slightly lachrymose.

In September, 1944, Vassiltchikov moved to Vienna, where she served as a nurse. Here again she endured heavy bombing. Most harrowing, however, was her flight from Vienna just days before it fell to the Soviets. The war's end found her in the American-occupied Austrian Tyrol.

History is not kind to losers, and the failure of the July 20 plot has brought much criticism down upon its perpetrators, especially from the

Left: They were too timid, too incompetent, some of them compromised by early Nazi sympathies; they opposed Hitler not because they found his policies morally repugnant but because those policies had failed; they were more concerned with the fate of Germany than the fate of the Jews; they were aristocrats completely without popular support who looked backward rather than forward. Whatever the merit of such criticisms, these ungenerous thoughts are far from mind by the time one finishes this diary, and one is filled with admiration for these men and women who, whatever their shortcomings, in the end had the courage to act on their convictions. They have found a fitting memorial in the diary of Marie Vassiltchikov, whose unpretentious decency and humanity shine through on every page.

Paul B. Kern

Sources for Further Study

Booklist. LXXXIII, April 15, 1987, p. 1247.
Kirkus Reviews. LV, January 15, 1987, p. 121.
Library Journal. CXI, February 15, 1987, p. 143.
National Review. XXXIX, February 27, 1987, p. 48.
The New York Review of Books. XXXIV, April 9, 1987, p. 7.
The New York Times Book Review. XCII, April 5, 1987, p. 6.
The New Yorker. LXIII, May 25, 1987, p. 113.
Publishers Weekly. CCXXXI, January 16, 1987, p. 66.
Time. CXXIX, April 13, 1987, p. 75.
The Times Literary Supplement. July 18, 1986, p. 777.
The Washington Post Book World. XVII, March 29, 1987, p. 1.

BEYOND OUR MEANS
How America's Long Years of Debt, Deficits, and Reckless Borrowing Now Threaten to Overwhelm Us

Author: Alfred L. Malabre, Jr. (1931-   )
Publisher: Random House (New York). 175 pp. $17.95
Type of work: Economic history
Time: 1945 to the mid-1980's
Locale: The United States

A brief historical description and analysis of the post-World War II American economy and its problems

Alfred L. Malabre, Jr.'s, new book, *Beyond Our Means: How America's Long Years of Debt, Deficits, and Reckless Borrowing Now Threaten to Overwhelm Us*, is an example of the contemporary genre of gloom-and-doom predictions or speculations about the future. In his commentary in *Newsweek* magazine, environmental scientist S. Fred Singer wrote, "Old-time favorites like famine, war and pestilence now take a back seat to such man-made ecological disasters as nuclear winter and ozone depletion, with fresh catastrophes close behind." In the economic arena, Malabre's book must be reviewed, along with Geoffrey Abert's *After the Crash* (1979), Ravi Batra's *The Great Depression of 1990* (1985), and Paul E. Erdman's *The Crash of '79* (1976; updated in 1987 and renamed *The Panic of '89*, since the "crash" did not come in 1979, though the author continues to predict it) as an analysis predicting economic collapse. Although part of this gloomily popular approach to economic predictions, of which readers must be skeptical, *Beyond Our Means* has much to commend it.

First, Malabre's book is a rather good, nontechnical description of post-World War II economic history. Second, the book briefly describes the major postwar economic systems or theories—Keynesianism, industrial policy, monetarism, and supply-side theory—and demonstrates how none of these can provide a satisfactory explanation of or solution to modern economic problems. In fact, Malabre points out that economic theory neither comprehends nor can solve the contemporary predicament, a fact supported by Chemical Bank of New York's firing of its staff of forty economists in August, 1985. Third, Malabre attempts to discern the nature of the problems confronting the American economy. Fourth, having rejected conventional economic theory to explain the economy, the author attempts to apply economic cycles to the economy and describes the nature of the business cycle and some of its manifestations—the Kondratieff Wave, the Jugler Cycle, and the Kuznets Cycle. Finally, *Beyond Our Means* discusses what is likely to happen to the American economy, what *should* be done to deal with contemporary economic problems, and what *will* be done to cope with those problems. Within a rather small compass, *Beyond Our Means* is a comprehensive, interesting, and important economic survey and analysis.

Beginning with a description of efforts to cope with the Great Depression of the 1930's, Malabre attempts to document "the long, dismal record of our post-World War II extravagance." Malabre holds that as Americans have "persistently, stubbornly lived far beyond our means . . . it is beyond our means to put things right readily" and that "our predicament" is such that "painful choices . . . now confront us."

Malabre contends that the New Deal programs of President Franklin D. Roosevelt were appropriate at the time. The Federal Deposit Insurance Corporation (FDIC) and federal bank licensing, as examples, protected the banking public and restored faith in the nation's banking system. While the FDIC "continues to be appropriate," other New Deal-initiated problems have simply transferred tax-collected money to individuals on the basis on need.

Americans have come to believe that they are "entitled" to receive money from such programs, even though the entitlements are, in many cases, really not based on need. The food-stamp, Social Security, Medicare, Medicaid, school-lunch, public-housing, Supplemental Security Income, and Aid to Families with Dependent Children programs all support many people who are well off and receive but do not need the benefits. In spite of President Ronald Reagan's expressions about reducing deficits, entitlement payments have continued to increase, and, since the 1960's they have risen "from 24 percent of federal spending to 41 percent." Federal support of benefit programs for corporations has also been very generous, as has federal support of military pensioners—"among the wealthiest 20 percent of all U.S. households." In the past, the wealthy have been able to take advantage of low-interest student loans, often investing the money to receive high returns rather than using it for educational purposes. Farm-subsidy payments benefit far more wealthy than poor farmers, because the payments are based on production and thus mostly go to larger producers. In other words, transfer-payment or entitlement programs have grown enormously (from $1.5 billion in 1930 to nearly $500 billion in the 1980's) and have often benefited prosperous rather than needy Americans.

A second problem that Malabre describes is the enormous growth of debt. The entitlement and transfer-payment programs have contributed to the growth of the federal debt. Federal programs to build bridges, roads, and public facilities are another source of debt, as is the costly military establishment. While the rate of increase in debt has accelerated in the 1970's and 1980's, productivity, which could help pay the debt, has declined along with per capita savings (which have been discouraged by a tax climate that has succeeded in stimulating spending). The effect of "the tendency to spend too much and save too little" has limited economic growth in these two decades.

The spectacular growth of the federal debt has had a counterpart in the significant rise of corporate and private debt. The result has been a substantial growth of borrowing and an increasingly problematic borrowing situation. Delinquencies in the repayment of debts have increased: "Consumers are assuming more and more debt and encountering more and more difficulty servicing it." Corporate debt and the numbers of corporate failures have significantly increased in the 1980's. Under the pressure of this very great growth of debt, banks and savings and loan associations have been under considerable pressure, and publicity about their failures has been disturbing. Bank failures have, however, not represented a problem for the customers of banks, who are covered by FDIC. The federal government, in turn, has handled FDIC payments by increasing the money supply, which, along with taxes and borrowing, is a major source of debt coverage. As debt has increased, the Federal Reserve Board has authorized the continued growth of the money supply to cover not only the debt but also the very great increase in the interest payment on the debt. None of the traditional methods of raising money—increased taxation, borrowing, or printing more money—seems very satisfactory in the light of the present debt level. Increased borrowing would increase indebtedness and the interest rate. Printing more money would stimulate inflation. Changing the tax laws to discourage borrowing and to pay off the debt more fully might not be politically wise for the party in power.

The result of America's cumulative debt is that the standard of living has been adversely affected. Malabre predicts that "the coming generation of Americans won't be able to afford the standard of housing enjoyed by their parents." In education, other nations are clearly ahead of the United States, both in the percentage of the population being educated and in the quality of education. American productivity has been declining and has contributed to a growing trade imbalance. This has meant a lower standard of living. America's highway, transit, sewers, bridge, and water systems are all deteriorating more rapidly than money is available to repair them. Moreover, there has been underinvestment in the manufacturing industries, which has resulted in plant obsolescence. A declining standard of living may be seen in all these areas as well as in the consequences of an increasing investment in defense. Defense spending "puts more money in the hands of thousands of workers who make the bombs but does nothing to increase the supply of goods and services available for consumption."

All these post-World War II economic changes have combined to produce a service-oriented economy. Indeed, more than 70 percent of all jobs in the United States are service-type positions, in contrast with the two-thirds of all jobs in the 1920's that were in manufacturing. Malabre characterizes the activities of this service economy with the terms "underinvestment," "overborrowing, overspending, and undersaving," and, above all, "overindulgence." Moreover, productivity continues to decline even in manufacturing, while increases in salary continue for workers and, especially, for management, whose salaries have reached the level of obscenity. Since Americans are no longer competing effectively in the world market, they have turned, instead, to protectionism.

Protectionism has been supported in industry after industry by both management and labor. Rather than improving their products, reducing their costs, or increasing productivity, protectionists have refused to compete and have chosen to reserve the American market for themselves. The philosophy of protectionism is to force American consumers to purchase inferior products at higher prices than would be charged in competitive markets. Protectionism does nothing to enhance competitiveness and may threaten to "trigger painful countermeasures abroad," as may be seen in the consequences of the Smoot-Hawley Tariff of 1930, which helped turn a bad depression into something worse. For Malabre, however, like growing debt, excessive borrowing, a declining standard of living, declining productivity, and a service economy, protectionism is simply another example of living "beyond our means."

Having defined the economic situation through a complex analysis of the postwar economy, Malabre then describes the major economic theories that have sought to comprehend the economy and solve its problems. This is one of the author's most interesting sections. Keynesianism holds that taxation and government spending should be employed to stimulate or reduce economic activity, thereby keeping the economy at whatever level the government wishes. This system may have worked at one time, but, by the 1970's, as former Chairman of the Federal Reserve Board Arthur Burns said, "Confidence in Keynesian ideas began collapsing." The economy in the mid-1980's is so problematic that Keynesianism is no longer a popular solution.

A second solution, offered by Professor Robert Reich of Harvard University, is known as industrial policy. This system advocates strong central planning, but such central planning is already partly in place and clearly is not working. A third economic formula is monetarism, advocated by Nobel laureate Milton Friedman of the University of Chicago. Friedman supports manipulation of the money supply by the Federal Reserve Board as the key to economic stability. In the words of Friedman's Keynesian opponent, Walter Heller, however, "Friedman's ideas are wonderful, but unfortunately they work only in heaven."

The fourth major theory is supply-side economics, which President Reagan and his advisers have advocated. It simply seeks to cut taxes to encourage more earning, savings, and investment to expand economic activity and therefore the total taxable national income, thus solving all America's economic problems. Malabre speaks of supply-side theory as "hokum" and reinforces his view by pointing to increasing deficits. Supply-side theory is not a workable theory but merely a utopian promise for political advantage. It is the logical extension, in theoretical form, of living beyond our means.

What an analysis of economic theory reveals is that no present theory has come to grips with Malabre's view of the American economic situation. The economy, according to Malabre, is, however, conforming to the business cycle. Although he really offers no explanation for the cause of business cycles, the author insists that they have operated in the past and very likely will continue in the future. The patterns of boom and bust are probably linked to the optimism and pessimism inherent in human nature. In the normal course of events, an economic downturn makes real contributions to economic well-being. In times of prosperity, much luxury, economic mismanagement, inefficiency, and living beyond our means is possible. An economic downturn purges the economy and contributes to strengthening recovery. The long period of sustained growth since World War II, often supported by government intervention, has prevented the purging of the American economy. This means that any economic downturn will probably be very severe, very painful, and very troublesome.

Malabre does not not say precisely when such a downturn might be expected, but he suggests that forecasters "should watch a variety of leading indicators." While the author believes in the validity of the business cycle, he is rather skeptical about specific cycles. Somewhat supportive of Kondratieff Wave theory—long, slow business cycles—he is less certain of the shorter Jugler or Kuznets cycles. It is only through the painful process of an economic downturn, however, that the economy will eventually correct itself.

The real question to be answered is, will Americans, having for almost half a century lived beyond their means, have the will to live within their means? In his book, *The End of the American Era* (1970), Andrew Hacker replied in the negative. There is little that politicians have done to support any but a negative reply. Malabre recommends severe cuts in the entitlement or transfer programs, no matter how painful this may be, but politicians have little courage for such action. Politicians and government officials have also been reluctant to deal with federal debt by curtailing any major programs such as defense. So, the difficulties of bank failures, farm debt, Third World debt, and other problems continue to mount. Malabre believes that the debt issue alone is beyond the capacity "of even governmental agencies to cope."

Given the present economic situation, what is likely to happen? Malabre offers four possible scenarios. The least likely is that the American government and people will wake up, realize the fault of living "beyond our means," reduce spending and the debt, and stabilize the economy. A second improbable scenario is hyperinflation. A third possibility for which Malabre gives a 30 percent likelihood is deflation. The scenario to which Malabre gives a 50 percent likelihood is strong government intervention in the economy. The result will be "the prospect of greatly increased governmental control over all aspects of economic activity." This may well put an end to the Reagan Administration's version of a deregulated economy that has encouraged living beyond our means.

A closely reasoned, and thoughtful analysis, Malabre's rather pessimistic *Beyond Our Means* is undoubtedly one of the better descriptions of the American economy. What it lacks in detail—fuller descriptions of contemporary economic theory and its failures, cycle theory, and consequences of economic downturn—it makes up in comprehensiveness and clarity, while avoiding a simplistic approach. This volume is recommended for both lay readers and advanced students of economic history.

Saul Lerner

Sources for Further Study

Barrons. LXVII, May 4, 1987, p. 83.
Booklist. LXXXIII, March 15, 1987, p. 1081.
Fortune. CXV, May 11, 1987, p. 189.
Library Journal. CXII, April 1, 1987, p. 143.
Los Angeles Times Book Review. April 19, 1987, p. 4.
The Nation. CCXLIV, May 2, 1987, p. 584.
The New York Times Book Review. XCII, April 12, 1987, p. 7.
Publishers Weekly. CCXXXI, February 6, 1987, p. 80.
The Wall Street Journal. March 24, 1987, p. 34.
The Washington Post Book World. XVII, March 8, 1987, p. 6.

BLUEBEARD

Author: Kurt Vonnegut (1922-   )
Publisher: Delacorte Press (New York). 300 pp. $17.95
Type of work: Novel
Time: 1987, with flashbacks
Locale: Long Island, New York

The fictitious autobiography of Rabo Karabekian, an unsuccessful, one-eyed abstract expressionist painter of Armenian descent

> *Principal characters:*
> RABO KARABEKIAN, a painter, a minor character in Vonnegut's novel *Breakfast of Champions* (1973)
> CIRCE BERMAN, a widow who moves into his house and becomes his roomer and chaste companion
> PAUL SLAZINGER, an eccentric would-be novelist who lives next door to him and scrounges off him

Rabo Karabekian lives in a mansion on Long Island with a woman who cooks for him and her teenage daughter. His friend and neighbor is a novelist, Paul Slazinger, who is suffering from writer's block. Rabo, a failed artist, is bonded to Slazinger by their experiences in World War II, in which Rabo lost an eye and Slazinger suffered a severe wound when he fell on a Japanese grenade to protect his fellow soldiers. Rabo despairs of them both, saying, "We look like a couple of gutshot iguanas!" Rabo's first wife divorced him, and he is alienated from their two sons. His beloved second wife, Edith, died and left him the nineteen-room mansion in East Hampton, where he lives in slothful widower comfort. His life takes a sudden turn when he meets Circe Berman, a widow who at forty-three is twenty-eight years younger than Rabo. Circe, a very successful writer of novels for juveniles, is a woman of great spirit and charm. She moves into Rabo's mansion and goads him into writing the autobiography that makes up the novel.

The plot of *Bluebeard* develops three major themes. First, Rabo is an Armenian, and Armenians and Armenian history are at the novel's center. Second, Rabo is a talented illustrator who became closely involved with the major figures of Abstract Expressionism but failed as an artist. Finally, the Turkish genocide against Armenians is seen as a forerunner of the broader genocide perpetrated against Jews and other minorities in World War II. Uniting all these themes is Rabo's search for a family and community, a search satisfied for him twice—once as a soldier and once again as a member of the Abstract Expressionist movement.

Rabo's father escaped the Turkish slaughter by hiding in the ordure of a privy, his mother by pretending to be dead in a pile of corpses. As his mother lay among the corpses, she noticed in the pile an old woman whose mouth was gorged with jewels, and she took those spilled on the ground in the hope of financing a new life. When Rabo's parents eventually reached Cairo, they met another Armenian survivor, Vartan Mamigonian, who quickly bilked them into buying a bogus deed to a nonexistent house in San Ignacio, California. Thus, Rabo was born in San Ignacio rather than, for example, in Fresno, which had a warm, supportive Armenian community.

The atrocities in Armenia and the hoodwinking by Vartan Mamigonian made Rabo's father bitter. A talented man who could have pursued a career teaching and writing, Rabo's father chose instead to become a cobbler. Finally, at the end of his life, he began making beautiful cowboy boots and selling them door to door, a development that failed to please Rabo because it changed his father's life so completely. Rabo says of his father's new occupation, "It gave me the creeps, actually, because I would look into his eyes, and there wasn't anybody home anymore." Terry Kitchen, one of Rabo's artist friends, had the same look when he became converted to Abstract Expressionism, and Circe Berman explains the phenomenon to Rabo this way: "Maybe they had started picking up signals from another station, which had very different ideas about what they should say and do."

Rabo has never forgiven his father for several things. First, he resents his father's failure to move to Fresno, where Rabo could have had the advantage of growing up in a settled community of Armenians. Still more intensely, he resents his father's becoming a cobbler instead of the teacher and writer that he might have been. Again, Circe Berman explains that his father had been victimized by Survivor's Syndrome: excessive guilt over having lived through an ordeal that killed so many others. Circe becomes Rabo's salvation. She leads him to an understanding of his problem with his long-dead father and rescues him from any of his own tendencies toward Survivor's Syndrome by gently nagging him into writing his life's story.

Rabo's life before World War II revolved around his relationship with a famous illustrator, Dan Gregory (whose original Armenian name was Gregorian), and Dan's mistress, Marilee Kemp. Hoping to curry favor with a prosperous fellow Armenian, Rabo's mother insisted that he write to Dan and seek his patronage. The result was a long correspondence—from 1927 through 1933—between Rabo and Marilee, who saw in Rabo a suitable correspondent and a way to ease her loneliness through writing. Marilee was ten years older than Rabo and a former Ziegfield Follies showgirl. She eventually awakened his sexuality, when he was nineteen years old.

It was Marilee's clever manipulation that resulted in Dan Gregory's very grudging acceptance of Rabo as an apprentice of sorts. Dan was a brilliant illustrator for magazines but was explosively contemptuous of modern art and defensive about the range of his talent. He forbade Marilee and Rabo to visit the Museum of Modern Art, and when he saw them there he banished them—his children fallen into sin—from the paradise they had enjoyed under his sponsorship. It was then that Rabo and Marilee made love for the one and only time before separating. Thus ended Rabo's apprenticeship period: He had lived in New York City during his adolescence, perfected his talents as an illustrator, had a love affair with a beautiful older woman, and, in general, learned much about the ways of the world. When he was banished by Dan, he had had his last significant experience with Armenians.

Left homeless and friendless in New York City, Rabo had a significant insight into American life: "I learned the joke at the very core of American self-improvement: knowledge was so much junk to be processed one way or another at great universities. The real treasure the great universities offered was a lifelong membership in a respected artificial extended family."

After a brief job for a New York advertising agency, Rabo escaped the Great Depression by joining his first extended family—the United States Army. Adolf Hitler had already invaded Poland, but the United States was not yet at war, and Rabo's first duty detail was to do an oil painting of the commander of the Corps of Engineers. He was so successful that the grateful general made him a master sergeant and put him in command of a new camouflage unit.

When the United States went to war, Rabo was commissioned a lieutenant and served in North Africa, Sicily, England, France, and finally Germany, where he lost an eye and was captured. Meanwhile, Dan Gregory, who had left the United States to support his idol, Benito Mussolini, was shot to death in Egypt. At the same time, Marilee, as Rabo learned in 1950, had married Mussolini's Minister of Culture, Count Bruno Portomaggiore. Count Bruno, a homosexual who appeared to be a vain, effeminate coward, was actually the head of British Intelligence in Italy. When Marilee and Rabo were reunited briefly after the war, she was the recently widowed Countess Portomaggiore: "Thus did a coal miner's daughter become the Contessa Portomaggiore."

The climactic event of Rabo's military experience was his release from the prison camp at war's end. He describes the scene in a passage that becomes significant later:

> Our guards vanished one night, and we awoke the next morning on the rim of a great green valley on what is now the border between East Germany and Czechoslovakia. There may have been as many as ten thousand people below us—concentration camp survivors, slave laborers, lunatics released from asylums, and ordinary criminals released from jails and prisons, captured officers and enlisted men from every Army which had fought the Germans.

Although little of Rabo's military experience is actually described, he reverts to the theme frequently in explaining how he, as the son of displaced Armenian survivors in a foreign country, sought a family to which to belong; he describes his feelings as he surveyed the thousands of survivors in his camp and remembered the experience of his mother and father and all the other persecuted Armenians.

His discharge from the Army freed Rabo for membership in the second important family in his life—the Abstract Expressionist movement in modern art. His close friends were such figures as Mark Rothko, Jackson Pollock, and, closest of all, the fictitious Terry Kitchen. His marriage suffered from his intimacy with his friends, who were then mostly unknown artists whose paintings he accumulated on a casual basis and which eventually become a considerable treasure for him. Rabo's own canvases were covered with Sateen Dura-Luxe, and he was quite successful until the paint eventually disintegrated and he became, in his own eyes, a terrible laughingstock of the art world. He was left with a sense of himself as a failed creative artist with only a craftsman's skill at clever trompe l'oeil illustrations. The suicides among his artist friends and his failure as a husband and father combined with his professional debacle to defeat his sense of self-worth. His only happiness came with his second marriage, but when his second wife, Edith, died, he was left alone with the other "gutshot iguana," Paul Slazinger, to stew in his spiritual decrepitude.

So the adventitious appearance in his life of Circe Berman proves his salvation. Rabo has a big potato barn on his property, and he keeps it securely padlocked because it contains a secret not to be disclosed until his death. He compares himself facetiously to Bluebeard, the fictitious character who married a series of child brides who are told they may enter any room in the castle but one. For the infinitely curious Circe Berman, the potato barn is a tantalizing mystery that none of her charms can beguile Rabo into sharing with her. Finally, when Circe is about to give up for good her residence with Rabo he tells her that he cannot show her what is in the barn because, "I don't want to be around when people say whether it is any good or not." When she replies that he is a coward and that is how she will remember him, he realizes the justice of her charge and takes her to the potato barn.

What Rabo shows Circe is a huge mural, eight feet by sixty-four feet, painted on eight canvases from which the Sateen Dura-Luxe had faded. It depicts in minute detail the scene that greeted Rabo the morning he was freed from the German prison camp. It is, Rabo explains, where he was "when the sun came up the day the Second World War ended in Europe." It is a stunning re-creation that reveals Rabo's superb craftsmanship at the same time that it transcends mere craft to become an artistic vision of human love. The people in the mural are of all races, but one of the most striking figures is a dead Gypsy queen from whose mouth trickle rubies and diamonds. Circe is greatly moved by Rabo's disclosure, and their mood afterward is, as Rabo says, "postcoital."

Rabo entitles his mural "Now It's the Women's Turn"—the women's turn, perhaps, to create a better world. In his final commentary on the Abstract Expressionist movement, Rabo tells Circe that in their nonrepresentational creations they were seeking a "pure essence of human wonder," an art that turned away from the pursuit of worldliness and sought to be "surely apart from the universal human impulse among painters and plumbers alike toward inexplicable despair and self-destruction." Abstract Expressionism was, then, in one sense a world-hating phenomenon that perhaps explains the tragic lives of such painters as Mark Rothko and Arshile Gorky. "Now It's the Women's Turn" represents Rabo's affirmation of humanity and his escape, under the loving tutelage of Circe Berman, from the guilt of Survivor's Syndrome.

Frank Day

Sources for Further Study

Booklist. LXXXIII, August, 1987, p. 1699.
Chicago Tribune. September 27, 1987, XIV, p. 1.
Kirkus Reviews. LV, August 1, 1987, p. 1113.
Library Journal. CXIII, January, 1988, p. 101.
Los Angeles Times Book Review. October 4, 1987, p. 10.
The New York Times Book Review. XCII, October 18, 1987, p. 12.
People Weekly. XXVIII, October 19, 1987, p. 22.
Publishers Weekly. CCXXXII, September 25, 1987, p. 95.
Time. CXXX, September 28, 1987, p. 68.
The Washington Post Book World. XVII, October 4, 1987, p. 9.

THE BONFIRE OF THE VANITIES

Author: Tom Wolfe (1931-   )
Publisher: Farrar, Straus and Giroux (New York). 659 pp. $19.95
Type of work: Novel
Time: The 1980's
Locale: New York City

A sumptuous comedy of manners and rudeness among the varied social circles of contemporary New York

> *Principal characters:*
> SHERMAN McCOY, a patrician investment banker whose world is demolished by a foolish indiscretion
> CAMPBELL McCOY, his six-year-old daughter
> JUDY McCOY, his socially ambitious wife
> MARIA RUSKIN, his married lover
> LARRY KRAMER, the frustrated assistant district attorney of the Bronx
> PETER FALLOW, a hard-drinking, unscrupulous British journalist working for a New York tabloid
> THOMAS KILLIAN, Sherman's street-smart defense attorney
> THE REVEREND REGINALD BACON, a black demagogue and charlatan

In 1972, Tom Wolfe was hailing a movement that "would wipe out the novel as literature's main event." What he championed as "the New Journalism" was an attempt to deploy the stylistic resources of fiction in the service of recording actualities. Wolfe later collected works of such writers as Joan Didion, Truman Capote, Norman Mailer, and Hunter S. Thompson into an influential anthology called *The New Journalism* (1973). As much as anyone else, Wolfe himself, in such tours de force of observation and articulation as *The Kandy-Kolored Tangerine-Flake Streamline Baby* (1965), *The Electric Kool-Aid Acid Test* (1968), *Radical Chic and Mau-Mauing the Flak Catchers* (1970), and *The Right Stuff* (1979), was demonstrating that nonfiction can be as artful as fiction, and even more urgent.

The New Journalism did not, however, quite wipe out the novel as literature's main event. Evidence of that appears in the form of *The Bonfire of the Vanities*, a richly textured, exuberant tale of New York that is the first novel that Tom Wolfe has published. A foolish consistency need not hobble major authors. In one big book, Wolfe establishes himself as the leading candidate for the title of the Balzac of contemporary America.

The Bonfire of the Vanities is the story of Sherman McCoy, a thirty-eight-year-old blue-blooded prince of Park Avenue who can barely afford his $2.6 million apartment and his $1,800 British suits on his $980,000 income as the top bond trader at Pierce & Pierce, a Wall Street investment bank. McCoy must also post bond when he is arrested for reckless endangerment. Lost in the South Bronx, he and someone else's randy wife, Maria Ruskin, flee the scene when his Mercedes hits a black youth. The resulting scandal is urban theater whose *dramatis personae* include a freeloading alcoholic writer for a sleazy local tabloid, a cynical black demagogue, an anxious, love-starved prosecutor, and a supporting cast of hundreds. Sherman McCoy's life becomes the stage for every raw conflicting ambition in a turbulent city where opportunity knocks—often ruthlessly.

Canny Abe Weiss, eager to be reelected district attorney from a borough that is now 70 percent black and Latino, refers to the Bronx as "the Laboratory of Human Relations." The New York City that Wolfe depicts might pride itself on being a melting pot, but the contents are an immiscible stew of rival classes and ethnic groups. A social satirist and student of the woeful human comedy, Wolfe brings a keen ear to the motley accents of a contemporary metropolis. He is attentive to the speech patterns, clothing, diet, habits, and obsessions of the disparate denizens of what McCoy considers "the city of ambition, the dense magnetic rock, the irresistible destination of all those who insist on being *where things are happening*."

McCoy is intent on rearing his six-year-old daughter Campbell within the shelter of "the Best School, the Best Girls, the Best Families, the Best Section of the capital of the Western world in the late twentieth century." Yet Wolfe provides a convincing portrait not only of life at the top, but of existence at the bottom and in the middle of the social hierarchy as well. In recounting the fatuous fall of Sherman McCoy, *The Bonfire of the Vanities* is an exuberant and poignant examination of the fragility of fortune. It mocks the temptation to define identity by the very social coordinates that this novel is so adept at rendering. "Your *self*," says McCoy to his street-smart Irish criminal lawyer, Thomas Killian, "is *other people*, all the people you're tied to, and it's only a thread." The unraveling of that thread constitutes the plot and theme of *The Bonfire of the Vanities*.

The courthouse in which Sherman's fate is decided is located in a run-down section of the Bronx that is so forbidding to middle-class municipal employees that they regard the courthouse as an island citadel from which they dare not emerge, not even for lunch. Wolfe is forever crosscutting between Park Avenue, the South Bronx, Wall Street, Harlem, City Hall, and the offices of a shabby newspaper and a sleazy lawyer. He provides as convincing a portrait of Larry Kramer, an underpaid Jewish prosecutor who feels trapped in a cheap apartment and a dull marriage, as he does of the macho Irish cops whom Kramer emulates.

Wolfe's first novel is so compellingly dense because the author has reappropriated for fiction those devices that he had praised New Journalism for adapting from it originally: scene-by-scene construction, realistic dialogue, penetration of characters' minds, and use of status details—that is,

everyday gestures, habits, manners, customs, styles of furniture, clothing, decoration, styles of traveling, eating, keeping house, modes of behaving toward children, servants, superiors, inferiors, peers, plus the various looks, glances, poses, styles of walking and other symbolic details that might exist within a scene.

Wolfe is acutely aware of every distinguishing feature of his characters, down to, and especially, the precise kinds of shoes they wear. They speak with Yiddish, black, British, Irish, and Southern inflections exaggerated into lampoon by their caustic author. Wolfe describes the "pimp roll" with which black youths strut through a courtroom as well as he depicts the gait of a millionaire out walking a dachshund named Marshall.

The novel excels in set pieces. Of particular interest are two elaborate, pretentious dinner parties that Sherman and his arriviste wife Judy attend before and after his public humiliation. A scene in which vulgar tycoon Arthur Raskin, who has made his fortune chartering jets to fly Muslims to Mecca, is obsequiously welcomed into a fancy restaurant but then carelessly disposed of after suffering a fatal heart attack is Proustian in its disdain for social contempt.

"Daddy," asks little Campbell McCoy, "what do you do?" The question is meant to be occupational, not metaphysical, but it is still not an easy one. One of the most striking moments in the novel occurs when Sherman attempts to explain to his young daughter just what it is that he does in an office set thirty stories above "the gloomy groin of Wall Street." *The Bonfire of the Vanities* takes the reader inside business in a way few other late twentieth century American novels do, and we see the complicated transactions by which Sherman's firm, Pierce & Pierce, acquires six billion dollars' worth of a twenty-year bond. Campbell's ingenious question, however, is one that troubles Sherman.

Though his private epithet for himself is "Master of the Universe," how can Sherman explain to a six-year-old what it is that he does, and how can he explain to himself that it has any value other than monetary? Bond speculation seems immensely profitable, but it appears as much of a sham as the Reverend Reginald Bacon's scheme to wrest $350,000 out of a philanthropic foundation by exploiting the directors' liberal guilt over black misery. Judy McCoy, who is perfectly loyal to her husband as long as her loyalty does not have to be tested, belittles the otiose activities of her conjugal investment commando who spends his days aggressively buying and selling certificates. "Even if it's for people who are shallow and vain," she says of her own work as an interior decorator, "it's something *real*, something describable, something contributing to simple human satisfaction, no matter how meretricious and temporary, something you can at least explain to your children." Wolfe places his readers in the skeptical position of children, to whom the events in the novel can be explained, but not justified.

The coda with which the book concludes is New Journalist-turned-novelist Wolfe's fictional sneer at the old journalism. The epilogue purports to be a

New York Times article published one year after the events of the narrative, summarizing what has happened in the interim. Written in the magisterial deadpan of *The New York Times*, the article dispassionately records the triumph of scoundrels. The final paragraph—surely an echo of the conclusion to Gustave Flaubert's *Madame Bovary* (1857), in which the reader is told that the pompous fool Homais has been elected to the Legion of Honor—announces that Peter Fallow, the sleazy journalist who broke the McCoy story, has been awarded the Pulitzer Prize.

With gossips named Rawthrote and Bavardage, *The Bonfire of the Vanities* lurches toward caricature, but many of the other characters seem drawn, and quartered, from life. Fallow, the raffish and bibulous English reporter who need abandon no scruples to sensationalize the McCoy story because he has none, regards journalism as "a cup of tea on the way to his eventual triumph as a novelist." It is difficult to imagine Fallow achieving the fertility of Tom Wolfe. "Like every writer before him who has ever scored a triumph," the reader is told, "Fallow was willing to give no credit to luck." Wolfe's *Bonfire* blazes in triumph, but it is the product of research, imagination, and compassion.

Steven G. Kellman

Sources for Further Study

The Atlantic. CCLX, December, 1987, p. 104.
Booklist. LXXXIV, October 1, 1987, p. 170.
Library Journal. CXII, November 15, 1987, p. 92.
The Nation. CCXLV, November 28, 1987, p. 636.
National Review. XXXIX, December 18, 1987, p. 46.
The New Republic. CXCVII, November 23, 1987, p. 42.
The New York Times Book Review. November 1, 1987, p. 1.
Newsweek. CX, October 26, 1987, p. 84.
Publishers Weekly. CCXXXII, October 2, 1987, p. 82.
Time. CXXX, November 9, 1987, p. 101.
The Washington Post Book World. XVII, October 25, 1987, p. 3.

THE BOTTOM TRANSLATION
Marlowe and Shakespeare and the Carnival Tradition

Author: Jan Kott (1914-   )
Translated from the Polish by Daniela Miedzyrzecka and Lillian Vallee
Publisher: Northwestern University Press (Evanston, Illinois). 165 pp. $22.95; paperback $10.95
Type of work: Literary criticism

Jan Kott's essays collected in this volume explore how certain plays by William Shakespeare and several of his contemporaries are animated by imaginative transformations of sixteenth and seventeenth century literary and festive traditions

The Bottom Translation: Marlowe and Shakespeare and the Carnival Tradition is not so much a unified analysis of the "carnival tradition" in the work of William Shakespeare as a far-ranging continuation of *Shakespeare Our Contemporary* (1964). This is no cause for alarm or disappointment, though, because like that deeply influential study, *The Bottom Translation* is filled with illuminating, though often fleeting and loosely arranged, meditations on the art and thought of Shakespeare and several of his contemporaries. The essays collected here—on Christopher Marlowe's *Doctor Faustus* (1604), Shakespeare's *A Midsummer Night's Dream* (1600) and *The Tempest* (1623), the plays of John Webster, and *Ran*, Akira Kurosawa's 1985 film adaptation of *King Lear* (1608)—examine these works in their original setting but also collapse distinctions of time and place to view them as existing in a kind of continuing present moment. In this way, Jan Kott is able to disclose how the best dramatic art of the seventeenth century is simultaneously a commentary on earlier times, a reflection of its own, and an often harrowing premonition of centuries to come.

The use of the term "carnival tradition" in the subtitle is an acknowledgement of Kott's large general debt to the writings of Mikhail Bakhtin, the Soviet scholar whose works are becoming more influential now that they are available in English translation. Although it is difficult to summarize Bakhtin's subtle and often complicated theories about language, art, and society in a brief space, some knowledge of his central terms and concerns is useful as background to Kott's approach to Renaissance drama. Kott draws especially from *Rabelais and His World* (begun in the 1930's, published in 1965, and translated into English in 1968), in which Bakhtin defines "carnival" and the "carnivalesque" in opposition to official, authoritarian culture. Carnival stands for exuberance, freedom, gaiety, physical enjoyment, and the subversion or inversion of traditional laws, rituals, and habits. For Bakhtin, the riotous laughter and disorder of holidays represent not so much a social safety valve—a way for the lower classes to let off steam, preventing a possibly dangerous buildup of tensions and resentments—as an enactment of truly revolutionary impulses that at least for the moment fulfills basic, irrepressible human needs for liberty and laughter.

Bakhtin focuses primarily on the way this spirit of carnival animates François Rabelais' novel *Gargantua and Pantagruel* (1567), but he makes clear that such an approach is vital to a full appreciation of many other works as well. Kott takes off from this point. Like C. L. Barber, whose *Shakespeare's Festive Comedy: A Study of Dramatic Form and Its Relation to Social Custom* (1959) stands as a remarkable breakthrough in this field, he pays particular attention to the role of holiday customs and folk entertainments in various plays, but he goes beyond Barber to embrace all kinds of transgressions as part of the carnival spirit. For example, Kott spends much time discussing Doctor Faustus in Marlowe's play as a magician and philosopher, but he notes that throughout the play, "There is seriousness in the laughter and laughter in the seriousness." Faustus' attempts to go beyond the allowable limits of human perfection and knowledge are earnest, and ultimately tragic, but they are viewed in part from the perspective of "carnival laughter and popular wisdom," and Kott points out how the stage actions choreographed by the devilish Mephostophilis include processions of the Seven Deadly Sins and visions of Hell drawn almost directly from popular folk pageants. Shakespeare's *A Midsummer Night's Dream* provides an even better example of a play inextricably rooted in carnival, which typically turns the world upside down. The union of the bewitched Queen Titania and Bottom the Weaver, transformed into a beast, is a perfect image of the meeting of high and low, a theme that recurs throughout the play. Kott echoes this scene in the title of his book, not only to call attention to the importance of metamorphosis in Renaissance drama but also to emphasize that these plays must be read, as it were, from the bottom, from Bottom's perspective: He represents "a language of the earth," a language that is carefully poised against that of the court and that conveys an altogether different message and mood.

Kott's focus on the dialogue of languages or voices recalls another key element of Bakhtin's theories, his stress on the "dialogic" nature of speech, especially literary speech. Simply stated, according to Bakhtin, works of literature contain various words that are constantly echoing, modifying, or somehow reacting to other words, as though the work is a continual dialogue of a variety of voices. The inherent ambiguity or multiple levels of meanings of words—heteroglossia, to use Bakhtin's term—complicates but also enhances a literary work, insofar as the artist's task is not to communicate truths simply and directly but to create polyphonic texts containing many voices, tones, and meanings. Kott uses these concepts very shrewdly when he discusses the overall structure of several plays. For example, he praises *Doctor Faustus* as a fine example of " 'polytheatrical' drama," in that it is composed of elements drawn from many literary forms, including tragedy, morality play, farce, interlude, and metaphysical poetry. While this undermines an interpretation of the play as thoroughly consistent and unified, it points out the richness of the materials from which Marlowe crafted the play and underscores the way that *Doctor Faustus* structurally as well as thematically conveys "man's predicament at the threshold of the seventeenth century," almost literally bombarded with irreconcilable ideas and forms. Kott's interpretation of *The Tempest* is an even more compelling elaboration of how polyphonic a play can be: He describes it in musical terms, as a fugue, and shows how the key words "torment," "trouble," "wonder," and "amazement" recur, sometimes simply echoed, other times subtly modulated. For Kott, the music in and the musical structure of *The Tempest* prove to be among its most critical dimensions.

While the essays in *The Bottom Translation* are thus deeply influenced by the work of Bakhtin, they also demonstrate Kott's versatility and independence. He is always ready to approach a work from a variety of critical perspectives, and his readers must be prepared for quick shifts of subject and point of view. Kott's interest in close structural analysis is matched by his constant attempts to uncover new contexts of interpretation. He has a scholar's fascination for tracking down sources and analogues, not as an antiquarian exercise but as an integral part of his demonstration of the dynamism of Renaissance playwrights, revealing how they adapted what they adopted. For example, Kott examines how, in *A Midsummer Night's Dream*, Shakespeare drew heavily from an unlikely pair of sources: Lucius Apuleius' *The Golden Ass* (c. A.D. 100), a comic tale about the adventures of a man while transformed into a beast; and Saint Paul's first Epistle to the Corinthians, a line of which—"the Spirite searcheth all thinges, ye the botome of Goddes secretes" (Geneva Bible translation, 1557)—may have prompted Shakespeare to give his character the name Bottom. The linking of these two strikingly different types of texts is part of the "riddle" of the play and is basic to its success as a work which dramatizes the union of high and low, the sacred and the ridiculous. For Kott, the subtle nuances of tone in a play may be noticeable only when the artist's imaginative manipulation of sources is analyzed closely. When he turns to *The Tempest*, the most-discussed play in the volume, Kott emphasizes Shakespeare's constant echoes of Vergil's *Aeneid* (c. 29-19 B.C.), not as a model for imitation but as a model for transformation: "The Virgilian myths are invoked, challenged, and finally rejected," he notes. Shakespeare's romances are usually treasured for their consoling powers and visions of harmony and restoration, but placed in contrast with the *Aeneid*, which embodies a successful journey from the destruction of Troy to the founding of Rome, *The Tempest* seems to be a bitter tale of renunciation and failed magic.

What is distinctive about Kott, already fully displayed in *Shakespeare Our Contemporary*, is his unalterably somber way of interpreting Shakespeare and his contemporary dramatists. To be sure, Kott is not blind to wit, playfulness, and comic celebration. In fact, in this volume he gravitates toward characters who are energetically creative, imaginative, and above all theatrical: Puck and Bottom in *A Midsummer Night's Dream*, Prospero in *The Tempest*, and Doctor Faustus, these last two not only magicians but also stage managers and directors of great skill. For Kott, however, these comedians and directors preside over a world that remains bleak, resistant to their best efforts: Faustus' joy in the world is only momentary and illusory, and his death marks the end of Renaissance optimism over the power of human reason and the possibility of attaining freedom and knowledge; the carnivalesque comedy of Puck and Bottom is never able to bridge the gap between high and low, and the play ends with "a strange and piercing sadness"; and Prospero ends where he began, released from the island and about to return to Naples, but—to paraphrase Jacques' melancholy recital of man's fate in *As You Like It*—sans magic, sans daughter, sans everything.

Kott's taste for the dark side of Shakespeare is apparent also in his two short essays on modern productions. He is fascinated by the energy of Giorgio Strehler's production of *The Tempest* (first performed in 1978) in Milan, Italy, especially by the way it captures both the transcendent realization that art can transform the world into a wondrous place and the desperate awareness that such transformations are fleeting. Ultimately, however, this production is not to Kott's liking, because it "has almost nothing of the Shakespearean bitterness and renunciation." Predictably, he is much more enthusiastic about *Ran*, Kurosawa's magnificent and disturbing adaptation of *King Lear*, which confirms in its unforgettable images, Nō theater and Kabuki conventions, and even in its title ("chaos") that the world is mad, painful, and absurd, a judgment linking Kurosawa's depiction of the medieval time period, Shakespeare's age, and Kott's twentieth century.

The world of Lear pervades the essays in *The Bottom Translation*, and Kott insists that comedies and romances, no less than tragedies, may show that the "wheel of fortune" has been replaced by the "wheel of torture." One must test this vision by looking at life as well as literature, as Kott does in *Shakespeare Our Contemporary* by summoning up images of world wars, refugees, and concentration camps to help translate *King Lear* for a modern audience. These images are not repeated in *The Bottom Translation*, but they are never far from Kott's mind, as one sees in two haunting paragraphs near the conclusion of the volume, where he merges a description of the end of *Ran* with a description of the "stark desert" surrounding his own home. Kott lives, abstractly and concretely, in Lear's world. One must know this to appreciate fully how his criticism is a work of admirable courage as well as persuasive scholarship.

Sidney Gottlieb

Sources for Further Study

Choice. XXV, October, 1987, p. 311.
Library Journal. CXII, February 15, 1987, p. 148.
The New York Times Book Review. XCII, June 14, 1987, p. 27.
The Village Voice. XXXII, June 23, 1987, p. 57.

BRENDAN

Author: Frederick Buechner (1926-   )
Publisher: Atheneum (New York). 240 pp. $17.95
Type of work: Historical novel
Time: Early Middle Ages, mainly the sixth century
Locale: Ireland and the New World

A linguistically inspired and theologically profound fictional account of the life of Saint Brendan the Navigator, the Irish priest who may have been the first European to visit the New World

> *Principal personages:*
> BRENDAN, a zealous monk, seafarer, and evangelist
> FINN, the narrator, his lifelong companion
> SAINT ITA, who rears Brendan in her community
> SAINT BRIGIT, who sustains Brendan in the faith
> SAINT COLMAN, a bard converted by Brendan
> SAINT MALO, a Christ-hating figure who becomes Brendan's confessor

Frederick Buechner may well be the finest self-consciously Christian novelist in the United States. While the late twentieth century is certainly no golden age for artists of this description, Buechner runs in good company: Walker Percy, Reynolds Price, Will Campbell, and Madeleine L'Engle are names that come immediately to mind. With *Godric* (1980), Buechner turned away from the realistic mode of the novels in the Bebb series (*Lion Country*, *Open Heart*, *Love Feast*, and *Treasure Hunt*) to treat the life of a twelfth century saint. *Brendan* also concerns a saint, but now the setting is even further removed from the present. The subject of the novel was born in 484 near what is now Tralee, Ireland. Brendan intrigues some historians because of the claim that his famous voyages brought him to the New World (he may indeed have gotten as far as Florida). Buechner, however, wishes to see the voyages in another light: how they both hindered and advanced Brendan's progress toward sainthood.

This task is clearly a very difficult one, for sainthood is extremely difficult to comprehend, let alone to portray convincingly in fiction. It cannot be sought, for to seek sainthood would mean attempting to earn a status which must be imputed—that is, attempting to exert control over God. Yet comprehending that sainthood is an unseekable gift can lead one to even subtler perils, for the properly humble would-be saint is tempted to take pride in the very humility he or she is "required" to possess. As if these pitfalls were not enough, Buechner's subject forces him to cope with other problems. Saints are Christian heroes, but ours is the age of the antiheroic. Saints perform wonders and miracles, but modern science produces miracles sufficient to most of our needs. Saints are celibate and chaste. How can they possibly offer us a thrilling enough story?

Despite these obstacles, Buechner has written a thoroughly compelling novel about Saint Brendan. A major reason for the novel's success has to do with Finn, its narrator. He tells nearly the entire tale, and Buechner provides him with qualities which evoke the reader's trust and loyalty. Two years younger than Brendan, Finn comes to know him at the school of Abbess Ita in County Limerick. Brendan had been taken from his peasant parents at the age of one and placed there by his kinsman Bishop Erc, a former druid converted by Saint Patrick himself—"at the mere sound of whose name the high angels wet their holy breeches," says Finn. Ita prepared Brendan for a priestly vocation, but earthy, skeptical Finn takes no vows. To be sure, his is a reverent skepticism—he crosses himself to ward off the Devil, checks his ruminations on the nonexistence of the soul, and is an empathic observer of Brendan's spiritual development. Yet he never becomes Brendan's follower, though the two finally become friends. Whether Finn ultimately accepts the new faith is an interesting question, the answer to which depends on one's interpretation of the last sentence of the novel.

In any case, Finn is Buechner's bridge from modernity to the rough, faith-saturated, impoverished world of sixth century Ireland. Buechner supplies Finn with a startlingly pungent, densely metaphorical, and completely Irish narrative language in which to chronicle a vast tale filled with remarkable characters, strange adventures, and madly improbable events. Brendan's birth is attended by a huge brush fire which leaves no trace of its destruction. A doe (was it Saint Ita transformed?) suckles him when his mother's milk ceased. Brendan converts the heathen king Bauheen by reading in the old man's eyes the name of his beloved dog Fiona. With one prodigious spit, Maeve, the warrior woman of Irish legend, splits a rock in two. More impressively, she keeps her virginity while ascertaining whether Hugh the Black has two testicles or one. The Abbess Brigit dries her wet cloak by laying it over a sunbeam. Brendan heals a man who has received a deep spear wound and conjures a mist in order to forestall a battle.

The most celebrated adventures of Brendan occur on his two great voyages. Finn narrates only the second of these, for he is washed overboard near shore at night just as the first begins. The tale of the first voyage is related through Brendan's journal, recorded on parchment and later copied by Finn. For a brief space (twenty-six pages), the reader is thus given direct access to Brendan's consciousness. Not everyone will appreciate this break in the novel's narrative consistency. Brendan's voice is distinctive but far too modern. Excluding the lovely prayers addressed to God, "my dear," it could be mistaken for the voice of Ernest Hemingway or F. Scott Fitzgerald. Also, Brendan records much more dialogue than one would expect of a diarist.

Yet the power of the narrated events allows the reader to overlook these flaws. Buechner's historical end note explains that he relied heavily on Tim Severin's *The Brendan Voyage* (1978), a description of his forty-five-hundred-mile journey in a leather-covered curragh (or coracle). Severin reached Newfoundland, substantiating the claim that Irish monks might indeed have discovered America. Severin did not, however, camp on the back of the black great whale Jasconius, who cries out his own name. Nor did he meet Judas, banished to a rock in the far Atlantic and no longer able to shape his lips to speak Christ's blessed name.

Brendan's first journey lasts five long years. His second voyage commences more than a decade later, after he has been made a priest, founded his own company of monks at Clonfert, built churches, and spread Christianity. The goal of this voyage is again Tir-na-n-Og, the Country of the Young, the Land of the Blessed. Also called Hy Brasail, it is pictured by bards as a place where the righteous go after death, where sin is unknown, and where "gentle men and handsome women lie together in the shade . . . without shame or sorrow . . . and all you've ever prized and lost is once more found." Brendan yearns to meet Erc there, as well as to find his parents. Finn seeks his dead son. Each of the fifty crew members of the large vessel longs for some profound reunion, completion, transcendence of finitude.

The tropical paradise that they find, however, does not yield such treasures. Surprisingly, it is ruled by a long-lost, merrily crazy Irish monk whose faith has gone sour—his pets are named Saint Patrick and Paraclete. The sacred mud from its river does not heal Crosan, Brendan's beloved, godly clown. The journey results in Maeve's final disillusionment with Christianity. Hy Brasail is not the Kingdom of Heaven, but rather a confusing place of sensuous beauty and tempting perversions of true faith.

The "failure" of the second voyage forces Brendan to intensify an inner journey already commenced. A series of deaths culminates in Brendan's self-banishment to an island in the River Shannon. On the first voyage, a crew member is burned to death when the curragh veers too close to a volcanic eruption. About the same time, Finn's only child (whom he had named Brendan) dies, and so do Brendan's neglected parents and his saintly teacher, Jarlath. Later, a monk's drowning is indirectly caused by an angry, heedless order from Brendan. Crosan is the victim on the second voyage. These innocents, Brendan believes, suffered because of his obsession with Tir-na-n-Og and worldly glory. He begins to listen to the taunts and accusations of Malo, a bitter fellow whom Ita assigned to him as a continuing source of penance.

Malo represents the costliness of Christian discipleship. Just before a harvest, he converts to the new faith. When his grain fields are consumed by fire, his kindred rape and strangle his wife and then torture his children to death before his eyes. From that day forth, Malo torments believing Christians, especially Brendan. In his river hermitage, Brendan accentuates the antagonisms by using Malo as his confessor. Yet the men begin to be drawn together. They are linked through their mutual affection for Crosan and for the blind sage, Mahon. Watching Brendan pass through a long night of the spirit provokes some pity in Malo, thus softening him. Malo finally ceases warring with believers. Near the end of the novel, he says, "All at once I saw in myself the helplessness of Christ. . . . That's when I forgave him. . . . He's so helpless he's got no hands to help with save our own."

Christ's powerless hands are emblematic of the relation of deep dependency in which Christians—even saints—stand one to the other. Throughout the book, Buechner builds up successive layers of symbols to communicate this insight. There are recurring images of corporeal incompleteness and blemish. Ancient Ita suckles Brendan to give him strength for the second voyage. Finn is deaf in one ear. Mahon is blind. Hugh the Handsome cannot become king at Cashel because he has only one "stone." The chronicler Gildas is missing a leg. There are several heads along the wall at Cashel, and Brendan yearns to restore them to their bodies in Tir-na-n-Og. This symbol of beheading is the book's most persistent, negatively suggesting Paul's meditations on the Church as Christ's body. Buechner hints that Christians are led by a blemished yet victorious king who relies for his life on blemished yet faithful subjects.

Noncorporeal symbols are also present, but they convey a similar meaning. Brendan senses that he is responsible for Maeve's loss of faith. Mahon explains to him that the king in chess is the weakest and most dependent piece, yet he is the most precious of all. To this Brendan responds that "Christ too is just such a king in his weakness, meek and lowly of heart and like a sheep dumb before its shearers."

Thus sainthood in *Brendan* is discovered to be a communal achievement. For all men and women are cripples, reliant on the completing efforts of others and of the power of God. "To lend each other a hand when we're falling," remarks Brendan. "Perhaps that's the only work that matters in the end." That Malo only becomes *Saint* Malo by learning how to embrace Christ's weakness is an apt indication of the paradox Buechner's art illumines.

Of all the artistic virtues on display in *Brendan*, none is more conspicuous than its use of language. Buechner has provided Finn with verbal gifts of the highest order. He speaks in a slightly ungrammatical folk idiom rich in metaphor, alliteration, hyperbole, and irony. Buechner has clearly listened well to the lovely rhythms of contemporary Irish English—and perhaps Gaelic as well. At the same time, Buechner's fluent appropriation of and acquaintanceship with *Beowulf*, Geoffrey Chaucer, William Shakespeare, John Milton, and Edmund Spenser is evident throughout. Gerard Manley Hopkins' alliterative style is strongly evident in particular sentences in *Brendan*: "It dazzled Dismas's eyes with the basin till his eyes themselves went silver," or "There's shield-makers and smiths, cobblers and tinkers for keeping the king's strength strong."

Brendan thus begs to be read aloud, declaimed, even memorized. The glories of the non-Latin side of the English language are wonderfully displayed. Gnarled, strange, arresting words find their way into Finn's narrative: flummery, wen, moil, cairn, taradiddle, cockalorum. Further, the book is positively cluttered with startling similes and metaphors. Says Finn: "I once saw a man trussed in a wicker cage for burning. Brendan's face was like that." Or, "His eyes filled slow as cow prints in the rain with the sight of us." Or, "His tongue wobbled like a crab claw in a hole as he tried to get a greeting out."

It is important to see that this vibrant language is related to Buechner's theological intention. Nothing stifles contemporary Christianity more than its linguistic fatigue, the meaninglessness of "God-talk," the clichéd formulas of televangelists and popular piety, the invasion of terms drawn from sociology. *Brendan* is another effort in Buechner's long quest to loosen and enliven theology's tongue. It comes at a time when literary scholars and theologians are recovering the integrity of biblical narrative and the possibilities of experiencing the Bible in aural terms, as a compendium of dramatic, enactable stories by which living communities and synagogues and churches are sustained. Significantly, the word "Jesus" almost never appears in this deeply Christian novel, nor are there abundant references to "God." Yet in a manner curiously surprising to modern ears, Buechner's sixth century speech is alive with references to the Messiah. He is "King Christ," "Prince of Light," "King of Stars and Waves." Ita prays over her fosterlings: "May the shadow of Christ fall on thee. May the garment of Christ cover thee. May the breath of Christ breathe in thee." Gildas says, "They hold once Christ has cocked his holy eye on you, you're helpless to flee him as a bird in a net." Of a deathbed conversion, the horse-loving Brigit reports: "I slipped Christ's bridle on him, the Holy Mother be praised."

In the world of Buechner's story, words (and the Word) are not cheap. Readers of the novel are thus subjected to a process of training in an earlier form of Christian sensibility, one which took words and oaths and curses very seriously. One becomes sufficiently schooled in this sensibility to recognize a very serious moment in the novel. The monk Gestas, having lost his only friend overboard, cries to the heavens: "Thou holy bleeding God, I piss for spite into your lovely eyes." These words cause the very sun to pause in its setting. Brendan is haunted by them to his death. It is not the blasphemy that shocks, but the rejection of the tenderness that lies deep within the heart of creation. Gestas is doomed not to Hell but to life apart from all that would sustain him in his loss. For God's eyes are lovely and loving. They call men to an unfathomable intimacy. In their gaze, the true costliness of things is revealed. Thus, when Brendan petitions God, it is with this form of address: "Pray do not forget, my dear, how thou didst mark me once for thy precious." In *Brendan*, "my dear" is a phrase used both in prayer and in everyday speech. The reader is disarmed by it, as its users disarm themselves in its usage. Malo's conversion begins when he can finally say to his beloved, dying Crosan, "You deserve far better, my dear."

What more can one expect from a book than such practical teaching in how to speak anew of the ways of God to humanity? Buechner is an ordained Presbyterian minister and one of the finest preachers of our time. Perhaps his literary aim is the conversion of his audience. Surely such a statement puts the matter too simply, however, with too much emphasis on the teller and not the tale, the result and not the mysterious process that yields it. Though Finn does not convert to Christianity, he does grow sufficiently in the faith to utter a profound judgment on Brendan. If he were called upon to "sentence" Brendan, he says, "I'd sentence him to have mercy on himself. I'd sentence him to strive less for the glory of God than just to let it swell his sails if it can." "If it can..." expresses the doubtful hope with which many will approach *Brendan*. Buechner seems to be saying that such a hope is good enough and that our friend Finn will try to pray for us now and at the hour of our sentencing.

Leslie E. Gerber

Sources for Further Study

The Atlantic. CCLX, July, 1987, p. 99.
Booklist. LXXXIII, May 15, 1987, p. 1407.
Christianity Today. XXXI, December 11, 1987, p. 58.
Kirkus Reviews. LV, April 1, 1987, p. 489.
Library Journal. CXII, June 1, 1987, p. 127.
Los Angeles Times Book Review. September 6, 1987, p. 13.
The New York Times Book Review. XCII, August 9, 1987, p. 15.
The New Yorker. LXIII, September 28, 1987, p. 97.
Publishers Weekly. CCXXXI, April 10, 1987, p. 84.

A CENTURY OF THE SCOTTISH PEOPLE, 1830-1950

Author: Thomas Christopher Smout (1933-   )
Publisher: Yale University Press (New Haven, Connecticut). Illustrated. 318 pp.
  $25.00
Type of work: Social history
Time: 1830-1950
Locale: Scotland

A lucid history of many elements of Scottish society, concentrating on the rural poor and the industrial working class

Currently Professor of Scottish History in the University of St. Andrews, T. C. Smout has, in the present volume, written a worthy successor to and continuation of his earlier, well-received *A History of the Scottish People, 1560-1830* (1969). Though the volume is presented as social history, its concentration on the rural and industrial poor and working class is clearly the result of Professor Smout's long interest in those classes in such earlier work as *Scottish Trade on the Eve of Union, 1660-1707* (1963), *Comparative Aspects of Scottish and Irish Economic and Social History, 1600-1900* (edited with L. M. Cullen, 1977), *Scottish Population History from the Seventeenth Century to the 1930's* (1977), and *The State of the Scottish Working Class in 1843* (1979).

The focus of the present study is slightly more limited than the simple title might indicate. First, this is social history; while politics are inevitably mentioned, there is no attempt to provide a consecutive recounting of the ins and outs of various political parties and governments. Second, the book does not attempt to deal comprehensively with the full spectrum of society; as mentioned above, Smout concentrates upon the poor and the working classes, to the extent of having virtually nothing to say of the life of the upper or landed classes, of those who might usually be classed as the opinion makers of the period. The middle classes receive only slightly more attention. Finally, there are certain elements of what would normally be called "social life" which are either not addressed or treated only briefly, for example, the artistic and intellectual life of the period, the popular literature of the period, transportation, or sports other than football (soccer). Had the author attempted to cover all these topics and classes, the result would have clearly been unwieldy. Thus, if the reader wishes to know about Scottish baronial architecture, the growth of Scottish industry, the life of the clans, or details of Scottish relations with the central government in London, this is not the book to which to turn.

What the author does do—and that is still considerable—he does very well indeed. After a brief general introduction on the state of Scotland in the 1830's and 1840's, the author looks at his social history under a number of different topics, rather than attempting to juggle the different topics within a straight chronological narrative. Thus Smout presents separate chapters on such topics as the tenement city, working conditions in industry, drink, sex, churchgoing, and education; within each chapter he deals with the particular topic on a generally chronological basis, though it must be said that the majority of his material deals with the years before 1900 rather than after. The reader is, in effect, presented with a series of very sharp essays on particular elements of Scottish social history within the period covered.

To concentrate as Smout does upon the lower orders of Scottish society is certainly understandable, if for no other reasons than that the upper classes have certainly been adequately covered in the traditional history books, and that, after all, the classes under discussion here in fact form the great majority of the population. This concentration upon the lower orders, however, does present the historian with a practical problem, namely, that the lower classes, especially of the nineteenth century, are relatively inarticulate. It is difficult for the historian to have specific, firsthand documentary evidence from people of whom many could not read and write, and most of whom were far too busy earning a living and keeping body and soul together to be able to take time out to describe their lives and circumstances. The inevitable result is that the book leans heavily on statistics and government papers and reports to speak for those who were generally unable to speak for themselves. It is a measure of the author's ability that he has used these materials judiciously, telling a story that is firmly grounded in hard evidence yet not lacking in the human touch, even occasionally moving.

From the viewpoint of the casual modern reader, the story which is told in these pages is a horrific one. Page after page, report after report, statistic after statistic lay bare, as more impressionistic or anecdotal narration could not, the wage slavery, the appalling sanitary conditions, the almost barbaric housing, and the fear of unemployment. Though the writer is by no means a Marxist historian, his work will certainly give no comfort to staunch supporters of the proposition that unrestrained capitalism and free enterprise (much praised in nineteenth century Scotland) are good for all, owner and workingman alike. Smout realizes the effect his recital will probably have on readers and warns, early in the work, that the assumptions of the present may not always be appropriate criteria for judging events of another period. What we may regard as insupportable or even immoral was not necessarily insupportable or immoral to those experiencing it. While life must certainly not have been particularly pleasant, it is difficult if not impossible for twentieth century readers to say at this distance that the people of the lower orders were or were not "happy"—whatever that word may have meant at the time. Smout is writing history and not a tract. Thus he tends not to moralize or read lessons, though the conclusions from the evidence he presents are often inescapable.

One of Smout's themes which may surprise readers is the depth and strength of the fear that the lower classes inspired in the middle and upper classes. Quotation after quotation from the Victorians themselves reveals not only a widespread loathing of the lower orders, especially the urban working class, but also the actual physical fear with which such people were regarded. If one listened only to the voice of middle-class Scotland, one could easily gain the impression that the lower classes were concerned only to revolt, hang every "aristo" from the nearest lamppost, and plunder every shop and mansion in the country. (Though the author does not say so, this attitude certainly suggests a remarkably bad conscience upon the part of those well-off and in authority.) Further reinforcing this fear was the assumption by the middle classes that they were not only economically superior to the lower classes, but morally and spiritually superior as well.

In this light it is paradoxical that, in spite of the conditions faced by the workers, in spite of the fear of unemployment, the lower classes never, in fact, boldly threatened to rise against the middle class. No doubt it looked somewhat different at the time, and there were certainly protests and petitions, but the fears of the middle classes were never to be actualized. In the final two chapters of the book, Smout analyzes the working-class radical tradition and the rise and fall of socialist idealism. Several factors seem to have prevented any particularly violent uprisings against the status quo. First, the largest and best organized movement, that of the Chartists, typically preached the power of moral force rather than violence. Second, while Scots of all classes were loyal to the memory and traditions of Scotland, their patriotism did not have in it much of an urge to separatism or nationalism. Smout notes that the radical tradition, descending from the working-class Liberals of the late nineteenth century, insisted strongly on no government intervention and a tradition of self-help which lasted almost until World War II. The working class itself presented difficulties to organized programs of change or protest; the divisions within the working class, such as that between craftsmen and ordinary laborers, caused many of the same attitudes as existed between the middle classes and the working classes generally. (In this context, it was always possible for the Scots lower classes to look down upon the growing number of Irish immigrants—perhaps there is something in human nature which requires everyone to have someone to look down on.) Finally, Smout documents the power of the urge to "respectability" which, reinforced by kirk and educational system alike, influenced all classes of society, and not least the lower classes.

Another theme which emerges from the book is the way in which government intervention came about, when it did come. In the earlier part of the period, a number of farsighted individuals and organizations attempted to ameliorate some of the worst effects of slums, bad housing, and poor sanitation. It quickly became evident that the problems were far too large for individuals, however wealthy, or voluntary organizations, however well-meaning, to achieve any substantial or lasting reforms. The only forces that could realistically handle the organization and capital requirements of slum clearance were, first, city governments and subsequently, central governments. Thus, elements of socialism or of the welfare state were introduced because it finally became evident that a certain job had to be done (for whatever reasons—economic, religious, humanitarian) and that the only authority with sufficient power and resources was the government. To the people of the day and to the present reader, no doubt such reforms and interventions came too slowly and perhaps not on a sufficient scale, but they did come, however, gradually and grudgingly. They arose from necessity, not from political ideology.

The most controversial views espoused by Smout in this book will no doubt be those in his chapter on education. Scots have traditionally afforded a great respect to education, and Scottish education has often been praised, not least in England, as a sort of model. Smout finds this respect exaggerated: "It is in the history of the school more than in any other aspect of recent social history that the key lies to some of the more depressing aspects of modern Scotland." The general spirit of Scottish education aimed

> firstly at providing, as cheaply as possible, the bulk of the population with the bare minimum of elementary education combined with adequate social discipline, and secondly, at giving a small number of children of all classes, but especially of the higher classes, a more respectable academic education, to qualify them for their role as a controlling elite.

The myth of democratic education in Scotland, whereby any young lad of parts could rise, is, in fact, merely that—a myth. The reasons for the gap between myth and reality are not surprising. A goodly number of people continued to believe that to educate the laboring classes was wrong because to do so would cause them to be less content with their lot, making them bad servants. The continuing demand for child labor was probably the greatest enemy of school attendance. (In Glasgow in 1857, fewer than 50 percent of the children between five and ten years of age were attending school.) Religious differences, too complicated even to summarize here, also militated against universal, quality education; for example, during much of the nineteenth century, many of the Irish Catholic children received little education because of the choice of other sects to have as little to do with them as possible. Under Smout's critical eye, the great reputation of Scottish education is shown to be totally unjustified.

In such space as here provided it has only been possible to summarize and generalize. The reader should be aware, however, that Smout is most discriminating; he makes numerous qualifications of his interpretations; he distinguishes between regions and between cities. Clearly, not everything he says is always true of all places—and Smout knows it and tries to explain.

The book is furnished with extensive notes and most useful annotated bibliographies at the end of each chapter for further reading. This book is not only informative but also wise and thoughtful. It is to be hoped that the author does not wait too long before bringing his social history of Scotland forward from 1950.

Gordon N. Bergquist

Sources for Further Study

Booklist. LXXXIII, February 15, 1987, p. 871.
British Book News. February, 1987, p. 73.
Choice. XXIV, May, 1987, p. 1457.
Chronicle of Higher Education. XXXIII, January 21, 1987, p. 6.
Contemporary Review. CCXLIX, September, 1986, p. 166.
The Guardian Weekly. CXXXV, July 13, 1987, p. 21.
History Today. XXXVI, October, 1986, p. 57.
London Review of Books. IX, January 22, 1987, p. 19.
The Observer. June 29, 1986, p. 22.
The Spectator. CCLVI, June 14, 1986, p. 27.

CHAOS
Making a New Science

Author: James Gleick (1954-   )
Publisher: Viking (New York). Illustrated. 354 pp. $19.95
Type of work: Current history and history of science
Time: 1960-1986

A report on the development of the mathematical study of turbulent systems and the interdisciplinary scientific cooperation that produced a startling reappraisal of the nature of chaos

> *Principal personages:*
> MICHAEL BARNSLEY, an Oxford-educated mathematician who developed a new technique using chaos to model nature
> MITCHELL FEIGENBAUM, who at the Los Alamos National Laboratory in 1976 developed the theory of universality
> MICHAEL HÉNAN, an astronomer at the Nice Observatory in France whose work on mathematical "attractors" deepened insight into chaos
> ALBERT LIBCHABER, an experimental physicist at the École Normale Supérieure in France, who in the late 1970's showed that chaos theory applied to actual behavior of fluids
> EDWARD LORENZ, a meteorologist at the Massachusetts Institute of Technology (MIT) whose primitive computer models of weather laid the foundation for chaos in the early 1960's
> BENOIT MANDELBROT, a mathematician, who as an IBM researcher developed and named fractal geometry and the Mandelbrot set
> ROBERT MAY, a biologist at Princeton University, who in the 1970's used chaos models to explore population biology and epidemiology
> STEPHEN SMALE, a topologist at the University of California, Berkeley, who in the 1960's helped picture the chaotic behavior of dynamical systems
> JAMES YORKE, a mathematician at the University of Maryland in the 1970's, who gave chaos its name

Underneath the rubric "chaos" lurks a revolution in science. James Gleick, a science writer for *The New York Times*, sets for himself the task of chronicling that revolution in progress. Though there is far from universal agreement on the boundaries of the new science, or even that it should be called chaos, most critics acknowledge fundamental breakthroughs in the mathematical understanding of turbulent systems. Until the advent of chaos research in the 1960's and 1970's, and the development of high-speed computers, there were no adequate scientific ways to describe phenomena as common as the turbulence produced by boiling water, mixing cream into coffee, or the collision of air masses. Chaos studied these systems in process. Mathematicians and physicists, ecologists and astronomers, physiologists and those in fluid dynamics—all learned to "see" in a new way, not piecemeal and locally, but systemwide and globally.

The revolutionary character of chaos is not limited to new ways of evaluating systems. Gleick borrows insights from science historian Thomas Kuhn and *The Structure of Scientific Revolutions* (1962, enlarged second edition 1970), picturing chaos as a threat to the old ways of doing science, as well as a risky undertaking for its pioneers: "A few freethinkers working alone, unable to explain where they are heading, afraid even to tell their colleagues what they are doing—that romantic image lies at the heart of Kuhn's scheme, and it has occurred in real life, time and time again, in the exploration of chaos." Gleick's report on chaos is in part the story of such freethinking scientists and how the interdisciplinary nature of the study of nonlinear systems encroached upon their colleagues' well-guarded turf. Each of the chapters in *Chaos* follows one or more pioneers of the new science as insight is added to insight. Swirled into the mixture of personalities is Gleick's explanation of the fundamentals of chaos and its applications. A fitting kind of turbulence prevails throughout the book as each chapter explores new lines of research, which mix with and reinterpret earlier data. Gleick's account is enlivened by dozens of anecdotes derived from extensive interviews. There is the image of Mitchell Fiegenbaum thinking deep thoughts on long walks at Los Alamos National Laboratory in New Mexico, and the four rebellious researchers who constituted the "dynamical systems collective" at the University of California's Santa Cruz campus.

The text is supplemented with sections of color and black-and-white illustrations and graphs, though oddly text and illustrations are not always closely coordinated (the detailed index, however, does refer to the appropriate picture under the appropriate concept). Gleick's prose is simple and basically nonmathematical as he conveys the feeling as well as the content of what it means to "make a new science." As a result, *Chaos* has been widely praised; it was chosen by *The New York Times Book Review* as one of the best books of 1987.

One of the foundations of chaos research is that nonlinear systems are sensitive to and dependent upon small changes in initial conditions. Linear or straight-line relationships can easily be graphed with a ruler, because the values in a linear equation are proportional to one another. As Gleick notes, if friction did not exist, a simple linear equation could describe how much energy is required to accelerate a hockey puck. Once friction is introduced, however, the straightforwardness in equations disappears. Friction plays a part in how fast the puck is moving, but it is not a constant, linear, factor because friction is more or less significant depending on the present speed of the puck. A nonlinear equation is required. "Nonlinearity means that the act of playing the game has a way of changing the rules."

This insight was forcefully brought out in the early 1960's with the work of meteorologist Edward Lorenz. When Lorenz attempted to capture the essence of atmospheric convection using three simple, but nonlinear, equations, he found that tiny changes in the numbers he was using at the beginning produced wild variations as the equations were iterated (that is, as numerical values produced by each equation were plugged back into the equation to simulate constantly changing weather patterns). Perhaps a difference of a degree or two in initial atmospheric temperatures, for example, might mean the difference between a placid day and the advent of a hurricane a month in the future. The difficulty for long-range weather forecasts, however, was that even the most sensitive temperature gauges had only finite accuracy, and only so many could practically be placed in the atmosphere. Thus, small temperature changes overlooked by the instruments, or changes outside the range of the instrument, might be the determinants of the development of a storm weeks ahead. Though it sounds obvious, Lorenz's discovery violated a basic scientific credo, a kind of modified Newtonianism, that imperfect measurements in the beginning could nevertheless produce close approximations of future events.

Yet while small changes at the beginning produced vast differences later on in a system of nonlinear equations, the variations were not random. Hidden within Lorenz's three nonlinear equations was an elegant "butterfly" pattern: As lines showing the progress of the system were graphed in three dimensions, two "wings" emerged with the pattern traced over and over again, yet never exactly the same as any other pattern. Lorenz found that a small change in the initial values used in his equations meant a complete reshuffling of the wing pattern as the equation was iterated. Thus, though different initial values of nonlinear equations could produce chaotic differences later, at a deeper level the system was patterned, even though the pattern might be reshuffled. In the midst of chaos locally, as others later put it, the system was stable globally. The Great Red Spot in the Jovian atmosphere is a case in point. In the light of chaos, older theories that tried to account for the Red Spot's stability by tying it to a surface feature can be discarded. "The spot is a self-organizing system, created and regulated by the same nonlinear twists that create the unpredictable turmoil around it. It is stable chaos."

Robert May began his career as a theoretical physicist in Australia, but it is as a biologist that he made his mark on the emerging science of chaos. In a mathematical exploration of changes in the boom-and-bust cycles of wildlife populations, May discovered that when the boom-and-bust parameter is low, the population becomes extinct. There may not be sufficient animal population to overcome predators or establish its own niche, and so the population is doomed. As the parameter increased, however (as May expected), the population increases at a steady rate. If the system is driven harder, (that is, if the parameter is increased), the boom-and-bust rate breaks in two, indicating an alternating higher and lower population in alternating years. The system is still regular, though more complex, when at a higher parameter there appear four alternating population levels. As the parameter is increased, the number of population levels doubles, then doubles again. At a certain parameter value, chaos intervenes. That is, in nonlinear equations governing the rate of animal population, changes from year to year appear to be totally random. Yet as the parameter was further increased, out of "randomness" emerged new areas of periodicity. The population would have three stable levels, then six, then twelve, with an eventual return to chaos—only to be followed by new areas of stability or patterned behavior. Another old scientific intuition—that order gave rise to order, randomness to randomness—had been dashed. In May's first crude work with a hand calculator, it seemed that even simple nonlinear equations gave rise to chaos, which appeared random but which was infinitely finely structured.

May's findings were not mere theoretical curiosities. Gleick points out that records of measles epidemics in New York display a similar kind of "deterministic chaos." When inoculations were first introduced, the number of measles cases, contrary to intuition, did not slowly subside but rather took on a pattern of seeming random oscillation. An inoculation program could actually produce a short-term increase in the disease, even while the disease was being eliminated over the long run.

The mathematical investigation of the patterns within chaos drew on what became known as fractal geometry. First developed by Benoit Mandelbrot at IBM, fractal (for fractional dimension) geometry became a tool of nonlinear dynamics, used alike by seismologists and Hollywood's special effects artists. Robert May had discovered a patterned chaos in population behavior equations; Mandelbrot was working on the problem of noise during computer interfaces. Whenever one computer talked with another computer over telephone lines, it seemed that little random bursts of noise would produce transmission errors. Mandelbrot, working on the problem in the 1960's, discerned that no matter how short a time span, the noise was never continuous. Between one burst of noise and another there were always times of clean transmission. It was that way on the largest and the smallest scales. Mathematically speaking, the "dust" of noise was infinitely small but ever present. (Mandelbrot's advice to IBM was to increase the redundancy in a transmission and not to try to overpower the noise which seeped in everywhere.)

Mandelbrot found that the noise in the circuits, while seemingly random, nevertheless formed an elegant mathematical pattern. The idea that there was a scattering of noise, no matter how finely sliced the time period, had a spatial analogy. One might imagine observing an entire coastline, and then examining a tiny portion of the coastline with a magnifying glass. The same kind of protrusions and inlets are present at both scales. The roughness of the coastline extends at least down to the atomic level, and perhaps beyond.

A given stretch of coastline is thus, paradoxically, infinitely long. Mandelbrot was able to calculate the degree of roughness of objects and found that, whatever the scale, the degree of roughness remained constant. Degrees of roughness were measured in what Mandelbrot called fractional dimensions. The curve of a snowflake, or a cloud, or a coastline, "implies an organizing structure that lies hidden among the hideous complication of such shapes." A simple triangle, and a formula that adds a triangle half its size to each side of the original triangle, and so on, when iterated enough times produces the kind of roughness that mimics the real coastline, or the real snowflake. Simplicity yields complexity.

In the late 1970's, Mandelbrot plotted a strange fractal shape that now bears his name. The Mandelbrot set is infinitely complex but based on the iteration of a simple nonlinear equation. Plotted on the complex plane (with real numbers on one axis and imaginary numbers on the other), each dot represented the behavior of each number, regardless of whether in the iterated equation the values tended toward infinity. Those numbers that did not were in the set; those that did were outside. High-speed computers were needed for the plotting, for only after, say, ten thousand iterations might it be apparent the equation tended toward infinity. It was like determining which volume levels produced the squeal of microphone-loudspeaker feedback and which did not. When plotted as groups of colored points by a computer, the Mandelbrot set resembles a buglike object with what seem to be wisps of fine hair emanating from its body. Yet the computer can perform ever more calculations, thus "magnifying" any portion of the set, revealing a strange world of infinite complexity and pattern. Here are bizarre seahorses, diamond-studded starfish, fiery plumed squid. And yet, as "magnification" between any two points increases, "one picture seemed more and more random, until suddenly, unexpectedly, deep in the heart of a bewildering region, appeared a familiar oblate form, studded with buds: the Mandelbrot set, every tendril and every atom in place." The lesson in these abstract pictures was twofold: First, engineers could no longer simply assume that some approximation of the ideal in a nonlinear equation was sufficiently "safe"—the Mandelbrot set demonstrated that in some equations, chaos may be only an infinitely small point away.

The other lesson had to do with "universality." This discovery is credited to Mitchell Feigenbaum, who in the mid-1970's found that, as one researcher put it, "there were structures in nonlinear systems that are always the same if you looked at them the right way." The reappearance of the Mandelbrot set, deep within the Mandelbrot set itself, was a good example. Some of the structures in nonlinear equations were independent of the particular equations. Again, this was more than theory. In the late 1970's, when Albert Libchaber experimented with the turbulent behavior of liquid helium, he observed "the universal Feigenbaum constants turning in that instant from a mathematical ideal to a physical reality."

The message for researchers was that while Nature may be chaotic, she is chaotic only in certain ways, only in or through certain patterns. Leaves, clouds, coastlines, all look as they do through the outworking of relatively simple patterning. Evolution itself might be explained as "chaos with feedback." As chaos has shown, incredible beauty and complex orders can come out of "randomness." The new scientific credo is this: "Simple systems give rise to complex behavior. Complex systems give rise to simple behavior. And most important, the laws of complexity hold universally, caring not at all for the details of a system's constituent atoms."

As a report on science-in-the-making, Gleick's account necessarily lacks historical perspective. He seems to take most of his sources at face value and succeeds in involving the reader in the social and political struggles that produced chaos. Whether chaos will become merely another discipline, with its own well-guarded turf, or the face of science will truly be changed and barriers shattered must be left to future historians. For his part, Gleick is a compassionate and reliable guide through the turbulent beginnings of a new science.

Dan Barnett

Sources for Further Study

Chicago Tribune Books, November 22, 1987, p. 10.
The New York Times, October 15, 1987, p. 11.
The New York Times Book Review. XCII, October 25, 1987, p. 11.

CHARLES FOURIER
The Visionary and His World

Author: Jonathan Beecher (1937-   )
Publisher: University of California Press (Berkeley). Illustrated. 601 pp. $49.50
Type of work: Historical biography
Time: 1772-1837
Locale: Besançon, Bugey, Lyons, and Paris, France

A historical biography of Charles Fourier that emphasizes the influence of the French Revolution and Restoration upon his thought

> *Principal personages:*
> CHARLES FOURIER, a utopian social theorist
> JUST MURION, one of his chief supporters and disciples
> VICTOR CONSIDÉRANT, his disciple, the founder of a Fourierist colony in Texas
> ROBERT OWEN, an industrialist and social theorist
> HENRI SAINT-SIMON, a social theorist

Charles Fourier was the nineteenth century's complete utopian. A social critic who advocated "absolute deviation" from established philosophies and institutions, he surpassed Rousseau in the intransigence of his rejection of the society in which he lived. A psychologist who celebrated the passions as agents of human happiness, he carried to its ultimate conclusion the rejection of the doctrine of Original Sin that had been the hallmark of utopian thinking ever since the Renaissance. A social prophet whose blueprints included everything from color schemes for work uniforms to designs for nursery furniture, he was more concerned than any of his radical contemporaries to give precise definition to his conception of the good society. A visionary who foresaw an age in which oranges would grow in Warsaw and sea water could be turned into lemonade, he had a faith in the power of human beings to shape their own world that was remarkable even in the age of Napoleon.

This description of the wide-ranging interests of Charles Fourier provides a framework for examining Beecher's portrait of the man in *Charles Fourier: The Visionary and His World*. The excerpt from the preface only touches upon the subjects in which Fourier was interested and upon which he theorized. What Beecher seeks to accomplish in this work is not a recapitulation of Fourier's utopian system but an examination of how his life experiences influenced his intellectual development and contributed to the formation of his utopian vision. The recounting of the man's life and development of his social system is presented in three broad sections.

The first of these, "Provincial Autodidact," relates Fourier's formative years in provincial France (Besançon). His experiences with revolutionary change—especially the Jacobin terror—and with economic difficulties—loss of an inheritance and difficulty earning a living as a commission merchant (traveling salesman)—started Fourier thinking about a better way of life. As Beecher relates, Fourier's ideas developed largely in reaction to political events and socioeconomic realities of the Revolutionary period and age of Napoleon. These excesses and abuses of power left him with a lasting hatred of revolution and social turmoil and directed his thought toward an evolutionary rather than revolutionary social system. Within this section, Beecher details many of the encounters and experiences that had a direct influence on Fourier's writing and on his theoretical system. For example, Fourier's futile efforts to secure a position as a recognized commission agent at the Paris Bourse had the effect of poisoning him against organized capitalism and providing a case for eliminating the stock exchange and its functions in the society of the future—"Harmony," as Fourier termed it. From a consideration of Fourier's formative years, the book moves to a discussion of his middle years and the development of his theories and utopian writings.

"The Theory" builds upon the preceding section, as Beecher shifts his focus from Fourier's interaction with the world to his reaction to it. Here the main themes of Fourier's work are presented in relation to those experiences. In this section are discussed such aspects as Fourier's critique of civilization, his concept of the passions, the basis for an ideal community, reform of the education system, work, sexual liberation, and his scheme of history and cosmology. To a great extent, Fourier's thoughts on "passion as a force 'attracting' human beings to their predestined ends" and a harmonious world order were influenced by his reading and interpretation of the work of Sir Isaac Newton. It was the idea of an orderly system similar to that envisioned and described by Newton that formed the framework of his theory.

The final section of the book, "Parisian Prophet," returns to an examination of Fourier and the world of Restoration France. After spending years in Besançon and Lyons eking out a living and writing his treatises, Fourier moved to Paris in an effort to gain wider dissemination of his ideas and also to find a backer to underwrite an attempt at putting his theories into practice. This section also discusses Fourier's relationships with contemporary social theorists, notably Robert Owen and Henri Saint-Simon, and his interactions with the small group of disciples that he managed to gather. The work ends, naturally, with the death of Fourier in October, 1837.

Beecher has succeeded admirably in his presentation of the visionary and his world. A self-taught theorist whose ideas were quite advanced for the age in which he lived, Fourier's reality was often at odds with his theory, although his theories often sprang from his experiences. For example, in his views of sexual relationships, Fourier was far ahead of even the "liberal" French. A lifelong bachelor who was apparently celibate by choice, he advocated sexual liberation and the satisfaction of all sexual proclivities and erotic fantasies. Later theorists espoused a guaranteed minimum income for all; Fourier set a new standard with his "sexual minimum" for all. In his speculations on the future world of love and sex—the "nouveau monde amoureux"—he took the Catholic Church as his target:

Fourier's Court of Love, with its female pontiff, its priests and confessors, and its fakirs and fairies, is on one level certainly a parody of the Catholic religious hierarchy. These officials had the power to issue "indulgences," to impose "penances," and to exact "amorous tithes" from the faithful. . . . Just like the Catholic church, Harmony would also have its saints and angels and crusades. But the saints would acquire holiness through amorous and gastronomic prowess. . . . As for angels, they would generally come in pairs, the highest rank being occupied by the angelic couple, those "angels of virtue" who would minister to the sexual needs of the poor, the elderly, and the unattractive.

Emancipation from constraints was an underlying theme of Fourier's message. Indeed, he insisted that continued progress toward future Harmony was dependent upon the complete emancipation of women—a revolutionary idea for one who favored evolutionary change.

Beecher set out to provide a portrait of "the visionary and his world." To this end he has succeeded. Fourier is rescued from the anonymity of "utopian theorist" and revealed as a living, breathing, idiosyncratic human being. His experiences and thoughts ranged from soaring heights to abysmal depths, yet he never lost sight of the end—the achievement of his system of Harmony. Fourier failed to complete the exposition of his theory. In his writing, he frequently became carried away with minute detail at the expense of the broad picture. He wrote assiduously, promising that one day he would put it all together. Unfortunately, he never did; it was left to his few disciples, and to later historians of utopian thought, to provide the concise, ordered statement of his system that had eluded its creator.

While Beecher has done an excellent job with the biographical aspects of the work, the discussion of Fourier's theories and their development would have been better served with a chapter giving a concise statement of the Harmonian system. Thus, an intelligent reading of this book requires some knowledge of the French Revolution, the Napoleonic era, and the Restoration and an acquaintance with the basics of Fourier's utopian system. Those seeking an understanding of Fourier's system would do well to turn to Nicholas Riasanovsky's *The Teaching of Charles Fourier* (1969).

Beecher is to be commended for his thorough research. He has made excellent use of available sources to provide a revealing look at a very complex and interesting individual—one who might feel somewhat at home in today's world.

Steven A. McCarver

Sources for Further Study

Choice. XXV, September, 1987, p. 196.
Library Journal. CXII, May 15, 1987, p. 80.
The New York Times Book Review. XCII, May 17, 1987, p. 22.

CHAUCER
His Life, His Works, His World

Author: Donald R. Howard (1927-1987)
Publisher: E. P. Dutton (New York). Illustrated. 636 pp. $29.95
Type of work: Literary biography
Time: 1340-1400
Locale: England, France, Spain, and Italy

This book presents the facts about the life of Chaucer, while setting him in the context both of the English royal court and of contemporary European literature

> *Principal personages:*
> GEOFFREY CHAUCER, poet and courtier
> PHILIPPA CHAUCER, his wife
> JOHN OF GAUNT, the Duke of Lancaster, Chaucer's patron
> EDWARD III, King of England, 1327-1377
> RICHARD II, King of England, 1377-1399

Donald R. Howard remarks at the beginning of *Chaucer: His Life, His Works, His World* that one could almost believe there were "two Geoffrey Chaucers" in late fourteenth century England. One was the famous poet, author of well-known and now much-studied works such as *The Canterbury Tales* (1387-1400), *Troilus and Criseyde* (1382), *The Parliament of Fowls* (1380) and half a dozen more. The other was the courtier and civil servant, who is known, for example, to have been captured by the French in 1359, to have been employed in later life on a variety of missions in Spain and Italy, often important and sometimes secret, and to have been if not involved, at any rate very much present during such critical events as the Peasants' Revolt of 1381 or the long faction struggles which led to the deposition and murder of Richard II at the century's end. Scores of surviving documents refer to civil-servant Chaucer, telling about his career, income, and connections. None of them, however, says a word about his poetry, which to the royal bureaucrats who made appointments and paid expenses was clearly of no significance. Nor does Chaucer, in his poetry, say anything about his work as a "secret agent," whatever stimulus it may have given him. Except for a very few tantalizing references in the poetry to daily life and daily duties—vital because they confirm that the two Chaucers really were the same man—the gap between poet and courtier appears total. What Howard's book tries to do is to bridge the gap, reconstructing Chaucer's life and suggesting how political and personal crises did in fact affect his writing.

There is certainly an amplitude of provocative and dramatic material in Chaucer's life. Of all English poets, he was the one who was closest, for the longest, to the political center stage. Although he was the son of a London merchant, he could in the end even claim to be related to the English king, though in a typically strained and uncertain fashion. In 1366, Chaucer married Philippa de Roet, daughter of one of the queen's retainers. Only a few years later, his wife's sister Katherine became the mistress of John of Gaunt, Duke of Lancaster, the son of Edward III, uncle of Richard II, and father of Henry IV. For many years, this liaison was well-known to the entire English court, and after the death of his second wife, Gaunt even went so far as to marry his long-term mistress, the mother of several of his acknowledged children.

Near the end of his life, then, Chaucer could claim to be the king's uncle's brother-in-law. This relationship must have been at once useful and embarrassing. In the affecting elegy known as *The Book of the Duchess*, written to commemorate the death of Gaunt's first wife in 1368, Chaucer appears to be urging Gaunt to cease mourning and recover from grief. Can he have meant Gaunt to do this by seducing Katherine? Many years later, Chaucer received many marks of favor from Richard II, yet the man who deposed Richard was Gaunt's son Henry Bolingbroke, whom Chaucer must have known from birth; in addition, the man who, in some accounts, actually murdered the deposed king in 1400 was Henry's half brother, Sir Thomas Swynford, Gaunt's illegitimate son by Katherine and Chaucer's nephew.

Other aspects of Chaucer's "official" life are as thought-provoking. When the mob stormed London during the Peasants' Revolt, they entered by the gate over which Chaucer was actually living. They would almost certainly have killed the poet-courtier if they had caught him—he was by then a senior customs officer, almost as bad as a tax collector to the mob—but in some unknown manner he escaped. Earlier Chaucer seems to have been given tasks as varied, difficult, and responsible as persuading English mercenaries not to act against English interests in European wars and negotiating a vital loan from Florentine bankers to pay for royal campaigns. This last assignment must have been especially difficult as the Crown had ruined bankers a generation before by inventing the device of "debt repudiation."

Closer to home, Chaucer can be seen in other documents giving evidence to a heralds' court, being robbed by highwaymen twice in one week, and being accused of rape. That accusation is of particular curiosity and danger in that the lady complaining was the stepdaughter of Edward III's mistress (the notoriously corrupt and influential Alice Perrers). Howard finds this last fact especially hard to square with Chaucer's poetry, which he sees as the work of a man always sympathetic to the plight of women in a man's world. The accusation could have been spurious, and Chaucer was never convicted, but rape is a charge on which it is notoriously hard to convict. All round, one may say that Chaucer's career hung perpetually on the edge of violence, whether it be rape, lynching, war, murder, or death on the block. Could Chaucer have afforded to be the traditionally sensitive poetic soul?

The picture which Howard offers is that of a man of great utility but uncertain status, who had learned above all to fill a role at court without ever venturing beyond it. He was allowed, and may even have been encouraged, to comment on events but not to influence them. Thus, there can be no doubt that the early *The Book of the Duchess* is a reaction to the death of Blanche, Duchess of Lancaster, at once memorial to the dead and consolation to the living. What can be said, though, of *The House of Fame* (1372-1380), an unfinished poem which many have believed to be the working out of some inner and personal problem? Howard argues that it was left unfinished to commemorate a royal flop, the failure to arrange a marriage between the young King Richard and the Italian heiress Caterina Visconti. This belief is based on the mention of "December the tenth" in the poem, the date on which news appears (in 1379) to have arrived of the termination of negotiations. Howard even describes a scene in which the poem could have been read to an audience "in the know," breaking off with a mild jibe at the Italian nuncio then present.

Yet there are many doubts as to this interpretation. The poem may not have been written in 1379, and December 10 may have had some other significance. The poem's main concern is fame, not marriage. Chaucer may in other words have written it solely for himself, not for the court. Much the same could be said of Howard's analysis of *The Parliament of Fowls*, clearly a Valentine's Day poem, but one set in the spring, while February 14 in England is still quite definitely midwinter. Howard suggests that Chaucer had learned in Genoa of the Genoese Saint Valentine, whose feast day is May 3, and had in consequence introduced a new spring festivity to the English court. May 3 is mentioned several times by Chaucer in different poems. It is also the date on which Richard II was eventually betrothed to Anne of Bohemia. Was *The Parliament of Fowls* then written for that betrothal and the betrothal arranged to fall on that day? This conclusion would give Chaucer a major role at court. Nevertheless, one could object that in Chaucer's poem there is no betrothal, making it an odd compliment to a prospective bride. Some of Howard's further suggestions, such as that the translation of Boethius' *The Consolation of Philosophy* (523) was for the young king and commissioned by his tutor, rest on no evidence at all.

The problem is, once again, one of status. Was Chaucer a professional, writing always to order? Or did he just write in his spare time, circulating his poems only to such friends as he thought would appreciate them? Either view is plausible. Howard prefers the former, which does admittedly place Chaucer near the center of events. The latter is indicated simply by the fact that no court document ever mentions that Geoffrey Chaucer was a poet.

There is also the problem of *The Canterbury Tales*, Chaucer's major work, one in many ways singularly uncourtly. Howard explains this discrepancy by date, and by the modern theory of "age-crises," mentioned several times in this book. He points out that in later life Chaucer seems to have drifted away from major affairs, resigning his posts and accepting smaller payments. This withdrawal may have been a sensible reaction to the dangerous faction-fighting in which several of Chaucer's acquaintances were executed, but it can be seen also as a typical reaction of the fifties, a period when men are alleged often to go through attacks of unfulfillment and despair. In this view, Chaucer is seen as having been left alone by the death of his wife, and demoralized by English politics and the violent deaths of colleagues, turning in reaction to a style of comic and detached writing which had not been present before. These conjectures are made to dovetail well with a central problem of Chaucer's career, namely the fact that Chaucer never at any time mentioned his contemporary, the Italian poet Giovanni Boccaccio, though they had almost certainly met and though Chaucer used Boccaccio's works as the basis for his two longest and most ambitious poems and arguably also for the entire concept and framework of *The Canterbury Tales*. Chaucer admired Boccaccio as a poetic technician, Howard suggests, but despised him for his uncourtliness on the one occasion when they could have met. Chaucer reacted to Boccaccio both as imitator and as rival; it was thus an especially significant moment when Chaucer moved away from his normal courtly environment and on (or, he might have thought, back) to the relatively bourgeois milieu of the Italian writer.

Donald Howard's achievement in this biography is significant, as was posthumously acknowledged when *Chaucer* received the 1988 National Book Critics Circle Award for Biography/Autobiography. Howard has presented a deep and well-based account of Chaucer's background, very strong on dates, documents, and literary coincidences. (For the general reader, the text is supplemented by a chronology, a discussion of Chaucer's pronunciation, a guide to further reading, and brief discussions of the order of *The Canterbury Tales* and the evolution of Chaucer's reputation; the scholar will find almost one hundred pages of notes.) Howard has also given Chaucer's life a shape which modern readers can recognize and to which they can relate their own experiences. It is no disservice to Howard to add that the book contains flaws which he surely would have corrected had he lived to see it through to publication. A number of passages of historical background and narrative substantially repeat information given in earlier sections, often with similar wording.

Given the scope of his attention to Chaucer's life and times, Howard makes no attempt here to provide full or close readings of the major Chaucerian works such as he undertook in *The Idea of the Canterbury Tales* (1976) and other studies. In his concentration on Chaucer-the-courtier, Howard has furthermore had to leave aside, not Chaucer-the-poet (for the author thinks that this poet's job was usually to be a courtier), but Chaucer-the-private-individual—even though most twentieth century Chaucer critics have stressed the private humor of Chaucer's writing. Did Chaucer never mean to be fully understood? Or has the key to his intentions been lost, a key plain to the inner circle of his own day? If the latter is true (and it may not be), then Howard's book comes closest to the key's rediscovery.

T. A. Shippey

Sources for Further Study

Booklist. LXXXIV, September 15, 1987, p. 104.
Chicago Tribune. December 20, 1987, XIV, p. 4.
Kirkus Reviews. LV, September 1, 1987, p. 1293.
Library Journal. CXII, October 15, 1987, p. 82.
Los Angeles Times Book Review. December 20, 1987, p. 12.
The New York Review of Books. XXXV, February 4, 1988, p. 33.
The New York Times Book Review. XCII, December 13, 1987, p. 43.
Publishers Weekly. CCXXXII, September 4, 1987, p. 57.
The Wall Street Journal. January 14, 1988, p. 24.
The Washington Post Book World. XVII, December 13, 1987, p. 3.

THE CHILD IN TIME

Author: Ian McEwan (1948-   )
Publisher: Houghton Mifflin Co. (Boston). 263 pp. $16.95
Type of work: Novel
Time: Unspecified; sometime not long after the 1980's
Locale: England

After his three-year-old daughter disappears in a supermarket, a young writer attempts to deal with her loss through an extensive reconsideration of his life and the meaning of love

> *Principal characters:*
> STEPHEN LEWIS, a successful writer of children's books
> JULIE, his wife, a musician
> KATE, their child, who is abducted while accompanying Stephen to the supermarket
> CHARLES DARKE, the publisher of Stephen's books and a member of Parliament
> THELMA DARKE, Charles's wife and a professor of physics
> DOUGLAS and
> CLAIRE LEWIS, Stephen's parents
> THE PRIME MINISTER OF ENGLAND, unnamed

The Child in Time is a remarkable book, one which balances social criticism and satire with a sad, compassionate story of loss and redemption. Stephen Lewis, the protagonist, is a successful writer of children's books, an occupation he assumes almost by accident. As a young man without purpose, he at first decides to write a novel to be entitled "Hashish," "about hippies stabbed to death in their sleeping bags, a nicely brought-up girl sentenced to a lifetime in a Turkish jail, mystic pretentiousness, drug-enhanced sex, amoebic dysentery." Instead, he writes *Lemonade*, a novel derived from his experiences as an eleven-year-old in the company of two girl cousins. This book is seized by Charles Darke, a young publisher who tells Stephen that it is brilliant because, like the best children's stories, it "spoke to both children and adults, to the incipient adult within the child, to the forgotten child within the adult." Stephen is very soon both wealthy and famous; he and his wife, Julie, are friends of Charles and Thelma Darke, a professor of physics, and enjoy the benefits of the socially privileged in England.

The Lewises' lives are devastated, however, several years later when Stephen takes their three-year-old daughter, Kate, with him to the supermarket one morning while Julie sleeps. There Kate simply disappears as they stand together in the check-out line, magically removed in the blink of an eye, snatched away in an instant of inattention. For months, Stephen searches for his lost daughter, posts bulletins, follows leads, and wanders the streets looking at faces, convincing himself that these actions give order to the chaos his world has become. Finally, however, his movement ceases, and he gives himself over to his grief, withdrawing into an alcoholic attenuation of purpose.

Two years later, Stephen lives alone in his London flat, Julie having moved to the countryside to confront her own grief. Stephen has been appointed to the Subcommittee on Reading and Writing, a part of the Prime Minister's Official Commission on Child Care. The commission has been given the task of creating *An Authorized Child-Care Handbook* for the government. Stephen is involved in this undertaking, in part because of the influence of Charles Darke. Darke had left the publishing business to become a member of Parliament, but after several years of increasing influence and growing promise, he has abruptly and mysteriously resigned, leaving London with his wife Thelma for a life of seclusion. Stephen cares nothing about the commission and spends his time there dreaming, sleeping, or thinking of Kate who, in his mind, continues to exist, to grow.

During this year, several events occur which change Stephen's life. On a rare visit to Julie's cottage, he experiences an almost mystical out-of-time moment. Walking through the wet countryside, he comes to a tavern, The Bell, and looking within he sees a young couple engaged in serious conversation. The girl looks at him through the window, but it is as if she sees him and sees through him at the same time. Stephen recognizes this couple as his parents. Later, in talking with his mother, he learns that she and his father had indeed had such a conversation before they were married, although she was then pregnant with Stephen. The question Stephen watches them discuss is whether to abort the unexpected child. According to his mother, it was the sight of a child's face—Stephen's face lost in time—at the window of the pub which resulted in her decision not to undertake the abortion.

Other events occur. Stephen receives a rather urgent invitation from Thelma to come for a visit. Since Thelma had cared for him in the traumatic months following Kate's disappearance and had nursed him back to some semblance of health, he feels an obligation to attend her summons. On the way he witnesses an accident and acts to save the life of a man trapped in a wrecked lorry. Once he reaches the Darke estate, he finds that Charles has in effect regressed to the childhood he had never been allowed to experience. While Thelma works on her research, Charles has created for himself a giant playground, complete with an elaborate treehouse. He insists that Stephen, the writer of childhood things, climb with him to the top of the treehouse, although Stephen is terrified of doing so. Still later, having returned to London and his work on the commission, Stephen is called upon by the Prime Minister, who wants to know what has happened to Charles and who seems to have an unusual interest in Darke's reasons for leaving public office.

The setting of this story is England of the very near future, presented in a slightly absurd manner. Beggars roam the streets, becoming progressively more demanding and abusive as the book continues. The United States and

Russia almost go to war over a dispute at the Olympic Games. The Prime
Minister (whose sex is left ambiguous) is a manipulative, somewhat sinister
figure in love with Charles Darke. His/her government is strongly right-wing
and moving toward a kind of tyrannical rule, an extension of the Thatcher
reign. This political state is best illustrated by the commission on which Stephen serves. Its announced goal is to create a handbook for British parents,
a guide for rearing children:

> "Their real function, it was said cynically, was to satisfy the disparate ideals of myriad
> interest groups—the sugar and fast-food lobbies; the garment, toy, formula milk, and
> firework manufacturers; the charities; the women's organizations; the pedestrian-
> controlled crosswalk pressure group people—who pressed in on all sides. . . . It was
> generally agreed that the country was full of the wrong sort of people. There were
> strong opinions about what constituted a desirable citizenry and what should be done to
> children to procure one for the future."

Stephen's father tells his son that it is all a sham, that the handbook has
probably already been written, which, as Stephen later discovers, proves to
be the case. McEwan prefaces each chapter with an excerpt from this handbook, and the general tone makes clear that, in the government's view, children need less freedom and more discipline:

> "It should be remembered that childhood is not a natural occurrence. . . . Childhood is
> an invention, a social construct, made possible by society as it increased in sophistication
> and resource. Above all, childhood is a privilege. No child as it grows older should be
> allowed to forget that its parents, as embodiments of society, are the ones who grant this
> privilege, and do so at their own expense."

Throughout the book McEwan parallels the government's responsibility for
its citizens with that of parents for their children. The government has
turned its back on its children, who now roam the streets begging. Stephen
has lost Kate, who now may be among the street people, who may be anywhere, or nowhere, at all.

Running through the novel is a meditation on the nature of childhood and
time, of memory and reality. Stephen captures childhood in his books by re-
creating memory, but he is unable to protect the life of his own child, who is
lost in memory. When his friend Charles tries to construct his own childhood, tries to force the past into the present, his efforts lead only to madness and a petulant death. Once Kate disappears, time becomes equally
skewed for Stephen. Months pass in an alcoholic continuum; he is often lost
in terrible reveries which are more real than the life around him. Thelma,
the physicist, lectures him on the theoretical identities of time, but in his
own life, he experiences them at firsthand. On odd occasions, time warps
into slow motion, as when he witnesses the auto wreck, or loops back on itself, as when he watches his still-young parents discussing his impending

birth. For much of the book Stephen is convinced that his life has been for nothing, that all life is for nothing, but in its marvelous conclusion, when time loops once again into a kind of everlasting present, he discovers that "all the sorrow, all the empty waiting, had been enclosed within meaningful time, within the richest unfolding conceivable."

The Child in Time ends in magic, with the lost child in a sense reborn, swept back into Stephen's world. *"Had you forgotten me? Did you not realize it was me all along? I am here. I am not alive,"* Kate seems to say to Stephen through the newly born child. Stephen then realizes in his joy, "This is really all we have got, this increase, this matter of life loving itself; everything we have has to come from this." Thus the book ends in celebration, with the confirmation that childhood, innocence, and love are redeemable, that time can be recaptured, that all is not lost. Pain is resolved, tragedy given meaning. In its realization of hope and wonder, McEwan's book stands as one of the most accomplished of the year.

Edwin T. Arnold

Sources for Further Study

Booklist. LXXXIV, September 1, 1987, p. 28.
Kirkus Reviews. LV, August 1, 1987, p. 1102.
Library Journal. CXII, September 1, 1987, p. 200.
Los Angeles Times Book Review. September 20, 1987, p. 19.
The Nation. CCXLV, October 31, 1987, p. 491.
New Statesman. CXIV, September 18, 1987, p. 28.
The New York Times. September 26, 1987, p. 14.
The New York Times Book Review. October 11, 1987, p. 9.
Publishers Weekly. CCXXXII, August 7, 1987, p. 436.
Time. CXXX, September 21, 1987, p. 77.
The Times Literary Supplement. September 4, 1987, p. 947.
The Wall Street Journal. September 15, 1987, p. 30.

CHILE
Death in the South

Author: Jacobo Timerman (1923-   )
Translated from the Spanish by Robert Cox
Publisher: Alfred A. Knopf (New York). 134 pp. $15.95
Type of work: Current history
Time: 1973-1977
Locale: Chile

Jacobo Timerman reports on life in Chile under the regime of General Augusto Pinochet and speculates on the country's future

> *Principal personages:*
> JACOBO TIMERMAN, an Argentine newspaperman, returning to Chile after a fifteen-year absence
> SALVADOR ALLENDE, first president of Chile (1970-1973); removed from office by a military coup
> AUGUSTO PINOCHET, a Chilean army general and leader of the ruling junta since the coup
> ANDRÉS ALLAMAND, a leader of the democratic opposition to Pinochet

"The last Prussian army in the world" began to rule Chile in September, 1973, when a military coup deposed socialist president Salvador Allende. The army's chief general, Augusto Pinochet, has ruled effectively and harshly. The armed forces direct every aspect of daily life and control political life. Thousands of leftist activists, intellectuals, and leading citizens have been arrested; some have been executed, and many others have simply disappeared. Pinochet claims that his country is now a "protected democracy," safe from the threat of Communist subversion. Civilian politicians describe the Pinochet regime as fascist and self-aggrandizing. In 1989, Chile will hold its first presidential election in almost twenty years, and questions abound. Will Pinochet be the only candidate, or will he tolerate a rival? Will the election be a ceremony that crowns a king or a competition that shows a healthy democracy?

To assess the country's chances of returning to civilian, democratic government, Jacobo Timerman visited Chile in early 1987. Long a political reporter in neighboring Argentina, and himself the victim of repression by a military regime in his native country (in April, 1977, Timerman was arrested and tortured for publicizing the disappearance of Argentine citizens), Timerman empathized with the plight of ordinary citizens as well as political leaders of the left and the center. Personal memories of two men who died in the coup also drew him to Chile: Allende, a good man but perhaps a politician out of his depth as president of a volatile country, and Augusto Olivares, an honest man and a journalist sharing Timerman's hopes for Latin America's democratic future.

Timerman found much to depress him about life in Chile. The army rules firmly and keeps the cities as well as the countryside outwardly serene. The "economic miracle" of the mid-1970's (much praised by North American economists for its capitalist principles) has benefited military officers whose houses, cars, and vacations are symbols and rewards of loyalty to Pinochet. Even sergeants and corporals prosper, secure in the knowledge that suppressing Communists is good, steady work: It provides subsidized housing, free education for their children, and fringe benefits. These benefits include the profits to be made on street patrol: ignoring prostitution, winking at traffic violations, and authorizing street vendors—all for a fee.

Timerman had no trouble finding the torture and the terror which underpin the outward calm. He punctuates his political analyses with first-person accounts of arrests, beatings, and disappearances. Many chapters conclude with a Chilean's "testimony" about the suffering which the soldiers inflict officially by arrest or in secret dungeons by interrogation. Timerman lets speak the actor terrorized by a rat thrust into his face or down his pants, the college student impregnated in a gang rape by policemen, the exiled intellectual witnessing fellow expatriates commit suicide. As appalled as he is by physical brutality, Timerman is most fascinated by the regime's ability to force its victims to remain silent. For him, the archetypal incident is the massacre at Calama. Here, in 1973, a commando team visited several villages and killed political prisoners as well as apolitical farmers. The women and children of the victims subsequently pretended that their husbands and fathers were not dead. The massacre went long unremarked until one woman went into counseling and broke the silence as well as the illusion. The revelation prompted not mass protest, but group therapy to help the victims' relatives accept the reality of their loss.

Timerman found General Pinochet as well entrenched in his office as his army is in the street. He delayed for seven years a plebiscite promised during the coup, then limited it to approving a constitutional provision for an unopposed election in nine years thence; this election will provide an eight-year term of office. Thus the modern dictator is to stay in power for twenty-four years. Pinochet has also proven a skillful manipulator of image. He meets foreign VIPs and domestic visitors early in the morning to show that he is physically fit and mentally alert. He ingratiates himself with the United States by proclaiming that his regime is a bulwark against Communism: His survival of an ambush by Marxist guerrillas is portrayed as a providential sign that he is succeeding. After many years in power, Pinochet ceased to make public appearances in full uniform, shedding the regalia of military discipline for civilian paternalism. Surrounding himself with reporters and cameramen from state-run media, Pinochet visits poor villages to bestow supplies and a few luxuries, projecting the image of a kindly grandfather or rich uncle. Timerman is convinced that Pinochet is too crafty to make the mistake which brought down the Argentine military dictatorship in 1981:

military adventurism. Chile has no Falkland Islands to covet.

Yet Timerman believes that he detects signs of hope. True, many individuals appear as bland and listless as the patrolled streets of Santiago, but they are only "submarining." Submerging their natural passion and curiosity, they keep their distance from one another, they sleepwalk through each day's routine, and they avert their eyes from the military presence. They wish only to go unnoticed and avoid scrutiny. Like other twentieth century citizens who lived under Fascism—Italians under Benito Mussolini, Jews under Adolf Hitler, Spaniards under Francisco Franco—Chileans have learned the arts of subterfuge and adaptation. Their symbol of hope is the poetry of Pablo Neruda, winner of the 1971 Nobel Prize in Literature. His sensuous, erotic verse epitomizes Chilean spontaneity and passion. During the coup, his house—a veritable shrine—was destroyed, and his poetry (which had drifted into leftist political commentary toward the middle of his life) was banned. The death of Allende and the successful coup caused the collapse and death of the aged, ailing poet. Yet his verse lives on in the memories of educated Chileans, a consolation from another life, as well as its anthem. Though Neruda's readers do not go on open pilgrimage to his house, casual passersby often linger at the site for a moment's reflection.

Timerman finds indications that political life, so long dormant, now has the chance to revive. The visit of Pope John Paul II to Chile in April, 1987, put the military government on the defensive. Though appearing publicly with Pinochet and preaching reconciliation, John Paul withheld any sign that might indicate endorsement of a regime that killed priests. Without directly condemning all government action, John Paul nevertheless showed that he sides with the oppressed more than with the oppressors: He received with open arms—literally—men, women, and children scarred and maimed by torture. The papal visit justified and invigorated the activities of the Vicarate of Solidarity, Chile's most prominent human-rights organization, which is sponsored by the Catholic Church. By giving his approval to the Vicarate, the Pope endorsed its efforts to find missing persons as well as to protest the torture of political prisoners; by giving the Vicarate his imprimatur, he enabled it to work openly with less fear of government reprisal. Timerman calls the papal visit a healthy dose of realism for a people who have had to submarine for so many years.

An equally positive sign is the emergence of Christian Democrat politicians such as Andrés Allamand who are developing a political center which might provide a genuine alternative to military dictatorship and Communist insurgency. The hope of this democratic center is to convince the army that someone other than Pinochet can lead Chile—perhaps an army officer, perhaps a civilian. Even if the new movement cannot affect the presidential election of 1989, it may preserve the traditions and ideals of Chilean democracy. Thus, when the dictatorship ends—as it inevitably must—there will be democratic forces to prevent anarchy or civil war. Timerman points to the Spanish politicians who persevered while Franco ruled; after the Generalissimo's death, they returned the country to democracy.

This hopeful gradualist approach to political change is Timerman's rebuttal to those who despair that Chile can return to democracy. Some worry that military control has been so successful that a generation is now politically inert, its will paralyzed. Timerman offers the gradualist approach as an alternative to guerrilla warfare by leftist parties which imagine that a heroic uprising could topple the Pinochet regime. The army is too entrenched, as Timerman shows; rebellion only confirms the military's determination to rule. Even if a revolt had a chance to succeed, it would bleed white an already desolate populace. Better to be patient and work in quiet ways. Though little consolation to those who have been tortured and whose loved ones have been executed or have disappeared, a gradualist approach is the counsel of age and wisdom. The maimed and the dead cannot really be avenged; they are better remembered as models of hope and courage.

Chile: Death in the South is the first notable book in English about Chile in the 1980's. In the 1970's, numerous books debated the role of the Central Intelligence Agency in Allende's overthrow and the economic theories of the "Chicago School" which Pinochet professed to implement. In 1983, two studies of the military's repression, one by Amnesty International and one by Americas Watch Organization, gained attention by publicizing stories of execution and disappearance. While these reports caused brief outrage, they stirred little curiosity about future prospects. Most political analysts ignore Chile to focus on other critical, unsettled problems. Compared to the pugnacious Sandinistas in Nicaragua, the guerrilla war in El Salvador, and the cocaine trafficking in Colombia, Pinochet's tranquil though unhappy Chile shows little change which could attract outsiders' attention. Timerman's book recalls North America's attention to an ongoing, unfinished chapter in Latin American politics.

Chile is Timerman's third work. His previous books, *Prisoner Without a Name, Cell Without a Number* (1981) and *The Longest War: Israel in Lebanon* (1982) dealt with other nations in which military arrogance played havoc with democratic traditions and personal integrity. The first concerns the military coup in Argentina, the second deals with the Israeli invasion of Lebanon in 1982. Coming of age in the 1930's and hating the Fascism which plunged the world into war, Timerman is acutely sensitive to the resurgence of its ideology. Born from fear, addicted to military ritual, trusting only in ruthless violence, the fascist mentality always lurks on the fringes of democracy and awaits a moment of crisis. Democratic men and women must speak out against fascism, oppose it, and—if they lose the fight—outlast it.

Timerman's previous books were intensely personal. His account of his own incarceration in an Argentine jail details the sights, sounds and sensations of imprisonment and torture. His book about Israel depicts movingly the tension between his dislike for a reckless military adventure and his love for this unique, struggling, Jewish nation. *Chile* lacks such personal intensity. Being a neighbor of the country under discussion is simply not the same as being its citizen or coreligionist. Timerman works to overcome the inevitable distance; he recalls memories of old friends, interviews Chileans at home and abroad, gives space to their accounts, and observes events for himself. About events of the previous year Timerman writes with his familiar vivid intensity. His absence of fifteen years, however, makes his account of Pinochet's early regime seem thin and vague. For this period he clearly relies on what he has heard informally rather than on careful reading.

Chile is a journalistic rather than a scholarly analysis. Timerman skillfully re-creates each individual's speech or character. Adeptly he spots the image which sums up the nation's experience, or the instance which crystallizes its history. Effortlessly he communicates the mood, the mien, the subtle shades of daily life. He is a master of the simple, dramatic, summary phrase: The returning expatriate, rediscovering his land, concludes that "Santiago is more beautiful than ever." Of Pope John Paul's sermon on mercy and love before a huge crowd, Timerman remarks simply, "Pinochet will never forget those words." These stylistic virtues, however, will alienate some readers. Timerman assumes an audience as familiar with the events and personalities as he is; anyone looking for an introduction to Chilean history will need a companion volume to fill in the background. Nor does Timerman's book encourage further reading: It has no notes or bibliography to guide readers to the best source. Since Timerman often writes without specifics (the date or location of events, the names of witnesses), the reader is unable to do research that might verify or amplify the author's account.

From one perspective, then, *Chile: Death in the South* is flawed. It is a mix of ingredients of memoir and political analysis which never quite blend. From another perspective, it is an honest work, flawed and incomplete as all attempts to describe a society in crisis and predict its political future must ultimately be.

Robert M. Otten

Sources for Further Study

Chicago Tribune. December 13, 1987, XIV, p. 6.
Kirkus Reviews. LV, December 1, 1987, p. 1621.
Library Journal. CXIII, January, 1988, p. 76.
Los Angeles Times Book Review. December 20, 1987, p. 3.
The New York Times Book Review. XCIII, January 10, 1988, p. 10.
The Washington Monthly. XIX, January, 1988, p. 58.

CLOSE QUARTERS

Author: William Golding (1911-   )
Publisher: Farrar, Straus and Giroux (New York). 281 pp. $16.95
Type of work: Novel
Time: The early 1800's
Locale: The Atlantic Ocean

The continuing journal record of a young, early nineteenth century English aristocrat's sea voyage from England to Australia

> *Principal characters:*
> EDMUND FITZHENRY TALBOT, a minor English aristocrat
> WHEELER, his servant
> MISS CHUMLEY, his beloved
> LIEUTENANT DEVEREL, an alcoholic ship's officer
> FIRST LIEUTENANT CHARLES SUMMERS, Talbot's friend
> CAPTAIN ANDERSON, the captain of the ship
> LIEUTENANT BENET, a ship's officer, a poet and seducer

William Golding's *Close Quarters* follows his *Rites of Passage* (1980) as the second in a proposed trilogy of novels in the format of a journal written by the main character, Edmund FitzHenry Talbot, a young aristocrat traveling by ship from England to Australia, where he plans to pursue, it seems, a career in the colonial government. The novel borrows from the eighteenth century adventure story, the most famous example of which is Daniel Defoe's *Robinson Crusoe* (1719). Defoe's hero, like Talbot in Golding's story, finds that nature is not benign but frightening and learns to cling to the human walls that surround him.

In the guise of an antique adventure story, *Close Quarters* records the mistakes of its main character; if its format links it to popular fiction in that it concentrates on plot, its intention links it to serious or "novelistic" fiction in that it concentrates on character.

The premise of the novel is a simple one: The former warship on which Talbot has taken passage is becalmed in equatorial waters west of Africa—a condition worsened by the seaweed that has accumulated on the ship's hull and keel and by the loss of the ship's top masts. This latter event occurs when Deverel, one of the ship's lieutenants, leaves his watch to an inexperienced midshipman and gets drunk. Partially crippled, the ship later encounters the English frigate *Alcyone*; Captain Anderson, his crew, and the passengers take it for an enemy ship at first and prepare for battle. They soon discover their mistake and are told by the crew of the *Alcyone* that the war with Napoléon Bonaparte is over. At this point, Talbot falls headlong in love with Miss Chumley, the ward of Captain Henry Somerset and Lady Somerset of the *Alcyone*. The resolution of this romance, another ingredient of traditional adventure, is left uncertain—perhaps to be taken up in the concluding volume of the trilogy. After a dinner with the Somersets on the *Alcyone* and a ball put on by the two ships featuring songs, a poetry recitation, and dancing, the ships part, and Talbot has no chance to pursue his love, let alone to prove it by undertaking the risky deeds typical of the classic romantic hero.

The next development in the adventure aspect of the plot occurs when, moving into the stormy seas between Africa and Antartica, the ship, ill-constructed to begin with and old, as well as hampered by the previous accident with the masts and by the weed clinging to the hull, threatens to fall apart. Talbot, as when the ship was preparing for battle with the *Alcyone* before it was identified, has little to do with opposing this threat. He barely knows the construction of the ship and has no experience as a seaman. It is Lieutenant Benet (who had been forced to leave the *Alcyone* because of his passionate flirtation with Lady Somerset) who devises a way to increase the ship's speed, setting up a drag-rope system to clear the ship of the seaweed weighing it down. By the end of the novel, in fact, the ship is still in danger, and though the reader knows from the Postscriptum that it reaches its destination, Talbot notes that he left off his journal during the danger, thus extending his impotence from what he cannot do (which is to overcome the threat) to what he can (which is to write about it).

Thus, taken strictly as an adventure story, *Close Quarters* features little action, and as an adventurer, Talbot is incompetent—comically so. Yet to the extent that the plot focuses on the relationships between Talbot, his setting, and other major characters, it provides a richer texture to the novel than the larger action does. The story is at pains to follow Talbot's misman-aged attempts to assert himself in relation to his surroundings and to other characters in the story. Because he is tall and unaccustomed to the roll of the ship, he constantly bumps his head in the cramped quarters in which he moves about. Thus he spends a substantial amount of time in his bunk, drugged and asleep. He moves into the cabin of Pastor Colley (who died in the preceding novel, *Rites of Passage*) in order to absorb some of the latter's flair for writing, but he ends up as ill and confused there as he was in his own cabin, unaware that it is not one's setting that defines one, but oneself. He is also unaware of his effect on First Lieutenant Charles Summers, whom he regards as a close friend; Summers has misconstrued Talbot's friendship as the patronage of an aristocrat because of an idle word from Talbot, and Talbot is confused by Summers' increasingly sour attitude to-ward him until the end of the novel, when they make up. Talbot further shows his lack of perception in his dealings with Wheeler, his servant who, having been lost overboard in *Rites of Passage*, turns up on the *Alcyone* in this novel. Like Captain Ahab's cabin boy Pip in Herman Melville's *Moby Dick* (1851), Wheeler has been unhinged by his ordeal at sea, but Talbot, ir-ritated by Wheeler's clinging to him after their reunion, as well as by Wheeler's inability to explain his experience, constantly orders him to get away from him.

Indeed, Talbot makes one mistake after another in dealing with his ship-mates. He lets Lieutenant Deverel convince him to act as his emissary to Captain Anderson, who has restricted Deverel to his quarters and forbidden him to drink because he is responsible for the loss of the ship's top masts. Talbot thus disrupts the protocol between a captain and his officers, and his failure is underscored when Deverel, attempting to lure Anderson into a duel, is restrained in irons and finally traded to the *Alcyone* for its more charming but equally disruptive officer, Lieutenant Benet. When Talbot agrees to represent a committee of passengers concerned with the fate of the ship, he bungles his role badly, ending up in collusion with the officers in concealing from the committee the ship's real danger. It is unclear whether Summers and Benet have fully described the danger in any case.

In many ways, Talbot seems to be everybody's fool, including his own. This becomes most apparent when he meets Miss Chumley on the *Alcyone*. His instant infatuation with her controls not only his feelings but also his view of everything else. She is callow behind her good looks and takes little risk in teasing men since she is under the protection of Captain Somerset and Lady Somerset, but these facts escape him. Waking up from another of his sick spells to find Miss Chumley gone with the *Alcyone* on its way to In-dia, he befriends Lieutenant Benet because of his romantic looks, his skill at poetry, and his proximity to Miss Chumley while he was trying to seduce Lady Somerset. Talbot fails, in short, to see the real Benet, who is an op-portunist, instead seeing him through the aura of his longing for Miss Chumley—a longing as doomed to failure as Talbot's wish to control what is happening to him in general.

The comic stupidity, if not meanness, of Talbot's "adventure" is vividly highlighted by Wheeler's suicide and brought full circle by Talbot's business with Mr. Jones, the ship's purser. The dead Colley's cabin is a kind of coffin that Talbot misreads as a place of inspiration. He witnesses Wheeler killing himself there with the stolen blunderbuss of Mr. Brocklebank (a fellow pas-senger, an alcoholic painter of ships and the sea), and this has the usual effect of anything important on him: He gets sick and escapes into uncon-sciousness. When he awakens, he is as mystified as ever by Wheeler and as unaware of his own part in his servant's despair. A comic note is struck when Talbot bargains with the purser for a barrel in which to store his jour-nals in case the ship sinks. The other passengers and the crew enhance this comic deflation by urging Talbot to include their letters and bric-a-brac with his journals in the barrel.

If Golding has a point to make in this novel, it may concern writing itself. Writing is the one thing at which Talbot is successful, and he talks about it constantly, from the dead Colley's style (which he envies) to his own style (which he misreads as awkward), from the prose he thinks alien to the sensibility of women to the poetry he thinks native to it, and finally from the time he has to write to the time he has lost for doing so.

It is uncertain, however, what Golding means by this emphasis on writing beyond defining his main character's goal (which seems less to survive his journey than to record and understand it). Imagination itself in the form of writing may be the issue; that is, Golding may be trying to show how the writer's power is to disguise himself in layers of imagined formats—in this case, a type of adventure story borrowed from another time, and in the sensibility of a character appropriate to that time. Further, in exercising this power convincingly, he may be saying that the writer's power is also to show that nature and human character, despite changes in technology and language, are constant. Time disappears to the extent that Golding makes his readers feel intimate with the main character and the events of his story, and thus nature becomes as vast and dangerous for the moment as it was in the period in which the novel is set, and youth is revealed once more as what it was then—idealistic and foolish, pompous and miserable.

If nothing else, indeed, Golding has reasserted in this novel a kind of legendary status for the charming fool, the lovable amateur, and may in addition be calling attention to the role of the writer's imagination and skill, and therefore importance, in making this kind of character authentic.

Mark McCloskey

Sources for Further Study

Chicago Tribune. June 14, 1987, XIV, p. 6.
Kirkus Reviews. LV, April 1, 1987, p. 496.
Library Journal. CXII, April 15, 1987, p. 98.
London Review of Books. IX, June 25, 1987, p. 9.
Los Angeles Times Book Review. June 7, 1987, p. 3.
New Statesman. CXIII, June 12, 1987, p. 27.
The New York Times Book Review. XCII, May 31, 1987, p. 44.
The Observer. July 19, 1987, p. 23.
Publishers Weekly. CCXXXI, May 15, 1987, p. 267.
Time. CXXIX, June 8, 1987, p. 80.
The Times Literary Supplement. June 19, 1987, p. 653.

THE CLOSING OF THE AMERICAN MIND
How Higher Education Has Failed Democracy
and Impoverished the Souls of Today's Students

Author: Allan Bloom (1930-   )
Publisher: Simon and Schuster (New York). 393 pp. $18.95
Type of work: Intellectual and social criticism

A passionate indictment of the modern American university for its promulgation of faddish values and its production of shallow graduates

The Closing of the American Mind: How Higher Education Has Failed Democracy and Impoverished the Souls of Today's Students is a publishing anomaly, an erudite biopsy of the soul of American culture that became a popular success. Six months after the book's release, it continued to reside on the hardcover best-seller lists of *The New York Times* and *Publishers Weekly*. Explanations of this performance were legion. The publisher suggested a happy coincidence with the rise of public interest in educational issues, pundits discovered an articulate conservative spokesman, and critics found a bellwether antirelativist, while wags delighted in the irony of a book about the decay of liberal education being devoured by the masses.

In the popular press, the book has been mined for its broadsides against rock music, casual sex, and the 1960's. Yet, while attention has focused on Allan Bloom as a curmudgeon from the ivory tower, much of his central message has been missed, or misapprehended.

"Civilization or, to say the same thing, education is the taming or domestication of the soul's raw passions—not suppressing or excising them, which would deprive the soul of its energy—but forming and informing them as art." It is Bloom's contention, at least for students in the twenty or so greatest universities in the United States, that their passions have been co-opted by mindless music, while within the university, students are exposed only to the denatured, Disneyized thoughts of the greatest minds. Rock music has unleashed the passions; what passes for liberal education has excised them. The result, according to Bloom, is a whole catalog of woes. Students have become isolates, lacking any ideological reason for commitment to one another. There is among them a psychological return to the "state of nature," before civilization, and it is expressed in the loss of fidelity in the love relationship, a casual openness to ephemeral values, a lackadaisical approach to truth, all aided and abetted by the modern academic smorgasbord, the university. Ultimately what is lost is the community of those in dialogue, as exemplified in the richness and magic of the *Symposium* (c. fourth century B.C.) of Plato, and thus the bedrock on which American democracy exists, that of the responsible, informed citizen. Writes Bloom,

This is the American moment in world history, the one for which we shall forever be judged. Just as in politics the responsibility for the fate of freedom in the world has devolved upon our regime, so the fate of philosophy in the world has devolved upon our universities, and the two are related as they have never been before.

Bloom writes from the academic trenches, looking back on three decades as an instructor at Cornell and Yale universities, the University of Toronto, and most recently as a professor in the Committee on Social Thought at the University of Chicago. He characterizes *The Closing of the American Mind* as a "meditation on the state of our souls." The soul is the seat of a person's reason and the domain of the passions; it is that which aspires to virtue. The passions are what energize the reason; they are far different from mere bodily desires. Bloom's lament is that in the last quarter century, students at the very best American universities have ceased caring for their souls and instead have substituted the idea of the self as worthy of all their attention. This is a monumental and devastating shift in perception. For the ancients, the soul was the locus of man's aspirations and nature's showcase. Nature herself was purposive; thus, the varied aspects of the soul mirrored the hierarchy of nature, and the flourishing of the human soul, the practice of virtue, was in full accord with natural teleology. Virtue, however, cannot be practiced in isolation; human society must exist and with it some form of government that, ideally, would serve to promote flourishing in the community of souls. As Aristotle had it, man's nature is to be political.

With the Enlightenment of the seventeenth and eighteenth centuries, however, triumphant science could find in nature nothing but matter in motion. Stripped of its teleology, nature no longer provided a reasonable explanation of the origin of society. Nature, in fact, was inimical to the individual, as political philosopher Thomas Hobbes maintained, and it followed for John Locke to suggest that man in the "state of nature" surely would trade that existence for life in society, even though it meant becoming law abiding (rather than a law unto himself). Self-preservation was the great gain.

As Bloom points out, Locke's conception demanded too much from a demythologized nature. Nature, given Locke's assumptions, could only be expected to produce men who were slaves to their desires, brutish beasts and not the rational individuals who seemed to populate Locke's state of nature. This was the insight of Jean-Jacques Rousseau. Locke had invented the self as a kind of unifying factor for the individual, a holding device for the welter of sense impressions bombarding the person. Without the self, as distinct from nature, man simply collapses back into nature, and his development of society and political institutions cannot be accounted for.

The dualism of René Descartes further cemented the bifurcation of self and body, with modern psychology staking its claim to knowledge of that self. What distinguishes man from mere nature is the self, and the self is ego centered, selfish. Rousseau, contrary to Locke, viewed nature not as man's enemy but as a surcease from the artificiality of the city; for Rousseau there was at least some hope that the rift between nature and society might be overcome. Man must plumb the self, tapping into that yearning for pristine nature, for the self to live in harmony with the body.

Twentieth century America is heir to the Locke-Rousseau controversy. Bloom finds the Lockean in those who call for mastery of nature, who adjust easily to civil society. The Rousseauvian knows that adjustment to modern society is difficult indeed; his is the domain of the melancholy psychoanalyst. The selfishness of the Lockean is found in his conception of nature as raw material, useful for the building up of his own property. That of the Rousseauvian is found in those who pursue pleasure to satisfy the self. The nature-society distinction has thus in the twentieth century triumphed over the ancient tension between body and soul. "For Aristotle, good regimes have rulers dedicated to the common good, while bad ones have rulers who use their positions to further their private interest"; by contrast, the modern state is charged with overseeing the selfish interests of those who make it up.

Bloom's students mirror the modern state. They are pluralists with a vengeance, uncritically open to each new cultural deviation or fad but always reserving the right at any moment to turn their attention to a yet newer innovation. This is not a quest for truth or virtue, but proof of historicism's supremacy. Historicism says that not only are the great thinkers of the past so molded by their own times that they have nothing to say to the present generation, but also that what the present generation values may be altered willy-nilly to suit the circumstances. "Openness used to be the virtue that permitted us to seek the good by using reason. It now means accepting everything and denying reason's power." Such openness constitutes the closing of the (rational, critical) American mind.

Bloom devotes the first third of his book to a detailed description of the ethos of the university student. It is dominated by rock music. While students in France, for example, are steeped early in Descartes or Blaise Pascal and thus are shaped by their country's literary tradition, American students are gyrating to the rhythms of Mick Jagger "tarting it up on the stage." The deepest feelings of young people are not being given over to an examination of the literary and philosophical tradition that formed their psyches but instead are drained by the incessant drumbeat of sex. Rock is no more countercultural than a business degree; young people with their Walkmans are caught up in a "nonstop, commercially prepackaged masturbational fantasy."

In the sexual lives of the students, it is all freedom and equality; gone are the charms of romance, the roles of male and female in marriage, the taste of infinity in intercourse. Sex is all very businesslike; one's biology is one's destiny. The new freedom has replaced traditional family commitment; the idea of sexual tension being mastered by the higher soul, in a mix of education and eros, is simply foreign. The passions are drained, the "flat soul" is made universal. Students are indulged by their society and their university experience finds them increasingly deaf to the wisdom of others.

Bloom, however, is not disingenuous when he maintains that his purpose is not the production of a conservative tract: "I am not arguing . . . that the old family arrangements were good or that we should or could go back to them. I am only insisting that we not cloud our vision to such an extent that we believe that there are viable substitutes for them just because we want or need them." This is a key to the understanding of much of *The Closing of the American Mind*; Bloom inveighs against relativism only insofar as it voids consideration of more ancient explanations of the quandary of man. "A serious life," he writes, "means being fully aware of the alternatives, thinking about them with all the intensity one brings to bear on life-and-death questions, in full recognition that every choice is a great risk with necessary consequences that are hard to bear." A student may indeed choose nihilism, despairing that all the answers have come to nothing, but the cry of despair must come from the passionate soul. In the United States, nihilism takes a far different form from that taken on the Continent. Americans who find nothing at the center are candidates for therapy "to put them back in touch with themselves." "It is nihilism with a happy ending," says Bloom, " . . . nihilism without the abyss."

The center section of the book is in fact entitled "Nihilism, American Style," with Bloom describing how the German thinkers Friedrich Nietzsche, Martin Heidegger, Sigmund Freud, and Max Weber have all cast long, dark shadows on American culture. The shadows, however, have produced not fear of the darkness; students, true to the American genius, have simply turned on a light. The brooding faces of Nietzsche and Heidegger, Freud and Weber are no longer wrapped in darkness; in the American light they are peaked, washed out. Yet their influence lives on in certain fundamental modern catch phrases. Heidegger's existential dread (angst), Freud's sexual motor, the id, Weber's fact-value distinction, Nietzsche's "God is dead" are all the lingua franca of modern American university students. The dread is shallow, however (it is easily overcome by another rock concert or a taste of the id), and students are free to be self-creative (the mere facts of nature offer no basis for any prescribed values), as, indeed, they are free to be the very creators of their world (God has been displaced). Historicism rules the day, and the Continental terror at man's loss of the old, exhausted values is entirely missed by the American. Values become simply life-styles.

The German connection underlined the insights of Rousseau that reason itself, divorced from teleological nature, is never large enough to define man. Reason itself prescribes an end to reason. The implications of such a harrowing conclusion are lost on the American mind: "It is not the immorality of relativism that I find appalling," writes Bloom. "What is astounding and degrading is the dogmatism with which we accept such relativism, and our easygoing lack of concern about what that means for our lives." It is left to "The University," the third and last section of the book, to present perhaps the only counterforce to a final closing of the American mind. Yet in Bloom's thinking, the prospects of the university again becoming the domesticator of the passionate soul are dim indeed.

The university must always put the great questions at the forefront, and do so by keeping alive the grand Western tradition found in the old books. Historicism must be banished not because a serious soul might find it tenable, but because it denies man access to his past. The university must keep reason alive, keeping alive as well the tension between the philosopher and the demands of the state. Whereas the project of the Enlightenment was to see the rule of the scientist-philosopher, Socrates in *The Republic* (c. fourth century B.C.) knows otherwise. "What *The Republic* actually teaches is that none of this is possible and that our situation requires both much compromise and much intransigence, great risks and few hopes. The important thing is not speaking one's own mind, but finding a way to have one's own mind."

Bloom's observation of the university in the 1960's does not lend itself to hope. He accuses Cornell, where he was then teaching, of promulgating slogans in place of thought and of turning out homogenized students, emotionally committed to values that had floated in on the wind—equality, freedom, peace, world citizenship—and that could equally well float away again. Those instructors who sought to continue to transmit the content of the Great Books found themselves embattled and then made irrelevant.

The 1960's fragmented the university, and it has yet to recover. Philosophy is only another subject arranged alphabetically in the catalog. Bloom hopes not for reform but that those who still cherish the books may continue to touch a few students. The translator and interpreter of *The Republic* (1968) and of Rousseau's *Émile: Or, on Education* (1762; Bloom's translation was published in 1979), both preeminent treatises on education, is certain that

> The real community of man, in the midst of all the self-contradictory simulacra of community, is the community of those who seek the truth. . . . In fact this includes only a few, the true friends, as Plato was to Aristotle at the very moment they were disagreeing about the nature of the good.

Bloom, then, writes not as an apologist for conservative politics, an absolute moral system, or even a rigorous Platonism, but rather as one who yearns to pursue the true and the good in an open university, where the old thinkers are taken seriously and where students once again may engage in passionate dialogue as their souls are formed and informed by a liberal education, preparing them for the "American moment." Novelist Saul Bellow, in the foreword to Bloom's book, is perhaps the optimist: "In the greatest confusion there is still an open channel to the soul."

Dan Barnett

Sources for Further Study

The American Spectator. XX, August, 1987, p. 14.
The Christian Century. CXIV, July 29, 1987, p. 659.
Commonweal. CXIV, July 17, 1987, p. 422.
The Nation. CCXLIV, May 30, 1987, p. 714.
The New Criterion. V, May, 1987, p. 24.
The New Republic. CXCVI, May 25, 1987, p. 38.
The New York Times Book Review. XCII, April 5, 1987, p. 7.
The New Yorker. LXIII, July 6, 1987, p. 81.
Psychology Today. XXI, August, 1987, p. 70.
Publishers Weekly. CCXXXI, February 20, 1987, p. 67.
Time. CXXIX, April 13, 1987, p. 79.
The Washington Post Book World. XVII, April 19, 1987, p. 1.

THE COLLECTED LETTERS OF KATHERINE MANSFIELD
Volume II: 1918-1919

Author: Katherine Mansfield (1888-1923)
Edited by Vincent O'Sullivan with Margaret Scott
Publisher: Oxford University Press (New York). Illustrated. 365 pp. $29.95
Type of work: Letters
Time: January, 1918-September, 1919
Locale: Bandol and Paris, France; London and Cornwall, England; and Hampstead, England

In the second of five volumes of her collected letters, meticulously edited and sensitively introduced by Vincent O'Sullivan, Katherine Mansfield struggles with failing health and the stresses of separation from loved ones and friends, yet continues her creative activity culminating in the publication of Prelude *(1918) and the near completion of* Bliss and Other Stories *(1920)*

> *Principal personages:*
> KATHERINE MANSFIELD, a British short-story writer and poet
> JOHN MIDDLETON MURRY, her lover and later her husband
> LADY OTTOLINE MORRELL, her friend
> DOROTHY BRETT, her friend
> VIRGINIA WOOLF, a British novelist

The Collected Letters of Katherine Mansfield, Volume II: 1918-1919 covers less than two years in Mansfield's life, from January 1918 until September 1919; this period was characterized by isolation from John Middleton Murry, lyrical introspection, and, finally, tragic foreboding as her health continued to decline. Always driven by a powerful will, more finely controlled than her frail body already weakened by tuberculosis, she had hoped, early during her twenty-ninth year, that a few months of the Mediterranean climate would restore her well-being. Her doctor had urged upon her this vacation. When she left England on January 7, 1918, she did not know that tuberculosis was already established in her left lung, and she hoped to return home in the spring, when she planned to marry Murry. The couple had stayed at Bandol, France, for several months in 1917—a happy and artistically productive interlude—and Mansfield now supposed that her spirits would revive among the familiar scenes. Murry, assigned to intelligence duties at the War Office in London, could not join her, so letters were their means of communication. Because of World War I—always the war and the convulsions caused by that massive war effort—letters were often slow to arrive, with the effect that the lovers were separated by both space and time constraints. Finally, to complete their sense of isolation, they were often struggling with financial burdens that they concealed from each other.

Letters from this period in southern France—January to April, 1918—reflect Mansfield's varying moods, from depression (January 11) to occasional elation (January 20). Signing her letters "Wig" or "your little wife Tig," she poured out to Murry ("My own Bogey" or "My dear life" or "Dearest of all") a passionate recital of her fears, dreams, and longings. Always independent, she urged Murry not to send her money, although her financial situation was often precarious. Instead, she usually tried to cheer him up with amusing gossip (January 24, 25), anecdotes of her domestic tasks (February 6), or literary chitchat (February 23). Curiously, her letters from this time rarely concern her own literary ambitions. Yet at Bandol she composed one of her finest stories, "Je ne parle pas français." Darkening her vision of a life involved in love and art was the specter of approaching death. On February 19, she recorded in her notebook the onset of her first hemorrhage. She determined not to share the news with Murry: "I don't want to be ill, I means [sic] 'seriously' away from Jack. . . . How unbearable it would be to die, leave 'scraps,' 'bits' . . . nothing real finished."

On March 21, Mansfield left the south of France, expecting to be in London shortly. She was detained in Paris, however, for the day after she arrived, the Germans began their bombardment of the city from positions in the Forest of Crèpy, near Laon. German aircraft also intensified bombardment, so that the city was virtually a besieged fortress. Foreigners were discouraged from travel. On March 23, Mansfield wrote to Murry of her distress; she had applied for police permission to leave the city but had to wait for instructions. By March 29, all civilian travel had apparently been halted. Along with the constant bombardment (April 6) and the delay in receiving letters, Mansfield suffered from privations and from witnessing scenes of horror (April 2). By April 9, she reported feeling "desperate." This torment, however, was soon to end. On April 11, she telegraphed Murry that she would arrive at Waterloo Station in the morning.

Mansfield moved in with her lover at 47 Redcliffe Road and, in her letter to Dorothy Brett (May 1), she announced that she had received an Order of the Court declaring "the Decree Nisi to have been made absolute." With more legal delays, the couple married on May 3. But the condition of her health frightened Murry, so they left his Fulham flat for Cornwall. To Ottoline Morrell, Mansfield wrote (May 12) that she seemed "always renewing a marriage with Murry." To Brett (May 12), she described her visit to Virginia Woolf, whose industry and artistic devotion she ruefully contrasted with her own: "My poor dear Prelude is still piping away in their [sic] little cage and not out yet. I read some pages of it & scarcely knew it again." *Prelude*, not published until early July—by Leonard and Virginia Woolf's Hogarth Press—caused little stir, for the book was distributed unreviewed, and most of Mansfield's friends appeared to be unenthusiastic.

During the spring and early summer of 1918. Mansfield exchanged many letters with Murry (who was staying at the Headland Hotel, Looe, Cornwall), but also corresponded at length with others, especially with Ida Baker ("Jones"), who served her well as confidante, soundingboard, and helper. To Ida she wrote (June 25) asking for spare "tea"—her code word for money—since she could not bear to ask Murry. Her letters to Woolf were much less confiding, more formal. After all, Woolf was more than a friend: She was a literary rival. More relaxed with Brett and Morrell, Mansfield could speak freely on such matters as the death of her mother (letters of August 11 and August 14). She admired in her mother "*courage—spirit—poise*"—qualities that she herself had to draw upon from her reserves, as her strength flagged.

Toward the end of August, the Murrys moved to Hampstead, to a home (Portland Villas, East Heath Road) that they loved. For once, they appear to have established roots. They now had permanent servants, and their bohemian existence seemed behind them. By January 1, 1919, Mansfield could wish Brett a happy new year and report: "We had a superb Xmas. . . . Oh, I did *love* it so—loved everybody." During this time, Frieda and D. H. Lawrence are often Mansfield's concern, along with mutual friends of the Murrys and Lawrences, including S. S. Koteliansky, who collaborated with her on a series of translations of Anton Chekhov's letters. Although her literary, domestic, and financial prospects appear to have brightened (Murry took over the editorship of *The Athenæum* in February 1919), her health remained precarious.

By the summer of 1919, Mansfield's illness forced her to seek medical intervention. Dr. Victor Sorapure, her friend and physician, advised her to go to the Italian Riviera, and by August 13, in a letter to Morrell, she reported: "It has determined me to go into a Sanatorium next month & to stay there until April. . . . But oh—this agony of ill health & worry is too much." She wrote an informal will and left England on September 11. Her last letter prior to departure, to Murry ("My darling Boy"), is heartbreaking: "Thats all. But don't let anybody *mourn* me. It can't be helped. I think you ought to marry again and have children. If you do give your little girl the pearl ring." The letter is signed: "Yours for ever, Wig."

As both a record of literary history and a human document, Mansfield's collection of letters from 1918 to 1919—taken as a unit—represents one of the most impressive achievements of her career. Indeed, she must be ranked among the undeniably great English letter-writers of the first part of the twentieth century, along with George Bernard Shaw, John Millington Synge, Woolf—and a few additional notables. Rich in reference to important literary people (especially those of the Bloomsbury Group—the Woolfs, Lytton Strachey, Clive Bell, Roger Fry—and those associated with Lawrence—Brett, Mark Gertler, Koteliansky, Morrell, Bertrand Russell, J. W. N. Sullivan), the letters are useful in rounding out a scholar's sense of major literary personalities and their interconnected relationships during the post-World War I era.

Equally important, the letters are valuable records of a great-souled woman in love. Without question, the romance between Murry and Mansfield is one of the most touching love stories of the first half of the twentieth century. Murry has left for readers his own poignant account of these years with Mansfield (*Between Two Worlds*, 1935). Now the letters of his wife tell her side of the story. In their depth of moral courage, tenderness, intelligence, wit, playfulness, and poetic sensibility, they are quite simply extraordinary in the literature of love-correspondence. Among women correspondents, perhaps only Anaïs Nin, a decade later, rivals Mansfield in range, fluency, and psychological acuity. Among artists in letters, there is none that surpasses Katherine Mansfield for pathos.

Leslie B. Mittleman

Sources for Further Study

Booklist. LXXXIV, September 1, 1987, p. 21.
The Observer. February 8, 1987, p. 29.
The Spectator. CCLVIII, February 28, 1987, p. 31.
The Times Literary Supplement. February 13, 1987, p. 156.

THE COLLECTED POEMS OF OCTAVIO PAZ
1957-1987

Author: Octavio Paz (1914-   )
Edited by Eliot Weinberger
Translated from the Spanish by Eliot Weinberger and various hands
Publisher: New Directions (New York). 669 pp. $37.50
Type of work: Poetry

  A bilingual collection that brings the achievements of Latin America's foremost poet into sharper focus

  The Collected Poems of Octavio Paz: 1957-1987 is a virtually complete gathering of Paz's poetry from *Piedra de sol* (1957; *Sunstone*) to his first new book of poems in eleven years, *Árbol adentro* (1987; *A Tree Within*). As Eliot Weinberger notes, the latter "appears in translation here simultaneous to its Spanish edition, perhaps a 'first' for a book of foreign poetry." In this handsome volume, the Spanish text appears facing the English translation, so that even a reader who has had nothing more than a bit of high school Spanish can get a sense of the sound of Paz's poetry. More than half of the poems in the collection are appearing in English for the first time. Most of the translations are Weinberger's, and they read very well; also included are a handful of translations by other poets, contributed chiefly by Charles Tomlinson and Elizabeth Bishop. In his preface, Weinberger provides an overview of Paz's career; the text is also supplemented by twenty pages of notes supplied by the poet himself (quite helpful), a list of Paz's works available in English translation, and indexes of titles in both Spanish and English.

  While Paz has received a generous amount of critical attention, his own wide-ranging prose remains the best guide to his poetry. Particularly valuable is the revised edition of *El arco y la lira* (1967; *The Bow and the Lyre*, 1973), part treatise on poetics, part literary history, part manifesto. There, Paz connects poetry with "the perception of the spark of *otherness* in each of our acts." Awareness of otherness is variously manifested in poetry, religion, and love: "Hidden by the profane or prosaic life, our being suddenly remembers its lost identity; and then that 'other' that we are appears, emerges." In calling poetry to the recovery of the sacred, Paz chides modern rationalism for its denial of this entire realm of human experience, yet at the same time he rejects religion's claim to it: "The experience of the divine is more ancient, immediate, and original than any religious conception." Above all, he rejects the emphasis which Christianity and other religions place on a life after death: "I am not concerned about the *other life* elsewhere but here. The experience of *otherness* is, here and now, the *other life*."

  Poetry as a revelation of the other life: This is the recurring theme that gives continuity to Paz's massive and multifaceted body of work. It can be

traced over the entire span of the present volume through a group of remarkable poems that strongly resemble one another in subject and form.
While Paz has ranged from haiku to book-length poems such as *Sunstone*,
the poems in this group are of intermediate length, roughly five to ten
pages. Like most of his work, they are written in free verse.

These poems are linked by other similarities as well. They are firmly in
the lyric tradition: The poet speaks in the first person, and the voice is
consistently his own, so that the reader is not inclined to make any distinction between the speaker of the poem and Paz himself. Most of these poems
begin at night or in twilight, at a time when the ordinary world is transformed; many of them take as their point of departure the act of writing, reflecting on their own composition as they progress.

One of the first poems of this group is "Same Time." It is set in Mexico
City, at night; the opening lines establish a contrast between the natural
world, which is "at rest," and the city,

> turning on its shadow
> searching always searching itself
> lost in its immensity
> never catching up
>   never able to leave itself

The city is an emblem of consciousness, and the poet feels the contagion of
its restlessness:

> I close my eyes and watch the cars go by
> they flare up and burn out and flare up
> burn out
>   I don't know where they're going
> All of us going to die
>   What else do we know?

These lines hint at what is later made explicit: The poem records the play of
the poet's mind as he sits writing. Eyes closed, he can still perceive the sudden brightness of headlights; that is the literal meaning, but the paradox of
"I close my eyes and watch" suggests interior vision, the vision that will yield
poetic revelation. While these opening lines produce an image of futility—
life as traffic, an aimless coming and going—the remainder of the poem will
provide an alternative, culminating in lyrical ecstasy:

> This afternoon from a bridge I saw
> the sun enter the waters of the river
> All was in flames
> the statues the house the porticoes burned
> In the gardens feminine clusters of grapes
> ingots of liquid light

> the coolness of solar vessels
> The poplars a foliage of sparks
> the water horizontal unmoving
> beneath the flaming earths and skies

The concluding section of the poem shifts from this tumbling intensity to a poetry of statement reminiscent of T. S. Eliot in *Four Quartets* (1943): "There is another life within this life," Paz affirms, and "there is another time within time."

The same movement from bleakness to affirmation, from quotidian reality to poetic revelation, can be seen in "Clear Night" (dedicated to surrealists André Breton and Benjamin Péret). The title of the poem has a straight-forward meaning—it is a clear night; the stars are visible—yet it is also (like "I close my eyes and watch") a paradox: For Paz, the clarity of darkness is a recurring image associated with poetic vision. The poem opens in Paris, in the Café d'Angleterre; it is ten o'clock, and only Paz and his two friends remain in the café. The first section announces the theme of revelation—"Everything is a door/ all one needs is the light push of a thought"—and introduces the poem's refrain: "Something's about to happen."

Like "Same Time," "Clear Night" confronts futility and desolation, in Paris and also in London, to which the poet shifts for a time in memory. Again, too, he experiences ecstatic vision; in this case, the transformation is prompted by the sight of an unsentimentalized teenage couple:

> On her jacket the color of strawberries
> was emblazoned the hand of a boy
> the four letters of the word Love
> burned on each finger like stars

It is the crude image of that hand (a drawing of which appears in the text of the poem) that galvanizes Paz's imagination: "hand full of eyes in the night of the body/ tiny sun and cool river/ hand that brings resurrection and dreams." From the memory of that afternoon in London, the poet shifts back to the Paris night. He and his friends leave the café, and again the poem turns to images of desolation: "century carved into a scream/ pyramid of blood." Yes, the poet concedes, "we have lost all the battles," yet he immediately follows that concession with a paradoxical affirmation: "each day we win one/ Poetry." On the strength of that affirmation, the poem concludes with an erotic catalog in the manner of the Song of Songs ("your hair unpinned is a storm on the terraces of dawn/ your belly is the breath of the sea and the pulse of day") in which the poet identifies the city with his love, and identifies both city and woman with elusive, indefinable otherness: "City Woman Presence."

The group of poems represented by "Same Time" and "Clear Night" includes several which Paz wrote in India in the 1960's during his tenure as ambassador (notably "Vrindaban" and "A Tale of Two Gardens") as well as several written in the 1970's after his return to Mexico ("Return," "In the Middle of This Phrase . . . ," and the great poem "San Ildefonso Nocturne"). It is fitting that the poem which concludes *A Tree Within*, "Letter of Testimony," the very last poem in the book, should also be of this number. All of these poems deal explicitly with poetic revelation; together they constitute the richest vein in Paz's work.

For English-speaking readers, this volume of collected poems makes abundantly clear the scope of Paz's achievement. ("Those members of the Nobel Prize committee who do not know Spanish," Charles Tomlinson remarks in *The Times Literary Supplement*, "can now think again and the next time round do what they chose not to do in 1987.") More so than before, it is possible to see how Paz's recovery of the sacred sets him apart from the bleak chorus of contemporary literature. His sense of the otherness that is "here and now"—not simply asserted but repeatedly embodied in poetry— is a reproach not only to casual materialists but also to Christians and other religious believers who by deadening custom have restricted their experience of the sacred to neatly demarcated zones, hardly interfering with their daily lives. Yet this recognition may obscure another truth about Paz's version of the sacred: that it stops short of the hope without which all intimations of "the other shore" may finally seem to be mere delusion.

John Wilson

Sources for Further Study

Library Journal. CXII, October 15, 1987, p. 83.
Los Angeles Times Book Review. December 27, 1987, p. 3.
The New Republic. CXCVIII, March 14, 1988, p. 36.
Publishers Weekly. CCXXXII, October 30, 1987, p. 59.
The Times Literary Supplement. January 15-21, 1988, p. 55.

COLLECTED PROSE

Author: Robert Lowell (1917-1977)
Edited, with an introduction, by Robert Giroux
Publisher: Farrar, Straus and Giroux. 377 pp. $25.00
Type of work: Essays, reviews, and memoir

A posthumous collection of reviews, essays, prefaces, eulogies, interviews, and memoirs by the most celebrated poet of his generation

When he died at the age of sixty in 1977, Robert Lowell had published only one widely known piece of prose, the autobiographical "91 Revere Street," an unblinkered, unflattering, and yet oddly affecting scrutiny of his Brahmin-yet-embarrassing upbringing in Boston during the 1920's. While Lowell did contribute an occasional review, particularly in the earlier part of his career, he was in no danger of being taken for, or compared with, the brainy poet-critics he so obviously surpassed in the intensity and architecture of his poetry, Randall Jarrell and John Berryman—both friends of Lowell (and the subjects of essays in this volume). Yet the pieces collected here, admirably edited by Robert Giroux, reveal for the first time the extent to which Lowell was a critic of astute insight, as well as a master of American prose, a prose filled with enough wildly surprising and knowing evaluations and asides to put whole schools of academic critics to shame.

Giroux divides the *Collected Prose* into three parts. The first consists essentially of reviews and occasional pieces, the earliest being a 1943 paean for the just-published *Four Quartets*, the most recent a 1974 eulogy of John Crowe Ransom. There are also essays on Robert Frost, Wallace Stevens, William Carlos Williams, Yvor Winters, Stanley Kunitz, Robert Penn Warren, W. H. Auden, Elizabeth Bishop, Andrei Voznesensky, and Sylvia Plath, as well as essays on the poems of critic I. A. Richards and of novelist Ford Madox Ford. There is also a charming and characteristically self-deprecating remembrance of his first visit to the Allen Tates, when, misinterpreting his hostess' remark that there was no room for an unannounced guest unless he "pitched a tent," Lowell, with "adolescent heedlessness," traveled to Nashville, returned with a Sears, Roebuck umbrella tent, and pitched it for a watershed summer.

In assessments that are as nervously precise as they are respectful and at times reverent, Lowell's method is to dart directly to the poet's "matter" and then to spiral back, hastily nailing in qualifying planks and historical handrails that will constitute a stairway. In addition, it is characteristic of Lowell, with his wide personal acquaintanceship and affinity for biography, to punctuate his criticism with ad hominem comments meant to enlarge and enrich the image of the creator focused beneath the lens. He could familiarize the peripatetic, cosmopolitan Ford effortlessly to American imaginations as a "large, unwieldy, wheezy, unwell" man who "looked somehow like a

British version of the Republican elephant," and shake the wool off Robert Frost by observing, "He was almost a farmer. Yet under the camouflage there was always the Brahma crouching, a Whitman, a great-mannered bard." An early essay on Stevens recognizes what is surely an unspoken caveat for many—especially American—readers, who have come to expect at least a whiff of the midnight oil, if not of scandal and self-torment, from their poets: "There seems to be something in the poet that protects itself by asserting that it is not making too much of an effort." In a later piece, a more mature and fellow-feeling Lowell grants Stevens the largeness and originality whose presence renders niggling pointless. He was "a large poet with the ear of Shakespeare" who could "express the inexpressible and loosen the constriction of sense." "The constriction of sense" is a fine and far-reaching phrase that tilts at the empirical bias manifest in the judgments of art's self-appointed gendarmes during the twentieth century.

One of the handsomer essays in this section, on John Crowe Ransom, works from within the matrix of Lowell's tutorial association with the Agrarians, while reflecting the critical distance that subsequent years and influences—particularly that of Williams—were to build. Certainly one of the central questions concerning Ransom the poet, as opposed to Ransom the doyen of the New Criticism, has to do with the poet's stingy output. We have only the slight *Selected Poems* (1974) and that to a debatable extent vitiated by the poet's "revisions" of an earlier *Selected Poems* (1963). While finding some of the revisions "disastrous," Lowell points out that not all are so, as the first, influential reviewers suggested. (In an interview with Frederick Seidel collected here, Lowell, asked if he revises much, answers "Endlessly.") He sees a virtue in the ability of Ransom's poems "to stick apart; and refuse to melt into their neighbors. They seem few until one tries to discover as many in some favorite, more voluminous author." Of their whole significance, Lowell concludes, "Man goes creased and sometimes finds a puzzling joy."

If Tate and Ransom were Lowell's early mentors, whose influence can be seen to preside over the burled, tortured, seven-layered early poems, William Carlos Williams can be credited with providing Lowell with a looser structure and more off-the-cuff technique, one more suited to negotiating the autobiographical left-turn the poet made in the 1950's. Lowell's sensible and schematic reading of *Paterson* (1946-1958) before his actual correspondence and friendship with the good doctor shows an awareness of that ambitious poet's need to fashion a homemade American oeuvre based on a dovetailing of his own experience and his reading of the cranky, prolix American colossi who lurk intimidatingly at the beginning of American literature. Citing analogies in William Wordsworth's *The Prelude* (1850), Lowell finds Williams on the trail of his own American myth, according to which "we must unavoidably place ourselves in our geography, history, civilization, institutions, and future." Yet, he admits, "How hollow, windy, and inert this [the American myth] would have seemed to an imaginative man of another culture!" On the other hand, "America *is* something immense, crass, and Roman." Williams' insight, which would in turn be taken up in the postwar Lowellian cosmos, is into "Whitman's America, grown pathetic and tragic, brutalized by inequality, disorganized by industrial chaos, and faced with annihilation." Lowell admires this engagement with America yet cannot fully emulate it: Williams' is "a Dantesque journey, for he loves America excessively, as if it were *the* truth and *the* subject; his exasperation is also excessive, as if there were no other hell. His flowers rustle by the super-highways and pick up all our voices."

The second section of the book contains more general, belletristic essays, including an insightful, if somewhat schoolboyish, essay on Homer's *Iliad* (c. 800 B.C.), written when the poet was eighteen. The most impressive piece—and one of the most surprising—is "New England and Further," an unfinished, unrevised essay begun in the late 1960's and taken up infrequently until the poet's death. What is most remarkable about the essay, a compendium of brief, impressionistic feuilletons on New England writers, is that it was composed from memory without recourse to library or sources while the poet was vacationing in Maine. Presented here are Cotton Mather, Benjamin Franklin, Ralph Waldo Emerson, Nathaniel Hawthorne, Henry David Thoreau, Abraham Lincoln, James Russell Lowell, Herman Melville, Henry Wadsworth Longfellow, historians Francis Parkman and John Lothrop Motley, Henry James, Henry Adams, Emily Dickinson, George Santayana, Frost, Steens, and Eliot. The display of erudition toward this formidable, frequently crusty pantheon of ancestors is as astonishing as the effects of cursory, yet intimate, judgment, obviously the result of a lifetime's private rumination and confrontation.

Franklin was "a New Englander whose every breath denied the spirit; an American who wasn't even a colonial but an eighteenth century European, a prophet whose mild sociable Quakerism was stubbornly worldly, and a writer whose writings sought only ease and clarity and shunned soaring." Hawthorne "died depressed, . . . he found life too long for comfort and too brief for perfection," while Emerson ("Frost's sweeter, thinner, more celestial forerunner") "lingered through twenty or more years of amnesia. For one, unlit self-confinement; for the other, a gentle *tabula rasa*." Lowell's ancestor, James Russell Lowell, he finds "amiably student-Byronesque," though "most of [his] literary judgments are local and overstated." By contrast, Longfellow is "our cultured metrical technician. Tennyson without gin." While Dickinson is "steadily alive and original—strangely like the late Henry James's recklessly strenuous prose," she also strays "into shagginess, purposeless bad grammar, [and her] meaningless dashes spread like bird shot." On the other hand, "she made the language of her contemporaries obsolete." In keeping with the time, Frost had been recommended by Lowell's mother as "understandable to everyone . . . no nihilist of the middleclass." Yet he "survived this recommendation of everything I hated" by writing of "the heart . . . we must care for—a heart of stonemason darkness." Stevens is

> more solitary than a Prufrock, but happy to turn our human flesh, and the sun itself, into metaphor, his eternal metaphor. His great cloud of figures and shadows sops up moisture from the earth. Some woman or lovely thing is forever casting its crystal X-ray on him . . .

Eliot's *The Waste Land* is "sex gone haywire," while "Gerontion" is "a miracle of invention and magnificent upholstery to anyone who has tried to write of dejection." *Four Quartets* is "Eliot's furthest stretch, his greatest and most compassionate poem, written in a revolutionary and lax language."

The third and final section of the volume includes prefaces, interviews, and autobiographical pieces. Almost from the start of his career, Lowell submitted his privileged circumstances to the glare of ironic scrutiny. Disaffected from his blue-blooded ancestors, unimpressed by the tony Beacon Hill address ("the hub of the hub of the universe"), he chose as his subject the vacuity behind the brownstone façade. "91 Revere Street" treats his claustrophobic upbringing during his father's long career slide into professional and social irrelevance. A navy man who was second in command at the "defunct" Boston Naval Yard, Commander Lowell had "begged" for the assignment as a concession to his wife, whose separate residence, set up in defiance of the one provided free of charge at the Yard, was a source of personal and professional humiliation, as he packed up to return and spend each night at the Yard by command of the Admiral. The poet's arch, domineering mother, who "hated the Navy, hated naval society, naval pay, and the trip-hammer rote of settling and unsettling a house every other year," had "violently set her heart on [her husband's] resignation." The young Lowell used to "look forward to the nights when . . . I would awake with rapture to the rhythm of my parents arguing." An only child, Lowell naturally fell prey to his mother's manipulations against her husband, though in his early resistance to the flaws in both parents one may see prefigured his later career as an angry leveler of pretensions. Imagining himself as a "master of cool, stoical repartee," Lowell responded to his parents' battles by means of point-of-order verbal minimalism. When his father was called back to the Yard one Christmas Eve, his mother exclaimed, "Oh, Bobby, it's such a comfort to have a man in the house," to which Lowell replied, "I am not a man . . . I am a boy."

There are three principal impulses that can inspire the writing of an autobiography: recording memoirs, justifying oneself, and creating a personal mythology. Lowell, in each of his autobiographical fragments, has chosen, like a good postmodernist, to stand the last reason on its head. Yet for all his debunking, and despite his flirtation with an alien, if more accessible, poetics in the 1950's, he inherited plenty from his patrician background, a debt most apparent in the inclinations and disinclinations—Puritan, yet cultured, independent, public-spirited—that strove to possess his allegiance.

At the same time, Lowell was subject to the menacing, life- and sanity-threatening bouts of acute mania during which his imaginative powers would operate under a protracted siege of mental inflation at the expense of his physical tolerance. Several of these attacks necessitated his removal to the hospital. One especially steamrolling episode, which occurred shortly after his mother's death in Italy, is recorded here as "Near the Unbalanced Aquarium," a horrifically deadpan threnody to his own problematical poise:

> At Occupational Therapy there was the room of the loom and the room of the potter's wheels. I spent several mornings in each, inquiring. But when the loom or the wheel was put in my hands, I excused myself by explaining Charles Collingwood's theory that art could never be merely craft, "despite all the attacks made on inspiration by our friends the anti-romantic critics." I pretended that my doctor had given me permission to read *Kim.*

Lowell intersperses his account of this episode with flashbacks, first to his trip to Italy to retrieve his mother, who died half an hour before his arrival in Rapallo. He arranged for her funeral, doing everything "that Father could have desired," including purchasing a "black-and-gold baroque casket that would have been suitable for burying her hero Napoleon at Les Invalides," so that propriety was affronted only by the misspelling of her name, which was reproduced as L-O-V-E-L. "I could almost hear her voice correcting the workmen: 'I am Mrs. Robert Lowell of One Seventy Marlborough Street, Boston, L, O, W, E, *double L*.'"

Near the end of the account of his hospital stay, Lowell relates a story concerning a self-styled "Israelite," a black fellow-prisoner whom he encountered while serving his sentence for resisting the draft in World War II, whose sect, "among the many eccentrics" there, "took the prize," believing that "the people of the Old Testament were Negroes" and that "modern Jews were impostors." As Lowell sat with this "most venerable and mild of the Israelites" contemplating the town of Danbury, "which consisted of what might be called filling-station architecture," his friend stretched out his arm and said, "Only man is miserable." Lowell's response: "I told my doctor that this summed up my morals and my aesthetics." The clear implication is that his misery, despite prison and the asylum, was a home-grown malaise, born and nurtured in the domestic caldron of what Sigmund Freud quaintly called "the family romance." Lowell's autobiographical eulogy for his parents ends on a Freudian note:

The last autobiography I looked into was a movie about a bullterrier from Brooklyn. The dog's name was, I think, House on Fire. The district he came from was so tough that smoking had to be permitted in the last three pews at High Mass. House on Fire's mother had been deserted by his father. House knows that his father is a great dog in the great world, either as a champion fighter or as a champion in exhibitions. House on Fire keeps saying with his Brooklyn accent, "I want to be a champ so that I can kill my father." In the end there is peace.

Lowell's own father was suited neither to fighting nor to exhibition, and perhaps that is the problem—that, in respect to engaging the aggressive, simmering aspects of his son's character, he declined the challenge. Lowell concludes puzzlingly, "My own father was a gentle, faithful, and dim man. I don't know why I was agin him. I hope there will be peace." That Lowell grew to be House on Fire, however, is indisputable.

David Rigsbee

Sources for Further Study

Booklist. LXXXIII, March 1, 1987, p. 975.
Chicago Tribune. April 7, 1987, V, p. 3.
Kirkus Reviews. LV, January 1, 1987, p. 40.
Library Journal. CXII, March 1, 1987, p. 77.
The Nation. CCXLIV, April 11, 1987, p. 475.
National Review. XXXIX, March 13, 1987, p. 50.
The New Republic. CXCVI, March 30, 1987, p. 30.
The New York Times Book Review. XCII, July 12, 1987, p. 22.
Publishers Weekly. CCXXXI, January 30, 1987, p. 78.
USA Today. April 10, 1987, p. D8.

THE COMPLETE NOTEBOOKS OF HENRY JAMES

Author: Henry James (1843-1916)
Edited, with introductions and notes, by Leon Edel and Lyall H. Powers
Publisher: Oxford University Press (New York). 633 pp. $30.00
Type of work: Notes and diary entries
Time: 1870-1915
Locale: Primarily London, England, and the northeastern United States

A meticulously prepared edition of all the extant notebooks and pocket diaries used by American writer Henry James to collect and record impressions for stories, plays, and novels

The Complete Notebooks of Henry James will certainly take its place on the shelves of James scholars, and perhaps of many others seriously interested in American literature and literary history. Its 633 pages of quality paper, bound in thick black boards handsomely gold lettered, will no doubt be squeezed in between other equally impressive tomes, such as the volumes that constitute the New York edition of James's works, those two dozen or so revisions of his works that Henry James himself shepherded through the press. If the purchaser of this new edition of the notebooks has been truly serious about assembling a "must-have" collection of works by and about this important American author, he is sure to have already on this same shelf more than a dozen books about James which bear a second name—that of Leon Edel.

For half a century, the scholarly world has benefited from Edel's devotion to James's life and works. Several editions of James's novels and stories bear Edel's imprint. His meticulous scholarship and graceful style have produced a detailed, multivolume edition of James's letters and an award-winning, four volume biography. With the distinguished critic Lyall H. Powers, Edel has brought out this new edition of James's famous notebooks, a work that certainly supplements, and will probably replace, the 1947 edition, *The Notebooks of Henry James*, edited by F. O. Matthiessen and Kenneth B. Murdock.

The title of this collection is actually somewhat misleading, since the volume contains much more than the title suggests. Less than half of the book is devoted to reproducing the nine notebooks that have survived and are now part of the James papers at the Houghton Library of Harvard University. Included also are detached notes that were discovered with the notebooks; notes for various works with which James struggled during the later years of his life; proposals he submitted to various publishers for some of his works, including his famous "Project for a Novel," the draft outline of *The Ambassadors* (1903); the pocket diaries James kept from 1909 until 1915; and his "deathbed dictations."

Surprisingly, even in a volume of this size, editorial intrusion is slight. Edel and Powers offer separate introductory remarks, the former on the discovery of the notebooks and on James's method of note taking, the latter on the method of editing. The headnotes to each section sketch out the general content and provide sufficient information to place each notebook biographically. Edel's essay offers some revealing insights into the way in which James's changes in his writing style—near the end of the nineteenth century he hired a secretary to take dictation, and he eventually dictated directly to a typist—affected his note taking, changing the notebooks from confidential commentary to more cryptic jottings, often made in his pocket diaries.

Within that portion of the book that reproduces the notebooks and diaries, editorializing is so infrequent that it surprises. For example, remarking on James's inability to produce a story from notes on which he obviously worked long and hard, the editors observe: "The thing [the story] never did come, probably because of HJ's [James's] inherent inability to manage the details of *macho* male sexuality." Readers who expect much of this kind of assessment, however, will be disappointed. Instead, James's comments are left to speak for themselves.

That editorial method seems most appropriate. The nine notebooks themselves are, of course, invaluable as clues to the creative process that underlies James's work as a writer, and it is on the text itself that the reader's primary interest is focused. In the first American notebook, one of two that he kept on separate visits to the country he abandoned for the more inspirational shores of Great Britain and the European continent, James writes to himself that he "ought to endeavour to keep, to a certain extent, a record of passing impressions. . . . To catch and keep something of life—that's what I mean." At least in the early notebooks, James felt that when he made his entries he was "tak[ing] a sheet of paper, as it were, into my confidence." As a result, many of these notes read as if they were addressed to another person, one who is alternately addressed as a "dear friend" or "confidante." The style is often one of direct address.

On occasion, James uses the notebooks as a kind of diary, and one can glean from autobiographical revelations his reaction to a variety of personal situations—hopes fulfilled or shattered. The two American notebooks make particularly interesting reading for the social historian, as they are filled with anecdotes of New England cultural and intellectual life.

James was a voracious observer and recorder of the life around him, and he made ample use of suggestions for stories provided by friends both American and European. The notebooks alternate between plot outline and criticism, with a steady running commentary in which James explains to himself the methodology he must follow to turn this raw material into art. Infrequently, but dramatically, James is likely to burst into apostrophe: "Oh art, art," he writes in 1885, "what difficulties are like thine; but, at the same time, what consolation and encouragements, also, are like thine? Without thee, for me, the world would be, indeed, a howling desert." Once in a while, James uses his notebook as a commonplace book, copying out important passages from other works which he found particularly interesting.

If one reads the notebooks from beginning to end, one can follow the progress of dozens of James's stories from conception to finished product. Most appear initially as brief observations, which James mulls over until he finds a suitable theme and method for presenting it. Some stories appear only once; others take shape in the course of several passages, as characters and incidents change and assume more definite form.

Readers of *The Complete Notebooks of Henry James* who are well versed in James's oeuvre will experience frequent pleasurable shocks of recognition, as they see the seeds that sprouted into the literary flowers for which James is acclaimed. Amid long lists of characters, lists which James had a habit of making, presumably to provide himself with a ready stockpile from which to choose, one finds (interspersed among entries that have no apparent significance) such evocative entries as "Marcher" and "Strether." Similarly, one needs no footnote to call attention to the relationship between the "ghost story" which James heard from the Archbishop of Canterbury and *The Turn of the Screw* (1898), or that between Jonathan Sturges' remarks about William Dean Howells' impressions of European life and *The Ambassadors*. Such discoveries will sustain the interest of the aficionado of James's fiction.

It is also possible to trace in these entries several recurring themes that reveal something of the artist and his concerns. For example, stories of James's disappointment over failing as a dramatist are corroborated in his notes. An 1881 entry in the first American notebook displays his eagerness for such a career: "After long years of waiting . . ." he notes, "I find myself able to put into execution the most cherished of all my projects—that of beginning to work for the stage. . . . None has given me brighter hopes," he confesses to himself, "none has given me sweeter emotions." "The field is common," he reminds himself in a note eight years later, "but it is wide and free." Sometimes he finds himself frustrated that the necessity to meet the demands of publishers hounding him for his fiction prevented him from mounting a "genuine and sustained attack on the theatre."

The poor showing which he made as a dramatist, culminating with the closing of *Guy Domville* on its opening night in January, 1895, may have driven him from active work for the stage, but it did not quell his passion for wanting to make all his work dramatic. Perhaps it was the sense of completeness, a sense that the drama was a carefully knit form, that appealed to James. From his earliest notes, he seems obsessed with the idea of form in his fiction. He admires Guy de Maupassant as a master of the short story because the Frenchman is able to shape his incidents carefully, building toward a single effect. Many of James's musings in the notebooks are over his own methods, as he moves from the discovery of an idea to its

final embodiment in a story where an appropriate action illuminates the social or moral theme he wishes to illustrate in the work. A surprisingly large
number of the entries deal with his concern for working out his ideas within
certain mechanical limits: The pages of *The Complete Notebooks* abound
with reminders that stories must be a certain length, or that a certain number of chapters (and no more) must be given to moving forward specific elements of the plot.

The notebooks also afford the discerning reader some moments of amusement. Interspersed amid the comments on mechanics and the detailed plotting of the stories, novels, and plays are James's observations of various
people and professions that have earned his admiration—or his disdain.
One of the latter professions is—perhaps predictably—the publishing industry, especially the popular press. Adding to the outcry over an open letter
about Venetian society written by Mary McClellan for the New York *World*,
James lashes out at her for being "irreflective and irresponsible." He goes
on to note that, as a chronicler of his age, he must deal in his fiction with
people such as McClellan, who in her role as a journalist is symptomatic of
a sad phenomenon: "the invasion, the impudence and shamelessness, of the
newspaper and the interviewer, the devouring *publicity* of life, the extinction
of all sense between public and private." Paradoxically, though, he writes on
more than one occasion of the limits to which he can go with his stories if
they are to appear in American magazines, where a false sense of morality
has resulted in needless prudery. For journals such as *Harper's Magazine*, he
has nothing but contempt; there the editors refuse to accept works on difficult or delicate subjects, preferring to stick with "slighter," "safer," and
hence "inferior" materials. One writes for *Harper's Magazine*, James notes
sadly, for no reason "save the sole pecuniary one," since "the company one
keeps in their magazine is of a most paralysing dreariness." One need only
survey a newsstand today to see that not much has changed.

To turn from the notebooks to the pocket diaries may be something of a
letdown. These small books served a dual function for James. Most of the
entries are short memoranda of meetings and appointments, or reminders
of presents to send or money to repay. They are of greater interest to the
biographer than to the literary critic. Even so, the claims of the editors that
one can construct an "entire Edwardian and post-Edwardian social and literary history" from these "brief and hasty jottings" seem a bit farfetched.
Nevertheless, those wishing to know all there is to know about Henry James
will be grateful for their inclusion in this volume, as they will be for the editors' decision to print the various dictated notes, notes to publishers, and
the unfinished story "Hugh Merrow." While it may be hard to imagine
another biographer retracing the ground that Leon Edel has so carefully
covered, the history of the scholarly profession suggests that such will be the
case—perhaps not in the near future, but certainly within a century. When

that happens, the new biographer will find *The Complete Notebooks of Henry James* an invaluable sourcebook.

Laurence W. Mazzeno

Sources for Further Study

Booklist. LXXXIII, November 15, 1986, p. 467.
Choice. XXIV, May, 1987, p. 1396.
Library Journal. CXI, December, 1986, p. 112.
Los Angeles Times Book Review. January 18, 1987, p. 9.
The New York Times Book Review. XCII, December 28, 1986, p. 10.
The New Yorker. LXIII, March 9, 1987, p. 101.
Publishers Weekly. CCXXX, October 24, 1986, p. 66.
The Washington Post Book World. XVI, December 28, 1986, p. 1.

A CONFLICT OF VISIONS

Author: Thomas Sowell (1930-   )
Publisher: William Morrow and Company (New York). 273 pp. $15.95
Type of work: History of ideas
Time: The seventeenth century to the twentieth century

An experienced ideological warrior attempts to identify historically crucial, competing visions of human nature and society

Any new book by Thomas Sowell is likely to cause a stir among politically oriented readers. In a dozen or so books, Sowell—a model of the contemporary ideological warrior—has combined engaging scholarship with a fervently held political point of view. He has also been a contributor to the editorial pages of many newspapers and periodicals and occasionally appears as public speaker.

Educated as an economist under the tutelage of free-market advocate and pioneer monetarist Milton Friedman, Sowell has provided sympathetic guides to free-market economics (for example, *Classical Economics Reconsidered*, 1974), advocated the free market as an antidote to racism (for example, *Markets and Minorities*, 1981), raised doubts regarding the value of political responses to racial inequality (*Civil Rights: Rhetoric or Reality?*, 1985), and associated black poverty in the United States with values promoted in black churches (*Ethnic America*, 1983).

These positions alone would probably be enough to afford Sowell some measure of notoriety, but he has become an especially controversial figure because he is a black man. Sowell brings to the conservative cause the advantage of rather special credentials. Well educated, articulate, and sincere, Sowell can champion individualism as opposed to affirmative action, free-market prosperity as opposed to massive jobs programs, and formal as opposed to substantive justice—all this without being branded a white supremacist. For liberals and black activists, on the other hand, Sowell constitutes a particularly dangerous enemy, one who can easily be seen as a traitor to his own kind or at the very least an "Uncle Tom."

Sowell's professional career has reflected this controversy. Upon finishing his graduate work at the University of Chicago, Sowell, perhaps naïvely, decided to take a position at Howard University, one of the nation's most prestigious black schools. Unfortunately, there was very little tolerance of Sowell's unorthodox ideas at Howard, and he ultimately moved on to the Hoover Institute, a well-respected conservative think tank. Sowell has produced most of the essays, editorials, and books noted above as a Hoover scholar.

In recent years, Sowell has shifted the main focus of his attention to the history of ideas. In *Marxism: Philosophy and Economics* (1985), he presented an overview of Marxist theory. In *A Conflict of Visions*, Sowell explores this area of interest more broadly. Defining "vision" as a sort of "gut feeling" which supplies the basic premises undergirding positions on various political and social issues, Sowell claims to have isolated two persistent, radically opposed visions of human nature and society. Categorizing these visions as "constrained" and "unconstrained," Sowell argues that much of the political turmoil of the modern era has been rooted in the conflict between the two.

Though he distinguishes vision from "theory," Sowell illustrates the two visions by citing the work of representative theorists. His prime exemplar of the unconstrained vision is William Godwin. Godwin, an anarchist who experienced very brief popularity at the close of the eighteenth century, blamed the ills of his time on existing social arrangements and the brute force of government, which conspired to blunt the full potential of human nature and, thus, the natural harmony between human beings. According to Sowell, Godwin's is an unconstrained vision because it sees human nature as malleable, so much so that altruism can be made the ordering principle of society. In addition, Godwin and other believers in the unconstrained vision suggest that knowledge exists with which it is possible to engineer a society that will bring out the best in mankind. Thus, there are two crucial elements here: first, the belief that it is possible to transcend the apparent limits of human nature, allowing man's innate goodness to emerge, and, second, the belief that the knowledge which would direct this transformation is indeed accessible.

To this basic framework, Sowell attaches a number of more or less likely corollaries. For example, he notes a tendency for believers in the unconstrained vision to be elitists, since it takes expertise to engineer a truly egalitarian and just society. He also suggests in passing that the unconstrained vision can be associated with deception, ruthlessness, and a lack of patriotism. All these points are arguable; none is central to Sowell's argument. What is essential, however, is the assertion that the unconstrained vision seeks and expects to find rationally based "solutions" to a full range of social problems.

The constrained vision is exemplified by three primary figures: Thomas Hobbes, Edmund Burke, and Friedrich August von Hayek, the latter with a strong assist from Adam Smith. It emphasizes the limitations of human nature and human knowledge. Thus Hobbes, writing in the mid-seventeenth century, against the background of the English Civil War, paints a picture of human nature that emphasizes man's selfishness and inability to live harmoniously without stable government. Burke, a contemporary of Godwin and the most prominent conservative theorist of his time, emphasizes the value of tradition as an antidote to the frailties both of human conduct and human reason. Hayek, a twentieth century economist, offers a comprehensive social theory which utilizes the free marketplace as the prime source of order.

When these various strains are combined, what emerges, according to Sowell, is a common vision which takes human nature as severely limited and argues that humankind lacks the capacity to conduct successful social engineering. Instead, alternative sources of acceptable social order, independent of human rationality, are put forth. Proponents of a constrained vision defend tradition and the free market in this light. These more or less spontaneous mechanisms are not likely to achieve perfection, and they cannot be manipulated to accommodate every social goal, but neither are they static. Problems which arise, though likely to elude rational solutions, are subject to judicious "tradeoffs."

According to Sowell, these competing visions of human nature and society lead to radically different conceptions of equality, justice, and power. Where believers in the unconstrained vision seek nothing less than radical equality and uncompromising social justice, believers in the constrained vision see no safe or practical way to achieve such a result, opting instead to accept the tradeoff of procedural (or formal) equality and a concept of justice based on rules or processes. Where the unconstrained vision sees cooperation and good fellowship as the way to world peace, the constrained vision sees the need for pragmatic power politics. And so on, until one sees in these competing visions the roots of conflict over such issues as redistributive social programs, nuclear deterrence, affirmative action (and other forms of judicial activism), freedom of the press, and crime.

Sowell does not choose between the two visions. His purpose, he tells his readers, is to shed light on the origins of various political conflicts, and he restricts himself to identifying the two distinct visions and demonstrating their role in producing and shaping selected political debates. This circumspection may seem curious to longtime Sowell watchers, since he has clearly been a proponent of what he would categorize as a constrained, free-market vision. On the other hand, he has also usually tried to preserve the appearance of objectivity.

Still, there does seem to be an ideological message implicit in the book. In Sowell's account, conservatives and free-market advocates are presumed to be compassionate rather than callous toward poverty and other social ills which they are hesitant to address with direct political solutions. Indeed, Sowell rejects the widely encountered distinction between constrained and unconstrained visionaries in terms of compassion. There is disagreement over causation—that is, whether inequality, for example, results despite or because of the social system—and there is disagreement over what remedies will actually be safe (from potential political tyranny) and effective, but Sowell denies the unconstrained vision the moral high ground. Both sides care—they simply have different beliefs about what can realistically be done to provide relief.

While Sowell's distinction between two radically opposed global visions is a powerful analytic tool, his approach has serious liabilities as well. First, Sowell's schema does not convincingly explain much political conflict. Nationalism, Fascism, and even interest-group liberalism receive little or no treatment in the book. Thus, big chunks of the political universe are not even considered. In the conflicts which Sowell does explicitly mention, it simply is not clear that the debate centers on the relative presence or absence of constraints. For example, judicial activists who pushed forward desegregation and affirmative action were definitely opting for "trade-offs." They wished to preserve the basic structure of American society without turning a blind eye to racism and its consequences. Indeed, in the years following World War II, as the world struggled to grasp the enormity of the Nazis' racial policies, some move in this direction seems to have been inevitable. Likewise, supporters of redistributive policies in the United States appear to have a thoroughly constrained vision of what is humanly and socially possible. They have, indeed, usually been relatively conservative and "capitalist." Again, in the debate over crime, both sides can point to constraints ignored by their opponents. Law and order advocates can make a good argument that liberals have been unrealistic about the importance of punishment, given the unruliness of human nature, but liberals can point out in response that their opponents are just as unrealistic with regard to the importance of crime-producing social conditions and the limited effectiveness of deterrence.

In short, while there is widespread disagreement about the exact nature and extent of the constraints facing contemporary society, one is hard put to locate a coven of advocates for anything remotely resembling Godwin's vision or any other that might correctly be called unconstrained. This suggests that Sowell's categories are imprecisely defined. Indeed, he admits that no vision—not even Godwin's—is completely unconstrained; he also points out that some of the most interesting social theorists, among them Karl Marx and John Stuart Mill, rely on what he calls "hybrid" visions of human nature and society. The fact is that a more accurate classification would focus on elements of *constraint* and *transcendence*, present in different forms and doses in virtually any compelling vision. It is not clear what conclusions would be drawn from such an analysis; a dualism not unlike the one described in Sowell's book might well emerge. If it did, however, it would be more precise and more sensitive to varieties of constraint.

Another problem with Sowell's categories is that he lumps together some widely disparate visions under the banner of constraint. Hobbes is a social contract theorist for whom tradition plays a secondary role. Hayek (as well as Friedman) went to pains earlier in his career to point out that he was not a conservative. Further, the innovation that fuels a market society seems to be at odds with both the continuity sought by conservatives and the stability valued by Hobbes. It seems possible, therefore, that a great amount of political conflict could be traced to such differences within the constraint camp.

Finally, a major omission in this book is the role of history as an agent both of constraint and transcendence. The theories of Marx and Mill revolve around a fluid conception of circumstances framing the human condition. This is especially crucial in an age of constant change and conspicuous discontinuity, an age when utopianism of the mean is just as likely as that of the extremes. Thus, supposedly moderate and realistic American policies in Iran and Vietnam have led to disaster. What may have seemed to be a reasonable sense of constraint only yesterday becomes a flight of fancy today.

The late twentieth century is an unstable time—a time in which, for most of the world's people, tradition has either been shattered or never existed in any acceptable form, market mechanisms are socially disruptive, and even Hobbesian absolutism is politically untenable. In such a world, might it not be the traditionalist (or conservative), the advocate of a free-market society, or secular absolutist who misunderstands the constraints on human action? Might it not also be that, in such a world, transcendence—the ability to stretch the limits of what is possible—becomes not an idle hope but a necessity of survival?

Ira Smolensky

Sources for Further Study

Booklist. LXXXIII, January 15, 1987, p. 734.
The Christian Science Monitor. February 4, 1987, p. 23.
Commentary. LXXXIII, March, 1987, p. 78.
Kirkus Reviews. LIV, November 15, 1986, p. 1713.
Library Journal. CXII, January, 1987, p. 92.
National Review. XXXIX, February 13, 1987, p. 52.
The New Republic. CXCVI, February 9, 1987, p. 46.
The New York Times. January 24, 1987, p. 13.
The New York Times Book Review. XCII, January 25, 1987, p. 14.
Publishers Weekly. CCXXX, December 12, 1986, p. 44.
Time. CXXIX, March 16, 1987, p. 79.
The Wall Street Journal. February 6, 1987, p. 19.
The Washington Post Book World. XVII, January 4, 1987, p. 7.

CONGREGATION
Contemporary Writers Read the Jewish Bible

Editor: David Rosenberg (1941-   )
Publisher: Harcourt Brace Jovanovich (San Diego, California). 526 pp. $29.95
Type of work: Literary, social, and theological criticism and autobiography

Reflections by leading contemporary American Jewish writers and critics on the individual books of the Jewish Bible

For *Congregation: Contemporary Writers Read the Jewish Bible*, editor David Rosenberg encouraged thirty-seven contemporary American Jewish writers and critics to reflect on a book of the Bible in the light of his or her own lifelong experience as a Jew and a writer. The result is an uneven but ultimately engaging mosaic of emotion-edged insight, sometimes into the biblical texts, but more tellingly into the hopes and fears of the modern world.

As might be expected, there is a great range both in the quality of these essays and in their basic approach to the task. Some of the essayists treat their chosen books in great detail, showing themselves familiar with the thousands of years of commentary and controversy that surround their particular texts. Others take books only as starting or ending points for their own general reflections about the human condition. David Evanier writes a short story as his response to Zechariah. Gordon Lish does not mention his particular biblical text at all; instead, he produces a hysterical attack on the Bible, apparently regarding it as a threat to his very existence.

The most common and effective approach is, as the editor urged, autobiographical. Sometimes this approach is almost embarrassingly personal, as when Phillip Lopate uses his essay on Judges to expose the deficiencies of his still-living but enfeebled parents. Most of the powerful moments in these essays, however, result from personal reflection on the intersection of a Jewish upbringing, exposure to the Bible, and careers as largely secular writers and thinkers.

One of the best examples of the effective use of personal history to deepen reflection on an ancient text is the poet Robert Pinsky's essay on Isaiah. The opening lines of Isaiah call attention to an eternal problem: rebellious children, in this case the people of Judah, who have turned away from those who reared them, in this case the Lord. Judah's sin, in Pinsky's view, is idolatry and empty worship.

To the contemporary mind, idolatry is a practice of remote primitive people before graven images. Pinsky rightly points out, however, that it is actually the common practice of our society, embodied for him in the colorful, sometimes violent life of his Grandpa Dave. Idolaters, says Isaiah, "please themselves in the children of strangers" and "worship the work of their own hands, that which their own fingers have made." This definition, says Pinsky with more affection than judgment, fits his grandfather, a rough and totally worldly man who "stood for the immense beauty and power of idolatry, the adoration of all that can be made and enjoyed by the human body, with breath in its nostrils."

If Grandpa Dave, with his secular and sensuous love of the world, was an idolater, then Pinsky's own immediate family, nominally Orthodox and observant, was guilty of that other sin of Judah in Isaiah's time—empty or misguided worship. Pinsky suggests that he, taught as a young boy by pious but narrow men to chant words that he did not understand, was unknowingly participating in an idolatry as offensive to God as his grandfather's. His ignorant chanting was not simply the temporary condition of a young boy too young to understand the significance of his words, Pinsky suggests, but emblematic rather of modern worship generally. Not only do people of the twentieth century no longer understand how to worship God, but they have also lost the desire to do so.

The power of Isaiah, in fact, comes from the realization that prophets, for all their fierce truth, will not change anything. It is the fate of the prophet to this day to be ignored even when his words are believed. The standards of God, observes Pinsky, are such that even the devout slip quietly away even as they acknowledge them.

What is God to do with such children, self-absorbed idolaters and practicers of empty worship? In Isaiah's time and ours, Pinsky argues, God's will is at the same time "punitive and urgent" and "impenetrable and mysterious." It must be done, but it cannot be understood. The God of Isaiah destroys sinners, but the images of a restored Jerusalem are maternal and joyous. Only the structure of prophetic poetry, says Pinsky, is able to contain these apparent contradictions, and poetry is something which his boyhood synagogue and modern religion generally neither value nor understand.

As Pinsky's essay would suggest, this collection inevitably reveals more about the contemporary world than it does the ancient one. Modern readers bring to the Bible their modern prejudices, insights, and concerns. Most of these writers are at pains to make it known that they see these books not as revelation from God but as stories of individual beings and an ancient tribal nation. In his essay on Leviticus, Leon Wieseltier's accurate observation applies equally well to the entire collection: "Realism in history and immanence in theology have captured Jewish intellectuals, and perhaps cowed them."

This modern sensibility at work can be found in Jerome Charyn's fine essay on I Samuel. With his opening words, Charyn identifies a problem as pressing for Jews today as for their ancient forebears—and, more widely, for the entire modern age:

> The first book of Samuel is about the presence and absence of voices, the history of a tribe that has become tone-deaf. The Hebrews have forgotten how to listen. They cannot hear God's voice. The Lord is absent from their lives. They go into battle with the

Lord's own Ark and lose it to the Philistines. It's a sad and evil time for the Hebrews. "And the word of the Lord was rare in those days; there was no frequent vision" (3:1).

Charyn's essay explores a topic that many in the collection explore in one way or another: the painfully ambiguous nature of communication—among human beings, certainly, but especially between humans and a God who might not be there, or at least is not answering. In Saul, the man Samuel picks to satisfy the ungodly desire of the people for a king, Charyn finds a man the modern age can understand. Saul is "always melancholic, afraid to rule. He is perhaps the first schizophrenic king. Saul's *disease* is the terror of a man who's lost the voice of God. He seeks God and finds only demons."

The Renaissance, Charyn points out, loved and celebrated the intelligent, handsome young David: musician, warrior, faithful friend. Yet who is there to love Saul? David tried, but it availed Saul nothing; he was a man who shared everyone's low opinion of him. Not until the modern age, Charyn argues, has there been a time that seems as defeated, as abandoned by God, as Saul was.

Charyn expresses his preference for Saul, "as bewitched as our own century," to the "Boy Scout" David. Like Saul, people in the modern age do not hear the voice of God that David seemed to hear so frequently. As a representative of his time, Charyn acknowledges that he shares Saul's feelings of diminishment and perhaps inevitable doom: "If David is history's darling, then we, all the modern fools—liars, jugglers, wizards without song—still have Saul."

This sense of the absence or silence of a God who is reported to have once spoken with and directed his people is common to many of these essayists. Some of them lament this seeming silence and seek evidence that the ancient dialogue is still possible; most take it for granted that such a dialogue never really existed.

Along these lines, Wieseltier's intriguing essay on Leviticus explores the effect that the "pastness of God's presence" has had on the historical development of Judaism and on Western religion generally. Western religion's characteristic emphasis on revelation, Wieseltier argues, "disguises a fatalism, a willingness to settle for something less than experience in a relationship with God." Such religion is founded on a revelation which is over, leaving its religious leaders as "managers of revelation."

It is no wonder, then, that history became the life-blood of Judaism (and, to a lesser extent, Christianity). History preserves the memory of God's direct communications to His people. It also presents the challenge of how that miracle of miracles, God speaking to His creation, can be adequately transmitted to those who have not had the experience itself. The answer of Leviticus, of Judaism, is the Law, the Tradition.

Tradition is the attempt to provide structure for that which defies structure—miracle, transcendence. In preserving the memory of the time when Jews had both tradition and experience with God, it encourages the hope that God will speak again. Memory and hope characterize Judaism since the voice of God went silent, but the price, according to Wieseltier, is an ongoing present that seems always incomplete.

Two specific events of the present are mentioned repeatedly in these essays. The first is the Holocaust. For many Jews and non-Jews, it is the primary evidence of the silence of God in the twentieth century. Norma Rosen opens her essay on Jonah with words that others in this collection echo less directly:

> Show me a text that speaks of God's unbounded mercy, and images of the Holocaust appear before my eyes. It's not anything I can help. *Theology* doesn't help. This is visceral. I don't imagine I'm alone in this. Perhaps my generation will have to die out in the desert before God can appear again on an untarnished mercy seat. Such a return is essential for the healthy nurture of the human religious impulse. I understand that. But I can't be of any help there.

The other contemporary historical reality that surfaces throughout *Congregation* is the state of Israel, particularly as it struggles to find a way to combine survival and justice in its relationship with Arabs both inside and outside its borders. For some of these writers, the survival of Israel would seem to be paramount; for others, survival without justice would be meaningless.

In his essay on Ezra, Jay Neugeboren explores not only the question of ancient and present-day Israel among hostile neighbors, but also the larger problem of maintaining an ethnic or religious identity in an aggressively pluralistic world. Ezra, he says, saved his people from corruption and assimilation not by teaching the common ethical principles to which any moral person could ascribe, but by insisting on the specific laws and customs of Judaism. Neugeboren acknowledges the powerful logic and attraction of pluralistic culture, in which he participates, but wonders how Judaism can survive if it does not resist it.

As the book of Ezra is followed in the Bible by Nehemiah, so Neugeboren's reflections on the difficulty of preserving ethnicity are followed by Anne Roiphe's exploration of the darker side of the quest for ethnic purity. She does not share Nehemiah's certainty regarding who should be inside and who outside the walls of the rebuilt Jerusalem:

> The history of this small oasis in the Middle East is one of siege and casting out, of taking what has not been yours and defending it against all claims. It is a benighted, blood-filled history that we in the twentieth century cannot see as an expression of our God's success against their God or Gods but as a misfortune for us all, as a calamity of human misunderstanding, cycles of woe and broken pride.

There is much gloom in these essays. It comes from the terrible revelations of human weakness in these books of the Bible, from a diminished belief in the God who can overcome those weaknesses, and from the sense that the modern age is, if anything, even more corrupt than those against which the prophets thundered. Yet amid this gloom there is, strangely, also a kind of hope, the kind found paradoxically in the message of the prophets. Elie Wiesel sees in Ezekiel's vision of life returning to the dry bones a recurring and inextinguishable hope: "That vision, that consolation, is offered to every generation, for every generation needs it—and ours more than any before us."

Daniel Taylor

Sources for Further Study

Library Journal. CXII, November 15, 1987, p. 85.
The New York Times Book Review. XCII, December 20, 1987, p. 1.
Newsweek. CXI, January 18, 1988, p. 72.
Publishers Weekly. CCXXXII, October 9, 1987, p. 74.

CONVERSATIONS WITH CZESŁAW MIŁOSZ

Author: Czesław Miłosz (1911-   )
Translated from the Polish by Richard Lourie
Edited by Ewa Czarnecka and Aleksander Fiut
Publisher: Harcourt Brace Jovanovich (San Diego). 332 pp. $27.95.
Type of work: Interviews
Time: 1911-1986
Locale: Wilno, Warsaw, Paris, and California

A series of informative conversations on Miłosz's life, works, and philosophy with journalist Ewa Czarnecka and scholar Aleksander Fiut

What is the fate of a great poet who writes in a little-known language? How does he make his work accessible to foreign readers? How does the Eastern European writer bridge the enormous cultural and political gap that defines his concerns but separates him from his Western audience, particularly after the Holocaust, the destruction of Warsaw, and the Soviet domination of Poland after World War II? These are but a few of the questions that Lithuanian-born poet Czesław Miłosz addresses in a series of extended conversations about his life, his writings, and his beliefs.

This volume combines in English translation, two books of interviews published independently of each other in Polish by Aleksander Fiut (1981) and Ewa Czarnecka (1983). In addition, Czarnecka's volume included a section of critical analysis, omitted here. In part 1, Miłosz responds to questions about his life, reflecting on what he has already presented in his memoir, *Rodzinna Europa* (1958; *Native Realm: A Search for Self-Definition*, 1968); in part 2, he addresses critical and interpretive questions about his works; and in part 3, perhaps the most interesting, he discusses literary and philosophical influences in his work.

Miłosz makes it clear that for the Eastern European poet there can be no artificial separation of life and art, no retreat into aestheticism or the cultivation of self, no Modernist elitism, and no luxury of ignoring unpleasant political realities. There has been a long tradition in Eastern Europe of linking politics with poetry and expressing patriotic feelings openly and fervently, so that, for the poet, there is no real distinction between public and private sensibility. For Miłosz, as for Hungarian critic György Lukács, every act is ultimately political. This does not mean that Miłosz is merely a political poet, especially in any ideological sense. Rather he is a nature poet, a philosophical poet, and ultimately a religious poet, with his images and mental landscapes deeply rooted in his native Lithuanian soil and in the Roman Catholic faith of his childhood. Most of all, his poetry derives its strength from the rhythms and cadences of his native Polish language.

Being an émigré or exile is unquestionably the worst fate that can befall a writer such as Miłosz. Like the giant Antaeus, the poet loses the power of his eloquence when he is separated from his native language. For Miłosz, the exile has been twofold, first from his native Lithuania and later from Poland. In 1951, he requested political asylum in Paris after becoming disenchanted with the postwar Stalinist regime in Warsaw. Eventually he emigrated to the United States, where he had served as cultural attaché from 1946 to 1950, and accepted a position as professor of Slavic languages and literatures at the University of California at Berkeley in 1961. There he continued his career as a poet, projecting through his poems the dual consciousness of Old World and New, contrasting images of wartime Poland with the California coast in poems such as "Dithyramb," and evoking a deep sense of nostalgia for the Lithuanian countryside of his youth. Yet Miłosz touches upon the universal experience of exile from the paradise of childhood in a way that allows one to empathize with his particular situation.

Though Miłosz has been writing poetry since the 1930's, when he was a member of a group of young "catastrophist" poets in Warsaw, he first became known in the West through his brilliant study of totalitarianism, *Zniewolony umysł* (1953; *The Captive Mind*, 1953), which could have earned for him a position on any political science faculty. He is also a novelist of some note, having published *Zdobycie władzy* (1953; *The Seizure of Power*, 1955) and *Dolina Issy* (1955; *The Issa Valley*, 1981), with its echoes of Adam Mickiewicz's *Pan Tadeusz* (1834; English translation, 1917), as well as his memoirs, *Native Realm*. It was primarily for his poetry, however, that he was awarded the Nobel Prize in Literature in 1980. A noted literary historian as well, Miłosz has written *The History of Polish Literature* (1969, 1983) and translated a number of contemporary Polish poets into English, including Tadeusz Różewicz, his friend Zbigniew Herbert, and Aleksander Wat. Miłosz has also served as his own translator, earning high praise for the precision and lucidity of his translations.

In the first two parts of these conversations, Miłosz traces the development of his career as a poet. He recalls travels with his parents, childhood memories of Wilno, studies at the King Stefan Batory University, prewar travels to Paris, the influence of his uncle, the French poet Oscar Milosz, and his work for Polish Radio in Warsaw. He notes that in an early poem, "Slow River," written in the 1930's, he unwittingly foreshadowed the Holocaust in his image of the "crematoria rising like white cliffs," and that his second volume of poetry, *Trzy zimy* (1936; three winters), contains a clear premonition of war.

The experience of having one's entire world overturned and destroyed is one that few Western poets have known. Miłosz recalls rescuing precious books and manuscripts before his Warsaw apartment was destroyed by German artillery shells. Not only were homes and possessions lost in the destruction of Warsaw, but people lost faith in the possibility of civilized behavior. They discovered the fragility of social norms and the thin line that separates civilization from barbarism. Throughout the war years, Miłosz remained active in the Polish underground, holding literary readings, publishing clandestine works, and even translating William Shakespeare's *As You Like It* for the underground theater. After the war, Poland literally had to rebuild a society from ashes and ruins. Initially Miłosz sympathized with the task of constructing a socialist Poland, but he gradually became disillusioned with the Gomułka regime. The culminating incident that led to his decision to seek asylum in the West occurred in the summer of 1949. As Miłosz was leaving an evening reception in Warsaw, he noticed thinly dressed prisoners being driven away to prison by warmly dressed soldiers and realized in what kind of society he lived.

Miłosz has commented that when a poet is overwhelmed by strong emotions, his form tends to become simpler and more direct. This observation is certainly true for Miłosz's wartime poetry, particularly in the cycle "The Voices of Poor People." The poem "A Poor Christian Looks at the Ghetto" expresses both the eloquence of grief and the guilt of the survivor in its image of the "guardian mole" tunneling beneath the heaps of debris and the broken, mangled bodies, keeping count of the dead. Another poem, "Café," records the disbelief of the poet that he has been spared and is among the survivors. For others, less reflective, like the drinking, card-playing rabble described in the poem "Outskirts," who gather in a sandpit outside of the wartorn city, life continues, despite the appalling destruction around them.

Even Miłosz's postwar poems show a profound awareness of the "doubleness" of civilization, with the decorum and order on the surface masking the decadence and violence below. His poem "Child of Europe" implicitly condemns the duplicity and barbarism of modern European history, including the actions of the Polish Stalinists, who justified their brutal seizure of power in the name of historical necessity, yet Miłosz finds the American indifference to history just as disturbing in its own way, with its hedonistic self-absorption and its facile assumption that America will not be affected by the social and political problems of Europe.

In his Charles Eliot Norton lectures at Harvard University, published as *The Witness of Poetry* (1983), Miłosz observes that all poetry is ultimately eschatological, concerned with "final things." European man has always turned his eyes toward Heaven as the ultimate source of spiritual hopes and aspirations, and Miłosz regrets the loss of the Christian mythos and its replacement by the future-oriented historical utopianism of Marxism. The Western loss of faith in the future is reflected, according to Miłosz, in the nihilism and pessimism of the modernist poets and their preoccupation with the past. The articulation of hope links poets with the human family; without hope, they retreat into aestheticism and formalism, the preoccupation with form rather than content. His war experiences have not left Miłosz bereft of hope, though they have instilled his poetry with a strong Manichaean bent, a sense of the irreconcilable dualism of good and evil in the spiritual and material world. He is particularly fascinated with the concept of *apokatastasis*, or the hope after the Final Judgment of the restoration of humankind to the innocence that existed before the fall from grace. Some Polish critics have pointed to Miłosz's "Arcadian tendencies," but he counters that poets must offer some contrast to the pervasiveness of evil in the twentieth century with images of peace and beauty. "It's difficult to be a poet only of despair, only of sadness," he remarks. "An element of joy, located somewhere in an imaginary future, is the other side of catastrophism."

Philosophically, Miłosz describes himself as a realist, fascinated by the ineluctability of life, yet he is haunted by the elusiveness of reality, the lack of substantiality of ordinary things. For him art is mimesis; it takes its models from nature, rather than from the artistic forms themselves. He condemns the formalistic tendency of modern writing, which feeds on itself, as anti-mimetic. His poems celebrate "a Dionysian ecstasy with the world," but he never becomes lost among the minutia, describing physical details for their own sake, as he has accused some American poets of doing. "American poets aren't sure what to write about, so they describe whatever life hands them," he observes. "They fail to understand that poetry is an act of enormous distillation." The fact that so much human experience eludes description—despite poetic distillation—is a recurring theme in Miłosz's poetry.

Although he is aware of its limitations, Miłosz shows a particular veneration for language, affirming that language, rather than more tangible cultural institutions, may be the essence of civilization. His interest in language extends beyond writing and translating poetry. Recently he has begun translating portions of the Bible into modern Polish in order to render the poetic beauty of the ancient Hebrew and Greek Scriptures in contemporary form.

In his Nobel Prize speech in 1980, Miłosz acknowledged his debt to two thinkers, Simone Weil and Oscar Milosz, and, in the third part of these conversations, he discusses their influence on his work. Oscar Milosz introduced him to the visionary literature of Emanuel Swedenborg and William Blake, whose influence is apparent in the poems in *Ziemia Ulro* (1977; *The Land of Ulro*, 1984). Miłosz's own theological outlook has been much influenced by Simone Weil, the brilliant French religious thinker whose life and thought he found so attractive. In her own way, she experienced a "dark night of the soul" comparable to the despair of the Warsaw Resistance fighters; she too knew the attraction to and disillusionment with Marxism; and she demonstrated that a life outside the Church may be closer to the love of God than the unexamined faith of some Christians. A philosophical poet himself, Miłosz found Weil's presentation of the problems of necessity and determinism close to his own views. Weil believed that God has subjected Nature to an absolute determinism, but though the created world is marked by an ironbound necessity, it is also inexpressibly beautiful. For Miłosz, the Fall and Original Sin are key mysteries because of the contradictions between free will and determinism, grace and necessity. The Fall alienated humanity from God, but made Redemption possible through the intervention of Divine Grace. Miłosz finds the interpretation of these theological mysteries a central theme in his own work.

In his concluding remarks, Miłosz downplays his accomplishments, commenting that all of his writing has stemmed from a "desire not to appear other than I am." He was especially disconcerted at being treated as a heroic figure when he returned to Poland in 1981, after receiving the Nobel Prize, realizing how badly he might have disgraced himself had he remained in Poland rather than emigrating to the West. The intellectual range of *Conversations with Czesław Miłosz* supports critic George Steiner's observation that some of the most important contemporary literature is coming from writers of Eastern Europe.

Andrew J. Angyal

Sources for Further Study

Chicago Tribune. September 6, 1987, p. 6.
Kirkus Reviews. LV, July 15, 1987, p. 1041.
Library Journal. CXII, September 1, 1987, p. 182.
Los Angeles Times Book Review. September 13, 1987, p. 14.
The New York Times Book Review. XCII, October 11, 1987, p. 3.
Publishers Weekly. CCXXXII, July 31, 1987, p. 62.
World Literature Today. LXI, Summer, 1987, p. 467.

CONVERSATIONS WITH NIETZSCHE
A Life in the Words of His Contemporaries

Editor: Sander L. Gilman (1944-   )
Translated from the German by David J. Parent
Publisher: Oxford University Press (New York). Illustrated. 276 pp. $26.00
Type of work: Biography
Time: 1844-1900
Locale: Germany, Switzerland, and Italy

A compilation of contemporary accounts by friends and acquaintances of encounters with the philosopher Friedrich Nietzsche

Principal personages:
FRIEDRICH W. NIETZSCHE, the German philosopher
ELISABETH FÖRSTER-NIETZSCHE, his sister and chief apologist
LOU ANDREAS-SALOMÉ, his friend
FRANZ OVERBECK, his colleague at Basel
IDA OVERBECK, his friend, wife of Franz
MALWIDA VON MEYSENBUG, his friend, a philosopher

Conversations with Nietzsche: A Life in the Words of His Contemporaries contains eighty-five extracts from works by fifty-eight different memorialists of the philosopher's life. As the editor reveals in his introduction, it is a much-reduced version of his *Begegnungen mit Nietzsche* (1981; revised edition, 1985). All periods of Friedrich Nietzsche's life are covered, including his boyhood years and the years of his insanity. While the coverage is chronological, the different periods are labeled—for example, "Childhood and School Days (1844-1858)," "Migrant Years (1879-1889)." The table of contents, as well as the headnotes in each chapter, provides a chronological sense of the material. A thorough familiarity with the table of contents will prove helpful for readers unfamiliar with the trajectory of Nietzsche's career: The chapters are not interrupted to mark the passing of the years. The book's apparatus includes a list of sources for all contributions and biographical notes on all the contributors.

In one case, chapter contents do not entirely conform with chapter heading: In "University and Military Time (1864-1869)" there is no material directly from Nietzsche's stint in the army, though references to his attitude toward the service, as well as to the German imperial ideal to which it gave significant embodiment, occur later. The shortest chapter is the one recounting Nietzsche's childhood, while the longest details his "Migrant Years"—his various journeys as well as his stay in the Engadine district of Switzerland. In general, there is a wealth of fascinating and sometimes contradictory evidence about Nietzsche's life and times which, quite apart from its intrinsic interest, is all the more welcome for being, for the most part, translated into English here for the first time.

The range of contributors to *Conversations with Nietzsche* is wide. Beginning, inevitably, with the philosopher's sister, Elisabeth Förster-Nietzsche, who did so much work to propagate her brother's name (not all of it by any means beneficial; she has been thought of as one of the primary reasons that Nietzsche's name became associated with Nazism), the book has a large *dramatis personae*. It includes Nietzsche's mother; boyhood, school, and undergraduate friends; colleagues and comrades from his academic career at the University of Basel; visitors and acquaintances to Sils-Maria, the philosopher's domicile in the Engadine; and, not least, a somewhat ghoulish parade of the curious who came to see him when, after his mental collapse, he was under the care first of his mother, then of his sister at Weimar, where he died.

This last phase is discussed in the chapter "On Display at Weimar (1897-1900)," a title that reveals as much of an editorial slant as may be found in *Conversations with Nietzsche*. Such a slant is a means of drawing attention to the growing cult of Nietzsche, a phenomenon which embodied a mordant irony, since the one from whom these votaries presumed to learn was on his deathbed, incapable of the vivifying conversation on which the bulk of the other recollections is based.

One of the most interesting features of this book's cast of characters is that so many of those with whom Nietzsche conversed were female. Not only does this reveal an important aspect of the philosopher's intellectual life, but it is also revealing about the intellectual climate of Nietzsche's day. Undoubtedly, many of these women were formidable in their educational attainments, conceptual propensities, and cultural commitments. The best-known of them is that intellectual femme fatale Lou Andreas-Salomé, who would be famous for her connections with Sigmund Freud and Rainer Maria Rilke even if she had never been closely associated with Nietzsche. Yet, in the company which she is obliged to keep in *Conversations with Nietzsche*, she seems more biographically significant than intellectually impressive. Intellectually, she is eclipsed by both Ida Overbeck, wife of Nietzsche's most loyal Basel colleague, and Malwida von Meysenbug, herself a philosopher and free spirit—rather freer in spirit than Nietzsche found it possible to be. In addition to these two women, Helen Zimmern, the philosopher's first translator into English, deserves mention, not only because of her linguistic skills, but also because of the fresh, direct character of her contribution.

Ida Overbeck's commentary on Nietzsche's Basel years shows an almost unsettling degree of psychological insight, which may be one reason why it has been preferred for this collection over her husband's reminiscences, from which only one selection is made. Frau Overbeck writes as one reflecting on conversations with Nietzsche after the effect: hence the strongly analytical character of her insights, which in turn has given rise to a somewhat impenetrable style. Meysenbug, in contrast, attempts in her accounts to re-create her conversations with the philosopher, which feature her own wit and intelligence as much as Nietzsche's. The claims made on Nietzsche's behalf by these two particularly interesting memorialists have, because of their less than worshipful attitude toward him, an authenticity, responsiveness, and thoughtfulness which do not always mark the dispositions of members of the Nietzsche circle.

Thus, for example, important as Meta von Salis-Marschlins was to Nietzsche (she rented the Villa Silberblick in Weimar where he spent his last years and which is the site of the Nietzsche Archive), it seems that she had little to offer the philosopher by way of intellectual empathy. It is from her pen that torrents of essentially hagiographical sentiment descend. Such downpours are quite revealing in the context of *Conversations with Nietzsche*, since the book is premised on materials that are to provide the intimate portrayals of the philosopher. Thus, in contrast to the image of Nietzsche as a monster of *Übermenschheit*, there is a strong and consistent emphasis throughout on the purity of Nietzsche's spirit, his sensitivity, his emotional refinement, his gentlemanliness. Contributors such as Salis-Marschlins (and they are by no means all female) protest too much about the prominence of such qualities in the man they knew. Nevertheless, there is no doubting the value of such testimony.

One reason for the seeming extravagance and air of unreality about some of the statements made in praise of Nietzsche may be the translation. This is not merely a matter of questioning the translator's competence. The text does contain a number of minor stylistic solecisms, though sentences such as the following are rare: "I was making my first independent journey in still very young years." The problem, rather, is the difficulty of finding a reasonably familiar idiom in English that would convey the exalted view of Nietzsche ardently held by many of his devotees. Such a problem has to do with more than Nietzsche's uniqueness as a philosopher, a fundamental component of which is his dazzling ability as a stylist and prosodist. (Part of Nietzsche's fascination for modern philosophers such as Martin Heidegger and Jacques Derrida lies in his being a philosopher of language.)

In addition, however, Nietzsche's uniqueness seems to have created verbal problems for his adherents, the literalness and reality of whose attachment prevented them from resorting to parable and parody as means of communicating their perceptions. *Conversations with Nietzsche* thus clearly demonstrates, particularly for the nonspecialist reader, how Nietzsche's being difficult is a primary, inescapable, and all-important fact. As this book brings out, his difficulty was evident in every phase of his existence—health, thought, personal relationships, career, sexuality, reputation, and achievement—and it is the main reason that his position in European culture is so significant. What is difficult in and about Nietzsche prefigures many of the difficulties—psychological anxieties as well as epistemological adventurism—that typify twentieth century thought.

In the unobtrusive but inescapable manner in which *Conversations with Nietzsche* brings the reader face-to-face with the philosopher and the reality of his life, it performs an invaluable service. Moreover, in viewing Nietzsche in the round, it also provides interesting documentary material in a variety of other areas—the state of German music, the state of German academic life, and medical matters (including the treatment of the insane) in this period of German history. It must be pointed out, however, that there is no direct evidence from the two outstanding intellectual presences in Nietzsche's life, Jakob Burckhardt and Richard Wagner. Burckhardt, the pioneering cultural historian, was a colleague of Nietzsche at Basel. Wagner, of course, whose music-drama Nietzsche championed and then denounced, is one of the most celebrated figures in late nineteenth century European cultural life.

The omission of such figures is revealing in a number of ways. In the first place, it maintains a balance and unity among the contributors, not because of the uniformity of their testimony, but because they all achieved a degree, however minor, of unproblematical intimacy with Nietzsche. This achievement may have been facilitated by their relative lack of fame. Secondly, the reader can have few if any expectations of testimony provided by unfamiliar witnesses. Such openness would be less likely if the contributors were famous. In addition, the fame of a Burckhardt or a Wagner might tend to overshadow the authenticity of, say, a Paul Deussen or Resa von Schirnhofer (to name two important contributors not previously mentioned).

The obvious connection between composition and omission in *Conversations with Nietzsche* is not merely of interest in its own right. More important, it draws attention to the questions of genre which the book raises and which increase its interest and value. The nature of such questions can be understood in part from the following remarks by the editor at the end of his introduction:

> No attempt has been made to clarify contradictions between the various views of specific incidents, as no single view is most probably "correct." *Conversations with Nietzsche* presents (as did its German source) a "new" Nietzsche in that the contradictions in the perceptions of those who knew him are made manifest. Thus the volume can serve as a biography in contradictions of this most contradictory of thinkers.

Incompleteness, lack of ostensible editorial or authorial finality, selectivity, and omission are therefore the preeminent features of *Conversations with Nietzsche*. Explicit formal deficiencies in the text are offered as a means of more direct access to the subject than the mere orthodox, or at least the more familiar, requirements of the single-author biography. Just as Nietzsche's own aphorisms evoke the art of the lacuna, the vignettes and meditations included here evoke the art of silence. The reader of the aphorism extends its thought, filling in its various implications, providing it with the structure of which it is the keystone. Comparably, the auditor of these conversations completes and integrates what he overhears.

In one sense, *Conversations with Nietzsche* offers an extremely sophisticated account of a familiar aesthetic option, "less is more." In another sense, however, the book provides a stimulating challenge to assumptions about the nature of biography, its use of a central coordinator and its perhaps arrogant, unnecessary, and irrelevant pretense to a final, singular point of view. Even if such a challenge is not taken up, the reader who considers *Conversations with Nietzsche* as a text will be obliged to acknowledge the paradox that the raw materials of biography, presented without the intervention of the biographer's shaping hand, produce a more vivid, complex, and intimate portrait than conventional biographical methods provide, whether or not they are applied to Nietzsche.

Such an outcome may well be a tribute to Nietzsche's gifts as a conversationalist and to his arguably more uncanny ability to inspire commitment and loyalty in those who came into contact with him. These considerations may tend to give credence to clichés about the mystique of a given subject's personality. In this case, however, the mystique is replaced by evidence of those intangible qualities that show a Nietzsche who is human, all too human. This view is the most unexpected and most instructive which *Conversations with Nietzsche* conveys. It arises from the subtle, challenging, and finally simple harmonization—between subject, material, and method—which this book achieves.

George O'Brien

Sources for Further Study

Kirkus Reviews. LV, June 1, 1987, p. 835.
Library Journal. CXII, August 20, 1987, p. 119.
The New York Review of Books. XXXV, February 4, 1988, p. 35.

THE COUNTERLIFE

Author: Philip Roth (1933-   )
Publisher: Farrar, Straus and Giroux (New York). 324 pp. $18.95
Type of work: Novel
Time: 1978
Locale: Newark, New Jersey; Israel, the West Bank; and Gloucestershire, England

The fourth novel in which Philip Roth's persona, Nathan Zuckerman, attempts to cope with his family, his Jewishness, his art, and his life

> *Principal characters:*
> NATHAN ZUCKERMAN, a forty-five-year-old novelist
> HENRY ZUCKERMAN, his forty-year-old brother, a dentist
> CAROL ZUCKERMAN, Henry's wife
> MARIA ZUCKERMAN, Nathan's wife
> WENDY, Henry's assistant and mistress
> JIMMY BEN-JOSEPH, a fanatical terrorist

Philip Roth introduced Nathan Zuckerman in a 1974 stock-taking novel entitled *My Life as a Man*. In that work, Nathan is a fictional creation of Roth's own fictional creation, Peter Tarnopol, who used him as a persona in two stories within his novel to exorcise the effects of a bad marriage and to help define himself as a man and an artist. In Roth's next novel, *The Ghost Writer* (1979), Tarnopol disappears and Nathan takes the stage as Roth's own immediate persona, an aspiring young writer who pays a visit to his artist mentor to be confirmed in his own work and to find an intellectual father figure. In the next work in the series, *Zuckerman Unbound* (1981), Zuckerman is thirty-six and trying to cope with the fame (and the infamy) of writing a notorious best-selling book on growing up Jewish. Finally, in *The Anatomy Lesson* (1983), Zuckerman is forty and suffering from a sense of having lost his subject and his ability as an artist.

Now in this, Roth's fourth Zuckerman book (he published the first three in a single volume in 1985 under the title *Zuckerman Bound*, which also included a novella, *The Prague Orgy*, featuring Zuckerman as protagonist), Zuckerman is forty-five and caught not only in his desire to be a father and to have a family, but also, more centrally, in the web of his own fictionality, for in this novel Roth becomes even more self-consciously concerned with the artifice of his craft and his role as an artist than in the first three. *The Counterlife*, which was awarded the National Book Critics Circle Award in the category of fiction, begins conventionally enough with a brief introduction focusing on Nathan's brother Henry, who, because of medication he must take for heart disease, is impotent. This italicized section ends rather abruptly with Henry's decision to have heart surgery rather than face a sexless life. When the reader discovers that the opening section has been written as a eulogy for Henry by Nathan himself, however, the novel shifts from the conventional to the metafictional. The rest of Part 1 focuses on Nathan at his brother's funeral, reconstructing from his notes the sexual dilemma that led to Henry's death.

Much of Henry's reason for risking unnecessary surgery centers on his assistant Wendy, with whom he is having an affair, and a beautiful, blonde Swiss woman he met ten years previously named Maria. Although Henry fantasized running away to Basel to live with Maria, he denied himself this romantic escape from middle-class Jewish respectability only to sacrifice himself (much to Nathan's astonishment and dismay) for his purely sexual desire for potency with Wendy.

This first section, however, entitled "Basel" (after Henry's fantasy of running away to Switzerland with Maria), is undercut by the second section, entitled "Judea," which presents Nathan on a trip to Israel to visit Henry, who has, in spite of his announced death in Part 1, survived the surgery and run away to Israel to reaffirm his Jewishness, which he has discovered is the root of his life. Even more confusing is the fact that in this second section, Nathan is married to an English woman, who, like Henry's earlier Swiss lover, is blonde, has a young daughter, and is named Maria. Nathan is living in England in this section, having fulfilled his desire, after four childless marriages, to have a home and a family.

Much of the "Judea" section consists of conversations about being Jewish, held first in England between Nathan and Maria's friends (whom Nathan finds anti-Semitic) and then in Israel with Henry and his new companions, who are powerfully pro-Israel. In this Israeli section of the novel, the focus is primarily on the difference between American-Jewish intellectuals in the West, such as Nathan, who enjoy a comfortable and secure existence, and the freedom fighters in Israel. Henry's presence in Israel is seen by Nathan as primarily the result of Henry's romanticized fascination with, particularly, the guns and the power of the Jewish state. Indeed, Henry is presented as having become what Nathan calls a "born-again Jew." So much of the "Judea" section is taken up by discussions about the Arab-Israeli conflict and the Jewish position in the world that it is less narrative than discursive polemic. Henry now sees his stress back in the United States as the result of what he calls "Diaspora abnormality," exemplified by his fantasy about Maria—the Jewish dream of escape to Switzerland with the blonde and beloved shiksa. All of this makes Nathan think about what might be the thematic focus of the book itself—that is, the kind of stories that people turn life into and the kind of lives that people turn stories into. Thus Nathan sees Henry's journey to Israel as simply another attempt at escape from his hedged-in, middle-class life.

The novel shifts once again in the third section, entitled "Aloft," this time from straightforward polemic about the Jewish struggle in Israel to a madcap and manic flight which Nathan takes back to London. Inserted into this section is a long letter from Nathan to Henry, in which he points out the irony of Henry becoming a Jewish activist while Nathan has become a bourgeois husband, and a long phone conversation, recorded in Nathan's notebook, with Henry's wife Carol, who resents Henry's quest for his Jewish roots.

The narrative of this third section, however, focuses on a young man with a thick beard who is sitting beside Nathan on the plane reading a Hebrew prayer book—a young man who turns out to be Jimmy Ben-Joseph, whom Nathan had met earlier in Israel. He announces to Nathan that he is going to hijack the plane in support of a doctrine he calls "Forget Remembering," which mainly centers on the need for Jews to forget the Holocaust and Jewish suffering. Jimmy calls Nathan his idol, his father figure, who has revealed in his novels that he really has the inside track on how not to be a Jew. When Jimmy pulls out a hand grenade and a gun, however, he and Nathan are immediately attacked by undercover antiterrorist guards on the plane. Both Jimmy and Nathan are searched, grilled, lectured by the guards on the universal loathing of the Jewish id, and taken back to Israel.

In turn, the fourth part of the novel, "Gloucestershire," calls the entire hijacking episode into question, for it begins abruptly by making clear that it is Nathan rather than Henry who is on drugs for a heart disease and therefore impotent. This chapter focuses on Nathan's romance or fantasy with his Maria, a twenty-seven-year-old Englishwoman with a baby girl named Phoebe. Nathan says he no longer wants to spend his life writing, for he feels that he has practically written himself out of life, to which Maria retorts that he now wishes to write himself back in. Indeed, this entire novel might be seen as Nathan's effort to write himself back into life.

Midway through this section, the narration shifts to the point of view of Henry, who takes up the story after Nathan's death from surgery. It is here that the reader finally gets a clue to the significance of the title of the novel, for Henry recalls receiving Nathan's abhorred books and how he would sit down and try to compose in his head a "counterbook" to redeem from distortion the lives of his family, about whom Nathan wrote.

After the funeral, Henry goes to Nathan's brownstone and pillages his filing cabinets, removing the pages from Nathan's notes which depict Henry's affair ten years earlier with his own Maria. Even more interesting, Henry finds the manuscript of a novel, the first chapter of which is "Basel." Here the reader realizes that this unpublished novel is the very novel that he is now reading. Henry is furious when he reads about his own death, knowing that Nathan has used Henry to conceal his own vulnerability while disguising himself as responsible, sane, and reasonable. Henry also reveals that he never went to Israel, that it is Nathan's own fantasy which is embodied in the second section of the novel. The last chapter, entitled "Christendom," is what Henry calls Nathan's magical dream of escape from Jewishness, from his heart disease, and from the world of Nathan's own inescapable character. Henry removes the chapters "Basel" and "Judea," as well as the opening of the hijacking chapter, which Henry says has as little relation to the real world as anything else in the book.

The final section of "Gloucestershire" recounts an interview with Maria after Nathan's death. Maria tells of her own reading of parts of the manuscript of *The Counterlife*, particularly the final chapter entitled "Christendom," in which she says Nathan put all his own feelings about Christian women into a Christian woman's feelings about a Jewish man. At the end of the interview, the reader discovers that the interviewer is a ghost of Nathan himself, perhaps invented by Maria, as invented by Nathan, who is, after all, the author of his own novel.

The final section, "Christendom," picks up this tangled web of fictionality when Nathan returns to London after his visit with Henry in Israel; there is no reference in this section to the fantastic attempted hijacking. "Christendom" begins, appropriately enough, with Nathan at a church service with Maria and Phoebe, during which Nathan makes fun of the Disneyland nature of the Christian celebration of Christmas. Later, after the service, Nathan has a conversation with Maria's sister, Sarah, who lectures him on English anti-Semitism; later still, he and Maria have dinner at a restaurant, marred by a grotesque encounter with an anti-Semitic woman. In the emotional aftermath of that incident, Nathan and Maria have the first real fight of their marriage, and he leaves the house they are renting, taking a taxi to the house they have bought and are having remodeled: a symbol, Nathan recognizes, of the domestic warmth and "mundane concreteness" promised by marriage and family, from which he now feels alienated.

There, at the house by the river, Nathan ponders the strange events of this day that began in Jerusalem. He imagines returning to find Maria gone, having left a letter. In this imaginary letter, a fiction within a fiction within a fiction, she says that she is leaving him and the book into which he has written her. Speaking as a character rebelling against the author who created her, she says that she fears for Phoebe; after all, as an author, he was not above killing his brother, killing himself, and grandiosely amusing himself in a lunatic hijack attempt. Who knows what fate he will imagine for Phoebe? She scolds him for never being able to forget that he is a Jew and insists that she will not participate in his primitive drama, not even for the sake of fiction.

The novel then ends with Nathan's response to Maria, in which he asserts that there is no Maria and no Nathan, only a way they have established themselves over the months of performing together. Being Zuckerman is one long performance, says Nathan, in an admission that might be made by any fictional character if indeed it were possible for a fictional character to know that he is fictional. Roth's use of this extended metaphor of fictionality, however, cuts deeper than this notion of reflexivity, for in the last two pages of the novel, he, by means of the persona Nathan, lectures Maria, and thus the reader, about the fictional nature of all human lives. Nathan argues that for certain self-aware people, imagining themselves to be real and authentic has all the aspects of hallucination.

It is all impersonation, says Nathan/Roth, and in the absence of a self, one impersonates selves, finally impersonating best the self that best gets one through life. He asserts that he has no self, only a variety of impersonations. He tells Maria, in this last letter to her, that she should come back to him so that together they can play the most interesting game of trying to get a handle on their own subjectivity—becoming *Homo ludens* and wife, inventing the imperfect future.

Each time Roth publishes another Zuckerman novel, he seems to bring Nathan to a dead end, and thus the reader suspects it is the last novel in the series, but each time Roth brings his favorite persona back for another ultimate encounter with his own identity. Now that in *The Counterlife* one has Zuckerman coming so close to admitting that he is a fictional character—a creation of his own invention—one wonders if indeed Roth will choose to carry this self-consciousness further, perhaps next time casting aside any attempts at presenting Nathan as an "as-if-real" person in the phenomenal world and instead enmeshing him completely within the metaphysical tangles of pure fictionality.

Charles E. May

Sources for Further Study

The Atlantic. CCLIX, February, 1987, p. 89.
Christian Science Monitor. LXXIX, January 7, 1987, p. 19.
Library Journal. CXII, February 15, 1987, p. 163.
Listener. CXVII, March 12, 1987, p. 25.
London Review of Books. IX, March 5, 1987, p. 3.
Los Angeles Times Book Review. January 11, 1987, p. 1.
The New Republic. CXCVI, February 2, 1987, p. 36.
The New York Review of Books. XXXIV, March 26, 1987, p. 40.
The New York Times Book Review. XCII, January 4, 1987, p. 1.
The New Yorker. LXIII, March 2, 1987, p. 107.
Newsweek. CIX, January 12, 1987, p. 69.
Time. CXXIX, January 19, 1987, p. 78.
The Village Voice. XXXII, January 27, 1987, p. 51.
The Wall Street Journal. CCIX, January 14, 1987, p. 20.

COUNTERPOINTS

Author: Rodney Needham (1923-   )
Publisher: University of California Press (Berkeley). 251 pp. $25.00
Type of work: Anthropological theory

This book considers notions of opposition from antiquity to the present day and points out that even so apparently natural a concept leads to serious difficulties of theoretical and practical analysis

The study of "binary opposites" has for some time been a major feature of modern anthropology, being applied by many scholars to matters as diverse as kinship, myth, and the structure of societies. Opposition has been believed to be a basic feature of human understanding, one of the few concepts which can safely be said to be noncultural, universal, ubiquitous. In this book, Rodney Needham turns to question all these assumptions, doing his best to prove them false. *Counterpoints* is in fact one in a sequence of works by this author dedicated to considering the very foundations of anthropology including the issue of whether anthropology may be considered a science, or separate field of knowledge, at all.

Needham begins with a cartoon which figured as a cover for *The New Yorker* in 1963. It pictures a thick, three-dimensional capital letter E, and above it, in the bubble that in cartoon convention means "thinks" or "dreams," a thin, two-dimensional capital E with a French acute accent over it. On the lower letter sits a cat, and at its foot lies a dog. A hen with a chicken on its back, and another following, walks from right to left. In the foreground is a border of plants, with a blooming potted plant among them. What, one may ask, does this cartoon mean? What kind of opposites does it include?

Needham draws from the picture a list of opposites including some of those mentioned above, such as cat/dog, chick/hen, three-dimensional/two-dimensional, but significantly omitting or rephrasing others. For example, Needham makes little of the acute accent (though it might be thought, on the cover of *The New Yorker*, to suggest French/English and, by association, elegant/plain). He does note the bubble convention but interprets it as ethereal/terrestrial, and decides that the plants in the border stand to the potted one as weed to flower and as untended to cultivated. The point is that even a drawing as bounded as this one may include more oppositions than a casual list can enumerate, and that any two observers will almost certainly draw up slightly different lists.

Can the oppositions produced by the drawing, however, be sorted or categorized? Are they random and personal or, as has so often been assumed, implicitly basic and universal? Needham turns from the cartoon, in his first few chapters, to consider early attempts to categorize the very notion of opposition. He notes, for example, that while the notion does appear to exist in many if not all languages, the words used for it are almost bewilderingly various. In English one may speak of antitheses, contraries, counterparts, dualities, polarities, even syzygies, not to mention other terms, and all of these appear to mean slightly different things. The English lexicon is in any case strongly Latinate, though the word "against" is related to the German word *Gegenteil*, the normal translation for "opposite." Both English and German have a strong sense of space in their terms. Needham notes again that in common speech one readily talks of "the opposite side of the street," meaning the other side of the street and anywhere along it, not merely the bit at right angles to where one happens to be standing. He asserts, however—at this point rather strongly conditioned by the communal dining habits of Oxford colleges—that one would be much more reluctant to say that someone is sitting "opposite" one at table if he or she were even slightly displaced to right or left. Meanwhile, there is no difficulty in talking about opposite banks of rivers, even if the river is winding so much as to make right-angle placements impossible. Moreover, in other languages, such as Chinese or Hebrew, the words usually used for opposition have different associations and come from different roots.

Such difficulties of classification have been around for a very long time. Needham considers the attempt by Aristotle to classify oppositions and notes that the Greek philosopher saw them as falling into several distinct categories. Opposites may, for example, be correlative, as in "double/half" or "mother/child": Each term is what it is in relation to the other. Or they may be contrary, such as good/bad, which is not quite the same thing: The mother is the mother of the child, but the good is not the good of the bad, nor black the black of the white. Contraries may furthermore have intermediates, as black and white have gray, or they may not: For Aristotle, at least, there was no intermediate between an odd and an even number. One may also see categories arising out of privation, as with sighted/blind, or out of logical statements of affirmation and negation. Aristotle's work is at least an attempt to consider the subject, as Needham points out. Yet how well does it work on *The New Yorker*? Returning to his own list of opposite qualities found in the cartoon, Needham finds some of them covered by Aristotle, some not. However one takes the results, it is plain that there are at least five different modes of opposition in Needham's own reactions to the drawing.

Classification might have been expected to advance since Aristotle's time, but actually Needham finds little on which to comment until he comes to C. K. Ogden's book *Opposition*, published in 1932. Ogden begins with twenty-five pairs of words said to have opposites in the "ordinary" sense of the term (as Ogden rather optimistically puts it). These include black/white again, but also hot/cold, right/left, town/country, and even (a pair which hardly anyone would find ordinary, British or not) British/alien. Ogden broods over such questions as why the opposite of black is white, while the opposite of visible is invisible; inside and outside suggest to him the notion of a "cut," a line which may be arbitrary, but which may also have considerable force—as in English common law, where the transit from being outside to being inside a house has major bearing on offenses for which a person may be charged. Ogden's views, in Needham's opinion, are interesting and varied, but in the end create more confusion than clarity; they suggest on the whole only that the world has grown more complex since Aristotle's day.

After dealing with Aristotle's and Ogden's theories, however, Needham takes on other anthropologists, and at this point his book takes on a strongly (and not altogether attractively) polemic note. In 1973, Needham edited a volume of essays on the subject of *Right and Left: Essays on Dual Symbolic Classification*, as this particular opposition is seen in different cultures. While he is quite prepared to extend this issue further and to concede that the notion of "complementarity" used by several contributors to the volume requires deeper analysis, he clearly finds himself irritated by recent French responses to that work, especially those of Louis Dumont and Serge Tcherkézoff. The argument here becomes extremely technical, but in brief it may be said that Dumont introduces a concept of "encompassment" (*englobement*) which Needham finds unconvincing. Dumont also tries to argue that social hierarchies are often arranged on bases of opposition and inversion—as in the notion that a king is superior to a priest in matters of public order, but that the converse is true in matters of religion (a distinction, it might be noted, more appropriate in Catholic France than in Anglican England, where the monarch is *ipso facto* head of the church and defender of its rights). Dumont's pupil Tcherkézoff takes matters further—and applies the question at last to classical anthropology—by trying to apply such theories to analysis of African societies such as the Meru and the Nyamwezi. Can anything revealing be said about "the left hand of the Mugwe" (a religious personage among the Meru) as a result of hierarchic analysis? Needham concludes that it cannot. More generally, and probably more interestingly, he raises the wide question of what one might call "the diagrammatic fallacy" among anthropologists: the belief that clear diagrams, on paper, often with arrows, dotted lines, and other diacritics, can in any real way represent the inner beliefs, or even customs, of human beings living in societies.

Needham clearly has a strong point here in indicating the specious attractions of this technique to what he calls the "reificatory" type of mind. Rather extending what he himself says, one could argue that many analyses of *la pensée sauvage*, "the savage mind," have become little more than mechanical extensions of a spatial metaphor, which insistently represents natural features on a two-dimensional scale. Needham points out that even night and day—a clear pair of opposites in most systems—are well-known to have all kinds of gradations in real life and to real people, including first light, twilight, broad day, and dusk. The same could be said even of male and female; as for other oppositions beloved of modern anthropology, such as raw and cooked and natural and cultural, most of them dissolve into ambiguity when confronted by even small amounts of skepticism. Moreover, how can any of these theses manage against the complexity of even a simple cartoon such as the one from *The New Yorker*? If a theory cannot cope with something well understood by the man in the street (so the reasoning goes), it should at least not be trusted before further refinement.

Counterpoints is a difficult work which often appears over-elaborate. Its merit is that it exposes the beliefs of one field (anthropology) to the challenges of others, including philology and philosophy. It also demonstrates what can be done, without technical language, by the exercise of an elementary, if Anglo-Saxon pragmatism.

T. A. Shippey

Sources for Further Study

Choice. XXV, December, 1987, p. 636.
The Times Literary Supplement. December 4-10, 1987, p. 1356.

THE COURT AND THE CONSTITUTION

Author: Archibald Cox (1912-   )
Publisher: Houghton Mifflin Company (Boston). 434 pp. $19.95
Type of work: Legal history
Time: 1787-1987
Locale: The United States

The author describes how the United States Supreme Court, as the final interpreter of the Constitution, has built its authority by linking each decision to that document while responding to new realities and changing social needs

As the bicentennial of the Constitution, 1987 was a year of intense interest in that historic document. Public ceremonies commemorated the signing two hundred years ago by the "Framers." Chief Justice Warren Burger published a widely read series of newspaper columns outlining the development of the Constitution and its underlying principles. A bevy of books appeared, approaching the subject from all angles, some serving as new, indispensable scholarly sources. There was the ambitious, critically acclaimed *Documentary History of the Supreme Court of the United States, 1789-1800: Volume 1* (1985), edited by Maeva Marcus and James R. Perry. David P. Currie's *The Constitution in the Supreme Court: The First Hundred Years, 1789-1888* (1986) treated significant early cases not widely remembered in the twentieth century except by legal scholars.

Other books on the Constitution ranged from philosophical investigations to polemics; most of them, however, like Burger's columns and Currie's book, acknowledged a profound historical connection between the Constitution and the Supreme Court, and some tried to characterize the work of the Court in that role. Michael Kammen, for example, in *A Machine That Would Go of Itself: The Constitution in American Culture* (1986), portrayed the Court as so aloof from public opinion (to maintain an impartial attitude) that the justices seldom answer or even read letters from citizens about a pending decision. On the other side, Eva R. Rubin, in *The Supreme Court and the American Family: Ideology and Issues* (1986), asserted that the Court has been committed to traditional concepts of the family and thus has generated conflict with those who consider those concepts obsolete. Whatever they may have thought of the Court, most of these authors declared their faith in the Constitution as a plan of government and, with its amendments, as a bulwark of civil liberties. An exception was Christopher Wolfe, who asked in *The Rise of Modern Judicial Review: From Constitutional Interpretation to Judge-Made Law* (1986) whether the Constitution is really an adequate basis for modern government.

Archibald Cox would answer with a resounding "Yes!" As he makes clear in *The Court and the Constitution*, however, Cox also believes that the Supreme Court is the most effective instrument for ensuring that the Constitution continues to provide this adequate basis for modern government.

Cox's book has something in common with the scholarly publications occasioned by the bicentennial as well as with the polemical. Yet as a writer on this subject, he also has one unique qualification: a certain kind of direct experience. As Solicitor General from 1961 to 1965, and as the first Watergate Special Prosecutor, he has witnessed constitutional principles being tested, approved—and evolved. Indeed, in the latter capacity, he was party to a showdown over the quasi-constitutional doctrine called "executive privilege"—a crisis that he deftly sketches in his prologue. Sworn to pursue the Watergate break-in investigation wherever it led, even to the presidency, Cox subpoenaed the taped conversations of President Richard M. Nixon after testimony by Alexander Butterfield, a former Nixon aide, revealed the existence of these tapes. Cox was sure that they would establish whether or not Nixon and others in his administration had engaged in a cover-up to hide the responsibility for the Watergate burglary.

Until 1973, no American president had ever been forced to give evidence in response to a subpoena. Nixon, who did not intend to break with that tradition, vowed to keep the tapes confidential and claimed two legal grounds for his refusal to comply with the subpoena: immunity from legal process (based on separation of powers) and executive privilege, the right to decide what information and documents in the executive branch should be kept confidential. Though it is not generally acknowledged, precedents for both of Nixon's arguments reached as far back as the administration of James Madison, and, more important, no court had ever forced a test of executive privilege. Nevertheless, the Watergate judge, John J. Sirica, would accept neither of Nixon's claims. According to Cox, the ruling by Sirica, subsequently upheld on appeal, "settled the principle that even the President of the United States is subject to the Constitution and other legal obligations as interpreted by an independent judiciary." Perhaps because this was a landmark resolution, it appears not to trouble Cox greatly that he himself was a casualty of the battle: Nixon had him fired by then-Solicitor General Robert Bork in the infamous "Saturday Night Massacre" of October, 1973.

It may seem astonishing that the legal question involved in this conflict—whether an American president is really subject to legal or judicial mandate—should not have been answered until the nation was almost two hundred years old. Yet executive privilege is only one of many Constitutional issues whose slow, painful evolution Cox delineates. More significant to him, in this particular case, is that twelve ordinary citizens on the Watergate grand jury stood up to the President by publicly voting to subpoena the tapes. While noting that "all our liberties depend on compliance with the law" by both ordinary citizens and the highest public officials, he is led to ask: "Why do the people support constitutionalism and the rule of law, and, as their instrument, the courts? Will the support continue?"

Part of his answer is that "law, as it binds public officials, is seen as a check on both executive oppression and bureaucratic caprice." He also cites an ancient belief that some individual rights are, or ought to be, "beyond the reach of any government, even the majority. . ." One suspects, however, that to Cox the most important reason is that "law is reaching for equal justice."

The operative word is "reaching," and it is as evolutionary instruments that Cox portrays both the Constitution and the Supreme Court. To demonstrate how far both have come, he takes the reader back to a time when neither they nor the way of life they have contributed to could be taken for granted. Before the Constitutional Convention at Philadelphia in 1787, the nation was merely a loose union of thirteen former colonies, strung out along the eastern seaboard, with a thinly scattered population of three million (where, in the 1980's, seventy million live). The federal government had no power to impose taxes, raise an army, or enforce any laws; given intense sectional rivalries and the difficulty of communication, it was not clear that this federation would ever get any stronger.

Of the many divisive issues faced at Philadelphia, says Cox, none was more difficult than "the conflict between the demands of unity and diversity." The Framers' solution was the unique invention called federalism, a state-federal partnership with each assigned its own powers and functions, with a unified economy, and with a single document—the Constitution—embodying the supreme law of the land.

Again, none of these principles could be taken for granted, even after the Framers signed their names to the governing instrument. Not only did these principles have to be enforced, but also, as Cox points out, the Framers deliberately avoided overdefining the powers granted to any branch of state or federal government. This, he says, was attributable to "their remarkable capacity for saying enough but not too much—just enough to give those who would come after them a point of reference and a strong foundation on which to build, but not so much as to inhibit their successors, who would live in changed and changing worlds."

Who mediated these changes and gave them shape? The Supreme Court, says Cox. Adopting a conceit from the medieval physician Galen, Cox calls the Court a "great ganglion of the nerves of American society, receiving messages from all parts of the body politic, appreciating their meaning and its needs . . . and sending back the critical impulses to shape the body's growth." Cox also leads his readers through the cases that fashioned the Court into this nerve center: the first tests of presidential powers (such as *Marbury v. Madison*, 1801); the years of building a nation with a truly unified economy through the Interstate Commerce Clause (as in *Cooley v. Board of Port Wardens*, 1851); the evolution from laissez-faire to recognized collective-bargaining rights (*West Coast Hotel v. Parrish*, 1937); the use of constitutional adjudication as an instrument of egalitarian reform (as in *Brown v. Board of Education*, 1954); and finally, the debate over the role of the Supreme Court in the final quarter of the twentieth century. In each instance, he shows the Court striving to interpret the sometimes meager evidence of the Framers' intent in the light of vastly changed circumstances in American life. Along the way, the Court evolves its own style from "judicial supremacy" to "judicial restraint" to what some now call "judicial activism."

As Cox chronicles each historical issue and relives the debate, he also relates stories of ordinary citizens who provided the occasions for these great debates. As a stylist, he is at his best when telling in vivid, pithy sentences of the events that led up to landmark cases. As a legal expositor, he provides much valuable information on subjects widely taken for granted in contemporary society.

The book has many excellent qualities, but also some major flaws. Most notable is Cox's seeming confusion about his intended audience. Is the book directed primarily to common citizens like those whose landmark cases it chronicles? If so, Cox's exposition would have benefited from a more consistent style: Despite his lively portrayal of the "facts" in each case, his sentences often run to several hundred words when expounding the legal issues; moreover, some of these lengthy pronouncements are not so much complex as frustratingly obscure. Such detailed discussions suggest that Cox was also writing for other legal scholars—a supposition bolstered by the case-number citations at the end of the book. Addressing two such distinct audiences, Cox is unable to reconcile conflicting demands.

Indeed, while generally providing a balanced presentation, Cox sometimes reveals biases of his own. An example is his assumption that without federal restraint, state and local governments would automatically be "selfish"—that is, they would seek economic gain or solutions to local problems at the expense of other communities. The historical evidence he provides does not seem sufficient to warrant such an assumption.

It would be unrealistic, however, to expect such an ambitious undertaking as Cox's book to be free of flaws. He does in the end prove his point regarding the spirit behind constitutional adjudication in the face of social change: "Continuity is essential to law as a whole, but the continuity must be creative." The question that remains for Cox and his readers is whether the American people will continue to support "constitutionalism and the rule of law." It depends, he answers, on "the spirit of tolerance and cooperation." It also depends on the consent of the governed, a term Cox uses to include not only the governed, but also those governing. The Watergate case may have been part of the passing show, but it contains a central message.

Thomas Rankin

Sources for Further Study

Booklist. LXXXIII, August, 1987, p. 1702.
Choice. XXV, November, 1987, p. 543.
Kirkus Reviews. LV, June 15, 1987, p. 902.
Library Journal. CXII, August, 1987, p. 136.
Los Angeles Times Book Review. September 13, 1987, p. 20.
National Review. XXXIX, August 28, 1987, p. 46.
The New York Times Book Review. XCII, September 20, 1987, p. 3.
The New Yorker. LXIII, September 28, 1987, p. 98.
Publishers Weekly. CCXXXI, July 10, 1987, p. 60.
The Washington Post Book World. XVII, August 23, 1987, p. 10.

CROSSING TO SAFETY

Author: Wallace Stegner (1909-   )
Publisher: Random House (New York). 277 pp. $18.95
Type of work: Novel
Time: Early 1930's to early 1970's
Locale: Madison, Wisconsin; rural Vermont; and Florence, Italy

The friendship of two couples survives the accidents of three and a half decades and brings happiness and sustenance to their lives

> Principal characters:
> LARRY MORGAN, a writer, the narrator of the novel
> SALLY MORGAN, his wife, crippled by polio in 1938
> CHARITY LANG, who is dying of cancer in the summer of 1972
> SID LANG, her husband of forty years, a professor of English
> AUNT EMILY, Charity's mother

Crossing to Safety is an old-fashioned novel about a traditional subject, friendship, and what it means in the lives of four people who experience it over several decades. The novel is dedicated to Wallace Stegner's wife and "to the friends we were both blessed with," and one suspects that there is a strong autobiographical strain in the book.

The novel is narrated in the present of the summer of 1972 by Larry Morgan, a writer who, with his wife Sally, has returned to Battell Pond, Vermont, to pay a last visit to their friends Sid and Charity Lang. Most of the novel works as a series of flashbacks, as Larry describes the relationship that has developed between the two couples, especially in their first year in Madison, Wisconsin, when Larry and Sid were young English professors at the University of Wisconsin, and then in the following summer, when they all congregated in Vermont and spent three idyllic weeks together. Now, in 1972, Larry and Sally are in Vermont again—after intermittent summer visits and a winter together in Florence, Italy, in 1958—because Charity is dying of cancer and has asked for one last visit with friends and family.

When the Morgans first meet the Langs in Madison, in the fall of 1937, all four people are full of energy and expectation, for life is a continuing series of possibilities. The Langs are wealthy, through Sid, and they share their happiness and their plenty, in these last days of the Depression, with their new friends the Morgans. Both wives are pregnant, Sally with her first child and Charity with her third. Their pregnancies, however, hardly keep the two women from an exciting round of activities—parties and picnics— usually arranged by Charity:

> a charming woman, a woman we couldn't help liking on sight. She raised the pulse and the spirits, she made Madison a different town, she brought life and anticipation and excitement into a year we had been prepared to endure stoically.

Larry is only a one-year replacement at the university, while Sid is nearing the end of a three-year contract, and, at the close of the academic year, with the births of both their children, the dream ends. Larry's contract is not renewed, and Sid is only given a three-year extension (not tenure or promotion). In an attempt to forget their troubles, the four go sailing but capsize in the still-freezing waters of Lake Monona. The accident hints at greater disasters to follow.

Charity's name is not lightly chosen, for the Langs are the embodiment of love and generosity. They take Sally and her baby (named Lang in their honor) back to Vermont for the summer and let Larry stay in their Madison house, where he can teach and save money. At the end of the summer, he joins his family in the Lang summer compound in Vermont for three idyllic weeks, until the real tragedy hits: On a hiking trip, Sally is struck down by polio and crippled for life.

Now, in 1972, the Morgans have survived thirty-five years of a different kind of life. In a sense, Larry has been in bondage to his wife, but Sally has made the most of her disability, and Larry now thinks that "my chains are not chains," for "Sally's crippling has been a rueful blessing" that "has taught me at least the alphabet of gratitude." In fact, Larry has become a famous writer, and the couple has traveled widely in the intervening years. Sid has also been fortunate. When he was finally denied tenure at Wisconsin, he and Charity retreated to the isolation of their Vermont home, but after World War II, Larry was able through a connection of his own to get Sid a job in the English Department at Dartmouth College, where he has been teaching successfully ever since.

Life has now caught up with the Langs, and Larry and Sally have come at Charity's last beckoning. It is not an easy scene, for Charity is never a simple or patient woman.

> All her life she has been demanding people's attention to things she admires and values. She has both prompted and shushed, and pretty imperiously too. But she herself never needed or accepted prompting in her life, and she is not going to be shushed, not even by cancer. She will burn bright until she goes out; she will go on standing on tiptoe till she falls.

Charity wants to die her own way, which naturally is not everyone else's, and Sid especially feels excluded by her last plans. The tension between Sid and Charity is not new, however, for it has been the "serpent," as Larry Morgan calls it, in the otherwise paradisiacal relationship among the four characters since almost their first meeting.

Charity Lang is the center of the novel and the source of much of its strength and drama. A tall, beautiful, exuberant woman, she overflows with love of life and generosity for those with whom she shares her vision. Charity organizes events to throw Larry together with her Uncle Richard, an editor who soon helps to launch Larry's own editorial career; the Langs pay for many of the Morgans' medical expenses following Sally's disastrous accident. Charity's life is a series of good deeds for others, deeds that usually result in real benefit. In her marriage, however, she is too often the mother to Sid, and it damages their relationship.

Sid is himself large and handsome, a man of energy and charm, but he is not as ambitious as Charity would have him. The daughter of a renowned academic, Charity would like Sid to be more assertive in his professional career. Sid, of no small talent, would rather write poems than scholarly articles and is probably denied tenure at Wisconsin because of this limitation. Charity treats him at times like a child and, when he fails her, turns childish herself and withholds her love.

At the end, when Charity is orchestrating her own last scene, Sid is barely considered; it is as if he is given a bit role in a last tragic act. Her compulsive control will even extend beyond the grave: She has given him a list of five women she approves of his remarrying. Yet Sid has needed that "direction and reassurance" throughout his life, Larry thinks, and, in the end, Larry is the one who is providing needed friendship to the stricken Sid. One important aspect of the novel is that Charity is a complex character: a woman who is capable of untold amounts of love, who can also be a manipulative tyrant. Both are true, and readers must hold both truths simultaneously.

The larger meaning of the novel is conveyed in the title from Cicero that Larry introduces early in the novel: *De amicitia*, concerning friendship. This is a novel concerning friendship and the love and happiness it carries. "They're the only family we ever had," Sally says in Vermont in 1972. "Our lives would have been totally different and a lot harder without them." The novel deals also—because of friendship's setting here—with marriage, that institution of mutual addiction and dependence, and with what it does to the individual partners—Sid and Charity and Larry and Sally.

Finally, the novel speaks of survival, of "crossing" life to safety. During their early years of struggle, the four friends love to repeat to one another a line from William Faulkner: " 'They kilt us but they ain't whupped us yit.' " *Crossing to Safety* is thus a novel dealing with the survival of the human spirit as it prevails, as Faulkner might say, over the vagaries of life. The title is taken from a poem by Robert Frost entitled "I Could Give All to Time," the last stanza of which serves as the epigraph to the novel:

> I could give all to Time except—except
> What I myself have held. But why declare
> The things forbidden that while the Customs slept
> I have crossed to Safety with? For I am There
> And what I would not part with I have kept.

What are the things "forbidden" by "Customs" that the poem's narrator has "crossed to Safety with"? The image seems to be of Charon poling the ferry across the river Styx to Hades—some customs gate in the last journey of life. Yet the characters of Stegner's novel have crossed to safety, have survived life with love, and charity, and friendship. They need pay little duty to Time.

The classical allusion in the Frost poem is reflected elsewhere in Stegner's novel. Charity is described as Demeter, Greek goddess of marriage, at one point; later she is compared to Achilles, the hero of the Trojan War. The drama here reads like a Greek tragedy: Characters (particularly Sally) are struck down by the Fates. Yet there is another level of allusion here, and it is more Christian. In one powerful scene in Florence, the four drive a workman with a mangled hand for help, after viewing Piero della Francesca's painting of the resurrected Christ, and the images get tangled together. At the end, Charity's death is likened to the death of Christ, and there are several other allusions to communion and crucifixion in the novel. The story of the Langs and the Morgans, in short, is wrapped in an allusive language that elevates it to greater drama and meaning.

In other ways, the novel is quite traditional. *Crossing to Safety* contains three sections, and mostly they comprise flashbacks to earlier times the Langs and Morgans spent together, in Madison, at Battell Pond, in Florence. The novel is thus built around a series of episodic scenes—their first dinner in Madison, preparations for Charity's last birthday/"deathday" picnic—and often years pass between episodes. Stegner's descriptive prose is lean, and he evokes the events of his novel with both detail and atmosphere. There are few pyrotechnics, but readers experience the lives here with exactitude and fullness.

Crossing to Safety is an important contribution to the opus of work by one of America's most distinguished novelists. From *The Big Rock Candy Mountain* (1943) through *Angle of Repose* (1971, winner of the Pulitzer Prize for Fiction), Wallace Stegner for some decades has been telling us about ourselves, about the customs and mores and meaning of American life. *Crossing to Safety* is a significant addition to a remarkable body of work in American literature.

David Peck

Sources for Further Study

Booklist. LXXXIV, September 1, 1987, p. 2.
Chicago Tribune. August 2, 1987, XIV, p. 3.
Commonweal. CXIV, November 6, 1987, p. 630.

Kirkus Reviews. LV, July 15, 1987, p. 1029.
Library Journal. CXII, October 1, 1987, p. 110.
Los Angeles Times Book Review. September 6, 1987, p. 3.
The New York Times Book Review. XCII, September 20, 1987, p. 14.
Publishers Weekly. CCXXXII, July 31, 1987, p. 66.
The Washington Post Book World. XVII, October 4, 1987, p. 1.

CULTURAL LITERACY
What Every American Needs To Know

Author: E(ric) D(onald) Hirsch, Jr. (1928-   )
Publisher: Houghton Mifflin Company (Boston). 251 pp. $16.95
Type of work: Current affairs

Hirsch describes the decline of literacy in the United States, analyzes the causes of this trend, and offers a solution for reversing it

The Victorian historian Thomas Babington Macaulay confidently asserted, "Every schoolboy knows who imprisoned Montezuma, and who strangled Atahualpa." Whether or not such knowledge was widespread in nineteenth century England, it most assuredly is not in twentieth century America. In the October 3, 1983, issue of *The Washington Post*, Benjamin J. Stein reported on what he called "The Cheerful Ignorance of the Young in L. A." According to Stein,

> I have not yet found one single student in Los Angeles, in either college or high school, who could tell me the years when World War II was fought. Nor have I found one who could tell me the years when World War I was fought. Nor have I found one who knew when the American Civil War was fought. . . . None has known how many [senators] Nevada or Oregon has.

Stein adds that a junior at the University of California, Los Angeles, thought that Toronto "must be in Italy," and a junior at the University of Southern California placed Washington, D.C., in Washington State.

Such ignorance is not unique to Los Angeles. A 1978 study by the National Assessment of Educational Progress reported a significant recent decline in American children's knowledge of civics. Average verbal Scholastic Aptitude Test (SAT) scores are considerably lower in 1987 than they were in 1970, with an especially sharp decline among the supposedly best-educated high-school students. E. D. Hirsch's son teaches Latin; when he informed his class that Latin is no longer spoken, one of his students challenged his statement because she believed that it is the language of Latin America. A group of community college students in Richmond, Virginia, the capital of the Confederacy, could not identify Ulysses S. Grant or Robert E. Lee.

Many factors have been blamed for this sorry state of affairs: television, the breakup of the traditional family, low pay or low standards for teachers. According to Hirsch, though, the cause is more fundamental—nothing less than the philosophy underlying contemporary American education. Hirsch describes this attitude as formalism, the belief that literacy is a skill, like riding a bicycle or driving a car. According to this view, if one learns to ride a Schwinn, one can also ride a Peugeot; if one can drive a Chevrolet, one can drive a Ford, too. Similarly, once a student learns to read a text about friendship, he can understand a passage of equal difficulty about the Civil War.

Together with David Harrington, Hirsch tested this assumption using just such a pair of essays, comparing the reading ability of students at the University of Virginia and a community college in Richmond. The two groups did equally well when they had to read the piece requiring no special information beyond vocabulary recognition. When confronted with an article about Grant and Lee, though, they showed markedly different abilities. The university students, who had sufficient background knowledge of the Civil War, again read the essay easily. The community college students, who did not know who Lee and Grant were, found the writing difficult, even though the vocabulary was no more challenging than in the piece about friendship. So, too, a group of literate Americans can more readily grasp a description of an American wedding than of an Indian ceremony, whereas literate Indians find the account of their native customs more comprehensible.

Such results are consistent with what linguists have learned about language acquisition. Comprehension requires a knowledge of both the lexical and structural meanings of a sentence. That is, one must indeed possess the skill to combine sounds into words and to interpret the dictionary meaning of those words. Here American education, with its formalist philosophy, does very well; American first graders read at least as well as their European and Asian counterparts. As early as the second grade, though, American children begin to lag behind, with those from culturally poor environments falling further behind than their culturally richer classmates.

These differences arise because grasping lexical meaning is not enough. "Meet me at the green" is a sentence any third grader can read, but it is not one every third grader can interpret. A child growing up in New England will immediately recognize that "the green" refers to the grassy plot in the center of town where sheep grazed in the eighteenth century. To a Californian, however, the sentence would be meaningless, because he would lack the knowledge of what "the green" is, even though he could easily pick out a green shirt.

Before the triumph of formalism, children learned lexical and structural meanings at the same time, for their school readers dealt with American history, and their curricula included literary classics. John Dewey and his camp changed all that. In *Schools of To-morrow* (1915) he urged the teaching of "a small number of typical situations with a view to mastering the way of dealing with the problems of experience, not the piling up of information." Dewey's schools of tomorrow became the schools of today, emphasizing current fiction that deals with social issues. High-school graduates may be better able to cope with death and divorce, but they have trouble communicating information. Furthermore, they are ignorant in fundamental areas.

As Hirsch points out, this ignorance is a political and economic as well as a cultural problem. In a totalitarian society, illiteracy is a personal tragedy; in a democracy it is a national disaster. In a letter to Colonel Edward Carrington dated January 16, 1787, Thomas Jefferson wrote:

> Were it left to me to decide whether we should have a government without newspapers, or newspapers without a government, I should not hesitate a moment to prefer the latter. But I should mean that every man should receive those papers and be capable of reading them.

Whether one relies on television, radio, or printed matter for one's news, the need for cultural literacy remains. Otherwise, one cannot grasp the nature of domestic debates or international conflicts. One of the realizations that prompted Hirsch to write his book was that a typical newspaper article would be unintelligible without a considerable amount of assumed background knowledge.

Cultural illiteracy also leads to political fragmentation. The Constitutional Convention almost foundered on sectional mistrust resulting from ignorance. General Charles Cotesworth Pinckney observed toward the end of the four-month session in Philadelphia, "I had myself prejudices against the Eastern states before I came here, but I will acknowledge that I have found them as liberal and candid as any men whatever." National cohesion demands a trust based on a shared body of knowledge.

Prosperity, too, requires cultural literacy. The story of the Tower of Babel illustrates the impossibility of accomplishing a task when coworkers cannot communicate. Many companies find an analogous situation in the 1980's, as midlevel executives seem unable to share information.

To combat cultural illiteracy, Hirsch urges curricular reforms that will again emphasize "factual information and traditional lore." A sixty-three-page appendix lists the specific content of such a revised course of study. In teaching these forty-five hundred people, places, concepts, phrases, texts, and titles, teachers should, Hirsch says, be flexible. Everyone should recognize the name Henry David Thoreau, but not everyone needs to read *Walden* (1854). The distinction Hirsch makes is between extensive knowledge, which asks only a superficial understanding of Thoreau as an advocate of civil disobedience and a lover of nature, and intensive knowledge, which might include an understanding of Transcendentalism, Thoreau's relationship with Ralph Waldo Emerson, or his response in *Walden* to Benjamin Franklin's version of the American Dream.

While the proposed changes are far-reaching, they are not excessively demanding. According to Hirsch, "Only a few hundred pages of information stand between the literate and the illiterate, between dependence and autonomy." In the near future, Hirsch plans to publish a dictionary containing that information.

The problem that Hirsch addresses is real. Millions of Americans lack even minimal literacy, the ability to complete simple forms or read road signs. Hirsch reports that "only two thirds of our citizens are literate, and even among those the average level is too low and should be raised." His proposals, however, raise numerous questions.

For example, there is the list in the appendix. Despite Hirsch's disclaimer that it "is provisional" and not definitive, it illustrates the problem of defining cultural literacy. According to this list, the ideal schoolchild will know who imprisoned Montezuma but not who strangled Atahualpa. He will know the dates of the Civil War, World War I, and World War II, but not of the French and Indian or Spanish-American War. He will know about Thor but not about Woden. Even though cultural literacy is a worthwhile goal, the road to it is not as clear as Hirsch would suggest.

Nor is it as painless. As an example of what he considers cultural literacy, Hirsch notes that his father, in giving financial advice to his associates, would write, "There is a tide," assuming that his readers would recognize the reference to Brutus' speech in William Shakespeare's *Julius Caesar* (1623). Here Brutus is urging immediate action. Although the elder Hirsch intended the allusion to support his recommendation, someone familiar with the play might consider that Brutus' eloquence leads to disaster at Philippi and so choose another counselor. A little learning is a dangerous thing. To suggest that a few hundred pages of any book will create cultural literacy is to raise unrealistic expectations.

Moreover, it is unfair to place the entire responsibility of cultural education on the schools. If Americans in the nineteenth century were culturally literate or shared common knowledge, the school curriculum was hardly the only reason. For in 1890, only half the children between the ages of five and seventeen were attending classes, and fewer than 10 percent of the population had been graduated from high school. Thus, if Americans in the 1980's are culturally illiterate, the schools cannot assume all the blame. Stein's audiences in Los Angeles had heard about the Civil War, but students resemble Huck Finn, whose interest in Moses declined sharply when he learned that the Jewish leader "had been dead a considerable long time." As Huck explains, "I don't take no stock in dead people." Students in 1987 recognize the name Madonna, but their association is with the living rock star, not the mother of Jesus, who has been dead a considerable long time.

Third graders from culturally rich homes read better than third graders who lack that background because the former not only learn in school but also have information reinforced or introduced through books in the house and trips to museums or historical sites. Once one abandons the delusion that cultural literacy is a matter of learning a few isolated facts about a limited number of arbitrarily selected items, one will see that all elements of society must join the enterprise; parents, media, and libraries cannot shirk their obligations by insisting that a place where students spend one-eighth of their year bear total responsibility for acculturation. One will also recognize that acquiring cultural literacy is a lifelong process, not one that ends at age seventeen.

Finally, Hirsch's standards of cultural literacy are ethnocentric. Panama appears on the list but not Argentina, 1776 but not 1789, ukulele but not the Ukraine. In a global economy, in a world that will survive only if people from different nations can communicate with one another, a program of national rather than international acculturation is both myopic and dangerous.

Whatever its shortcomings, though, *Cultural Literacy: What Every American Needs to Know* raises important questions about contemporary education and points out failings that require remedy. If the answers are not as simple as Hirsch implies, one should not despair but rather work the harder to speed the day when all inhabitants of the global village, rich and poor, black and white, Hispanic and Anglo, Russian and American, can sit down together at the table of mutual understanding, when the Earth shall be as full of knowledge as the waters that cover the sea.

Joseph Rosenblum

Sources for Further Study

Booklist. LXXXIII, April 15, 1987, p. 1234.
Choice. XXIV, July, 1987, p. 1736.
The Christian Century. CXIV, July 29, 1987, p. 659.
Commentary. LXXXIV, July, 1987, p. 45.
Los Angeles Times Book Review. May 17, 1987, p. 1.
The Nation. CCXLIV, May 30, 1987, p. 710.
The New York Times Book Review. XCII, March 15, 1987, p. 12.
The New Yorker. LXIII, June 1, 1987, p. 106.
Science. CCXXXVI, May 22, 1987, p. 973.
Time. CXXX, July 20, 1987, p. 72.
The Washington Post Book World. XVII, April 19, 1987, p. 1.

DANCING AT THE RASCAL FAIR

Author: Ivan Doig (1939-   )
Publisher: Atheneum Publishers (New York). 405 pp. $18.95
Type of work: Historical novel
Time: 1889-1919
Locale: Montana

Recounting the first two decades' settlement of a sheep and cattle ranching area called "Scotch Heaven," this novel—the second in a projected trilogy—dedicates itself both to delineating a historical period and to creating characters who shape and are shaped by that place and its history

Principal characters:
ANGUS ALEXANDER MCCASKILL, a homesteader, a schoolteacher, and the narrator
ROBERT BURNS "ROB" BARCLAY, a fellow immigrant and homesteader
ANNA RAMSAY REESE, a schoolteacher and Angus' beloved
ADAIR BARCLAY MCCASKILL, Angus' wife
VARICK ALEXANDER MCCASKILL, Angus and Adair's son
LUCAS BARCLAY, Rob Barclay's uncle
STANLEY MEIXELL, a United States Forest Service ranger

Henry David Thoreau once remarked that mythology precedes poetry, and between them must lie a long enough stretch of history to challenge the fixed forms of the mythological with the flux of particulars. The American West has its fossilized and formulaic mythology, the stuff of countless films and pulp novels that have produced a strange kind of poetry, and it has been Ivan Doig's purpose to bring a new vision to challenge it, both in his novels and in such nonfictional works as *This House of Sky: Landscapes of a Western Mind* (1978). Doig, who has a doctorate in history, emphasizes the complex reality of the West: The region is more than a cultural vacuum into which can be placed the good-versus-evil fantasies that have come to take on a kind of specious reality because of their sheer number.

Dancing at the Rascal Fair, the second novel of a projected trilogy about the McCaskill family and the Two Medicine region of Eastern Slope Montana—note that within the saga's chronology, this story comes before *English Creek* (1984)—is above all an attempt to create an intensely particular historical account of the early homestead era there and to elicit a complex and poetic reality from those particulars. The narrative gives a lively catalog of event. fact, and expression, of the kind that only the most intimate knowledge of a place can provide: a failed summer's hay crop ("I could cover the width of each windrow with my hat"), an argument at poker ("Goddamn you and the horse you rode in on"), the idea of national forests ("lines of logic laid upon the earth").

Dancing at the Rascal Fair is also (and this is not at all usual for novels of the American West) informed by an intensely ironic vision of life. Despite the conviviality of Doig's first-person narrator Angus McCaskill, and despite the fact that Doig shares some of his narrator's biases, there is no single authoritative spokesperson in this novel. Doig plays with the stock elements of Western fiction—sheepmen versus cattlemen, government versus the individual, man versus nature—but he employs them to his own ends: His cast of characters includes not a single outlaw, and his invented scenes show not a single gun pointed in anger from one man to another. The struggles and violence are of a much subtler kind, and prove the characters to be not stereotypes but mixtures of the rational and passionate, of order and confusion.

Doig begins the novel not with Americans, and not in America. When Angus McCaskill and Rob Barclay walk down the quay toward their ship on the River Clyde, they react as Scotsmen, and the narrator approximates a Scottish brogue he will later lose:

> The Atlantic Ocean and the continent America all the way across to Montana stood as but the width of a cottage threshold, so far as [Rob] ever let on. No second guess, never a might-have-done-instead out of [him], none. . . . Man, man, what I would give to know.

Doig's West is a land of immigrants whose seemingly mundane lives are a far cry from romantic stereotypes.

Doig departs from the conventional expectations of the Western in other ways as well. Fiction set in the West has seldom emphasized women and settled society, and even the most mature work in this area, such as Wallace Stegner's novels *Angle of Repose* (1971) and *The Big Rock Candy Mountain* (1943), hews close to the traditional line of women wanting to settle down while men want to keep moving. Doig deviates from that line; he recognizes that the key social element is the presence of women, but one of the strengths of his novel is the variety of their portraiture: They are as likely as men to upset any status quo.

At the outset, women are present in Montana only as synecdoche: The teamster Herbert speaks of "the calico situation," meaning in most cases the availability of prostitutes. The desolate architecture of Gros Ventre which Angus and Rob find when they arrive in the spring of 1890 is emblematic of the lack of true society there: Angus notes that the "raggle-taggle fringe of structures was the community entire." Repeatedly, Doig undercuts images of the West that hide its harsh realities. The town's favorite prostitute is a Slavic immigrant who has been dubbed Bouncing Betty: Her surname, Mraz, means "ice" in her native language.

As the narrative progresses, increasingly populated by women, one cannot help but notice that there is much coldness in the male-female relationships. Angus remembers his parents' marriage as "locked in ice." The novel's safest marriage, that of Rob and Judith Barclay, is free of mutual passion, for as Uncle Lucas notes, Rob's love is for himself. Angus' lack of feeling for Rob's sister Adair stands in sharp contrast to his futile and all-consuming passion for Anna Ramsay, and his marriage to Adair seems not much warmer than his parents' had been. Anna repeatedly manipulates Angus by telling him, after her own marriage, that if she ever sees that she and Isaac are not right for each other, she will know where to turn for better. His holding on to hope for twenty years because of this implied promise illustrates one of the novel's themes: the destructive force of passion.

Greed is another kind of passion working itself out in the open possibilities of settlement, and Doig examines that antisocial force in several lives. Most obvious is Rob himself. His desire for more and more sheep, more and more profit, pairs him with the Williamson clan of the Double W; in this ironic doubling of sheepherder and cattle baron, both are eager to graze the land bare. Furthermore, Rob's automobile and his steam-tractor plowing on the dry benchlands link him with the exploitive forces of industry— the machine in the garden. His opposition to the national forest plan comes from his greed as well, the stereotyped frontiersman's opposition to any institutional restraint on the individual's exploitation of the land.

In the stereotyped West, this sort of rapacity is exclusively male, but in Doig's richly ironic novel the blame is spread around: Anna Ramsay marries Isaac Reese in good part because of her desire for economic ease; Angus gets involved in the land-locator business with Lucas and Rob in part because Adair wants more money and in part because having more will mean her departure for Scotland and the possibility of Angus' marriage to Anna. In Doig's hardheaded view of the world, the complicated web of individual desire, both male and female, creates the patterns of social order and social error; no one is totally innocent. Society plainly consumes its own members just as it exploits the physical world. While those in the Old World they left behind battle through the Great War "like rabid dogs," Angus and Rob share a boundary on the land and feel a hatred that has expressed itself in a bloody fight and that often seems to threaten gunfire as well. One of the strengths of the novel is that it keeps the general and particular constantly reflecting each other.

Again in the economic sphere, Doig's novel tests ideas of community as they relate to major but conflicting notions of order: populism and capitalism. Scotland exists in Angus' memories as a place of exploitation designed to favor the owners of factories (those "shrines of toil"), with "the accusing spire of a church" overseeing all. This similarity of images is no coincidence. Pounding an anvil took his father's hearing but not his sense that Angus should spend his life doing the same work. Throughout the narrative, Angus shows an instinctive dislike for the favor of money, and in that he expresses Doig's own dislike of his own youth, "the economic uncertainties of running sheep on shares—sort of sharecropping for rich ranchers who owned all the land."

Angus' intense guilt for having joined Lucas and Rob as real estate agents for dry-land farmers who they know will fail is another expression of the populist urge that subsides only when he is in the schoolroom, where some of the novel's finest vignettes and some of its most lyrical prose detail his relationships with the students and his pleasure in their learning. In truth, nowhere outside the four walls of the school is there true satisfaction to be had for Angus McCaskill—even his beloved Anna, soon to be married to another man, is truly his only once, and that too in a schoolroom. Therein lies Doig's supreme irony in *Dancing at the Rascal Fair*: his handling of the old theme of society versus nature as the proper place for the pursuit of happiness.

On one hand, nature is a constant in all Doig's books, nonfiction and fiction. If there is one instantaneous change in Angus as a new arrival in America, it is his Thoreauvian love of the wildness of nature. This he shares with Doig, and shows in every part of the narrative:

> [The mountains] were my guide now, even the wind fell from mind now in their favor. Seeing them carving their canyons of stone into the sky edge, scarps and peaks deep up into the blue, a person could have no doubt where he was. The poor old rest of the world could hold to whatever axis it wished. . . .

Like every other element in this many-voiced novel, however, this one has its counterpoint, and it is spoken frequently by Adair: Why would anyone wish to spend a life in such a powerful and unpredictably destructive country? Even after an emergency trip has taken her with Angus to the highest mountain vistas and brought them closer together than they have been for years, she nevertheless tells him:

> There is so much of this country. People keep having to stretch themselves out of shape trying to cope with so much. Distance. Weather. The aloneness. All the work. This Montana sets its own terms and tells you, do them or else.

The novel holds both views. Doig himself loves Montana but lives in Seattle, and he has made clear in *This House of Sky* what ambiguous feelings he holds for the country and what living there cost his parents. It is important to note that he has chosen to end the period covered by *Dancing at the Rascal Fair* with the summer drought and five-month killer winter of 1919: There is something glorious in the perseverance of the survivors and something sad in their intention to remain and continue being stretched by the demands of such a place.

Doig's own response to this dilemma is the irony found throughout the novel, extending even to the distance between him and his narrator Angus.

Those who take Angus to be Doig's spokesman on all issues miss the truths spoken about Angus by other characters such as Rob, who for all of his weaknesses is true to his wife and is justifiably outraged at Angus' treatment of Adair (though not justified in poisoning the mind of Angus' son Varick).

Certainly, Angus has many strengths, and a moral earnestness inseparable from his conduct, but it could be said that the champion of kindness and perseverance and adaptability is Adair herself. Near the end of the novel, she takes on a new and crucial role in the relationship between Angus and Rob. Some readers might not like the Penelope role she ultimately assumes, but remembering that she is not always the quiet sufferer helps balance that reservation. The discussion comes full circle: Women are the crucial complement. The final irony of the novel is that Angus and Adair deserve each other; between them, they ask all the right questions and provide a full range of sensible responses. Doig does not instruct his readers on the correctness of these choices; like Anton Chekhov, he is content to pose the questions well.

Kerry Ahearn

Sources for Further Study

Booklist. LXXXIII, July, 1987, p. 1625.
Chicago Tribune. December 10, 1987, p. 1.
Kirkus Reviews. LV, August 1, 1987, p. 1090.
Library Journal. CXII, September 15, 1987, p. 93.
Los Angeles Times Book Review. October 18, 1987, p. 15.
The New York Times Book Review. XCII, November 1, 1987, p. 3.
Publishers Weekly. CCXXXII, July 31, 1987, p. 70.
The Washington Post Book World. XVII, October 18, 1987, p. 1.

DARKNESS AT NIGHT
A Riddle of the Universe

Author: Edward Harrison (1919-   )
Publisher: Harvard University Press (Cambridge, Massachusetts). Illustrated. 294 pp. $25.00
Type of work: History of astronomy
Time: The sixth century B.C. to the 1980's

For centuries astronomers have pondered the riddle of the dark night sky, and the quest for a solution abounds in strange and interesting ideas and personalities

> *Principal personages:*
> JEAN-PHILIPPE LOYS DE CHÉSEAUX, the French astronomer who first quantitatively analyzed the problem of the dark sky
> EDMOND HALLEY, the English astronomer who discovered a geometric solution to the problem
> WILHELM OLBERS, the German astronomer who gave his name to the paradox of the dark sky
> EDGAR ALLAN POE, the American poet and short-story writer who gave a qualitative solution to the paradox
> WILLIAM THOMSON, LORD KELVIN, the Scottish physicist who presented a modern mathematical resolution of the paradox

Edward Harrison, a professor of physics and astronomy at the University of Massachusetts at Amherst, became intrigued by the riddle of the dark night sky more than twenty years ago. To the uninitiated, the riddle's answer seems simple: The sun has set and now shines on the Earth's other side. If one thinks of infinite space as uniformly populated with stars, however, then the entire night sky ought to be ablaze with light, because the more distant stars, though fainter, are correspondingly more numerous. By adding the light of the fewer near stars to the light of the more numerous far stars, one finds that the night sky should be intensely illuminated. Nevertheless, the night sky is dark. Why?

Astronomers have proposed two basic solutions: Either the dark gaps are filled with stars that remain unseen and the missing starlight must be explained (the covered-sky interpretation) or the dark gaps are mostly devoid of stars and the missing stars must be explained (the uncovered-sky interpretation). For Harrison, the riddle has an answer falling within one of these interpretations, and surprisingly, the first person to give a qualitatively correct solution was not a scientist but a poet.

Harrison divides *Darkness at Night: A Riddle of the Universe* into three parts. In the first part he traces the emergence of ideas in the ancient and medieval periods that led to the origin of the riddle of darkness. Three systems of natural philosophy dominated the pre-Christian period: the atomist system of infinite space populated with numberless worlds composed of atoms; Aristotle's orderly geometric system of celestial spheres; and the Stoic system of a finite cosmos of moving worlds surrounded by an infinite void. Harrison suggests that the Stoic worldview, which pictured a place where the starry universe ends, offers a natural explanation of the night sky: The dark spaces between the stars are the darkness of the infinite void.

During the medieval period, ecclesiastical authorities were concerned about the spread of pagan beliefs involving the nature of the universe, and the condemnations of Aristotle's ideas in the thirteenth century led to new cosmologies, such as Nicholas of Cusa's unbounded universe. Nicholas Copernicus wrote much about a sun-centered universe but little about what lay beyond the sphere of fixed stars. Shortly after Copernicus, Thomas Digges, an English mathematician, thought that the stars were not affixed to a sphere but scattered throughout endless space. He confronted the riddle of darkness and answered it by proposing that the most distant stars, despite their great numbers, were too faint to be seen. The true nature of the riddle could not emerge, however, until new systems of astronomy were developed, particularly through the work of Galileo Galilei and Johannes Kepler. By using the telescope, Galileo made visible unseen stars that greatly outnumbered the stars observable with the naked eye. Kepler, an early Copernican who discovered the elliptical orbits of the planets, believed passionately in a finite universe. He argued that the large number of new stars discovered by Galileo proved that the fixed stars must be less bright than the Sun, otherwise the night sky would be more luminous than the Sun. Kepler therefore believed that the sky was dark at night because the universe simply contained too few stars to cover the whole sky.

In the second part, Harrison shows how the development of the great systems of modern science, particularly the Cartesian and Newtonian, revealed new solutions to the age-old riddle. In René Descartes' system, space extended in all directions to indefinite distances, and continuous matter under the aegis of mechanical laws pervaded the whole of space. The Cartesian system rejected the existence of space by itself along with the atomicity of matter, but it accepted the unlimited extent of space. Sir Isaac Newton rejected an unlimited expanse of stars, but he accepted space by itself (the vacuum) and the atomicity of matter. Although he began by believing in a finite cosmos, he accepted, later in his career, an infinite, star-filled universe. The reason for this belief derived from his theory of gravity: If stars formed a finite system, then they would all be attracted into the middle of the universe. Since that is obviously not the case, the stars must be uniformly distributed throughout infinite space.

Edmond Halley, Newton's friend, explained the darkness of the night sky by the great decrease in apparent luminosity of the stars with distance, but his argument lacked clarity and accuracy. For example, he assumed correctly that rays from distant stars are much too weak to be seen on the Earth, but he assumed incorrectly that the same is true of the combination of rays from large numbers of stars.

A way out of this confusion was found by a young Swiss astronomer, Jean-Philippe Loys de Chéseaux. In 1744, he explained that starlight is slowly absorbed while traveling across the immense distances of interstellar space and that the cumulative effect of this loss of light during the long journey is sufficient to account for the dark night sky. Wilhelm Olbers built on Chéseaux's work in the nineteenth century. Olbers, who practiced medicine by day and astronomy by night, pointed out in 1826 that the reason the night sky is dark is that dust obscures most of the light. His proposal that interstellar space is permeated with a thin fog that absorbs the light from distant stars was the same as that already given by Chéseaux some eighty years before, and so the paradox, because of Olbers' failure to acknowledge Chéseaux's work, has unjustly become known as Olbers' paradox.

During the nineteenth century, huge telescopes operated by such astronomers as William and John Herschel revealed objects called "nebulae" that some interpreted as interstellar gases and others as island universes composed of myriad stars. John Herschel was convinced that this galaxy, the Milky Way, was all-encompassing. Olbers did not accept Herschel's single-galaxy idea but instead believed in a universe populated with many galaxies. The long controversy over extragalactic nebulae finally ended in 1924, when Edwin Hubble of the Mount Wilson Observatory proved that the Andromeda Nebula consisted of individual stars. He was even able to determine the distance of the stars and thus establish that this spiral nebula is indeed a stellar system far distant from the Milky Way galaxy.

The third section of Harrison's book develops the implications for the darkness-at-night puzzle of the new hierarchical picture of the universe that surfaced in the nineteenth century and for a time was energetically championed in the twentieth century. This hierarchy consisted of stars grouped into clusters, clusters into galaxies, galaxies into clusters of galaxies, and so forth. By cleverly clumping stars together and surrounding these clumps with vast expanses of empty space, an astronomer could explain the dark-sky problem. Nevertheless, there were difficulties with the hierarchy solution: It required that clustering occur on progressively larger scales, escalating to infinity in an endless universe. Hierarchy had a further drawback: It ignored the speed of light and assumed that all parts of the universe, no matter how remote, were immediately connected with the observer. A solution to these difficulties was available in the nineteenth century, if astronomers only knew where to look. The problem was that most astronomers did not read poetry.

In 1848, the year before he died, Edgar Allan Poe published *Eureka,* a prose poem, in which he visualized a universe rhythmically expanding and collapsing. The work was too metaphysical for scientists, but it did contain an interesting contribution to cosmology, for just twenty-five years after Olbers wrote his paper on the riddle of darkness, Poe proposed the correct solution. He knew that light rays, though unimaginably fast, traveled at a finite speed. He also recognized that the stars, though incredibly long-lived, shone for a finite time. Poe therefore proposed that the light from the most distant stars, those whose cumulative power was needed to turn the dark night brilliant, had not yet had time to make the journey to Earth.

Poe had solved the problem qualitatively, but what was needed was a rigorous quantitative solution. The man who provided this was William Thomson, later Lord Kelvin, who spent most of his career at Glasgow University. Thomson proved mathematically that, because of the finiteness of light's speed and because of the finite lives of stars, only a very small proportion of all the starlight in the universe would be reaching the Earth at any one instant. Hence the sky is dark at night.

Although Lord Kelvin's solution is essentially correct, it did not mean the end of the story, for he solved the riddle for a universe that would later be shown not to exist, that is, a universe filled with an etheric medium. In the nineteenth century, scientists believed that light could not propagate without a medium. Some even contended that, far away from this galaxy, the etheric medium might vanish, leaving space as an etherless void incapable of transmitting light. In the twentieth century, Albert Einstein's theory of special relativity doomed this marvelous substance, the ether. Furthermore, Einstein's theory of general relativity showed that gravity is the consequence of the curvature of four-dimensional space-time. These new ideas had implications for the nature of the universe. Willem de Sitter, a Dutch astronomer, discussed these implications for a spherically closed universe, and this discussion created complications for the darkness riddle. Other astronomers suggested that a finite, unbounded universe, enclosed within spherical space and containing a finite number of stars, solved the darkness riddle. Harrison, on the other hand, points out that the curvature of space cannot solve the riddle of cosmic darkness. The random gravitational fields of stars continually deflect rays of light, and so light rays traveling around the universe tend to spread out.

When the expansion of the universe was discovered in 1929, this expansion in turn was put forward as a solution to Olbers' paradox. The expansion shifts the wavelength of light coming from distant stars into the invisible frequencies of the infrared. When the British cosmologists Hermann Bondi and Thomas Gold proposed their steady-state theory of the expanding universe and the continuous creation of matter, it stimulated renewed interest in the darkness-at-night riddle. Because the steadystate universe expands, starlight from distant galaxies arrives at the Earth feeble and red, and the feeblest starlight from the farthest galaxies is shifted into invisibility. When Bondi first proposed this solution, valid in the steady-state theory of continuous expansion, it seemed to many scientists sufficiently plausible to be accepted as a general solution, even for universes of finite age, such as the now-accepted "big-bang" universe. Nevertheless, Harrison criticizes Bondi's theory. Harrison thinks that the sky is dark at night because of missing stars, not because of missing starlight. He favors an energy solution to the paradox, that is, there is not enough energy in the universe to create a bright starlit sky. He agrees with Poe and Lord Kelvin that the stars needed to cover the sky cannot be seen because their light has yet to reach the Earth. There was a time, near the beginning of the universe, when all really was brilliant light, but this light is now gone, cooled by cosmic expansion and transformed into an infrared gloom invisible to the naked eye.

Robert J. Paradowski

Sources for Further Study

Booklist. LXXIV, October 1, 1987, p. 194.
Choice. XXV, February, 1988, p. 928.
Kirkus Reviews. LV, August 15, 1987, p. 1211.
The New York Times Book Review. XCII, September 27, 1987, p. 32.
The New Yorker. LXIII, January 25, 1988, p. 112.
The Sciences. XXVIII, January/February, 1988, p. 57.

DAVID BOMBERG

Author: Richard Cork (1947-   )
Publisher: Yale University Press (New Haven, Connecticut). Illustrated. 344 pp.
   $85.00
Type of work: Biography and art history
Time: 1900-1957
Locale: England, Palestine, and Spain

   A study of the life and work of one of Great Britain's most important but neglected modern painters

   Principal personages:
      DAVID BOMBERG, a near-forgotten British artist whose landscapes are among the century's finest
      LILIAN BOMBERG, his widow, who championed his work
      ISAAC ROSENBERG, his friend, a fellow artist who achieved greatness as a poet in the trenches of World War I
      WYNDHAM LEWIS, the founder of *Blast* and a prominent culture critic of the 1930's and 1940's
      HERBERT READ, an important twentieth century critic of arts and letters

   David Bomberg belongs to that haunting circle of artists who spend their lives in relative obscurity but rise after death to greatness and belated fame. One thinks of Amedeo Modigliani and Vincent Van Gogh. Like these two masters of modern art, Bomberg was a man of passionate dedication and tortured temperament. Hardened by anti-Semitism and Edwardian snobbery, Bomberg became fiercely self-reliant and often offended those who might have helped him. Such behavior represented the self-destructive side of the same quality that finally proved the secret of his power—a courageous integrity.
   Bomberg's early experiments in Cubo-Futurist composition attracted the attention of Wyndham Lewis, the enigmatic and controversial founder of the famous Vorticist journal *Blast: The Review of the Great English Vortex*, which identified with Filippo Marinetti's radical doctrine of Futurism and its glorification of machines and technology. In 1914, Lewis thought Bomberg, who was only age twenty-four at the time, one of the most vigorous new forces in English art. Richard Cork speculates that Bomberg could have been introduced to Ezra Pound in 1913 by either Lewis or sculptor Jacob Epstein. A bold experimental painting by Bomberg entitled *Ju-Jitsu* depicts what looks like a disintegrating chessboard, but in fact, it records with kaleidoscopic intensity a geometrical transformation of squares into triangles. The painting could well have inspired Pound's poem "Dogmatic Statement on the Game and Play of Chess": "This board is alive with light/ These pieces are living in form,/ Their moves break and reform the pattern."
   Lewis offered to include Bomberg's work in *Blast* in July, 1914, but

Bomberg hesitated. He feared domination by Lewis. In this resistance of patronage, he recalls William Blake, an artist whose obscure origins and defiant independence provided an important model. Like Blake, Bomberg had to remain true to his own "system" to avoid enslavement by another man's ideas.

Bomberg's reluctance to side with Vorticism and its celebration of machines and abstract design had much to do with his love of man and nature, a love that resisted the growing abstractionism of modern art. Although he felt constrained by representational conventions, Bomberg never lost his sense of the representational foundation or referent. When T. E. Hulme, another important supporter of Bomberg's pre-World War I experiments, described a drawing of his as being uninterested in "figurative significance" (the phrase is Richard Cork's), he was going too far. It is true that Bomberg was persuaded by Hulme's insistence that a dedication to geometric line was essential in order to overcome the tendency toward impressionistic vagueness characteristic of the time. Nevertheless, although the legs in the painting Hulme admired look like cylinders, Bomberg was primarily interested in dramatizing human movement in abstract forms; he was not, as Hulme suggested, interested in completely deserting literal representation.

Why was Bomberg too committed to representation to forge ahead with abstraction and take his place with the Cubists and their followers, who were about to change the face of modern art? The answer is complex, but a look at Bomberg's beginnings in the East End of London provides some clues. Cork writes that Bomberg belonged to a talented group of writers and painters who called themselves the Whitechapel Boys. Between 1900 and 1914, there was a cultural explosion in the East End. In the midst of poverty and a shabby urban congestion only a shade away from slum life, the first English-born generations of Jewish immigrants from Russia and Poland were beginning to make their mark in professional schools and literary and artistic circles.

A close friend of Bomberg at the Slade School of Fine Art was Isaac Rosenberg, the brilliant poet and painter who was encouraged by Edward Marsh, Winston Churchill's secretary. Rosenberg was killed in the trenches in 1918 just as his poetry, shocked into maturity by the horrors of the war, showed signs of the genius posterity has fully recognized. Rosenberg had turned to poetry after important efforts in painting and drawing. In the summer of 1914, he had secured a job teaching painting in South Africa and gave there an important lecture on modern art. Like Hulme, Rosenberg extolled the importance of line but noted that modern English painting was dominated by Blake's drawing, which for all of its power and genius was essentially crude. As a result, English painting, said Rosenberg, was cut off from the magisterial authority of the Italian line, most powerfully exemplified in the drawings of Leonardo da Vinci. Rosenberg concluded his address with a critical remark about his friend and fellow painter David Bomberg, who "has crude power of a too calculated violence—and is mechanical, but undoubtedly interesting." Rosenberg was Bomberg's conscience; the poet represented the deeply ethical and life-revering sentiment at the heart of Jewish consciousness that held Bomberg back from losing himself in abstractions.

Before he was killed, Rosenberg wrote several letters to a mutual friend asking for news of Bomberg. The painter-turned-poet sensed that his friend would suffer the evils of the war with no less a protesting passion than his own. He was right. Bomberg enlisted in the Royal Engineers in November, 1915. It is significant that he did this shortly after agreeing after all to exhibit his work in a Vorticist show and after visiting wartime Paris with Alice Mayes, his future wife. The visit rekindled his admiration of and sense of solidarity with French abstractionism or near-abstractionism in Pablo Picasso, Georges Braque, and Fernand Léger. The war was to change all this utterly. The ceaseless pounding and callous bombardment at the front disillusioned whatever faith he still had in the glories of Marinetti's Machine Age. After Hulme was blown to pieces by a huge shell at Nieuport, Bomberg despaired and shot himself in the foot as an act of protest. To make sure that no one might accuse him of cowardice or shirking, he insisted on confessing to his intentions and risked severe punishment. Refusing to call the incident an accident, even after his adjutant suggested that he do so, Bomberg was treated leniently. Nevertheless, after recovering, he was given the dangerous assignment of running messages under fire. Eventually, he landed a position in the drawing office, but an anti-Semitic brigadier refused to trust him with section mapping, and he was sent back to the trenches.

Cork introduces an ink drawing from this period, *Figures Helping a Wounded Soldier*, which powerfully reflects Bomberg's conception of the interrelationship of representation and abstraction. Two orderlies hover over the inert body of a soldier close to death. Although the whole drawing consists simply of a frenzy of intersecting lines, there is no mistaking its representational intention. The blurred motion conveyed by the sketchy lines is pregnant with the pathos of the orderlies' attempts to save the dying man, who is represented by little more than a bodiless profile with eyelids closed.

Like Léger, who went through an even more sweeping conversion from abstraction to representation than Bomberg after the war, Bomberg found new inspiration in the longings of the common people. In Bomberg's case, this entailed a look at Palestine. He accepted a commission from the Zionists to paint the new settlements that were changing an ancient wasteland into a modern homeland for the Jewish people. What Bomberg discovered, however, was not ideology but landscape. This was the turning point of his life in art. Shortly before leaving for Palestine, he declined the opportunity to go to the Netherlands and participate in further Cubist experiments: "I had found I could more surely develop on the lines of Cézanne's rediscovery that the world was round and there was a way out through the sunlight— this I have followed and matured in ever since."

The rest is history—and sadness. After discovering the sun in Palestine, as Paul Cézanne and Van Gogh had discovered it in Provence years before, Bomberg went on to paint English and Spanish landscapes that are now recognized as his masterpieces and among the best landscapes of twentieth century art. After painting Jerusalem in the 1920's with what seemed, at first, a Pre-Raphaelite precision, he went on later in life to paint the sun-drenched landscapes of Toledo, Cuenca, and Ronda with a free and impassioned brush that reminds one more of Joseph Turner than Blake. Landscape had largely replaced portraiture, but his postwar commitment to a more "figurative style" never wavered. His landscapes were alive with the vision and fervor of the Jewish prophets.

That is the history, but the sadness lies in the neglect Bomberg's work suffered. He earned the reputation of a legendary teacher and his students achieved acclaim, but Bomberg himself was ignored by exhibitions and passed over during World War II by military art commissions. Critics such as Herbert Read forgot their enthusiasm about his work during and immediately after World War I and ignored him entirely in their retrospective histories. His second wife, Lillian, fought to save his reputation after he died. With her help, Cork has produced a magnificent volume filled with Bomberg's work. Many important paintings and drawings are presented here for the first time. Cork's commentary is informative, but there is no doubt that the pictures themselves constitute the book's greatest value. Here is a giant who walked among us unseen.

Peter A. Brier

Sources for Further Study

Choice. XXIV, July, 1987, p. 1684.
Listener. CXVII, April 16, 1987, p. 37.
London Review of Books. IX, March 5, 1987, p. 8.
New Statesman. CXIII, March 27, 1987, p. 30.
The Observer. February 8, 1987, p. 28.
Publishers Weekly. CCXXXI, April 3, 1987, p. 62.
The Times Literary Supplement. February 6, 1987, p. 133.

THE DAY OF JUDGMENT

Author: Salvatore Satta (1902-1975)
First published: Il giorno del giudizio, 1979
Translated from the Italian by Patrick Creagh
Publisher: Farrar, Straus and Giroux (New York). 300 pp. $19.95
Type of work: Novel
Time: Late nineteenth century and early twentieth century
Locale: Nuoro and its environs, Sardinia, Italy

An imaginative reconstruction of life in the author's hometown, punctuated by arresting and moving meditations on love, work, and death

> *Principal characters:*
> DON SEBASTIANO SANNA, the protagonist, a notary and landowner
> DONNA VINCENZA, his wife
> LUDOVICO, one of their seven sons
> MANCA, a teacher
> DON RICCIOTTI BELLISAI, a teacher and politician who is an enemy of Don Sebastiano

The Day of Judgment is a remarkable work in several respects. The first of these may well be the very fact of the novel's existence. The manuscript was found among the author's effects after his death, a hitherto unsuspected work that was written during the last thirty years of his life. Its presence, not to mention its distinction, was all the more surprising since its author, Salvatore Satta, was not a literary man. On the contrary, he had earned an illustrious reputation for himself as a jurist, in particular for the work he carried out reconstructing his country's penal code after the Mussolini era and World War II. As is sometimes the case in such literary discoveries, the novel is incomplete, and in this translation it comes without evidence of the author's further intentions with regard to a work which, judging by this segment of it, was perhaps unfinishable. As various reviewers have pointed out, its history strongly resembles that of another long-lost important Italian novel, Giuseppe di Lampedusa's *The Leopard*, set amid the generation immediately preceding that dealt with in *The Day of Judgment*. *The Leopard* also came to light posthumously, and was also greeted rapturously: It was published in Italy in 1958.

Another remarkable feature of the work is its setting, the author's native town of Nuoro in Sardinia. Some of the novel's landscape will perhaps be recognized by readers familiar with D. H. Lawrence's travel book, *Sea and Sardinia*. Indeed, Lawrence's work may be used as an introduction to *The Day of Judgment*, particularly since Lawrence visited Sardinia during the period covered by Satta's novel. Yet the Lawrence book, can only perform a scene-setting function. The strangeness of Sardinian life, and within that (as Satta continually emphasizes), the strangeness of life in and around Nuoro, is simply not amenable to depiction by an outsider. In *The Day of Judgment*, this strangeness is evident in the frequent, though never confusing, use of the local dialect, such as in some of the lower-class characters' names, and also in various references to local cuisine, superstitions, costumes, and songs. Such references, together with a certain fondness on the author's part for terms such as "mystery" and "dream," create a superb sense of Nuorese reality, even while Satta insists on the nullity of it all.

The setting's strangeness is not, however, simply a matter of picturesque detail, but also extends to features which have a more general significance. Nuoro is isolated in almost every conceivable way. Before the days of mass communications (the novel is set at the turn of the twentieth century, in the years leading up to Benito Mussolini's ascent to power), the town was geographically isolated. This condition evidently bred a marked lack of curiosity among the inhabitants concerning the world at large. Thus, Nuoro (and presumably Sardinia in general) was a historical backwater. Indeed, although not even Nuoro could avoid involvement in World War I, the author does manage to tell his story, or rather to paint what he calls his "fresco," without incorporating a single date.

Nuoro's isolation from the world created isolation within itself, or so it seems. The town's sense of community is stilted and constrained by virtually feudal connections of blood and classifications of rank. Moreover, in the realm of personal relations there is little openness and generosity. Public institutions such as the school system and the church are, perhaps predictably, useless for engendering wider awarenesses or opportunities for progress. The town feeds on its isolation, projects an aura of benightedness, seems paralyzed and static. *The Day of Judgment* produces effects of intense claustrophobia and a genuinely morose atmosphere of lives damaged irreparably by the stultifying consequences of living in such a place. It is not a novel to read for fun.

The Day of Judgment may not be a novel. For want of a better classification, however, it has been placed in that category. In some respects, it does conform to the conventions of fiction, such as in its employment of a protagonist, Don Sebastiano Sanna. He is the town's most distinguished notary (Nuoro being the kind of place that is filled with functionaries who earn a living shuffling meaningless pieces of paper). In certain respects, the book may be considered a fictional biography of Don Sebastiano and, through him, a depiction of a desolate place at an inert time.

Although Don Sebastiano happens to be a notary, his occupation is not particularly germane to the biographical perspective chosen by the author. Some detail of the protagonist's work enters into the narrative, but it is not crucial to the story. Instead, the narrative proceeds digressively to deal with his private life, his inner life, and his life as a landowner. Land is a constant in the world of Nuoro and its surrounding area. Although Satta is somewhat restrained as to the amount of attention which he devotes to Don Sebastiano's activities as a landlord, there is no denying the quality of the attention which he does give. Some of the best sustained passages in the book are devoted to the land: viniculture, the wonderful vista of oleanders, and the author's pleasure in the sensory delights of growing things. In addition, there is a bond between landlord and worker which is more durable and dependable than any other bond in the story; it is all the more authentic since the parties to it are hardly aware of it, accepting it as the natural order of things. This bond is exemplified in the various vital services performed by Don Sebastiano's bailiff, Ziu Poddanzu.

In contrast, Don Sebastiano's house in the town has been pretentiously designed and built so inexpertly as to seem grotesquely misshapen. The latter description also applies to the protagonist's relationship with his wife, Donna Vincenza, and their seven sons (two daughters died young). His marriage, in particular, crystallizes the unnatural and disinterested isolation which typifies the world of the novel. The fate of Donna Vincenza—the insidious onset of her immobilizing arthritis, the inevitable departure into the wider world of her beloved sons, her husband's paralyzingly authoritarian remoteness—is conveyed with great feeling. More obliquely, the lack of attachment between Don Sebastiano and his sons has the ultimate effect of nullifying them as personalities, since it denies them direction and encouragement. *The Day of Judgment*, insofar as it may be considered a novel of family life, must be the most silent one of its kind: It lacks dialogue to a virtually provocative degree.

Similarly, in its depiction of life in the wider society, the novel dwells on what characters jealously guard from each other and on their insufficiencies in dealing with one another. Again, the lack of dialogue is a clue, as is the impoverished language in which characters address one another in public. Only in moments of drama—which for the Nuorese arise at times of death and of the subsequent property entailments—do characters shake off their inarticulateness. Otherwise, in café life, for example, interaction occurs in terms of japes, maudlin songs, the conferring of nicknames, and other acts of idleness. In the abortive political campaign of Socialist Don Ricciotti, his audience does not understand his rhetoric, and he is disgraced by gossip. Neither school nor church can provide a basis for individuation such as distinctive powers of articulation, as the graphic portrait of Manca, the alcoholic court jester to Nuoro café-society, makes clear.

In some obvious respects, therefore, *The Day of Judgment* is a novel. It conforms to the genre by having a strong focus on family. It possesses an abundance of realistic, ethnographical, and quasi-anthropological detail. It conveys a sense, however imperfect, of time elapsing, and it portrays an individual in relation to society. Yet the term "novel" does not begin to do justice to the richness of the book's unifying preoccupation, which, as its title indicates, is with death. At the same time, however, the book's form handicaps it, preventing it from attaining its full potential as a novel.

Because *The Day of Judgment* is an unfinished work, criticizing its form may seem inappropriate. Throughout, however, the book seems to resist the conception of artistic form. This resistance can be seen in two basic areas. First, the novel's development is problematic. Rather than a straight-forward, chronologically based exposition of certain problems pertaining to the protagonist, which is what the novel traditionally offers, *The Day of Judgment* provides a series of set pieces—scenes, vignettes, exchanges, and developments through which a cross section of Don Sebastiano's life, and life in Nuoro, may be perceived. The descriptive term "fresco" is applied by Satta to his approach: the term "frieze" also comes to mind. Inevitably, questions of connections between chapters (which lead to questions about overall artistic objectives) are raised by the use of this method, particularly since within each set piece there are digressions of various kinds.

The second challenge to the claims to fictional status made by *The Day of Judgment* is provided by Satta in person, so to speak. From time to time— and again, without following the principle of repetition and development upon which the novel form depends—the author himself interrupts the narrative to reflect on his enterprise. Such a strategy is hardly unfamiliar to readers of contemporary fiction. The difference here is that it is difficult to construe Satta's appearances as strategy: If they were, then one would expect *The Day of Judgment* to be artistically more sophisticated in other respects. On the contrary, these interruptions have a certain naïvete about them, and, while never egregious, they reveal a basic indifference to artistic finesse—which suggests that they are the product of a mind which, for all its undoubted expository skill, is finally not the mind of an artist.

What Satta achieves by his interventions is a reminder that his aim is not to tell a story, or at least not to impart to his material the neatness and completeness of stories. His sense of finality is animated by less artificial concerns: The reason the author does not speak as an artist is that he desires to speak as a moralist. His treatment of the Nuoro of his past—its quality of life (or rather, its lack thereof), its deficiencies and vicissitudes, and the very fact that it sustained itself on its own hollowness—adds up to the author's own day of judgment. Toward the close of the book, Satta mentions the difficulty of continuing in the face of his own mortal illness. These asides make explicit his book's unifying theme, which is death. Seldom has there been a work which has so blatantly and so successfully lived in the shadow of death, not merely in its final sequences but throughout.

The author's remorseless awareness of this shadow's presence—that it is a shadow cast by the condition of Nuoro in those years, and that his formative years were spent under it—gives *The Day of Judgment* its somber majesty. The characters' lives are cast into bitter relief by the shadow of death: They all submit, in the author's imagination, to the grim democracy of the grave-yard. By virtue of this dimension, this brooding preoccupation with mortality and with Nuoro as the nullity which seemingly collaborates with it, *The Day of Judgment* becomes rather more than a mere novel and transforms itself into a different kind of text. The term for this alternative kind of text is "an anatomy," along the lines of Robert Burton's *Anatomy of Melancholy* (1621), or of the essays of Michel de Montaigne. To invoke such precedents for *The Day of Judgment*, however, is merely to emphasize its grandeur and to draw attention to its contemplative seriousness. To encounter the total commitment of an author's mind is rare. To discover a work which grows richer and more daring with each rereading is rarer. *The Day of Judgment* is a book to live with.

George O'Brien

Sources for Further Study

Kirkus Reviews. LV, July 1, 1987, p. 956.
New Statesman. CXIII, June 26, 1987, p. 30.
The New York Times Book Review. XCII, October 4, 1987, p. 13.
The New Yorker. LXIII, October 19, 1987, p. 115.
The Times Literary Supplement. August 28, 1987, p. 930.

THE DISCOVERY OF SLOWNESS

Author: Sten Nadolny (1942-   )
First published: Die Entdeckung der Langsamkeit, 1983
Translated from the German by Ralph Freedman
Publisher: Viking/Elisabeth Sifton Books (New York). 325 pp. $19.95
Type of work: Biographical novel
Time: 1796-1859
Locale: England, Lisbon, Copenhagen, Cape of Good Hope, Australia, Cape
Trafalgar, Northern Canada, Tasmania, and the Arctic Ocean

Using documentary sources, Nadolny re-creates the life and character of the nineteenth century English explorer Sir John Franklin

> *Principal characters:*
> SIR JOHN FRANKLIN, an English naval officer and explorer
> TOM BARKER, his boyhood antagonist
> SHERARD PHILIP LOUND, his boyhood friend
> MATTHEW FLINDERS, his uncle, a naval captain
> DR. ORME, his teacher, an amateur scientist
> ANDREW BURNABY, his teacher
> MARY ROSE, a prostitute, his first erotic attachment
> ELEANOR PORDEN, his first wife
> ELEANOR ANNE FRANKLIN, his only child
> JANE GRIFFIN, his second wife
> SOPHIA CRACROFT, his niece
> PETER MARK ROGET, an amateur scientist and inventor
> GEORGE BACK, a naval officer on his expeditions
> ROBERT HOOD, a member of the first of his overland expeditons

Three years before its original publication in German, Sten Nadolny's novel *The Discovery of Slowness* captured a major literary award given by the Austrian city of Klagenfurt, the Ingeborg Bachmann Prize for Literature. When the novel appeared on the market in 1983, the initial reviews seemed to bear out the confidence of the award jury that had reached its decision solely on the basis of a public reading of the fifth chapter. The novel's author, born into a family of writers, lives in Berlin and in addition to writing fiction has taught history and worked in film production. Both of these occupations have left a visible imprint on his literary work.

The creative exploitation of history in *The Discovery of Slowness* recalls the techniques of writers of the 1960's such as Peter Weiss and Rolf Hochhuth, who turned to documentary sources as a factual base to support their critical view of the recent German past. The reasons behind the turn to historical fact, however, change with the times. In his fictional re-creation of the life of the nineteenth century British naval officer and explorer John Franklin (1786-1847), Nadolny no longer uses history to produce sociopolitical commentary. "History is intercourse with greatness and duration," one of the minor characters remarks to Franklin. Nadolny's novel serves as the vehicle of this interchange and, as a quasi-historical document, "allows us to rise above time." The author has, moreover, written a work that bears closer resemblance to the German *Bildungsroman* than to an adventure novel, to which his sources lend such a wealth of material. The documentary evidence of Franklin's various expeditions and journeys to Australia and into the frigid land- and seascapes above the Arctic Circle provide the mere structure for the central focus of the novel, the depiction of an inner development of character. In an author's note appended to the work, Nadolny lists the substantial historical sources to which he is indebted for many details of characterization, yet admits that the historical Franklin must have differed in many ways from his fictional creation.

The story of John Franklin that Nadolny tells begins in the small village in rural England where he spends his childhood years, long before becoming the celebrated explorer and chronicler of two land expeditions in search of the Northwest Passage. As a boy, Franklin's sluggish temperament puts him at a natural disadvantage in the fast-moving games of his companions. To participate at all he seeks out roles in which he can remain stationary, often amazing the others by his ability to stand motionless for long periods of time. The boys he admires most, however, taunt and torment him because of his inability to move, respond, and speak at a normal speed. Much of the time he spends concocting ingenious methods to accelerate his phlegmatic disposition, fantasizing about new friendships with the quickest boys or, at the depths of his depression, giving in to the soothingly regressive desire "to slow down until he died."

An instinct for survival, however, draws him one day the few miles across the fields from his village to the sea, which seems to hold out the promise of an existence free of the pressures of time that make his life so miserable on land. Although Franklin ultimately gains the highest honors that a seafaring nation can bestow on a remarkable career, he achieves them not because conditions at sea are tolerant of his slowness, but because he successfully adapts his natural disposition to these conditions. It is the process of maturation and adjustment through which he learns to compensate for his slowness and to make the best use of it that lies at the center of Nadolny's novel. As a man, Franklin no longer rejects time as he had in his boyhood, but finds his proper relationship to its inevitable flow. In this fictionalized account, the inner voyage and the discovery of his unique tempo for living take precedence over Franklin's voyages and discoveries around the globe.

For a man of Franklin's temperament, sudden change brings confusion, whether on the small scale of a naval battle's duration or on the larger ones measuring the periods of his absences from London. While he is away in corners of the world untouched by the rhythms of the West, changes in England take place at the rapidly increasing rate of the industrial revolution. At every return, new sights and sounds overwhelm his senses, new pressures seem to be at work behind the compulsive haste of his countrymen. Following his first land expedition into the northern territories of Canada, he remarks that "reaching for one's watch chain had become a more frequent move than reaching for one's hat." Franklin's slow rhythm becomes increasingly out of synchronization with the accelerating tempo of his western contemporaries, yet he takes a passionate interest in various gadgets and inventions, holding discussions with men at work on ideas that foreshadow modern calculating machines and motion pictures.

Both in his associations with other contemporary thinkers and in his own work, Franklin champions progressive ideas in education as well as in political and social reform. As governor of the British penal colony Van Diemen's Land (Tasmania), he attempts to improve the lot of the prisoners sent to the island as well as that of the aborigines who had been driven off their land to make room for white settlers. Under difficult circumstances, he liberalizes and democratizes a previously autocratic legislative council. He loses any hint of the reactionary or anachronistic and becomes exemplary in his slowness, the very quality that sets him apart from the hurried life rhythms of his countrymen. For Nadolny, whose first novel *Netzkarte* (1981) argues the benefits that slowness might bring to his own society, the merits of Franklin's pace should be as self-evident to his readers as they prove to be within the fictional setting of nineteenth century England.

Impatient and suspicious of him in the beginning, each new crew learns to respect Franklin for his thoroughness and tenacity in finding solutions to problems and for his prodigious memory. To the questions of subordinates and superiors alike, he may reply hours after they are originally posed, but his answers are invariably accurate and often save lives. Realizing that for the common good he must impose his own speed on those under his command, he gradually gains the courage to request from impatient crew members that statements be repeated which are not immediately intelligible to him. Even as an adolescent on board a warship shortly before the Battle of Trafalgar, his naturally deliberate rate of comprehension seems to be the basis of a higher wisdom, since it resists the enthusiasm for battle and the willingness for self-sacrifice that infect his comrades.

Much later in life, his patient, unhurried observation of the behavior of the aborigines in Australia and the Eskimos in North America helps bridge the mutual incomprehensibility of cross-cultural encounters. His slowness enhances his capacity for empathy with the native populations and insulates him against the ethnocentrism that grips his European countrymen. The Indians of Northern Canada remark on his "wealth of time," a sign of great distinction and even immortality to a people unacquainted with the quicker rhythms of an industrial society. When a prominent citizen of this society congratulates him after his first overland expedition and graciously informs him that his slowness must surely be an illusion, Franklin rejects at least silently the intended compliment. As he matures, he learns to value above all else what in the eyes of others is a handicap. Late in his career, he begins to make plans for passing on his insights. He places the discovery about himself at the core of an educational philosophy which, however, he is never able to realize in practice: "The pupils must learn how to discover things. Above all, their own way of seeing and their speed, each for himself."

At certain points in the novel—particularly conspicuous at the beginnings of chapters 8 and 10—Nadolny's narration breaks with the historical chronology, injects the reader at a forward point on the time line, and only belatedly fills in the intervening actions and events necessary to understand the sequence. This acceleration of time leaves a gap to be filled in by the reader, who initially finds himself in a state of perplexity parallel to the confusion of the main figure when events outrun his comprehension. Nadolny turns the reader into a participant observer; the reading process itself duplicates Franklin's relationship to the flow of time. At other points the author limits the details of a fast-moving scene to those which Franklin himself might perceive and passes over those which he would likely miss, involving the reader directly in his mode of perception. Nadolny employs this technique particularly effectively in a scene on board ship during the Battle of Copenhagen, when Franklin becomes involved in a life-and-death struggle with an enemy sailor without knowing how he finally defeats his foe. An omniscient perspective would have given a richer external narrative of the struggle, but the limited view tells the reader more about Franklin's own experience of the episode.

In May, 1845, at the age of sixty, the historical Franklin set out on his final exploratory voyage of the Arctic region in command of two ships and a crew of 138 officers and men. The expedition was last sighted north of Baffin Island by a whaling ship in July of the same year. When two years later no further word had been received in England about the fate of the expedition, a search was begun that was to remain largely unsuccessful until 1857. A mission financed by Franklin's second wife in that year found enough physical evidence among the Eskimos of the region and a written account of the expedition through spring, 1848, to be able to reconstruct the tragic events that finally took the lives of the entire crew. Franklin himself had died on June 11, 1847. Despite its potential for fictional amplification, Nadolny abridges this entire episode in the two brief last chapters of his novel. By his restraint and the foreshortening of the twelve-year period, the author allows his fictional figure to recede abruptly from the view of the reader, as did his model in real life from the view of his contemporaries. In both life and fiction, a paucity of information about these years creates an impenetrable sense of mystery about a man who may have lagged behind the accelerating tempo of his age, yet paradoxically serves as an exemplary figure for an electronic age that shows even less patience for slowness.

Francis Michael Sharp

Sources for Further Study

Booklist. LXXXIV, October 15, 1987, p. 362.
Kirkus Reviews. LV, September 15, 1987, p. 1345.
Library Journal. CXII, September 15, 1987, p. 96.
Los Angeles Times. October 14, 1987, V, p. 6.
The New Republic. CXCVII, December 7, 1987, p. 39.
The New York Times Book Review. XCII, December 20, 1987, p. 15.
Publishers Weekly. CCXXXII, August 21, 1987, p. 56.

DOROTHY DAY
A Radical Devotion

Author: Robert Coles (1929-   )
Publisher: Addison-Wesley Publishing Co./A Merloyd Lawrence Book (Reading, Massachusetts). 182 pp. $17.95
Type of work: Biography

A profile of Dorothy Day, the Catholic activist who devoted her life to God and the American poor and working classes

Robert Coles is famous for his listening. Reading any of his books of psychiatric research, one is amazed at the harvest of voices Coles takes from people on the edge, in one sense or another. Children in slums, Eskimos, migrant workers, the aged, wealthy but troubled children—what they say, Coles has always found to be revealing and important. As a psychiatrist, Coles's presence, as projected in his books, is that of empathizer, seeker, and, in its comprehensive spiritual sense, lover. He is rich in respect for the people he comes to visit. He approaches them as a learner and as someone always ready to admit ignorance and receive instruction. His trademark as a psychiatrist is the constant reminder that theories about why people do what they do are never conclusive. Life evades theory.

In his work, Coles is ever conscious of the fact that he is a stranger to those he meets and questions. From the privileged world of intellectual culture, he descends into one place after another where intellect is present but not institutionalized. This intellect, and Coles would say, soul, is directed toward survival. The books which result from these visitations speak admiringly of the power distressed people have to live their lives, and Coles's success as a witness to this power rests on his ability to retain, in his writings, the actual voices he has heard.

Dorothy Day, cofounder of *The Catholic Worker* daily newspaper and hospitality houses, was an acquaintance of and inspiration for Robert Coles while he was attending medical school in New York early in the 1950's. He worked as a volunteer in her hospices during that time and developed a friendship with Day which remained close until her death in 1980. Over those more than thirty-five years he recorded fifty hours of their conversations and filled notebooks with more. *Dorothy Day* is another product of his listening. His subject is someone more like himself intellectually and culturally than those he usually interviews, a journalist and thinker who, for Coles, had still to be reached through a descent of the kind earlier noted. The young Robert Coles appeared for his first visit at a hospitality house and observed Dorothy Day sitting at a table speaking to a drunk, one of the hopeless her ministry was designed to serve. The impatient young man was noticed at last and Day asked if he wanted to speak "with one of us?" Day's proposing her equality with the drunk made an impression: "*One of us*: with those three words she had cut through layers of self-importance, a lifetime of bourgeois privilege, and scraped the hard bone of pride: 'Vanity of vanities; all is vanity.'" In Day, Coles met a woman for whom the descent was a permanent fact—everyday contact with the oppressed from the early days of the Depression until her death fifty years later.

Written for the Radcliffe Biography Series, *Dorothy Day* is not a conventional biography but rather, as Coles says in the preface, something to give "readers the benefit of her distinct, compelling point of view." The major share of the text is long quotations from Day responding to a line of questions about her life—her early pre-Catholic days as a journalist and activist in 1920's New York, her common-law marriage and the birth of her daughter, her conversion, and her part in the formation of the Catholic Workers movement. The book is a dialogue. Coles preserves the nuances of their shared company over those thirty years—the incessant tea drinking, Day's occasional silences, and his own feelings as a young psychiatrist attending to an older person for whom he feels admiration as well as no small share of psychiatric curiosity. While sharing her temperamental inclinations and understanding her vision for the poor, Coles presses for clarification when he cannot understand the radicalness of her position, such as her lifelong celibacy since the conversion, and especially the turn to celibacy while still a young and attractive woman. The pleasure of the book is in Coles's admitting fear at bringing up the topic. He is no Barbara Walters, out to savage another interviewee, and his sensitivity is rewarded by searching answers: "I wanted to die in order to live," and "I loved [God], in other words, and like all women in love, I wanted to be united to my love."

Coles's first chapter dispenses necessary biographical data. Though a young and beautiful intellectual involved in the social scene and with aspirations for a career as a novelist, Day felt a demand to look at other people each day of her life and ask: "Could I live that way?" She came as close to others as she could, at first through a political activism which landed her in jail and earned for her the label "whore" for affiliation with the Industrial Workers of the World (IWW), and through her ongoing satisfaction of the urge to be in close contact with anyone she met: "Dorothy Day was constantly noticing people, constantly ready to engage with them and let them become . . . part of her life." Late in the 1920's, wanting to settle down, living with Forster Batterham, she gave birth to a girl, Tamar, who became the occasion for the common-law marriage to end. Batterham, a biologist, anarchist, and atheist, resisted his wife's widening quest for spiritual meaning. Day's conversion to Catholicism ensued. Batterham believed that she needed the attentions of a psychiatrist, since she was making a bond with the invisible, contentless proposals of religion.

Day makes it clear to Coles that the split with Batterham, the man she loved, even craved, was a separation caused by her sense that even their unsurpassable love was insufficient as the basis for a life. The church offered a relationship with the eternal. Day's explanation was unconvincing to other friends, as well, and her sanity became an issue.

Coles, who studied the motivations of young political activists fighting for black freedom in the 1960's, knows as well as anyone can the psychological motions which can lead a young person to dedicate his life to a "greater cause" than mundane existence and domestic happiness. Day denies that her conversion and subsequent founding of the Catholic Worker movement was simply a substitution of something more heroic for conventional happiness with a man. She makes it clear that her idealism was always part of her nature and was based on what she calls her lifelong curiosity about life and how people manage to live. Coles terms her motivation "inquiring idealism," to emphasize the element of curiosity which is seemingly an odd rationale for taking up the cause of the poor. Day calls this urge to know and involve herself with others an inspiration, planted within her by God. Yet it had to be founded in conversion. Young radicals without God can be terrific hypocrites, she says, remembering how things were before the conversion in her activist circles: "A lot of the time we'd say these beautiful things about justice and fairness and equality, but we weren't so nice to each other." Spiritual transformation was the basis for the succeeding decades of devotion to the poor.

In back to back chapters, "Conversion" and "The Church Obeyed and Challenged," Coles presents the two conflicts Day faced when her life changed. Entering the church, she alienated her radical friends who thought that the conversion signified mental illness. "After I became a Catholic I began little by little to lose track of my friends. Being a Catholic, I discovered, put a barrier between me and others; however slight, it was always felt." Day entered into a period she called "the long loneliness," which is also the title she gave to the book she wrote on her new life with God. The loneliness was both distance from her former society and a distance from the society she had entered—the Church. Her friends were dubious because entering the Church was joining to the enemy position. The Catholic Church was not known for humanitarianism. It was not waiting for communists and socialists to fill the pews. It was not a generous place, but was notorious for taking from the poor and building for the rich. Yet something, or Someone, called her to the Church and she went, "poor, chaste, and obedient." She took with her, however, all the political sensitivity of her radicalism. She looked through the history of the Church's hypocrisy back to the first hypocrite, Peter, who was the founder of an institution which has made plenty of trouble for people through the centuries. With Peter the denier as its foundation, the Church was the best that God could do for reclaiming humanity. "Jesus compared the Church to a net cast into the sea and hauled in, filled with fishes, both good and bad. 'Including,' one of my non-Catholic friends used to say, 'some blowfish and quite a few sharks.'"

Coles focuses at length on the loneliness and alienation which characterized Day's life, but he devotes his final chapter to her "spiritual kin," writers
secular and sacred, who she read all of her life for inspiration. Like Coles
himself, who works face to face with troubled people in crisis but also writes
books on the likes of William Carlos Williams, Walker Percy, and Flannery
O'Connor, Day was always alert to the two domains—the real world and
the imaginative, intellectual response to the real world in literary creations.
Typically, she was closest to those writers who wrote about the poor—
Ignazio Silone, Charles Dickens, George Orwell, Leo Tolstoy, Fyodor Dos-
toevski, and Anton Chekhov. Yet, as Coles leads her to admit, the company
she sought was not the writer or intellectual but the poor working-class person whose presence the great writers sustained visions of in books. When
she wrote her innumerable articles, she tells Coles, the audience she was
addressing was always the "factory workers and farmers" to whose existence
it was her destiny to attend. Thus, Day was not really lonely, since the family of the poor was always at her doorstep and eating the food she provided.
Poverty and religion were inseparable. She saw the Church's failure to care
for its greatest treasure, the poor worker, in whose person she believed she
could daily meet Christ. She meant to have real intimacy with her brothers
and sisters, a "companionship," which Coles points out literally means "the
sharing of bread." The writers she admired she knew to be looking for the
same person—God—she was seeking, and the company of the poor gave
the nearest approximation.

Robert Coles's portrait of Dorothy Day is the result of such close
companionship. Years of talking, letter-writing, and praying for the life of
the other, are now arranged into a book which shows that Dorothy Day
knew her family instinctively. She did not need to marry and rear children.
Her family was there immediately, numberless, reaching out for food, and
desperate beyond words. Robert Coles, though a father and husband in
fact, will similarly be remembered. He awaits his listener and biographer.

Bruce Wiebe

Sources for Further Study

Booklist. LXXXIII, June 1, 1987, p. 1476.
The Christian Century. CV, January 6, 1988, p. 28.
Library Journal. CXII, July, 1987, p. 72.
The New Republic. CXCVII, August 31, 1987, p. 9.
The New York Times Book Review. XCII, September 6, 1987, p. 10.
Publishers Weekly. CCXXXI, May 1, 1987, p. 58.

THE ELIZABETH STORIES

Author: Isabel Huggan (1943-   )
First published: The Elizabeth Stories, 1984, in Canada
Publisher: Viking (New York). 184 pp. $15.95
Type of work: Short stories
Time: 1946-1970
Locale: Southwestern Ontario, Canada

Eight connected stories, tracing the life of Elizabeth Kessler from childhood through high school

   Principal characters:
   ELIZABETH KESSLER, the protagonist and narrator
   FRANK KESSLER, her father, a banker, later a hardware distributor
   MAVIS KESSLER, her mother, a housewife

Although Isabel Huggan's *The Elizabeth Stories* was published in Canada in 1984, it has just been released in the United States. Critics and reviewers have welcomed this collection of frank, intimate stories; indeed, there is much to praise in the author's first published volume. The eight stories here range widely in length and structure, but all center on the author's alter ego, Elizabeth Kessler. Like most protagonists of the *Bildungsroman*, Elizabeth is sensitive and misunderstood by adults in general and by her parents in particular, but unlike many others, she is often an unlikable, even nasty child. Not until midway through high school, when she blossoms on the basketball court and begins to like herself, does she become a fully sympathetic character. Herein lies one of the clues to the stories and perhaps the central message of the book.

Treating this collection of stories as a kind of loosely structured novel is a difficult trap to avoid, since the stories are arranged in chronological order and form a nearly seamless portrait of the artist as a young woman. The short-story sequence is by no means a novel idea, having been practiced by writers as diverse as Ernest Hemingway, William Faulkner, Virginia Woolf, H. E. Bates, and V. S. Pritchett. Connecting stories this closely, however, pushes the form to its limits and creates some of the stresses that weaken particularly the longer stories.

The shortest and in many ways the most effective story is the first, "Celia Behind Me." Celia is short, fat, nearsighted, and diabetic, not at all the sort of seven-year-old that other children like to be around. Elizabeth's mother, however, has dutifully instructed her to be nice to Celia, since "she won't live forever." Elizabeth grudgingly tries to comply with what she regards as misplaced sympathy, but Celia is too whining and stupid to like, let alone protect, as Elizabeth's mother insists. Elizabeth's real fear, however, is that in defending Celia she will become the next target of ridicule, "For I knew, deep in my wretched heart, that were it not for Celia I was next in line for humiliation." This is the kind of insight and honesty that distinguishes *The*

Elizabeth Stories throughout, and especially the first one, for at the end, Elizabeth rages against Celia, beating her head against a culvert in rage and exasperation. The righteous anger of adults eventually subsides, but Elizabeth is never able to forgive Celia. "She made me discover a darkness far more frightening than the echoing culvert, far more enduring than her smooth, pink face."

The cruelty of children, especially that of little girls toward one another, is a constant theme in the earlier stories. There is also enough childhood sexuality to satisfy the most rabid Freudian. The adult measures taken to repress violence and sex are appropriately severe, for this is postwar, small-town Ontario, where social activity revolves around the church and where the virtues of "grace, tidiness and frugality" form a kind of unholy trinity. When, therefore, in "Sawdust" three-year-old Elizabeth is caught doing unseemly things with a teddy bear, she is turned over to grandmother for a talking to. Elizabeth does not stop "greeting" as she calls it, and in fact introduces the practice two years later to her five-year-old friends. Eventually "greeting" gives way to rougher sexual games, in which boys capture girls or vice versa. Unfortunately, Elizabeth and her friend Trudy Shantz are humiliated when the two of them are caught mutually "greeting" on the sawdusty floor of Mr. Shantz's butcher shop. So complete is their shame that the Shantzes are forced to leave town.

For Isabel Huggan, one of the chief emotions of childhood is humiliation, and one of the book's most touching stories concerns Elizabeth's shame at having to dance the part of a boy in the annual ballet. Her mother tries to alleviate the pain by buying Elizabeth her first brassiere, but she does not want a bra, she wants her mother to hold her tight and sympathize. Her father, like many of his generation, believes that toughness is better than kindness and sees the role as a chance for his daughter to develop character. Elizabeth interprets his reaction as betraying his desire for a son. The bitterness of this story is offset by a parallel narrative line in which Mavis Kessler's sophisticated friend from Toronto comes to visit and, when the Kesslers are out, teaches Elizabeth to play poker. "Aunt" Eadie is Elizabeth's Auntie Mame—wealthy, worldly, and abominated by Frank Kessler because she is safe from him and his kind. This visit ends in Eadie's humiliation, however, because she nips from her whiskey bottle while teaching Elizabeth to play poker and falls asleep on the couch. At least Elizabeth has seen that it is possible for adults to be shamed, too, though her sympathies lie entirely with the freedom-loving and disgraced Eadie.

Childhood and adolescent sexuality, humiliation, parental injustice, and the problems of being accepted are the chief themes of these stories. "Into the Green Stillness" deals with these in a particularly harsh way, as Elizabeth is blamed by her cousins for stealing from Mavis' purse. In fact her cousin Charlene is the culprit, and her older brother uses his knowledge of the theft to force his younger sister into performing fellatio. The final injustice comes when they accuse Elizabeth of making their youngest sister Gracie help clear a path in the woods, when in fact both have enjoyed the game immensely. The ending of this story is perhaps the most poignant in the collection. "Queen Esther" begins as a story about the Mennonite girl who does Mrs. Kessler's ironing, but ends as a study of innocent adolescent homosexual kissing, which is the chief thing Elizabeth learns at Bible camp. In "Sorrows of the Flesh," Elizabeth discovers her talent for science and basketball through the help of a young American teacher, whom she loves and idolizes until he is convicted of beating his wife. "Secrets" finds the adolescent Elizabeth being included in the feminine world of keeping secrets from husbands, but her enjoyment of the game is spoiled when she suspects that her mother is having an affair. Mavis' affair turns out to be only an infatuation with the Anglican Mass—a secret Elizabeth decides she must keep. The final story, "Getting Out of Garten" depicts a more confident and mature Elizabeth, secure with her Platonic boyfriend Dieter, eager to leave behind the small town of Garten to begin a new life at a university. The story ends at the "shotgun" wedding of her friend Trudy. Ironically, Elizabeth herself might be in this predicament but for Dieter's impotence on the one occasion when she tried to seduce him.

As these brief analyses suggest, the stories in this collection are frank, sometimes brutal, in their depiction of children and adolescents. No one can read them and come away with a faith in the natural goodness of children unshaken. Adults—the usual villains in stories about children—come off no better, although often the reader sympathizes with their clumsy attempts to deal with the confusing and sometimes arbitrary emotional needs of their offspring. Frank and Mavis Kessler are earnest, hardworking, and well meaning. They also possess the usual blindness, limited imagination, and hypocrisy of adults, trying hard to be good parents and succeeding as much or as little as most.

Playing as large a part as any character is the small town of Garten. It is narrow, church-bound, gossipy, and unforgiving, making comparisons between these stories and Sherwood Anderson's *Winesburg, Ohio* (1919) inevitable. Indeed, Garten is one of Huggan's targets, and she often skewers the town with deadly accuracy. Yet Elizabeth kicks against more than just the traces of small-town life; like all youngsters, no matter where they live, she is eager to experience everything life holds. It is perhaps difficult to call a girl who masturbates at three and who has witnessed fellatio, intercourse, and wife-beating "innocent," yet she is—innocent in the way today's tough, pseudosophisticated, and streetwise teenagers are innocent—of the consequences of life's actions and choices.

Huggan's skill as a writer lies mainly in her ability to draw character. Elizabeth is at times whining, sneaky, untruthful, mean, and selfish, but she is also intelligent, obedient, sensitive, alert, and likable. She becomes more attractive as the stories progress, the turning point coming during that awful ballet. Her anguished, defiant cry at the end of the dance, "I'm really a girl, I'm really a girl!" shocks both her parents and friends into an awed respect for her pain. The reader's sympathies turn to her entirely at the end of "Into the Green Stillness." When struggles in high school with a clumsy, oversized body yield to the coaching and friendship of Jerry Wheeling, there will be few readers who will not wish that someone such as he had touched their lives. Even as a likable teenager, however, Elizabeth is not without faults and foibles. She smokes out of sheer defiance and frequently lies. Nevertheless, the reader feels a twinge of pain when she tries to revive what she believes is her parents' failing marriage by suggesting a night out and her father suspects her of wanting to get rid of them. Mavis is drawn with less detail than Elizabeth but with no less sharpness of insight. At first she seems to be an overly strict mother, too worried about what the neighbors will think. She emerges gradually, however, as conscientious and loving, frustrated by life in Garten, when what she wants is the Toronto of her single youth. Frank hovers in the background, seldom seen, and when he does emerge it is generally to disappoint either mother, daughter, or both. Much of the instructive value of these stories is to watch these three ordinary people try to understand one another.

As a composer of stories, Huggan needs to practice greater economy and compression. "Celia Behind Me" is deftly and economically structured, and the sexual theme of "Sawdust" is sufficient to hold it together. "Jack of Hearts," with its parallel narratives, works reasonably well, but Eadie's humorous disgrace takes some of the emotional edge from Elizabeth's humiliation. "Into the Green Stillness" is tightly woven in all aspects, but "Queen Esther" is diffuse and "Sorrows of the Flesh" contains enough material for a novel. Long patches of this are stitched in to bring together disparate elements, so that in spite of moments of emotional intensity, the impact of the story is attenuated. "Secrets" and "Getting Out of Garten" work well in the context of the collection but would be hard to separate from their predecessors.

Huggan writes in a clean, uncluttered style that makes no attempt to be literary or call attention to itself. What distinguishes these stories, however, is less the manner of their telling than the honesty of their explorations of the human heart. In the analysis of Elizabeth, and beyond her in the creation of the town of Garten, Huggan presents her readers with a remarkable picture of what it is like to grow up in a small town. Between Sherwood Anderson's anger and Garrison Keillor's sugary fantasies lies Isabel Huggan's wise understanding.

Are these Canadian or simply North American stories? Certainly the place names, such as Toronto, Guelph, and Stratford, help root Garten in a specific locale, and a few tricks of speech are characteristically Canadian. Beyond this, there is in the social ambiance something certainly not American, though precisely what is hard to define. Perhaps it is the quiet solidity of the town, with its peculiar mixture of German and English elements, or the provinciality of its residents that seems particularly Canadian. Otherwise, what is peculiarly Canadian is too subtle for analysis. As with the short story generally, nationality matters less than insight. On this basis, Isabel Huggan is a new and talented writer to watch.

Dean Baldwin

Sources for Further Study

Booklist. LXXXIII, April 1, 1987, p. 1177.
Kirkus Reviews. LV, March 1, 1987, p. 326.
Library Journal. CXII, April 1, 1987, p. 163.
Los Angeles Times Book Review. August 2, 1987, p. 3.
Ms. XV, June, 1987, p. 18.
The New York Times. May 23, 1987, p. 11.
The New York Times Book Review. XCII, July 12, 1987, p. 11.
The New Yorker. LXIII, August 31, 1987, p. 97.
Publishers Weekly. CCXXXI, April 3, 1987, p. 63.
Time. CXXX, July 27, 1987, p. 67.
The Washington Post Book World. XVII, August 2, 1987, p. 9.

ELLEN FOSTER

Author: Kaye Gibbons (1960-   )
Publisher: Algonquin Books (Chapel Hill, North Carolina). 146 pp. $11.95
Type of work: Novel
Time: The 1970's
Locale: The rural American South

A poignant, honestly written, and highly accomplished first novel narrated by its eleven-year-old heroine

> *Principal characters:*
> ELLEN FOSTER, the narrator, an orphan
> STARLETTA, her young black girlfriend
> BILL, her father, an abusive drunkard
> "MAMA'S MAMA," her wealthy grandmother
> NADINE NELSON, her aunt, one of her mother's sisters
> DORA, Nadine's daughter
> JULIA, an art teacher who serves briefly as Ellen's foster parent
> "NEW MAMA," Ellen's foster mother

Ellen Foster is the first novel by twenty-seven-year-old Kaye Gibbons, a North Carolina native and recent graduate of the University of North Carolina at Chapel Hill. Although one chapter from her novel was published in the initial issue of *The Quarterly*, Kaye Gibbons was virtually unknown until *Ellen Foster* achieved praise and national recognition in *The New York Times Book Review*. The praise is well deserved. *Ellen Foster* is an accomplished first novel, written with honesty, compassion, and humor, and offering a vividly realized plot, conflict, and central character.

Set in the rural South, where the author grew up, the novel is narrated by the title character, an eleven-year-old orphan who adopts the surname Foster after she begins living with a foster family. Ellen's story concerns her arduous and painful search for a safe, loving family with whom to spend her adolescent years. The novel alternates segments from Ellen's present life with her foster mother, whom she calls only "my new mama," with harrowing recollections from her earlier life: the death of her ailing, abused natural mother, Ellen's harassment and physical abuse by her drunken father and, following his death, a vengeful grandmother, and brief stays with both of her mother's sisters, neither of whom wishes to rear Ellen. Details of Ellen's life at her foster home introduce and close each chapter. Thus, throughout the novel, the isolation, hardship, and fear Ellen experienced in her early years contrast sharply with the security, warmth, and dignity she has found in her new home. In the hands of a less talented novelist, this plot might have led to sentimentality and morbidity, but Gibbons is so skillful in interweaving past and present and in the consistency with which she handles the first-person point of view that *Ellen Foster* emerges as a triumphant story of survival, growth, and the endurance of human will.

Guided by Ellen's feisty good nature, honesty, and strong determination, the reader is thrust into the world of destructive family life with the opening sentence of the novel. "When I was little I would think of ways to kill my daddy," Ellen startlingly announces at the opening of the novel. Despite the shocking content of the sentence, Ellen's is a voice the reader trusts, that of the adult-child forced to fend for herself. Contemplating the murder of her father was a practical necessity for Ellen, an issue at the core of her struggle to survive. The reader is immediately engaged. He knows to take Ellen seriously, to trust her determination and survival instincts.

In some ways, Ellen bears comparison with that famous orphaned adolescent of American literature, Huck Finn. Both speak their own stories in their own language, making the books that result triumphs of realistic use of the vernacular. Ellen, however, has none of the resistance to education that Huck exhibits. School and reading are important to her; she is eager to see the library bookmobile arrive weekly. A precocious and voracious reader, she had already read Geoffrey Chaucer's *The Canterbury Tales* in modern English and the novels of the Brontë sisters. Unlike Huck, moreover, Ellen does not resist the idea of God or church attendance, although she is intelligent enough to question a god who would make someone as mean as her father.

In this last respect, her struggle to escape the abuse of a drunken father, Ellen most resembles Huck. In one poignant scene, she locks herself in a closet for safety when her father brings home a number of drinking buddies, black men who make fun of the frozen dinners Ellen has stored for herself and drink themselves to sleep on the living-room floor. (As a sensible child, Ellen spots her narrative with survival tips, advice on buying food in bulk to save money and on saving time when shopping for school clothes.)

Like Huck also, Ellen faces a conflict over the racial prejudice she has been taught as a child in the South. Early in the novel when Ellen visits the home of her black friend Starletta, she is unwilling to drink from the same cup as Starletta or to eat the food the family offers. Though uneducated and poor, the black family is compassionate and willing to offer Ellen shelter from her abusive father. It is Ellen's own stubbornness that keeps her silent about her father's abuse and sexual advances, and part of her growth and maturing comes from the loosening of the blinders of prejudice she has placed on herself. Through her own hardship and suffering, the goodness and generosity of Starletta and her family, and, when Ellen is living with her grandmother and forced to work in the cotton fields, the kindness of Mavis, a black farmhand, Ellen changes. She comes to recognize the guilt she bears for her prejudice toward Starletta as well as the deep love she feels for her friend. She sees finally that a person need not worry about whether someone is black or white. "I am old now," she comments near the end of the novel, and know it is not the germs you cannot see that slide off her lips and on to a glass then to your white lips that will hurt you or turn you colored. What you had better worry about though is the people you know and trusted they would be like you because you were all made in the same batch. You need to look over your shoulder at the one who is in charge of holding you up and see if that is a knife he has in his hand. And it might not be a colored hand. But it is a knife.

It is a measure of Ellen's growth that by the end of the novel, when she invites her friend Starletta for the weekend and sees her sleeping in her white friend's bed, she recognizes that it is Starletta who has come "even farther" than Ellen herself.

This racial conflict and the emphasis on familial and racial relationships remind the reader that *Ellen Foster* is a deeply Southern novel, though it is by no means a regional work, limited in its appeal. Rather, the novel exhibits a number of those traits and concerns that have come to be identified with the body of Southern literature published in the twentieth century. Besides the focus on familial and racial relationships, and the guilt and sense of sin that racism has instilled in many Southern whites, the novel evinces a rootedness in the details of everyday life and a strong sense of place common to Southern literature. Ellen frequently comments on clothing and money and thinks compulsively about food—perhaps mirroring in her physical hunger her deep emotional needs. She is a keen observer also of the smells, objects, and living conditions in the different homes she visits. Many of her descriptions focus on luxury or its absence, calling attention to the class and racial divisions that still prevail in many parts of the South. For example, while Ellen's grandmother, her "mama's mama," has a home filled with expensive furniture and antiques, what Ellen calls "Egyptian type candy jars," Starletta and her family live in a one-room house with no inside toilet, a dirty place with "little sticks all between the floorboards." Their house with its "fried meat" smell offers a realistic look at the poverty of rural blacks in the South at the same time that it calls attention to the social and racial injustices that linger in the region.

Perhaps the two most strongly Southern characteristics of *Ellen Foster* are its vivid, fresh language with heavy reliance on colloquial Southern speech patterns and its use of the grotesque. From the beginning of the novel, Ellen's language is honest and direct. Her voice is clearly that of an adolescent white girl who always refers to her father as "daddy" and blacks as "colored." Moreover, there is no direct dialogue in the novel; everything is related in Ellen's own words, giving the novel authenticity and, at times, humor. In describing her parents, Ellen speaks of her father as a "big wind-up toy of a man." Her mother, who dies of an overdose of heart medication, "has not had a good heart" since suffering from "romantic fever" in her youth, an apt linguistic play on "rheumatic fever" in the light of her marriage to an abusive husband. When Ellen must go to court for the question of child custody to be settled, the art teacher, Julia, who acts as temporary guardian with her husband, dresses Ellen in "lace stockings and black patting leather shoes." Later, when Ellen spots the woman she wants as her "new mama" at church and learns that she has a foster family, with characteristic honesty Ellen says she has heard that the woman takes in everything from "orphans to stray cats," which "fit my description perfect." Such descriptions add poignancy as well as humor to the novel and offer ample evidence of the author's keen ear for fresh, witty language and the patterns of everyday Southern speech.

This same ear is also evident in the uses of the grotesque that occur in the novel. Since the deaths of close relatives repeatedly haunt Ellen's life, quite expectedly her attention focuses frequently on the details of dying. After her mother dies in her arms, Ellen builds a strong resentment toward her father and a determination not to be found with another dead person. When her father does not come home the Christmas following his wife's death, Ellen comments that maybe he "drove off in the ditch somewhere and froze to death. Nobody would be out on Christmas to find him before he got blue and solid." Then, when her father does die of a ruptured blood vessel, Ellen says "he had a vein or a head fuse explode so he died." Perhaps the most grotesque details describe her grandmother's death in bed while Ellen is living with her. "Too smart to let somebody find" her "with a dead lady the second time around," Ellen decorates her grandmother's body and bed, putting a Sunday hat on the dead woman's head and arranging artificial flowers around the body so "she looked set off like a picture." "I stood over her," Ellen comments, "hoping she was the last dead person I knew for a while."

The central struggle of Ellen's life resurfaces with the death of her grandmother: the quest for a safe home with "somebody good" to love her. It is this theme which gives *Ellen Foster* its power and universality. Driven from her home first by an abusive father, Ellen seeks refuge with her Aunt Betsy, only to be sent home again after one weekend. When she is rescued from her father temporarily by one of her teachers, Ellen is comfortable but wary, and justifiably so since the courts quickly place her in the custody of her grandmother, a cruel woman who abuses her grandchild in order to avenge her daughter's death. When Ellen's father dies, her grandmother forbids her to weep or grieve, punctuating her command with repeated slaps. With her grandmother's death, Ellen is thus once more at the mercy of her mother's family and the courts. This time she lives briefly with her Aunt Nadine and her spoiled daughter, Dora. When an argument with her aunt leads to her being thrown out of the house, Ellen seeks shelter with the foster family she has seen at church. In a heartrending scene, she arrives on foot at her "new mama's" house on Christmas Day and offers to pay for her stay with the money she has saved. She has even dressed herself in her fanciest outfit so that she would look like she is "worth something." Though at first Ellen cannot believe that she will be able to stay, she has at last found a home she will not have to leave, a place where children are respected and loved, where there is laughter, play, and compassion.

The end of Ellen's quest drives home two of the novel's central concerns: the pain and hardship of a childhood without loving parents and the meaning and importance of good parenting. The good people in this novel who care for Ellen—Starletta's parents; Julia, the art teacher, and her husband; Mavis, the black farmhand; Ellen's "new mama"—all share traits of tolerance, compassion, and a willingness to support and encourage children regardless of financial limitations. Ironically, those with the most material wealth—Ellen's grandmother, her aunts Betsy and Nadine—appear as selfish, petty women. They are unaware of or unconcerned with the fact that what each child needs, as Ellen says, is "somebody decent to love her good." It is this theme, so vividly and skillfully conveyed through the heroine's own story, that makes *Ellen Foster* a valuable contribution not only to the tradition of Southern letters but also to American literature at large.

Stella Nesanovich

Sources for Further Study

Chicago Tribune. May 22, 1987, V, p. 3.
Kirkus Reviews. LV, March 15, 1987, p. 404.
Library Journal. CXII, April 15, 1987, p. 98.
Los Angeles Times Book Review. August 16, 1987, p. 4.
The New York Times Book Review. XCII, May 31, 1987, p. 13.
Publishers Weekly. CCXXXI, March 20, 1987, p. 70.

THE EMBARRASSMENT OF RICHES
An Interpretation of Dutch Culture in the Golden Age

Author: Simon Schama (1945-   )
Publisher: Alfred A. Knopf (New York). Illustrated. 698 pp. $39.95
Type of work: Cultural history
Time: The seventeenth century
Locale: The Netherlands

Drawing upon a remarkable array of sources both literary and graphic, Simon Schama finds the essence of seventeenth century Dutch culture in its superabundance and in popular anxieties over the precariousness of such good fortune

The Dutch nation was an anomaly in seventeenth century Europe. It was a republic in a world of monarchy, governed by a bourgeois elite and nurtured by a very middle-class society. Against all odds, the seven loosely confederated provinces of the northern Netherlands made good their claim of independence from imperial Spain, fought wars against England and France as well as Spain, and became the leading commercial nation of Europe. The necessity of war and trade further disciplined the Dutch people, already long accustomed to struggling against the sea. Their success in trade brought them great riches, the highest standard of living in Europe, and a vibrant culture that was the envy of their aristocratic neighbors. Who were the Dutch, what did they believe, and what made them a separate people? Looking at the United Provinces at the zenith of its political, economic, and artistic powers, Simon Schama answers these questions in truly masterful fashion. Relying largely on travel accounts, popular literature, paintings, and prints, Schama succeeds in illuminating that complex of core values which gave the Dutch their distinctive identity. With his use of paintings and prints, he has put together a model of creative scholarship, valuable not only for its historical craftsmanship but also for its literary excellence.

The Embarrassment of Riches: An Interpretation of Dutch Culture in the Golden Age is a long book, divided into four parts, eight chapters, an epilogue, four appendices, and a wonderfully complete annotated bibliography. It is beautifully, and very meaningfully, illustrated and gracefully written. Its 698 pages read easily and quickly. Schama's focus is largely on Holland, particularly Amsterdam, but his knowledge of popular literature, the graphic arts, custom, and folkways takes him into the countryside and hinterlands of the Netherlands. His analysis is impressionistic, but it is informed by encyclopedic knowledge and keen intellect and is very convincing. Although concerned largely with Dutch thought and sensibility, Schama necessarily describes basic social institutions and the material artifacts of Netherland culture. He refers only obliquely to political and economic history, concentrating instead on the psychology and emotions of the people.

Part 1, on the emergence of the Dutch nation, emphasizes the relationship of the people and the sea. As Schama so artfully points out, the moral geography of the Dutch was defined by their diligence in maintaining dykes, building new ones, and draining off water to redeem more land from the sea. In part because they literally made so much of their land themselves, the Dutch, unlike most other Europeans, never experienced the full rigor of feudalism. During the Middle Ages, the authority of the dukes of Burgundy rested lightly on the Netherlands, limited by customary freedoms of villages and towns. The local nobility, primarily the Houses of Orange and Nassau, found it in their interest to resist any effort to limit traditional freedoms. Hence, the centralizing efforts of Philip II met with a remarkably unified response from Netherlander burghers, lords, and farmers. In fact, Philip's attack upon the ancient freedoms endangered the customary methods of holding back the sea; the Dutch themselves would break the dykes to foil the Spanish and other invaders. The war for independence fed their sense of separateness and aided the spread of Protestantism, especially Calvinism, and that in turn joined with an already strong Hebraic tradition in Christian Humanism to lead to a popular identification of the Dutch people with the children of Israel. Yet religion, especially militant Calvinism, was moderated significantly by Humanism, pragmatic materialism, and local government. Hence, despite the Reformed *predikants*, religious toleration prevailed in practice, downplaying religious and ethnic differences in the interest of economic and political advancement.

Part 2 looks at the style of Dutch life. It is here that Schama fully develops his central thesis of the Dutch republic as a remarkably communal society, based largely upon familial economic ambitions. Caught between the Spanish and the sea, as it were, the Dutch thrived in terms of commerce and manufacturing. They reveled in material success, for it signaled the vitality of the republic, of Dutch society as a whole. Still, there were deep anxieties, produced as much by the Christian humanism of Desiderius Erasmus as the Reformed faith of John Calvin, both of which warned of the corrupting influence of material success. Another factor exacerbating Dutch anxieties was the unparalleled rapidity with which the United Provinces had reached the pinnacle of economic and political leadership in Europe. Such bounty and power seemed almost too good to be true, as if a whale had run aground and obligingly surrendered its blubber and bone to nearby villagers. As Schama makes clear, however, the beached whale, commonly portrayed in Dutch art, was considered portentous of hardships to come. To become too enamored with material success was to court well-deserved disaster. Not riotous indulgence but temperate consumption, preferably in a family setting, was the ideal portrayed in Dutch paintings and prints. Epidemics, stock speculations that crashed, and invasions were all portrayed as punishment for abandonment of the golden mean and civic virtue in favor of self-indulgent materialism.

The Dutch enjoyed their riches but were embarrassed by them because they knew that materialism ultimately corrupted. Their predicament was complicated because they were the subjects of the intense jealousy, even hatred, of their monarchical neighbors. The Netherlands' geography and politics, according to the conventional wisdom of the day, dictated failure, and yet the bourgeois republic had achieved unbelievable wealth and success. Not surprising, the Dutch developed a sense of being a chosen people, and their neighbors hated them for having the impertinence to survive and prosper. Based on his understanding of Dutch economic enterprise, Schama doubts that Max Weber's thesis regarding Calvinism and capital formation adequately explains Dutch economic success. Schama argues convincingly that the Dutch enjoyed spending for consumer goods, did not save much, and accumulated capital not because they were frugal but because they simply were making vast profits on commerce. His descriptions of various lifestyles, from that of the rich merchant to that of the middling artisan, make it clear that Dutch prosperity was founded at least in part upon heavy consumption. Dutch people spent heavily, if they could, on furniture, clothing, and silverware. Perhaps indicative of its consumer-oriented economy, it was in the Dutch republic that paintings became common household items for the first time.

Part 3 finds in the family the heart and soul of Dutch culture. Indeed, the family was the model for the commonwealth, and civic duty simply reflected familial responsibility. The Dutch housewife's fetish for cleanliness, Schama claims, signaled the centrality of the family in nurturing the virtues that would protect both the family and the nation. The household was to be separate, kept pure of corrupting outside influences, and therefore scrupulously clean. Its literal spotlessness reflected its ethical and spiritual significance. The role of the housewife in all of this was of the utmost importance, though Dutch males harbored their share of distrust toward women, and misogynistic images of the shrewish wife, the adulterous wife, and especially the domineering wife were common in popular art and literature. Prostitution was especially condemned in popular literature, and the prostitute was portrayed as a grave threat to the family, while the good wife was sanctified in verse and portrait as the keeper of the household and the guardian of the family. Comparing family size, Schama notes that the Dutch family of two or three children was the smallest in Europe. He further agrees that Dutch husbands and wives, for the most part, were forming "companionate marriages" in the seventeenth century. All of this strongly suggests that in the United Provinces the family was taking on characteristics usually associated with the modern family of the industrial age.

Another sign of modernity was the focus upon the child in the Dutch family. Indeed, Dutch art was the first to portray children in realistic terms, as babies who cry and smile and mess their diapers rather than as the stylized putti found in so much religious art. The Dutch recognized childhood as a distinctive stage of human development, and the evidence is that Dutch parents were rather indulgent and bound by the affectionate attitudes toward their offspring that are associated with modern times. Rather than dwell on that significant point, however, Schama makes it clear that the Dutch projected their own fears about their world onto their images of childhood and child care. Child rearing manuals were remarkably modern in urging patience toward children and the maximum amount of freedom for them. They recommended breast-feeding and warned against nurses' or servants' influence on children. There is a striking parallel between the vigilance required of the parents over the child and that required of the people over the virtues of the republic. In a very real sense, the two—children and civic virtues—came together, because the children were the future of the commonwealth. The well-ordered family and the mannerly child presented in paintings represented the ideal. The disorderly schoolroom or the mean and hurtful play of rowdy children represented more than mere juvenile misbehavior. It aroused deep-seated fears for the future of the republic.

Part 4 examines the weakening of the communal ethos of the golden age after 1700, during what is called the "age of the periwigs." Schama seems to be saying that as long as the upper and middle classes looked upon themselves and most of those below them as part of the same community, then Dutch culture remained vital. That attitude required civic virtue; it required the prosperous to pay heavy taxes and the not so prosperous to accept the leadership of their economic betters. It required the wealthy to recognize their connection to the poor. Indeed, benevolence and philanthropy provided much of the glue that kept Dutch society together. That began to change. Ironically, it changed in part because the foreign threat to the republic lessened. Europe was becoming more like the once-anomalous Dutch state just as the members of the Dutch elite were becoming more attracted to the style of the French court. Suspicions of internal corruption led to renewed oppression of people existing on the fringes of society such as the Gypsies, and a hysterical persecution of persons accused of homosexuality began in 1731-1732. The cattle plague and the collapse of North Sea dykes in the winter of 1731 were seen as divine punishments calling the people to repentance and atonement for falling away from their national covenant.

The Dutch character is still suspended, Schama claims, between worldliness and homeliness, consecrated wealth and corrupting materialism. It can be traced back to the sea, which supplied the riches and yet always threatened everything. One does not have to agree fully with Schama to recognize that he has written an intriguing book probing the very essence of a people's character. He does not say everything that should be said about the Dutch character. What he does say, however, is most insightful because it brings together both material culture and the mind and heart of the Dutch people.

The Embarrassment of Riches is a brilliant commentary that will surely influence scholarship for years to come.

Ronald W. Howard

Sources for Further Study

Booklist. LXXXIII, May 1, 1987, p. 1331.
History Today. XXXVII, December, 1987, p. 51.
Kirkus Reviews. LX, April 15, 1987, p. 626.
Library Journal. CXII, May 15, 1987, p. 83.
Los Angeles Times Book Review. June 14, 1987, p. 12.
The New Republic. CXCVII, August 24, 1987, p. 28.
The New York Times Book Review. XCII, July 5, 1987, p. 1.
The New Yorker. LXIII, September 14, 1987, p. 130.
Publishers Weekly. CCXXXI, April 3, 1987, p. 62.
The Washington Post Book World. XVII, June 28, 1987, p. 1.

EMBATTLED COURAGE
The Experience of Combat in the American Civil War

Author: Gerald F. Linderman (1934-   )
Publisher: The Free Press (New York). Illustrated. 288 pp. $22.50
Type of work: Military and cultural history
Time: 1861-1865
Locale: The United States and the Confederate States of America

A study of American concepts of courage in 1861 and 1862 and the ways in which they had changed by 1865

> *Principal personages:*
> JOSHUA L. CHAMBERLAIN, the commander of the 20th Maine and hero of Little Round Top; later governor of Maine and president of Bowdoin College
> JACOB D. COX, the commander of the Ohio militia, who served under generals William Starke Rosecrans and William Tecumseh Sherman; a major general who was later governor of Ohio, secretary of the interior, and president of the University of Cincinnati
> GEORGE A. CUSTER, a brilliant cavalry commander, the youngest major general in the Union army; he died at Little Big Horn
> OLIVER WENDELL HOLMES, JR., an officer in the 20th Massachusetts who was wounded five times; later a justice of the United States Supreme Court
> JOHN S. MOSBY, a cavalry officer under General Jeb Stuart; he organized irregular forces attacking the Union rear
> ROBERT G. SHAW, the commander of 54th Massachusetts, the first black regiment; he was killed at Charleston in 1863

Only in the mid-twentieth century has it been widely understood that courage is a cultural virtue which changes its meaning from age to age. Courage is still often equated with fearlessness, but Plato said that fearlessness must be combined with compassion, justice, and moderation to be called courage. Gerald F. Linderman demonstrates that Americans in the 1850's had developed a code of fearless courage based on the duel: They prized the "cool courage" of the gentleman who could face a pistol or a ruffian without any display of concern, much less fear. Following the demands of this code and its relentless endorsement by the public, including their families and friends, the volunteers of 1861 exposed themselves willingly to enemy fire. This code, Linderman contends, lay at the foundation of Civil War military tactics as much as did the theories of Henri de Jomini taught at the United States Military Academy at West Point or the experience of the Mexican War.

Even professional officers subscribed to this concept of courage, though they knew that mass infantry warfare required, not would-be gentlemen, but ordinary men who could be formed through discipline, pride, and fear into soldiers. Volunteers could not, however, be trained swiftly along the lines of the regular army, not solely because of their numbers but also because they and the public rejected the process as undemocratic and unbecoming. Enthusiastic volunteers from North and South alike believed that courage was a matter of character and will. The war, for them, was less a contest of systems and ideologies than a test of courage, and they forced their ideas upon the officers whom they elected.

The chivalric romanticism of the combatants apparent in the gaudy uniforms and florid speeches became manifest throughout the armies, North and South. Had the volunteers had their way, they would all have been knight-errants, besting their opponents in single combat before the gaze of friends, parents, and admiring ladies. Holding firmly to their notions of propriety and individualism, they undermined all the efforts at discipline by which their officers tried to make raw recruits into soldiers who would follow orders without questioning.

Commanders were able to form effective units and fight as an army only by manipulating the code of manly courage. They appealed, not to political causes or to patriotism, but to bravery, duty, self-respect, and the opportunity to prove one's manhood. They could win their troops' respect only through personal example. The resulting casualties ultimately forced soldiers and officers alike to modify their beliefs. The public, however, was slow to realize the change. Even at the end of the war, there was a general cultural lag in this respect. The public still valued "cool courage" above proper caution, endurance, patience, good weapons, and plentiful supplies. Consequently, a valuable lesson was soon forgotten.

To an extent almost incomprehensible today, the widespread belief in foolhardy courage as the supreme value remained dominant past 1914; it was only slowly changed after the machine gun had ripped apart the serried ranks of charging soldiers and artillery had pounded the miserable trench-bound armies into an awareness of the meaning of cannon fodder. Officers of the Great War nevertheless continued to defend their use of mass formations in the belief that individual soldiers would seek shelter if deprived of the example of comrades and allowed to believe that efforts to survive would not be observed. The change in attitude came in 1918, after the Germans had developed techniques of training small special units which could operate on the modern battlefield without murderous losses. It was this lesson as much as the introduction of tanks and other vehicles which made World War II so different from the Great War. A second lesson from the trenches was that every soldier has a breaking point which can be predicted with statistical regularity. Fear is normal, and it can be controlled through training and by temporarily withdrawing hard-hit units from combat. Some politicians and old-fashioned generals (such as George Patton in the famous slapping incident) never did learn this lesson; others, however, learned to limit the amount of stress (potential combat fatigue) imposed on any unit or individual, thus preventing a breakdown of armies such as had occurred between 1914 and 1918.

These lessons had been partially understood by the American organizers of armies as early as 1863. Linderman explains the massive reenlistment of Union troops in that year not as an outburst of patriotic feeling, but as a response to the offer of an immediate furlough home. Soldiers contemplated the odds of surviving the remaining six months of their enlistment and chose reenlistment with a furlough over the possibility of dying without seeing family and friends again. As the concept of courage changed, soldiers dug shelters without prompting and accepted brutal discipline in the belief that draftees and substitutes were not gentlemen and could not be molded into soldiers in any other way; moreover, they wanted to win the war quickly and go home. Combat was no longer a contest of courage. Soldiers respected their battlefield opponents. The war was now against the opposing system—and they approved of every means that could weaken it. They stole food, burned barns and houses, and made no secret of their hatred of civilians on both sides. As the war spread across the countryside, small-unit encounters became commonplace.

During World War II and the Korean War, students of small-unit warfare discovered that, although the average soldier could be trained to overcome fear, he remained a reluctant killer. S. L. A. Marshall's sandbox reconstructions indicated that only 15 percent of American infantry fired their weapons, but that almost 100 percent of the machine guns and artillery were discharged. The 85 percent were not cowards (they did not run away, wound themselves, or surrender), but they never saw the silhouettes of target practice in combat, they disliked picking out individual men to slay, and they universally assumed that everyone else was shooting, so that their failure to join in would not be noticed (whereas members of weapons crews had no such illusions). Interestingly, that percentage apparently applied to all the enemy armies as well.

In *The Warriors: Reflections on Men in Battle* (1959), Jesse Glenn Gray provided an understanding of this phenomenon and others, thus establishing the basic foundation for Linderman's reinterpretation of Civil War combat. Courage, Gray says, is not a simple virtue. Normal men are all afraid. Most learn to deal with it. The "cowards" who cannot adapt may simply be aware of the consequences of fighting; they certainly are more aware than the immature teenagers who enter combat with a profound belief in their own invulnerability. Courage, indeed, may be better demonstrated by those who are willing to accept ridicule and punishment for their efforts to escape danger than by those who merely follow along, doing whatever their fellows do. American soldiers of the Civil War came to understand this. Originally intolerant of cowards, they ultimately saw that courage alone was no match for rifled muskets and artillery. They became reluctant to punish deserters, stragglers, or even those who fled the scene of combat. They could not acknowledge openly the fear that all experienced, but neither could they condemn the "weakness" of fellow soldiers with the fervor that they employed on stay-at-home patriots, especially those who continued to praise the now-outmoded code of courage. They voiced open hatred of pacifists, war profiteers, and the indifferent public. They took revenge on enemy civilians.

Upon returning home, the veterans found it necessary to conceal their true feelings. Family and friends admired their wounds, praised their patriotism and manliness, and deferred to them as pillars of the community, but they could not and did not want to understand what the veterans had endured. When the former soldiers saw that it was impossible to explain what they had undergone, they lapsed into silence. For almost two decades, veterans' organizations languished and few individuals spoke about their experiences. In the 1880's, as memories of wartime emotions faded, as the responsibilities and boredom of peacetime became tiresome, and as middle age brought them to reflect on the meaning of their lives, veterans preferred to remember their earlier code of courage; they praised it as the fundamental test by which they had proved their worthiness—a test that many powerful industrialists and businessmen had not even tried to pass.

Thus was the code passed on to the next generation. Theodore Roosevelt could envision himself on a horse at San Juan Hill, pointing his sword at the enemy and leading his volunteers to victory. The fact that he had no horse and was rescued at a critical moment by black troops made no difference. The public wanted to believe in the code of courage and did so enthusiastically.

William Urban

Sources for Further Study

AB Bookman's Weekly. LXXIX, June 29, 1987, p. 2906.
American History Illustrated. XXII, November, 1987, p. 10.
Choice. XXV, September, 1987, p. 206.
The Christian Century. CIV, October 7, 1987, p. 866.
The Guardian Weekly. August 30, 1987, p. 18.
Kirkus Reviews. LV, March 1, 1987, p. 354.
The New York Times Book Review. XCII, July 5, 1987, p. 67.
The New Yorker. LXIII, September 14, 1987, p. 135.
Publishers Weekly. CCXXXI, March 13, 1987, p. 78.
The Washington Post Book World. XVII, August 2, 1987, p. 4.

EMPIRE

Author: Gore Vidal (1925-   )
Publisher: Random House (New York). 487 pp. $22.50
Type of work: Historical novel
Time: 1896-1906
Locale: Washington, D.C.; New York; Newport, Rhode Island; Philadelphia, Pennsylvania; Saint Louis, Missouri; New Hampshire; England; and France

A spirited account, mingling fictional characters with historical figures, of that moment at the turn of the century when the United States ceased to be a republic and set up shop as an empire

> *Principal characters:*
> CAROLINE SANFORD, an ambitious young woman reared in France and determined to conquer Washington, D.C.
> BLAISE SANFORD, her half brother
> JOHN APGAR SANFORD, her cousin and lawyer
> WILLIAM RANDOLPH HEARST, the newspaper magnate
> THEODORE ROOSEVELT, the twenty-sixth President of the United States, 1901-1909
> JOHN HAY, secretary to Abraham Lincoln and secretary of state under Theodore Roosevelt
> DEL HAY, John's son and Caroline's fiancé
> JAMES BURDEN DAY, a Democratic congressman and Caroline's secret lover
> HENRY ADAMS, a melancholy historian and scion of the presidential Adams family
> HENRY JAMES, the expatriate American novelist

"History does not enjoy too close an examination of its processes," observes the author of *Empire* following Theodore Roosevelt's terse speech seconding William McKinley for the presidential nomination. In his latest novel, the fifth in a cycle tracing American history, Gore Vidal provides an elaborate examination of political developments at the turn of the century, and, if history itself does not enjoy it, it is likely that his readers will. Vidal, who grew up in Washington, D.C., in a distinguished political family, himself ran twice, unsuccessfully, for public office. *Empire* follows *Washington, D.C.* (1967), *Burr* (1973), *1876* (1976), and *Lincoln* (1984) in Vidal's continuing attempt to provide fictional shape for American history and to debunk the most fatuous national myths. His contemporary contempt for an imperial presidency and for Yankee arrogance is projected nine decades into the past.

Set during the administrations of McKinley and Roosevelt, the novel records that moment when, militarily triumphant in Cuba, Panama, and the Philippines, the United States ceased to be a republic and set up shop as an empire. Puerto Rico, Guam, the Philippines, Panama, the Dominican Republic, and Cuba came to be ruled out of Washington, D.C. Though *Empire* focuses on a period that is perhaps less intrinsically colorful than those of *Lincoln* and *Burr*, it manages to convey a detailed sense of life at the social and political top in Washington, New York, and Newport, Rhode Island. It mingles invented characters, such as Caroline and Blaise Sanford, with such historical figures as William Randolph Hearst, John Hay, and Henry Adams. The worldly, urbane voice of its author is intent on demystifying the birth of American imperialism.

The novel's theme is power, and, while warriors and diplomats are busy offstage extending United States dominion to the edge of Asia through chicanery and brutal massacres, Caroline Sanford is busy taking control of her own life by subduing those in her way. Defying social conventions, she insists on bearing the child of her married lover. Beautiful, intelligent, and manipulative, she is a melodramatic creation.

As the book begins, in 1896, Caroline is twenty years old and has been deprived of a considerable inheritance through the machinations of her half brother Blaise until she reaches the age of twenty-seven. Through a technicality in their father's will, Blaise manages to maintain temporary stewardship of fifteen million dollars. While he can, Blaise makes use of it to bankroll and then rival Hearst's journalistic empire.

Caroline refuses to accept the gilded cage to which the Gilded Age has consigned women of her class. Establishing herself in Washington, she becomes the owner of the feeble *Tribune*, and she uses her new position as newspaper lord to become a fierce competitor to Hearst not only in reporting events but also in contriving them. *Empire* chronicles American history as a pageant of scoundrels and fools, and, when Hearst, whose yellow journalism fabricates and promulgates the myth of San Juan Hill, asks President Roosevelt, "After all, I made you up, didn't I?", there is no question but that he did. Those who, like Hearst, Sanford, and Vidal, create the narrative control history. The rest are feckless and pathetic.

Caroline is affectionate toward Hay, the ambitious young presidential secretary in *Lincoln* now become crepuscular secretary of state, and toward the elderly Adams, who nurses his private grief with public melancholy. She becomes an intimate of the aging survivors of a secret, select group calling itself the Five of Hearts. She refuses, however, to share their debilitating sorrow over historical entropy. Like several actual figures corrupt even in their fashionable crusades against corruption, Caroline is a dynamo of amoral energies. Determined to be an active agent of history, she earns the awe of Adams, the wistful historian.

Caroline's actions in the scene in which her fiancé Del Hay falls out a window to his death are worthy of Marcel Proust's Madame de Guermantes, who is more concerned about the color of her shoes than about the news her friend Swann brings of his own imminent demise; indifferent to the corpse sprawled on the ground, Caroline intently searches the pavement for Del's opal ring. Later, she cunningly enters into a marriage of convenience with her lawyer cousin John Apgar Sanford, a union that proves much more convenient to her than to her hapless spouse.

Beyond the historical melodrama and the naughty reinterpretation of national icons, *Empire* delights with stylistic niceties that are almost an homage to Henry James, who puts in a cameo appearance in the novel. When, for example, Blaise, who has just learned that Congressman James Burden Day is Caroline's secret lover, is shown trying to impress Day with his understanding of his half sister, Vidal writes one brief line that telescopes the man's vanity, presumption, and blindness: " 'I know her,' Blaise lied. 'Better than myself,' Blaise told the truth."

Built into *Empire* is an awareness of its own fictionality and of its place within the Vidal canon. Adams, who wrote a book about Aaron Burr but then burned it, as he tells John Hay ("Hay had always thought Burr an ideal scamp to write about"), and Hay, who wrote about Abraham Lincoln, are clearly surrogates of their own sly author. In *Burr*, Charles Schermerhorn Schuyler, the roguish vice president's law clerk, becomes convinced that he is also his illegitimate son. In *Empire*, Schuyler is Caroline's late grandfather, and, when she reads the diaries for his time spent with Burr and, written much later, for the year 1876, she might as well be reading two earlier volumes by Vidal.

Empire already has a sequel in *Washington, D.C.*, which is set during the Truman Administration, but fertile territory still remains between Theodore Roosevelt and the successor to Franklin D. Roosevelt. In the closing pages of *Empire*, Elihu Root, who has succeeded Hay as secretary of state, is making dinner conversation with Alice Roosevelt Longworth. "The new president of Princeton said that nothing has spread socialistic feeling in this country more than the use of the automobile," quips Root. When Alice asks what the new Princeton head's name is, Root cannot remember but volunteers that someone has predicted that he will be president of the United States. " 'Fat,' said Alice, 'chance.' " Vidal's next installment might well be called *Wilson*.

"Truth is bizarre enough for the mere historian," says Adams to deny the suspicion that he is writing another novel. *Empire* parades its historical truths about, for example, the moment that the Executive Mansion began being called the White House and that a telephone was first used in it. Much of *Empire*'s attraction is as a wax museum of familiar figures sculpted with salient warts—Roosevelt as a jingoistic blusterer, Hearst as a cunning megalomaniac, and so on. In the empire of Vidal's narrative, these figures occupy the same verbal space as the author's invented characters. *Empire* is Vidal's magisterial revision of the American history written by his predecessors.

Vidal's hefty novel is strictly history from the perspective of the rich, famous, and powerful, and, despite the recent historiographical emphasis on examining the past for structures of ordinary experience, his narrative of America at the turn of the century ignores the massive immigration, the growth of labor unions, and the rapid urbanization that were having at least as significant an effect on American life as the political salons he chronicles. The novel is not as ostentatiously bizarre as some of its author's other books, but it is bright enough to create the impression that the sun never sets on Vidal's *Empire*.

Steven G. Kellman

Sources for Further Study

Kirkus Reviews. LV, May 1, 1987, p. 673.
Library Journal. CXII, July, 1987, p. 99.
Los Angeles Times Book Review. May 24, 1987, p. 1.
The New Republic. CXCVII, September 14, 1987, p. 49.
The New York Review of Books. XXXIV, September 24, 1987, p. 31.
The New York Times Book Review. XCII, June 14, 1987, p. 1.
Newsweek. CIX, June 15, 1987, p. 70.
Publishers Weekly. CCXXXI, May 1, 1987, p. 53.
Time. CXXIX, June 22, 1987, p. 73.
The Washington Post Book World. XVII, May 24, 1987, p. 1.

ENIGMA
The Life of Knut Hamsun

Author: Robert Ferguson
Publisher: Farrar, Straus and Giroux (New York). Illustrated. 454 pp. $30.00
Type of work: Literary biography
Time: 1859-1952

Robert Ferguson examines the life and literary career of Knut Hamsun, the acclaimed Norwegian novelist who was disgraced after World War II for his support of Norway's collaborationist government

> *Principal personages:*
> KNUT HAMSUN, a Norwegian novelist
> BERGLJOT BECH, his first wife
> MARIE ANDERSEN, his second wife

Knut Hamsun, who is Norway's most important novelist, was born Knut Pedersen on August 4, 1859, at the farm Garmotræet in the district of Lom, Norway. His father, Peder Pedersen, was a tailor and small farmer, and his mother, Tora, was also of peasant stock. In 1863, the family moved to Hamarøy in Nordland, Norway, there to settle on the farm Hamsund, from which Hamsun later took his surname.

Hamsun's childhood was happy until he was sent to live with his maternal uncle, a wealthy merchant and landowner, who also owned Hamsund. Though he treated Knut harshly, financial pressures forced the boy's parents to consent to the arrangement. Leaving his uncle's home in 1873, Hamsun began a long series of odd jobs. He clerked in several country stores and became by turns an itinerant peddler, a shoemaker's apprentice, and even a sheriff's deputy. He also worked as a country schoolmaster.

During these years, Hamsun began writing; his first novel, *Den gådefulde* (1877; the riddle), was published when he was only eighteen. Eventually, he managed to secure the patronage of a wealthy merchant and thus to focus more fully on his writing. Still, this support did not make Hamsun's way smooth. He traveled to Copenhagen to offer a new manuscript to Scandinavia's best-known publisher, Hegel of Gyldendal. To his dismay, his work was rejected, and he spent a difficult winter in the city of Kristiania, Norway. Later, this experience would provide him with the material for the novel that would become his first critical success: *Sult* (1890; *Hunger*, 1899).

Prior to the publication of *Hunger*, however, Hamsun lived for several years in the United States. Working in a variety of jobs, he read widely in both European and American literature and presented lectures on literary topics to Norwegian immigrants. In 1888, he returned to Scandinavia, taking up residence in Copenhagen, where the first chapter of *Hunger* was published anonymously in a periodical. Suddenly, though his identity remained a secret, Hamsun began receiving much attention in literary circles. The following year, he addressed Copenhagen's Student Society in a series of lectures that were published as *Fra det moderne Amerikas aandsliv* (1889; *The Spiritual Life of Modern America*, 1969).

The publication of *Hunger* in its complete form created a literary sensation and is regarded as a milestone in Scandinavian literary history. It is the first psychological novel in Norwegian literature, one which has influenced many later writers. In an 1890 article, Hamsun explained the principles and framework that he had employed in constructing the novel. This article, "Fra det ubevidste sjæleliv" ("From the Unconscious Life of the Mind"), was followed by a series of lectures in numerous Norwegian cities during 1891. Attacking earlier Norwegian literature for focusing on social conditions, Hamsun called for an exploration of the inner life of the exceptional individual.

During the 1890's, Hamsun wrote *Mysterier* (1892; *Mysteries*, 1927), *Pan* (1894; English translation, 1920), and *Victoria* (1898; English translation, 1929). Many critics consider *Pan* his most important work of the period, and some term it his masterpiece. Its point of view is complex, for the bulk of the story is narrated by the main character, the lieutenant Thomas Glahn; this section is followed by an epilogue narrated by Glahn's unnamed hunting companion and killer. Issues of power and love surface repeatedly in all Glahn's relationships; the ultimate message of the book is that power corrupts and love kills.

Although Hamsun enjoyed his growing reputation and traveled widely, he longed for more stability in his life and sought it in his relationship with Bergljot Bech, whom he met in 1897 and married the following year. The novel *Victoria* presents a fictionalized version of their romance. Unfortunately, conflicts arose between them, leading to the dissolution of the marriage in 1906.

During the years following the divorce, Hamsun wrote novels such as *Under hostsjærnen* (1906; *Under the Autumn Star*) and *En vandrer spiller med sordin* (1909), which were translated into English in a 1922 volume entitled *Wanderers*. These works, which feature middle-aged protagonists whose wanderings and ruminations on the nature of existence give the stories their shape, are not regarded as among Hamsun's best, but they are important for what they tell about his artistic development. After the novelist's 1909 marriage to the young actress Marie Andersen, however, his writings took a different turn.

In his literary lectures of 1891, Hamsun had expressed scorn for what he considered the dull social literature of his contemporaries and had advocated a kind of fiction that would explore the exceptional consciousness. After his second marriage, however, he began to produce works in which he attempted to balance the social and the psychological, emphasizing unusual men in their social setting. *Børn av tiden* (1913; *Children of the Age*, 1924) and its sequel, *Segelfoss By* (1915; *Segelfoss Town*, 1925) have as protagonists exceptional men, yet through them Hamsun analyzes the workings of society. In *Segelfoss Town*, for example, the aristocratic Willatz Holmsen embodies certain traditional values that eventually give way to those of the modern entrepreneur Tobias Holmengraa; here Hamsun appears to defend the traditional against all that is new in both intellectual and material culture.

In 1911, Hamsun bought the farm Skogheim in northern Norway, where he lived as a farmer and writer. In 1917, he moved to the southern part of the country. He drew upon his experiences at Skogheim to write what became his best-known book, the novel *Markens grøde* (1917; *Growth of the Soil*, 1920), for which he received the Nobel Prize in 1920.

After the publication of *Growth of the Soil*, Hamsun began searching for a new and permanent home. Eventually, he settled at the farm Nørholm, where he lived for the rest of his life. During this period, he farmed and also published two more novels, *Konerne ved vandposten* (1920; *The Women at the Pump*, 1928) and *Siste Kapitel* (1923; *Chapter the Last*, 1929).

Through the mid-1920's, a difficult time for Hamsun, he struggled against the fear that his creative powers had begun to fail him. During the winter of 1926, he availed himself of the services of a psychiatrist, and in the fall, he began one of his finest works, the novel *Landstrykere* (1927; *Vagabonds*, 1930). It is the first volume in a trilogy which was completed with the publication of *August* (1930; English translation, 1931) and *Men livet lever* (1933; *The Road Leads On*, 1934). The trilogy follows the adventures of August, a dreamer and eccentric, and shows how his actions destabilize the lives of others. These novels continue Hamsun's critical examination of modern society.

At the time of the publication of the last book of his August trilogy, Hamsun was well into his seventies. He was aging physically, and his hearing was failing. He produced only one more novel, *Ringen sluttet* (1936; *The Ring Is Closed*, 1937), and would probably have remained in retirement were it not for political developments. Hamsun had always admired Germany and German culture and detested the British. After the German invasion of Norway and the flight to England of King Haakon, Hamsun supported the collaborationist government headed by Vidkun Quisling and encouraged Norwegian soldiers not to resist the invaders. After the war, he was arrested and tried. In the course of the trial, his mental condition was examined; he was found not to be senile, but to have permanently impaired mental faculties. Nevertheless, he was convicted of treason and heavily fined, the result of which was that he was financially ruined. His last book was the poignant memoir *På gjengrodde stier* (1949; *On Overgrown Paths*, 1967), which abundantly demonstrated that his mental faculties were anything but impaired.

Hamsun passed his final years quietly. By tacit agreement, no critical attention was paid to his work, and he had nothing further to say. The author died on his farm on February 19, 1952.

Ferguson's *Enigma* is the first full-length Hamsun biography in English, and the major biography of the author in any language. It is a well-written and well-balanced work. The biographer pays an appropriate amount of attention to each of the major periods in Hamsun's life: his youth, his literary breakthrough, the renewal experienced during his middle years, and the tragedy of his old age, and he strikes a fairly good balance between Hamsun's personal life and the activities of Hamsun the author as well. Ferguson's biographical research, however, goes into greater depth than does his critical consideration of Hamsun's works; the bibliography is, in regard to literary criticism of Hamsun, rather disappointing. Ferguson has clearly had to privilege biographical concerns over in-depth literary analysis, perhaps in order to prevent the book from becoming too long.

Ferguson's enthusiasm for his subject has also led him to adopt a more tolerant attitude toward Hamsun's Nazi sympathies than is appropriate. One may inquire at length into what led Hamsun to his pathological social and political views, but no amount of explanation should be allowed to overshadow the fact that Hamsun's actions during World War II essentially constituted treason to both his country and humanity. These objections are, however, minor ones. Ferguson's biography of Hamsun constitutes a major achievement.

Jan Sjåvik

Sources for Further Study

Booklist. LXXXIII, April 15, 1987, p. 1245.
Kirkus Reviews. LV, April 1, 1987, p. 529.
Library Journal. CXII, May 15, 1987, p. 85.
Listener. CXVII, March 26, 1987, p. 30.
Los Angeles Times. May 28, 1987, V, p. 1.
The New York Times Book Review. XCII, June 7, 1987, p. 28.
The Observer. March 15, 1987, p. 26.
Publishers Weekly. CCXXXI, April 17, 1987, p. 57.
The Spectator. CCLVIII, April 18, 1987, p. 28.
The Times Educational Supplement. April 24, 1987, p. 23.

THE ENIGMA OF ARRIVAL

Author: V. S. Naipaul (1932-   )
Publisher: Alfred A. Knopf (New York). 354 pp. $17.95
Type of work: Novel
Time: 1950-1984
Locale: A village in Wiltshire, England

An autobiographical novel which centers on the mental journey of one man, a traveler and an exile, who unexpectedly finds peace of mind after many years in a foreign land

> *Principal characters:*
> THE NARRATOR, a middle-aged writer
> JACK, a farm worker
> BRAY, a local man who runs a car-hire business
> PITTON, a gardener
> MR. and MRS. PHILLIPS, the managers of the country estate
> ALAN, a writer
> UNNAMED, the landlord of the estate and a recluse

The journey has been a recurring motif in the Western literary and religious tradition, from Homer to T. S. Eliot, from the Bible to the medieval Christian mystics. The journey of the hero, in which he undergoes difficult trials before returning home triumphant, occurs in many mythologies around the world. Such examples might not at first glance seem relevant for a review of a novel by V. S. Naipaul. Although Naipaul frequently does write about journeys, they are usually journeys into exile and hopelessness, and his work is permeated by a sense of irrevocable loss. This was one of the themes, for example, of Naipaul's last work of fiction, *A Bend in the River* (1979). In his autobiographical novel *The Enigma of Arrival*, however, familiar themes emerge in an unexpectedly fresh and positive light.

The novel is about the separation of a man from his homeland, and from himself, followed by his eventual recovery of wholeness and integrity, in which he feels connected with nature and its rhythms. It is a story about death and rebirth, about the gaining of wisdom, and of calm insight into the complex mystery of things. As such it is one of the most optimistic and profound of Naipaul's works.

The story covers a period of nearly thirty-five years (although, characteristically, Naipaul does not approach his material chronologically, but loops forward and backward at will until the tapestry is complete), beginning with the narrator's first journey from his home in Trinidad in 1950, at the age of eighteen, to take up a scholarship at Oxford University. He has already decided that he is going to be a writer. The events of this first trip—arrival in New York, passage by sea to Southampton, a two-month stay at a boardinghouse in Earl's Court, London—are less important than the young man's state of mind. He has a preconceived idea of what a writer should be like and of what constitutes suitable material about which to write. Without realizing it, he is being false to himself, not responding truly to the experiences he is accumulating. He later attributes much of this to the abstract education he had received in Trinidad (for example, he could write an essay on the French cinema but had never seen a French film). It is only later that this split between man and writer is healed.

After twenty years in England, he finds himself mentally exhausted, haunted by the fear of failure (although he has also had his share of success), and dogged by a recurring nightmare in which his head seems to be exploding and he is certain that he is about to die. In this depressed frame of mind, he moves to an isolated country setting in Waldenshaw, a village near Salisbury in the southern English county of Wiltshire. Living in a cottage on the grounds of an old manor house which had been built at the height of Britain's imperial wealth and power, initially he feels out of place, a foreigner from another hemisphere.

In the more than ten years he spends there, however, his life takes an unexpected turn. He experiences a rebirth. For the first time in his adult life, he finds that even though he remains in an alien land, he is at peace. He learns to absorb the contours of the landscape, to appreciate the changing of the seasons—which forms a constant background in the novel—the fruits that each season brings, and the sacredness of the land. It is as if he were learning a second language and seeing things for the first time. He journeys back to a "simplicity and directness" of perception. It is almost like a return to Eden, a "second, happier childhood . . . the second arrival (but with an adult's perception) at a knowledge of natural things, together with the fulfillment of the child's dream of the safe house in the wood." This is a remarkable journey for an author who has so frequently chosen to depict alienation and rootlessness, the incompatibility between men and their environment.

It is through the narrator's daily walks, which take on something of the quality of a spiritual pilgrimage, that this new life grows. Much of what he learns comes from his observation of the simple integrity in the life of Jack, the farm worker, and the manner in which he cultivates his garden. The narrator senses the contrast between Jack and himself—Jack fits his environment, and he seems to have found fulfillment in the routine of life that he has cultivated, in tune with the seasons. His life appears like a "constant celebration." It is because he knows how to live that he also knows how, when the time comes, to die. The narrator sees one of Jack's final acts—rousing himself, when mortally sick, to drive down to the public house to spend a Christmas evening with his friends—as heroic and life-affirming. Learning how to cope with death is one of the underlying themes of the novel, and Jack is held up as an example.

Jack remains a strong presence in the novel even after his death. Although his garden is turned into allotments and later concreted over, there is something eternal about the man, and the narrator permits himself the belief that "below all that concrete over his garden some seed, some root, would survive; and one day perhaps, when the concrete was taken up (as surely one day it would be taken up, since few dwelling places are eternal) . . . some memory of Jack, preserved in some shrub or flower or vine, would come to life again."

This sense of the continuity and interpenetration of all life pervades the novel. The land itself is not isolated from human life, but "partakes of what we breathe into it, is touched by our moods and memories." The shrub of flower may contain a memory of Jack. The continuity is seen also in the narrator's strong sense of history and of antiquity, of the different civilizations which have occupied the land—from the ancient Britons who built Stonehenge, to the Romans, to the Anglo-Saxons who founded the local town of Amesbury in the tenth century. Nothing is ever entirely new; there is always something that has gone before it, leaving its traces.

This continuity of life, maintained through the passing of countless human generations, has immediate consequences for individual life: "It is as if we all carry in our makeup the effects of accidents that have befallen our ancestors, as if we are in many ways programmed before we are born, our lives half outlined for us." In passages such as this, one traces echoes of Naipaul's Indian heritage (although born in Trinidad his parents were Indian): the strong sense of the ways in which humanity bears a collective Karma, the legacy for good or ill that the dead bequeath to the living. He also shares the Eastern sense of the cyclic nature of human life and history. Patterns tend to repeat themselves in individual lives, and Naipaul keenly perceives the odd ways in which these cycles may meet or intersect, as if all humanity is locked into a series of interconnected Karmic wheels. He notes, for example, the quirks of history which brought him to occupy the same grounds as his landlord, the strange way in which two lives so outwardly different ("at opposite ends of empire and privilege") come sympathetically to touch.

The importance of pattern is seen in one incident which takes place in 1950, when the narrator leaves home for the first time. As the plane soars into the sky, he sees the landscape of his childhood from the air. At ground level, it had always seemed so poor and messy, but from the air he could see a larger pattern which had its own logic. It was as if he had never seen his childhood environment until this point. It is a significant moment to which the narrator twice returns, and it encapsulates one of the main themes of the novel. The larger one's vision, the more one can see beyond the chaos of the moment to a wholeness which possesses its own validity and its own special kind of beauty.

This larger perspective also enables one to connect the past and the present, which is another recurring motif in the novel. It is striking to observe how much of the novel revolves around memory. Meeting an old man, the narrator immediately reflects that the man must have known in his youth people whose memories went back to the early years of the nineteenth century; the narrator's memories of his boyhood in Trinidad continually interact with the present scene, and many of the people he encounters live in their memories of the past. Memory too is an aspect of continuity.

It is the recognition of such patterns which mitigates the narrator's recurring awareness of flux and change. Although he now lives in an area of England which to the casual observer seems timeless, it is his temperament "to see the possibility. . . of ruin, even at the moment of creation," and the Indian cast of his mind comes out again when he meditates on a world in flux: "the drum of creation in the god's right hand, the flame of destruction in his left." Yet this gives him no cause for grief; on the contrary, it lends a poignancy and beauty to each moment.

Against this background of mature reflection, the narrator encounters the local Wiltshire people, a somewhat undistinguished collection of English folk made interesting by the acuteness of his insight into their lives. He has the gift of seeing from their points of view, and they in turn respond to his interest in the routine of their lives. For the most part, their stories make up the warp and woof of ordinary life, with its conflicts, its established routines, its hidden miseries and small satisfactions. In addition to Jack (who in a sense is the hero of the book), there is the car-hire man, Bray, opinionated, arrogant, and self-reliant, a man who enjoys being the odd man out. He surprisingly finds a new dimension to his life in religious faith, which he had previously scorned. Ironically, his illumination comes about through the influence of a woman with whom he has an adulterous affair. Bray's next-door neighbor, whom he dislikes, is Pitton, the gardener. Pitton, always punctual and meticulous, dresses like a gentleman and looks anything but a gardener. Indeed, in the opinion of the managers of the estate, Mr. and Mrs. Phillips, Pitton does not "know" about gardening; he is a kind of impostor, ignorant of the subtle mysteries of his art. These four characters live close to one another "in a net of mutual resentment." In addition, there is the promising but unproductive writer Alan, who commits suicide, and the narrator's reclusive landlord. The narrator never speaks to him and glimpses him only twice, but he nevertheless feels a silent bond with him and enjoys piecing together the story of his life.

The final three chapters of this five-chapter novel increasingly focus on death. The ivy which gives chapter 3 its title is responsible for destroying many of the trees in the grounds of the estate, and the narrator calculates that it first took hold when the landlord retreated into solitude—it symbolically represents his denial of life.

The flock of rooks which descend on the estate in chapter 4 are omens of death (the chapter contains two deaths, as well as a remembered death).

The short final chapter, which serves as both climax and epilogue, begins with the narrator, in the wake of a serious illness, subject to increasing melancholy and given to the contemplation of death. The death of his sister, and his return to Trinidad for a memorial service, force him to come to terms with death. It is as if V. S. Naipaul has journeyed, like Edgar in *King Lear*, to the realization that "Men must endure/ Their going hence, even as their coming hither:/ Ripeness is all." It gives him, he relates, the impetus to write *The Enigma of Arrival*, with its theme of a man coming to peace with himself and with his environment. The narrative ends where it began, with the focus on Jack and his garden.

Bryan Aubrey

Sources for Further Study

Booklist. LXXXIII, January 15, 1987, p. 729.
Kirkus Reviews. LV, January 15, 1987, p. 89.
Library Journal. CXII, March 1, 1987, p. 93.
London Review of Books. IX, April 2, 1987, p. 16.
Los Angeles Times Book Review. March 22, 1987, p. 3.
The New Republic. CXCVI, April 13, 1987, p. 27.
The New York Review of Books. XXXIV, April 9, 1987, p. 3.
The New York Times Book Review. XCII, March 22, 1987, p. 11.
The New Yorker. LXII, August 11, 1986, p. 26.
Publishers Weekly CCXXXI, January 23, 1987, p. 62.
Time. CXXIX, March 2, 1987, p. 75.

THE ESSAYS OF VIRGINIA WOOLF
Volume I: 1904-1912

Author: Virginia Woolf (1882-1941)
Edited, with an introduction, by Andrew McNeillie
Publisher: Harcourt Brace Jovanovich (New York). 411 pp. $19.95
Type of work: Essays
Time: 1904-1912

Most of the pieces included in this first volume of Woolf's complete essays have not previously appeared in book form

Decades after her death, Virginia Woolf continues to be served well by admiring critics and editors, much to the advantage of those who wish to study this great writer systematically. The first of these admirers was her husband. Leonard Woolf gave to this woman of precarious physical and mental health the support and encouragement that enabled her to publish regularly for a quarter century; after her death, he gathered many of her best uncollected essays and short stories in book form as well as an excellent selection of excerpts from her diary.

Since Leonard Woolf's own death in 1969, a number of valuable works have appeared, including Quentin Bell's candid but tactful biography of his aunt, *Virginia Woolf* (1972), and Nigel Nicolson's six-volume *The Letters of Virginia Woolf* (1975-1980). The complete diary has been edited in five volumes by Anne Olivier Bell (1977 to 1984), enabling Woolf's readership to trace her reflections on her art from 1915 until 1941. B. J. Kirkpatrick's *A Bibliography of Virginia Woolf* (third edition, 1980) has kept up with a continuing stream of Woolf material.

In *The Essays of Virginia Woolf, Volume I: 1904-1912*, Andrew McNeillie, who assisted on the diary, presents in chronological sequence all the essays and reviews Woolf is known to have written from 1904, when, as twenty-two-year-old Virginia Stephen, she began to write for the periodical press, until her marriage to Woolf in 1912. Clearly these years were crucial ones, not only in the sense of being apprentice years but also in determining whether she could overcome the mental disorders to which she was subject. She had suffered her first serious breakdown in 1895 when she was only thirteen; the second occurred in the spring of 1904. The first essays in this book were undertaken in the fall of that year as part of her convalescence. It must be remembered that her illness followed upon a long period of ministering to her father, Sir Leslie Stephen, a noted writer who had finally died the preceding February. As a young woman who had inherited his literary aptitude and grown up among books and writers—James Russell Lowell was her godfather, for example, and young Virginia was accustomed to seeing Henry James in the house—she lacked an outlet for her talent. She keenly missed the university education which both of her brothers received as a matter of course. Her pursuit of private lessons in Greek beginning in 1902 signifies her desire to achieve an education equivalent to that which well-bred young Englishmen, whether academically inclined or not, regarded as their birthright.

A kind friend of her early years, Violet Dickinson, cared for her during her most difficult months and encouraged her to submit reviews and essays to the editor of the women's pages of *The Guardian*, a weekly clerical newspaper. Shortly thereafter she began to teach in an adult education program in London. Writing was clearly her vocation, and within a matter of months she branched out into other publications. Most of the early reviews were of ephemeral books. An exception in 1905 was Edith Wharton's *The House of Mirth*, which she praised in a mere one-paragraph notice. An essay on Jane Welsh Carlyle's letters anticipates the kind of subject she came to relish: the personal revelations of people—especially women—in a literary milieu. Although the *Guardian* reviews were usually brief, they were not perfunctory. She generally contrived a shrewd assessment of a book's weaknesses and closed with such praise as she could honestly bestow. She apparently regarded a plot summary of a novel as her duty and sometimes gave away more of the denouement than readers likely would have wanted.

Denied degrees and convinced by her teaching experience that her talents lay elsewhere, she had no inclination to academic criticism. The approach she favored insisted on no sharp divisions between book review and personal essay. Her pure essays—this volume contains a few with titles such as "On a Faithful Friend," "Street Music," and (significantly) "The Decay of Essay-writing"—are early work and represent what she accurately judged a dying convention. Her assignments from Bruce Richmond, editor of *The Times Literary Supplement*, gave her more room to develop her own ideas, to use the book at hand as a base from which to launch observations drawing upon her already extensive reading. She began early to develop the style familiar to the "common reader" she later addressed in two collections of her mature years—a boon to her bibliographers, incidentally, who must establish her canon amidst piles of yellowing periodicals filled with unsigned articles. Publications such as *The Times Literary Supplement* afforded her the chance to exercise her wit. Thus, in a 1907 review of a new edition of a life of Sir Philip Sidney by his friend Fulke Greville, she finds the author "often closely throttled in the embraces of a sinuous metaphor." Later that year, she harpoons "tedious and prolix people much at the mercy of their pens."

Especially when she enjoyed a biography, she focused much more on the life than on the book. Her interest in biographical theory, well known from previously published essays and from her novel *Orlando* (1928), surfaces early. She chastises William Bayard Hale, author of *A Week in the White House with Theodore Roosevelt* (1908), which purported to be an intimate portrait of Roosevelt but relied heavily on a long string of observations of his daily routine: "Words were never meant to take the place of eyes, but to interpret what they see." She is often found objecting to biographers who merely gather information in large batches and fail to select, arrange, and interpret their material; she especially laments literary biographers who cannot significantly relate biographical facts to artistic achievement. This daughter of the editor of *The Dictionary of National Biography* (1921 to 1922) suffered through a life of Maria Edgeworth which failed to seize "the opportunity of getting at the truth at the risk of being dull," a risk she herself had to take late in her career in *Roger Fry: A Biography* (1940). A competent life, such as Wilbur L. Cross's of Laurence Sterne, elicits from Woolf a batch of critical insights concerning both fiction and biography.

None of the essays before 1909 found its way into the *Collected Essays* which Leonard Woolf issued in 1966 and 1967, but McNeillie's chronological sequence showed her talent ripening in 1908 with a perceptive review of a biography of Thomas Hood, an acerbic assessment of *The Reminiscences of Lady Dorothy Nevill* (1906), and a review of *Letters of the Wordsworth Family* (1907) which nimbly sketches the relationship between the poet's rather commonplace letters and his best poetry. The aforementioned book on Roosevelt, also from that year, demonstrates one of Woolf's enduring prejudices. While she acknowledged Americans of genius, her general attitude toward the United States was condescending, and she never deigned to cross the Atlantic. To her, Theodore Roosevelt exemplified American complacency and insensitivity to finer thought and emotion. In a note, McNeillie quotes a private Woolf letter expressing her glee at what she took to be her success at deriding, while seeming to praise, the president. American readers today, however, may be inclined to think that she underrated the intelligence of their grandparents, as indeed she underrates Roosevelt, for she did not see through the façade he erected to deflect public attention from his intellectual and artistic interests (he was, for example, one of the earliest patrons of Edwin Arlington Robinson) and toward the presumably more acceptable machismo and democratic sympathies he also radiated.

In 1909 she wrote her best essays yet, three of which—"Sterne," "A Friend of Johnson," and "Oliver Wendell Holmes"—Leonard Woolf reprinted. McNeillie's entries for that year also include a perceptive essay on James Boswell at a time when Thomas Macaulay's judgment that Samuel Johnson's biographer was merely a fortunate fool still precluded general recognition of Boswell's genius. Yet another fine essay nominally reviews a biography of Richard Brinsley Sheridan but actually paints a fascinating portrait of Sheridan as playwright, politician, and husband.

After more than five years of steady reviewing, Woolf published only four essays from the spring of 1910 until her marriage two years later. One possible explanation for this sharp decrease in productivity is illness. The year

1910 took her again to the brink of madness, and she turned ill again for several months early in 1912. Woolf is normally the sanest of essayists, but a review published early in 1911 of a book about the first Duke and Duchess of Newcastle-upon-Tyne has an uncharacteristically morbid tone. Another factor—probably related to her illness, for creative work strained her nervous system to its limit—was her increasing attention to "Melymbrosia," her working title for her first novel, begun perhaps as early as 1907 and finally published in 1915 as *The Voyage Out*. For whatever reason, after establishing herself as a considerable critical talent, she exercised that talent very little for a number of years, for when McNeillie's second volume appears, it will undoubtedly show that the hiatus continued through the first years of her married life, when she endured her most prolonged and dangerous breakdown.

In addition to the three 1909 essays mentioned above, twenty-three of the other more than one hundred essays in this volume have been previously reprinted, most of these in Mary Lyon's *Books and Portraits* (1977). Few of the essays uncollected by Leonard Woolf rise to the standard of her better mature work. Nevertheless, McNeillie has performed a signal service to all lovers of Virginia Woolf. Now for the first time it is possible to trace her development as critic and essayist, and it is no small pleasure to see in this volume the unfolding of a first-rate critical intelligence.

The editor has also provided an extensive apparatus. The notes include not only the publishing history of the inclusions, where relevant, but also references to Nicolson's edition of the letters, to others of Woolf's writings on the same subjects, to her "reading notes" in the Sussex University Library, and to pertinent Woolf manuscripts in the Berg Collection of the New York Public Library. McNeillie has attempted to identify allusions in the essays. Occasionally he is overzealous; it is doubtful, for example, that many readers of this book need to be informed that *The Faerie Queene* was the work of Edmund Spenser. He has also performed the laborious task of referencing Woolf's quotations from books under review, from which labor the reader can discover that she was often careless, though seldom misleadingly so, in quoting her sources.

Since most of Woolf's reviews were unsigned, the determination of her authorship has been an ongoing process. Only at the last minute did McNeillie determine her responsibility for one 1906 *Guardian* review; as a result it has been relegated to an appendix. The editor has included several essays termed "doubtful" by Woolf's bibliographer and has summarized the evidence in favor of the attributions in an editorial note. Another appendix prints seven reviews McNeillie considers apocryphal; a last-minute note, however, claims one as "almost certainly" Woolf's.

The present volume can profitably be read against the background of Woolf's letters and existing biographies. If McNeillie includes citations to

Bell's edition of her diary (which she did not begin to write until 1915) in future volumes, he will have taken another notable step in facilitating the understanding of Virginia Woolf's achievement as an essayist.

Robert P. Ellis

Sources for Further Study

Booklist. LXXXIII, February 15, 1987, p. 870.
Encounter. LXVIII, January, 1987, p. 57.
Kirkus Reviews. LV, January 1, 1987, p. 52.
Library Journal. CXII, March 1, 1987, p. 78.
London Review of Books. IX, April 23, 1987, p. 14.
Los Angeles Times Book Review. February 8, 1987, p. 3.
New Statesman. CXIII, January 2, 1987, p. 23.
The New York Times. January 30, 1987, p. 20.
The New Yorker. LXIII, April 13, 1987, p. 100.
Publishers Weekly. CCXXXI, January 9, 1987, p. 73.
The Times Literary Supplement. December 12, 1986, p. 1393.

EVELYN WAUGH
The Early Years 1903-1939

Author: Martin Stannard (1947-   )
Publisher: W. W. Norton and Co. (New York). Illustrated. 537 pp. $24.95
Type of work: Literary biography
Time: 1903-1939
Locale: Great Britain

The first volume of a two-volume biography of novelist Evelyn Waugh, containing a discussion of Waugh's ancestors, his childhood, his schooling, and his career—from his earliest success to his establishment as a major writer

> *Principal personages:*
> EVELYN WAUGH, the English novelist
> CATHERINE WAUGH, his mother
> ARTHUR WAUGH, his father
> FRANCIS CREASE, an illustrator and book designer
> J. F. ROXBURGH, Waugh's schoolmate
> EVELYN "SHE-EVELYN" GARDNER, Waugh's first wife
> LAURA HERBERT, his second wife

The reputation of Evelyn Waugh as a major literary artist continues to grow. The wildly inventive comic novels and the more heartfelt fiction of his later years have been established as landmarks of twentieth century English literature. Waugh's importance will be further enhanced by this excellent study of the life of the artist.

The major accomplishment of the work is that it lays to rest the vision of Waugh as an improbable clown, turning out witty but shallow satires. Waugh insisted that he was not a writer of satire, because satire could only flourish "in a stable society and presupposes homogeneous moral standards." He maintained, rather, that he was creating "little independent systems of order of his own." This serious purpose in the creation of his fiction has often been ignored, partially because of the similarities of the works to the light comedy of such writers as Ronald Firbank and P. G. Wodehouse, but also because of Waugh's own deliberate transformation in his later years into an eccentric Colonel Blimp-like character. Stannard's biography uncovers the depths in the man. Here, Waugh emerges as a man possessed by a monklike devotion to his craft while driven by a revulsion to the isolated act of writing into the bright whirl of society, a world where he could never be at home, for he loathed everything modern that that social banquet offered.

Stannard begins with a discussion of Waugh's ancestry and of his early childhood days and complicated relationship to his parents. His mother represented devotion, care, and predictability. Arthur Waugh on the other hand, was often histrionic, devoted to the publishing business of Chapman and Hall and absorbed in cricket and the manly world it represented. In short, he was the embodiment of those qualities of the upper-middle-class

Edwardian gentleman that Waugh came to loathe. The young Evelyn felt isolated when sent to school at Lancing College, an establishment he viewed as inferior and somehow demeaning. He never shook this sense of social stigma, but these early school days did provide him with the models of two different ways of life that would dominate his later years.

During his years at Lancing he came under the influence of Francis Crease and J. F. Roxburgh. In his autobiography, *A Little Learning* (1964), Waugh states that these two men were his "mentors," and they stood for the widely divergent lives of the isolated aesthetic craftsman and the flamboyantly extroverted man of the world. Francis Crease lived near Lancing and worked as an illustrator and book designer. In 1919, the young Evelyn had won first prize in the school's art exhibition for an illustrated missal. As a result of this demonstrated talent, Evelyn became a pupil of Crease, and a friendship developed between the older, delicate, and artistic man and the isolated schoolboy. From Crease, Evelyn received a profound lesson in the essential nature of craft and design, structure and form. For the rest of his life, Waugh insisted that structure defined true art.

At about the same time as the lessons with Crease began, J. F. Roxburgh returned to the school with a distinguished war record. Roxburgh and his personality dominated Lancing. He was a classical scholar of impeccable taste—elegant, refined, worldly. Waugh came to appreciate Roxburgh's outgoing personality and individual charm. He began to create a "personality" for himself—disdainful, sharp, critical. These two figures and what they represented drove Waugh along contradictory paths.

Waugh's Oxford years, from 1922 to 1924, were not years of intense scholarly endeavor. In fact, his tutor at Oxford, C. R. M. F. Cruttwell, became his nemesis and in later years was pilloried in novel after novel, as a succession of unpleasant characters appeared under the name of Cruttwell. As Stannard notes, at Oxford Waugh again faced the prospect of two ways of life, neither of them concerned with the traditional pursuit of learning. One side of his nature tempted him to make the best use of his "faun-like appearance" and become a wise clown, amusing his friends and annoying the authorities. The other side of him sought to become the serious artist, respected by friends and the Oxford world at large for his genius and craft. Close friendships with men such as Sir Harold Acton, Henry Yorke, and Brian Howard developed his aesthetic sense and gave him an abiding respect for the artistic life.

Leaving Oxford behind him after years of revelry and further artistic refinement, Waugh found himself unsure of his purpose, unclear as to his future. The years after Oxford were filled with failures as a schoolmaster and a socialite, even a failure at suicide. Waugh lacked concern for the majority of his pupils, lacked the resources for a life in society, and even lacked the determination to end it all when his attempt to drown himself was foiled by a school of jellyfish. Waugh later stated that he turned to writing reluctantly because he was a failure at everything else.

Having met and become entranced with a young woman named Evelyn Gardner, Waugh married her. He and his wife ("He-Evelyn" and "She-Evelyn") shone as stars in the world of the Bright Young People who dominated the London panorama—beautiful, witty, frivolous. Waugh lacked the resources to maintain such a life and was always on the edge of financial doom, but he clung to the festive life no matter what his circumstances. Having interviewed Evelyn Gardner, Stannard gives a balanced account of the subsequent collapse of the marriage. She tells her side of the separation, a separation that occurred when she fell in love with John Heygate and, without warning, left Waugh to live with another man. Stannard seems to defend her on the grounds of Waugh's sexual inexperience and inadequacy, a "modern" view of the marriage state that Waugh would have found contemptible. (Waugh stated at one time that the notion that you could not lead a happy life unless your sex life was happy was "mischievous nonsense" that led to the divorce courts.)

The marriage had spurred him into writing as a profession. He attempted to finance the high life through essays, reviews, and books. The first important work was a biography of Pre-Raphaelite painter Dante Gabriel Rossetti. The biography, *Rossetti: His Life and Works* (1978), offers a vision of Waugh's early aesthetic tastes and his dislike of "interpretation," unless such judgments be supported by a series of facts or a coherent system of aesthetic principles. Waugh the stern, uncompromising novelist was already being formed in this early book. The biography was a critical success, but it did not generate the anticipated revenues.

Waugh proceeded to begin work on *Decline and Fall* (1928), his first major work of fiction and an undisputed masterpiece. This novel of the misadventures of Paul Pennyfeather in the labyrinth of modern life embodies those principles and ideas that Stannard shows slowly coalescing in Waugh's imagination—cool objectivity, high fantasy, raucous absurdity, stern criticism, impeccable design. Waugh's first novel remains such an impressive piece of work because the artistic bases for it had been laid slowly and deliberately from Waugh's schoolboy days—the aesthetics of the fiction are clear and concise because they are inseparable from the life.

As with the Rossetti book, *Decline and Fall* was a critical success, but it provided only modest financial rewards. Ironically, Waugh found himself writing for Chapman and Hall, his father's publishing firm. The ironies multiplied when, with his next volume, *Vile Bodies* (1930), he became one of their most successful authors. *Vile Bodies*, a biting portrayal of London's Bright Young People and the barrenness of their world, created a sensation on its appearance in January, 1930. Waugh in later years never spoke approvingly of the work, most likely because the memory of its creation was not a pleasant one. In the midst of its composition, his wife deserted him. Waugh found himself more alone than ever. His obsession with the whims of "Fortune" and the emptiness of a haphazard, uncontrolled, patternless life intensified. As Stannard states, he was more filled than ever with a "hunger for permanence."

The pivotal event in Waugh's life was his conversion to Catholicism in 1930. A superficial account of the event might say that he sought refuge from the failed marriage within the Church, but the fact is that Waugh still desired a wife, a family, and a home; by entering the Church, he was effectively closing off for himself any chance of such happiness, as the Church did not recognize divorce and thus the union with Evelyn Gardner was still in force. One of the few weaknesses of Stannard's biography is his inability to focus on the clear reasons for this conversion. In the space of this first volume he offers many reasons for Waugh's decision. At one point, he sees it as generational despair in the face of the postwar world, in its way analogous to W. H. Auden and Christopher Isherwood's acceptance of Socialism. Elsewhere he states that Waugh had a "mystical habit of mind" that seems to have settled finally into the Catholic church. There are also hints that Waugh was attracted by the exuberance of the Mediterranean as opposed to the "pinched and parsimonious culture" of the Northern Protestant countries. Later, he speaks of the "meticulous institutional organization" that appealed to Waugh and, again later, of Waugh's belief that the Church was the only hope of civilization to fend off barbarism.

While these ideas were all held by Waugh, the simple fact is Waugh joined the Catholic church because, in his own words, "it is true." There was no sense of sentimentality, no appeal of high aesthetics. Waugh simply came to believe that the Church embodied a true and concise philosophical system and therefore he must be a part of it. Father Martin D'Arcy, who gave Waugh instruction in the faith, states that few converts could have been as matter-of-fact as Waugh. D'Arcy says that Waugh entered the Church with "little emotion" but "on firm intellectual conviction," even if that conviction meant he might be barring himself from future happiness.

For Waugh, life finally had permanence and order. The vagaries of modern life could be viewed even more vividly in all of their absurdities, for they were no longer real; the supernatural was now the real. Waugh had also freed himself from fortune and the governance of chance. In his mind, he had found the truth and, in doing so, could now comprehend his place in the divine plan, the role that had been created for him that only he could fill—the objective reporter of the horrors of the modern world. The subsequent novels of the 1930's, *Black Mischief* (1932), *A Handful of Dust* (1934), which many believe is his masterpiece, and *Scoop* (1938), grew out of this assurance. Stannard also provides a generous discussion of Waugh's biography of Edmund Campion, which presents a comprehensive vision of

Waugh's philosophy and his understanding of the meaningful life, the soul in harmony with God. Stannard restores the book to its central place in the Waugh canon.

The 1930's also saw Waugh embarking on his many travels and assuming his role as travel writer and reporter. His expeditions to Africa, Spitzbergen, and Latin America are documented here with great precision. The reader is also given a feel for Waugh's contained restlessness and profound boredom. If the real purpose of life commenced after death, death was not to be feared. What was daunting was the prospect of continued years of dealing with the grotesqueries of the modern age. As a result, Waugh kept in motion, seeking the range of the world, making new friends in the world of society. Fortunately for him, he did find a measure of happiness and stability with his marriage to Laura Herbert in 1937. After years of waiting, Waugh was granted an annulment by Rome on the grounds that neither he nor his first wife had possessed "serious intent" when entering the marriage. This freed Waugh to wed a charming young woman with whom he had fallen in love. The marriage endured until his death.

The first volume of Stannard's biography concludes on the eve of World War II, with a changed Waugh. The happiness provided by his marriage impelled him to a new direction in his art. He was no longer satisfied with the comic vision of the earlier novels. He sought a more rounded and more heartfelt aesthetic in what is now known as *Work Suspended* (1949). The fragmentary nature of the work results from Waugh's correct perception that the world he was attempting to display in this work was about to vanish forever in the rush of oncoming events. He abandoned the novel and prepared himself for his role in the looming cataclysm. The second volume of Stannard's biography, if it upholds the precision and excellence of the first, should provide fascinating reading.

David Allen White

Sources for Further Study

Booklist. LXXXIII, March 15, 1987, p. 1089.
Commonweal. CXIV, October 23, 1987, p. 602.
Contemporary Review. CCXLIX, November 1986, p. 278.
Library Journal. CXII, April 1, 1987, p. 150.
London Review of Books. VIII, December 4, 1986, p. 14.
National Review. XXXIX, July 31, 1987, p. 48.
The New York Times Book Review. XCII, August 30, 1987, p. 1.
The Times Literary Supplement. November 7, 1986, p. 1237.
The Washington Post Book World. XVII, August 16, 1987, p. 1.

EVERY FORCE EVOLVES A FORM
Twenty Essays

Author: Guy Davenport (1927-   )
Publisher: North Point Press (San Francisco, California). Illustrated. 171 pp. $16.95
Type of work: Essays

These essays examine work by particular painters, poets, and other writers to explore questions of form and meaning in art

Looking at the economic forces in American life that have banished the supermarkets in Lexington, Kentucky, to a beltway, and the post office to the next county, Guy Davenport claims, "Every building in the United States is an offense to invested capital. It occupies space which, as greed acknowledges no limits, can be better utilized." Davenport makes this remark at the start of "Making It Uglier to the Airport," an essay review dealing with books about architecture, utopianism, the history of cities, and family identity in the twentieth century. The range of topics and Davenport's willingness to make challenging assessments are typical of the twenty essays found in *Every Force Evolves a Form*, and so is his interest in the factors accounting for particular phenomena.

Davenport takes his title from a statement by Mother Ann Lee, the founder of the Shakers. Focusing chiefly on the work of painters, poets, and other writers associated with twentieth century modernism, he explores in one essay after another questions relating to the ways in which meaning arises from the achievement of aesthetic form. "A work of art," he says, "is a form that articulates forces, making them intelligible." In some instances, such as the essay in which he examines Vladimir Nabokov's lectures on *Don Quixote de la Mancha* (1605, 1615), Davenport deals with a scholar or critic intent on restoring for a contemporary reader the ideas shaping a particular text. In others, he focuses on the ideas themselves and traces their transformation through one or more creative minds, as he does with the notion of birds as daimons in poems by William Wordsworth, Edgar Allan Poe, Walt Whitman, and Gerard Manley Hopkins in the essay giving the collection its title. Whatever the subject at hand, however, Davenport examines the ways in which ideas take shape for poet, scholar, or painter, tracing both the origins of the materials with which he works and the particular formulation he gives them in his work. This focus gives *Every Force Evolves a Form* both unity and persuasive power.

Davenport opens the collection with "The Champollion of Table Manners," on the surface a review of *The Origin of Table Manners: Introduction to a Science of Mythology*, 3 (1978), by Claude Lévi-Strauss. He says it is an "ungivingly tedious book" but celebrates Lévi-Strauss' skill, and influence, as an interpreter of culture.

The primitive mind sees disorder in itself and enlists every discipline to keep from contaminating the world. We, says Lévi-Strauss, see all disorder outside ourselves, in the

world and in other people; our anxiety is that they will contaminate us: botch our
composure, snatch our opportunities, queer our luck.

Davenport's statement is a key both to his analysis of Lévi-Strauss' impact
on the ways we look at our culture and to Davenport's own reasons for
exploring the ways in which creative minds work. He agrees with Lévi-
Strauss in seeing structuralism, expecially in its application to the analysis of
literary texts, as faddish. Nevertheless, his own work as scholar and critic
betrays the influence of Lévi-Strauss, whose research lies behind so much
literary criticism of a structuralist sort, as an interpreter who sees human
behavior as central to the significance of any work of art.

The central behavior of the artist, Davenport suggests in "What Are
Those Monkeys Doing?," an essay dealing with French primitive artist
Henri Rousseau, is a fusion of idea and form that transforms his materials
into a self-referential artifact. "What he was after with all his work was a
buzz of interest, talk, the generation of texts. Ironically, what we got was
anecdotes (a good half of them suspect) about the man, not the work. We
have a debt to pay Rousseau." Davenport is alert to inaccurate scholarship,
which in its simplest form is a failure to see the evidence on the page—in
this case, the canvas. The Rousseau monkeys referred to in the essay's title
are not two, as credentialed commentators claim, but five; they are not tip-
ping over a milk bottle in the foreground of the canvas, for the object is
clearly a soda siphon; and they stare out of the painting, Davenport argues
from details in the picture, at the European explorer who approaches to
investigate what they are doing to his African campsite. Davenport points
out ways in which certain Rousseau paintings reflect the sensibilities of fellow Frenchmen, the poet Arthur Rimbaud and the novelist Gustave Flaubert. All three, he suggests, see the world in similar ways, regardless of
whether they are aware of common traditions.

Davenport sets out to find the traditions behind work by the American
poet E. E. Cummings in "Transcendental Satyr" and by the Irish novelist
James Joyce in "Ariadne's Dancing Floor." Both essays trace the ancestry of
particular texts back to the Greeks, in the case of Cummings to the typog-
raphy of the textbooks from which he studied the Greek language, and to
the mythic labyrinth of the Minotaur in the case of Joyce. The sentimentality of Cummings and the difficulties readers have voicing his poems, Davenport suggests, derive as much as anything from his decision to make the
poems look like fragments of Greek literature. The textual richness of
Joyce's fiction, on the other hand, here the Daedalian knots in books such
as *Ulysses* (1922) and *Finnegans Wake* (1939), derives from "the imaginative
bonding of images in an harmonic pattern. . . . This is the method of all art,
and one artist differs from another in the quality of invention with which he
bonds one image to another." As Davenport suggests, artists such as Joyce

and Cummings invent themselves out of the influences they choose, not always consciously, for their work. The artist and the work come to be seen, however, almost permanently in relationship to the elements going into the making.

Davenport is good at explaining the why and how of this identification of artist and tradition. His essays on Cummings, Joyce, and Rousseau explore the generation of particular texts. Three other essays, originally the Arthur and Margaret Glasgow Lectures for 1985 at Washington and Lee University, are the most interesting pieces in *Every Force Evolves a Form*. They are also the most challenging, for in them Davenport examines in specific terms the differences in approach to a text that characterize the artist, the scholar, and the critic. In "The Artist as Critic," he advances the hypothesis that the artist creates within the context of the work of other artists. It is a statement recalling T. S. Eliot's seminal "Tradition and the Individual Talent" (1920), for Davenport argues that the sculptor, poet, or novelist is "answering other creators" when he works. "Spontaneous generation is as uncommon in art as in nature." The generalization is less striking than the linkages he finds among works by Auguste Rodin and Constantin Brancusi; Ezra Pound and Eliot; Homer, Joyce, Marcel Proust, and Nikos Kazantzakis. Especially striking is Davenport's suggestion that the series of poems by William Butler Yeats about the character Crazy Jane derives from a long poem about a similar figure by George Meredith. The connection has not been noted, Davenport comments, because scholars are constrained by the artificial boundaries of a discipline that puts Meredith in the Victorian period and Yeats in the modern.

Davenport is at his most outspoken, as "The Scholar as Critic" demonstrates, when faced with wrongheaded scholarship. He challenges Richard Ellmann's designation of the manuscript of "Giacomo Joyce" as a novel by Joyce, finding it instead the sort of notebook any writer uses when working out his ideas. Davenport argues this case at length because he casts the scholar as "the transmitter of texts. He functions as a critic of the highest order because of his attention: what he chooses to edit, restore, annotate, reclaim." When the text the scholar transmits is flawed, the result is bad commentary and worse criticism. What good scholarship enables one to see, Davenport argues, is the interaction between text and context. He makes this point clear by tracing his own efforts to read and annotate a particular poem by Charles Olson.

Davenport's reading of Olson is an effort to enable a reader, any reader, even himself, to recognize the contexts in which the poem was placed by its author and understand the meanings deriving from them. Based on scholarship, this is the activity of the critic. Davenport argues, in "The Critic as Artist," that the critic collaborates with the artist to give the reader a way to read a particular text. Citing the excellent work done by Hugh Kenner on the poetry of Ezra Pound, he insists that this is merely one way to read Pound, and not the only way. A critic's interpretation will be flawed, however, if he approaches the text with a predetermined method of analysis. Davenport insists that the method appropriate to reading each particular work is to be found in the text itself, and it is the responsibility of the critic to discover it. In the process, the critic reconstructs the world the writer sees, commenting on and explaining it.

Davenport is engaged in this process of discovery and reconstruction in his essays on Rousseau, Joyce, and Cummings in *Every Force Evolves a Form*. He does the same thing when he reviews Samuel Beckett's novel *Company* (1980), Richard Rollins' *The Long Journey of Noah Webster* (1980), or an edition of *Mary Chestnut's Civil War* (1981) edited by C. Vann Woodward and Mary B. Chestnut. Even in these shorter pieces, constrained by the necessity every reviewer feels to provide some sense of the content of the books he writes about, Davenport's primary interest is in seeing how writers communicate a sense of the world. He also makes clear how he responds to these books by placing each in a context of his own making. He begins his essay about Mary Boykin Chestnut's Civil War diary with the receipt for the purchase of a slave by Davenport's own great-grandfather in Abbeville, South Carolina. He follows it with the fact that at a meeting of the American Academy and Institute of Arts and Letters, he received a scribbled note from Ralph Ellison in which the black novelist noted the fact that his own ancestors came from Abbeville.

These facts are not irrelevant to Davenport's purpose in reviewing Chestnut's diary. They appear in his essay to suggest contexts firmly rooted in human experience which enhance his assessment of her account of the Civil War in South Carolina. In every one of the pieces in *Every Force Evolves a Form*, Davenport tries to write criticism that conforms to a statement by George Santayana that he quotes in his Glasgow lectures: "To understand how the artist felt, however, is not criticism; criticism is an investigation of what the work is good for."

Davenport's essays explain what particular pictures, poems, and books are good for; they tell readers something about human beings living in worlds they recognize as not unlike their own. He does this with a certain crankiness that adds to the appeal of his writing. It is no surprise that he is fond of the Reverend Sydney Smith, a nineteenth century British clergyman and cofounder of the *Edinburgh Review*, who said, concerning a proposal to put a wooden sidewalk around Saint Paul's in London, "Let the dean and Canons lay their heads together and the thing will be done." Davenport is equally intolerant of blockheads, but he admits to limitations. In the essay "Pergolesi's Dog," he traces the cause of a misunderstanding between the artist Joseph Cornell and film director Stan Brakhage to the conclusion that no man is ever so certain of his knowledge as when his facts are wrong. Nobody respects the facts more than Davenport, and he clearly works hard to muster them.

Nevertheless, Davenport is more a clear thinker than an original one. He derives theoretical underpinnings from Lévi-Strauss, and behind that influence looms the shadow of Pound. Davenport's fondness for Greek literature and culture, and his tendency to locate sources in it for twentieth century writers, suggests the influence of the author of *The ABC of Reading* (1934) and a *Guide to Kulchur* (1938). Less combative than Pound, Davenport is equally intolerant of the deadening technocracy which reviews books, designs buildings, and relocates the supermarkets in city after American city to the edge of town. Pound would have appreciated Davenport's struggle to renew his passport at the Lexington post office.

Every Force Evolves a Form confirms the evaluation of *The Geography of the Imagination* (1981), an earlier collection of essays prompting reviewers to welcome Davenport as a fresh voice in American criticism. He addresses fundamental questions concerning the way a text reveals itself, and in the process he makes the things he writes about interesting. Davenport's essays indicate just how few are the common references Americans share, and they suggest that public education in the United States does little to prepare people to read with the skill so many texts require. At the same time Davenport points out the problem, he is taking steps to remedy it. *Every Force Evolves a Form* is lively, invigorating, and fascinating reading. It deserves serious attention.

Robert C. Petersen

Sources for Further Study

Booklist. LXXXIII, February 15, 1987, p. 868.
Kirkus Reviews. LV, February 1, 1987, p. 187.
Library Journal. CXII, February 1, 1987, p. 78.
National Review. XXXIX, February 13, 1987, p. 49.
Publishers Weekly. CCXXX, December 26, 1986, p. 50.
The Wall Street Journal. May 12, 1987, p. 32.

FAITH, SEX, MYSTERY
A Memoir

Author: Richard Gilman (1925-   )
Publisher: Simon and Schuster (New York). 253 pp. $16.95
Type of work: Memoir
Time: The 1950's
Locale: Primarily New York City, also Colorado Springs and New Orleans

The noted drama critic and Yale professor describes his conversion to Catholicism at the age of twenty-nine, and his subsequent falling away from the church

> *Principal personage:*
> RICHARD GILMAN, a drama critic and professor at Yale University

Richard Gilman grew up in a Jewish family who did not follow strictly the precepts of that faith, and by the time he reached his late twenties considered himself an atheist. A series of miraculous-seeming events, however, forced him to reconsider his view of the divine, and at the age of nearly thirty he was baptized as a Catholic. For a period, a mysterious grace seemed to hover over his life, but within three years he began to suffer what a priest told him was spiritual aridity. Before long he ceased attending Mass and eventually lost his belief in God, although not his more generalized conviction that a spiritual realm exists.

Gilman's narrative consists of more than a recounting of the events suggested in the preceding paragraph. The book also includes intermittent passages of spiritual meditation in which Gilman tries to recapture how, as a newly converted Christian, he had come to terms with such mysteries as the incarnation of God in Christ, transubstantiation, and the Devil. In doing so, he provides readers, Christian or not, with a yardstick against which to measure their own approach to religious questions. It is hard to imagine a reader who could finish this book without engaging in some reflection about his or her own relation to traditional religious dogma. Gilman commands attention by his willingness to reveal his layman's resolution to complex theological issues.

In a sense then, *Faith, Sex, Mystery: A Memoir* is two books in one: a theological discourse and a very personal account of some strange and not-so-strange occurrences. The personal history is of special interest and includes events in which a hand from another world seems to have nudged Gilman toward faith. For example, one evening after a conversation with a sympathetic priest, Gilman finds himself reciting the Hail Mary, a prayer he has never heard or read before. The most spectacular such occurrence, however, is the first, in which a casual library visit becomes an unexpected entry into the spiritual world.

On this occasion, against his normal practice, Gilman decides to visit the Cathedral branch of the New York Public Library. Inexplicably he is drawn to the religious section, and then to a book called *The Spirit of Medieval Philosophy: The Gifford Lectures, 1931-1932* (1936) by Etienne Gilson. Riding home on the bus he feels an aversion to the book, so much so that he is tempted to throw it out the window but refrains because he cannot afford to replace the volume. Once home, he reads the book in a compulsive day and night, and when he is finished he finds that he believes everything it says: He has been intellectually persuaded of the truth of Catholicism. Later he discovers that this experience precisely mirrors that of Thomas Merton as described in his autobiography *The Seven Storey Mountain* (1948), including the discovery of Gilson's book at a particular branch of the New York Public Library and the impulse to throw the book out the window of a Lexington Avenue bus. By the time he learns of Merton's parallel experience, Gilman has already come to see "the supernatural as real, not a myth, not a human construction out of longing."

Gilman's conversion, then, has an intellectual basis, but at the same time a mystical foundation which contradicts all his prior expectations about how things come to be known. His own skeptical temperament pulls the like-minded reader into Gilman's experience: Grace does seem to be operating in his life. In this category of special events, Gilman includes his friendship with a woman named Ruth, who serves as a spiritual mentor to him in the months prior to his formal conversion. Ruth helps him in practical ways—for example, she explains to him the use of the missal—but she is also a model in larger matters. Herself celibate, she encourages Gilman to practice a similar restraint. To Gilman's distress, he is sexually attracted to Ruth herself, making her teachings on this subject that much harder to bear. Ultimately he finds that he must tear himself away from this relationship and its disconcerting ambivalences. Nevertheless, Ruth remains in his memory a friend and guide through the phase of his introduction to Catholicism. (In a disturbing episode later in the book, Gilman encounters Ruth after years of separation and finds her unwilling to acknowledge that she knows him.)

As the episode of Ruth suggests, and the title of the memoir emphasizes, Gilman found it difficult to reconcile his sexuality with what he perceived as church teachings. He found that the rosy picture of wholesome sex within the context of marriage was not a plausible ideal for him. At the time when he first became intrigued with Catholicism, Gilman was married, and he admits that his sexual habits had alienated his wife. With evident embarrassment Gilman recounts his obsessive fantasies about dominant, muscular women. He made a fetish, for example, of a poster of Marlene Dietrich showing her muscular thigh encased in a garter belt and stocking. This dream of female aggression in turn made Gilman a passive lover; he seems to feel it natural that his young wife was disappointed in him.

Already guilty about his sexuality, Gilman became all the more concerned with the problem after his conversion. In one section of *Faith, Sex, Mystery,* he considers the relationship among the seven capital, or deadly sins, and he concludes that lust is of a different color than the others. He finds that he is able to rationalize away most of his sins: For example, when he feels worldly ambition or pride he reminds himself that the greatest achievement is to serve God. Yet he cannot drive away desire in a similar way. Lust, he concludes, springs from the unconscious and is not subject to man's deliberate control. Eventually one of Gilman's major frustrations with church practices stems from what he sees as the failure of most priests to understand the nature of his sexual concerns. Repeatedly he steels himself to confess his sexual sins only to find that the priest listens without apparent response, assigning him a mild penance and advising cold showers. Gilman's near despair about these matters is finally largely relieved by the words of a sympathetic English-speaking French priest who reminds him that God's love is ineffable and does not depend on obedience or even on scrupulous practice of Catholicism. That God's love is mysterious is a source of wonder for Gilman throughout his life, even after his repudiation of the conventional trappings of Catholicism.

As suggested in the preceding paragraph, Gilman felt more successful at conquering his ambition than his lust. Yet an important part of this story is the growth of Gilman's career as a journalist, eventually specializing in the drama criticism that led him to his prestigious position at the Yale School of Drama. Other aspiring writers will take comfort in noting that Gilman did not begin to write professionally until he was in his thirties, and that his first position, for the Catholic magazine *Jubilee*, was earned only after a stint selling subscriptions. Working at *Jubilee* was eye-opening in one important respect. At the time of his conversion, despite his love for Catholic doctrine, Gilman had what can only be called a snob's attitude toward most practitioners of the faith. Whenever he went to Mass, he found himself surrounded by people whom he assumed to be his intellectual inferiors, and he believed the Church administrators to be "at best indifferent to social and political injustice and oppression and, at worst, frankly aligned with the most reactionary and even fascist forces everywhere." At *Jubilee*, however, Gilman learned about a more liberal Catholicism, one concerned with the rights of the oppressed and engaged in social activism. Writing retrospectively, Gilman now sees himself and his fellow workers as naïve for hoping to make a difference either in the prevailing philosophies of the Church or in the larger world, but at the time it was a cleansing experience for him to be associated with people of such good will.

In the long run, though, his stint at *Jubilee* helped Gilman in his career, since it provided his entrée to *Commonweal*, another Catholic magazine but one with a much wider audience; it was there that he began to write drama criticism, teaching himself as he went along the theater history necessary for the position. As his status in the literary world became more secure, he found his attachment to religion slipping away. *Newsweek* magazine offered him a post at four times the salary he had earned at *Commonweal*, and his move to the secular world was apparently complete. He began to be what he had long wished to be: "well-known."

Another issue that Gilman takes up is the meaning of having become a Catholic after a Jewish upbringing. He felt no need to repudiate Judaism, since to him the religion had always connoted an ethnic identity rather than a specifically religious one. And in fact, although he felt Catholicism to be true as a religion in a way that Judaism was not, he had what he calls an instinctive sense that Jews as people were superior to most of the ethnic groups typically associated with Catholicism, including Italians, Poles, and Irish. Ironically, as a child Gilman believed that all Christians were his enemies, and never informed his parents of his conversion, and although he can never quite explain it to himself, he has been proud to be a Jew— throughout the period of his active Catholicism and afterward.

In his foreword, Gilman expresses embarrassment at the arrogance of autobiography. He seems possessed of an ambivalence about his own status: Is he so unimportant that no one will care about his experience, or so well-known that he risks an incapacitating scrutiny if he reveals his story? He resolves his ambivalence by suggesting that our present secular society (secular despite what he calls "the fundamentalist twitchings on the surface") is ready for a consideration of the spiritual, and that he can speak as one who, for a time, took instruction and comfort from an otherworldly realm. He speaks also of a kind of freedom to be found in exploring a subject that is so patently unfashionable as religious belief. He finds it liberating to address himself to a subject that his professional peers consider outside their realm of interest; as Gilman astutely points out, people may appear to lose interest in things which are mysterious and unknowable, yet the possibility of renewed interest is very close to the surface.

By the time one comes to the last pages of the book, moreover, one has the sense that Gilman, in his sixties, twice divorced, is looking for the meaning of his life beyond the real, but limited, fame he has achieved as a theater critic and professor. He genuinely believes that he was singled out, in that long-gone day in the Cathedral Branch of the New York Public Library, but he has never been able to come to terms with the meaning of his selection. When he writes the last words of his book he is still awash with bemused uncertainty.

Diane M. Ross

Sources for Further Study

Commonweal. CXIV, February 13, 1987, p. 85.

Kirkus Reviews. LIV, November 15, 1986, p. 1700.

Library Journal. CXII, March 1, 1987, p. 71.

Los Angeles Times Book Review. February 22, 1987, p. 11.

National Catholic Reporter. XXIII, May 15, 1987, p. 13.

The New Leader. LXIX, December 1, 1986, p. 11.

The New Republic. CXCVI, February 16, 1987, p. 37.

The New York Times Book Review. XCII, January 18, 1987, p. 1.

Publishers Weekly. CCXXX, November 21, 1986, p. 44.

The Washington Post Book World. XVII, March 1, 1987, p. 11.

THE FALL OF THE HOUSE OF LABOR
The Workplace, the State, and American Labor Activism, 1865-1925

Author: David Montgomery (1927-   )
Publisher: Cambridge University Press (New York). 464 pp. $27.95
Type of work: Social and economic history
Time: From the end of the Civil War to 1925
Locale: The factories, mines, and workplaces of America

A comprehensive history of the development of the working class from the point of view of the craftsmen, operatives, and laborers in the workplace and their attempt to secure justice in their conflicts with management

In 1904 the German sociologist/economist Werner Sombart visited the United States to observe the functioning of American capitalism. The question he posed in his 1906 book *Why Is There No Socialism in the United States?* had a formative impact upon subsequent scholarly attempts to understand the working class and working-class consciousness (or lack thereof) in this country. For Sombart, American "exceptionalism" was explainable in terms of social mobility, high living standards, and political democracy, which he summed up at one point: "All Socialist utopias came to nothing on roast beef and apple pie." Though replete with many observations that later proved less than accurate and some omissions—he neglected the importance of immigration as a major factor in the study of conflict between labor and management—Sombart's work did try to examine workers as active agents in creating their own lives.

For the next fifty years, American labor historians, mostly ill-equipped intellectually to use Marxist methods of class analysis, studied the subject from the lofty vantage point of the great leaders and institutions. In the 1960's, New Left historians influenced by the groundbreaking work of E. P. Thompson, *The Making of the English Working Class* (1963), began to study "history from the bottom up," that is, from the viewpoint of the laborers themselves. From this dialectic there emerged the new labor history led by such scholars as Herbert G. Gutman, Alan Dawley, David Noble, and David Montgomery.

David Montgomery, a professor at Yale University, came to the study of history only after his political activities as a machinist and union organizer resulted in his being blacklisted. He was thus forced out of the workshop and into the university. In a 1981 interview he emphasized that his studies of shop-floor struggles "underscored . . . that the working class has always formulated alternatives to bourgeois society in this country, particularly on the job." "When you come right down to it," he concluded, "history is the only teacher the workers have." To understand the labor process, the historian must explain the workers' activities in the workplace, their activities to secure "a democracy, industrious and political, based on enduring justice," and the role of the state in hindering or assisting them in obtaining their goals. This is an ambitious task, but the one that Montgomery sets for himself in *The Fall of the House of Labor*.

In this work he attempts to do for American labor history what E. P. Thompson had accomplished for English labor history. Where Thompson studied the development of a working class and a corresponding class consciousness in the years leading up to the Reform Bill of 1832, Montgomery traces the similar development in the United States from the Civil War to 1925. With astonishing detail he describes the day-to-day toil of iron rollers, puddlers, machinists, longshoremen, coal miners, textile workers, light bulb assemblers, and many others within the context of a nation in the process of rapid technological change and industrialization. As craftsmen and journeymen sought to defend their traditions, privileges, and ways of work, the new immigration from Southern and Eastern Europe and the enduring questions of race and sex created problems which hindered organization along class lines. The ensuing struggle between worker and management for control of the workplace is the core of Montgomery's study. As management sought to exploit workers' skills and knowledge, the worker, bound by tradition, resisted; it was they who had "the manager's brain under the workman's cap." Master metal workers in some instances were contracted to plan the work process and subcontract the hiring of laborers to assist them. Labor here had complete control. On their side the factory owners had Frederick Winslow Taylor and scientific management to wrest this skill from labor.

With their stopwatches, measuring tapes, and slide rules in hand, Taylor and his followers centralized planning and routing in the factory, divided plant operations into small and distinct parts, provided detailed instructions (taken from the workers themselves) and supervision of each task, and established wage payments based on workers' compliance with the above. Within a comparatively brief time span, but not without a struggle, the skilled craftsmen were reduced to efficient operatives, paid by the piece. This too created an arena for conflict, for now the workers had new sources of grievances based on pay rates, speed of production lines, and means of measuring efficiency. The debates over hours, work safety, and even worker ownership of the means of production still remained. The transition also involved costs to the plant owners: It took time and money to train operatives, and there was a high level of absenteeism and turnover as the skilled craftsmen found little value in their jobs. As Adam Smith noted (and Karl Marx quoted), "The man whose whole life is spent in performing a few simple operations . . . has no occasion to exert his understanding. . . . He generally becomes as stupid and ignorant as it is possible for a human creature to become."

While employers sought to reduce wages and production costs, "workers, whose powers of resistance were strengthened by familial, gender, ethnic, and community loyalties, and especially by the decisive role of skilled craftsmen in the existing relations of production," fought back. Workers countered the prevailing ideology of acquisitive individualism "which explained and justified a society regulated by market mechanisms" with an ideology of mutualism, "rooted in working-class bindings and struggles." Americanism and prohibition drives against saloons (legitimate gathering places for workers), combined with support and sponsoring of religious revival movements, served management well in socializing the workers to the ways of the newly industrialized America—and in the era of World War I, these tactics were well supported by a period of ferocious Red-baiting. For example, a Mexican immigrant, Jesus Romo, and his entire family were deported for merely writing a letter defending the Industrial Workers of the World against newspaper charges of being bomb-throwing anarchists.

It is clear that in these struggles class alliances with a developing class consciousness were being created. The employers, armed with the full power of the state behind them, attacked striking workers and their unions on the picket lines and in the legislative halls and courtrooms. Montgomery traces the development of labor organizations from the Knights of Labor and the American Federation of Labor to the Industrial Workers of the World and the myriad trades unions (the sea of initials at times is overwhelming) and their war against capitalism. In no country was the conflict so bloody as in the United States: As labor historian Steven J. Ross notes, "In the two decades after the Centennial Exhibition of 1876, with its grand celebration of American industry and progress, there were more strikes and more people killed or wounded in labor demonstrations in the United States than in any other country in the world." Industrial accidents were commonplace; one historian noted that twenty-five thousand workers were killed and one hundred thousand injured in the year 1913 alone—and hundreds more died as they walked the picket lines, the victims of private detective agencies, uniformed police, and the National Guard.

While Montgomery makes no attempt at a comprehensive history of American labor struggles, he does give detailed accounts of the strikes at such places as Turtle Creek Valley in Pennsylvania; Lawrence, Massachusetts; Homestead, Pennsylvania; and Ludlow, Colorado (where sixty-six people were killed when National Guard troops opened fire with rifles and machine guns on striking workers, their wives, and children). Other, less well-known chapters in the experience of American workers of various trades receive proportionately more attention. Despite the effects of racism, sexism, and ethnic rivalry—the divisive potential of which management was more than willing to exploit—and despite the exclusionary tactics of the American Federation of Labor and other unions and political party organization which served to emasculate labor's growing power, the workers were able to stand together in many instances as a class to fight for their rights and a future which gave them control over their own lives and labor.

As *The Fall of the House of Labor* demonstrates, the revolutionary tide that appeared in the second decade of the twentieth century was engulfed in an undertow of government reaction. The 1919-1920 Palmer raids drove radical leaders from the country. The Immigration Bureau of the Department of Labor in cooperation with local police, employers, and patriotic societies routinely scrutinized foreign-born workers; by the end of the 1920's the groups were expelling in excess of thirty-eight thousand workers per year. In the factories, the Rockefeller plan of management created company unions, promoting a form of corporate welfarism supported by conservative employees that detracted from radical trade unionism. More and more, machinery replaced men and women in the production of goods, and the position of labor continued to decline. Most new jobs were created in services and sales—not manufacturing—again deskilling labor with the concomitant lower pay, a historical process which continues today

The collapse in the 1920's of worker militancy which David Montgomery describes was but a hiatus in the story of labor's struggles in the United States, just as Werner Sombart had predicted in the first decade of the twentieth century:

> All the factors that till now have prevented the development of Socialism in the United States are about to disappear or to be converted into their opposite, with the result that in the next generation Socialism in America will probably experience the greatest possible expansion of its appeal.

In the depression-ridden years of the 1930's, radical unionism and working-class militancy were revitalized and once more played important roles in attempting to transform the American work system based on material plenty for the few and poverty for many to one that is more equitable, Based on that experience and subsequent labor history, there is reason to believe, with David Montgomery, that the workers' struggles will be revitalized in the post-Reagan years, and that the ultimate goal of the "House of Labor" may one day be reached.

Norman S. Cohen

Sources for Further Study

The Atlantic. CCLX, September, 1987, p. 100.
Library Journal. CXII, June 15, 1987, p. 68.
The Nation. CCXLV, September 5, 1987, p. 201.
The New Republic. CXCVIII, February 8, 1988, p. 35.
The New York Times Book Review. XCII, November 29, 1987, p. 30.
The Washington Monthly. XIX, November, 1987, p. 59.
The Washington Post Book World. XVII, August 30, 1987, p. 1.

THE FATAL SHORE

Author: Robert Hughes (1937-   )
Publisher: Alfred A. Knopf (New York). 688 pp. $24.95
Type of work: History
Time: The late eighteenth to mid-nineteenth century
Locale: Primarily Australia, occasionally England

An admirably evocative description of the founding of present-day Australia by 160,000 convicts sent by an England that treated the new continent as a penal colony

Principal personages:

CAPTAIN ARTHUR PHILLIP, the first royal governor of New South Wales

MAJOR JOSEPH FOVEAUX, the first in a series of sadistic penal commandants of Norfolk Island

WILLIAM REDFERN, a naval surgeon who protested unhygienic conditions aboard transport vessels

CAPTAIN ALEXANDER MACONOCHIE, a penal reformer who investigated mistreatment of convicts in Van Diemen's Land

COLONEL GEORGE ARTHUR, the lieutenant governor in charge of Van Diemen's Land from 1824 to 1836

LIEUTENANT COLONEL LACHLAN MACQUARIE, the governor of New South Wales from 1810 to 1821

LORD JOHN RUSSELL, the colonial secretary of Great Britain from 1839 to 1841

In contrast to the United States, Australia as it is known today was founded not in hope but in despair. During a period of sixty years England shipped approximately 160,000 men and women convicted of crimes to a continental concentration camp, the world's first gulag. It treated Australia as an opportunity for a dreadfully oppressive experiment, populating this obscure and wild land with what it regarded as a human trash heap of unwanted criminals.

Robert Hughes is almost the first historian to explore his native land's convict origins, terming them "a moral blot soaked into our fabric." Official amnesia and academic evasion marked Australia's embarrassed nonrecognition of this story of suffering, shame, and brutality until C. M. H. Clark published in 1962 the first volume of *A History of Australia*, a monumental but dryly written work. Hughes deserves enormous credit for grasping his painful subject with passion, clarity, grace, boldness, and remarkable eloquence. His book unites the solid information derived from a decade's painstaking research with a masterful command of narrative and scenic description. It will undoubtedly become what too many texts are undeservedly called—a classic.

Hughes was born and educated in Sydney, Australia, and studied art and architecture at Sydney University. In the 1960's, he lived in London, working as an artist and writing *The Art of Australia* (1966). Since 1970, he has lived in the United States and served as *Time* magazine's art critic. He both wrote and narrated the public television series on contemporary art, "The Shock of the New." His background and training have come to full fruition in this epic account of his country's anguished settlement, enabling him to emphasize the story of his country's history in prose of verve and robust resonance, demonstrating an unerring eye for the moods of landscape and climate and for arresting anecdotes of individual ordeals.

In his opening chapters, Hughes renders an unforgettable description of Georgian England's social stratification: London was not only the world's greatest city, boasting beautiful parks, elegant townhouses, magnificent cathedrals, and the presence of Edmund Burke, David Garrick, James Boswell, and Samuel Johnson; it was also the ugliest and worst-smelling of cities with sewers running into open drains, armies of rats foraging through warrens of shacks, children put to labor as soon as they reached the age of six, and one resident in eight estimated to be living off crime. Under the stresses of a soaring birthrate and dehumanizing industrialization, many English workers were unable to find employment in a saturated labor market. Hence a "swinish multitude"—Burke's phrase—engaged in theft, forgery, and prostitution; hence the Establishment enacted draconian laws to protect itself against what it regarded as serious assaults on social order, particularly property rights. Hence England's jails proved inadequate for absorbing a swelling horde of prisoners. Where to put them? Transportation overseas was the obvious solution: "It conveyed evil to another world."

After 1776, the former American colonies could no longer serve as a dumping ground for Britain's undesirables. On the other hand, Captain James Cook had in 1770 discovered southeastern Australia, naming the territory New South Wales while calling his particular landfall harbor Botany Bay. By 1786, the cabinet of William Pitt the Younger decided to found a penal colony at Botany Bay, located near Sydney. Captain Arthur Phillip was appointed New South Wales's first royal governor. He outfitted a transportation fleet of eleven small, aged vessels, which turned out to be undervictualled by a crooked contractor. More than seven hundred convicts went on this first fleet, their average age twenty-seven. Typhus broke out after two months at sea; no antiscorbutics were aboard; each prisoner received two slices of bread per day. When the boats landed at Botany Bay after 252 days at sea, forty-eight people had died en route.

Relations between the convicts and Aborigine tribes were bad from the beginning. The former, as England's lowest social class, desperately needed even lower scapegoats; the natives of the new continent answered that need, and Australian racism began its virulent history from this encounter. The marines and sailors of the first fleet, in their turn, hated both the inhospitable new land and the convicts for being the cause of their coming to it. By 1790, the new settlement had sunk into the torpor and agony of slow starvation, since the land proved difficult to cultivate and no promised relief supplies had arrived. Food theft became endemic; punishment for it became extremely cruel: One man received three hundred lashes and six months in chains for having stolen twenty ounces of potatoes. Most of a second fleet was shipwrecked in 1790; a third fleet finally arrived in 1791, with many of its convicts too emaciated to work hard.

That year Governor Phillip gave a convict whose term had expired, James Ruse, the land and minimal equipment to set up a farm of his own. Ruse thereby became the ancestor of Australian agriculture, the founding member of what was to become a powerful new class: the Emancipists.

In 1800, the first of a series of horrendously sadistic penal commandants took charge of Norfolk Island: Major Joseph Foveaux. He ordered that after his flogging sentence—say, two hundred lashes—a prisoner's back be splashed with salty seawater. Convicts' leg irons were made smaller each month, so they would pinch flesh more severely; for slight infractions prisoners would often be locked into subterranean water pits for forty-eight-hour periods, alone, naked, unable to sleep for fear of drowning. No record of Foveaux's viciousness was permitted to find its way into either prisoners' letters (censored) or official reports. Norfolk Island was a sealed zone of ruthlessness; no civil law applied.

One of Hughes's most illuminating procedures is to quote extensively from the testimony of the convicts themselves—letters, depositions, petitions, and memoirs. He describes the nature of their transportation voyages largely through their voices on these papers. Many wives wanted to accompany their husbands into overseas exile; usually their requests were refused; thus, transportation often destroyed the family unit. Many transportees were brutalized during their journey: Fourteen-pound irons were riveted to their right ankles; some were even confined in double fetters, unable to bribe their warders for an "easement of irons." Convicts were ordered to give their money and good clothes to the ships' officers for safekeeping; they often lost both. Food aboard ship was inadequate and abominable; the cells were dark and stank with foul air; discipline was savage; usually only a minority of transportees landed in even fair health. After 1815, conditions did improve somewhat in response to reports made to the authorities by a surgeon, William Redfern, who stressed the need for cleanliness, ventilation, disinfection, fumigation, exercise, and decent food.

Who were these convicts? Year after year, Hughes indicates, the same proportion held. Four out of five had been convicted for theft, and at least half were repeat offenders. Almost none were political prisoners, and men outnumbered women six to one. In the early nineteenth century, a new, class-conscious vocabulary permeated English society: Respectable people spoke heatedly of a "criminal class," quite different from law-abiding Britons, which needed to be torn out of the social fabric. Hence transportation was intended to excise a cancerous growth from England's body politic by uprooting it. It is not surprising that this aim miscarried, since transportation did not address the causes of crime. Hughes cites the example of a clerk, Isaac Nelson, sentenced to seven years' transportation: He had stolen silverware from an employer after he had been out of work for a year, his wife seriously ill, their infant dead of malnourishment. Mrs. Nelson's plea for mercy to George III, asking His Majesty to mitigate Nelson's sentence by permitting it to be served in England, or at least allowing her to accompany her husband to Australia, was refused.

Hughes distinguishes four phases of transportation. About twelve thousand convicts from England and Ireland were banished in the first phase, from 1787 to 1810, with relatively few ships available for transport because of the exigencies of the Napoleonic Wars. In the second stage, between 1811 and 1836, about fifty thousand people were transported, as England's runaway unemployment created runaway crime rates, while Australia's growing farming economy demanded an increasing supply of convict labor. In the third stage, 1831 to 1840, the system peaked at the rate of more than five thousand transportees annually. Most English citizens had by then accepted transportation as the most convenient response to criminal conduct. The last phase, from 1840 to 1868, saw diminishing use of convicts as laborers, with native-born Australians favored by the job market.

Of the prisoners transported, about twenty-four thousand were women—eighty percent of them sent out for theft, but none (despite legends to the contrary) for prostitution, which was not a transportable offense. Nevertheless, notes Hughes, ". . . the whore-stereotype, accepted by the upper layers of a rigid little colonial society, wielded immense power." At sea the female convicts were immediately taken over by sexually aggressive seamen; then, as soon as a women-bearing ship docked in Australia, female convicts were mustered on deck in what amounted to a slave market, with shore officers getting first choice, then other military personnel, and lastly those former convict settlers who had obtained gubernatorial permission to have a female servant. Since these liaisons were not legally binding, a settler could simply evict a convict woman when he tired of her. Thus English sexism was imported to Australia and there amplified by penal restrictions, with many women becoming prisoners of former prisoners—a degraded, doubly colonized class.

As for homosexuality, it naturally abounded in a territory whose male-to-female proportion varied from four to one in cities to twenty to one in the bush areas. Sodomy was a capital crime, loathed by the English and Irish working class. Nevertheless, the practice was utterly pervasive in hulks and penal settlements, with new prisoners routinely raped. Yet, since Australian landowners stood to lose their assigned convict labor in the case of convictions for this offense, they almost invariably agreed to overlook or deny its existence.

Every convict's career ran along the following prescribed course: He or she served the Crown directly, or some private master designated by the Crown, for the allotted prison term. Then he was released from bondage in one of three ways. An absolute pardon from the governor—extremely rare—would restore all of his rights, including the prerogative of returning to England; a conditional pardon would give the former convict citizenship in the Australian colony but no right to return to England; or a ticket-of-leave enabled him to work for himself as long as he stayed within the colony, a permit which had to be renewed annually and was subject to revocation for such vaguely defined actions as insolence, idleness, or overcharging. Despite its precarious nature, every convict craved a ticket-of-leave.

The Fatal Shore is grimly effective in evoking the frightful drama of penal Australia, with one prison commander after another competing in savage sadism. Thus Norfolk Island, under the loathsome Lieutenant-Colonel James Morissett, became a living hell of convict degradation, an infernal machine for extinguishing human hope. Its prisoners were kept half-starved by corrupt guards; informers were encouraged to splinter convict solidarity; the slightest infraction of incredibly despotic regulations, such as those that prohibited mislaying shoelaces or smiling while working, resulted in floggings of at least one hundred lashes; torture was customary. In despair, a group of prisoners plotted suicide by lottery:

> A group of convicts would choose two men by drawing straws: one to die, the other to kill him. Others would stand by as witnesses. There being no judge to try capital offenses on Norfolk Island, the killer and witnesses would have to be sent to Sydney for trial—an inconvenience for the authorities but a boon to the prisoners, who yearned for the meager relief of getting away from the "ocean hell," if only to a gallows on the mainland.

From 1835 onward, sentiment against such circles of hell as Norfolk Island took an increasing hold among morally outraged liberals who sought to abolish the transportation system as iniquitous. One humane penal reformer, Captain Alexander Maconochie, investigated the treatment of prisoners in Van Diemen's Land, a pendant island off Australia's southern tip. He roundly denounced transportation as a cruel debasement of both convicts and jailers, resulting in crushed, resentful, embittered, and vindictive humans. His reports to the Colonial Secretary, Lord John Russell, ultimately cost him his administrative post in Australia but caused a sensation in the British press. Russell was delighted to obtain ammunition for his long-held view that transportation was an outmoded system, that England should keep its prisoners in penitentiaries on English soil while encouraging free emigration to Australia.

Transportation to New South Wales ended in 1840, not before monstrous acts of extreme terror had been visited upon convicts by commanders and

governors. In 1851, gold was found in the territory, and regiments of emancipated convicts rushed to dig for more, flooding particularly into and near
Melbourne. These freed settlers agitated throughout Australia against the
police-state horrors of what they termed "the Stain." In England, the press,
led by *The Times*, solidly opposed further transportation. Free men from
England and Ireland were booking passage to join the gold rush; they re-
sented having to share their get-rich-quick chances with recently released
offenders. In 1853, Van Diemen's Land ceased to be a penal colony and
renamed itself Tasmania. Western Australia, the most arid third of the continent, remained the last area to receive overseas convicts. On January 10,
1868, the last prison ship from Great Britain landed its convict cargo in
Australia.

What did the transportation system achieve? As social amputation of England's criminal class, it failed. As a model of deterrence, to frighten the innocent away from crime, it also failed. As a means of reforming criminals
and restoring them to society, however, it succeeded. Hughes concludes
that, "For all its flaws . . . the assignment system in Australia was by far the
most successful form of penal rehabilitation that had ever been tried in English, American or European history." It fostered self-reliance and rewarded
endurance and competence. Perhaps most significantly, the system hastened
Australia's pace of colonization by half a century. To ask what the continent
would have amounted to without the influx of convicts is, Hughes maintains, "existentially meaningless" speculation—the truth is, Australia was
built largely by criminals. This anguished reality is one that most Australians have long wanted to forget or deny. Hughes's powerful work will not
permit such an evasion.

Gerhard Brand

Sources for Further Study

The Atlantic. CCLIX, January, 1987, p. 86.
Kirkus Reviews. LIV, December 1, 1986, p. 1778.
Library Journal. CXI, November 1, 1986, p. 93.
London Review of Books. IX, March 19, 1987, p. 15.
The New Republic. CXCV, February 9, 1987, p. 33.
The New York Review of Books. XXXIV, March 12, 1987, p. 3.
The New York Times Book Review. XCII, January 25, 1987, p. 1.
The New Yorker. LXIII, March 23, 1987, p. 92.
Newsweek. CIX, January 26, 1987, p. 78.
Publishers Weekly. CCXXX, December 5, 1986, p. 59.
Time. CXXIX, February 2, 1987, p. 72.
The Washington Post Book World. XVII, January 11, 1987, p. 3.

FIASCO

Author: Stanisław Lem (1921-   )
Translated from the Polish by Michael Kandel
Publisher: Harcourt Brace Jovanovich (San Diego, California). 322 pp. $17.95
Type of work: Philosophical science fiction
Time: The future
Locale: Quinta, a planet in the Harpy system

Fiasco *describes the failure of an Earth expedition to communicate with aliens*

> *Principal characters:*
> ANGUS PARVIS, a spaceship pilot
> MARK TEMPE, a pilot, who may be Parvis resurrected a century
> after his death
> FATHER ARAGO, a Dominican monk
> STEERGARD, the captain of the Quinta mission

Stanisław Lem has said that he would prefer not to visit any of the futures he has imagined or any of those that may actually come to be. For his lack of enthusiasm, he gives two reasons: "the distant future could resemble a cemetery, or it could be incomprehensible to me."

Fiasco represents both of these possibilities. The main story in *Fiasco* concerns an expedition from Earth to the distant planet of Quinta, where there is a civilization of aliens at the right stage of development for communication. This expedition fails to communicate, however, and at the center of this failure is the problem of human nature so vividly illustrated by the arms race. The expedition fails to understand the Quintans because humans can understand aliens only in human terms, just as on Earth one culture has difficulty understanding another.

Mark Tempe is the sole member of the expedition to gain a brief glimpse of the Quintans, before he is mistakenly destroyed by his comrades. The Quintans appear to be a kind of treelike fungus, both aerobic and anaerobic. Tempe cannot grasp this utterly alien biology, and he never has a chance to imagine what their intelligence must be like or how they would develop and use technology and for what purposes. Before he lands and briefly examines Quinta, however, he and his shipmates believe that they discover quite a bit about Quintans. In fact, they discover virtually nothing verifiable, nothing that is likely to be true.

Lem's point is partly that the alien cannot be known. In mankind's fantasies about encounters with alien intelligence, there is usually an assumption that alien biology either will not affect understanding or will be so similar to human biology that the passions and intelligences of the two species will coincide enough to make communication possible. *Fiasco*, in a gripping fiction, though it is without deeply interesting characters, explores the reasons humanity should not be so optimistic about contact with the alien.

The Quintans remain essentially mysterious throughout the novel. Their main functions are to be present and to be silent. Their presence draws the expedition to them and provides physical evidence about which the men can reason. Their silence licenses the men to read freely the meanings of the evidence. The result of this freedom is that the men read their own human attitudes and history into the Quintans' artifacts and visible activities. The majority of those in the expedition see the Quintans as involved in a highly technological civil war that has yielded an arms race currently in a stand off. The expedition sees itself as a possibly unwitting player in this game. Factions on the planet may deal with them separately in an attempt to gain advantages over other factions.

Much of the central portion of the book consists of various members of the expedition adding their twists and angles to this attempt at interpretation, each trying to account for new or as yet unexplained physical evidence. The only serious opposition to this general approach comes from two interesting directions.

First, Tempe wants above all "to see the Quintans." He shows a practical man's desire to keep explanations simple, to withhold conclusions, and to try different approaches. What little success the expedition achieves is largely the result of his resistance to theorizing.

Second, and more important, is the Christian opposition of Father Arago. He is the only member to argue seriously that the Quintans' silence most likely means that they would rather not communicate. This possibility is a central tenet of the theory about alien civilizations that brought the expedition to Quinta. After centuries of hearing nothing while monitoring radio signals from space, Earth scientists concluded that while it was likely that there were many intelligent species "out there," only a few at any given time met the conditions of being close, sufficiently advanced for radio communication, and not so advanced as to wish to avoid contact with primitive civilizations such as Earth's.

Father Arago believes that for some reason the Quintans would prefer to be left alone. He and Steergard, the captain of the expedition, seem to agree at the beginning of the journey that they must respect such a desire if the Quintans show it. When they are on the scene, however, only Father Arago is able to maintain this position. Steergard and the rest feel driven to force communication upon the Quintans. Why the expedition feels so driven, why they push onward toward the completion of a fiasco, is another significant theme of Lem's novel. Lem not only shows that aliens are likely to be incomprehensible and that they may not desire contact from humans, he also shows why humans are yet driven to seek contact.

The fiasco at Quinta results from the escalation of a confrontation between the expedition and the planet. This confrontation is understandable only from the human side. Placed on guard by changes in Quintan behavior as the *Hermes*, the mission's vessel, approaches, Steergard is especially cautious about opening communication. He feels challenged and threatened from the beginning, and his human response is therefore aggressive and defensive. He and his crew, as mammals, are predisposed to see an approach of strangers as probably issuing in battle or flight. They never seriously deviate from this predisposition.

Quintan responses to Steergard's initiatives are really incomprehensible. No Quintans show themselves. There are, at first, no replies to various kinds of broadcasts. Only a few mysterious artifacts are found. A probe ship from the *Hermes* is intercepted, but since the probe ship destroys itself and its interceptors unexpectedly, their purpose cannot be known. A mass of matter suddenly appears next to the *Hermes*, causing a discomforting automatic defense maneuver. Out of these events, the crew spins its elaborate theories of Quintan history and intention. The central irony of these theories is that they are based upon and amount to a picture of Earth in the late twentieth century. Each theory is based on a massive, energy-draining race to perfect and build arms. Each theory ends in, if not mutual destruction, at least depletion to virtual helplessness and futility. Each also is grounded in human biology, in the natural tendency to see the power to kill as the way to safety from the unknown stranger. The irony is that the expedition is creating its own mirror image and remains blind to the Quintans.

A second irony is that in doing so, the crew completes the fiasco it hypothesizes. Reading the Quintans as aggressive, the *Hermes'* response is aggressive. After being shaken up by his own ship's automatic defensive maneuver, a purely technological response, perhaps not even necessary, to an unexpected event, Steergard decides on a show of force. All he is supposed to want is to communicate, but if the Quintans' antipathy to communication is so strong that they will try violence to drive him away, then he must show that he is too tough to be defeated so easily. Thus his reason fails him as he translates the lack of mere communication into violence, as if one would destroy a person's house because he refused to answer his telephone.

First the *Hermes* destroys Quinta's moon. Further attempts at communication lead to further acts of aggression from the *Hermes*, though the ship itself is never attacked. In the midst of this escalating violence, Tempe comes up with the only really successful means of communication. He suggests projecting cartoons on the planet's clouds. The result of this is a reply cartoon, one of the clearest messages of which is that the Quintans, like humans, want to survive. Beyond this, little of significance passes between the two species in this or subsequent communications. This nonaggressive interlude in the series of attempted contacts highlights the degree to which the humans must seem mad if the Quintans are at all able to make sense of them—destroying a moon one day, showing cartoons on clouds the next. The humans can hardly be more understandable to the Quintans than the Quintans are to the humans.

The central cause of the fiasco, then, is human nature, especially its biological base in a mammal that has achieved dominance of its planet largely through aggression. Lem explores several facets of human nature that contribute to the fiasco. That the desire simply to communicate is subsumed into the pattern of aggressive/defensive behavior leads to the fiasco, because humans read themselves into the silence of the Quintans. This failure points to fundamental failures of humanity to understand itself. Only Father Arago sees how they are falling victim to habitual and unconscious ways of thinking. Other aspects of the novel show other ways in which humanity fails to know itself.

The novel opens about a century before the Quinta mission with an adventure on one of Saturn's moons, Titan. This adventure yields a smaller fiasco that reveals elements of human nature which contribute to the larger fiasco of the book: Humans are driven by irrational passions and they are imperfectly social animals.

That humans are driven by irrational passions rooted in human biology is clear in Angus Parvis' decision to rescue friends lost on the deadly moon. Some passions are admirable, for it is friendship that draws Parvis into this dangerous attempt and the desire for greater self-knowledge that draws the *Hermes* mission to the stars. Other passions are useful, but not always admirable—overweening pride in mankind's habitually technological solutions to complex problems makes Parvis think that he can succeed and, therefore, leads to his death. Likewise, the expedition's pride in technology leads to errors at Quinta, one of the more serious being to refuse to take responsibility for the accidents caused by their own machines doing exactly what they were designed to do.

The first fiasco on Titan results also in part from the imperfections of human society, as shown in the competition between business and political factions. One result of competition entering into a situation where cooperation is critical is having two bases when there should be one; this results in frequent mix-ups of supply and personnel deliveries. These bureaucratic confusions lead, in turn, to frequent attempts at deadly surface travel and Parvis' fiasco. This problem is more subtle on the *Hermes*, for the crew's factional disagreements about how to interpret some details of the Quintans' behavior and about how to respond mask their essential agreement about the aliens' warlike intentions and the appropriateness of aggressive responses.

That humanity is both individual and social is a source of human beauty and pain. The desire to be social stands behind and makes possible the Quinta mission, and individualism leads to the variety and flexibility of response that has also made such achievements possible. The internal conflicts of the species, however, produce inefficiencies and disasters and, furthermore, come to seem so normal that Steergard and his crew, without second thoughts, attribute similar conflicts to the Quintans.

Lem has written about the human longing to meet aliens in several other works, including *Solaris* (1961; English translation, 1970) and *One Human Minute* (1985; English translation, 1986). In such works, he sees this longing as expressive of mankind's desire for self-knowledge and meaning. *Fiasco* is typical of Lem's work in expressing this longing, as well as in asserting that the universe probably does not hold the answers for which people so avidly hope.

Terry Heller

Sources for Further Study

Booklist. LXXXIII, May 15, 1987, p. 1412.
Chicago Tribune. July 12, 1987, XIV, p. 7.
Discover. VII, December, 1986, p. 56.
Kirkus Reviews. LX, April 15, 1987, p. 598.
The Missouri Review. VII, 1984, p. 218.
The New York Times Book Review. XCII, June 7, 1987, p. 1.
Publishers Weekly. CCXXXI, April 10, 1987, p. 86.
Time. CXXIX, June 1, 1987, p. 70.
The Village Voice Literary Supplement. June, 1987, p. 12.

THE FITZGERALDS AND THE KENNEDYS

Author: Doris Kearns Goodwin (1943-   )
Publisher: Simon and Schuster (New York). 932 pp. $22.95
Type of work: Family biography
Time: 1863-1961
Locale: The United States

An intimate history of the life and times of America's most famous twentieth century political family

Principal personages:
JOHN FRANCIS "HONEY FITZ" FITZGERALD, Mayor of Boston, 1906-1907 and 1910-1914
P. J. KENNEDY, a Boston neighborhood boss
JOSEPH P. "JOE" KENNEDY, a banker, speculator, and ambassador to the Court of Saint James's
ROSE FITZGERALD KENNEDY, his wife, the mother of nine children
JOSEPH P. "JOE" KENNEDY, JR., their eldest son, killed during World War II
JOHN F. "JACK" KENNEDY, their second son, thirty-fifth President of the United States, 1961-1963
KATHLEEEN KENNEDY, their second eldest daughter

Although in many ways a brilliant psychoanalytical portrait, Doris Kearns Goodwin's first book, *Lyndon Johnson and the American Dream* (1976), relied so heavily on extensive interviews with the former president that it was colored by Johnson's subjective memory. Eight years in the making, Goodwin's new book is meticulously researched, combining oral history with a thorough combing of primary and secondary sources.

The Fitzgeralds and the Kennedys is very well organized—not only in its overall conception but also in the selection of which episodes to emphasize and which details to accentuate. Add to these strengths Goodwin's graceful style and her acute historical insights, and the result is an engrossing, definitive book.

Goodwin is one of a growing number of social historians who have recognized the legitimacy of interviews as primary source materials. Her book touches on such important subjects as the immigrant experience, the role of the Church and of political machines as socializing agencies, the growth of American business, and the changing nature of the family.

"American Dream" would have been a fitting subtitle to Goodwin's second book, as well as her first. Instead the phrase "An American Saga" appears on the dust jacket, implying an edifying narrative of almost legendary proportions—containing elements of glory and degradation, triumph and tragedy. In Goodwin's words, this family saga "was both symbol and substance of one of the most important themes of the second century of American life: the progress of the great wave of nineteenth-century immigration, the struggle of newcomers to force open the doors of American life so zealously guarded by those who had first settled the land."

The American Dream meant different things to the male and female members of these two Irish clans. Goodwin describes the environmental and cultural influences which allowed male talents a wide orbit, while women were expected to nurture the bonds of family—no small task in the face of the disintegrating forces of modern society. Consequently, while this saga describes a family's rise from obscure poverty to the center of the world stage, it also documents the tension and trauma caused by the male-oriented cult of competition and success.

The book's central character is, in fact, Rose Kennedy. Her complex relationships with her father, her husband, and her children are the threads that tie the narrative together. Often portrayed by the media as virtually a saint, Rose Kennedy emerges here as multifaceted—feisty and free spirited, devout and devoted to her offspring, yet pragmatic and not totally selfless.

Beginning with the baptism of John Francis Fitzgerald, *The Fitzgeralds and the Kennedys* spans almost a hundred years, culminating with the inauguration of John F. Kennedy, America's first Catholic president. Book 1 documents the rise of the Fitzgeralds from the poverty of Boston's North End to the political triumphs and travails of the president's maternal grandfather. Book 2 concentrates on the marriage of Joseph P. (Joe) and Rose Kennedy, the amassing of the family fortune, and the mixed results of Joe Kennedy's forays into government service. Book 3, entitled "The Golden Trio," focuses on three of the four eldest Kennedy offspring—Joseph, Jr., John, and Kathleen. Daughter Rosemary was retarded, and Goodwin's account of how she was lobotomized and institutionalized is one of the most harrowing parts of the book.

With such a large cast, Goodwin does well to make the central family members come alive by concentrating on the character-molding aspects of their lives. Thomas "Cocky Tom" Fitzgerald was a fish peddler, one of that small minority of Irish immigrants who made slow progress out of the tenement slums. With the help of his brother, he opened a grocery and groggery; in time he became a property-owner and slum landlord. His wife Rosanna gave birth to twelve children and was again pregnant at the age of forty-eight when she apparently died of shock after hearing a false report that her family was in a train accident. No photographs of her survive. Writes Goodwin: "Hers is the familiar story of countless immigrant women who defined their worldly possibilities entirely through their husbands and their children. She was indispensable in life, but only vaguely remembered in death." On her tiny cemetery marker is the simple epitaph "Mother."

Tom and Rosanna Fitzgerald's son John overcame physical and intellectual inadequacies with energy and charm. A newsboy, he obtained the best corner in Beacon Hill, home of Brahmins such as Henry Cabot Lodge, whose palatial home he examined after helping the cook with her packages.

The beautiful wooden toys he beheld in the Lodge children's room symbolized a world he longed to enter. After his father's death, Fitzgerald went to work for neighborhood boss Matthew Keany, "the most respected man in the district," who dispensed aid and advice like a spider spinning a web. Heeler, checker, speaker, and ever the loyal lieutenant, Fitzgerald had no compunction at betraying a friend's uncle who dared vote against the machine candidate. Taking over Keany's turf when the boss died, Fitzgerald was a congressman by age thirty-one and mayor by age forty-two.

Josephine Fitzgerald, John's wife, was a withdrawn woman molded by Catholic dogma, Victorian ideals, and childhood tragedies which cast a dark shadow over her personality. Bitterly resentful over the demands of politics on her husband's time, she was also jealous of his utter devotion to their headstrong daughter Rose. When his administration was embarrassed by revelations of corruption, Fitzgerald bowed to pressure from the bishop and sent Rose to the Convent of the Sacred Heart. Rose's heart had been set on going to Wellesley College; it was the most bitter disappointment of her life. Later Rose's father would oppose her courtship with Joseph P. Kennedy—even arranging a Florida vacation to coincide with Harvard University's Junior Dance—because he regarded the suitor as "a dark threat to his exclusive attachment to her."

The flagstone contract scandal, which cost Fitzgerald reelection, involved the noncompetitive awarding of contracts in violation of city regulations and, in some cases, at twice the necessary cost. At the trial of Superintendent of Supplies Michael J. Mitchell, Fitzgerald provided damaging testimony that contributed to his old friend's incarceration. As Goodwin concludes, Fitzgerald "was one of those rare men who could demand sacrifice of others without making them feel he was using them for his own ends." Mitchell died a broken man; Fitzgerald made a triumphant return to city hall in 1910, climaxing campaign speeches by singing "Sweet Adeline" (hence the legend of the golden voice of "Honey Fitz"). Mitchell's defense lawyer, Daniel Coakley, got his revenge by circulating rumors about the mayor's flirtations with a woman nicknamed Toodles—an allegation which James M. Curley used with devastating effect to force him out of the 1914 mayoralty race. In a chapter entitled "The Balance Shifts," Goodwin describes how Fitzgerald's ebbing political fortunes coincided with the marriage of daughter Rose to Joseph P. Kennedy and the latter's meteoric rise in the banking industry.

The son of ward politician P. J. Kennedy, whose surprise defeat in a race for street commissioner demonstrated the vicissitudes of politics, Joe Kennedy pursued power through wealth. Slighted by Harvard's most exclusive clubs and rejected for membership in the Cohasset Gold Club, he was extremely sensitive to the prejudice of Boston's governing elite. Charming but ambitious, Kennedy, in Goodwin's words, "did not honestly care for a single soul beyond the circle of his friends and his family. If he found it convenient he could be as tactful and as dignified as the next man; yet, if it suited his purposes, he could be brutal, relentless and cunning." In short, he "united in his person both inexorable self-will and the capacity for deep attachment, both appalling ruthlessness and unswerving fidelity."

Goodwin's recounting of Kennedy's entrepreneurial career recalls the central theme of Abraham Cahan's novel *The Rise of David Levinsky* (1917), in which success comes at a high ethical price. Goodwin provides exactly the right amount of detail except on the matter of Kennedy's alleged bootlegging activities.

During World War I, while Kennedy's friends fell sway to patriotic urgings to enlist, Kennedy managed the building of ships for Bethlehem Steel Company. Next, joining a prestigious brokerage firm, he mastered the intricacies of stock-market speculation. In 1923, he brilliantly orchestrated an aggressive buy-and-sell strategy which saved John Hertz's Yellow Cab Company from a hostile takeover. The episode left Kennedy a wealthy man and established his reputation as a financial wizard.

As Goodwin makes clear, Joe Kennedy's talents and personality exemplified the self-interested spirit of the 1920's. Fascinated by the motion-picture industry as a veritable gold mine, he took control of Film Bookings Offices of America (FBO), which turned out low-budget melodramas, and helped form Radio-Keith-Orpheum (RKO). He openly romanced actress Gloria Swanson, even finding a job in Europe for his lover's husband. While other speculators scoffed, Kennedy began to liquidate his holdings in the spring of 1929; when the market plummeted, he profited by selling short.

Rose Kennedy adjusted to her husband's absences and infidelities with remarkable equipoise. "From her earliest childhood," writes Goodwin, she "had been taught to believe that marriage was to be her great adventure, her journey's end." Even so, at one point she left Joe and her three preschool children. The separation lasted three weeks. Thereafter, she resolved to bind the family together through excursions and other rituals. Her marriage became a partnership based on devotion to the children. She apparently maintained the Catholic view that sex was meant exclusively for procreation. After nine children, she demanded separate bedrooms. Devoting most of her maternal efforts toward Rosemary, she refused to admit that her daughter could not make normal progress. As for the rumors about Swanson, she tolerated them so long as the family was secure.

As the eldest of what Goodwin labels children of privilege, Joe, Jr., was cocky and rather overbearing. In this family of high expectations, he outshone his sickly younger brother John (or Jack, as he was called by the family) in everything except charm and mental facility. Both boys attended Choate School in Connecticut rather than public or parochial school, as Rose would have preferred, because Joe, Sr., appreciated the social contacts which accrued to those who were part of an aristocracy of talent. Both brothers courted excitement and danger. Jack almost got expelled for organizing a Muckers Club and lost his virginity to a Harlem prostitute. Joe, Jr., loved bobsledding and risked injury in the vain hope of winning a Harvard football letter. Similarly, a ruptured disc sustained on the gridiron left Jack in pain for the rest of his life. Daughters Kathleen and Eunice were perhaps the most talented siblings of them all, and Goodwin implies that they might have made the best politicians had women enjoyed more rights.

During the early 1930's, Joe Kennedy, Sr., came to realize, in Goodwin's words, that "the center of gravity in America would shift from big business to big government." He contributed heavily to the 1932 Democratic campaign, even traveling with the Brain Trusters on the Roosevelt Special. When his hopes for an important governmental post were foiled by presidential adviser Louis Howe, he even considered suing the Democratic National Committee for repayment of a loan. Finally, in June, 1934, came an offer, the chairmanship of the Securities and Exchange Commission. As Franklin D. Roosevelt chortled, sometimes it took a fox to police the barn. Kennedy provided exemplary leadership for the new agency, steering a middle course between those who sought punitive measures and opponents of strict regulation. Ironically, his actions helped make Wall Street respectable again.

Joe Kennedy's next major assignment would not end so well. After a stint on the United States Maritime Commission, Roosevelt appointed him ambassador to the Court of Saint James's, the first Irish-American so honored. It was not a post suited to his temperament. Writes Goodwin: "Standing at the summit of his powers, he was revealed as a man whose source of greatness, his absolute confidence in his ability to tackle anything, became his fatal flaw."

When World War II erupted, Kennedy feared its effect on his family, on his financial fortune, and on freedom (in particular, freedom from centralization, from government authority). He became increasingly pessimistic about Great Britain's chances against Germany; he was quoted as saying that democracy was finished in England and perhaps also in America. His isolationist views, out of step with the Roosevelt Administration, led to his resignation shortly after the 1940 election. It was a humiliating climax to his public career.

Thereafter, Joe Kennedy's ambitions were transferred to his eldest sons. When Joe, Jr., was killed on a dangerous combat mission in 1944, his father was devastated and inconsolable. For Jack it meant sudden responsibility and an unwanted end to the sibling rivalry that had so defined his personality. "I'm shadowboxing in a match the shadow is always going to win," he said.

Having pulled strings to get Jack stateside following the PT 109 incident (Kennedy's ship had to be abandoned after a Japanese destroyer rammed it), Joe Kennedy lobbied to get him decorated as a hero. In 1946, the elder Kennedy wanted Jack to run for lieutenant governor of Massachusetts, but Jack preferred a seat in Congress, which would allow him to address national issues. His grandfather Honey Fitz frequently accompanied the successful candidate on campaign trips throughout Boston's Eleventh District. The congressman later refused to sign a petition to have Fitzgerald's old rival Mayor Curley pardoned, even though his father initially favored it. The entire family contributed to Kennedy's triumphant Senate race in 1952. The patriarch secured the endorsement of the Boston *Post* with a timely loan, while his wife hosted a series of tea parties. Several years later, "Papa Joe" even lobbied to get his son a Pulitzer Prize for *Profiles in Courage* (1956).

Goodwin does not gloss over Jack Kennedy's obsessive sexual appetite, claiming that it masked a fear of intimacy. Like his father, for whom he sometimes procured young escorts, he was a woman chaser. "They were a dime a dozen," one friend remarked. One of Jack's most lasting infatuations was with Danish reporter Inga Arvad. Goodwin does not speculate whether she was, as the Federal Bureau of Investigation suspected, a Nazi spy. Neither does the author offer much insight into the relationship between Jack and his wife Jacqueline, other than to assert that they were attracted by mutual loneliness. In addition to the deaths of brother Joe and sister Kathleen (in an airplane accident), the precariousness of his health also influenced Jack Kennedy's behavior. The family covered up the fact that he suffered from Addison's disease, claiming that the symptoms were periodic recurrences of malaria. Kennedy became very dependent on the drug cortisone, which altered both his appearance and his mental state. In 1954, he almost died from blood loss during a spinal operation. Back pain bedeviled him most of his life.

If Jack Kennedy entered politics in part to heal his father's sorrow over Joe, Jr.'s, death, by 1960 he was his own man, gregarious but calculating. With television transforming politics into theater and public relations, Kennedy had an ideal image of youth, glamour, and charisma. A secular leader who lacked a principled ideology, he had no trouble burying the issue of his Catholicism and winning the crucial debates with Richard M. Nixon in 1960. His ascendency, concludes Goodwin, signaled the completion of "the great immigrant revolution." The day after the election, father and son made their first public appearance together in more than a year. At the reviewing stand during the Inaugural parade, Joe Kennedy stood and took off his hat in a gesture of salutation when his son approached. In turn, the president-elect tipped his hat to his father, the only time he did so all day.

Goodwin ends her book on a triumphant note, explaining that Kennedy's presidential years have been amply documented by others. Nevertheless, there is a tragic side to this American saga; as Goodwin acknowledges, "the very nature of their search was for success of such towering proportions that . . . a terrible price was paid." While Goodwin does not uncover much material not previously known to Kennedy scholars (the best chapters are the early ones about the Fitzgeralds), her objectivity, lucid prose, and keen insights deserve high praise and a wide readership.

James B. Lane

Sources for Further Study

Boston Magazine. LXXIX, February, 1987, p. 74.
Kirkus Reviews. LIV, December 1, 1986, p. 1775.
Library Journal. CXXII, February 15, 1987, p. 142.
Los Angeles Times Book Review. March 1, 1987, p. 4.
The New Republic. CXCVI, March 16, 1987, p. 36.
The New York Times Book Review. XCII, February 15, 1987, p. 11.
Newsweek. CIX, February 9, 1987, p. 72.
Publishers Weekly. CCXXX, December 12, 1986, p. 46.
Time. CXXIX, February 16, 1987, p. 69.
The Wall Street Journal. March 24, 1987, p. 24.

FLESH AND BLOOD

Author: C(harles) K(enneth) Williams (1936-   )
Publisher: Farrar, Straus and Giroux (New York). 82 pp. $12.95
Type of work: Poetry

C. K. Williams' poems build by refinement and qualification of an observation or idea, capturing in their hesitations and modifications the very process of a subtle mental and emotional instrument struggling to register its experience

C. K. Williams is one of the foremost practitioners of a brand of poetry that is in many ways indistinguishable from prose. This status does not make him an outcast—far from it. Instead, he is working in a paradoxical mainstream of American poetry, a stream that goes back to Walt Whitman and flows through the work of such representative twentieth century figures as William Carlos Williams, Robert Creeley, and John Ashbery. These figures, and others, have helped to define—by practice more than precept—a literary form that still wears the label poetry but bears few of the traditional characteristics of that genre. By stripping his work not only of patterned sound and rhythm but also of concrete imagery and typographical play, C. K. Williams dares one to discover just what the essence of poetic expression may be.

Each poem in *Flesh and Blood* is eight lines long, apparently a severe discipline, but the lines themselves average twenty-two syllables—far longer than the lines in any established form of versification. In fact, on the page, these poems require sixteen lines of type, because each line is so long that it needs to have its last few words tucked underneath the margin-busting opening thrust. The typical specimen, then, is perhaps 176 syllables long, against the 140 of a standard sonnet.

As readers turn the pages of this collection, they confront four heavy and equal blocks of type on each pair of facing pages. This vehicle—or grid—is an equivalent, in a prose mode, to the long stanza of verse. Williams' long lines, and longer sentences, fight off any further resemblances to traditional poetry—or do they?

One consequence of the Romantic revolution in English poetry was to usher in an age of the lyric: a (usually) short poem of emotional intensity that slowly usurped the whole space of poetry at the expense of narrative and meditative types. The novel emerged as the dominant narrative genre, and meditators were left the prose essay. The emotive qualities of lyric poetry were, for a long time, connected to its ancient association with song and music, but just as characteristic is the lyric's special way of focusing experience: its ability to crystallize and personalize moments of feeling, perception, thought, or memory. An intensity of concentration in response to what the world has to offer became the lyric's special domain, the response more essentially the subject than the stimulus for the response. In recent criticism, this area of response has come to be called "affect," defined as the conscious, subjective dimension of emotional feeling separate from any physiological change. The focus on affect, in the utterance of the speaker as transferred to the experience of the reader, became the hallmark of the lyric, even as the mnemonic, structural, and decorative aspects of poetic art fell away. As affective writing, then, Williams' work remains lyrical, even as he pushes out toward the flexuous manner of prose, even as he wanders into discursive uses of language and into long patches of abstract diction.

Rhetoric and syntax, as Jonathan Holden has observed (in *The Rhetoric of the Contemporary Lyric*, 1980), have become the communicative heart of much contemporary poetry, and it is in these terms that the poetic art of C. K. Williams is best understood and appreciated. The devices of persuasion and sentence construction, along with the framing or focusing activity of each poem, need the kind of careful analysis one is accustomed to giving to meter, line break, imagery, sound patterns, and figures of speech.

At one extreme of Williams' practice is a poem such as "Dignity," a poem that syntactically rolls on, accumulating clauses and phrases until it comes to rest at its only and final period. There are a number of poems like this one, poems that build by refinement and qualification of an observation or an idea, capturing in their hesitations and modifications the very process of a subtle mental and emotional instrument struggling to register its experience. A mobile intelligence that looks closely at everything and at its own responses finds everything hard to pin down, and yet the act of trying to pin things down—the process—is what is most sharable. Williams is most successful in such endeavors, though a stretch of these poems can wear out a reader. His twisting sentences remind one of the style Henry James used in novels such as *The Ambassadors* (1903), works in which the same kind of restless scrutiny of experience and reflection occurs.

Williams is able to adapt his instrument, his own book-length convention, to a number of purposes. Some of his poems could find their way into a collection of short short stories. They read like story treatments waiting to be fleshed out but are confined by the eight-line regime to suggestive essentials. "Will" is one such poem, and it is followed by "Pregnant," a canny character sketch waiting to be elaborated in a plot. (In many ways, the whole of *Flesh and Blood* reads like a poet's novel, an unplotted series of illuminations of the speaker's psychic territory.)

Other poems are given over to scene painting, meditation, or dramatic outlining. Indeed, almost every one of Williams' poems, freed as they are from verse anchors, rushes off to embrace another genre. In this way, the writer seems to keep asking—where are the boundaries? Is this poetry? Dose it really matter what we call it?

Flesh and Blood is divided into three sections. The first section, which comprises two-thirds of the book, displays the wide range of Williams' subjects in a surprisingly random fashion. Although every so often, two poems are placed consecutively for their obvious relationship, such as "Drought" and "End of Drought," more frequent is the habit of arranging by contrast. Williams' pages look as though they hold stanzas or units in a long poem, but the sense the reader gets is like that of looking at a collage in which there is no overriding figure. Since the material would easily lend itself to larger thematic groupings, one must assume a purposefulness on Williams' part. Perhaps he did not want the impact of individual poems lost in arrangements that would link them together. When the reader does come across companion pieces ("Alzheimer's: The Wife" and "Alzheimer's: The Husband" or "Snow: I" and "Snow: II"), the paired poems offer an assurance, like road markers, that the traveler is making progress.

In the second section, sequences prevail and no poem stands alone. It is difficult to tell if the individual poems were written as parts of a planned sequence or if the sequences were arranged retrospectively. In any case, some of Williams' most attractive work is here. The accumulating observations around a central idea or image give Williams the room that the single poem does not, and the workings of his imagination benefit from this opportunity for dilation. The six-part sequence in which each title begins with the word "Reading" reveals Williams' healthy sense of humor. The sequence turns on the centrality or marginality of the act of reading in a series of settings dominated by other activities and concerns. It is a powerful stretch of social satire.

The other sequences—"Suicide," "Love," "Good Mother," and "Vehicle"—have a richness of observation and compassion that does not emerge anywhere near so fully in the independent poems of the first section. "Love" in particular is noteworthy for the range of tones delivered and styles acutely rendered. Williams' special success with these sequences leads one to hope for an even more extended effort, and the third section fulfills that expectation. "Le Petit Salvié," an elegy for Paul Zweig in eighteen of Williams' characteristic eight-line passages, answers any remaining questions about the expressiveness of this prosy poetic vehicle. It is among the most powerful sustained efforts of its decade.

Like the classic elegies of Western tradition, "Le Petit Salvié" takes the occasion of a particular loss and transforms it into a meditation on the sources of life's meaning. Though details of setting, character, and relationship speak of Williams' deep ties with Zweig, the questions raised by his dear friend's death are the old questions. The theme, as ever, is the movement of Williams' own intelligent heart from grief to something larger that lets the grief go. Williams tries to reject the notion of an afterlife, one traditional consolation, but his feelings are ambiguous. On the one hand, he insists that "Redemption is in life" and that "we're compressed into this single span of opportunity/ for which our gratitude should categorically be presumed." On the other hand, these honed utterances on the eternal here and now go stale as soon as spoken: "this without conviction, too."

The poem embraces memories of time shared overcoming the inevitable jealousies that two talented poets, however friendly and supportive, would feel toward each other: the mutual need for admiration, the mutual "suggesting and correcting and revising," and the "tellingly accurate envy sublimated into warmth and brothership." All this is lost to Williams now, but in another sense it is never to be lost.

"Le Petit Salvié" is an astonishing performance, the other side of the prideful masculinity and urbane wit expressed in dozens of other poems. Not that it is Williams' only poem of the heart—far from it. *Flesh and Blood* shows a compassionate man's reactions on numerous occasions. In many of these cases, however, one suspects that Williams is exercising compassion for the sake of making a poem. Here, the poem is the inevitable result of feelings; as Walt Whitman put it (in "When Lilacs Last in the Dooryard Bloom'd"): "Death's outlet song of life."

The C. K. Williams of *Flesh and Blood* is no longer the angry young man of *Lies* (1969) or *I Am the Bitter Name* (1972). Mellower notes were introduced into Williams' work when he turned to the long, prose line in *With Ignorance* (1977), and his art reached a fullness of vision in *Tar* (1983).

In *Flesh and Blood*, which was honored with the National Book Critics Circle Award for Poetry, we have the work of a keen, mature intelligence striving for an impossible clarity and completeness. The rolling, qualifying sentences reveal that intelligence at work, heaping disclaimer upon assertion as the world is broken down into eight-line segments of experience and reflection. It is, finally, a shrewd formal combination of open-endedness and restraint that Williams has discovered to organize and release his prodigious talent.

Philip K. Jason

Sources for Further Study

Library Journal. CXII, May 1, 1987, p. 72.
The Nation. CCXLIV, May 30, 1987, p. 734.
The New York Times Book Review. XCII, August 23, 1987, p. 20.

FOE

Author: J. M. Coetzee (1940-   )
Publisher: The Viking Press (New York). 157 pp. $15.95
Type of work: Novel
Time: Unspecified, but presumably the early eighteenth century
Locale: A barren island and England

This retelling of Daniel Defoe's Adventures of Robinson Crusoe *from the point of view of a female castaway goes well beyond the range of mere parody to explore the relationships between male and female, black and white, master and slave, fact and fiction, art and life*

> *Principal characters:*
> SUSAN BARTON, the castaway and narrator
> CRUSO, the possessor of the barren island on which Susan finds temporary refuge
> FRIDAY, Cruso's slave
> FOE, the author to whom Susan both writes and tells her story, hoping that he will turn it into a book at once interesting, saleable, and true

John Coetzee may very well be the finest allegorical novelist writing today, a South African writer whose works evidence a deep but decidedly oblique political commitment, one whose fictions cannot be reduced to mere dogma but which instead open out to explore in the widest sense possible the basic concerns of human freedom and dignity in ways that clearly pertain to and yet nevertheless steadfastly transcend the political situation in his native land. In doing so Coetzee makes plain the importance of novel-writing in an age which has witnessed the growing estrangement of the novelist from his world both in England and the United States, where fiction has come to occupy a more and more marginal place.

While *Waiting for the Barbarians* (1980) and *The Life and Times of Michael K* (1983) may be Coetzee's most clearly South African novels, *Foe*, his fifth and perhaps best novel, is by far his most troubling, both in subject and structure; it is a fiction that engages the reader's sympathy and intelligence even as it defies his or her efforts to understand the text in some final, definitive way. It is impossible to decide whether *Foe* is the story of or, alternately, the story told by Susan Barton, the "female castaway" whose quest for her abducted daughter comes to nothing and whose return voyage to England leads to her being cast adrift by a mutinous crew, an ordeal that ends (to the extent that anything may be said to end in this novel) when she reaches an island inhabited by two earlier castaways, Cruso and Friday. Any comfort the reader may feel upon discovering himself on so familiar a narrative ground is short-lived, however, for Coetzee quickly moves to defamiliarize Defoe's text and the cultural and narrative conventions upon which it is based. Coetzee's revisionist telling of Susan Barton's suppressed story— of "herstory" to parallel, oppose, and modify Defoe's fictive "history"—

would undoubtedly have provided a different kind of novelist with sufficient material for parody or pastiche, but Coetzee's interest lies in another direction.

Even as Susan's straightforward language lulls the reader into accepting her narrative, Coetzee's larger structure serves to unsettle. The first two of the novel's four parts appear within quotation marks and, in retrospect, appear to consist of Susan's written accounts. The first is a memoir of her adventures, or more accurately of her lack of adventures, while on Cruso's island. Not until its closing pages does the reader discover that the "you" Susan has been addressing is "Mr. Foe," better known to readers by his adopted name, Daniel Defoe, author of *The Life and Strange Surprising Adventures of Robinson Crusoe of York, Mariner* (1719), a fiction which purports to be fact, its fidelity to factual truth being precisely what Susan's narrative calls into question, placing Defoe's entire novel in what the critic Mikhail Bakhtin would term figurative quotation marks. Defoe is not the only one to suppress information, however, each of the subsequent parts of Coetzee's novel coming to add material that serves to explain and qualify what came before, adding information but also raising new questions. Such is surely the case with Susan's letters to Foe (part 2), in which Foe is addressed in both the second and third person. The status of these letters, which the reader initially assumes have been sent to Foe, is clarified in the novel's third part, the first to appear outside quotation marks, a sign, perhaps, that it is intended (by Coetzee? by Susan?) as a spoken rather than written account.

In effect, then, each of the novel's four parts alternately clarifies and confuses. Far from merely fleshing out the skimpy, "artless" sections of Susan's narrative, the subsequent chapters create alternative versions, all of them possible, none of them verifiably true. This is especially evident and especially disconcerting in the brief part 4 with which the novel concludes. Here Susan views her own dead self lying at the bottom of the sea in the wreck (one assumes) of the ship that had rescued her and her two fellow castaways from their barren island and taken her to England, where (one again assumes) Susan wrote what the reader has just read in the first three parts. *Foe*, however, is a novel in which assumptions are always suspect. In the fictional world that Coetzee has so artfully conjured, like Shakespeare's Prospero conjuring his island, his fictive reality, alternatives and uncertainties abound, as do narrative "erasures" and "cancellations." What, the reader may well ask, is true, and how is the truth to be known?

Paradoxically, in a novel in which all versions are suspect, each a mere fiction, the fiction-making process remains necessary. Just as Robinson Crusoe lives in and through Defoe's tale, Cruso lives through Susan, and Susan in turn "desires" to live through Foe. Yet even this simple need, to tell and be told, is not without its own complication, for the relationship between character and author, between self and other, entails a risk, includes within itself its own deconstruction. For while to tell means to give story and therefore substance to the other, in effect to liberate the other from abstraction by giving him some one particular shape, his own narrative reality, this same process that liberates the other encloses him as well, defining the other too precisely, reducing to some one story what is in fact a plurality of stories, of narrative transformations. Equally dangerous, to give voice—to give a voice—to a Cruso or a Foe or a Susan Barton is to define the creation in terms of the creator's desires—a situation analogous to the interpretive process itself, particularly in this, the intertextual age of reader-response criticism in which the earlier authoritarian concept of the inviolable meaning— always singular—of the novel or poem to which the reader must defer has given way to at best an equality of text and reader or at worst a curious reversal by which the reader assumes ascendancy over the text. *Foe* does not impose its meaning on the reader, but neither does it yield passively to the reader's interpretive desires. Instead it remains beyond interpretation. A novel in which shipwrecks figure prominently, *Foe* is itself a narrative wreck, its journey forever incomplete, its meaning forever indecidable. It takes the form of intertextual wreckage, of narrative debris, of irreconcilable stories and the allusive bits and pieces drawn not only from Defoe's own works (including *Moll Flanders*, 1722, as well as *Crusoe*) but also from contemporary writers such as Roland Barthes, Jacques Derrida, and Adrienne Rich, whose poem "Diving into the Wreck" helps to explain the novel's final pages. *Foe*'s open-endedness and narrative contradictions lead to a rather surprising conclusion, for ultimately this is a remarkably hopeful book, a triumph of the redemptive imagination in which Coetzee gives an affirmative twist to Beckett's grimly comic existential claim, "I must go on I can't go on I'll go on."

As Susan comes to realize early in her narrative (if not early in the time of her narrative), "Cruso's island is no bad place to be cast away . . . if one must be cast away." But whereas Cruso is content with the emptiness of his barren island, unwilling or unable to imagine anything different or better, Susan is not. While he is indifferent to salvation, she has an "immoderate" desire to be saved, by which she at first means a desire to be rescued, but, as she later comes to understand, her real yearning is "to be elsewhere," to be other than what others (especially Cruso) say she is. Unlike the reductively self-sufficient Cruso, Susan feels compelled to record her experiences and in this way to authenticate and understand her life's adventures, or alternately, to have them recorded for her by Foe. Her account implies her need for and the existence of a listener/reader, a need that turns her monologue into dialogue, a barren island into a shared reality—so much so that Susan, speaking from the eighteenth century, comes to sound very much like contemporary critic Roland Barthes on the erotics of writing and reading, claiming for example, that "the desire for answering speech is like the desire for the embrace of, the embrace by, another being."

In the course of her narrated—or narrative—wanderings, Susan manages to embrace a number of lovers, bestowing on them both her sexual favors and her stories: ship's captains, Cruso, even Friday and Foe. But who is this "Foe"? And why is the novel named for him? Is he Susan's real subject, the reader/lover for whom she longs? Or is Foe the author of Susan Barton as Daniel Defoe is the author of Robinson Crusoe? Or is Susan her own Foe, the author of her own tale, at once creator and creation? Is Foe her creator or her lover or her foe, her rival and adversary? Is the author—any author, including Susan, Foe, and Coetzee—a foe, or worse, a cannibal (as Susan suspects Friday may have been)? In her ever-changing relationship with Foe, Susan plays the parts of source, subject, servant, usurper, lover, muse, and succubus astride the surprised and femininely passive writer. Theirs is a relationship marked by such odd reversals, by symbiotic equality—each needs the other—*and* by the typically sexist pattern of male dominance and female submission and neglect, as in Susan's wondering whether Foe will engage in a literary version of seduction and betrayal, taking her story but eliding her from his final version (as indeed is the case if the reader assumes that Susan is the source for Defoe's *Robinson Crusoe*). "Yet where would you be without the woman?" Susan asks.

Foe would be quite literally nowhere at all without Susan Barton, for he is her creation, a literary character in her story. Just as he is both author and character, so too is she: "When I reflect on my story," she explains in one of her letters to Foe (and therefore to the reader, another of her Foes), "I seem to exist only as the one who came, the one who witnessed, the one who longed to be gone: a being without substance, a ghost beside the true body of Cruso." Hers is a simple enough plaint on the part of a woman forced to play at best a secondary role in an otherwise all-male adventure fantasy, but at this point her plaint takes an odd turn, for what Susan laments most is not her absence as character in Foe's tale of Cruso but her absence as self-effacing author from her own narrative, the necessary but nevertheless lost authorial, or narrative, "I," the eye as witness and the I as teller of the tale. "Is that the fate of all storytellers?" asks Susan of her similarly self-effacing Foe. The author must remain unknown, substanceless, unless he or she becomes a character in his own fiction or in the fiction of another, a character that would not be the author him- or herself but that would instead by a version of him, as happens in *Foe* when Susan begets her own fictive self.

Susan, however, does considerably more; having displaced Foe, the male author, Susan strives both to affirm and displace her own self, choosing to tell the most impossible story of all, that of Friday, "consigned to a life of silence." If Cruso is the Defoe character so conspicuous by virtue of his relative absence from Susan's account, if Susan's significance derives from her emergence as author/narrator of a tale from which she had been unfairly cast away, and if Foe represents the male author whose self-effacement is meaningless insofar as the voice of Western fiction is traditionally and conventionally that of the white male, then Friday may be understood as the novel's silent center: "In every story," Susan explains, "there is a silence, some sight concealed, some word unspoken, I believe. Till we have spoken the unspoken we have not come to the heart of the story."

Friday is the still and silent point at the heart of Coetzee's whirling fiction: its central mystery, its best hope, at once the basis and the proof of Susan's "I believe." To be sure, there is a certain despair here as well, for as Susan well understands, "the only tongue that can tell Friday's story is the tongue he has lost!" Friday's secret may never be told, but what Susan realizes is that Friday does indeed have a secret. As Foe will rescue Cruso from his own indifference—as Defoe rescued Selkirk—so too does Susan wish to rescue Friday from the silence to which others have consigned him, depriving him of his freedom as well as his voice. The danger in such an enterprise is that Susan's words may well enslave as well as liberate, but this is a danger of which Susan is warned by Foe and for which she is prepared. More important is the fact that she chooses to tell Friday's story, to believe that he has a story worth being told, to make him a character, to lend him her voice, or, better, to speak in his voice, taking it as her own, to take this speechless black man as her own child. This is her most powerful transformation, the one at the heart of this, Coetzee's most powerful novel, a work that does not end but instead opens out, testifying to the inexhaustible power of fiction and of love: Susan, or what may be her ghostlike authorial self, seeing the sleeping Friday transformed into the drowned slave, pries his lips apart, and becomes witness (or conjurer) of this revelation: "His mouth opens. From inside him comes a slow stream, without breath, without interruption. It flows up through his body and out upon me; it passes through the cabin, through the wreck; washing the cliffs and shores of the island, it runs northward and southward to the ends of the cliffs and shores of the earth. Soft and cold, dark and unending, it beats against my eyelids, against the skin of my face." Thus ends Coetzee's *Foe*, with the story of the untellable story of the white South African's foe, the black man, still untold, still unspoken, but no longer either unspeakable or unimaginable. That is Coetzee's achievement.

Robert A. Morace

Sources for Further Study

Kirkus Reviews. LIV, December 1, 1986, p. 1741.
Library Journal. CXI, December, 1986, p. 134.
Los Angeles Times Book Review. February 22, 1987, p. 3.
The Nation. CCXLIV, March 28, 1987, p. 402.
The New Republic. CLVI, March 9, 1987, p. 36.
The New York Review of Books. XXXIV, May 28, 1987, p. 18.
The New York Times Book Review. XCII, February 22, 1987, p. 1.
Newsweek. CIX, February 23, 1987, p. 77.
Publishers Weekly. CCXXX, December 5, 1986, p. 64.
Time. CXXIX, March 23, 1987, p. 84.
The Times Literary Supplement. September 12, 1986, p. 995.

A FUGITIVE FROM UTOPIA
The Poetry of Zbigniew Herbert

Author: Stanisław Barańczak (1946-   )
Publisher: Harvard University Press (Cambridge, Massachusetts). 163 pp. $22.50
Type of work: Literary criticism

The first full-length study in English of the work of one of the most original and important poets of the twentieth century

This study of the poetry of Zbigniew Herbert is a major step in exposing the English-speaking reader to one of the most important contemporary European poets. In the United States and England, Herbert's reputation has been growing since 1968, when Czesław Miłosz, the winner of the 1980 Nobel Prize in Literature, and Peter Dale Scott published their translations of Herbert's poems, *Selected Poems*. Since then, as Herbert's oeuvre of both poetry and prose has continued to grow, new translations and critical articles have appeared in English in diverse journals. This book-length study is the work of the Polish poet, critic, and translator Stanisław Barańczak, Alfred Jurzykowski Professor of Polish Language and Literature at Harvard University. Barańczak describes the present volume as a "slightly abbreviated version" of a study published in Polish in 1984.

English-speaking readers have been able to appreciate Herbert by reading among the numerous translations of his works in print, but a critical study like Barańczak's performs a special function. Previously, information about Herbert and his work was hard to find, scattered in articles, interviews, or reviews in a bewildering variety of literary publications, languages, and countries. Barańczak's study, together with the bibliography and notes, gathers this information together for the first time. Students and critics who want to write about Herbert will turn to this book as an indispensable tool. It has two major ingredients: a wealth of information, some of it new, and, most important, an interpretation of Herbert's six collections of poetry by a first-rate critical mind.

There are different possible ways of writing about Herbert, and the choice of a method or approach is neither obvious nor inevitable. Two examples can be given. Is Herbert's life and biography important to an understanding of his poetry? Herbert has been moderately reticent in giving information about his life, but he has provided important information in interviews. He is neither a totally private poet nor by any stretch of the imagination a "confessional" poet. It would not be difficult for the critic to explore this background further, to interview Herbert's friends and acquaintances about his wartime experiences, his family, first jobs, relationships, and opinions. Herbert has a striking and original personality; this kind of anecdotal information would make fascinating reading. Barańczak has not followed this path; background information about Herbert is encapsulated in five pages in the brief introduction to the book.

A second decision about method is the treatment of Herbert's literary style or craftsmanship. This is harder for the English-speaking reader to appreciate because Herbert is encountered at a distance, through translation. Herbert's poems, especially in his first three collections, read extremely rapidly and succeed in making an immediate, seemingly spontaneous, highly synthetic impact. Herbert has encouraged the view that he pays little attention to self-conscious style. When an interviewer asked him why he wrote prose poems, he replied that when he devised this form he had no fixed domicile or convenient place to write. Consequently he chose a form to fit his living conditions, something that he could commit to paper in a very brief time. Many critics have followed Herbert's lead, emphasizing the content of his poems rather than their form. In addition, Herbert's verse (not his prose poems) has no punctuation. This, together with the awareness that they were reading Herbert's work in translation, led many English-speaking critics away from the close consideration of Herbert's craft and verbal artistry.

Some Polish critics, however, have looked closely at the texture of individual poems, and this is what Barańczak does. He gives many close reading, carefully analyzing metaphors, images, ambiguities, and "tensions." (Barańczak's critical vocabulary recalls on many occasions that of the New Critics of the 1940's and 1950's.) These are among the most rewarding parts of his book. His interpretations of poems are always well-informed and alert, with a sensitivity to subtleties of verbal texture as well as to mythical and historical connotations. Any student or critic who wants to test an interpretation of Herbert's well-known poems, such as "Apollo and Marsyas," "Pebble," "At the Gate of the Valley," "Preliminary Investigation of an Angel," or "Inner Voice," would do well to consult Barańczak's readings, as well as the footnotes in which he registers his disagreements with other critics. (These often make lively reading.)

A problem of still greater importance, encountered by any critic writing about Herbert, is that of the meanings of the poems, for Herbert is above all a poet of meanings. Miłosz wrote many years ago, "If the key to contemporary Polish poetry is the collective experience of the last decades, Herbert is perhaps the most skillful in expressing it." This "collective experience" is not just that of Poland but goes far beyond an individual nation and its fate. In a time when much poetry has become decorative or private—when, as Arthur Danto has forcefully stated in *The Philosophical Disenfranchisement of Art* (1986), many art forms since World War II have abdicated any direct engagement with either philosophy or history—Herbert deliberately confronts this subject matter in poem after poem. He is one of the contemporary poets who is most concerned with philosophical and ethical meaning. For example, the two poems "Elegy of Fortinbras" and "Apollo and

Marsyas" have an astonishingly broad frame of reference; the conflicts of idealism with practicality, and of victor with victim, are set in motion in terms that are both concretely specific and universal, reverberating throughout history.

Barańczak adopts a critical method that is reasonable but also has disadvantages. He presents Herbert as a poet of "antinomies," and details these: the West versus the East (the "heritage" of Western civilization versus the "barbarism" of the East), the past versus the present, myth versus experience. On the stylistic plane, these give rise to the lesser antinomies of white versus gray, light versus shadow, and air versus earth. In the domain of values, typical antinomies are the abstract versus the tangible, the perfect versus the imperfect, and the ornamental versus the truth. A thematic approach isolating these diverse strands in Herbert's poetry is scholarly, responsible, and useful. In discussing each separate theme, Barańczak ranges over Herbert's entire oeuvre, showing how the theme reappears in poem after poem. The method also has a schematism that probably inheres in any critical method but stands out in the attempt to account for Herbert's poetry. Barańczak's approach is analytical, separating the component parts and smaller units of meaning, yet Herbert's poetry is nothing if not highly synthetic. The poems present large, highly ramified wholes, and manage to be philosophical without using the technical language or jargon of contemporary philosophy. It might be overly demanding to ask the critic to account for this. Any analytical effort must share the limitations of discursive language and to some extent must increase the entropy described in the Second Law of Thermodynamics—as Norbert Wiener paraphrased it, "You cannot unscramble eggs." A similar process occurs when dealing with synthetic works of art.

Barańczak is probably aware of this disparity between analysis and synthesis. He uses different formulations to account for the coexistence of Herbert's antinomies: He refers to their "dynamic balance," to the "ambivalent tension between opposed poles," "Janus looking in two directions at once," an "insoluble contradiction," and antinomies that are "unresolved" or in "suspension." These concepts appear in different contexts, too. For example, when Barańczak discusses Herbert's use of historical personages in the poems, he refers to the "distance" between the persona and the poem's author or speaker. In the context of a poem's overall meaning, however, as opposed to its narrative technique, this notion of distance becomes more problematic. In one passage, Barańczak observes that Herbert simultaneously distances from and identifies with a persona. This is correct; it also points to a certain clumsiness in the term, which is a common tool of contemporary literary criticism.

A central chapter of Barańczak's book probes Herbert's unique use of irony. It makes a useful distinction between "classical" and "romantic" irony; Herbert's irony, Barańczak notes, is neither, and he introduces a new, fruitful concept of "mutual unmasking" that supersedes the old association of distance and irony. Yet the old problem of whether Herbert is to be called a classical poet remains unresolved. Barańczak criticizes several other critics for calling Herbert a classical poet, yet his own notions or dynamic balance point in this direction. Is it a balance or an imbalance? An equilibrium or a disequilibrium? There is a difference; this difference, that changes from poem to poem, is crucial in Herbert's poetry.

A difficulty in approaching Herbert analytically and isolating his themes is that the method does not show how they come together—how they cohere and form synthetic wholes. Herbert is above all an agile poet, and this agility takes on truly remarkable proportions. Herbert can shift his point of view, undercut it, mock it, mock those of others, then affirm it again, casting his voice and tonality like a ventriloquist in the space of only half a dozen lines with a dexterity that is the despair of the critic. The irony is often mixed with humor, so if we must associate irony with the concept of distance there are several types of distance at work, sometimes caustic and critical, sometimes rollicking. Yet these shifts, once again, cohere. They accumulate incrementally, building larger wholes of meaning which are expressive and which the reader spontaneously grasps. The critic can analyze out the constituent threads of meaning, as the French say they can be *décomposés*. To put them back together is, to be sure, a difficult task.

Barańczak's final chapter, "Imponderabilia," considers the larger meanings of Herbert's poetry, as well as the implications of his irony and his ethics. The analysis of the key poem "The Envoy of Mr. Cognito" is excellent, and Barańczak rightly observes that if there is any equilibrium in the poem, it is "a peculiar equilibrium indeed." In another important poem, "Mad Woman," irony is linked to schizophrenia. If Herbert is a stoic poet, he knows little of the Stoics' *ataraxia*. Herbert's relationship to nature, to natural forces and instinct, is problematic throughout his work and his ethics often come close to an imperative to resist human nature. As Barańczak points out, they are essentially tragic and have no external or institutional sanction. Nor is there a convergence between the notion of moral salvation and of physical survival—more frequently, there is downright opposition.

A major question in the book is whether Herbert himself chooses between the various antinomies he presents or whether he remains ambivalent, presenting a variety of answers with his different personas, sometimes opting for one solution and sometimes for another. Does the poem "Apollo and Marsyas" present one view about art and the poem "Fragment" another dialectically opposed to it, Herbert himself siding with neither, as Barańczak suggests? Herbert—we know from both his poems and interviews—detests dialectics. He is not a poet of what John Keats called "negative capability." A good argument could be made that Herbert is never really ambivalent when he presents his antinomies; he consistently opts for a solution. It must be granted that these solutions are never simplistic, but Herbert is always giving "a nudge to the balance."

Similarly, a good argument could be made that Herbert does not write "about" the themes and topics described in Barańczak's antinomies at all. Barańczak's emphasis on Herbert's technique is excellent, but Herbert's historical and mythological paraphernalia can also be taken as types of "metaphor," as topoi that always point to another deeper and more essential point of reference, usually ethical, sometimes practical, political, or critical.

Finally, it should be noted that there are some topics that *A Fugitive from Utopia* deliberately avoids. There is little discussion of literary influences on Herbert. To do this in an exact manner would be difficult. It is clear that Miłosz was an important influence, as was Józef Czechowicz ("one of the argonauts"), Constantine Cavafy, and T. S. Eliot. Barańczak does not enter the domain of Herbert's reading. In addition, there is little discussion of Herbert's evolution as a poet. A few turning points are briefly mentioned: Barańczak notes that after the 1961 collection of poems, *Studium przedmiotu* (study of the object), Herbert turned increasingly to the use of personas and the dramatic monologue. Yet the chronological sequence of the poems is generally downgraded; Herbert's techniques and attitudes are treated as if they were all of a piece. Perhaps this was a wise methodological decision on Barańczak's part. For more than a decade during the period of Joseph Stalin, Herbert was writing "for the drawer." Then he published his output almost simultaneously in two volumes in 1956 and 1957, when it seemed as if this new poet suddenly sprang, like Athena, from Zeus's brow. It makes little sense to speak of Herbert's poetic "debut," and it is very difficult to match an individual poem with a year of composition, establishing an accurate chronology. Perhaps as a consequence Barańczak provides no discussion of why Herbert's verse has no punctuation (a practice which continues to disturb many American and British critics), and way he writes prose poems or *bajeczki* with full, traditional punctuation.

It becomes increasingly clear that Zbigniew Herbert is one of the most significant poets of the century. It is satisfying to have, at last, a book that clearly describes the nature of his poetry, and that gathers together in a scholarly manner the various critical references and major insights into the poems which have accumulated over the past four decades. What Barańczak attempts to do, he does very well. This study will prove to be indispensable to those who want to read seriously and write about Herbert in the future.

John Carpenter

Sources for Further Study

The Christian Science Monitor. January 27, 1988, p. 17.
The Guardian. October 9, 1987, p. 21.

GEORGE C. MARSHALL
Statesman, 1945-1959

Author: Forrest C. Pogue (1912-   )
Foreword by Drew Middleton
Publisher: Viking (New York). Illustrated. 600 pp. $29.95
Type of work: Historical biography
Time: 1945-1959
Locale: The United States, Europe, Latin America, and the Far East

The fourth and final volume of the official biography of George Catlett Marshall, Jr., dealing with his last days as Chief of Staff of the United States Army, his postwar careers as Special Ambassador to China, secretary of state, president of the Red Cross, and secretary of defense, and his final retirement

> *Principal personages:*
> GEORGE CATLETT MARSHALL, JR., Chief of Staff of the United States Army, 1939-1945, and cabinet member, 1947-1951
> HARRY S TRUMAN, thirty-third President of the United States, 1945-1953
> ROBERT A. LOVETT, Under Secretary of State, 1947-1949; Deputy Secretary of Defense, 1950-1951; Secretary of Defense 1951-1953
> CHIANG KAI-SHEK, Generalissimo of China, 1928-1949; Head of the Kuomintang, 1949-1975
> CHOU EN-LAI, representative of Chairman Mao Tse-tung in negotiations with the Kuomintang and the United States mission, 1945-1946
> VYACHESLAV MOLOTOV, Soviet Minister of Foreign Affairs, 1939-1949 and 1953-1956

John Milton's sonnet "To the Lord General Cromwell May 1652" would serve as a pertinent epigraph for Forrest C. Pogue's *George C. Marshall: Statesman, 1945-1959*:

> Cromwell, our chief of men, who through a cloud
> Not of war only, but detractions rude,
> Guided by faith and matchless Fortitude,
> To peace and truth thy glorious way hast plough'd,
> And on the neck of crowned Fortune proud
> Hast rear'd God's Trophies and his work pursu'd,
> . . . .
> yet much remains
> To conquer still; peace hath her victories
> No less renown'd than war, new foes arise.

The emphasis on faith and fortitude, and particularly the phrase, "Peace hath her victories/ No less renown'd than war," fit well into the themes of the book; even the "detractions rude" are present. In this world, as in Marshall's career, new foes constantly arise.

Pogue's book has two important functions: It is the fourth and final volume of an excellent and monumental biography, and it is a thorough portrayal of world history, Eastern and Western, from 1945 through 1951. The remaining years, from 1952 to 1959, furnish an epilogue, necessary to the biography but less gripping as history.

A reader coming to *George C. Marshall: Statesman* after reading the first three volumes of the biography—subtitled: "Education of a General, 1880-1939" (1963), "Ordeal and Hope, 1939-42" (1966), and "Organizer of Victory, 1943-45" (1973)—will have some advantage over a reader who comes to this volume alone; the publishers, however, seemed to wish to separate this volume from the others, even by format and jacket cover, to indicate that it could well be read alone. The first three volumes were introduced with forewords by General Omar N. Bradley, whose death ended an assignment which he obviously treasured. The foreword to *George C. Marshall: Statesman* is by Drew Middleton, distinguished journalist and foreign correspondent, who covered the war in Europe from 1939 to its end, and the postwar period there until 1965.

Middleton begins his foreword with an account of a casual discussion of great men of the twentieth century by three Britons and two Americans. The five included a cabinet member, a diplomat, a historian, an editor, and a foreign correspondent, familiar with the great and the near-great in many parts of the world. There was unanimity on only two men of the century: Winston S. Churchill and George C. Marshall. According to Middleton, any reader of Pogue's book will understand the "unanimity of the five on Marshall." Middleton's foreword is an excellent composition: Anyone without the staying power to cope with the six-hundred-page book would do well to read it thoughtfully. It is a concise summary and critical essay combined. He enters a mild demurrer to what he thinks is Pogue's stress on Marshall's failure in China. He believes that the cards were so stacked against him that "Talleyrand, Metternich and Castlereagh could not have pulled it off." Middleton's position on the postwar crises with Russia, when the possibilities of a third world war called for a calculated risk, is that the United States was fortunate to have the secretary of state and the president that it did have. He considers Marshall's Harvard speech, which led to the European Recovery Plan, the high point of American diplomacy since World War II. He ends his foreword: "In the book Mr. Pogue has done more than record the final successes of George C. Marshall's career. He has restored the man to us in all his great dimensions. In war and peace he made a generation proud to be Americans."

In his preface, Pogue speaks of having spent at least thirty years with Marshall, as Douglas Southall Freeman spoke of living twenty years with Robert E. Lee. During those thirty years, Pogue's admiration and respect increased for the man he characterizes as "this giant of the twentieth century." He presents some of the problems of writing and publishing a biography composed over so many years. Apparently he began expecting to do three volumes: *Education of a General, World War II*, and *Statesman*; but the material on World War II got out of hand, and not even two volumes could do justice to it. When volume 3 went to press, the author considered devoting an entire volume to China, thus expanding the biography to five volumes. Washington Irving's *Life of Washington* (1855-1859) grew from two projected volumes to five completed ones. It certainly would have been easier for Pogue to cope with the enormous amount of his material in five volumes or six, instead of four. A reader can get some idea of the scope of Pogue's research by skimming the acknowledgements and the selected bibliography (twelve pages of small print).

The unity of volume 4 would have been improved if it had not been necessary to cover the close of World War II after the prologue; it is ungracious, however, to quibble over "what might have been" instead of praising the superb work that the author and the publishers have given to posterity. It will surely remain valuable to future generations.

The prologue could be produced as a one-act play for television. It begins with the announcement of Marshall's replacement as chief of staff by General Dwight D. Eisenhower, then shifts to a ceremony in the courtyard of the Pentagon, with appropriate music, including "The Spirit of V.M.I.," played by the army band. General Marshall delivered a brief farewell address, thanking the armed forces for their loyal service. He then pointed out the terrible conditions in Europe, where people were suffering hunger and cold. He urged the younger people to face the grim problems of the world and to dedicate themselves to alleviating them. The germ of the Harvard speech was in these words.

The next scene shifts to the domestic front. The general and his wife had left their quarters at Fort Myer and moved into an apartment, anticipating a peaceful retirement and relief from the weighty burdens the general had borne for so many years. The telephone rang just as Katherine Marshall was going upstairs for a nap. He answered it, but said nothing to her. When she woke up, she heard the radio announcing that the president had appointed the general a special ambassador to China and that he would leave immediately. The general explained that he could not bear to tell her until she had had her rest. She was hurt and bitter that another fearful burden had been laid on him just when rest seemed at hand.

Chapter 1 finishes the account of the war in the Far East and the development of the atomic bomb. It contains one of Pogue's typical brief biographical sketches, this one of General Leslie R. Groves, coordinator of the work of the scientists and the army in the Manhattan Project. Pogue comments on the controversy, which is "still noisy," over the decision to drop the atomic bomb. He believes the decision to have been a wise one, which saved many lives.

Chapter 2 begins with farewell good wishes from General Douglas Mac-

Arthur to General Marshall: "The entire command sends sincere greetings and hopes you will find full contentment in green pastures and by still waters." Marshall's laconic reply was: "Thanks for your message. My retirement was of rather short duration and the outlook does not indicate still waters."

The general took on the daunting mission to China with some hope that a unified China could be achieved. Characteristically, he set up an organization which he believed would work: field teams with representatives from the Kuomintang, the Communists, and the Americans. They were sent to trouble spots to try to prevent or end armed conflict. He dealt directly with Chiang Kai-shek, but on the Communist side he dealt with Chou En-lai, "the brilliant, dangerously charming representative of Chairman Mao Tse-tung." Chiang was unwilling to make any compromise; the Communists made no significant ones. Chiang, with considerable justification, thought that he had been treated badly at the Yalta Conference. He disliked General Joseph W. Stilwell and desired his removal. Stilwell was replaced with General Albert C. Wedemeyer, who had been one of General Marshall's planners for the cross-channel operation. Wedemeyer was a great admirer of his superior and strongly favored his appointment as secretary of state; but after his experience in China, he turned against America's China policy and against Marshall as supporting that policy. After the war, he published a bitter book, *Wedemeyer Reports!* (1958).

Pogue makes it quite clear that Marshall's mission to China was a failure; it would be hard to interpret it otherwise. Yet the China mission led to the appointment of Marshall as secretary of state, which changed the history of the Western world. Pogue is a shrewd observer of politics, as his account of the confirmation of Marshall by the Senate demonstrates. Democrats feared that the Republican party might nominate Marshall; Republicans feared that he might supplant President Harry S Truman as Democratic candidate. General Marshall spiked all guns by a forthright statement, as positive as General William Sherman's, that he would never run for any office.

When Marshall became secretary of state, he did not follow the frequent policy of sweeping out his predecessor's subordinates. He persuaded Under Secretary Dean Acheson to remain for a while, though the latter wished to resign. When Acheson did resign, he recommended Robert A. Lovett as his successor. Lovett became so important a figure in Marshall's careers as secretary of state and secretary of defense that Pogue dedicated *George C. Marshall: Statesman* to him. Pogue says that the rapport between Marshall and Lovett was remarkable. They had had some dealings when Lovett was Assistant Secretary of War for Air, and they began their work in the Department of State with mutual respect and liking.

In his interview with Pogue, Acheson stressed Marshall's "unmilitary approach" in the Department of State. In his organization of the communications within the department, however, Marshall did lean on his military experience.

Very soon after becoming secretary of state, Marshall had to attend the Moscow Conference of Foreign Ministers. He had not had time to study European problems thoroughly, and immediately he had the burden of Vyacheslav Molotov and Joseph Stalin laid on him. It was fortunate that he had had a baptism of fire with Chou and Mao to prepare him in part for what would be a main problem during the rest of his career. John Dryden accused his opponent Thomas Shadwell of never "deviating" into sense. Marshall found that neither the Chinese Communists nor the Russian Communists ever deviated into reasonableness.

Surely the climax of Marshall's career as secretary of state came with his so-called Harvard speech. The essence of it had been presented in his farewell address delivered in the Pentagon court. When he returned from Moscow, he delivered a report, on a national radio hookup, which amplified his ideas on the European situation. In 1947, Harvard University offered him an honorary degree and invited him to deliver an address. Though he declined the formal address at the commencement exercises, he agreed to make "a few remarks and perhaps 'a little more' at the alumni meeting." As Pogue puts it: "The 'little more' was to have global reverberations." In his citations, Harvard President James B. Conant called Marshall "an American to whom Freedom owes an enduring debt of gratitude, a soldier and statesman whose ability and character brook only one comparison [George Washington] in the history of the nation."

According to Pogue, Charles E. Bohlen and George F. Kennan were important contributors to the Marshall Plan, Bohlen actually furnishing a draft of the Harvard speech. "Bohlen was to insist later that the Marshall speech was born in the Kremlin—that it came after Marshall's interview with Stalin, following the frustrating negotiations with Molotov." Pogue points out that important contributions to history are made by unsung heroes. A principal point in the speech was that the initiative for European recovery should come from Europe, but that the United States would offer help if help were desired. The hand was extended to Russia and its satellites as well as to the rest of Europe. Stalin had no desire for the rest of Europe to make any recovery; he wanted it all. He allowed neither the Soviet Union nor any of its dominated countries to accept the offered aid.

Marshall's unimpassioned delivery and his clear picture of the desperate conditions in Western Europe were effective in gaining support for the European Recovery Plan. The Marshall Plan did save Western Europe from collapse and from being swallowed up by the Soviet Union. It did not, of course, bring sweet reasonableness and peace to a troubled world, then or later.

In the last years of Marshall's half-century of devoted service to his country and his fellowman, he was subjected to venomous attacks, to which he did not reply. Pogue believes that these criticisms may have helped him to decide that he had done enough and to leave his friend and staunch supporter Lovett to carry on the work of secretary of defense.

In 1953, President Eisenhower sent a commission to represent the United States at the coronation of Queen Elizabeth II. General Marshall, chairman of the commission, was received warmly. Pogue's account of the visit presents a charming picture. When Marshall entered Westminster Abbey, the entire congregation rose; puzzled, he looked around hastily to see what distinguished person was following him. Prime Minister Churchill, Field Marshall Viscount Alanbrooke, and Field Marshall Sir Bernard Montgomery stepped out of the procession to shake his hand. Pogue quotes excerpts from Marshall's letter to former President Truman giving an account of the trip. One shows "almost boyish pleasure":

> The banquet at Buckingham Palace was the most brilliant gathering I had ever seen. The Queen's party of about thirty was seated at an oval table in the center of the hall, surrounded by tables of twelve. I was included at her table with Princess Alice as my partner, and was, I think, the only commoner so honored. I sat between the Princess and the Queen Mother, and two chairs removed from the Queen.

After the banquet, Churchill took Marshall off for a long visit.

Soon after the return from England, Marshall was announced as the winner of the Nobel Peace Prize. In spite of influenza and perhaps pneumonia, he made the trip to Oslo and delivered his address of acceptance, written under the handicap of his illness. His health suffered from this trip, and his last years were dogged by illness. Pogue, who delights in human-interest bits, tells of Marshall's disappointment in being unable to attend a state dinner for Queen Frederika of Greece; but the Queen flew from New York to visit him in Walter Reed Hospital.

Pogue's epilogue sums up the general's whole career and supports his portrait with quotations from others. The four-volume biography presents an amazingly complete history of a period of world history and a portrait of an austere man, with "a quiet sense of humor and a passion for simple justice," a man of loyalty, integrity, and fortitude, not infallible, not free from errors in judgment, but free from malice and self-interest. Pogue quotes Thomas Jefferson's tribute to George Washington to underline Harvard President Conant's comparison of the two soldier-statesmen: "His integrity was most pure, his justice the most inflexible I have ever known, no motives of interest or consanguinity, of friendship or hatred, being able to bias his decisions."

George Burke Johnston

Sources for Further Study

The Atlantic. CCLIX, June, 1987, p. 78.
Booklist. LXXXIII, May 1, 1987, p. 1331.
The Christian Science Monitor. July 3, 1987, p. B4.
Library Journal. CXII, June 15, 1987, p. 67.
Los Angeles Times Book Review. August 9, 1987, p. 8.
The New York Review of Books. XXXIV, August 13, 1987, p. 11.
The New York Times Book Review. XCII, June 28, 1987, p. 3.
The New Yorker. LXIII, July 13, 1987, p. 89.
Publishers Weekly. CCXXXI, May 1, 1987, p. 57.
The Washington Post Book World. XVII, June 21, 1987, p. 1.

THE GOLD CELL

Author: Sharon Olds (1942-   )
Publisher: Alfred A. Knopf (New York). 91 pp. $14.95; paperback $8.95
Type of work: Poetry

Olds's treatment of female sexuality escapes the traditional stereotypes as well as the contemporary ones; everywhere, there is a sense of health, of sought and deserved satisfactions

The work of Sharon Olds is at once narrative and lyrical. Her gifts include a daring imagination for both subject and figures of speech and a sure sense of rhythm. This rhythmic sense gives momentum to the story elements in her poems, while the often-dazzling metaphors release the emotional values—the lyrical element. *The Gold Cell*, her third collection, solidifies her position as one of the major poetic voices to emerge in the 1980's. Following upon her startling debut with *Satan Says* (1980) and the widely acclaimed Lamont prizewinner *The Dead and the Living* (1984), *The Gold Cell* might have been a disappointment. It is, however, unquestionably a success.

This collection is focused on the issue of identity: the poet's first of all and, by extension, the reader's. Each of the four sections elaborates one of the key ways in which human beings find their identity. The first sequence in *The Gold Cell* contains poems about the speaker's relationship to the troublesome conditions of the world in which she lives. The reader finds here an urban self looking at a world filled with disasters, one who questions the social and personal meanings of the events and her responses to them. The self is defined as a sensibility that notices as only a single individual can notice and feels as only a single individual can feel.

The speaker witnesses a suicide, has a confrontation with a black youth in a subway car, records the discovery of an abandoned newborn, and imagines the trauma of a twelve-year-old girl who witnesses the rape of her friend and is brutally treated herself. In these poems and others, Olds gives the reader a series of harrowing portraits: tragedies usually brought to us through the news media rather than by the accident of personal proximity. Still, she makes them personal by her determination to move into the skin of the victim or perpetrator in order to register fully the impact of the tragedy on her own responding instrument. Who is she? She is the woman who pays attention to these events and feels this way about them. As significant aspects of her environment, these events help to define her.

The second group of poems identifies the self as the child of its parents. Olds links together the complex knots of emotion felt as the maturing daughter of this mother, this father, this couple. She defines herself as the inevitable sum of an eccentric genetic equation, seeing her imposing physicality as an inheritance from her father. More often, the analysis is in terms of conflicting emotions: the difficulty of loving the ones who hurt you, the ones you would not be like if you could help it. Olds's openness in these poems is frightening. There must be a pain returned upon the parents in such memories as are found here. The caring is in the intense scrutiny, the trust that such scathing directness can be beneficial and even healing.

"Saturn" opens with the lines:

> He lay on the couch night after night,
> mouth open, the darkness of the room
> filling his mouth, and no one knew
> my father was eating his children. . . .

The metaphor is carried out in horrifying detail. In the father's indifferent evening slumbers, the children's limbs are consumed one by one: "He took/ my brother's head between his lips/ and snapped it like a cherry off the stem." His passive absence is felt as an indulgence, an appetite, a cannibalistic betrayal. The poem complicates this reaction with some rationalizing forgiveness, but its center is in this reaction: what it felt like to be the child of this unconscious, snoring father.

In this way, through a powerful evocation of childhood scenes and moods, Olds unfolds an identity shaped by the parental household. The poems are both hostile and loving, true in each dimension because of the presence of the other. Moreover, Olds balances the re-creation of what-it-was-like-then with the registering of how-I-understand-it-now. The thoroughness and penetration of her investigation is admirable, though many readers will squirm. "Looking at My Father" and "Why My Mother Made Me" should not be missed, but surely they will sting.

Olds's third defining perspective is the sexual self. The opening poems of this section constitute a sequence in themselves. "California Swimming Pool" defines, in a ritual setting for young adolescents, the growth of sexual awareness. It is followed by "First Boyfriend," "First Sex," and "First Love," poems notable for their authentic detail and their sharable emotions. The speaker here is never shy, never an awkward experimenter, but a young woman eager and soon comfortable with her own sexuality, an actor defining herself through sexual behavior and pleasure.

These and other poems in section 3 of *The Gold Cell* will offend the prudish. Their eroticism will be labeled as pornographic by a narrow spectrum of readers. Yet, at the same time, they are examples of the kind of poem that Olds manages better than anyone else. There is never a hint of the reader being teased or manipulated, only a patient search for the right words and images to share an earthy woman's sense of who she is. These poems are unusual not because they treat sex from a woman's perspective, but because the voice is neither long-suffering, coy, seductive, nor outlandishly and threateningly aggressive. Olds's treatment of female sexuality escapes the traditional stereotypes as well as the contemporary ones; everywhere, there is a sense of health, of sought and deserved satisfactions.

The self-awareness reflected in these poems, a heightened version of that found throughout the collection, is also likely to be shocking at first, comforting and inspiring after the reader begins to accept what Sharon Olds has to offer. Poems such as "Still Life" and "I Cannot Forget the Woman in the Mirror" are Olds's most direct and obvious portraits of herself as a partner in lovemaking. In "This," she asserts that the individual body is the center of each person's identity. The risk here is one of egomania, but once again Olds's artistic sense and her trust that openness will win the reader over prevail. Her self-portraits are less invitations to voyeurs than lessons in coming to terms with what and who one is.

Finally, and perhaps predictably, Olds creates a section of poems defining herself as a parent. The poems here are among the most tender and most accessible in the collection. Few of them carry the edge of hostility or challenge found in so much of her work. Injury, sickness, and death are frequent subjects in this section; nevertheless, there is an optimistic tone that fights through the parental anxieties. As one might expect, Olds's poems about her son and her daughter become ways of finding herself. Nevertheless, the impressions of the children are so strong, the consciousness holding the impressions so much more selfless, that the poet's characteristic reflexive quality is muted. Olds will reach her widest audience with poems such as these, though they have less to make them distinct and memorable than the poems in the earlier sections. An exception is the childbirth poem, "The Moment the Two Worlds Meet," which is among the most memorable works in the book.

In "The Quest," a poem about finding the daughter after thinking her lost for an hour, Olds employs the phrase "gold cell" which she has taken to title the collection:

> I sit with her awhile and then I
> go to the corner store for orange juice for her
> lips, tongue, palate, throat,
> stomach, blood, every gold cell of her body.

The image, truly a generative one for the whole book, itself refers to generation: to the basic unit of making, nourishing, identifying, being. It is "gold" for its beauty, its value, its alchemical significance. The central significant fact of being, the locus of unique identity that is each person's gift found over and over again—this is the center and circumference of Olds's vision.

The separate recurrence of the words "gold" and "cell" throughout the book give the title a special power and a heightened lucidity by the time one reaches the poems in the final section. "Gold" appears in "Summer Solstice," "When," "What If God," "First Sex," "A Woman in Heat Wiping

Herself," and "This." It is variously connected to grace, a reborn sun, the body's sexual juices, and the yolk of an egg:

> was He a squirrel, reaching down through the
> hole she broke in my shell, squirrel with His
> arm in the yolk of my soul up to the elbow,
> stirring, stirring the gold? . . .

This passage, from "What If God," links the various associations that "gold" has and suggests the connection to "cell," the other half of the title image.

The various occurrences of "cell" as center, prison, defining limitation, biological sign or microcosm of self complete the network of associations that adheres to Olds's title. "In the Cell," "Alcatraz," "201 Upper Terrace, San Francisco," and "Greed and Aggression" are key poems in Olds's delineating of her book's ideational grid.

As a crafter of poetry, Olds has some questionable habits, one of which is to defy the convention of avoiding weak line endings. Over and over again, she places function words—articles and prepositions—under emphasis by breaking lines after them. In most cases, however, her practice is justified by the way in which such line breaks push the reader forward for the syntactical completeness that has been held off. Pushing the reader forward, also, is the effect of Olds's skill with rhythms and with her strategies for developing narrative material. Once the reader accepts certain mannerisms, Olds's power as a writer with a unique metaphorical imagination takes over.

In *The Gold Cell*, this constant metaphorical inventiveness enlivens every poem. There is always an element of expectation and surprise linked to Olds's virtuosity with figures of speech. Occasionally, wild connections may cause confusion or chagrin, but more often Olds is able to carry readers over the leaps her imagination takes.

Perhaps the greatest virtue of this collection is that in it Olds sounds like no one else. She makes her reading of life accessible and memorable in a highly distinctive voice. Given her themes, her celebration of individuation, it is important for her work to have its own stamp. The controlling image of *The Gold Cell* is like the seal on an envelope, the signature or sign of the voice and personality enclosed. Profound and powerful, it is truly a book of life.

Philip K. Jason

Sources for Further Study

The Georgia Review. XLI, Fall, 1987, p. 585.
The Hudson Review. XL, Autumn, 1987, p. 517.

Library Journal. CXXII, February 1, 1987, p. 81.
The Nation. CCXLIV, April 11, 1987, p. 472.
The New York Times Book Review. XCII, March 22, 1987, p. 23.
Poetry. CXLIX, January, 1987, p. 231.
Publishers Weekly. CCXXXI, January 23, 1987, p. 65
The Washington Post Book World. XVII, May 3, 1987, p. 8.

GONE TO SOLDIERS

Author: Marge Piercy (1936-   )
Publisher: Summit Books (New York). 703 pp. $19.95
Type of work: Novel
Time: 1939-1946
Locale: New York City; Washington, D. C.; Detroit, Michigan; London; Europe;
     and the Pacific

*A long and engrossing novel re-creates World War II through ten disparate points of
view which tell the story of individual lives while also revealing the forces that shaped
postwar history*

> *Principal characters:*
> LOUISE KAHAN, a journalist who writes women's magazine fiction
>   and becomes a war correspondent
> DANIEL BALABAN, a translator who decodes Japanese radio trans-
>   missions for the navy
> JACQUELINE LÉVY-MONOT, a young activist of the Jewish Resis-
>   tance in France
> NAOMI SIEGAL, Jacqueline's sister, smuggled out of France at age
>   twelve to live with relatives in Detroit
> RUTHIE SIEGAL, Naomi's cousin, who is able to get a good job as a
>   welder once factories gear up for war production
> DUVEY SIEGAL, Ruthie's brother, a seaman on Atlantic convoy
>   duty
> MURRAY FELDSTEIN, Ruthie's fiancé, a marine in the Pacific
> ABRA SCOTT, a graduate student at Columbia University who
>   begins to do research for the Office of Strategic Services
>   (OSS)
> BERNICE COATES, a young woman who is freed from keeping house
>   for her professor father when she joins the Women's Airforce
>   Service Pilots (WASP)
> JEFF COATES, Bernice's brother, an artist who is parachuted into
>   France as an OSS agent

It might seem that there have already been too many novels about World
War II. The cynical realists of the G.I. generation turned into the major
new writers of the 1950's while others produced romances—of both the
masculine and feminine variety—about patriotism and glory. Later, the
backwash of Vietnam bitterness aroused nostalgia for the home front and
battlefields of the "good war." In *Gone to Soldiers*, however, Marge Piercy
uses both sound historical research and telling new perspectives to follow
ten characters through disparate experiences of war at home and abroad. In
so doing, she re-creates the rhythm and totality of the war that wrenched
and changed individual lives and determined the shape of society for the
postwar generations.

Piercy gains control of this vast canvas by tapping readers' knowledge to
engage them in the tale, as well as through expert plotting and characterization. The first sections, which introduce the characters and make vivid the

texture of their lives, also provide clues to the date; readers know more than the characters, wait breathlessly to see what the onset of war will do to them, wonder how their lives will change. Piercy has done the research to provide much more than brand names and popular songs: she re-creates not only the physical but also the intellectual and ideological feel of place and time. Even attitudes that would destroy sympathy for a character of the 1980's become part of the inevitable social context.

Gone to Soldiers is a war novel about spies and jungle fighting and sub-marine attacks and how marines depend only on their buddies—all the traditional material is freshly and vividly handled. It is also a war novel about the comradeship of women working together in factories, writers striving to arouse patriotism, working stiffs on Atlantic convoy duty, and Jewish children smuggled across the Pyrenees to safety. Bernice Coates, a large, plain girl who feels trapped at home as her father's housekeeper, finds freedom and mastery as a pilot. Service with the Office of Strategic Services (OSS) in London gives Jeff a chance to paint, associate with art students, and recapture the youth he lost to the Depression. There is money in Detroit pockets and class mobility for men such as Daniel Balaban, who is sent to Harvard University to learn Japanese. Abra Scott and her friends have glamorous jobs in Washington, D.C. Professors break free of the dreary routine to do intelligence research. War breeds cash and excitement; it opens new opportunities and gives meaning to daily lives.

War also exposes the pervasive racism in American society, the sexual harassment of women who move into formerly all-male spheres, the stupidity and glory-hunting in high places, and the anti-Semitism everywhere (in the marine corps, Murray Feldstein is sometimes in greater danger from his sergeant than from the Japanese). Writers create tools to manipulate public opinion; workers die in unsafe factories. Even hardened fighting men are horrified by the mass suicide of Japanese civilians on Saipan. As victory finally draws near, the unspeakable degradation of concentration-camp life is made vivid—as is the Allied failure to bomb the railroad tracks that feed mounting numbers of Jews into the gas chambers.

By focusing on individuals and what they see, Piercy communicates the impact of war on daily life. Its constant presence, at some level of awareness, made every day exciting and agonizing, often at the same time. There are no grand set pieces, no moments of absolute triumph. The ambiguity is sharp, for example, in readers' intense concern for Murray, fighting across the islands of the Pacific as the Japanese defenses grow increasingly entrenched and suicidal. The atomic bomb comes as an immense relief: It will not be necessary to invade Japan at the cost of untold lives. Yet when Daniel and Abra visit Hiroshima (as part of a postwar survey providing the information to prepare for future wars), the effects of nuclear destruction— on a civilian population—are equally clear. Should the bomb have been dropped? There is no "right answer"; nothing in war, even in a good war, can ever be right.

Marge Piercy's fiction is more consistently political—in the broadest sense—than that of any other major contemporary writer in the United States. She conceived *Gone to Soldiers* soon after finishing *Woman on the Edge of Time* (1976), a book that imagined alternate futures which might grow from the seeds already visible in society. *Gone to Soldiers* uses the same technique in reverse. Just as Charles Dickens and George Eliot wrote about the world before railroads in an effort to understand how the immediate past influenced their own times, so Piercy has emphasized those elements in the World War II years that shaped the cultural and political context of the following generations.

The intertwined narratives of the various characters not only show the war as experienced by individuals but also emphasize the interconnections that make it no longer possible to lead separate lives. Daniel's work as a code breaker holed up in a fancy girls' finishing school in Washington, D.C., has an impact on marines facing the barren volcanic rock of Tarawa. Through the use of Naomi's viewpoint, the experience of Jews in France— both before and after the Nazi occupation—supplies an important context for the racial animosities of wartime Detroit.

Wartime ambiguities also reach deep into individual lives, casting light on both the domestic ideology of the 1950's and the new feminism of the late 1960's. Louise Kahan, at the beginning of the book, is a divorced leftist with a teenage daughter; she subscribes to the *Daily Worker* but earns her living writing slick-magazine romances, knowing full well that she is exploiting her readers' buried fantasies. Her initial wartime work—as a consultant feeding appropriate ideas to writers and editors—is ironically satisfying: Louise is very good at creating fiction to glamorize female independence and useful work. When the tide begins to turn, the message shifts, and Louise grabs the opportunity to advance her own professional future by going to Europe as a correspondent for *Collier's*. She rides on tanks, sleeps in foxholes, files a story from Paris even before the first troops arrive, and stays with the army through the disaster of the Ardennes. She sees farms, houses, whole villages destroyed; watches young men die; and covers the liberation of Buchenwald. It is wholly understandable—once Louise has seen the consequences of the games men play—that she begins to yearn for the world of romance and nurture, false though she knows it is.

The war enlarges even while it damages. A pretentious, snobbish, and self-involved adolescent such as Jacqueline can be transformed into a splendid hero of the Resistance. The G.I. Bill will give men a chance to break out of the working class into the American dream—yet they will not be the same men they were before learning to kill. Interviewing shipyard workers, Louise perceives that they were fighting for a higher standard of living. They were fighting their way out of the Depression. They were fighting for the goods they saw in advertisements and in movies about how the middle class lived. What these people saw in their future was not a new brotherhood of man (and certainly not of woman), but the wife back at home, a new car in the new garage of the new house in the new tract with grass this time. They saw themselves moving into an advertisement full of objects they had coveted, but never owned and seldom even touched.

Louise's own childhood in foster homes and her empathy for people who had always worked hard yet remained in want give the passage depth; it is not simply a criticism of 1950's materialism. In similar fashion, the growth of the OSS out of the old boys' network of the Ivy League suggests why power and secrecy were not easy to give up. Some reviews have criticized Piercy for representing a wide range of age, religion, class, background, and sexual orientation and yet omitting the black experience. Because she is a political novelist, however, Piercy knows full well that the omission of black Americans accurately represents the consciousness of the time. If black soldiers had been visible and black workers in Detroit had earned respect instead of resentment and fear, there would not have been any need for a civil rights movement in the 1960's. Because blacks were not "in" the society and period about which Piercy writes, the postwar world took the shape that it did.

Gone to Soldiers is packed with contextual understandings. Many of the women characters come to enjoy the easy comradeship of a world without men; some have, to an extent, given up sexuality—ceased to depend on or even crave male love. The growing animosity toward Women's Airforce Service Pilots (WASP) toward the end of the war grows from these and other factors:

> Congress was conservative, a product of the off-election of 1942 when rigid voting laws had prevented both the troops and the workers who had moved for defense jobs from registering. The Civil Service Committee said that there were already too many trained pilots who would be competing for scarce jobs as soon as peace came, when the Depression would immediately resume. They ought to be nurses or doing defense work or home with their families, like respectable girls. The general agreement seemed to be that WASPs, whatever they were, were not nice.

Gone to Soldiers is a long and demanding novel. At one level, it might be seen as an anthology of war fiction in its various guises. Jacqueline's story, for example, has echoes of Ernest Hemingway—except that Piercy changes the genders and carries the tale far beyond the pat, bittersweet ending. Louise Kahan might be the central figure in one of the World War II tales found on racks of paperback historical romances for women. Murray's misfit Jew in a combat unit is a character familiar from the books of the late 1940's; the story of Bernice, freed to fill a man's role and gradually learning to name her lesbianism, came to be told in later decades. In Piercy's hands, however, the individual stories enlarge one another and create contextual depths that make the book far more than the sum of its parts. Some of the characters are more interesting than others, but all are thoroughly realized—even the men, which is not always the case in Piercy's work. The complex structure is kept engrossing by intricate accumulations of detail about little-known aspects of the war, by the juxtaposition of sections to create ironic sidelights, and by deep emotional involvement with people worth caring about.

Sally Mitchell

Sources for Further Study

Booklist. LXXXIII, March 1, 1987, p. 948.
The Christian Science Monitor. May 29, 1987, p. 22.
Harper's Magazine. CCLXXIV, June, 1987, p. 30.
Kirkus Reviews. LV, March 1, 1987, p. 332.
Library Journal. CXII, April 1, 1987, p. 165.
Los Angeles Times. June 15, 1987, V, p. 1.
Ms. XV, June, 1987, p. 19.
The Nation. CCXLV, July 4, 1987, p. 24.
The New York Times Book Review. XCII, May 10, 1987, p. 11.
Publishers Weekly. CCXXXI, March 20, 1987, p. 68.
The Village Voice. May 19, 1987, p. 45.
The Washington Post Book World. XVII, May 3, 1987, p. 3.
Women's Review of Books. IV, July-August, 1987, p. 23.

THE GREAT TRIUMVIRATE
Webster, Clay, and Calhoun

Author: Merrill D. Peterson (1921-   )
Publisher: Oxford University Press (New York). 573 pp. $27.95
Type of work: History and biography
Time: 1812-1852
Locale: United States

A collective biography of three American statesmen whose careers were instrumental in shaping their country during the first half of the nineteenth century

> *Principal personages:*
> DANIEL WEBSTER, New Englander
> HENRY CLAY, Kentuckian
> JOHN C. CALHOUN, South Carolinian
> ANDREW JACKSON, seventh President of the United States, 1828-1836

In antebellum America, given the popular fascination with things classical, it is natural that a trio of dominant politicians, with careers linked by events, be given the sobriquet "the Great Triumvirate." Unlike their Roman precursors who helped bring about the collapse of a celebrated republic, Daniel Webster, Henry Clay, and John C. Calhoun played a significant role in molding a new, viable republican system. It is appropriate that Merrill D. Peterson, professor emeritus at the University of Virginia and winner of the Bancroft Prize, has chosen this subject. His most significant contributions to American historiography concern Thomas Jefferson, and this work becomes, in spite of its biographical foundation, an interpretive political history of post-Jefferson America—the end product of Jeffersonian ideology.

Clay, Calhoun, and Webster, each representing a different section of the country, assumed that they were the true heirs to Jefferson's legacy and sought to preserve the Republic from what they believed to be a contemporary version of Caesar: Andrew Jackson. In fact, the military chieftain from Tennessee becomes the fourth central character in Peterson's study. Yet by basing his analysis on Jackson's most important and enduring enemies, Peterson brings an important Whiggish dimension to modern understanding of the era, which is too often simply termed "the age of Jackson." From this perspective, Jackson is more important as a symbol than as a man. It was against the forces he represented and helped unleash that the triumvirs struggled for so long, and the dynamic tension between their versions of Jeffersonian ideology and the Jacksonians, who also claimed to be followers of Jefferson, completed the foundation of the American political system.

Peterson projects his narrative through a biographical lens, focusing on each of his characters in turn. With other historical figures, the approach would be limiting, but not in this case. At least one of the members of the Great Triumvirate always seems to be at center stage, allowing Peterson to construct a chronicle touching nearly every important national political issue from 1812 to 1852. The role of Peterson's heroes was essentially conservative. They sought to preserve what they believed to be the political structure of Jeffersonian America from the excesses of Jackson and his descendants. That conservatism, however, was based on their understanding of republicanism and the practical needs of a developing country. It called for the controlled growth of a national economic system and required a strong commitment to the role of the federal government.

In spite of their success at altering its course, the triumvirs themselves must share part of the blame for their ultimate failure to stem the rising tide of Jacksonianism. They proved to be no more immune to the siren call of sectionalism than were their enemies. Moreover, their own personal ambition, particularly lust for the White House, continually intervened to prevent long-term cooperation. Lastly, none of the triumvirs ever recognized that Jackson signaled the emergence of a new concept of political leadership in the United States.

The story begins with one of the great watersheds in American history, the War of 1812. In 1811, Clay and Calhoun had been elected to the House of Representatives as enthusiastic Jeffersonian Republicans and were soon recognized as potential heirs to a party leadership still dominated by the Virginia Dynasty. Both men also began acting with the so-called War Hawks, who were pushing for war with Great Britain. Whatever the individual reason for militancy, the overriding theme of this younger generation of politicians was an aggressive form of nationalism. Growing to adulthood after the revolutionary struggle, they represented the first generation of self-conscious Americans.

The third triumvir, Webster, did not arrive in Congress until eleven months after the war began. Unlike his colleagues with whom his name would be forever linked, the New Englander was no great admirer of Jefferson and certainly no advocate of war. As a leading light of Federalism in his section, he believed the struggle with Great Britain unnecessary and joined the opposition. Ironically, this stand against the War of 1812, which would haunt Webster throughout his political career, placed the declining Federalist Party, heretofore committed to a strong central government, in the uncomfortable position of advocating an extreme version of states' rights. Never at ease with extremes of any sort, Webster was overjoyed when the war's end allowed him to return to a more natural position.

Webster's feeling of relief at the ratification of the Treaty of Ghent was shared by Clay and Calhoun. The unsatisfactory results of the war helped unite all three in a vision of the country's future that temporarily overwhelmed specific issues and the ubiquitous irritations caused by sectionalism and personal ambition. Wartime failures plainly illustrated the limitations of what might be called the tendency toward negative government, which had always been part of Jeffersonian rhetoric, while it gave impetus to a movement toward positive government that had been growing since Jefferson's first administration. Action by federal authority became the primary thrust of the last years of James Madison's administration and was supported by a majority of the Republican Party as well as by many of their old Federalist enemies.

Webster, Clay, and Calhoun agreed with and participated in this commitment to a stronger central authority which fostered economic development and strengthened the United States as the chief bulwark of republicanism in the world. The immediate result was a new national bank, the maintenance of a moderate protective tariff, and the creation of a more effective national military force. Yet as this "Era of Good Feelings" moved into the Monroe Administration, postwar unity unraveled. Under Monroe, even the triumvirs went their separate ways. Clay remained Speaker of the House, but there his carping criticism of the administration made few friends. Calhoun joined the administration as Secretary of War, and Webster, always short of money, left Congress for private law practice. Nevertheless, each man, in his separate sphere, continued his support for national unity. Clay, in reality the political center of the triumvirate, emerged as the acknowledged master of the American legislative system. In Congress, he led in the struggle for the first of his great compromises, the Missouri Compromise, and lay the legislative foundation for his "American System," which became the program of economic nationalism for the next three decades. From his position as Secretary of War, Calhoun led in the push for internal improvements at Federal expense, and Webster in a series of famous cases before the Supreme Court, such as the *Dartmouth College* case and *McCulloch v. Maryland*, strengthened the power of central government.

The unity of the postwar era simply could not withstand the impact of personal ambition as a new generation of leaders replaced the old. Perhaps there was not enough room at the top. Moreover, the expansion of both populations and territory seemed to exaggerate the differences between sections and political factions. Ironically, the ultimate beneficiary of the collapse of party harmony was another product of the war, Jackson the military hero.

The situation came to a head in 1824, and Henry Clay's role was pivotal. Four candidates, Clay, Jackson, John Quincy Adams, and William H. Crawford, ran for president. No one of the four received a majority, and the election was thrown into the House. There Clay, eliminated because he received the smallest number of votes, gave his considerable support to Adams, who was elected. Jackson, the candidate with the most votes, was convinced that he had been cheated out of his due by a "corrupt bargain," and his suspicions seemed confirmed when Clay was appointed Secretary of State.

In fact, there was no real evidence that Adams and Clay had an arrangement in 1824; even if there had been a "bargain," it would have been clearly within the tradition of political give-and-take that had existed during the era of Republican dominance. Yet Jackson's fanciful charge appealed to the emotions of an unsophisticated and recently expanded electorate; its role in Jackson's victory marked the beginning of a period in American politics in which complicated issues were oversimplified and political appeals were more reaction to the voters than leadership. In this atmosphere, compromise seemed weakness rather than a necessary part of politics. The attitude may have always been part of American politics, but with Jackson it became primary.

Clay, Webster, and Calhoun spent the next two decades fighting against the forces that Jackson symbolized. Peterson carefully chronicles their struggles, and his story carries the reader through the squabbles of the Jackson Administration, including the bank war and "nullification," which culminated in the formation of the Whig Party. While the cooperation of the triumvirate behind the Whig banner temporarily checked the Jacksonian tide, the divisive issue of slavery, which had been submerged in the Jeffersonian era, combined with personal ambition to transform the Whig alternative into another version of Jacksonianism and eventually shatter the Whig party.

The impact and crucial importance of the slavery issue is most clearly illustrated by the tragic career of John C. Calhoun. In the beginning, the South Carolinian's commitment to national unity was as deep as that of his fellow triumvirs, but the excesses of the era's politics released the genie which Clay had tried to stuff back into the bottle with the Missouri Compromise in 1820. Following his conversion to the heresy of nullification, Calhoun's nationalism underwent a metamorphosis into an extreme variety of proslavery sectionalism. Yet even here the old nationalist tried to force his extreme sectionalism into a Jeffersonian mold and argued that he was trying to preserve the old system.

The triumvir's last hurrah, the so-called Compromise of 1850, found Clay and Webster struggling against their old ally in a vain attempt to "save the Union" once again. Though temporarily successful, this last effort was only a prelude to the Civil War. Fortunately, neither Clay nor Webster lived long enough to see the collapse of the system they had fought to preserve, and Calhoun's death spared him from the consequences of the doctrines he had come to advocate. Ironically, however, the "American System," which lay at the heart of Whig ideology and was based on the National Republicanism of the nineteenth century's second decade, emerged after the war to dominate the last half of the century under the banner of a new Republican Party, a party actually created by the slavery crisis. The United States of the twentieth century was erected on this foundation and is much closer to Clay's vision than Jackson's, even though the excesses of the Jacksonian style of leadership still haunt us.

While Peterson's methodology is traditional and his narrative breaks little new ground, his treatment is a fitting sequel to his earlier work. His major success consists in pulling together the various threads of nineteenth century politics, thus creating an understandable whole. Though the word "definitive" no longer has a place in modern historiography, *The Great Triumvirate: Webster, Clay, and Calhoun* is probably as close to that elusive goal as any contemporary historian is likely to come.

David Warren Bowen

Sources for Further Study

Booklist. LXXXIII, July 1, 1987, p. 1646.
Kirkus Reviews. LV, August 15, 1987, p. 1220.
Library Journal. CXII, August 1, 1987, p. 120.
Los Angeles Times Book Review. November 29, 1987, p. 1.
The New York Times Book Review. XCII, November 8, 1987, p. 65.
The New Yorker. LXIII, November 9, 1987, p. 151.
Publishers Weekly. CCXXXII, September 11, 1987, p. 75.
The Wall Street Journal. November 9, 1987, p. 25.
The Washington Post Book World. XVII, November 22, 1987, p. 3.

HAPPY HOUR

Author: Alan Shapiro (1952-   )
Publisher: University of Chicago Press. 45 pp. $16.00; paperback $7.95
Type of work: Poetry

Twenty poems present various angles on the unsuccessful relationships fostered by desire

Alan Shapiro's *Happy Hour* is a slim packet of dissent presented to an era which has believed it possible to practice a science called effective communication. To be seen and heard nightly inside a box in the living room—the dream of any communications major—is a metaphor Shapiro might have used in these poems for the estrangement he sees typifying human intercourse at the end of the twentieth century. In the poems, Shapiro graphs a self which is deeply structured to oppose others, not relate to them. The opposition is ontological, not volitional. Focusing especially on the relationship between a man and woman who set out to love each other, Shapiro's conclusion is that they are good to each other out of guilt and fear, primary feelings that are masked by a veneer called love. The images of communication breakdowns in these poems apparently derive from the poet's own experience. The first-person pronoun centers the poems on a forthright self-consciousness. The home lost is the poet's own; the failure to connect is the narrator's as much as it is the woman's. Loneliness is a theme, and, with it, bitterness toward the condition of false promise a relationship always brings. Thus, in a collection of poetry admirably written and sequenced, a humming of platitudinous angst sometimes is heard. Yet the pain presented does exist, and if no resolutions are offered by the poet, he does give the subject of loss and distance a cold solicitude and penetrating reflection which, in the best poems, make love seem as strange a condition as setting up permanent housekeeping on the moon.

One reason love fails, intimates Shapiro, is the deep rut a self grows accustomed to following and from which it is impossible to escape. The woman tries to climb out in the title poem, "Happy Hour," by drinking enough to "taunt him now/ to prove he doesn't love her/ and never could." Normally she is a "wife on ice," and she drinks to be bad. All the man offers her as she performs her bad girl act is his continuing circumspection, a priggishness which drives her to drink in the first place. How can his goodness be a badness, he wonders, and, as the poem concludes, he admits to himself that circumspection is his weapon, an armor the woman beats against to see if passion waits within. Insulted, the man merely *thinks* about throwing his glass in her face. Life has trained him to be careful, wary, to the extreme of pardoning all carelessness in others as a way to appear loving while gaining the less careful person's spurious respect and honor. The man is not fooled by his security operations and feels lousy: "Tomorrow/ will be *his* happy hour. There won't be/ anything she wouldn't do for him."

A sense of personal confession haunts several of these poems, a sense abetted by the direct description Shapiro employs, as if in pursuit of assimilable declaration rather than poetic artifice. Yet when Shapiro turns momentarily *imagiste*, as in "Lace Fern," the problems of love are presented in the acute fluctuations of sensitive perception. The poet is not simply relating a memory but processing the given, and a stronger poem results:

> For a moment the fern held you,
> your hair woven into the fine
> green netting, shining
> in the same light. And when you left
> the fern shaped what was past
> into a tracery of small innumerable spaces
> only the light can fill.

This is imagism strained through Wallace Stevens. Stevens posited a correlation between subjective volition and objective perception. This process of correlation, to which Shapiro gives an image, is the basis for love being lost. The fern is a brain; it "stirs suddenly," "like a word we need to say/ to remember." Shapiro attributes a similar Stevensian center to the lady his fern-brain arrests within its ganglion as she brushes her hair and sings:

> And I began to think that your long hair
> brightening where the brush would pass
> became the furthest edge of what you hummed,
> yourself hardly in the room.

When Stevens' famous blackbird flew out of sight, "It marked the edge/ of one of many circles" ("Thirteen Ways of Looking at a Blackbird"). What then is love if the object of desire is moments of process—the shine on brushed hair, a tune bespeaking an inviolable solipsism, and "a tracery/ of small innumerable spaces/ only the light can fill"?

Shapiro contends that a self plays at communicating but is denied communion, because the matter one intends to put across to someone else, someone close, is a package of fossils, or, as he puts it in "Familiar Story," an "accumulated separate lore." Even the sharing of disillusionment with someone who "understands" is a failure. (What then is a poem written to express this idea?) The speaker of failure in "Familiar Story," kindled by blind desire for monuments against the failure, is nevertheless inundated by a combination of his own fatigue and an all-conquering disillusionment which Shapiro—in a powerful inversion of traditional iconography—imagines as a blinding light. The communion candle is extinguished: "Desire in each other's all they see,/ and all else now is no more than the light/ hurting their eyes, too sudden and too bright."

Each poem testifies to isolation, and the shock-surprise that a person can so easily forget someone loved. Shapiro laments the absence of human presence. Another person, someone he intended to love, is disposable. Thoughts of that person are headed for the garbage disposal called time: "Suddenly for the first time I can imagine/ being years from my last thought of her,/ that past life, old intimacies, the small talk" ("Blue Vase"). The culprit for Shapiro is, again, desire, specifically a person's need to push in and inhabit another person. Even the faces on billboard advertisements "are gorgeous blanks/ desire fills in only as it will," while women seen during the day "are shills/ employed, he thinks, by this content-less/ longing after more and better." ("Neighbors"). Even the rabbit at school which he wanted to touch as a boy existed only to demonstrate that relating to something is really dominating it. When he finally has the rabbit in his grasp he roughs it up, so "there was no place now/ anywhere inside it that I didn't fill" ("Other Hands").

Rooms being redecorated, shapes left on matter by matter, recollected presences that memory tenuously retains—such is the melancholy duplicity of existence, the poet says. Man's instinct is to make places, to clear the forest and to inhabit. A woman then keeps the place, makes a home of it. Nature, however, covers and obliterates:

> The earth was all thick moss between the trees,
> giving off a muffled radiance
> placeless and unbroken, except for where
> the highest leaves rippled the sunlight down
> through the watery air.

> ("Otter Island")

In this poem, Shapiro is in Nova Scotia, where he finds evidence of a settlement, specifically an old trough covered with moss, "like some dream-struggling shape." One more container abandoned. Life, according to this poem, is a man pursuing butterflies with a ripped net. Things, like people, are better left unpossessed, or abandoned, before the self, like a sea anemone, sucks them in and renders them invisible or, like the "wife on ice," ossified. In "Rickshaw," a woman sells her bric-a-brac to the neighbors: "They're almost new again out here/ in this odd light." She dumps her accumulated novelties, intuiting in them "the trace of wishes that were vagrant as light."

So pervasive is the gloom in *Happy Hour* that a reader will suspect that it is partially a stage effect, an atmosphere the poet advances as a preconception and ground for his poetic perception. Some of the poems are convincing and draw a reader into their moods. Others proclaim the void too glibly, through the use of rhetorical crutches. Clichéd disillusionment ends the book's final poem, "Astronomy Lesson." Brothers stand outside their house, within which their mother and father attend separate televisions whose voices cancel each other,

> while the older boy
> goes on about what light years
> are, and solar winds, black holes,
> and how the sun is cooling
> and what will happen to
> them all when it is cold.

This would engage the mind more effectively if Shapiro directed a portion of his despair against the language he trusts to proclaim it. Is this simply a modern synthesis of Matthew Arnold's "Dover Beach"? The rhetoric of disillusionment has a considerable history, and if the reader hears echoes, the poet must make some excuses. Shapiro's excuse most likely is that the older boy is playing the prophet of doom, dramatizing the frightening universe for the wide-eyed brother, but Shapiro calls the two brothers "sad Ptolemies," thereby glazing the poem with the preciousness of adult hindsight. Reading the poem, one is not presented with a boy's awe and dawning knowledge but with an adult's gloomy reminiscence. The reader will want more—at least a poem or two specifying a distance between the poet and his own self-immolation, perhaps a poem about being a prisoner to language, an unwilling communicant at the altar of despair. Alan Shapiro clearly has the means of expression to go beyond the poetry in *Happy Hour*, but will he resist the pleasures of his despair mill to find them?

Bruce Wiebe

Sources for Further Study

The Hudson Review. XL, Autumn, 1987, p. 517.
The New York Times Book Review. XCII, July 26, 1987, p. 9.

HEMINGWAY

Author: Kenneth S. Lynn (1923-   )
Publisher: Simon and Schuster (New York). Illustrated. 702 pp. $24.95
Type of work: Literary biography
Time: 1899-1961
Locale: Chicago and Paris; Key West, Florida; Havana, Cuba; and Ketchum, Idaho

A remarkably subtle and well-crafted biography that goes beyond lavish praise or bitter vilification to show that the novelist's greatest creation was the enduring myth of himself

> *Principal personages:*
> ERNEST HEMINGWAY, an American man of letters
> GRACE HALL HEMINGWAY, his mother
> DR. CLARENCE EDMONDS "ED" HEMINGWAY, his father
> MARCELLINE HEMINGWAY, his sister
> HADLEY RICHARDSON, his first wife
> MARY WELSH HEMINGWAY, his fourth and last wife

The creative life of all great writers is undoubtedly grounded in the formative events of childhood, and this is especially true in the case of Ernest Hemingway, the first son and second child of Grace Hall Hemingway and Dr. Clarence Edmonds "Ed" Hemingway, an ill-fated couple who lived in the stuffy, middle-class community of Oak Park, Illinois. In 1906, they moved into a large house of Grace's own design, a dwelling that offered consulting rooms for Ed and a conservatory where Grace could continue her operatic singing and offer music lessons. Always the domineering figure of the family, Grace often humiliated her sensitive and insecure husband in front of the children (Marcelline, Ernest, Ursula, Madelaine, Carol, and Leicester). She had been an unusually assertive figure by the Victorian standards of her own upbringing, riding a bicycle, for example, at a time when that device was considered to be for men only. It was Grace who encouraged—and pushed—the children toward excellence, but it was also she who created the nightmarish contradictions that would forever torment the psyche of Ernest. These paradoxes, especially those relating to sex and gender, inform his best work, from *The Sun Also Rises* (1926) all the way to the posthumously published *The Garden of Eden* (1986).

It was Grace who insisted on dressing Ernest like a little girl—long beyond the time that this practice normally occurred. (Most boys of the period began their lives in dresses but changed fairly soon to trousers.) This sartorial confusion, however, was only the most obvious of a long series of strategies and schemes that confused the genders of Ernest and Marcelline, whom Grace treated as identical twins. Once they began school, Grace insisted on identical haircuts, coats, and hats for the two siblings. She engineered plots to have Ernest escort Marcelline to party after party (including the high school proms); in general, she promoted an entirely unhealthy relationship between her oldest children, one that would result in lifelong enmity between them, as illustrated in Marcelline's acerbic memoir, *At the Hemingways* (1962).

If this behavior on Grace's part were not enough to undermine and skew Hemingway's attitude and emotions toward women, then her treatment of her husband certainly furnished adequate evidence of the damage a wife and mother could cause. Never really sure of himself or his place in this large family, Ed Hemingway nevertheless displayed many admirable qualities. He had a passionate love for the outdoors, and when Ernest was still a child, Ed taught him how to fish and instructed him—as he did all the neighborhood children—in the art of identifying plants, birds, and trees. When Grace Hemingway thoughtlessly burned some of Ed's snake specimens, Ernest never forgave her. This particular event is echoed in his own work, as are the many facts about woods and watercourses which he learned during the annual family vacations around Lake Walloon and Horton Bay, Michigan (the setting and actual background for many of the Nick Adams stories). When Ed committed suicide in 1928, Ernest naturally blamed Grace for this tragic conclusion to his father's frustrated life. Ed's suicide also started a grisly tradition of sorts within the Hemingway clan: Ernest committed suicide in 1961 and the suicides of his younger sister Ursula, in 1966, and younger brother Leicester, in 1982, followed.

Perhaps the greatest real or imagined damage that became part of Grace's legacy was the inability of her son to reciprocate the love and affection shown to him by so many women (especially his four wives: Hadley, Pauline, Martha, and Mary)—or the kind and generous assistance of such writers as Sherwood Anderson, Ezra Pound, James Joyce, Gertrude Stein, Ford Madox Ford, John Dos Passos, and, especially F. Scott Fitzgerald. Kenneth Lynn is perhaps most convincing in his heavily Freudian reading of Hemingway's life when he shows the undeniable linkage between the novelist's betrayal by his mother and his lifelong tendency to betray his closest associates.

Again and again, Hemingway had to bite the hand that fed him, and this ugly trait is nowhere better shown than in his great novel *The Sun Also Rises*, a book in which Hemingway satirized and caricatured the most outstanding figures of the expatriate American literary community living in Paris in the 1920's (including Djuna Barnes). These bitter portraits of some of his closest friends—Hemingway's shabby way of redressing supposed slights and assuaging his powerful envy of fellow writers—continued in the short stories and in the posthumous *A Moveable Feast* (1964), where Hemingway depicted Fitzgerald as a bumbling fool and his wife, Zelda, as a vicious shrew.

These intemperate emotional outbursts were simply one side of a calculated campaign to buttress a sagging ego; the other (more successful) side of his strategy was to create the myth of Ernest Hemingway, a task in which he was unwittingly but consistently aided by various journalists (especially Malcolm Cowley) who believed and disseminated Hemingway's grandly inflated versions of himself. These dramatizations of himself had their beginning, apparently, during Hemingway's somewhat ludicrous service during World War I. Hemingway had volunteered for service with the American Red Cross and was struck by mortar fire when he was well behind the lines engaged in the rather nonmilitary act of passing out chocolates to the Italian soldiers. After this event, Ernest spent time in a military hospital in Milan, where he met and fell in love with Agnes von Kurowsky, his nurse. These bare elements formed the nucleus of the story Hemingway retells in his brilliant war novel *A Farewell to Arms* (1929).

Yet the ill-fated chocolates became the material for an ever-expanding fabrication which Hemingway commenced shortly after the incident by insisting that, in spite of his wounded legs (he did walk with a cane for several months), he had carried an Italian soldier on his back. Detail after spurious detail followed, including machine-gun bullets lodged in his body (an impossibility, as Lynn demonstrates), a number that rose to thirty-two penetrations when he told the story to the ladies of the Oak Park Memorial Committee in 1919. Yet, by a curious process of editorial alchemy the Hemingway myth became reality, as the self-made fables were represented as genuine facts in such books as Malcolm Cowley's *Portable Hemingway* (1944), Carlos Baker's standard biography *Ernest Hemingway: A Life Story* (1969), Jeffrey Meyer's *Hemingway: A Biography* (1985), and Michael Reynolds' *The Young Hemingway* (1986). Hemingway tried to live up to this myth for the rest of his life, proving his manhood as big-game hunter, pugilist, bull-fight aficionado, deep-sea fisherman, and womanizer.

Yet behind the Hemingway made up of newspaper pastiches and the pronouncements of feminists on the one hand and Freudians on the other, there stands a truly heroic writer struggling with an enemy more terrifying than any charging rhino or rogue elephant—the blank page. If Hemingway competed with other writers and tried to belittle their efforts, he did so only because he tried so passionately to perfect his art. He was filled with self-loathing when critics savaged one of his last books, *Across the River and into the Trees* (1950), but he rode a crest of euphoria when they praised his prize-winning gem *The Old Man and the Sea* (1952). After *The Old Man and the Sea*, Hemingway was never able to finish a major work or produce another masterpiece. He was beset by a variety of physical ailments, but these were insignificant compared to the nagging sensation that he had written all he could. Finally, fearing that he was losing his mind, Hemingway could stand the pain no longer, and on July 2, 1961, he blew his own head off with a shotgun. Tragically, as Lynn observes, "the battle he finally lost was with himself."

Hemingway was survived by Mary Welsh Hemingway, his fourth and perhaps most compatible wife. Given his complicated and confusing childhood, it is not surprising that Hemingway should have such stormy and unpredictable relationships with women, hating some (such as Zelda Fitzgerald and Margot Macomber, as demonstrated in his short story classic "The Short Happy Life of Francis Macomber") and preferring others, such as Duff Twysden (the model for Brett Ashley in *The Sun Also Rises*), precisely because of their unconventional sexuality. Hadley Richardson, Hemingway's first wife, was perhaps the simplest and most fragile of the lot, and Lynn gives an extraordinarily sensitive presentation of her plight, balancing the rather snide portrait painted by Hemingway in *A Moveable Feast*. Hemingway's second and third wives (Pauline Pfeiffer and Martha Gellhorn) are given somewhat shorter shrift, as befits their largely transitional roles. As Lynn makes clear, Hadley and Mary served as the anchors that held down the beginning and end of Hemingway's life as an artist.

With a character as large and complex as Hemingway, about whom theories and counter-theories abound, the temptation to simplify for the sake of easier reading always looms before the biographer. By focusing on the crucial importance of Hemingway's childhood—and its effect on his future life as man and artist—Lynn is able to weave a complex tapestry unified by a few principal designs (the Hemingway myth, sexual confusion, and the pattern of betrayal). Furthermore, Lynn is one of those rare biographers who writes beautifully on every page, combining the good, clear prose of journalistic writing with the color and imaginative verve of the novel. The result is a biography that reads well and engages the reader's head and heart simultaneously. Lynn's descriptive style is particularly effective, as in this evocation of a Hemingway party held for Ernest, Marcelline, and their teenage friends:

> Eighty-one invitations were sent out on pale blue stationery, dance programs were handed out at the door, an orchestra played peppy fox-trots and old-fashioned tunes for square dancing, and the table in the dining room was laden with dishes of tempting food. Ernest may have very well liked the food best of all, for his big feet and awkward coordination made him something of a menace on the dance floor. It had rankled him to be forbidden to dance, but he found that he could take it or leave it, once the prohibition was removed.

Equally readable are Lynn's clarifying statements of fact, as when he is dramatizing the genuine oddity of Ernest's wearing a dress:

> "On formal occasions, the typical boy might appear in a navy-blue sailor outfit with white piping, or in a buttoned military tunic that was worn with knickerbockers, leggings, and a campaign hat and was commonly known as a Tommy Atkins or Rough Rider suit, or in an elegant velvet jacket with matching knickers."

Lynn writes equally well about the Michigan woods; the Left Bank of Paris; Sun Valley, Idaho; Key West, Florida; Pamplona, Spain; and East Africa.

Despite all the outrageous blunders which Lynn exposes in Hemingway's tormented life, most readers will feel the tragedy of his death poignantly. He is, warts and all, an irreplaceable part of the American literary landscape, a giant whose work has never gone out of print. For Hemingway, that would surely be proof of success.

Daniel L. Guillory

Sources for Further Study

The Atlantic. CCLX, July, 1987, p. 91.
Booklist. LXXXIII, July, 1987, p. 1642.
Kirkus Reviews. LV, May 15, 1987, p. 776.
Library Journal. CXII, July, 1987, p. 79.
Los Angeles Times Book Review. July 26, 1987, p. 3.
The New Republic. CXCVII, July 13, 1987, p. 27.
The New York Review of Books. XXXIV, August 13, 1987, p. 30.
The New York Times Book Review. XCII, July 19, 1987, p. 3.
Publishers Weekly. CCXXXI, May 22, 1987, p. 61.
The Washington Post Book World. XVII, July 19, 1987, p. 3.

HERSELF IN LOVE AND OTHER STORIES

Author: Marianne Wiggins (1947-   )
Publisher: Viking (New York). 184 pp. $16.95
Type of work: Short stories
Time: The 1980's
Locale: Various places in the United States

In these stories, Marianne Wiggins examines the varieties of love and obsession, employing diverse styles and settings

Herself in Love is Marianne Wiggins' first collection of short stories, following three critically successful novels: *Babe* (1975), *Went South* (1980), and *Separate Checks* (1984). The thirteen stories in the new volume are remarkable for the range of styles Wiggins displays and for the variety of characters and situations she presents. Some of the stories combine fantasy with realistic detail, while others have a kind of gritty factuality.

The most memorable of these tales are those which manage to suggest far more about character and human relationships than they portray directly. The first story, "Ridin' up in Front with Carl and Marl," for example, is uneventful on the surface. Told in a kind of country accent by a third-person narrator, it concerns a young wife who is out jogging when her landlady comes by and insists that she get into a pickup truck. They talk as they drive, collect the landlady's husband after he is through work, and go to a fast-food restaurant. On the way home they find a woman photographer whose car has broken down and who is deeply suspicious of all of them. When they reach home, the young woman goes somewhat reluctantly to the house where her husband is waiting for her, wondering if she has brought him food.

This simple account constitutes the surface of the story. Beneath the surface, the narrator suggests considerable tension. Dolores, the young wife, is jogging to shake off the effects of one more in her series of quarrels with her husband. She resents the older couple and their interference in her life, but she lacks the strength to resist them. Dolores has an artistic streak which manifests itself in experiments with Polaroid photographs, but the landlady dismisses this interest and the professional photographer they encounter does not want to hear about amateur work. It is suggested that, when she returns home, Dolores may be beaten, or worse, by her husband.

"Ridin' up in Front with Carl and Marl" sets the tone for the entire collection. It indicates that Wiggins is interested in the interactions among people, that their emotions are central in her fictions, that there will be relatively little action in her stories but that their substance is to be found beneath the surface action, and that she is a superb stylist. The other stories show that she commands a wide variety of styles.

Wiggins' skill as a stylist and her concern with the emotional problems of her characters are demonstrated in one of the shortest of the stories, "Pleasure." Her descriptive power is shown in the setting: "Behind the women on the beach the russet cliffs rose, cosseting the dusty miller and the random vines. The shoreline was decaying. The clay that held the roots that held the shore was slipping to the sea like lava from the lip of an inferno." Two women, their children, and two dogs are on this windy beach when a whale beaches itself, to their amazement and horror. The older woman egocentrically conceives the idea that the whale is there to test her will, that if she can somehow get the whale to return to the ocean she will be allowed to rid herself of an obsession with love. She speaks to the whale, and it seems to listen. Eventually the whale slips back into the sea and disappears; it is probably dead. In a surprise ending, the woman appears to watchers as a pillar of salt, reminding the reader of Lot's Wife. In asking to be released from her obsession with love, she has lost her humanity.

Obsession, in Wiggins' stories, seems to be a center of interest. In "Pleasure" the older woman's obsession is destructive, as it is in such a story as "Kafkas." Here, the central character is a young woman named Fran Koslow, a Ph.D. who is living with her sister and her sister's husband. Her life is centered on the telephone calls she makes late at night, when her hosts have gone to sleep. She calls directory assistance in large cities and obtains a number for every man surnamed Kafka. As her conversations are reported, it is clear that her intention is to marry a man named Kafka so that she will become Fran Kafka, in imitation of the writer she admires. The men to whom she speaks are often angry at being awakened at a late hour with what they regard as nonsense, but some of them talk with her, and some of the conversations are amusing. Fran Koslow seems herself to be amusing in her quest.

At the end, however, it is clear that this amusing character is pitifully mad. Her sister comes to her with the previous month's telephone bill, demanding payment. It becomes evident that Fran Koslow has been making these calls over an extended period of time, that she has stopped looking for a job, that looking for a marriageable man named Kafka has become a destructive obsession. She is, by the end, hopelessly lost.

The character who takes the name Redcar in the story "Gandy Dancing" is subject to a more benign obsession. Redcar is an ordinary man, married and a father, who has the sense that life is changing around him and who on an impulse decides, one day, to take a long train trip:

> He would travel out to California, turn around and come right back. See the country, the whole sweep of it at once, by train, and be back home before the kids and Terry would have time to notice. The trip would take eight days. Which wasn't much, when you stop to think about it.

Redcar takes a flight from New York to New Orleans, where he will catch the train. The people he meets in airports and on planes are unpleasant and boring, but once he gets on the train he begins to form friendships. The fireman agrees to take Redcar along if he is called on to inspect the tracks in response to a warning signal. Redcar is fascinated by the landscape, the towns where the train stops, the deserted stations. He reaches California and starts back to the East Coast. On the return trip, the train is stopped in deep snow in Colorado and Redcar joins a fireman named Thayer in inspecting the tracks, far ahead of the stopped train. Thayer is a bit mad and a bit of a mystic, and in their tour of inspection Redcar has an experience of the life of a railroader. When they reach Chicago, he finally calls his wife, who calls him "Steve" and berates him for leaving without warning. His response is not given, but it is clear that the pull of "gandy dancing," of the friendliness he has found on the train, of the experience he has shared with Thayer, will all help him decide to keep his identity as "Redcar" and continue his life with the railroad.

In both "Pleasure" and "Gandy Dancing" there is an element of fantasy. In the former it takes the form of the character's delusion, while in the latter there is something mystical in Redcar's relationship with railroading. Self-induced fantasy is at the heart of "Among the Impressionists," whose central character, an older woman, spends her time at the National Gallery in London engaged in imaginary conversations with such French painters as Paul Cézanne, Pierre-Auguste Renoir, and Camille Pissarro. If she is not quite sane, she is happy.

Fantasy of another sort presents itself in "Stonewall Jackson's Wife," which seems to be the story of the final days in the life of the famous Confederate general, mortally wounded by accidental shots fired by his own troops. The apparent focus of the story is Jackson's wife, Mary Anna, mother of his daughter Julia. The Jacksons' slaves discuss his wound, and the narrator then describes Mary Anna and her reaction to the news, her preparations to go to her dying husband, the trip, Jackson's death, the funeral, and the progress of the train carrying the coffin from Virginia to Kentucky.

The narrator is present at all the events, speaks to the other characters but is not spoken to, and evidently detests Mary Anna, who is described in unflattering terms: "She learns by rote. She is a lumpy brown-eyed girl, not pretty. Her mouth is crooked and her face defies a symmetry. When she is crying, which she often is, she's positively ugly." It is only when Jackson is dying and in his delirium calls out the name of "Eleanor" that it becomes clear that the narrator is the ghost of his first wife, who died in childbirth. She has been the true love of Jackson's life, and now as a ghost she must endure what she regards as the insincere public grief of Mary Anna, her successor. That the ghost herself becomes maddened at what she sees becomes evident at the end. The funeral train makes one of its many stops, and the crowd, as always, cries out for a look at Jackson's infant daughter.

The ghost believes that she convinces the slave who carries the child to turn the little girl over to the crowd; it seems to be a measure of revenge against her successor, the child's mother.

Some of the stories in *Herself in Love* deal with more conventional relationships among more conventional people. They tend to be distinctly ironic fables about the pain humans cause one another, especially in love. "The Gentleman Arms" is told from the perspective of an American woman who has lived most of her adult life in England and who is traced down by a man who had almost been her lover twenty years before. He has since been a pilot in the Vietnam War, married, and fathered two daughters, but he tells the woman that he has always loved her. They become lovers, and he urges her to return with him to the United States, but she cannot accept all that he has done since their earlier acquaintance, and she is troubled by the attempt to revive, twenty years later, adolescent feelings. At the end, in an ironic twist, she finds that the landlady of the small hotel where they have stayed has had a similar unsatisfying relationship with an American soldier who was stationed in Great Britain in World War II and has returned only once to see her.

"Insomnia" is the brief first-person narration of a young woman whose fiancé returns from a trip to tell her that he has accidentally slept with another woman. Her thoughts, six months later, range from his friends, whom she has never liked, to the children in the class she teaches, to a conversation overheard in a restaurant, and finally to a cartoon she sought and intended to send to the other woman. In the end, she is sadly alone.

"Quicksand" is perhaps the most startling of the stories about men and women. A couple, long-married, travel by car through France, and the wife performs a strange ritual. On a snowy night, she makes her husband stop the car, strips to the waist, and gets out to stand in the headlights. Eventually, she gets back in the car and they continue their trip, arriving late at the house of a friend, Richard. There is a drunken conversation about truth. Years later, the wife tells the narrator that when she stood half-naked in the snow he should have run her over so that she would never have learned the truth. It turns out that the truth which now destroys them is that the husband and their friend Richard had been lovers; their deception had allowed the marriage to last.

"Herself in Love," the title story and the conclusion of the volume, is less grim than the other stories about men and women. The unnamed woman in the story almost accidentally takes as a lover a handyman named Killebrew. His visits to her are occasional and unscheduled, the lovers do not talk very much, and their lovemaking is usually brief. The relationship, however, is never strained and it provides the woman with a measure of happiness. In the end she knows that she loves him, but she refrains from saying so. In the context of the other stories about love, "Herself in Love" suggests that a successful relationship must be spontaneous and cannot be discussed directly. These lovers' willingness to accept each other as they are and their gratitude for their shared moments have held them together.

Marianne Wiggins' stories, in their use of fantasy, in their concern with ordinary people, and in their sometimes cryptic endings, suggest that she has been influenced by such contemporary writers as the Argentinian José Luis Borges and the Americans Robert Coover, Donald Barthelme, and Thomas Pynchon. At the same time, however, the realism of some of the stories shows that she is not limited to fictions that call attention to their fictitious nature. She succeeds superbly in creating complex and interesting characters in the brief pages of her stories. Even in the stories which involve fantasy, the emotions of the characters are strong and comprehensible. Most important, her skill as a stylist makes her work distinctive and thoroughly enjoyable.

John M. Muste

Sources for Further Study

The Christian Science Monitor. LXXIX, August 5, 1987, p. 17.
Kirkus Reviews. LV, June 15, 1987, p. 889.
Library Journal. CXII, July, 1987, p. 99.
London Review of Books. IX, September 17, 1987, p. 19.
Los Angeles Times Book Review. August 16, 1987, p. 3.
New Statesman. CXIV, July 3, 1987, p. 29.
The New York Times Book Review. XCII, October 18, 1987, p. 32.
Publishers Weekly. CCXXXI, June 5, 1987, p. 71.
The Times Literary Supplement. May 22, 1987, p. 558.
The Washington Post Book World. XVII, August 30, 1987, p. 6.

HEY JACK!

Author: Barry Hannah (1943-   )
Publisher: E.P. Dutton/Seymour Lawrence (New York). 133 pp. $15.95
Type of work: Novel
Time: The 1980's
Locale: A university town in Mississippi

A meditation on the state of American culture as reflected in the experiences of a Korean War veteran and his friend, Jack, an aging but perennially handsome proprietor of a community coffee shop

Principal characters:
> HOMER, the self-conscious narrator, a Korean War veteran experiencing, late in life, a genuine first love
> JACK LIPSEY, a man of integrity, moderation, and good taste
> ALICE LIPSEY, Jack's schoolteacher daughter who becomes involved in an affair with a rock star
> RONNIE FOOTE, an egocentric, rich, vulgar, and mindless rock star, who returns home to prey on women
> MA,
> PA,
> GRAMPS, and
> DOUBLE GRAMPS, shiftless members of the rock star's family
> A HYPOCHONDRIACAL PROFESSOR, whose death epitomizes the alienation of American culture
> DELIA, the professor's daughter, another victim of the rock star
> A DENTIST, who is disillusioned and suspicious, and who returns to the country to die "broke but happy"

Barry Hannah's seventh book *Hey Jack!* is something more and something less than a novel. It is an extended meditation on American culture as seen through the eyes of a survivor of the Korean War. The extremely self-conscious narrator is named Homer. During the course of the book, Homer travels, and he is guilty of infidelity to the woman he loves, but neither the content nor the manner of *Hey Jack!* invites comparison with the *Odyssey*.

The book opens with Homer's statement "I go back to Korea." His sensibility has been permanently marked by his wartime experiences at Chosun Reservoir, and allusions to those experiences, sometimes in quotation of printed sources, recur regularly. Homer's involvement with the life stories of people in his Mississippi university community comes across as compulsive but oddly detached. The book lacks both the epic and the novelistic quality because the narrator is more interested in expressing his views of culture and of assorted misfits than in showing people living their lives.

Hey Jack! is essentially lyrical, regularly undercut by comedic and satiric passages. The book is ordered as a poem might be, with the phrase "hey Jack" serving as a refrain. Other elements also recur. The book is a lamentation of sorts—a grieving condemnation of what the American South has become, though Hannah, like many Southern writers, is hopelessly ambivalent about his region.

One should not identify Homer with the author, or the unnamed Mississippi town with Oxford, where Hannah lives and teaches. Perhaps Hannah chose to focus on the Korean War precisely because he could know it only at second hand. Born in 1943, Hannah came of age in a culture deeply affected by that war and its veterans. *Hey Jack!* brings together remnants of a better time without glorifying The Old South, and it shows the merciless incursions of the cheap and tawdry which belie the pretensions of the increasingly commercialized Sun Belt.

Homer's comments about an incidental character named Harmon reveal his, and his community's, attitudes. No one, Homer says, enables him to gather his hatred into one space as Harmon does. Harm, as he wants to be called, thinks that he is a dude but is nothing; he is "Southern trash and would be Northern trash if he was up there." Harmon likes to beat women and he "likes to wallow around in mud in a pick-up truck." Harmon "doesn't have the guts to enlist in the service." Homer and his cronies agree that "people like young Harmon would better serve each other by going back up in the hills and committing incest man on man. Or having saw fights." Their judgment is that "the riffraff is on the increase."

The natty, aristocratic Jack Lipsey is the antithesis of Harmon—and of Ronnie Foote, the rock star who is equally trashy, but rich. Jack has written poems, he has taught at a college in Maryland, and he has been married three times. Jack remains close to his two living wives, for, with each, he has had a daughter. Homer notes approvingly that Jack is not the kind of man to make room for the likes of Harmon.

Homer tells his readers that he has "gone home, over and over, and written this down, so as to distinguish my life." He tells something also of his narrative method: "You will find me changing voices as I slip into the—let us say—*mode* of the closer participant." Almost instantly, he shifts to the young Ronnie Foote's voice questioning his Pa, then his Gramps, and finally his Double Gramps (a man so old he is "barely a scab demanding infrequent nutrients") about whether the old eat their young. Thus, without benefit of quotation marks, Hannah introduces three degenerate generations of Footes; then, he writes, "The kid grows up, a rock star, ageing at twenty-three. He's already eating the young by the thousand when the second thought hits him." For Homer, the word eat carries regular destructive and sexual overtones.

Even before the reader has an idea of who Jack is, Homer addresses him. Homer describes the lives and deaths of two friends of his and Jack's—the hypochondriacal professor and the epicene dentist. The professor had "height, indiligence, and nihilism," but nothing "finally came of it except the tired, infinitely tired loneliness that shook from his brows. . . ." Even his "select protégés" doubted sometimes that "he was energetic enough for despair." The professor dies, in a freak accident, after he has set fire to his house, and his only friends, "those dead book writers and composers," are going up in smoke. The professor's daughter Delia will be victimized sexually by Ronnie Foote only minutes after her father's burial.

The dentist's character seems more complex, but like all the people in Hannah's book, the dentist is "illustrative," not real. Most of what Homer tells about the dentist is clearly speculative. The dentist invested his money in a hog and potato farm, but when his workers abandoned him to seek work in Detroit, they left the gate open and the hogs gorged themselves to death on potatoes. Ambivalent about his attractive wife, ignored by his sons, and torn with hatred and guilt about the blacks who will not pay him their debts, the dentist drives to distant Meridian to seek help from a psychiatrist. Later, the dentist retreats to the country to die "broke but happy"; instead, he is disturbed by a tapping at his window and sees the son of a former employee. "Daddy's dead," the man tells him, "but I come back to mess with you." The dentist dies, and Homer's speculation tells more about him than about the dentist.

Though Homer tells his story to "distinguish" his own life, he calls on Jack to share the horrors of what he tells. He considers Jack a better man than he. Jack "never needs a drink and barely even smokes." He dresses well and, despite his age, is handsome. Jack takes Homer with him to the cemetery where they discover the dead professor's daughter and Ronnie engaged in sex. Jack becomes obsessed with hatred for Ronnie, who is carrying on an affair with Jack's daughter Alice—an apparently conventional schoolteacher whose husband came home from Vietnam (too sane, according to Homer), grew fat, and bored her. Homer attributes practically everything, including the Civil War, to boredom.

Much of the humor of *Hey Jack!* derives from the Foote family's white-trash behavior. Ronnie's favorite curse word is Yehudi Menuhin, the name of the famous violinist. He has given his family a mansion near the golf course, where they raise chickens and systematically destroy the house. Gramps, bored like everyone else, drops chickens from his window to see how far they can fly. He likes to gun them down with his .22, and a ricocheting bullet strikes Jack in the hand as he and Homer play a round of golf. In retaliation, Jack is content to slice golf balls into the Footes' house, but Homer steals Jack's .38 and opens fire on the house. Despite his avowed love for an unnamed woman, Homer shares an evening of drugs with the professor's daughter and, under the guise of expressing Jack's concern about Alice, he makes love with her. His fury at Ronnie appears partly to be the result of jealousy.

Jack retains his cool and his dignity. He refuses to talk about barraging the Foote house with golf balls, and after Alice's death (the result of

Ronnie's boredom), he does not kill himself, as Homer initially reports. The book's final scene effectively sums up the action and meaning, though with irony and understatement.

Ronnie Foote hangs himself in his jail cell and leaves behind a song to Alice which he wants delivered to Jack. Homer finds Jack on the golf course, and after Jack reads the song, he balls it up and chips it into the wind, "so high it came back to us and landed behind." The final words are Jack's: "No mercy."

Perhaps that is what Homer has learned, or needs to learn. Things keep coming back. There is no forgetting, no putting aside of pain and memory, whether it be the Korean (or any other) War, the senseless deaths of friends, the cheapening of one's culture or one's children. Hannah's book meets the definition of the novel as Henry Fielding expressed it in his preface to *Joseph Andrews* (1742): It is a long narrative poem in prose. *Hey Jack!* makes its point, and it reminds one that the novel is not a single kind of book. It, like the culture, is always in process.

Leon V. Driskell

Sources for Further Study

Booklist. LXXXIV, September 1, 1987, p. 27.
Kirkus Reviews. LV, July 1, 1987, p. 950.
Library Journal. CXII, October 1, 1987, p. 108.
Los Angeles Times Book Review. September 6, 1987, p. 3.
The New York Times. XCII, November 1, 1987, p. 26.
Publishers Weekly. CCXXXII, July, 1987, p. 52.

A HISTORY OF PRIVATE LIFE
Volume I: From Pagan Rome to Byzantium

Author: Paul Veyne (1930-   )
First published: Histoire de la vie privée: De L'Empire romain à l'an mil, in 1985
Translated from the French by Arthur Goldhammer
Publisher: The Belknap Press of Harvard University Press (Cambrige, Massachusetts). Illustrated. 670 pp. $29.50
Type of work: Social history
Time: The first century B.C. to the eleventh century
Locale: The Roman Empire, Europe, and the Byzantine Empire

A series of essays on private life in imperial Rome, medieval Europe, and the Byzantine Empire, this volume considers diverse aspects of personal and family life during the first millennium of the Christian era

This is the first installment of a projected five-volume series devoted to a history of private life from ancient Rome through the late twentieth century. The series, edited by the late Philippe Ariès and Georges Duby, reflects the general orientation toward social history encouraged by the French *Annales* school, and the particular interest in private practices evident in such monumental French studies as Numa Denis Fustel de Coulanges' *La Cité antique* (1864; *The Ancient City*, 1956) and Ariès' *L'Homme devant la mort* (1977; *The Hour of Our Death*, 1981). The focus of the series is upon private beliefs and everyday life, the backdrop to the great political and military events of which traditional history is made.

The text, accompanied by extensive illustrations depicting various aspects of ancient private life, is at its best when visual image and written word merge into a unified picture of private life. Roman hope in eternal rest in the afterlife, for example, is aptly supported by an illustration of a sarcophagus showing the deceased reclining on her bed in a bedchamber. Such coherence of text and illustration, however, is the exception rather than the rule in a book which lacks even a catalog of illustrations and in which words and visual images tend to create parallel rather than integrated impressions of the private life of humankind.

The first three chapters of this volume are devoted to pagan Rome, the fourth to Merovingian and Carolingian Europe, and the last to the Byzantine Empire in the tenth and eleventh centuries. The book, definitely francocentric, highlights Merovingians and Carolingians at the expense of Saxons, Tuscans, Iberians, and Scandinavians. Despite the limited geographic and chronological choice of subject matter, however, this volume creates an invaluable portrait of early European private life.

While there is a wealth of fascinating material on private life in this book, the nonspecialist reader, with minimal knowledge of the events of the period, will frequently find himself or herself lost in a sea of unfamiliar names and undefined terms. Knowledge of major political events and biographical information is often assumed; for example, the Merovingian sense of the public as private is illustrated by "the celebrated episode" of the vessel of Soissons, a tale retold only in an endnote. Similarly, while knowledge of such obscure works as Plautus' *Cistellaria* (third century B.C.; *The Casket*) and Procopius' *Polemon* (sixth century; *History of the Wars*) is not required of the reader, there are nuances of argument and interpretation which will be missed by the layman. Nevertheless, no reader will finish this book without being the richer for it.

The volume begins with a broad study of Roman life in the imperial period (c. A.D. 100-400). While evidence for private life in this period is unquestionably better than for earlier periods in Rome, many readers would probably have benefited from the historical perspective that a discussion of the evolution of Roman private life from prehistory through the Republic into the Empire would have provided.

In defense of his decision to begin the work with imperial Rome rather than with the Greeks, the Egyptians, or even Neolithic Europeans, Veyne argues in an introduction that the Greeks, at least, require no special attention because the Roman Empire was fully Hellenized. Yet there were significant differences between private life in imperial Rome and in classical Greece, specifically in fifth century Athens. The question of seclusion of women in Athens is a case in point. Since women in the Roman Empire of the first centuries A.D. were under no such restriction, the existence of this custom in the Byzantine Empire is better understood in the light of earlier Athenian practice.

In the first chapter, Veyne traces the life of a Roman in the imperial period from birth through death and considers basic features of Roman private life, such as marriage, the family, inheritance, slavery, and entertainment. Any overview of marriage in the imperial period requires some republican background, for there is solid evidence that several different forms of marriage evolved in the republican period. The oldest, and most aristocratic, was *confarreatio*, which had religious sanction and created a permanent conjugal bond. An early alternative to *confarreatio* was *conventio in manum*, in which the woman became the legal property of her husband. By the imperial period, a third form had become much more popular, *usus*, in which the woman retained more (especially financial) independence from her husband. Awareness of this conjugal evolution makes clearer Veyne's discussion of the transformation of Roman marriage from a civic duty to produce children and to run the household into an internalized code of the harmonious couple.

For the modern reader the Roman definition of a family is particularly striking. The Roman family was not the modern nuclear family but an entire household, including slaves and more distant relatives, living under the protection of the father, or head of the household. The unique Roman relationship between clients and patrons is, in a sense, a public extension of the family. Custom required clients to bring greetings every morning to the houses of their patrons, who were expected in turn to provide civic and legal protection for their clients. Confraternities, or clubs, constituted another significant Roman extension of private life into the public, eventually evolving into the medieval guilds. The elaborate public baths systems built throughout the empire further illustrate the fact that functions considered private in the modern world (such as hygiene) were part of the public realm in Rome.

Veyne also discusses the special class of "notables," that is, men of family, wealth, and power, whose values included both a contempt for manual labor and a parallel high regard for idleness, or *otium*, as a virtue. At the same time, these men were driven by a strong sense of entrepreneurism and private profit, and in their social code public office could readily be used for private financial gain. Such notables believed that they should use their time and wealth in euergetism, or public works and building projects for the benefit of the whole city. Emphasis was clearly on urban life and urban values, as well as on strong social pressure and conformity, supported by the Roman sense of tradition and by various pagan philosophies, such as Stoicism. These upper-class Roman values included a sexual puritanism which does not fit modern stereotypes of Roman orgies and sexual license. Both co-optation, the informal selection process whereby membership in the class of notables was achieved, and the elaborate system of bribery and extortion practiced by public officials demonstrate once again that an ancient Roman had a broader sense of the private domain than does a modern citizen.

The second chapter, by Peter Brown, is devoted to late antiquity, that is, to the Roman Empire in the third through sixth centuries and especially to the transformations caused by interaction between Christianity and the Roman world. In particular, Brown discusses the Judaic sense of tradition, of cultural solidarity, and of threatened community which Christianity transferred to the Roman world and which encouraged a sense of the private as negative and of the individual as dangerous to group cohesion. Christianity succeeded in popularizing moral values such as stoic virtue and fidelity advocated by the pagan philosophers and in establishing a middle-class morality in which sexual renunciation became a badge of male leadership in the Christian community.

During this period, the breakdown of the traditional Roman family was assisted by Christian praise of celibacy, and notables began to abandon their long-cherished duty to nourish the city through euergetism in favor of an almsgiving reflecting the Christian notion of the solidarity of rich and poor. Simultaneously, a reorientation away from the city toward the country was led by solitary hermits who existed in the no-man's-land outside the boundary and protection of the ancient city. Transformation of sexual values went beyond praise of celibacy (which, after all, had always existed in the Roman world in the persons of the vestal virgins). For Christians such as Augustine of Hippo, sexuality became concupiscence of the flesh, and the old idea that upper-class decorum in bed produced better children was replaced by a view of sex as an irrational and asocial moment in the life of a person.

The third chapter, by Yvon Thébert, surveys Roman domestic architecture in North Africa, where the organization of domestic space was apparently determined not by autonomous private needs, but by social ones. In this primarily urban culture, the most important aspect of house design was the arrangement of a public reception area around a colonnaded area called the peristyle. The custom of daily client visitation and the importance of the formal meal required the homes of notables to serve both public and private purposes. The difficulty in distinguishing between the archaeological remains of private and public buildings and the similarities between private house construction and the design of the Christian basilica reinforce the perception of the general Roman tendency to blur the boundaries between public and private. Trends in the opposite direction, marking an increase in social distancing on the part of the notables, were the proliferation of baths in the private homes of North Africa and an increasing tendency toward systematic compartmentalization of rooms, especially of the peristyle.

The fourth chapter, "The Early Middle Ages in the West" by Michel Rouche, considers especially "the invasion of privacy" which took place during the Merovingian and Carolingian period, when consideration of the public weal was replaced by the private interests of barbarians for whom the Roman concept of *res publica*, or the public interest, was totally foreign. Civic, urban life was replaced by a private life of violence in which individual right reigned at the expense of public law. The state, now a kingdom instead of a republic, came to be viewed as personal inheritance or patrimony. Private organizations, such as mercantile guilds and Jewish communities, modeled to a certain extent on the old Roman corporations, now flourished as self-protecting rather than semipublic institutions. The need for protected spaces evolved into the practices of asylum and hospitality, customs based in the ancient Mediterranean world on a belief in the rights of suppliants and of strangers.

The contradictory status of the body, the child, and the elderly, all simultaneously honored and despised, can be noted during this period, which was also marked by a gradual increase in monogamous marriages and a stronger sense of the indissolubility of marriage. The struggle to adapt barbarian ways to Christian beliefs caused Merovingian polygamy to be gradually replaced by Carolingian divorce, that is, killing one wife to marry another, a peculiar practice vividly reflecting the violence of the age.

Christianity, now the dominant religious force, also made an impact on private life. The old pagan anxiety about death, which was essentially private and personal, yielded to the calm felt by a Christian whose death was an entrance to the real community of God. Thus the custom of private entombment in family crypts on the outskirts of town was replaced by public burial in the churchyard. At the same time, there was a heightened sense of conscience and personal responsibility based upon a new Christian awareness of human community and equality under God. Finally, the medieval rejection of the old Roman ideal of *otium* is illustrated by the Benedictine life-style of prayer and work (*ora et labora*).

The last chapter, by Evelyne Patlagean, looks at private life in the eastern half of the Roman Empire during the Byzantine period, when the public interest became less that of the city and more that of the imperial government. As in the Roman imperial period, a strong urban bias is notable in the sources. The hermitic life was discouraged in favor of the monastic community, and an important feature of Byzantine society was apparently the founding of private monasteries by individuals and family groups.

In a throwback to the society of fifth century Athens, Byzantine society was marked by the rigid seclusion of women, the importance of betrothal, marriages arranged by parents for social and financial reasons rather than affection, and extended kinship groups outside the immediate family, such as the godparent-godchild relationship, which became an impediment to marriage. Attitudes toward the body and sex were affected by apparent links between medicine and asceticism, and great emphasis was placed upon the importance of dreams and visions, which were considered normal and common experiences of a religious rather than imaginary nature. The popularity of fictional works such as the equally edifying and entertaining *Alexander Romance* is another evidence of the Byzantine interest in the realm of the spirit or imagination. Attempts by public officials to control the proliferation of new religious cults are contrasted with the importance of personal devotion to icons and the peculiar practices of the Bogomile religious sect, which attempted to create a private form of religious life within the generally homogenous Byzantine society.

This book leaves the reader with the obvious but reassuring notion that every society creates its own definition and structure of the private, that what is private varies from one society to another and from one period to another.

Thomas J. Sienkewicz

Sources for Further Study

The Atlantic. CCLIX, May, 1987, p. 90.
Booklist. LXXXIII, April 15, 1987, p. 1234.
Choice. XXIV, June, 1987, p. 1546.

The Christian Science Monitor. March 11, 1987, p. 21.
Kirkus Reviews. LV, January 15, 1987, p. 122.
Library Journal. CXII, February 15, 1987, p. 144.
The New Republic. CXCVI, June 29, 1987, p. 39.
The New York Times Book Review. XCII, May 3, 1987, p. 14.
Publishers Weekly. CCXXXI, January 30, 1987, p. 374.
The Washington Post Book World. XVII, March 29, 1987, p. 1.

A HISTORY OF THE JEWS

Author: Paul Johnson (1928-   )
Publisher: Harper & Row, Publishers (New York). 644 pp. $25.00
Type of work: History
Time: Approximately 3000 B.C. to the 1980's
Locale: The Middle East, Europe, and America

This lively, insightful account of Jewish history from its origins to the present emphasizes the unique characteristics of Jewish history and the Jewish impact on the world

> *Principal personages:*
> ABRAHAM, the founder of the Jewish people
> MOSES, the Jewish leader who delivered the Ten Commandments
> ISAIAH, an important prophet and writer in the Jewish Bible
> MOSES MAIMONIDES, the most important Jewish medieval philosopher
> BENEDICT DE SPINOZA, a seventeenth century Jewish rationalist
> THEODOR HERZL, the founder of the modern Zionist movement
> SIGMUND FREUD, a Jewish physician and the founder of psychoanalysis

Paul Johnson is a British Christian writer, a journalist, and one of the most prolific historians of recent years. Among his major books are *Modern Times* (1983) and *A History of Christianity* (1976), both sweeping syntheses. Given the monumental histories of the Jews that have appeared in the last hundred years, the question could be asked whether a new synthesis of Jewish history was necessary, and whether a Christian historian could bring new insights to bear on it. The answer to both questions is a resounding yes. This major work is replete with refreshing insights, broad unifying themes, and striking historical illustrations.

While acknowledging his debt to the major works of Jewish history, Johnson provides four compelling personal reasons for embarking on his work. First, he came to realize the debt that Christianity owed to Judaism, while realizing that the Jews continued to develop their history and religion after the rise of Christianity, a fact to which many Christians remained oblivious. Second, the sheer span, drama, and excitement of the Jewish story captivated him. Third, he set out to explain the miracle of how the Jews obstinately retained their identity while adapting to and greatly affecting the world around them. Finally, he concluded that the Jews stood at the center of man's quest to give life a meaning, a purpose, and a dignity.

Much of the exhilaration this book offers seems to arise from the need of a brilliant and sympathetic Christian scholar to communicate his discovery of Jewish history. *A History of the Jews* provides the shrewd perspective of an outsider looking in, then attempting to re-create what he has experienced. In addition, what Johnson has done was to write a cross section of the history of the world from the standpoint of the Jewish experience, or as he puts it, from the viewpoint of a "learned and intelligent victim." He has written it very well, with verve, intelligence, and feeling.

This great synthesis predictably breaks Jewish history into major characteristic epochs. Johnson discerns seven of them: Israelites, Judaism, "Cathedocracy," Ghetto, Emancipation, Holocaust, and Zion. These periods represent for him a story of almost incredible drama and perseverance. The Jews began as a collection of west Semitic tribes, discovered man's destiny, established a kingdom, suffered crushing defeat, became powerless outsiders in the Middle Ages while managing to retain their uniqueness, surfaced and rose to the heights of modern civilization, experienced the greatest single crime in human history, then emerged again to restore their ancient dream and begin anew.

Johnson, however, goes beyond this overwhelming and enthralling story. Within the chronological narrative, he skillfully picks out and weaves in unifying themes that are unique to the Jewish experience. This ability to discern patterns is the mark of a fine historian; the resulting insights are greatly stimulating. Important themes include the invention of monotheism by the Jews, the internalization of morality, and the refusal of the Jews to worship man. This set of characteristics resulted in a people who on the one hand are intensely devoted to law and morality while on the other hand tend toward a critical and rationalistic point of view. According to Johnson, the Jews contributed to the "rationalization" of the world. That is to say, they were the great explainers of the unknown and some of the greatest problem-solvers in history. They developed notions of social justice and equality under the law, wrote the first meaningful histories, developed the idea of progress. Then they developed modern commercial techniques and produced towering giants of the intellect who sought to explain the mysteries of God, nature, society, and human nature. These important thinkers include Moses Maimonides, Benedict de Spinoza, Karl Marx, Sigmund Freud, and Albert Einstein. Characteristically, these great intellects were also great moralists. Above all, the Jews, says Johnson, were the only people in history to exist under a great system of law, yet without a state, for two thousand years. Johnson is surely correct in his perception that the historical and cultural development of the Jews cannot be categorized and remains unique.

Johnson begins his story with the theme of Jewish tenacity, with the passage of Abraham from Mesopotamia to Hebron, with his covenant with God and the promise of the new land. The central episode in the section on the Israelites comes with the archetypical figure of Moses, that great man of action and spirit, the lawgiver of ethical monotheism. Johnson rightly looks upon the Jewish adoption of the Law as one of the giant leaps of mankind, perhaps the greatest of all. With the Ten Commandments, life above all became sacred, and, with the making of the Torah, a body of laws and customs emerged to produce a portable religion and a veritable way of life.

With the aid of recent archaeological evidence, Johnson plots the story of the Israelites as they conquered the remainder of Palestine and established a kingdom with Jerusalem as its capital. The state was a mixed blessing, for it created a striking tension unique to the Jews: They distrusted the kingdom, which they regarded as man-made. This tension between religion and state has continued to the present day in modern Israel.

The destruction of the first Jewish Commonwealth at the hands of Assyria and Babylonia destroyed the unified Jewish state, yet produced Judaism. The prophets emerged as the truth-tellers and the conscience of the Jews. The Jews now based their religion on Holy Days, feasts, and festivals—above all on memory. Adversity greatly strengthened their faith and their resolve as they related their misfortunes to their role as the actors in God's vast drama. Along with many others, Johnson sees the Jewish Bible as possibly the grandest literature ever created. The Book of Job, for example, with its theme of human tragedy and absurdity, is a text for both ancients and moderns.

With the Greek and Roman conquest of the Middle East from about 300 to 30 B.C., the Jews entered into the history of Western civilization. Johnson wisely discerns a dual response of the Jews to Greek and Roman culture. They accepted some classical ideas on reason but fought to retain their uniqueness, for they drew an absolute distinction between the human and the divine. Thus, they refused to become Greeks or to worship the Roman emperor. Johnson makes the compelling point that while the Jews were conservative in terms of retaining their laws and identity, they repeatedly sought to reform the existing order when they deemed it unjust. Moreover, the Jews became divided into flexibilists and purists, those who accepted and those who rejected the host civilization. This division has persisted to the present.

Despite a brief period of independence in late antiquity, the Roman conquest ended Jewish rule in the area over which King David had reigned. This state of affairs lasted until the mid-twentieth century. The rise and success of Christianity was another important result of the Roman conquest. Johnson views Jesus as a universalist and as the creator of Christianity. This remains debatable, since there is no evidence that Jesus sought to create a new religion per se. A more plausible case can be made that the Hellenized Jew Paul of Tarsus was the true founder of Christianity as a distinct faith.

The Jewish catastrophes of A.D. 66 and 135 at the hands of the Romans put an end to the expansion of Judaism and assured the return of the Jews to their purist traditions and their turning to vast commentaries on their laws and traditions. The community and the Talmud became the pillars of Jewish life. The Jews became ruled by a "Cathedocracy," an elite of rabbis, scholars, and merchants. There was a price to be paid here in narrowness and parochialism, but it assured the survival of the Jews as a distinct entity.

Johnson asserts that this system served the Jews extremely well in the vast period of medieval adversity.

During the Middle Ages, Islam, the second great religion inspired by Judaism, conquered the Middle East and Spain. For a time the Muslims were tolerant and permitted a creative symbiosis of Jewish, Islamic, and classical culture. The Jewish philosopher Maimonides emerged as a great synthesizer of faith and reason. Still, Jewish mysticism developed in the same period; thus Judaism, like the other two great religions, displays both a rationalist and an irrationalist potential.

Though Johnson sometimes finds the phenomenon of anti-Semitism infuriating and inexplicable, he provides a good, concise discussion of why Jews have been hated throughout human history. He ascribes this hatred chiefly to Jewish persistence of identity, Jewish truth-telling, and the age-old charge of deicide. Johnson does well to stress the way in which medieval Christian anti-Semitism dehumanized the image of Jews as servants of Satan; he also discusses the rise of mass violence against Jews and the development of state anti-Semitism, of which the Spanish Inquisition is a prime early example. By 1500, anti-Semitism had assumed, in the apt words of Johnson, a "sinister and impersonal logic. . . . The historical record shows, time and again, that it develops a power and momentum of its own."

From 1500 to 1789, many Jews were restricted to living in ghettos. Despite the hardships of ghetto life, some Jews helped develop the techniques of capitalism and became advisers to kings and princes. In early modern times, both Jewish rationalism and Jewish messianism and mysticism continued to develop. Most Jews rejected the extremes of the would-be messiah Shabbetai Zevi and the pantheism of Spinoza.

Johnson does well to mark his fifth epoch, Emancipation, as a turning point in world and Jewish history. By 1800, the Jews had ceased to be outcasts and outsiders in the West. They scaled the heights of Western culture and helped to shape the modern outlook. Johnson provides fascinating and illuminating discussions of Reform Judaism, Jewish writers, politicians such as Benjamin Disraeli, financiers in the Rothschild family, and founders of Zionism, particularly Theodor Herzl. Johnson views Marx and Freud as pseudoscientists, theorists who unconsciously secularized and transformed the Jewish vision. His view of Freud as an "irrationalist" is too one-sided. Freud sought to explain, understand, and control the irrational, not to celebrate it.

Johnson's contrast between the emancipated Jews of the West and the oppressed Jews of Eastern Europe and Russia is well drawn, while his incisive characterization of the free American Jew as a new creation of history is superb. Despite such advances, anti-Semitism grew insidiously, grafting racism, conspiracy theory, and socioeconomic and political elements onto the old religious foundations.

The section on the Holocaust is probably the best available in a survey of Jewish history, for it effectively synthesizes the best of recent scholarship. It captures the unique combination of Nazi fanaticism and bureaucratic murder together with the deception and helplessness of the victims against the backdrop of an indifferent world. As Johnson says in one of his memorable statements, "The Jews, unlike the Christians, did not believe the devil took human shape."

Having relinquished their trust of the civilized world, the Jews proceeded to found a state of their own. Johnson skillfully sums up the complex forces and personalities that led to the state of Israel. The desperate efforts of Zionists coincided with the plight of Holocaust refugees, the decline of the British Empire, and the brief support of the United States and the Soviet Union. Israel was born in this brief opportunity. Johnson's sympathies lie with the beleaguered Jewish state. He points out that had the Arabs accepted either of the partition plans of 1937 and 1947, the size of the Jewish state would probably be a fraction of what it is today. Johnson concludes that, despite its problems, the state of Israel is necessary for Jewish survival. It remains a refuge, a symbol of rebirth, a deterrent to another Holocaust.

After a cursory survey of Jewish history since 1945, this majestic work concludes on an eloquent note. The great and sometimes onerous demands of Judaism, says Johnson, carried the Jews, gave them a purpose, and enabled them to survive and create with dignity. To paraphrase the words of Joshua, their conviction made them strong, of good courage, and unafraid, for they felt that God was with them. For Johnson, the Jews are the epitome of the human condition, for all of us are "strangers and sojourners" on this Earth. The Jews wrote the "pilot-project for the entire human race." Johnson would contend that the Jewish identity was God-given; others would say that the Jews believed so strongly that they were a special people that they became one. They wrote the existential script for themselves.

Even a survey as rich as this book must be selective, but some important omissions must be noted. There is very little detail on the long history of Jewish self-government that Johnson praises so highly. There is almost nothing on the travails and rewards of daily life, and on the history of Jewish women, children, and family life. The useful discussions of Jewish religious development are not followed up by a summary of trends since 1945.

Johnson's choice of terms is sometimes dated and misleading. The term "Old Testament" is a Christian designation that sometimes implies the obsolescence of the Jewish dispensation. "Jewish Bible" or "Scripture" might be an improvement. A more serious error is to call the Jews a race, as Johnson often does. Not only is this term inaccurate, but it also carries the negative overtones of pseudoanthropology. The term "Jewish people" would have been far better.

On the whole, however, Johnson's work is probably the best single-volume history of the Jews for the general reader. It is a joy to read, not merely because of its scholarship, its style, and its insights, but because it is written by a Christian historian who brings such intelligence and objectivity to his subject.

Leon Stein

Sources for Further Study

The Christian Science Monitor. June 11, 1987, p. 23.
Commentary. LXXXIII, June, 1987, p. 64.
The Economist. LXXXIII, March 1, 1987, p. 964.
Library Journal. CXII, March 15, 1987, p. 83.
Los Angeles Times Book Review. April 19, 1987, p. 1.
National Review. XXXIX, April 10, 1987, p. 48.
The New York Review of Books. XXIV, October 8, 1987, p. 7.
The New York Times Book Review. XCII, April 19, 1987, p. 11.
Publishers Weekly. CCXXXI, February 27, 1987, p. 158.
Time. CXXIX, May 11, 1987, p. 84.
The Washington Post Book World. XVII, May 24, 1987, p. 5.

HOMER
Poet of the *Iliad*

Author: Mark W. Edwards (1929-   )
Publisher: The Johns Hopkins University Press (Baltimore, Maryland). 341 pp.
  $29.50
Type of work: Literary criticism

This commentary on ten major books of Homer's Iliad *contains a first part on stylistic questions in both* Iliad *and* Odyssey *and assumes no knowledge of ancient Greek; thus, it can be used easily by both general readers and those who desire a more thorough grounding in Homeric criticism*

Mark W. Edwards' *Homer: Poet of the Iliad*, one of a series of commentaries on major literary works published by The Johns Hopkins University Press, sweeps away esoteric details which commentaries often include in order to provide a good grounding in stylistics as well as insightful comparisons which demonstrate the unity, logic, and coherence of the *Iliad*. Though part 1, a primer on Homeric style, deals with both the *Odyssey* and the *Iliad*, part 2 provides commentary on only ten of the *Iliad's* twenty-four books, those which Edwards considers essential to the poem's meaning. This focus allows sharper comparisons and illustrates that Homer often transcends formula through metaphor, sound, even symbolism and wordplay.

One distinctive feature of Homeric style is contraction of time. The *Iliad* covers a period of fifty-three days, the *Odyssey* forty. This is in marked contrast to other epics on the Trojan War. For example, the eleven books of the *Cypria*, written by some successor of Homer, considered events from the gods' decision to cause the war to the point at which the *Iliad* begins. The *Iliad*, on the other hand, considers only Achilles' departure from battle and his companion Patroclus' death, which causes Achilles to return. Since it ends with Hector's death, the *Iliad* does not even deal with Troy's fall. This was considered in another lost epic (the "Little *Iliad*") by another Homeratid (or "Little Homer") in its four books. (Richmond Lattimore discusses these lost works based on summaries, quoted fragments, and ancient commentaries in his translation of the *Iliad*, 1951.)

Homeric style expands these limited time frames by recounting the background of ongoing episodes. In the *Iliad*, this often occurs through a deity (such as Thetis, Achilles' goddess-mother, who reminds her son of the short but glorious life he is destined to live if he returns to battle). In the *Odyssey*, expansion appears in the six days of Telemachus' adventures (*Iliad* 1-4) as he searches for news of his father, Odysseus, later in Odysseus' relating of his own adventures to the Phaeacians, and later still in the dialogue of Odysseus and Eumaeus the swineherd, which occurs after Odysseus has returned to Ithaca.

Edwards makes valuable comments on the oral nature of Homeric verse.

How much did the rhapsodes, professional reciters of epic, alter the content of the poetry, and to what extent were such changes introduced in its codified (or written) version? What mnemonic devices (memory aids) were available to the rhapsodes, and how conscious was Homer of the rhapsodes' role in delivering his verses? Edwards notes the privileged place the rhapsode holds in the *Odyssey*. There are two named in the poem: Demodocus ("he who is received by the people") in *Odyssey* 8 and Phemius ("prophetic utterance") in *Odyssey* 22. Demodocus clearly has a privileged place at the Phaeacian court. A herald announces his presence (*Odyssey* 8.43-45; 62-63). Phemius appears, in contrast, to be a member of Odysseus' court. Though he has entertained the suitors in Odysseus' absence, his life is spared. A third rhapsode, unnamed, makes a brief appearance in *Odyssey* 3 and inspires tears at Menelaus' court with his song of the Trojan War. All this suggests that the rhapsode's role was a highly responsible one, perhaps akin to that of high priest and spokesman for the gods. Edwards provides useful references to the work of Denys Page and Milman Parry in this area.

Despite high social standing and relative independence in methods of presentation, it appears that the rhapsodes did not greatly increase the number of variants in the Homeric lines. This suggests that the poetry assumed an almost sacred character from a relatively early period. Though variations in dialect appear, those affecting content are rare. By the mid-second century B.C., the codifiers at Alexandria, Egypt, had established a written version, though to what extent their text was based on the oral version of the reciters is impossible to say. There may, Edwards suggests, have been a written version as early as the close of the sixth century B.C., that of Theagenes of Rhegium, one of the Homeridae, individuals who, obviously tenuously, traced their origins back to Homer.

Homer's own voice intrudes relatively little on the narrative he relates, as Edwards notes. This distance allows the principals to comment often on their own situations as events unfold. Though it is often written that Helen, presumably the world's most beautiful woman, remains undescribed, the fact is that, aside from brief epithets attached to the names of some of the poem's personalities ("ox-eyed Hera," "golden Aphrodite," "swift-footed Achilles," or "wily Odysseus"), there is next to no description of any individual's features in the *Iliad* and only occasional indirect descriptions of some of the more grotesque personalities who inhabit the *Odyssey*. Even so, Edwards writes, readers feel they know Homer and are comfortable with him, much the same as readers of Jane Austen feel they know their author.

Comments on meter and formula begin with comparison to the repetitions, formulas, and lengthy lines of Henry Wadsworth Longfellow's *The Song of Hiawatha* (1855). This analogy is well-founded. Longfellow intended an imitation of the Finnish *Kalevala*, an oral epic. Edwards provides sufficient examples to illustrate the regularity of the Homeric line, noting the consistency of epithets which fill it. Zeus is called "cloud-gatherer" when at ease, "thunderer" when active. Penelope, wife of Odysseus, is "noble" when complimented on her good sense, "sensible" in most other contexts.

Parataxis (subject-verb word order) allows the main idea to be understood before any qualification appears, and Homer usually follows such regular order. He does, however, also introduce lengthy periodic structure, most often to illustrate verbally confusion or disorder, as, for example, when Hector seeks in vain an escape from the pursuing Achilles. Likewise, enjambment (running a sentence from one verse to the next) is common, but it rarely separates sense units and so eliminates monotony and enriches naturalness in the narrative.

Type scenes abound in the Homeric poems, though with variety. These include visits from deities (Thetis to Achilles in the *Iliad*, Hermes and Athena to Odysseus in the *Odyssey*), ritual sacrifice (the Trojan victims on Patroclus' funeral pyre, Nestor's hecatomb in the *Odyssey*), eating meals, which are usually of immense size, and battle scenes, which are distinctive either because of grotesque deaths or because they increase dramatic tension. *Aristeiai*, moments of distinguished achievement in which heroes face ever more difficult opponents, appear throughout the *Iliad*. These usually are capped by speeches, brave words spoken by the victorious hero, and a vaunt over the body of his dead opponent. Lengthy similes inevitably have frames of reference which are as far from the scene of battle as possible; often they are pastoral.

Edwards emphasizes in part 2, the commentaries section, the special nature of the *Iliad*'s battle scenes. Though Homer clearly sees the Trojan War from the Greek perspective, there is no implication that the Greek side represents good and the Trojan evil. The *Iliad* focuses on the inner strength, the moral courage, and, at times, the pettiness of those on both sides. Agamemnon, for example, is "great-souled," but when he seizes Briseis, the woman given to Achilles as prize of honor, he reveals a lack of respect for his junior colleague. The gods, meanwhile, watch the human conflict and mirror human pettiness in their own actions. Achilles' anger drives him from battle after Agamemnon claims Briseis, and his anger appears in his mother Thetis' arguments among the Olympians. Zeus, as father of gods and king of men, presides over all this wrath and is ultimately responsible for all that fate brings; even so, he is strangely powerless to change it. Edwards takes each of these major scenes in *Iliad* 1 and illustrates these interrelationships, following with comments on *Iliad* 3, the combat of Menelaus and Paris.

Central in Edwards' comments on *Iliad* 3 is his consideration of Helen as she appears at the Scaean gate of Troy to watch the battle between her Spartan husband, Menelaus, and her Trojan lover Paris. Edwards compares the admiration she receives to that given Penelope by her suitors (*Odyssey* 1.328 and following, 18.206 and following) and Hera before Zeus (*Iliad* 14.292 and following). Edwards notes Helen's unhappiness, self-reproach, and desolation amid this outward approval. This emerges particularly in her mutually courteous words with Priam, King of Troy. The section concludes with analysis of the harsh criticism Helen has for Aphrodite when the goddess tells her to join Paris in his bedroom. She goes to the extent of suggesting that Aphrodite might choose to become Paris' concubine, if not his wife. Edwards rightly notes that Helen's words are far more taunting than those of Diomedes after he wounds Aphrodite (*Iliad* 5.348-5.351).

Edwards resumes his commentary with notes on *Iliad* 6, resumption of the pitched battle after the abortive duel of Menelaus and Paris. He writes that Diomedes becomes, in effect, a surrogate Achilles, the latter now having completely withdrawn from battle. Athena strengthens Diomedes for his *aristeia*. She then assists him in wounding the coward god Ares. The ensuing scene, in which Ares bewails his woes to his father Zeus, recalls for Edwards Aphrodite's complaint after having been wounded by Diomedes. The paradox here, rightly noted, is that both deities behave in exactly the same way, even though they preside over the opposite spheres of war and love.

Hector's farewell to Andromache (*Iliad* 6.369-6.529) establishes him as a loving husband and father and is distinctive because of its strong human emotions. Edwards compares this to the loveless household of Menelaus and Helen in *Odyssey* 3. He notes the irony of Achilles' providing a funeral and tomb for Andromache's father though he desecrates Hector's corpse. Edwards argues that this indicates the essentially self-centered nature of the Homeric hero whose first duty is to self.

Iliad 9 centers on the decision of the Greeks to approach Achilles in order to persuade him to return to battle. The book features oratorical skill (tact in publicly spoken words) and its absence. Diomedes' *aristeia* gives him credibility when he speaks in the assembly of chieftains, but his denunciation of the state of affairs under Agamemnon's leadership is uncompromisingly harsh as Nestor, sage counselor of the Greeks, is quick to note. The arguments of Odysseus, Ajax, and Achilles' respected tutor and retainer Phoenix at Achilles' tent do nothing to persuade the young man to reenter battle, but the scene is filled with forms of courtesy and respect. Phoenix enters first, and he remains after the others have left. Arrival of the envoys itself recalls the earlier embassy at which Briseis was claimed, and graceful courtesies contrast with the awkward abruptness of Briseis' seizing.

In his brief discussion of *Iliad* 13, Edwards attributes much of his insight to Bernard Fenik's *Typical Battle Scenes in the Iliad* (1968). He notes the preponderance of description in Poseidon's journey to the battlefield, the god's exhortation to the Greeks, the marshaling of ranks, and the *aristeia* of Idomeneus. The book continues with the catalog of Greek forces facing

Hector and ends with the abortive confrontation of Hector and Ajax. It is, in effect, a transitional book, leading to the council of the Greeks in *Iliad* 14 and Hera's seduction of Zeus in the same book. The war-love opposition thus continues. Edwards notes a parallel to the *Hymn to Aphrodite* 58-65, in which that goddess similarly prepares herself before setting out to seduce Anchises, Trojan father of the hero Aeneas. Hera even borrows Aphrodite's special girdle for the occasion. The effect will be to turn Zeus's attention from the battle so that, for a brief time at least, the Greeks may prevail. Zeus's passion resembles that of Paris for Helen, so seductive does Hera appear. The passage is filled with humor. No sooner does Hera believe that she has been successful than Zeus begins to enumerate for her a long list of his paramours.

No decisive change in the battle can eventuate, however, until Achilles reenters it. For this to happen, Patroclus must die at the hands of Hector and in Achilles' armor. This occurs in *Iliad* 16.684-16.867 and his death allows new armor for Achilles to be manufactured by the smith-god Hephaestus. Achilles' cruel sacrifice of the Trojan captives added to the desecration of Hector's corpse is somewhat mitigated by Achilles' deep affection for Patroclus and by his courteous return of Hector's corpse, now anointed and stainless, to Priam, the young Trojan's father.

No new ground is broken in Edwards' study, nor was his book intended to do so; nevertheless, his observations, particularly the comparisons he makes, are insightful, straightforward, and sound. The scholarship he cites and the judgments he makes about it are flawless, and he has produced a valuable companion to both of Homer's poems.

Robert J. Forman

Sources for Further Study

Choice. XXV, October, 1987, p. 302.
The Christian Science Monitor. September 9, 1987, p. 21.
Library Journal. CXII, September 1, 1987, p. 183.

A HOUSE OF TREES

Author: Joan Colebrook (1915-   )
Publisher: Farrar, Straus and Giroux (New York). Illustrated. 256 pp. $18.95
Type of work: Autobiography
Time: 1920-1937
Locale: Queensland, Australia

These memoirs trace the writer's passage from girlhood to womanhood and record how her closeness to family, formative years spent in Australia's exotic North, and life lived in a British colony combine to forge her identity

> *Principal personages:*
> JOAN HEALE COLEBROOK, the teller and subject of the memoirs
> HAZEL,
> MARGO,
> HELEN,
> ROBIN, and TRACY, her four sisters and one brother
> EDWARD and ROBINA HEALE, her parents

Joan Colebrook spent her girlhood during the 1920's in North Queensland, the upper part of an Australian state approximately one-sixth the size of the United States. Separated from the rest of Queensland by the unseen line marking the Tropic of Capricorn, this area was one of the last to be settled by white Australians, who started making their way north in the early 1900's, a little over a century after the original penal colony had been established along Sydney Harbor. The land they sought to tame took as its border the Coral Sea's glistening beaches and the Great Barrier Reef's underwater carnival of shape and color. Mountain ranges, holding immense mineral resources, rose from the coastal plains. In the rich volcanic soil nurtured by abundant rainfall and sunshine all things grew—blazing flowers, delicate fruits, a rain forest. Animals that had somehow skipped the demands of evolution wandered amid an almost prehistoric landscape framed by iridescent water. Yet heat and violent storms, crippling isolation, six hundred or so different poisonous snakes, flying cockroaches, crocodiles, fish with deadly stings, dense growth, and geological formations that defied passage—all of these and more combined to reveal the place's deceptive nature. Thea Astley, the contemporary Australian novelist whose fiction set in this region has gained international attention, captured the area's essence in her essay "Being a Queenslander": "Yes. It's all in the antitheses. The contrasts. The contradictions."

Of the early settlers, not many remained, but those who did developed an enviable strength of character forged from the hardships that so diabolic a paradise served up along with its elusive beauty and wealth. Colebrook celebrates this rare, remote place where she spent her girlhood and pays tribute to her parents, pioneers who stayed to build a home and community on the tablelands above the port town of Cairns. Now in her seventies, having lived in Europe and the United States for the past fifty years, she reinvents the long-ago days in North Queensland and thereby discovers the source of the emotional and intellectual reserves that have served her throughout the years. Astley, when called parochial for writing about North Queensland, replied: " . . . literary truth is derived from the parish, and if it is truth it will be universal." Much the same could be said of Colebrook's memoirs.

Colebrook commands a style as varied as the landscape evoked, as fragile as the faraway events recollected, as vivid as the fleeting emotions conjured up from the past. An analysis of a single sentence will illustrate the richness of her syntax, diction, and metaphorical language: "Then the tablelands would be swathed in a shroud of fine rain, and not until this lifted would the earth be disclosed with its old miracle of emerald grasslands and rich red roads." The land, dead from the long dry spell, seems ready for burial when the wet season arrives, swathing and shrouding it; then the miracle of resurrection occurs once more, its grandeur caught in the word "emerald," its lifeblood suggested by the "rich red roads."

Moreover, each chapter brims with memories of people, places, and events, all lent unity and meaning by titles such as "Thoughtless Heaven," "Over the Bump," and "Doomed to Happiness." The opening chapter, "On the Veranda," establishes both the family history and the landscape in which the family lives. As parents and children, and occasionally visitors, gathered there on hot afternoons during the dry season, they recalled old adventures, retold important events in the family's past, talked about politics, imagined the larger world, or tried to comprehend the dangerously beautiful world they inhabited; sometimes they read, sewed, or slept. During those afternoons, Colebrook suggests, she learned "that life was a kind of courage," so that the security embedded in the veranda and the knowledge gained "on one corner of that continent" permeate the remaining chapters, each one expanding like a tropical flower until the life of an ordinary, yet special, Australian girl opens in full bloom. Her progress toward this state was twofold: first, to know what being an Australian meant and second, to understand what being a woman constituted.

Educated in Church of England schools patterned after those from the "Mother Country," Colebrook wonders in retrospect about the value of such training for children living on the edge of Empire:

> We were slowly being conditioned to separate learning from our Australian life, . . . The school—with its core of Sisters and teachers, its small but well-chosen library, and its distant British goals—reflected one side only of our world.

Not until after World War II, during which England turned her back on the one-time colony and North Queensland in particular, did Australians begin to shed their emotional dependence on the country considered "Home" and in all respects superior. From time to time, during the 1890's for example, nationalism had made some inroads, but never enough. The private search

for her own Australianness that Colebrook carried out during the 1930's—
and records so exactingly—was far ahead of its time; such longings are
more familiar today in the literary, historical, and sociological writing of
Australian writers born after 1945. In this respect, then, *A House of Trees*
stands as a valuable social document about an individual seeking a national
identity when such a pursuit was considered irrelevant.

Traveling fifteen hundred miles southward to Brisbane, Queensland's capital, Colebrook completed high school, then entered the state's university,
where she neglected the prescribed course of study, consisting in large part
of British culture. Instead, she spent time reading Australian writing,
mainly realistic depictions of rigorous and often doomed struggles on the
inhospitable land. She also looked into the convict past, attempting at one
point to penetrate the lives of those forgotten men and women by examining
dusty files once so faithfully kept by the Empire's functionaries, but failing
to discover any humanity in such records. Brisbane itself began as a prison,
but Colebrook found scant reminders of its origins in the sprawling coastal
city; to obliterate a past perceived as disgraceful, even the original name of
the city, Moreton Bay, had been changed. Acutely conscious of what Australian historian Geoffrey Blaney was later to call "the tyranny of distance,"
Colebrook remembers that in those days "History was far away and ineffec-
tual, and separated from us by the glass of distance against which vague
fluttering ideas broke their wings like tired butterflies."

As the girl turned into a woman, she attempted to reconcile her divided
heritage: one part Australian, that told her "everything is beginning; everything is waiting for you"; the other part British, so restricting that she and
her friends scarcely knew who they were, "young women of the British provinces or young women of the great open spaces?" Looking back, Colebrook is thankful that the women of North Queensland's frontier society did
not live in a "prison of femininity"; nevertheless, she was reared in a society
that regarded women primarily as providers of masculine well-being and
pleasure. Escaping from reality through novels that depicted an expanded if
not an altogether truthful world, she harbored mixed expectations from the
male world. Her first romance and sexual experience—with a married
man—she records with candor, just as she does the self-discoveries brought
about by marriage.

By the time Colebrook reached her early twenties, she was moving farther from the veranda, its lessons still looming large, though, as she set out
to become a citizen of the world. She married Mulford Colebrook, an
American Foreign Service officer attached to the United States delegation
in Brisbane, and soon went with him to the United States, then to Europe
to begin life in the diplomatic service. The memoirs conclude with girlhood's end, and the woman Joan Colebrook sailing out of Sydney Harbor to
fulfill some of the half-defined ambitions of a provincial girl whose imagina-

tion overcame "the tyranny of distance."

A personal memoir is most often a record of the writer's search for identity, and that intention this book fulfills splendidly, first from a personal perspective, then from a wider view. Granted, the subject matter is mundane, composed for the most part of events experienced by generation after generation—family outings, classroom experiences, the discovery of a world outside the small one of childhood, the approach of womanhood, a first love, dreams of the future, the excitement great literature generates. What makes the commonplace extraordinary is Colebrook's talent in transforming her microcosmic experiences into universal ones, indeed to derive truth from the parish.

Robert Ross

Sources for Further Study

Chicago Tribune. December 20, 1987, XIV, p. 4.
Commonweal. CXIV, December 4, 1987, p. 707.
Kirkus Reviews. LV, September 15, 1987, p. 1360.
Library Journal. CXII, November 1, 1987, p. 108.
The New York Times Book Review. XCIII, January 17, 1988, p. 9.
Publishers Weekly. CCXXXII, October 23, 1987, p. 42.

HOW I GREW

Author: Mary McCarthy (1912-   )
Publisher: Harcourt Brace Jovanovich (San Diego, California). Illustrated. 278 pp.
$16.95
Type of work: Autobiography
Time: 1925-1933
Locale: The northwestern and northeastern United States

Recollections of adolescence by an important twentieth century novelist and essayist

Principal personages:
MARY MCCARTHY, an American woman of letters
HAROLD PRESTON, her grandfather
AUGUSTA MORGENSTERN PRESTON, her grandmother
ETHEL "TED" ROSENBERG, her closest high school friend
ADELAIDE PRESTON, the principal of the Annie Wright Seminary
HAROLD JOHNSRUD, an actor who was to become McCarthy's first
husband

In this collection of autobiographical sketches, most of which were published as separate pieces in magazines, Mary McCarthy extends the self-examination she began with her popular memoir, *Memories of a Catholic Girlhood* (1957). She assumes that readers of *How I Grew* will be familiar with at least the rough outlines of the childhood described in her earlier work: her pampered early days in Seattle, the death of her parents of influenza when she was six, the years of abuse she and her three brothers suffered at the hands of their guardians (a grandaunt and her husband), and her eventual rescue by her maternal grandparents. In the present volume, she describes the period following her return to Seattle, the years between thirteen and twenty-one, when she developed her identity as a thinking person. Earlier, as a result of the arbitrary, unpredictable behavior of the adults around her, she had made no attempt to "organize those painful experiences"; instead, she had retreated into dreaming. As she grew older, she was to use laughter as a way of dealing with her pain, but this, too, had its cost, as this work and her others show:

Laughter is the great antidote for self-pity, maybe a specific for the malady. Yet probably it does tend to dry one's feelings out a little, as if by exposing them to a vigorous wind. So that something must be subtracted from the compensation I seem to have received for injuries sustained. There is no dampness in my emotions, and some moisture, I think, is needed to produce the deeper, the tragic notes.

The organization of the work is roughly chronological. It begins with a chapter on her childhood reading, then moves on to her year at Garfield, a public high school, and three years at the Annie Wright Seminary, with an interlude recounting her first sexual experience—at fourteen—with a man nine years older than she. The second half of the book treats her years at

Vassar College and her relationship with Harold Johnsrud, the young actor whom she married shortly after her graduation from college. This chronological plan suggests a tighter organization than the book really has. Within each chapter, McCarthy incorporates character sketches of teachers and acquaintances, notes on her reading, brief passages of self-examination, details of social activities and clothes, and comments addressed in nineteenth century fashion to "Reader." At times the organizing principle seems to be free association; McCarthy occasionally has to draw herself forcibly back to the subject with which she began. While this narrative style establishes a casual, conversational relationship with her readers, it contributes to the impression that the book is a collection of fragments rather than a fully conceived autobiography. It is the reader's task, rather than the writer's, to pull together a rounded portrait of the young Mary from the details provided.

Perhaps the strongest impression that emerges is her essential solitude in the midst of a large circle of family members and acquaintances. In writing of her childhood, she makes note of "a crucial problem for my development, the real obstacle to the birth of a mind in my teeming brain—the fact that I had no friends." She was gradually to make friends, but as she describes her life even they seem rather remote. Her grandparents belonged to a different, stricter generation. She recognized and valued their devotion to her, but she could not confide in them and early learned to lie to protect herself from their disapproval of her social activities. Her young Uncle Harold and his friends paid attention to her but were just enough older not to take her seriously. Her intelligence and her early experiences separated her from most of her schoolmates, and certainly the men in her life offered her little beyond sexual exploitation.

Perhaps this detachment from others can be at least partially attributed to the fact that she always felt herself to be an outsider, though she made a place for herself at each of her schools. Her family's social position made her more privileged than most of her Garfield classmates but less so than the elite at Annie Wright; her Jewish and Irish blood, as well as her Western home, separated her from the New York and New England socialites of her Vassar "group." While she expresses regret over her youthful snobbery and anti-Semitism (she repressed her Jewish ties, particularly during the Vassar years), she still, writing in her seventies, devotes a surprising amount of attention to the social status of her acquaintances, suggesting that the issue has never been fully resolved for her.

One way she sought acceptance within the various circles in which she found herself was in relationships, both real and fantasized, with men. First it was twenty-three-year-old Forrest Crosby, who initiated her into sexuality in the back of his roadster in the fall of her sophomore year at Annie Wright. Then she announced to her classmates that she was engaged to a

friend of her Uncle Harold, a young college journalist named Mark Sullivan. Sullivan was fond of her and wrote to her regularly—she speculates
that he enjoyed an audience for his writing and was genuinely interested in
her intellectual development—but he planned to marry someone else. At
sixteen she carried on a clandestine affair with a Seattle artist. She met Harold Johnsrud between her junior and senior years at Annie Wright and considered herself more or less engaged all through her four years at Vassar,
though she dated others from time to time. In all these relationships she
depicts herself as the weaker, exploited partner, though she also describes
later encounters with both Sullivan and Crosby in which she takes considerable satisfaction in rejecting their advances.

Running parallel to this picture of a young woman craving social acceptance is the portrait of one growing intellectually into the future novelist,
essayist, and critic. It is this theme that occasions the musings on her early
reading in the first chapter and the frequent discussions of books and teachers throughout the work. Being "bright" was an essential part of her self-
image from her earliest childhood, and she acknowledges that she must
have used her abilities to win attention and praise even when her parents
were alive. The rationing of reading material by her uncle and aunt was thus
particularly painful, and one of her happiest memories of her move to Seattle was the acquisition of her first library card.

Though her grades were near-failing in her year at Garfield High School,
it was there, she asserts, that she learned what it meant to be an intellectual. She discusses at some length, though not with absolute clarity, her
sense that the American intellectual "is a product of mass culture," not of
an elite education. The latter, she feels, is designed not "to prepare a ruling
class to govern," as is the case in England, but "to represent in its curriculum the purest conspicuous waste." Her year at Garfield put her in touch
with mass culture and allowed her to profit from her boarding school and
college in ways that her more sheltered classmates could not.

Crucial to her identification of herself as an intellectual was her first real
friend, Ethel "Ted" Rosenberg. Ted, she says, "had picked me out as someone worth knowing. . . . Thus at a time when I was close to failing most of
my subjects, my real education was getting under way." Ted introduced her
to modern literature, and Mary quickly developed critical standards by
which she evaluated the works that her friend recommended to her. Ted
also, a year or so later, took Mary to meet Czerna Wilson, the center of
Seattle's bohemian set, a somewhat scandalous figure whose lesbianism and
sophistication fascinated her teenage visitor. When Czerna later mentioned
her acquaintance with Mary to the girl's lawyer uncle, she precipitated a
family row that put Mary—not for the first time—into "a nasty morass of
deception."

From Garfield, Mary went on to the Annie Wright Seminary, where the principal, Adelaide Preston, and a group of capable women teachers recognized and encouraged her abilities. The first to make a strong impression was Dorothy Atkinson, her sophomore English teacher, a Vassar graduate. She encouraged Mary to read and to write, and inspired her to go to her alma mater three years later. She read and praised Mary's first stories, though they did not, according to their author, show any literary promise. She provides a witty, caustic summary of several of these early efforts, which are chiefly about fat, vulgar, middle-aged women who persist in deceiving themselves. McCarthy ponders the significance of these plots, but she cannot call up any experiences to explain her "hatred of self-deception." She was a master at lying to others at that age, but so far as she can recall she was at least honest with herself.

She also pays tribute to her school principal and to her Latin teacher, Ethel Mackay, for pushing her on her way to Vassar. Recognizing with chagrin that she did not often live up to their image of her, she expresses regret that Preston allowed her to receive minor penalties for misdeeds that caused less bright and promising students to be expelled—and that she believed the tales Mary wove for her to explain her less savory activities. Guilt also colors her memories of Mackay, who recommended her to Vassar on the basis of "a strong will and plenty of ambition, and a magnetic and charming personality." After quoting this letter, McCarthy writes:

> Reading that, how can I fail to feel like a worm? Nobel Ethel Mackay! The kindly upright woman was greatly deceived in me. In her worst nightmares that dear Latinist could not have pictured my frequentations: Rex Watson in the woods . . . to say nothing of Forrie Crosby in the Marmon roadster sophomore year, before I even *knew* her, *when I was fourteen*. . . . Nonetheless I wonder. Invincible in her ignorance, she may have known me better than I knew myself. That is, *I* was deceived by the will-less, passive self I seemed to be living with, and Miss Mackay was not.

Teachers were crucial to her intellectual development at Vassar as well as at Annie Wright. She pays special tribute to two of her English professors, Miss Sandison and Miss Kitchel, to whose influence she attributes both an improvement in her literary judgment and greater willingness to stand on her own. Unlike their colleague, Miss Lockwood, who sought converts and disciples—and earned Mary's lasting dislike—these two encouraged independence of thought even as they worried about their students' personal lives. As a Vassar student, Mary increasingly identified herself as a writer, though she also harbored ambitions of an acting career until Johnsrud convinced her of her lack of talent. She wrote for the college literary magazine and participated with fellow students, including poet Elizabeth Bishop, in establishing a rival publication.

Yet her memories of her Vassar years, as related here, are much more social than intellectual. She recounts with pleasure her forays into eastern society, both Protestant and Jewish, and she offers her readers a rather overwhelming array of names to remember—classmates who were the models for characters in her popular novel *The Group* (1963), their friends and family members, the theatrical circle to which Johnsrud belonged, employees at an art gallery where she worked in the summer. McCarthy looks at her young self with a somewhat critical eye. "But what of me, Reader? Did nobody ever worry about the effect on a girl from the Northwest of exposure to the contagious disease of snobbery and the New York Social Register?"

The influence of Johnsrud was obviously a counterweight to the social pulls of Vassar, and he shaped many of her reactions from the beginning of her time there, when he told her she would find the college "brittle, smart, and a little empty." Rereading her letters to her Seattle friend Ted, she detects Johnsrud's influence; the letters are far more judgmental and negative than she remembers feeling at the time. She was, she deduces "trying to speak a language that he would approve of. And the courting of approval, I am sorry to say, *is* in my character."

The figure of Johnsrud dominates the last chapter, which focuses on Mary's senior year at Vassar and the summer preceding it. Their relationship was already a destructive one. She describes the summer month in which they lived together in New York City as "the worst month, I believe, of my life." He tormented her, making her cry daily, and she could never understand why. Though she does not make the connection, the pattern reminds the reader of her childhood with her Uncle Myer, who punished her erratically and irrationally. When Johnsrud went to California in the fall, she thought the relationship was over, but he returned to New York, stopping to visit her grandparents in Seattle, and they were married shortly after her graduation. She ends the book with the acknowledgment that her marriage was a mistake from the beginning, and that she realized it on her wedding night. Johnsrud had killed her feelings for him the previous summer. Most of her readers will recognize this marriage as the basis for that of Kay and Harald Petersen in *The Group*—though McCarthy emerged more or less whole from the experience that destroyed her heroine.

How I Grew offers its readers illuminating glimpses into the life of a relatively privileged young woman of the 1920's, with McCarthy's customary attention to details of daily living that add verisimilitude to her novels. Her brief character sketches of schoolmates, male friends, teachers, and acquaintances are lively and interesting, sometimes funny, often biting. There are short scenes that linger in the memory. One of the most vivid is the account of the evening on which fifteen-year-old Mary, dressed in a lovely new yellow chiffon gown, lurked in Mark Sullivan's backyard with a bottle of iodine, trying to work up her courage to drink it in despair over some now-forgotten pain. She concludes, more than fifty years after the fact, "All of a sudden it strikes me that my main motive for that theatrical suicide was to have an occasion to wear the yellow dress."

In this last comment can be seen that same dryness born of laughing at pain that was referred to earlier. McCarthy displays little compassion for her younger self, though the events of her life evoke considerable sympathy. A significant element of the growth registered here seems to be growth into a kind of stoic detachment from her own feelings—the mindset that characterizes much of her later writing and, in the opinion of some critics and perhaps of McCarthy herself, prevents her from reaching the highest levels of fiction writing.

This book is not likely to win many new readers for McCarthy. It presumes a familiarity with the author's life and work that not everyone will have, it almost overwhelms its readers with loosely connected details, and it never really comes together as a coherent self-portrait. It should, however, have considerable appeal for admirers of her work, both for its full depiction of a past era and for its candid self-revelation.

Elizabeth Johnston Lipscomb

Sources for Further Study

Booklist. LXXXIV, April 1, 1987, p. 949.
Kirkus Reviews. LV, March 1, 1987, p. 355.
Library Journal. CXII, April 15, 1987, p. 85.
The New Republic. CXCVI, May 11, 1987, p. 34.
New York. XX, April 20, 1987, p. 82.
The New York Review of Books. XXXIV, June 11, 1987, p. 19.
The New York Times. CXXXVI, April 13, 1987, p. 19.
The New York Times Book Review. XCII, April 19, 1987, p. 5.
Publishers Weekly. CCXXXI, March 6, 1987, p. 98.
Time. CXXIX, April 27, 1987, p. 82.
West Coast Review of Books. XII, March, 1987, p. 31.

I TELL YOU NOW
Autobiographical Essays by Native American Writers

Editors: Brian Swann (1940-   ) and Arnold Krupat (1941-   )
Publisher: University of Nebraska Press (Lincoln). 283 pp. $21.00
Type of work: Autobiographical essays

An extremely valuable and diverse collection of autobiographical essays, varying in length from five to twenty-four pages

> *Principal personages:*
> MARY TALLMOUNTAIN, a Koyukon Athabascan,
> RALPH SALISBURY, a Cherokee,
> MAURICE KENNY, a Mohawk,
> ELIZABETH COOK-LYNN, a Crow-Creek-Sioux,
> CARTER REVARD, an Osage,
> JIM BARNES, a Choctaw,
> GERALD VIZENOR, a Minnesota Chippewa,
> JACK D. FORBES, a Powhatan-Delaware-Saponi,
> DUANE NIATUM, a Klallam,
> PAULA GUNN ALLEN, a Laguna Pueblo,
> JIMMIE DURHAM, a Wolf Clan Cherokee,
> DIANE GLANCY, a Cherokee,
> SIMON J. ORTIZ, an Acoma Pueblo,
> JOSEPH BRUCHAC, an Abenaki,
> BARNEY BUSH, a Shawnee,
> LINDA HOGAN, a Chickasaw,
> WENDY ROSE, a Hopi-Anglo-Miwok, and
> JOY HARJO, a Creek, the eighteen Native Americans whose essays
> are included in this book

Most Americans probably believe that they know something about Indians, but a serious reading of *I Tell You Now: Autobiographical Essays by Native American Writers* is likely to disprove even this notion. The clichés in our minds about Indians are false or worse than false. Michael Dorris, in his essay "Indians on the Shelf," in *The American Indian and the Problem of History* (1987), has expressed this fact very well:

> For most people, serious learning about Native American culture and history is different from acquiring knowledge in other fields, for it requires an initial, abrupt, and wrenching demythologizing. One does not start from point zero, but from minus ten, and is often required to abandon cherished childhood fantasies of super-heroes and larger-than-life villains.

Dorris observes that for the non-Indian, discarding these clichés is accompanied by pain or a sense of betraying childhood fantasies; consequently, it is not a popular undertaking.

The differences among the eighteen contributors of *I Tell You Now* are extreme: Their origins range from the Eastern seaboard to the Pacific, from Alaska to the Mexican border. Jack D. Forbes includes a poem he wrote about the earth underneath the tarmac of the Dulles Airport in Virginia, once owned by his Powhatan ancestors, yet he grew up in South El Monte, a suburb of Los Angeles. To complicate matters, he is a mixture of many tribes and is also part African. Mary Tallmountain grew up in a bend of the Yukon River, while Simon Ortiz was reared in Acoma Pueblo near the Rio Grande. The ethnic origins of most of the writers are mixed; they are half-breeds. Perhaps this fact is not important, since full-bloodedness does not necessarily ensure full access to native culture: Wendy Rose's father was a full-blooded Hopi, but he was unwilling to share a sense of culture or tribal lineage with her. "His Hopi people . . . trace their lineage through the mother and I could never be more than the daughter of a Hopi man." Rose's essay, entitled "Neon Scars," is superb; it directly confronts the idea that she is "out of balance," even crippled by her difficult life.

If "Neon Scars" is the most extreme statement of the clash inherent in the lives of Native Americans, the other autobiographies describe varying forms of the same conflict. Its existence is inevitable. Elizabeth Cook-Lynn states that she feels a basic timidity and lack of confidence because she cannot "speak for my people." As a poet—especially a poet writing in English— she is only "self-appointed." Who are the real Indian poets?

> The "real" poets of our tribes [are] the men and women who sit at the drum and sing the old songs and create new ones. . . . Thus, when I hear the poetry of the Crown Butte Singers, the Porcupine Travelers, and the Wahpekute Singers, I have every confidence that they speak in our own language for the tribes, Oyate.

Many of the writers in *I Tell You Now* feel a sense of betrayal when committing words to paper. Simon J. Ortiz seems to believe that there is no basic conflict between oral traditions and writing, and that they naturally flow into one another; others such as Ralph Salisbury are less optimistic, and believe that Indian writers can only express a conquered people's awareness. Jimmie Durham states unequivocally that writing is always for whites: "Who reads all these things? The white folks. If we read—now here is a subtle point—if we read, we read like the white folks."

Reading and what one reads go hand in hand; reading interacts with culture. Durham has harsh words for those whom he calls the "intelligentsia." His statement clearly reflects a post-1960's mentality: "Our intelligentsia, the writers and artists, are such a bunch of stuck-up, apolitical, money-grubbing, and flaky ripoff artists, and our political leaders are usually crooks and pretentious bastards or . . . somebody's puppets." The content of language stretches far beyond what is written, extending to the electronic media. Barney Bush laments that "so many of our kin are marrying people attached to soap-opera mentality."

One of the most sophisticated descriptions of this clash at the very center of writing, and the act of communication, is given by Gerald Vizenor. For him, the mixedblood is condemned to the constant "mixing" or simultaneous use of the first- and third-person pronouns. He writes:

> The first and third person personas are me. Gerald Vizenor believes that autobiographies are imaginative histories; a remembrance past the barriers; wild pastimes over the pronouns.
> Outside the benchmarks the ones to be in written memoirs are neither sentimental nor ideological; mixedbloods loosen the seams in the shrouds of identities.

Vizenor's conclusion is that "Indianness" is ultimately artificial. Jimmie Durham also addresses the problem of pronouns, relating them to other concepts of possession, attitudes toward land ownership, and legal treaties. He notes: "In our own language the possessive pronouns can only be used for things that you can physically give to another person, such as, 'my woodcarving,' 'my basket.'"

Related to the problem of language and pronouns is that of genre. Poetry, writes Elizabeth Cook-Lynn, a Crow-Creek-Sioux poet, is not really an Indian genre: "Poets have a tendency to think too much of themselves. It is quite possible that we poets think we are more significant, more important than we are; that the events we choose to signal as important for one reason or another are, after all, something else; that the statements and interpretations we have given to these events are mistaken and/or irrelevant." One contributor made a similar observation about the genre of autobiography and how it encourages self-absorption: "You should realize that focusing so intently on oneself like that and blithering on about your own life and thoughts is very bad form for Indians. . . . I grew up and continue to live among people who penalize you for talking about yourself and going on endlessly about your struggles."

The editors, Brian Swann and Arnold Krupat, provide a historical sketch of Indian autobiography in the introduction to the volume; Krupat has written a book on the topic, *For Those Who Came After: A Study of Native American Autobiography* (1985). Autobiography is clearly a highly mixed genre, if it is a legitimate one at all. In *I Tell You Now* Jim Barnes claims, "The greatest autobiography is lie." No Native genre corresponds to autobiography, and the earliest examples were written by Christianized Indians, squarely in the European tradition of apologetic or conversion literature. The editors' belief that the 1834 *Life of Ma-ka-tai-me-she-kia-kiak, or Black Hawk* is an example of autobiography raises more questions than it answers, for Black Hawk knew little English and could not write. A genre must have a tradition, and if there is an Indian "tradition" of autobiography, it is largely a creation of the two editors of this volume.

This statement, however, is not intended to downgrade the genre or the essays included in *I Tell You Now*. It is time that white Americans become aware of the deep clash of cultures in the lives of Native Americans today. The clash at the heart of Swann and Krupat's concept of Indian autobiography lies at the heart of all Native American culture. Disharmony, bitterness, self-hatred—what Wendy Rose calls "lack of balance"—is the dominant impression produced by these autobiographical essays. The volume is suffused with rancor, anger, and open wounds, although some express the feelings more openly than others. Rose, Jimmie Durham, and Barney Bush are perhaps the most troubled and angry. Others such as Carter Revard and Paula Gunn Allen straddle two different worlds with greater ease. Revard and Allen both have an attractive sense of humor. Revard sets up his typewriter in his garage and establishes a pleasant rhythm as he writes. He can start a paragraph: "Let's see then. Earliest memories of small frame houses around the ragged edges of the Pawhuska, of mules and uncles and homebrew and whiskey." Allen writes in a semi-pop style: evoking the cafés and restaurants along old Route 66: "It's of course closed now. Has been most of the time since they retired a passel of years ago. . . ." The book's dominant tone, however, is that of bitter clashes.

The eighteen essays in *I Tell You Now* are varied, but other common features are apparent. As literature, it is above all a literature of suffering. Wendy Rose's "Neon Scars" is the prime example, but most of the other essays are also about dissolution, defeat, and open wounds. Clearly, the 1960's have come and gone, and with them has gone much of the swagger that one associates with Vine Deloria in *We Talk, You Listen: New Tribes, New Turf* (1970). As literature of defeat, it is intensely moving and human. It also provides a much-needed foil to contemporary American literature with its brash commercial hype.

The white American reader might be surprised at how many of these writers are not only half-breeds but also have only a small portion of Indian blood. Clearly, Indianness is a state of mind, combined with experience and culture. Ethnicity is not a simple matter and never is purely biological. In the United States, the 1960's had a crucial importance. Poets such as William Jay Smith or William Stafford could have become "Indian poets" because of their Native American blood but chose not to do so. Paula Gunn Allen, however, who comes from a very mixed ethnic background (she is Lebanese-German-Mexican-Indian), has a largely Indian consciousness; Diane Glancy, who is only one-eighth Cherokee, believes that "even that small part has leavened the whole lump." Duane Niatum made a very deliberate gesture in abandoning his former last name, Maginnis, and legally adopting the new Indian name of Niatum.

It is surprising, perhaps, that so many of these writers think of "white culture" in the United States as unified and monolithic. This idea will be news to those individual Americans attempting to maintain, against difficult odds, a knowledge of a European culture and language in the United States, often at the family level. Whether Swedish, Polish, Estonian, Greek, or Jewish, in the eyes of Native Americans, they are all "white." Is it a mistake to underrate the variety among these cultural and ethnic groups? Although the differences are of great importance, two sober realities buttress the Native American point of view. First, these European groups tend to abandon their original cultures and languages relatively quickly, often in a generation or two; some groups assimilate more and some less rapidly, but the final ethnic identity is often based on quite superficial features. Second, skin color turns out to be of huge importance. Most of the eighteen authors in *I Tell You Now* attest to the importance of lightness or darkness of skin; nearly every half-breed learned at a relatively early point in his life in what situations, and in which milieus, he could pass for a white.

The Native cultures have great value in themselves. Everything that can be saved and preserved is priceless. They also hold a mirror up to the dominant white American culture, one that is of great objective value. In what precise sense is it meaningful or significant to say that Columbus "discovered" America? Do white Americans have any real sanction for the preservation of the landscape? Barney Bush refers to "the atrocities that their own system secretly perpetuates"; are these atrocities actual, and why is there such difficulty in addressing them in past history? To what extent has the English language become distorted into a commercial tool? All of the contributors of *I Tell You Now* grapple with these problems, and American culture is the richer for it.

John Carpenter

Sources for Further Study

The Bloomsbury Review. November-December, 1987, p. 28.
Booklist. LXXXIV, January 1, 1988, p. 746.
Los Angeles Times Book Review. September 13, 1987, p. 8.
The Washington Post Book World. February 7, 1988, p. 9.

IN THE CITY

Author: Joan Silber (1945-)
Publisher: Viking (New York). 246 pp. $16.95
Type of work: Novel
Time: 1924-1927
Locale: Newark, New Jersey, and New York City

A novel about a young woman as she comes to maturity in the social world of New York in the 1920's

> *Principal characters:*
> PAULINE SAMUELS, the protagonist, a seventeen-year-old girl from Newark
> DEWEY FRANKLIN, her first lover, a would-be writer
> NITA, her friend, a violin player at a restaurant
> ROSE, a friend of Nita and Pauline
> MACK, her second lover, a reclusive scholar
> WALTER MICKELING, her friend, a well-known painter

Following the success of her first novel, *Household Words* (1980), which received critical praise for its delicate observation of everyday events and relationships (it also won the Ernest Hemingway Award), Joan Silber's *In the City* continues in the same vein. It is a coming-of-age novel about a young woman's first taste of independence and the adult world—in this case the artistic and literary set of 1920's Manhattan. Silber has commented on her novel: "I identified with that sense of starting out at a certain age— thinking you know what's going on and slowly realizing you don't." With an accurate and subtle skill, Silber captures the sensibilities of her young protagonist, who is at once self-assured and highly vulnerable.

Anticipating her high school graduation six months hence, seventeen-year-old Pauline Samuels is the daughter of first-generation Russian-Jewish immigrants. Her parents own a haberdashery in Newark, but Pauline does not get on with her taciturn father, and the narrow horizons of her mother are too limited to be of any help to her. Sufficiently intelligent and educated to choose to read Charles Baudelaire in French, Pauline wins the school prize for her essay on Lord Byron. She has earnest philosophical conversations with her chum Bunny, and she also has a high school sweetheart, with whom she is just beginning to explore her sexuality.

Sex for her is an infinitely enticing world of pure sensations which, she assumes, somehow contain the ultimate human experience. The innocent expectancy of youthful sexual awareness pervades the early part of the novel, and her three major sexual encounters reveal and reflect her growing maturity. First, while running an errand for her father in New York, she is partially seduced by a casual acquaintance who promises her work as a designer's model. Never suspecting that his story is untrue, she responds to him at first because she does not want to be thought timid, even though she does not like him or find him attractive. It is an awakening of a kind; it constitutes the first mark of her separation from the world of innocent youth and from her parents. The experience leads her, for example, to think that she now understands the world ("This went on all the time; the world was full of this") in ways that her parents do not. She tends always to think of herself as advanced and initiated.

When she leaves school, she becomes a file clerk for a ribbon manufacturer in New York and rents a bare, mildewed room in Manhattan. The work is unchallenging, and her social life is at first meager, amounting to cheap meals with her cousin Beatrice. She spends many evenings in her room or at the movies alone. Life warms up for her when she and Beatrice go to Vera's, a restaurant frequented by Bohemians, where she gets her first exposure to smart, artistic company. Pauline can well hold her own in the self-consciously clever and witty conversations in which she now finds herself taking part. Irony and a brand of playful sarcasm come naturally to her—just the sort of thing to make her accepted in her rather shallow new company. She develops a close friendship with Nita, an outspoken and self-confident young blonde who plays the violin in an all-women's orchestra, and with Walter Mickeling, an eccentric painter who hums arias to himself when drunk and professes to have a low opinion of women.

It is through this set that she meets her first lover, Dewey Franklin. Dewey works as a court reporter but also calls himself a writer. Pauline allows herself gradually to be drawn into a close relationship with him, even though she does not particularly like him: She is pleased to be getting involved with someone, and a little proud of how inexplicable their partnership appears to others. Eventually, she moves into his apartment. She does not, however, have the experience with which to evaluate the dangers of taking such a step. Her intellectual maturity is far ahead of her emotional maturity, and she fails to take notice of some early warning signs, such as Dewey's selfishness and his childish tantrums.

After a period of tranquillity, the relationship rapidly deteriorates. Dewey fails to finish any of his writing projects (Pauline never sees anything he has written, and she is rather glad of it). He spends an increasing amount of time loafing around the house, complaining about his friends, and behaving boorishly toward her. Events come to a head when he swindles a friend over the funding of a literary magazine. Pauline is goaded into standing up to him but gets a beating as a result.

After this she leaves him and soon takes up with Mack, a reclusive scholar who translates Epictetus from the Latin. He is sixteen years her senior. This time Pauline enters into the sexual relationship as an equal partner, no longer the young innocent. She is completely sure of herself. Although the relationship soon founders, there is a change in Pauline. After her experience with Dewey, she is more assertive, less willing to allow a bad situation to continue unchecked.

A few more events round out the story. There is a minor fire at Vera's while Pauline and her friends are there. One of the waiters, a former boxer called Adolfo, dies after being overcome by smoke when he returns to the restaurant to retrieve his shoes. Pauline attends the funeral with Nita. Then Pauline meets her old friend Bunny, a reunion which provides an opportunity for them to recall the people and events of three years ago. In this way Pauline gains a sense of perspective on her current situation. Finally, her friend Rose falls sick with influenza, and Pauline and Nita nurse her through it.

What is noticeable about *In the City*—and at the heart of Silber's technique—is that her heroine undergoes no great awakenings and no great disillusionments. It is the steady accumulation of small events, the relentless succession of the ordinary, not the infrequent eruption of the extraordinary, that shapes the course of her life. She discovers that as she makes certain choices (often without realizing that she is making them, or even that there is a decision to make), she is molding her own life—that every thought and act has its consequences, although these may not be immediately discernible. This attentiveness to the cumulative effect of the apparently insignificant means that, as in Silber's earlier novel, *Household Words*, there is no melodrama in her work. Nor is there any moralizing. The story is told, nothing is left out, yet no event is made to bear an importance that it does not merit. There is no climax, no grand conclusion.

Inasmuch as the novel can be said to have a guiding theme, it is perhaps Pauline's desire to extract from the apparently random jumble of events a sense of design, order, and progression in her life (even though the experiences she undergoes do not appear to reveal such a thing). She assumes that "even mistakes and failed experiments accrued toward a purpose, an eventual composite that was not random, and that everything had its later use." She is horrified by the apparent discontinuity in Dewey's life—the succession of dissimilar jobs and experiences. At Adolfo's funeral, she reflects that his life had been "unformed"; there had been no pattern to it. The events which he had undergone were now the sum total of his life, and there would be nothing more. No final, satisfying shape would emerge.

Linked to Pauline's desire for order and pattern is her desire for stasis, a kind of mental stillness. This was why, for example, she was attracted at first to the discipline of Latin—its calm logic appealed to her, even at the age of thirteen. The need for stillness is also one of the reasons she is attracted to the unworldly, reclusive Mack.

These two deeper instincts—the desire for order and the desire for stillness—lie just below the surface of her mind even when she is caught up in the social whirl she enjoys so much. Both imply a need and a facility for detachment, and indeed it is Pauline's moments of self-awareness, reflection, and observation that give the novel, which is told almost entirely from her point of view, much of its interest. She has a marked ability to stand back from the immediate pressure of her experience and observe the course of events, an ability that gives her a certain wisdom and maturity. Even in the midst of her ill-considered partnership with Dewey, for example, she realizes that she is only "living out the duration of a certain sequence... and that the conclusion could come of itself, as the term expired." It is also no coincidence that when she thinks about the happenings of her life, she feels as if she has been merely a reporter covering colorful events. The novel ends with her standing still, quietly observing her two friends.

She also has the ability to contemplate subtly the hidden or problematic aspects of her feelings, as when, for example, she reflects on the kind of men to whom she is attracted. "She didn't associate sexual attractiveness with direct discourse—she wanted obliqueness, fleeting impressions, hints at hidden mutualities." On another occasion, she thinks to herself that somehow she knows more than Mack, in spite of the fact that he is so much her senior. "She leaned very heavily on this idea of *knowing*—but what was it? it was so airy and inexact an accomplishment, and perhaps not even directly useful."

Intellectual speculation fascinates her. A painter's remarks about color set her thinking of the possibility "that there was some latent meaning overflowing even from the colors of things, and she had only to sharpen her own understanding to catch it." Later, as she strolls through the dockyards absorbing the colors of the landscape, she wonders about the heightened perception of painters, and "whether the pleasure they got from this was purely abstract, whether it carried with it an apprehension of natural law that was useful in ordinary life."

In the City is a refreshing novel in that it does not dwell overmuch on the negative aspects of a young person's growth into adulthood. Pauline, unlike the protagonists of many stories of initiation, does not have to endure a shattering experience which threatens her sanity or overwhelms her personality. She is not forced to discover or confront evil, and she never comes to regard the world as a dangerous and depressing place where dreams cannot be realized. Pauline is no helpless Jean Rhys heroine, exploited and dependent; her world is a quietly optimistic one. Perhaps as a consequence of this muted tone, the novel on the whole lacks intensity. When, for example, Pauline expresses horror at the "agonizing" or "excruciating disasters of her life" it is hard to believe her. The coolness of her detachment has made too strong an impression.

Bryan Aubrey

Sources for Further Study

The Christian Science Monitor. April 10, 1987, p. 24.
Kirkus Reviews. LIV, December 15, 1986, p. 1825.
Library Journal. CXII, February 1, 1987, p. 94.
Ms. XV, May, 1987, p. 17.
The New York Times Book Review. XCII, March 29, 1987, p. 8.
Publishers Weekly. CCXXXI, January 23, 1987, p. 63.
The Village Voice. XXXII, June 23, 1987, p. 56.

IN THE COUNTRY OF LAST THINGS

Author: Paul Auster (1947-   )
Publisher: Viking (New York). 188 pp. $15.95
Type of work: Novel
Time: An unspecified time in the twentieth century, possibly the future
Locale: An unnamed city that is falling apart

Paul Auster's In the Country of Last Things *is a vivid and allegorical portrayal of collapse on societal, individual, and artistic levels*

> *Principal characters:*
> ANNA BLUME, the narrator, a young girl in search of her missing brother
> ISABEL, a woman who befriends Anna and takes her into her home
> FERDINAND, Isabel's husband
> SAMUEL "SAM" FARR, a journalist with whom Anna falls in love
> VICTORIA WOBURN, a woman who runs a rescue mission and has a brief affair with Anna
> BORIS STEPANOVICH, a supplier for the rescue mission

How does the world end? According to Paul Auster's vision, it does so slowly, in a nightmare of dissolution and decay. In the nameless city that is the setting for *In the Country of Last Things*, a building that stands one day is gone the next, whole streets mysteriously disappear, thousands sleep in the gutters, prey to inclement weather and the vicious toll gatherers who charge for the privilege of crossing the rubble. Food is scarce, and some people are so thin that three or four will chain themselves together so as not to be blown away. Long lines may gather for merely the rumor of food or a newspaper to keep one warm. Even the weather is erratic and uncertain, sunny and hot one day and snowing the next, then fog, then several days of rain. The only sure thing is death, whose stench fills the streets.

Into this slowly disintegrating city comes Anna Blume, a young girl in search of her brother William, a journalist who has disappeared. The novel is her letter back home to an unnamed friend. She describes her education in the art of survival, how she avoids the dangers of the toll gatherers or the trickery of vendors who sell painted cardboard for food. She marvels how in such an environment one's humanity—feelings of compassion and grief—does not disappear altogether; but one must make compromises. How else, she asks, do you cope "when you find yourself looking at a dead child, at a little girl lying in the street without any clothes on, her head crushed and covered with blood?" She becomes an "object hunter," making a mean living by searching for usable objects to sell. In a society where nothing new is manufactured, things already made, the "last things," are the only commodity, even if they are only pieces of string or the peel of an orange. There is an undue reverence for the past and a prevalent sense that no matter how bad it was yesterday, it was surely better then than it is going to be today.

This bleak vision is what one might expect from an end-of-the-world novel, but there are some startling omissions. The narration, though vivid in description, is very abstract. Anna says little about what has caused this world to slowly self-destruct (there is simply a brief reference to "the Troubles"). Neither does she spend much time grieving over the irrevocable loss of life as we know it, nor offer a moral warning on how it could have been avoided—something that a reader will usually find in a book with an apocalyptic vision. This is because, for Anna, there is the persistent hope that she can eventually return to a world that still runs smoothly, one where the familiar laws of nature and economics still operate—the "home" to which she is writing. Like Dorothy in Oz or Alice in Wonderland, she is a temporary visitor to the country of last things, a world not meant to be fixed to a particular time or place—even to something so vague as an apocalyptic future. As strange as this world is, there is a nagging familiarity to it, suggesting that Auster is up to more than simply an end-of-the-world novel. Part of the richness of this excellent book is that it can be read as an allegorical commentary on numerous levels.

The plight of the homeless, gang violence, governments as repressive regimes and purveyors of misinformation, large-scale starvation—these are not simply outlandish visions of the future, but present-day realities. It is as though Anna, like Alice, has gone through the looking glass and seen not the future but the twentieth century itself in a heightened way. The strategies for personal survival that Anna sees around her become ironic commentaries on contemporary society. There is the imaginative suicide of the Runners, who submit to a rigorous discipline of physical training so that on the appointed day they may run in packs at full tilt toward their death. Others, with money, join Euthanasia Clinics, where after a few days or weeks of drug-induced euphoria they can pass out of the world with memories of bliss. There are the starving, who pack their clothes with newspaper to give themselves the appearance of being well fed so that no one will know their shame. There are the Smilers, who believe that everything, from the economy to the weather, would get better if people simply held positive thoughts. The message here is not the nobility and indomitability of the human spirit surviving under difficult conditions; rather, it is a picture of human powerlessness converted into strategies of denial or self-preserving ways out. At one point, Anna must escape from a human slaughterhouse. Again, this is not an outlandish vision of the future; in Nazi Germany human slaughterhouses were a reality. Here Auster is suggesting by what mechanisms the human race allowed it, through its own violence, its own pointless nostalgia, and its own head-in-the-sand unconcern. If there is an end to the world, he is saying, this may be how it comes about.

Yet Auster's vision of humanity is not strictly one-sided. Positive human qualities such as love and compassion play an important role in the novel. One day Anna saves the life of a complete stranger. She jumps without thinking to the rescue of another object hunter who is about to be run down. Anna moves in with this frail woman named Isabel, and her husband Ferdinand, a former sign painter who makes tiny ships inside miniature bottles and has not left their small apartment in years. Anna undergoes a self-acknowledged change in character, and, for the first time in her life, she commits herself to the care and safety of someone besides herself; she becomes the sole provider for this aging, weakened couple until, several months later, they die. Later, escaping from police after a food riot, Anna meets Samuel Farr, the journalist who had been sent as her brother's replacement. They commit to living together for practical reasons and then discover a profound love for each other. She helps him to work on the book he is writing, and she becomes pregnant (something unheard of in this city where nothing new is made), although she loses the baby when she makes a diving escape out a window at the slaughterhouse to which she had been lured. She becomes separated from Sam but is nursed back to health through the loving attentions of Victoria Woburn and the staff at Woburn House, a rescue mission offering medical care and shelter to the needy. While working there, Anna is reunited with Sam, who comes to the House looking for shelter. Though Woburn House must close down for lack of funds, Anna, Sam, Victoria, and Boris Stepanovich (the flamboyant trader who has kept the House going for as long as it has), make plans to escape the city.

In counterpoint to the self-centered and exploitative strategies of survival in the book, the plot reveals a persistent expression of community, of love and tenderness, of the recognition of man's essential interdependence. Simply put, to be human means to have the potential for both good and bad. What Auster shows is that hard times can be the litmus test that reveals which way a character will go.

On another level, the country of last things represents not so much a societal collapse as an individual one. The city can be read as a metaphor for an inner state of decline, the moment when one has lost the ability to build or believe in the future and is imprisoned in despair. The illogic of the weather, sunny one day and snowing the next, strangely altered "because of what happens below" it, confirms the subjective power of the inner world to change the things it sees. Indeed, there is much in the city of last things that suggests the dream world. It operates as a huge repository of memory and the past, using and reusing some objects with obsessive reverence, and losing (repressing) others when whole sections of the city mysteriously disappear or become cut off. The nonrational reigns over the rational, for each significant turn of plot can be attributed to chance, and every time something is supposed to happen, it does not. The rise and fall of various repressive and ultimately out-of-touch governments describe the mind's unsuccessful attempts to take charge of the situation and turn it around. Anna's letter to the friend back home, because "you know nothing," may be likened to the messages about itself sent to the unknowing conscious from the subconscious dream world. The pervasive images of starvation and death reflect a being in crisis.

More specifically, the crisis is a creative one. Anna has gone to this city to bring back a writer who has disappeared without sending back a single story. Isabel loses the power of speech before she dies, and the notebook Anna buys so that Isabel can communicate remains mostly blank pages. The book Sam is working on burns in a spectacular fire in the National Library before it can be completed. Art is dead in the city; nothing new is being created. The only music in the book comes from the sound of shopping carts hitting the chains that link them to their owners; books are not read but burned for their warmth. Survival supersedes art, but without art survival is just a slower form of death.

The novel itself, Anna's letter back home, represents the one successful creation in the book; it is the consummation of her brother's original purpose, to write about the country of last things. So on yet another level, the novel is about the passage from creative block to creative completion, the shaky interim between the "last thing" one has done and the next thing one will do. Male and female polarities represent significant ingredients of the creative process, both the logical and the intuitive sides of self. William, the logical, fact-seeking journalist, can write nothing on his own, and inspiration, his intuitive sister, goes in search of him. Anna first finds shelter in another pairing of male and female energies, Isabel and Ferdinand; so might the writer who cannot write read another author's work for inspiration. Yet there is no creative potential in this merging. Isabel loses the ability to speak; Ferdinand makes an unsuccessful attempt to rape Anna. The death of the pair is necessary; one cannot write from influence alone. Anna keeps Isabel's notebook and later will write her story within it. She meets Sam, who, like William, is a journalist; he is William's replacement, both literally and figuratively. Eventually this pairing makes it possible for Anna to write, but first there are false starts and misdirection, their lost baby and the burned book, and a separation that makes possible Anna's meeting with Victoria and Boris, the one a healer and the other a teller of tales, who complete her creative initiation.

She writes her book at Woburn House while they wait to make their escape to the next country. The last sentence of the book promises that when they arrive, Anna will write again, signaling that this creative process will begin anew. "The end is only imaginary," she writes, "a destination you invent to keep yourself going, but a point comes when you realize you will never get there." The life of the survivor and the life of the artist go on, even in an end-of-the-world novel.

Dana Gerhardt

Sources for Further Study

Boston Review. XII, April, 1987, p. 26.
Choice. XXV, September, 1987, p. 116.
Kirkus Reviews. LIV, December 5, 1986, p. 1812.
Library Journal. CXII, January, 1987, p. 104.
Los Angeles Times. June 18, 1987, Part V, p. 10.
The New York Times Book Review. XCII, May 17, 1987, p. 11.
Publishers Weekly. CCXXXI, February 6, 1987, p. 87.
The Village Voice. XXXII, June 30, 1987, p. 57.
The Washington Post Book World. XVII, March 29, 1987, p. 11.

IN THE SKIN OF A LION

Author: Michael Ondaatje (1943-   )
Publisher: Alfred A. Knopf (New York). 244 pp. $16.95
Type of work: Novel
Time: Early 1900's through 1938
Locale: The Canadian backwoods and the city of Toronto

The adventures of Patrick Lewis, from his youth in the Canadian wilderness at the turn of the twentieth century through his release from prison just before the start of World War II

Principal characters:
> PATRICK LEWIS, the passionate, poetic, and introspective son of a taciturn explosives expert
> ALICE GULL, his lover and closest friend, a former nun and skilled actress who is deeply committed to political principles
> CLARA DICKENS, his lover, a radio actress and Gull's spiritual sister, also the mistress of Ambrose Small
> AMBROSE SMALL, a bare-knuckled jackal of cutthroat capitalism
> NICHOLAS TEMELCOFF, an immigrant to Canada from Macedonia, master of midair construction work, baker, and mensch
> DAVID CARAVAGGIO, a dashing professional thief and political activist
> ROLAND HARRIS, the Commissioner of Public Works for Toronto

When an accomplished poet turns to prose fiction, there is always a danger that the intense concentration on the particulars of language necessary in poetry will divert the author's attention from the development of character and structure that a novel traditionally requires. If, however, the author is able to use poetic power to reveal character with compression and precision, to evoke mood with imaginative psychological insight, and to write scenes of action that blaze with intensity, the poetic aspect of the prose can become a source of strength rather than a distraction or diminution. For Michael Ondaatje, a Sri Lankan-born Canadian citizen, the poetic skills demonstrated in seven books, including the highly original *The Collected Works of Billy the Kid* (1970), are at the heart of a novel that projects a dynastic sweep of an important segment of Canadian history without any of the bloated, verbose, and formulaic writing common to inferior attempts to achieve historical significance.

In a sense, Ondaatje has rethought the entire concept of the historical novel. To begin, he discards the "Great Man" theory of history, substituting instead historical unknowns whose individual character has the true stuff of human greatness, although of a variety rarely recorded in official histories. Second, instead of beginning with a panoramic sweep of major historical forces viewed from the outside and from a distance of several decades in the future, he works from a series of tiny, apparently unnoticed incidents crucial to his characters: the basic building blocks of a huge cultural movement.

Then, by juxtaposing these short and apparently unrelated scenes, he holds many points of interest in a kind of narrative suspension which eventually coalesces into a whole of considerable dimensions when connections are established. In a philosophical aside typical of his authorial voice when he steps away from the action, he explains this strategy: "The first sentence of every novel should be: 'Trust me, this will take time, there is an order here, very faint, very human.'"

The trust he calls for has been earned by the seriousness of his tone and the authenticity of experience, and it is justified by the poetic intensity that grows through the restraint of immediate explanation, an intensity that creates a texture so tightly woven that a novel of 250 pages seems to have the depth of a thousand-page table crusher. The documentary realism that tends to overwhelm and then bore the reader in many long historical novels has been replaced by lyric invention, substituting piercing insight and acute observation of the critical detail for masses of factual matter. Paralleling the methods of modern film editing, which enable the audience to jump from scene to scene without sketching specific alignments, Ondaatje keeps exposition to a minimum and highlights those pieces of information he does provide. The occasional presentation of abundant technical material commands attention because of its rarity as well as by the clarity of its delivery.

Drawing on his own perspective as a double expatriate, Ondaatje, who moved to England from Sri Lanka (then Ceylon) at eleven to go to school and later to Canada to teach and write, has chosen the form of the historical novel to work toward his own version of Canadian history in the first half of the twentieth century. "Toronto is a city of immigrants but there is very little official history about who they were, what their lives were like," he comments. *In the Skin of a Lion* is designed to present a true picture of one of the essential aspects of Canadian cultural experience: the blending of diverse elements and forces into a dynamic, productive cultural matrix.

Not surprisingly, the position from which he begins is that of an outsider, but Patrick Lewis ("that's a brick of a name") is not a late arrival to Canada but a stranger in a vast land, disconnected from roots or current social relationships. His family has lived for generations in the rural wilderness, unconscious of their own history, attuned to the rhythms of the natural world but uncertain in any social situation, unschooled in standard methods of success, indifferent to politics, and intent on mere personal survival. Lewis represents something of the hidden spirit of the land, vaguely British in origin but acultural, his responses to phenomena marked by unpolished enthusiasm, his instincts sound and his inclinations humane.

After his father is killed in a blasting accident in spite of his exceptional skill with explosives, Lewis is "blown" out of his rut and into Toronto, where he is an immigrant in the city. As he quickly discovers, the qualities of mind and character he possesses do not suit him for anything particularly lucrative, and he becomes a "searcher" (an indication of his real nature), paid four dollars per week to look for the legendary millionaire Ambrose Small (a Howard Hughes figure, but more vicious than Hughes), who has vanished.

While Lewis remains the protagonist of the novel, the pattern of his life through four decades becoming the controlling thread of the narrative, other characters are interwoven as Ondaatje, speaking again as authorial consciousness, talks of "bringing together various corners of the story." Each of these other characters is an important element in Lewis' life, as well as a distinct person alive in the crux of their combined destiny. Like Lewis, they are part of a culturally diverse and rich mixture of people drawn to the New World so they would not have to "bow to priests and dignitaries." Yet they are still exploited by the old establishment, the British hierarchy that rules as the legacy of the colonial empire.

It is an important aspect of Ondaatje's plan to contrast the vibrancy and ardor of these people with their undervaluing and dismissal by official cultural histories. Nicholas Temelcoff, whose story is presented so vividly in the early stages of the novel that he threatens to usurp Lewis' central position, is a twenty-five-year-old refugee from the war in the Balkans. Arriving in Canada with no profession and no knowledge of English, he literally transforms himself into a symbol of power. His life is a positive paradigm for the immigrant experience: He learns English from the stage, earns enough money to open a bakery by his extraordinary ability to work in midair on a bridge project, and becomes a rock in the Greek community because of his warmth and quiet confidence.

David Caravaggio, for a short time also a bridge worker, eventually apprentices in a demanding, highly skilled profession open to immigrants, that of cracksman or thief. He has the special charm of a man who moves in an aura of menace but does not frighten because he is neither evil nor brutal. Although he works outside the official "law," he is respected in the ethnic community in which he lives with his family because his field of operation is the realm of the rich. He is seen as a version of justice as vengeance, balancing accounts and, like Temelcoff, involved in insurrectionist political action. Ondaatje captures the special qualities of each man through scenes of the two men at work—Temelcoff a wonder of spatial awareness, Caravaggio a creature of super-sensory development.

Similarly, in portraying the two women to whom Lewis is close, Ondaatje presents passionate experience as the culmination of human relationships. The intimate moments that Lewis shares with Clara Dickens and especially with Alice Gull are presented as expressions of lyric delight, Ondaatje operating in his métier as romantic poet but slightly modifying the mood with touches of humor—slightly ironic, slightly surreal. "Seduction was the natural progression of curiosity," he observes, and as Lewis and Alice Gull's relationship progresses from erotic obsession to the ripe love of mutual discovery, the entire cosmos seems to expand with possibility.

It is Alice Gull who introduces Lewis to a sense of himself as a political person, thus channeling his energy and decency toward a specific cause that gives him the direction to grow into maturity. "I don't believe the language of politics," Lewis says, "but I'll protect the friends I have." With Alice Gull's guidance, Lewis discovers that political action does not have to depend on familiar forms of political language and that friends can provide a community that increases the value of all experience. It is "no longer a single story . . . but a falling together of accomplices," Ondaatje says to describe the coordination of singular impulses, and it is this process that draws Lewis out of the "gap of love" that had previously existed for his family.

Each of these characters is "sewn into history" in the rather complicated but ultimately clear structure of Ondaatje's narrative. The separate units seem at first to be discrete entities of experience, but eventually the linear tracks begin to overlap and interweave. To fix a particular section amid complex coordinates, Ondaatje highlights that section with a set piece of unusual graphic power. In these brilliant descriptive passages, Ondaatje's poetic power is most evident. As the novel begins, introducing Lewis when he is about eleven years old, a scene in which Lewis and his father rescue a cow from a frozen lake exemplifies the experience of cold, animals, and landscape that defines boyhood for many rural Canadians. When Temelcoff uses his uncanny agility to gather out of the air literally a nun who has fallen off the edge of the bridge he is building, the scene captures the grandeur of human will compressed into a task that defies the limits of natural law. When Alice Gull performs as a mime in a puppet theater, her effect on Lewis and others recalls the ancient, mysterious power of art to inspire and elevate an audience to ecstasy. When Caravaggio moves through a house he is ransacking like an explorer in a strange landscape, so attuned to every stimuli that he is more at home than the sensation-stupified inhabitants of the house, his pattern of observation contains an implicit commentary on Ondaatje's own visionary style.

These heightened moments, while introducing and delineating character, are also preparation for the novel's dramatic climax. The special skills on display—inherent in these people, then cultivated through their labor—are harnessed for the purpose of dynamiting the heavily guarded water tunnel under Lake Ontario, a symbol of civic repression in a society that does not respect the work of its citizens. Constructed so that the suspense is pulse stirring, the plan does not exactly work out to the complete satisfaction of the participants, but Ondaatje's substitution of a situation that widens the moral issue for a conclusion that overwhelms everything with spectacular violence is an interesting choice. When Lewis and Roland Harris, the master builder of the Toronto Public Works Commission, meet in a confrontation between the champions of the underclass and the ruling class, there is at least a glimpse of a common position previously unsuspected and thus hope for a Canada that does not have to keep the classes in opposition.

"To relive those days when Alice was with him," Lewis tries to tell their story (the story of the novel) to Alice's daughter Hana, a story that recapitulates the past to prepare for the future. The sense of remembrance lends meaning to previous existence and, in turn, reaffirms the self as a sum of a life's experiences, which "in literature is the real gift," as Ondaatje explains. His novel is a direct challenge to those who have proposed that literature has exhausted its capacity for presenting that gift.

Leon Lewis

Sources for Further Study

Books in Canada. XVI, June, 1987, p. 16.
The Canadian Forum. LXVII, August, 1987, p. 35.
Kirkus Reviews. LV, August 1, 1987, p. 1105.
Library Journal. CXII, September 1, 1987, p. 201.
Los Angeles Times Book Review. October 4, 1987, p. 3.
The Nation. CCXLV, October 17, 1987, p. 421.
New Statesman. CXIV, August 28, 1987, p. 20.
The New York Times Book Review. XCII, September 27, 1987, p. 12.
The New Yorker. LXIII, January 25, 1988, p. 109.
The Observer. August 23, 1987, p. 24.
Publishers Weekly. CCXXXII, July 31, 1987, p. 70.
Quill and Quire. LIII, May, 1987, p. 21.
The Times Literary Supplement. September 4, 1987, p. 948.

JOHN CALVIN
A Sixteenth-Century Portrait

Author: William J. Bouwsma (1923-   )
Publisher: Oxford University Press (New York). 310 pp. $22.95
Type of work: Historical biography
Time: Late Renaissance (the sixteenth century)
Locale: Geneva, Switzerland

William J. Bouwsma's historical study examines the development of John Calvin's theology in the context of both Calvin's personal circumstances and the external historical events which shaped it

> *Principal personage:*
> JOHN CALVIN, the Protestant Reformer

William J. Bouwsma's study of John Calvin is, in a sense, not a biography at all, for it assumes a general knowledge of its subject's life and deals with what can reliably be said about Calvin's family history in fewer than forty of the work's more than three hundred pages. The work is, instead, a sensitive and sympathetic exegesis of Calvinist theology which traces its development through the peculiar historical circumstances of the late Renaissance. Bouwsma recognizes, as more traditional biographers of Calvin have not, that the religious movement generated by Calvin's ideas was of far greater consequence than the life of its namesake; moreover, Bouwsma steadfastly resists the understandable though tiresome tendency of contemporary biographers to psychoanalyze. Most remarkable, Bouwsma avoids overt analysis even as he argues that one may discern archetypal motifs in Calvin's theology. In short, what most informs Bouwsma's work is scholarly discipline and order, the two qualities Calvin admired most. Calvin would have been very pleased with this book; the general reader will find it enlightening.

Paradoxical though it is, Calvin's theology and inner life were quite separate. External circumstances forced his theology to grow and develop; his inner life never actually developed at all. His last years were plagued by the same doubts, confusions, and contradictory impulses which had bothered him as a young man. Actually, such precarious unease is inevitably characteristic of those who adhere to creeds which stress absolute certainty. Calvin was born July 10, 1509, into the episcopal traditions of Noyon, a cathedral town in Picardy, France. He founded a variety of Christian humanism derived from reading Desiderius Erasmus. The contradictions inherent in this unlikely mixing, which could never be fully reconciled within the man, produced limitless and inextinguishable anxieties: philosophy which ultimately denies intellect and humanism which distrusts human motives.

Though American Puritanism was founded upon an admixture of Separatist Calvinism (more properly called Browneism after Robert Browne) and Augustinian theology, Calvin himself rejected or was at least uneasy about dramatic conversions such as those of Paul and Augustine. He even distrusted elements of what in his own time had become a mythology surrounding the conversion of Martin Luther, though he clearly respected Lutheranism as a reaction to what he considered papist degeneracy. Calvin's reflexive hatred of the Roman Catholic papacy derives from his humanism. It is an irony that history often portrays him as the sullen patriarch of Geneva.

Bouwsma argues that Calvin's twofold homelessness (he was reared in a foster home after his mother's death and exiled from France as an adult) aggravated these feelings of anxiety. He notes Calvin's near-indifference upon being informed of his father's impending death. Bouwsma wisely does not push the argument to its potentially absurd conclusion: as a way to explain Calvin's visceral hatred of male figures of authority.

The real focus of this study begins to emerge after Bouwsma has set forth the facts of Calvin's life. Calvin was aware that anxiety indicated an imperfection in faith, a failure to trust in God's will; even so, he was haunted by the fact that one could take only a limited number of precautions to guard against disaster. He equated disaster with confusion and confusion with sin. Confusion characterized the world in general and intruded upon the lives of individuals in the form of sin. One could never hope to eliminate this intrusion; insistence on clarity and order in one's personal life was the only response one could make.

This conclusion had far-reaching consequences, for Calvin saw the conflict in almost Gnostic terms, a daily struggle to assert the primacy of orderly goodness over disorderly wickedness. He would have liked it to be the underpinning of his own cosmology. This drive led him to perceive the world's constituents in terms of mutually exclusive categories: white and black, elect and reprobate, stainless and defective. Still, he must have recognized the contradictions in such a scheme. If all human desires are evil, as he maintained, then clearly the only alternative for the elect is to eliminate them—clearly an impossibility.

Four hundred years before Swiss psychologist Carl Jung included it among his archetypes of the "collective unconscious," Calvin concluded that the labyrinth was a symbol of human powerlessness to extricate oneself from self-centered alienation from God. He declared that the kingdom of God is light and that those who are alienated from God wander a dark and endless maze. By extension, "up" and "uprightness" is erect posture (moral and physical), which leads to apprehending the light of goodness. For Plato in the cave allegory of *The Republic*, the journey moved from a prone position in dark ignorance to an upright posture in the sunlit world of philosophy; for Vergil's Aeneas, it was a journey from the Sibyl's cave to Elysium; for Dante, the journey began in the Valley of Doubt and ended when the Pilgrim reached the Celestial Rose. Calvin traversed the same intellectual territory as his predecessors.

Above all, Calvin sought a rational religion. Truth is objectively given by God, the source of objectivity; therefore, God can be objectively known. Consequently, Calvin rejected ecstatic mysticism in any form. This stand places him outside the tradition of Augustine, with whom he is often mistakenly aligned. Also unlike Augustine, Calvin was willing to accept secular literature as a teaching tool when it served to pave the way to a rational understanding of God. He drew frequently from his reading in the classics, particularly Plato and Aristotle, and derived his definition of philosophy from Cicero. The Gospel became his doctrine, though he shunned dogma, since for him it implied Romanism. By extension, he decried allegorical interpretation of sacred texts, since this approach introduced fallible human opinion where he believed there had to be certainty and firmness.

Though he would have been uncomfortable with the secular connotation of the term, there is no denying the influence of Humanism in Calvin's thought. Calvin's Humanism stemmed in part from his reading in Erasmus and the classics, in part from his lifelong interest in and simultaneous distrust of rhetoric. Rhetoric provided a means of answering the doubts and pretensions of philosophy. That many of the Latin Church Fathers had been trained rhetoricians gave rhetoric a respectability in the Renaissance which it does not enjoy in the twentieth century. For the Renaissance Humanist, language meant power, and eloquent sermons meant adherents. Calvin delivered more than two hundred sermons during each of his Geneva years.

One often-held misconception regarding Calvin's thought is that he necessarily considered "flesh" the lower half of the equation of being and "spirit" the higher. In actuality, though his cosmology usually posited dichotomies of superior and inferior, he shared with Augustine a surprisingly holistic view of the human personality. He was quick to assert that sensual gratification through food and drink was a good provided by God, a way to avoid the "abyss" of the external world. Though not an Epicurean in the modern sense, he was close to the classic conception of Epicureanism: that gratification implies moderation. Sexual gratification in the context of marriage was likewise a good; children born from the love of a husband and wife affirmed God's blessing upon the married couple and sanctified the married state.

As a corollary, chastity was unnatural and brought those who practiced it without sufficient reason to the edge of the abyss. To require that clergy remain unmarried was of no particular value, since it fostered unnatural practices; nor were women to be seen as either the exclusively sensual or the inferior half of the marriage partnership. Though such statements are so taken for granted as to seem patronizing in twentieth century context, they indicate a liberal humanism in Calvin which was by no means common among his contemporaries.

Interesting reversals which approach contradictions appear in Calvin's sermons. He could hardly deny that human beings are theomorphic, since Genesis notes that the first parents were created in God's image and likeness. Yet his theology forced Calvin to maintain human depravity from birth, a consequence of sin. The beacon of divinity shines weakly, therefore, through the deformed parody of God which human beings have become, and the human race has no right to call God its Father. Calvin could not, however, insist absolutely upon God's revulsion toward humanity, for it would remove the possibility of salvation for which human beings live. Here, in essence, is the reason for Calvin's ambivalent feelings about rhetoric. Even as he admired the effects it could produce in an audience, he realized that dramatic analogies inherently risked contradictions of logic.

Though Calvin was an accomplished classicist, read Greek, Latin, and Hebrew with facility, and recommended instruction in these ancient languages for all who would seriously study Scripture, he had a marked antipathy for Rome, particularly under the emperors. He hated what he considered its materialism and lust for power, the usurpation of senatorial authority by the emperors, and the progressive degeneration of its moral standards. Like many Humanist scholars of his time, he searched for historical continuities between antiquity and his own era and believed that he had found them in Catholicism's centralization of authority. For Calvin, the Pope was merely another emperor working his evils under the guise of religion. Calvin's own teachings constituted a reaction to such abuses, paralleling Cato's temperance and Curtius Montanus' courage against Rome's amorality.

Two pictures in Bouwsma's book show dramatically the man Calvin was and what he became. The first is the young Calvin teaching and wearing scholar's gown and tam; his right index finger is raised as though to emphasize an important point. He is in his early thirties with sensitive features, a kindly expression, and a neatly trimmed beard. The book's frontispiece is a portrait of Calvin thirty years older. He still wears a theologian's tam and ermine-trimmed scholar's gown, but is thinner with eyes that show deep sadness as well as profound spirituality. The artist of the second portrait has highlighted Calvin's figure with a glow that recalls a saint's charisma. Though certainly he would have rejected this imagery, one cannot but admire Calvin's sincerity, discipline, and conviction, however much one may object to what came from his ideas. Bouwsma clearly admires his subject; the honest and patient scholarship of his book shows how much.

Robert J. Forman

Sources for Further Study

Booklist. LXXXIV, September 15, 1987, p. 94.
The Christian Science Monitor. January 6, 1988, p. 17.
The Chronicle of Higher Education. XXXIV, January 20, 1988, p. A8.
Library Journal. CXII, October 1, 1987, p. 98.
Los Angeles Times Book Review. December 20, 1987, p. 5.
The New York Times Book Review. XCIII, January 10, 1988, p. 13.

JOHN DRYDEN AND HIS WORLD

Author: James Anderson Winn (1947-   )
Publisher: Yale University Press (New Haven, Connecticut). Illustrated. 651 pp.
  $29.95
Type of work: Literary biography
Time: 1631-1700
Locale: England

Placing Dryden within his cultural, political, and aesthetic milieus, Winn gives a full account of the poet's life and literary career

> Principal personages:
> JOHN DRYDEN, an English man of letters
> LADY ELIZABETH DRYDEN, his wife
> SIR ROBERT HOWARD, his brother-in-law
> THOMAS SHADWELL, the Whig dramatist, successor to Dryden as
>   poet laureate
> CHARLES II, King of Great Britain, 1660-1685
> JAMES II, King of Great Britain, 1685-1688
> GEORGE VILLIERS, Duke of Buckingham, the Restoration courtier

Seldom has a writer of any nation dominated the literary life of his own time to the extent that John Dryden dominated English letters during the Restoration, alternatively known to literary historians as "the Age of Dryden." For forty years he was recognized as England's foremost poet, dramatist, critic, and translator, and he inaugurated an age of neoclassicism in English literature that endured for a century. Unlike Abraham Cowley, whose reputation suffered an eclipse before his death, "Glorious Dryden," as Sir Charles Sedley called him, retained his exalted stature among readers and critics for decades after his death. Although his place in literary history remains secure, Dryden's reputation among the general reading public has declined. While literary scholars can ill afford to overlook him, general readers find that Dryden no longer speaks to them. Even Alexander Pope, his successor in the neoclassic tradition, enjoys a wider audience. To find people who can quote some of Pope's better known couplets is not unusual. Dryden is little quoted, and the only poems still known to a significant number of readers are his two odes on Saint Cecilia's Day.

The reasons are not far to seek. Dryden's plays, written with the intent of pleasing the audiences of his own time, now seem remote and artificial. His poetry is the poetry of reason, not emotion, an indispensable element since the advent of Romanticism. His satires, perhaps the best poetic satires in the language, are devoted to the literary and political events of his time, and their topicality now makes them difficult to read. His preferred verse form, the heroic couplet, though intricate, elegant, and complex, requires long study before its subtle effects can be appreciated.

Dryden's importance in literary history, however, can more readily be understood. As poet laureate for more than two decades, he found himself involved with the major political events of his time, so that his biography reflects, to a large extent, the history of his age. He has been fortunate in the biographers willing, even eager, to record his life. Following Samuel Johnson's *Life* (1779), the eminent Shakespearean scholar Edmond Malone devoted his formidable talents to Dryden and produced a monumental biography in 1800. Following Malone, Sir Walter Scott produced a more readable but less original account of Dryden in 1808. In more recent times, James M. Osborn of Yale University issued the results of his careful research on Dryden's life (*John Dryden: Some Biographical Facts and Problems*, 1940), and for the past generation, the standard biography has been the admirable work of Charles E. Ward, *The Life of John Dryden* (1961).

Writing within a strong scholarly tradition, James Anderson Winn, professor of English at the University of Michigan, has produced the most complete and best illustrated biography of Dryden thus far. Admirably qualified by his earlier research in Dryden's period, Winn makes numerous discoveries that escaped the notice of previous biographers. Winn's previous research on poetry and music prepared him to explore and record Dryden's debts to other arts, especially music and painting.

Like other biographers of early historical personages, Dryden's biographers have encountered formidable obstacles. There is often a dearth of material, and with Dryden the problem is especially acute. Unlike John Milton and John Bunyan, Dryden wrote impersonally, accepting the neoclassic attitude that art deals with objective, not subjective, reality. He could not help believing, as he himself expressed it, that "anything, though never so little, which a man speaks of himself, in my opinion, is still too much." His small collection of surviving letters reveals relatively little about his personal life. On the other hand, his contemporaries had much to say about him: He was the subject of more published attacks by literary rivals and political enemies than any other major poet in English. Since he normally refused to answer his attackers, a biographer must sift through accusations, slanders, and innuendos to try to judge which have any basis in reality.

Addressing the dearth of information about Dryden's youth, Winn has carefully examined available records. As an indication of how barren the record is, it includes not one anecdote about the poet's mother. As Winn points out, she was a clergyman's daughter, and she returned to her father's rectory for Dryden's birth. Scarcely more information exists about the poet's father, Erasmus, a local landowner living in the Northamptonshire village of Titchmarsh. To address these points, Winn describes the environment of Dryden's youth and recounts the way of life followed by his Puritan ancestors in the village. Winn includes a discussion of Puritan preaching in Titchmarsh and an explanation of Puritan attitudes toward child rearing. From his examination of family records, Winn corrects genealogical errors made by previous biographers. He describes the educational system at schools Dryden attended, with accounts of the influential teachers and headmasters such as Dr. Richard Busby of Westminster School.

To illustrate the advances Winn has made in providing additional information and analysis, a comparison with Ward is instructive. To Dryden's first twenty-nine years, including his childhood, schooling at Westminster, attendance at Cambridge, and employment in London, Ward devotes a single chapter of nineteen pages. For the same period, Winn provides four chapters and 118 pages. Although Winn is willing to offer speculation and conjecture when he encounters gaps in the record, he carefully employs the usual qualifiers—"perhaps," "may," "might," "I believe," and even "I should imagine." Yet his inferences and conclusions are clearly identified and appear plausible.

Once past the challenge inherent in a paucity of reliable testimony, a biographer must confront the question of Dryden's conspicuous changes in political and religious allegiance. From a Puritan who found employment in Oliver Cromwell's government, he became an Anglican Royalist under Charles II and a Catholic under James II. Because these changes appear to have coincided with Dryden's interest, his enemies accused him of timeserving. His literary production aggravated the charge, for he declared himself a loyal member of the Church of England in his long religious poem, *Religio Laici* (1682). Five years later he explained his conversion to Catholicism in an even longer poem, *The Hind and the Panther* (1687). The biographer Louis Bredvold, arguing that Dryden was basically a skeptic who found authoritarianism reassuring, noted that Dryden moved in a consistent direction. Following Johnson's example, biographers have been inclined to defend Dryden and to see his changes as sincere. Winn makes his contribution to the question by pointing out that categorical distinctions between Puritan and Anglican are not so clear as is often assumed. He suggests that Dryden's early Puritanism was tempered by the moderation of his own family and by the Arminian and royalist views of the strong-willed headmaster of Westminster, Dr. Busby. The Cambridge that Dryden attended, as Winn demonstrates, was more tolerant of Anglican views than is generally assumed, and, as a student at Trinity College, Dryden encountered a variety of religious perspectives. As for the conversion to Catholicism, Winn draws attention to numerous Catholic members of Dryden's family, especially among the Howards, the family of his wife, Elizabeth. Thus Winn ties Dryden's conversion more closely to his personal life.

While other biographers and scholars have studied the attacks on Dryden in detail, Winn's thorough reexamination adds to existing knowledge. The character John Bayes, a satiric portrait of Dryden in George Villiers' *The Rehearsal* (1671), has previously received adequate attention, and Winn finds little to add. On the other hand, Thomas Shadwell's character Drybob, from *The Humorists* (1670), though long recognized as a caricature of the laureate, has received relatively little critical attention. Winn calls attention to numerous similarities of manner and expression between Drybob and Dryden and, as a result, offers further enlightenment concerning the quarrel between Dryden and Shadwell.

As for his public life and involvement with public affairs, Winn provides a clear analysis of the major historical events of the Restoration. Dryden was involved in a minor capacity with the government in London as Cromwellian rule waned, and he rejoiced with the nation in the restoration of the Stuart monarchy. He produced a poem in the Vergilian manner on the Plague and Fire of London, 1665-1666. During the Anglo-Dutch Wars, he attacked the Dutch through numerous references in poetry and drama and produced one play, *Amboyna: Or, The Cruelties of the Dutch to the English Merchants* (1673), calculated to inflame public opinion against them. Following the Popish Plot, he employed his pen to promote the king's view of succession. With the rise of the two-party system, Dryden staunchly supported the conservative Tories against the more liberal Whigs. Under James II, he became a Catholic and defended the ill-advised policies of the king as fully as he dared, though not without reservations. Following the Glorious Revolution, Dryden lost all official support and was constrained to rely on his pen and his relations with publishers and booksellers for income. Even then he took every opportunity to cast unfavorable allusions against the government of William and Mary, whom he regarded as usurpers. Winn's narrative clarifies Dryden's involvement in all these events, as well as their effects upon his life.

In recounting historical developments in Dryden's time, Winn consistently enlightens readers more fully about their relevance to Dryden's life, to people who knew him, and to members of his family. A good example is the matter of Dryden's finances, which Ward had previously explored in some detail. Winn gives a thorough account of currency exchange rates in the 1690's to show that Dryden was not so affluent as scholars previously thought. Winn's account includes an explanation of the relative and fluctuating values of English coins at the time. The effect is to make more comprehensible Dryden's sometimes carping complaints in letters to his publisher Jacob Tonson.

Despite his willingness to offer tentative conclusions where the evidence warrants, Winn adheres to a somewhat conservative approach to scholarship. He accepts, as every biographer must, the fact that uncertainties remain even after careful analysis. For example, after examining the theories regarding the origin of the attack on Dryden in Rose Alley in 1679, he concludes that none can really claim probability. Occasionally he seeks to redress imbalances in previous scholarship. At one point, he cautions against reading too much into Dryden's dichotomies, or polarities, a hallmark of his thought, by pointing out that they are less conspicuous in his later writings.

Winn has made good use of the biographical discoveries that have been made since the publication of Ward's biography a generation ago, yet his most important contribution lies in his own scholarly discoveries. Among the most significant are those relating to Dryden's background, family, and early education. The new knowledge that he contributes exceeds any reasonable expectations for a subject whose life has been so fully explored by previous biographers.

The result is a fully developed portrait of Dryden as a professional man of letters. By including generous quotations from Dryden's work throughout his career, Winn leaves readers with a good grasp of Dryden's style and themes. His critical analysis goes beyond biographical significance to include aesthetics, yet he avoids excessively technical or arcane terminology. Above all, the book chronicles the history of the Age of Dryden, affording its readers a clear account of the political, religious, and aesthetic controversies of the time.

Stanley Archer

Sources for Further Study

The Atlantic. CCLX, November, 1987, p. 116.
The Christian Science Monitor. December 9, 1987, p. 19.
Library Journal. CXII, August, 1987, p. 127.
The New Republic. CXCVII, December 28, 1987, p. 32.
The New York Times Book Review. XCIII, January 24, 1988, p. 12.
The Spectator. CCLX, January 2, 1988, p. 26.
The Wall Street Journal. CCIX, October 27, 1987, p. 32.

JOYCE'S BOOK OF THE DARK
Finnegans Wake

Author: John Bishop (1948-   )
Publisher: The University of Wisconsin Press (Madison). 479 pp. $25.00
Type of work: Literary criticism

Starting from Joyce's own comments that Finnegans Wake *is a book about the night, John Bishop has written a comprehensive study of the modern novel most known for its obscurity, and in the process reveals valuable new approaches to the work*

Since its publication in 1939, James Joyce's *Finnegans Wake* has held the reputation as the definitive modern classic of obscurity, a difficult book that both demands and defies interpretation. The work has been both praised and denounced, explained and explicated by some of the finest literary critics. It has been abridged (by Anthony Burgess) to make it more readable, and filmed with subtitles to make it more comprehensible.

Finnegans Wake has inspired scholars to produce studies such as those elicited by no other modern novel: a census of its characters, a study of the book titles woven into its pages, a list of the river names it contains, a gazetteer of its landscape, and lexicons for the myriad languages that make up its strange, yet evocative, form of English.

For all this scrutiny, however, the book remains a puzzle, the last and perhaps crowning work of one of the greatest writers of the twentieth century, but a work which defies even definition, much less discussion. One might echo *Finnegans Wake* itself: "A hundred cares, a tithe of troubles, and is there one who understands me?"

Although there are many areas of disagreement concerning *Finnegans Wake*, two points of contention form the essence of the debate: Exactly what was Joyce attempting to do with *Finnegans Wake*, and was it worth doing? Those who admit their bafflement with Joyce's intent generally dismiss his book; those who believe that they have fathomed his purpose try, with varying degrees of persuasiveness, to explain its aim and affirm its value.

John Bishop certainly falls into the second category. Only a person who believes in Joyce's enigmatic production would spend the time and effort Bishop obviously has in first reading and rereading the book, and then writing so helpfully and entertainingly about it. In *Joyce's Book of the Dark: "Finnegans Wake"* Bishop has produced the clearest, most sensible, and most encompassing study of *Finnegans Wake* to date.

In his seminal study *James Joyce* (1941; revised and augmented, 1960), the noted critic Harry Levin correctly identified the circular process needed to understand the *Wake*: "The peculiarity of Joyce's later writing is that any passage presupposes a reading knowledge of the rest of the book. On the other hand, to master a page is to understand the book. The trick is to pick out a passage where a break-through can be conveniently effected." Thus, by the very "commodious vicus of recirculation" of Joyce's opening paragraph, the reader must continually construct and reconstruct the *Wake* in order to perceive its meaning.

This is the technique used by Bishop in *Joyce's Book of the Dark*, and while the underlying principle is not new, Bishop's assumptions and directions yield fresh and valuable insights into Joyce's curious volume.

In considering the *Wake*, Bishop takes Joyce at his word: It is a book about night, about sleep, and, to some extent, about dreams. The dream element has dominated most critical discussion of the *Wake*, but in his study Bishop subordinates the single aspect of dreaming to the entire process of sleep—a mysterious state itself, little understood, but well reflected in the prose of *Finnegans Wake*. "If one operates on the premise that *Finnegans Wake* reconstructs the night," Bishop writes, then the book makes sense on those terms, since "nobody's 'nightlife' make sense as a continuous linear narrative whole."

If not as a linear whole, then how should "nightlife" be depicted? To describe this largely unknown place or state, *Finnegans Wake* uses "representational mannerisms peculiar to the working of the night." Bishop argues persuasively that the language of these mannerisms is literal in its effects, but associative in its meanings. When Joyce writes of persons asleep, for example, his words mimic the state of sleep: They become vague and blurry, refusing to locate the reader in any definite place. As Bishop asks, just where is a person when asleep? The body may be in bed, but the mind (at least the conscious mind) is somewhere else, recalled only imperfectly in dreams.

Bishop makes the interesting and rather novel point that Joyce's writing is as literal as possible a re-creation of a person asleep, which means that the sleeper becomes, again literally, the entire universe of *Finnegans Wake*. Joyce's hero has a thousand names, but is best known as HCE, for Humphrey Chimpden Earwicker (perhaps) or Here Comes Everybody (certainly). Whatever happens in *Finnegans Wake* happens within HCE, and the key to the book is that a person asleep is both no one and everyone at the same time.

To capture this condition, then, Joyce's language is going to work by association, suggestion, and distortion. There will not be ongoing narrative, but an endless succession of states as the sleeper drifts from one half-submerged thought to the next. Nor will this succession be orderly, because the mind asleep does not proceed in an orderly fashion. The way to read *Finnegans Wake*, Bishop maintains, is not by a straight narrative line, but along a series of themes grouped together by the associations and etymologies of words and, above all, their sounds.

Here is where Bishop returns to Levin's earlier perception, that to understand a sentence presupposes a prior understanding of the book. Some might argue that sets up an impossible condition. Bishop would reply that by following the permutations of words and phrases as they are metamorphosed by Joyce, a number of definite and traceable themes emerge. By identifying and pursuing these themes, the *Wake* can be "read," although in a sense distinct from the way one reads any other book.

Bishop constructs his book around an exploration of these themes found in the *Wake*. The themes are diverse, because Joyce's seventeen years of work on the *Wake* left it not only obscure, but also packed and interleaved with an encyclopedic variety of interests. The use of language to mimic darkness and obscurity has been mentioned already; this is one powerful trail which wanders through the entire work. A closely related path follows language which captures and imitates nothing: the use of words in a paradoxical fashion to express the sort of nonexistence found in sleep. Anyone concerned with language use, as well as with Joyce or modern literature, will find the first two chapters of particular interest.

Bishop also examines the identity of the dreamer and the similar puzzle of "Finnegan," who gives his name to the particular wake under consideration, but who seems disinclined to participate except under a bewildering variety of pseudonyms. Bishop clears up these problems nicely through his thesis of the sleeper as everyone and no one. Although this may seem initially confusing, a moment's reflection should provide the reader with his own evidence of the mutability of identity found in our dreams.

One of the most fascinating chapters in the book concerns the links between *Finnegans Wake* and the Egyptian Book of the Dead. As Bishop's study implicitly acknowledges in its own title, Joyce was deeply influenced by the mythology and symbolism of ancient Egypt. When he came to write *Finnegans Wake*, he used what Bishop terms the "richly inflected hieroglyphy" of Egypt to convey one more sense of what it is like to be asleep. In addition, there is gained another layer to the work, for it can be considered that the Finnegans of the world will awake not from mere sleep, but from death itself.

A second chapter of particular interest touches on a subject not new to any student of Joyce: *Principii d'una scienza nuova* (1725; *New Science*, 1744) of Giovanni Battista Vico. Readers have long recognized that the theories of the Italian Renaissance thinker have an important part in Joyce's structure and concepts in *Finnegans Wake*. Generally, however, critics have reduced Vico's thought and Joyce's use of it to a crude system of repetitions, where all of human history is a series of cycles.

While this is certainly part of the *New Science*, it hardly accounts for Joyce's continued interest in the work, or his incorporation of its insights into *Finnegans Wake*. Previous commentators have not been totally incorrect about Joyce and Vico, but they often have been inexact or incomplete. Bishop's thoughtful and detailed discussion provides readers with a new and fuller understanding of this important topic.

This sampling of chapters makes Bishop's study sound diverse, perhaps even fragmented. Actually, it is not so, or at least no more fragmented than the *Wake* itself. As Bishop shows, the *Wake* is fragmented only if one reads it in the conventional sense. As he explains in his chapter on "Litters" (meaning, but not only meaning, "letters"), the *Wake*'s language is full of riddles and multiple meanings and mismeanings which must be comprehended by association.

Here, Bishop himself means association in a double sense: within the reader's mind, and across the pages of the *Wake*. The themes spread throughout the book and the phrases and words which carry them must also be carried from page to page. As in a dream, images rise, transmute, and reappear. Because Joyce is attempting a real reconstruction of our nocturnal life, his book acts in much the same way as that "nightlife." Just as dreams are like, but unlike, waking life, the "words" in the *Wake* are like, but unlike, conventional English, and their arrangement is like, but unlike, any style the reader may have ever encountered.

This is deliberate, Bishop would argue; this is Joyce's whole intent, to recreate the language of the day in the language of the night, and those who complain about distortions and confusions have simply missed what the book is about. (Along the way, it should be added, they seem also to have missed much of the humor in what is actually one of modern literature's wittiest books.) Bishop insists that the *Wake* stands (or perhaps lies, given the twinned topics of sleep and truth in the work) on its own, and must be approached on its own terms.

The underlying thesis of *Joyce's Book of the Dark*, that the *Wake* is about night and therefore is written in a language suited to night and dreams, will not be accepted by all Joyceans, but few will deny that Bishop has opened a new and valuable approach to the study of *Finnegans Wake*. Tribute is due as well to the University of Wisconsin Press, for presenting Bishop's text, and the intricate diagrams which supplement it, with clarity and elegance.

Michael Witkoski

Sources for Further Study

AB Bookman's Weekly. LXXX, August 3, 1987, p. 367.
The Antioch Review. XLV, Spring, 1987, p. 238.
Choice. XXIV, May, 1987, p. 1392.
Library Journal. CXII, May 1, 1987, p. 69.
The New York Times Book Review. XCII, January 18, 1987, p. 14.
Partisan Review. LIV, No. 3, 1987, p. 477.

THE KOREAN WAR

Author: Max Hastings (1945-   )
Publisher: Simon and Schuster (New York). Illustrated. 389 pp. $22.95
Type of work: History
Time: 1950-1953
Locale: Korea

A highly selective account of the Korean War, emphasizing the contributions made by British and other United Nations forces and particularly interesting for its use of material from Chinese military archives

The Korean War was indisputably a "frustrating, profoundly unsatisfactory experience," writes Max Hastings, the British historian and journalist whose new history of that war gives American readers a valuable, though limited and discomforting, perspective. It was, as Hastings and other writers have often noted, a war with marked parallels to the American involvement in Vietnam. The flood of books and films about Vietnam has served to keep that wound to the national psyche open and unhealed. Korea remains prominent because of its internal politics and its critical role as an American outpost in the Far East and for its dramatic and unrelenting war of words, and sometimes blood, with North Korea. Everything Korea is, and everything that happens there, including the 1988 Olympics, is directly connected to that series of events that began so unexpectedly on the night of June 25, 1950, and ended, more or less, with the armistice at Panmunjom on July 27, 1953. That war, known for a time as a "police action," until the term was ridiculed into oblivion, cost the United States 33,629 citizens, listed as dead and missing, in three years; some 55,000 Americans died in Vietnam over a much longer period, from 1963 to 1974. It does not diminish the tragedy of Vietnam to note that the Korean War may still claim the title that military historian S. L. A. Marshall gave it, "the century's nastiest little war," at least insofar as Americans have been involved.

Yet as another book, Clay Blair's *The Forgotten War: America in Korea, 1950-1953* (1987), points out, the intense involvement of the United Nations in Korea, and particularly that of the United States, seems to have been forgotten by the public. Did this happen because, as Rosemary Foot has argued, it was *The Wrong War* (1985)? Many of the veterans who talked to Hastings about their memories of Korea thought that it was: They had little sense of purpose or mission, unlike soldiers during World War II, and little fondness for the Koreans whom they were defending. The people seemed alien to the white Americans and Commonwealth soldiers, brutalized or corrupt, hardly worth defending and certainly not worth dying for.

It is interesting to note that Hastings disagrees profoundly with the historians who argue that the effort in Korea was a tragic waste of lives and fortune. The author implies that this is indeed the received opinion among historians by characterizing himself as a "revisionist." He concludes that for all of its difficulties, Korea was "a struggle that the West was utterly right to fight." In his foreword, Hastings elaborates on his certainty of "the rightness of the American commitment" in Korea. Who can doubt, he says, "looking at Korea today, that the people of the South enjoy incomparably more fulfilling lives than those of the inhabitants of the North? Civil libertarians may justly remark that the freedom of the South's 35 million people remains relative," yet there is no doubt that "North Korea is still among the most wretched, ruthless, restrictive, impenitent Stalinist societies in the world," while "South Korea is one of the most dynamic industrial societies even Asia has spawned in the past generation."

The Korean War, the author explains, "does not purport to be a comprehensive history." It does seem to have been considered by earlier reviewers as a comprehensive battle history, but the reader who wants to get the full sweep of the war, especially the role of the American army during the critical first year, will be much better served by Blair's immensely detailed account. Similarly, nothing in this book quite matches the drama of Robert Leckie's *Conflict: The History of the Korean War, 1950-1953* (1962) or of S. L. A. Marshall's classic *Pork Chop Hill* (1956). The politics that shaped American involvement in Korea are more fully examined in Joseph Goulden's *Korea: The Untold Story* (1982), than they are here. Since Hastings does not, in spite of his inclusive title, pretend to be comprehensive, these are not great flaws. There is a striking inconsistency in this book, however, between the author's optimistic conclusion and his narrative. What the United Nations in name, but the United States in fact, did in Korea was right, Hastings says, both for its reasons and for its results. How it was done, however, constitutes a sorry litany of errors, misjudgments, ineptitude, and culpable stupidity on the part of American diplomats, politicians, and soldiers. American achievements are diminished or ignored to such a degree that the reader is likely to think that the author suffers from British resentment of American hegemony and concentrates on American failures at the expense of truth.

This reaction, while justified, should not detract from the accomplishments of this book. Hastings' purpose is to show how an awareness of what happened in Korea can be heightened by a double perspective on the conflict not previously available. The first part of that perspective is the British view. The author is a newspaper editor in London and the author of two books about World War II, *Overlord* (1984) and *Bomber Command: The Myths and Realities of the Strategic Bombing Offensive, 1939-1945* (1979), and coauthor of *The Battle for the Falklands* (1983). Simply as an account of the war from the British perspective, *The Korean War* is a valuable record, full of insights that go beyond the merely political. Global politics had something to do with the hard feelings; the older British soldiers "found the experience of decline too recent not to gaze somewhat sidelong at the new dominant force on the globe and cherish unworthy thoughts about how much better the old team had done it."

Many of the British Tommies were draftees from remote English country villages and could see even less reason than did the GI's, National Guardsmen, and draftees from Nebraska and Pennsylvania for being sent so far from home to defend American interests in the Far East. Nevertheless, perhaps the most significant cause of disharmony between the two allies, and the most difficult for an American reader to accept, is the general contempt that the British had for American soldiers, especially after the humiliating headlong rout of the Sixth Army when the Chinese entered the war in November, 1950. Yet there seems to be little doubt that the performance of the American army in the first months of the Korean conflict was nothing short of scandalous. Only its overwhelming material strength—and the superior performance, admitted and admired by all, of the Marines, especially in their retreat from the Chosin Reservoir—allowed the United States to hold on long enough to turn defeat into not victory but accommodation; the British, like the other nations who helped defend South Korea, watched with amazement as the country that had built the world's mightiest military machine not a decade earlier fumbled its way back to competence. ·

The second perspective from which the author views his subject is that of the Chinese—those vast, inscrutable hordes with their bugles and white horses and insane willingness to mount "human wave" attacks against UN artillery and strongly entrenched infantry. At the time, as it was reported in the American press, the troops were savoring the remnants of their Thanksgiving turkey and pondering General Douglas MacArthur's pledge to have them home by Christmas, 1950. The war had in effect been won, insofar as repelling the North Koreans was concerned, only five months after it began—largely because of MacArthur's brilliant flanking maneuver at Inchon, which divided and broke the North Korean forces. The sudden appearance of hundreds of thousands of Chinese soldiers in North Korea was a startling surprise—so startling that MacArthur, who had consistently assured Washington, D. C., that the Chinese would not enter the war, found his forces driven to a toehold that became famous as the Pusan Perimeter, a tiny area on the southeastern coast of Korea. The introduction of the Chinese both astonished and appalled the UN command, which had trouble determining their motives. By comparison, the aims of the North Koreans were simple: They wanted to unify their country, under their control. It was less clear what the Chinese could hope to gain, except perhaps a few atomic bombs dropped on their major cities—a proposal, Hastings says, that was seriously considered by MacArthur and the threat of which brought the Communists to the final armistice agreement at Panmunjom.

It is now known that the Chinese saw Korea as a necessary buffer state, and that they would have attacked any power, perhaps even the Soviet

Union, that threatened to establish a presence in it. "To some degree, Hastings' moderate and understanding attitude toward the Chinese seems to be merely a reflection of the current Western rapprochement with China. Certainly the North Koreans, whom he (sensibly enough) did not approach for cooperation in writing his book, are depicted as unregenerate tyrants, the unambiguous villains of the drama. The Chinese, as Hastings sees them, were simply unwilling partners to a troublesome ally, in much the same way as the Americans and the UN were to South Korea. On another level, Hastings usefully corrects contemporary American views of the Chinese as either a bunch of contemptible "laundrymen" or as invincible robots. Instead, through his interviews with Chinese soldiers, the Chinese are seen as ordinary men—good soldiers with a clear sense of purpose, not minions of some Asian Darth Vader. One typical vignette explains how, after the American retreat in late 1950 and early 1951, the Chinese were "sustained" by the vast quantities of arms and supplies left behind. According to a Chinese officer who spoke to Hastings,

> Without the American sleeping bags and overcoats that we captured, I am not sure we could have gone on. Two thirds of our casualties were from the cold that winter, against one third from combat. The main problems were always—how to avoid American planes and artillery, and how to catch up with the Americans in their trucks.

Historians, military and otherwise, are always asking themselves if history offers useful lessons for the present and the future. Hastings quotes one of his most interesting sources, then-Colonel John Michaelis of the American Twenty-seventh Infantry Division, as saying

> I don't think, as an army or a nation, we ever learn from our mistakes, from history. We didn't learn from the Civil War, we didn't learn from World War I. The U. S. Army has still not accepted the simple fact that its performance in Korea was lousy.

Michaelis could find support for his argument in a number of areas covered by Hastings: Massive bombing raids over North Korea did not bring the North Koreans cowering to the bargaining table, any more than they were primarily responsible for victory in Germany and Japan during World War II or for forcing the North Vietnamese to negotiate an end to the conflict there. The efforts of the Central Intelligence Agency to infiltrate spies into North Korea were an embarrassing failure, as Hastings discloses in one of his more interesting chapters. The "point system," which allows men to return home individually after they accumulate a certain number of points, was introduced late in World War II and retained through Korea and Vietnam, in spite of evidence that it destroys unit integrity by treating men as interchangeable parts. Hardware, no matter how sophisticated, will not defeat people who are convinced that they are fighting for their homes—at best, it might keep them from winning.

These lessons seem not to have been learned, then or now. Others may have been learned but not fully accepted. One—not noted by Hastings—is that the United States needs a large standing army. It was humiliated in 1941 and in 1950, and there seems to be wide but by no means general agreement that anything, even paying to keep 35,000 men in South Korea and more than one-quarter of a million men in Europe, is better than being caught unprepared again. The author does note another lesson learned from Korea and reinforced in Vietnam: The pressure of public opinion in a democracy, or at least in the American democracy, will eventually force the government to settle rather than fight a war that does not directly threaten national security. The Communist strategy of "talk talk, fight fight" is one that works extremely well for them—and badly for the United States.

Yet in two important respects, the war in Korea was unprecedented and unlikely to be repeated; it therefore has less to teach than might be hoped. First, it was a clear-cut case of unprovoked aggression across well-defined borders, rather than a "popular uprising," an "insurgency," a "people's struggle," or any of the other euphemisms later and more adroitly used by the Communists to overthrow governments they disliked. It was a boot in the world's face, and it demanded a response. No Communist state, with the possible exception of the Soviet Union in Afghanistan, has since made such an egregious error. Even so, no response would have been forthcoming from the United Nations except for the unprecedented absence from the Security Council of the Soviet Union's representative, who had walked out some months earlier and was not present to cast his certain negative vote against the UN peace force.

The world and the UN are much different from what they were in 1950, but the essential elements of future American involvement in foreign wars remain—in the Philippines, the Middle East, Central America. Are there lessons to be learned from the Korean War that will guide the country in making the right responses in the future? Perhaps not. It is a certainty, however, that the less that is known of past American mistakes and accomplishments, the more likely the United States will be to make even more costly errors in the future.

Anthony Arthur

Sources for Further Study

Booklist. LXXIV, October 15, 1987, p. 346.
Economist. CCCIV, September 26, 1987, p. 115.
Kirkus Reviews. LV, October 15, 1987, p. 1497.
The Observer. September 27, 1987, p. 27.
Punch. CCXCIII, September 30, 1987, p. 71.

THE LAUNCHING OF MODERN AMERICAN SCIENCE, 1846-1876

Author: Robert V. Bruce (1923-   )
Publisher: Alfred A. Knopf (New York). Illustrated. 446 pp. $30.00
Type of work: Cultural history
Time: The nineteenth century
Locale: The United States

A synthetic analysis and description of the American scientific community in the mid-nineteenth century

> *Principal personages:*
> LOUIS AGASSIZ, Director of the Museum of Comparative Zoology at Harvard University
> ALEXANDER DALLAS BACHE, Director of the United States Coast Survey and head of the Lazzaroni
> JOSEPH HENRY, first Secretary of the Smithsonian Institution

At one time, historians of American science considered the nineteenth century to be a valley between the peaks of the outstanding individual efforts of Colonial scientists, exemplified by Benjamin Franklin, and the internationally respected community of the twentieth century. Beginning about 1960, however, scholars altered their view. The nineteenth century gained recognition as the period during which the institutional foundation of American science was built. It was this institutional foundation which supported the characteristic quantitative and qualitative growth of the American scientific community of the twentieth century. Instead of asking why there were so few great American scientists in the nineteenth century, as compared with the twentieth, historians began focusing on the demographics and characteristics of the community that did exist. They concentrated on questions of education, funding, organization, discipline building, and communication.

Robert V. Bruce's book synthesizes this historical research and summarizes it in a format accessible to the nonspecialist. He has read almost everything, if not everything, written on nineteenth century American science since the 1950's, most of the earlier secondary literature, and large quantities of the historical manuscripts and published primary material. Arguing that the national patterns and institutions in science established during the years 1846 to 1876 have endured into the late twentieth century, he describes the establishment and evolution of those patterns and institutions. Excluded from his discussion are medicine, the sciences of man, and the social sciences, such as anthropology and geography. Technology is viewed in relation to science. Throughout, he emphasizes the scientific process rather than the product.

The first two sections of the book, approximately the first half, set the stage. Bruce begins by discussing the European model of science which

Americans embraced and the efforts by Americans to learn at first hand what Europe had to offer. These "pilgrims," as Bruce calls them, ultimately became the leaders of the American scientific community. He then describes what life was like for an antebellum American scientist, including common educational and career patterns, and the contributions made by Americans to the various scientific disciplines during these thirty years. Much of this description is dependent upon a study Bruce made of more than one thousand scientists and technologists listed in the *Dictionary of American Biography* and active sometime between the years 1846 and 1876.

The first facet to be analyzed is the geographical distribution of scientists. Science was essentially an urban phenomenon, which meant that most of the scientific activity in the United States took place in New England and the Middle Atlantic states, the regions of large cities. Aiding the scientists in these regions were public support and a long tradition of scientific activity going back to Colonial days. The South and Midwest lacked these two essential ingredients as well as equivalent numbers of large urban centers.

Bruce characterizes American scientists as impatient, favoring research fields which required minimal training and expense and promised the most immediate returns and applications. They sought relatively unexplored problems and uncrowded fields. In a word, they were pragmatic, building on their strengths and compensating for their weaknesses.

They were a fairly uniform group—almost all of them were white males, typically college-educated and the sons of professionals. Most were professionals, dependent upon their science for their living. The majority taught, although one-third worked for either a state government or the federal government sometime during their careers. (The level of government support for scientific research during the antebellum period was not equaled until World War II.)

Technologists, a term under which Bruce lumps both engineers and inventors, are analyzed in only one chapter, yet they formed a group somewhat larger than the scientists'. His reason for providing so little space to this group is the lack of evidence of the application of science to technology. His technologists constitute a distinct group, less likely than the scientists to be college-educated or the sons of professionals. With the exception of engineering disciplines, notably civil engineering, scientists and technologists inhabited two very different and separate worlds.

The third section of the book is the centerpiece. Here Bruce describes and analyzes the governance of American science during the antebellum years. He focuses on the role of the Lazzaroni, an informal circle of leading science administrators and researchers. (The name of their group, a playful coinage which suggests an Italian secret society, signified that they were "beggars for science.") They were led by Alexander Dallas Bache, great-grandson of Franklin and the head of the United States Coast Survey, the largest government scientific bureau of its day. Bache was seconded by Joseph Henry, internationally recognized experimental physicist and director of the Smithsonian Institution; the Swiss-born naturalist Louis Agassiz, who had established the Museum of Comparative Zoology at Harvard University; and Benjamin Peirce, Harvard's professor of mathematics and astronomy. These four men formed a mutual admiration society. Together with a small coterie, they controlled, or attempted to control, the major institutional centers of scientific activity in the country, including the American Association for the Advancement of Science and the National Academy of Sciences (the latter was their creation).

Behind the machinations of the Lazzaroni was a dream: autonomy for the scientific enterprise in the United States. They wanted to ensure that scientific research would be supported in this country without scientists having to account for their actions to politicians or other nonscientists. They were seeking a solution to a fundamental problem in American society: In a democracy where the principle of majority rule reigns supreme, ultimate authority may lie in the hands of voters unable to evaluate properly the actions of scientists and other experts. The Lazzaroni saw the issue clearly. Society should not insist upon democratic principles in an arena where they were inappropriate. Science was a meritocracy, not a democracy. Right or wrong in science should not be determined by majority vote, but by the minority that was most qualified to evaluate the issues. If America desired to match the achievements of European science, then the leading scientists themselves had to have the final word on who was funded. As Bruce makes evident, such elitism did not sit well even within the American scientific community.

The final section of the book reports the tremendous negative impact of the Civil War upon American science and its subsequent recovery during Reconstruction. In contrast to the expansion during World War II, government support for science during the Civil War actually decreased, especially on the state level, weakening many state geological and natural history surveys that previously had served as significant sources of support for scientists. Also in contrast to later wars, the Civil War did not bring science into union with technology to produce better weapons, so science did not come out of the war with increased prestige or status. Other negative aspects of the conflict include casualties among scientists, the setting aside of research in favor of nonscientific war work, and the destruction of scientific facilities and collections in the South which left the South even further behind the rest of the nation in scientific productivity.

The only positive contribution of the war was the creation of the National Academy of Sciences, established in 1863 through Bache's machinations. Dominated by the Lazzaroni—they named the original fifty members—the National Academy was to be both an honorific society endorsing the standards of Bache and his friends and an adviser to the government on scientific issues. By the standards of the Lazzaroni, the academy was a failure. It neither continued to be dominated by the Lazzaroni nor was it often called upon by the government for advice, let alone provided with any government funds. As Bruce points out, however, this failure helped shape the future of the American scientific community. When the Lazzaroni lost control of the membership elections of the academy, it marked the end of the domination of American science by a single clique. The failure of the academy to become a partner of the government meant that it could not offer patronage, but only the prestige of election.

Bruce concludes his study with a survey of the state of American science in the centennial year of the United States. Among the developments he notes are the continuing geographical imbalance in scientific activity—the Northeast dominated and the South was insignificant—and the growing role of the federal government in the scientific enterprise, leading to the evolution of Washington, D.C., as a major scientific center. He also finds that the status of American contributions to world science varied by discipline. In fields such as geology and paleontology, America was a scientific power. Physics and mathematics were areas of rapid improvement. In other disciplines, such as chemistry or astronomy, Americans were competent but had clear weaknesses. The institutional structure, however, was in place. Growth could and would come.

The Launching of Modern American Science, 1846-1876 is an excellent synthetic introduction to a pivotal period in American science. Bruce presents opposing views when there is controversy and provides sufficient scholarly apparatus for the interested reader to delve deeper into the primary or secondary literature, yet ultimately offers a clear and concise exposition. Its accuracy and preciseness will induce the specialist to use it as a reference tool. The more general reader will come away with increased understanding of the human dimension of the scientific enterprise and of the roots of the most dominant aspect of modern life.

Marc Rothenberg

Sources for Further Study

Choice. XXIV, July, 1987, p. 1715.
Chronicle of Higher Education. XXXIII, April 29, 1987, p. 9.
Kirkus Reviews. LV, April 1, 1987, p. 525.
Library Journal. CXII, April 15, 1987, p. 90.
Los Angeles Times Book Review. August 9, 1987, p. 2.
National Review. XXXIX, April 10, 1987, p. 48.

The New York Review of Books. XXXIV, November 19, 1987, p. 17.
The New York Times Book Review. XCII, May 17, 1987, p. 26.
Publishers Weekly. CCXXXI, February 27, 1987, p. 154.
The Washington Post Book World. XVII, April 26, 1987, p. 1.

LAZAR MALKIN ENTERS HEAVEN

Author: Steve Stern (1949-   )
Publisher: Viking (New York). 249 pp. $16.95
Type of work: Short stories
Time: From the Depression to the 1980's
Locale: Mainly a Jewish neighborhood in Memphis, Tennessee, and its immediate
   environs

A grab bag of magic tricks composed of a surreal jumble of the real and the fabulous, the grotesque and the whimsical, the substantive and the spectral

Reaching toward the mythological, Steve Stern's stories of Jewish life invite comparison with the output of such writers as Isaac Babel, Isaac Bashevis Singer, and Bernard Malamud, whose artfully applied surreal techniques can blend the apocryphal and the real, horror and mirth into apocalyptic vision. Yet Stern insists on another comparison also. In "The Ghost and Saul Bozoff," the last of the nine stories in *Lazar Malkin Enters Heaven*, Stern's direct references to "Prospero's Cell" inevitably call to mind William Shakespeare's play *The Tempest* (1611) and Prospero's role as creator and director of all the characters on the enchanted island. Indeed, the Pinch, Stern's Jewish neighborhood on and around North Main Street in Memphis, can be seen as a kind of exotic island where the storyteller/artist can with a wave of the magic wand of language give form not only to humans but also to otherworldly spirits.

Artist figures are prominent in most of the stories. The first story in the collection, "Moishe the Just," introduces the collection's theme and a typical situation. Nathan Siripkin entertains his adolescent buddies and keeps them enthralled with his imagination. Nathan's mind is characterized as an overheated brain in an outsized head stuffed with demented creatures straining to break out and run about the streets of the neighborhood. Nathan's fabrications are given reality by the seriousness and intensity of his efforts and the collaboration of his audience. In the same way, Nathan spices up the real-life adventures of his neighbors. During the Depression, when times are becoming more dangerous for relatives across the seas, the boys spend night after night spying on their neighbors and, in response to Nathan's continuing questions, create with their leader a puppet play of people whose lives depend on an audience to give them significance.

The more Nathan feverishly invents, the more the boys demand, until finally Nathan makes a statement that can be proved only by putting a man's life in danger. Nathan knows this and his young disciples do, too, for only by showing that Moishe cannot die can Nathan prove that Moishe is one of the thirty-six truly just and innocent men who hold back evil in the world. Leader and disciples know the stakes, but they enter into a power struggle in which withdrawal would signify impotence and in which each side believes that the other will surrender. Together Nathan and his disciples rig a booby trap on the stage (floor) of Moishe's room, and then they all troop to the roof with their spyglass to watch the play enact itself.

Moishe does not physically die. At the very last moment, Nathan gives in and races to Moishe's side, arriving just in time to accept death himself as he saves Moishe. Moishe does die spiritually, however, when he realizes what has occurred, and the boys realize something more—that the death of one good and just man brings about the death of all. Simultaneously, war breaks out in Europe, North Main Street in Memphis is flooded by high waters, and the boys accept the signs foretelling the beginning of the end of the world.

The artist figure in "Lazar Malkin Enters Heaven" is Lazar himself, the quintessential Jewish peddler who refuses to accept ordinary conventions of behavior—a refusal that extends to the time of his death. For the inhabitants of the Pinch, Lazar comes to signify a great "beyond" which he regularly visits and from which he returns carrying gifts in a burlap sack for his neighbors. Lazar's refusal to die summons the angel of death, who must wrestle Lazar alive into his own burlap sack in order to get him to kingdom come. Lazar's son-in-law, the narrator, witnesses this passing and is convinced that Lazar will once again return carrying gifts. The hopeful note on which the story ends is only the latest gift Lazar leaves for his friends, the continuing promise of a wider world they have never seen.

In "The Book of Mordecai," Mordecai is the storyteller frantically trying to prolong his life by writing in a spiral notebook in reverse order all that he has experienced. Finally he conquers his fear of dying by reaching the point at which he is unborn. After Mordecai's death, his self-created holy book is salvaged by his nephew, who understands the importance of the text and its reverse chronology.

Bernard Rosen in "Leonard Shapiro Banished from Dreams" reminds his young cohorts that Jews are the people of the book. Bernard is a replica of other imaginative youths in this collection who call upon the Cabala, using tangled bits of language and lore to create spells and curses, to exorcise spirits, and even to resurrect the dead. His head teeming with ideas of the occult, Bernard curses scapegoat Leonard Shapiro, who becomes a homeless dybbuk doomed forever to walk the night. Aaron Bromsky in "Aaron Makes a Match" uses a bathrobe, a prayer shawl, a paper party hat, and an antenna (to substitute for a wand) in preparing to summon the angel Azrael to gain a husband for Aunt Esther; Nathan Siripkin in "The Gramophone" makes use of his brother Arnold's magic caldron to resurrect the dead and restore to his grandmother her old-fashioned gramophone.

Though the characters refer by name to such mystical tracts as *The Cabala Unveiled, The Testament of Solomon, and the Secrets of Abramelin the Mage as Delivered by Abraham the Jew unto His Son Laumech, A.D. 1458*, magic books are not exclusively ancient tomes. In the last, longest, and most artfully contrived story in the collection, "The Ghost and Saul Bozoff," the magic book is *Courts of Miracles and Last Resorts* by a fictitious contemporary writer named Leah Rosenthal.

For Saul, Rosenthal's book is composed of incantatory cadences; it has the feel of the forbidden, and he responds to it as though it were a mystical document. Indeed, what is striking about her book is that it contains stories whose summaries indicate a magical linkage with previous stories in Stern's book. Thus, Stern's story about writer Saul Bozoff links all the storytellers in the collection together, and further links the storytellers with Steve Stern himself. This literary device underlines the metafictional characteristics of Stern's collection and makes the ties among the stories a coherent aspect of theme. Rosenthal's stories, as described by Saul, combine the supernatural with the mundane, the archaic with the slapstick, the Old Testament with pagan themes, and turn-of-the-century locales with abstract mindscapes.

Saul has been experiencing writer's block undoubtedly tied to his plan to write what would be for him his life's achievement, a book of apocalyptic vision in which his protagonist, amnesiac after a nuclear exchange, would sit in a cellar buried under rubble trying to remember the world. With such a negative outlook, Saul finds that he cannot write, because he cannot think of anything worth remembering in view of the impending cataclysm which is the basis for his novel. Leah Rosenthal's book becomes for Saul a holy text, and his devotion to it seems to be a magic agent accounting for her appearance to Saul for the collaborative project they undertake. Saul becomes the medium through which Leah's additional stories are told, and Leah's stories, written by Saul, make up the contents of Stern's book. In retrospect, metafictional themes thus become dominant in the entire collection, distinguishing the postmodernist Stern from his modernist fathers Babel, Singer, and Malamud.

Working with basic surrealist techniques, Stern creates an immense assemblage of fantastic images startling in their visual impact. Moishe dances as if he were "being electrocuted in slow motion"; he buries "the hatchet of his face" in "crumb-strewn pages." Nathan's grandmother is "little more than a death rattle in a flannel nightgown." Returned from the dead, Nathan's brother has a stench "more acrid than burning grease"; his face is "tallowy and distended" like a "potato or a misshapen moon." Uncle Mordecai's hair and whiskers assume "the texture of smoke"; his face appears "to have been conjured out of his own cigar." The outraged butcher, Red Dubrovner, raises his huge wooden chopping block and lets "it fall on top of his head, rattling his teeth," which bite off the "the tip of his tongue." At the base of the surreal experience is the surreal image, composed of such wondrous and astonishing juxtapositions that a reader is impelled into instant recognition of the essence of the experience. Consequently, what readers have noticed most about Stern's writings on the basis of his as-yet small output are his highly charged images; his surprising prose; his outrageous metaphors; and his ability to comment on the living by referring to the dead, on the present by referring to the past.

Mary Rohrberger

Sources for Further Study

Booklist. LXXXIII, February 15, 1987, p. 875.
Kirkus Reviews. LIV, December 1, 1986, p. 1756.
Library Journal. CXII, January, 1987, p. 110.
Los Angeles Times Book Review. May 24, 1987, p. 6.
The New York Times Book Review. XCII, March 1, 1987, p. 11.
The New Yorker. LXIII, July 27, 1987, p. 77.
Publishers Weekly. CCXXX, December 12, 1986, p. 43.

LEAVING HOME
A Collection of Lake Wobegon Stories

Author: Garrison Keillor (1942-   )
Publisher: Viking (New York). 288 pp. $18.95
Type of work: Short stories
Time: 1974-1987
Locale: Lake Wobegon, Minnesota

In this collection of thirty-six sketches, Garrison Keillor continues his account, begun in Lake Wobegon Days, *of life in a small town in northern Minnesota*

> *Principal characters:*
> I, the narrator
> CLARENCE BUNSEN, the owner of Bunsen Motors, the town's Ford dealership
> ARLENE BUNSEN, his wife
> CLINT BUNSEN, the mayor of Lake Wobegon
> FATHER EMIL, the Catholic priest of Our Lady of Perpetual Responsibility
> ROGER HEDLUND, a farmer
> CINDY HEDLUND, his wife
> CATHY HEDLUND and
> MARTHA HEDLUND, their teenage daughters
> HJALMAR INQVIST, the president of First Inqvist State Bank
> VIRGINIA INQVIST, his wife
> CORINNE INQVIST, their daughter, a schoolteacher
> DAVID INQVIST, the Lutheran minister
> JUDITH INQVIST, his wife
> FLORIAN KREBSBACH, the seventy-two-year-old owner of the town's Chevrolet dealership
> MYRTLE KREBSBACH, his wife
> CARL KREBSBACH, their son
> CARLA KREBSBACH, Carl's daughter, the Homecoming Queen
> K. THORVALDSON, a former senator
> BYRON TOLLEFSON, the senator's nephew
> JIM TOLLEFSON, Byron's son
> DARYL TOLLERUD, a farmer
> MARILYN TOLLERUD, his wife
> LOIS TOLLERUD, their daughter

Each Saturday night for thirteen years, from 1974 to 1987, the fans of *A Prairie Home Companion* eagerly awaited Garrison Keillor's monologue on the news from Lake Wobegon. In 1985, he published a history of this imaginary northern Minnesota town modeled on his birthplace, Anoka (*Lake Wobegon Days*, 1985). The present book, published shortly after Keillor's final program on June 13, 1987, returns to Lake Wobegon to record further episodes in the lives of its citizens.

All the stories begin in the same way: "It has been a quiet week in Lake Wobegon," for at least on the surface Lake Wobegon is a peaceful town. In his monologues, Keillor noted that it is a place that time forgot, untouched by the vagaries of the economy, political scandal, or international turmoil. Conversation never strays far from the weather; the major issues that concern its inhabitants are whether to install a new furnace in the Lutheran parsonage, whether to go to Saint Cloud for the weekend. Its citizens are solid, stolid Scandinavians who, Keillor reminds the reader, "were brought up to work hard, not complain, accept that life is hard, and make the best of what little" they have. These people say, "Oh no thanks, it's too much really, I don't care for it." They must be forced to go to Paradise or Hawaii, and they cannot go away for even a few days without worrying about what is happening back home.

Their foods are simple: "meat loaf, whipped potatoes, string beans, bread, and tapioca pudding, . . . cream-of-mushroom soup and the many hot dishes derived therefrom," and they drink the local beer, Saint Wendell's— Wendy's for short—that has been brewed locally by the Dimmers for five generations. When Darlene makes Szechuan chicken one night, she uses more garlic "than she'd used in six years," and her marriage collapses as a result. Keillor's people also drive simple cars, Fords and Chevys—there are no foreign-car dealerships in Lake Wobegon—and drive them carefully. The biggest news one week is that Gary and Leroy have given someone—a nonresident, naturally—a speeding ticket. Now "if there was a law against pokiness, they could have made a mass arrest of the entire town."

Keillor meticulously details what Joyce Maynard in her review for *Mademoiselle* magazine calls this "life in the slow lane." Part of the appeal of Keillor's stories derives from their sense of nostalgia in the root sense of that word, a homesickness for the Norman Rockwell villages, where people sit on their porches on hot summer afternoons and sip lemonade—real lemonade—before returning to their chores, where a Carl Krebsbach will come over to help fix a leaky roof and the local teenagers will interrupt a party to get someone's car out of a ditch and then take up a collection for him.

Yet beneath this placid surface lurk the same deep passions and fears that stir people everywhere. If readers and listeners are drawn to Keillor's verbal portraits of a more innocent era most of them have never known, they also find here a countervailing force, a restlessness like their own that drives people away from the community, into the recesses of their basements or to Minneapolis and beyond. Many of the book's characters share the narrator's desire to leave home, either forever or only for a little while, and several of them finally act on that impulse.

Most notorious is David Tollefson, a carpenter who in 1946 left his wife to run away with Agnes Hedder, leaving behind his five children and her two, there in a town in which "a father was as permanent as the color of your eyes." Darlene, the thirty-eight-year-old waitress at the Chatterbox Café, also overcomes thirteen years of inertia to break away from a dead-end marriage and a dead-end job. Despite all of his relatives' objections, Dale Uecker is joining the navy and so exchanging the limited horizons of his local lake for the world's oceans.

Others, no less eager to escape, find leaving more difficult. Keillor ends his introductory "Letter from Copenhagen" with a narrative poem about two early settlers of Lake Wobegon, John and Ruth. They leave Newburyport for Oregon but stop in Minnesota, two thousand miles short. No one knows until after John's death that he never gave up his dream "of mountains by the ocean." That poem epitomizes the lives of many in the small town.

Roger and Cindy Hedlund set off for Grand Rapids to get away from the bad weather for a few days, but they soon return to check on the two teenage daughters they have left behind. Myrtle Krebsbach longs to live in a high-rise in Saint Cloud. She almost moved to Minneapolis in 1937, and since then she has wanted "to live someplace exciting." Clearly, though, her hopes are doomed. Myrtle's husband was born seventy-two years ago in the house they now occupy, and he has no intention of leaving his ducks for an eighth-story, three-room apartment. Daryl and Marilyn Tollerud had planned to go to Hawaii when their pig farming was prospering. Then they decided to wait another year so that they could afford to take Marilyn's parents, too. The pigs die, however, killing their hopes of a vacation. When Senator K. Thorvaldson sees Father Emil planting onions, he tells the priest, "I thought you were retiring and moving South." Father Emil replies, "I thought you were going to marry that woman out in Maine and move East." Instead both discover, "It's hard to leave here."

Some seek physical escape, others spiritual flight. Brian Tollefson reads about the Flambeaus and dreams of being part of that family rather than his own. His parents "sicken and disgust him; they are fat and lumpy and dreary and slow and determined to be dumb. Born to be boring." Not so the Flambeaus, who "live in large sunny rooms full of plants and piles of books and are easygoing and affectionate and talk intelligently about so many things." Jim Tollefson claims that he spent his allowance on pizza and a film in Saint Cloud because he thinks his father would not understand what he really did with the money: He went to Minneapolis to see the ballet and so satisfy a cultural craving. In an effort to erase the knowledge that his father has left his family for another woman, Val Tollefson destroys every gift the man has given him. Grace Tollefson and her three children live in her brother's trailer furnished with "a three-legged table, a very nice green sofa with large holes chewed out of it, some rickety chairs," all donated by the Lutheran church. Yet they spend their evenings talking about what they will do when they grow rich.

As Keillor reveals, what traps all these people is not a place or a heritage so much as personality. However far from Lake Wobegon one may go, life does not change. Grace Tollefson remains the same impoverished dreamer in St. Paul that she was in Lake Wobegon. Larry the Sad Boy, who repeatedly repented as a child, now as an adult spends eight hours apologizing for knocking over the Christmas tree. Eddie the Jealous Boy, who made his wife give up beauty pageants, is convinced that she has gone off into the woods with his brother-in-law Fred, forgetting that Fred has gone to Des Moines for the holidays.

In a sense, then, *Leaving Home* is about dreams unfulfilled and hopes deferred. For the most part, though, Keillor emphasizes the humor rather than the pathos of life, its sweetness rather than its sorrows, its small triumphs rather than its defeats. In "Eloise," for example, Keillor tells of Eloise Best, a divorcée with three children, who lives on welfare "in a two-bedroom tumble-down stucco house." To supplement her income she offers dancing lessons; Ella Anderson, a lonely old lady trying to care for her senile husband and herself, signs up simply to have some company. The story ends with "two women dancing, one with white hair and the other with red, smiling, turning" to the tune of the "Blue Skirt Waltz," each of them filling a void in the other's life.

As this story shows, *Leaving Home* does not eschew sentimentality. Still, its dominant mood is comic, Keillor indulgently laughing at the foibles of his creations. Roger Hedlund refuses to allow his daughter to bring her cat into the house on a cold night; then, feeling sorry for the animal, he goes out with his dog, Oscar, to find it.

> He walked naked except for his long T-shirt. . . . He pulled the T-shirt down to make himself decent, and thought he heard the kitten under the house. Bent over to look, and Oscar sniffed him. Roger jumped straight into the house, hitting the faucet with his thigh.

The next morning Roger agrees to let the cat live indoors. Daryl Tollerud befriends a skunk, hoping that it will fumigate Daryl's father, who aggravates Daryl by refusing to make commitments about anything, including a trip to Seattle even after the tickets are bought and the suitcases packed. The skunk does persuade Old Man Tollerud to go—by spraying Daryl. Wally's attempt to host a gathering of twenty-four Lutheran ministers on his twenty-six-foot pontoon boat leaves the clerics "standing up to their smiles in water, chins up, trying to understand this experience and its deeper meaning."

The book's structure emphasizes its comedic sense. The stories begin in late spring, with a threat of frost in the air, and move through the year, concluding in June as life-giving rain ends a monthlong drought. Keillor ends this work on a hopeful note, promising escape and discovery:

> And the river may rise so that you and I can push our lovely rafts from shore and be
> lifted up over the rocks and at last see what is down there around the big bend where
> the cottonwood trees on shore are slowly falling, bowing to the river, the drops glisten-
> ing on the dark green leaves.

Keillor has created a world and filled it with people who are ultimately not very different from his audiences. *Leaving Home* is a valedictory, a fare-well to his popular radio program and to Lake Wobegon. As his book dem-onstrates, though, exiles do occasionally return. Already Keillor has come back from Copenhagen to New York; perhaps his westward journey is not yet complete. Perhaps, *pace* Thomas Wolfe, he will go home again.

Joseph Rosenblum

Sources for Further Study

Booklist. LXXXIII, August, 1987, p. 1698.
Chicago Tribune. September 20, 1987, XIV, p. 1.
Kirkus Reviews. LV, August 1, 1987, p. 1100.
Library Journal. CXII, October 1, 1987, p. 108.
Los Angeles Times Book Review. October 11, 1987, p. 1.
Mademoiselle. XCIII, October, 1987, pp. 92-95.
The New York Times Book Review. XCII, October 4, 1987, p. 9.
Newsweek. CX, October 5, 1987, p. 82.
Publishers Weekly. CCXXXII, August 28, 1987, p. 67.
Time. CXXX, October 26, 1987, p. 118.
The Wall Street Journal. CCX, September 28, 1987, p. 30.
The Washington Post Book World. XVII, October 4, 1987, pp. 3-4.

THE LETTERS OF D. H. LAWRENCE
Volume IV, June 1921-March 1924

Author: D. H. Lawrence (1885-1930)
Edited, with an introduction, by Warren Roberts, James T. Boulton, and Elizabeth
  Mansfield
Publisher: Cambridge University Press (New York). Illustrated. 627 pp.• $59.50
Type of work: Letters
Time: June 1921-March 1924
Locale: Germany, Sicily, Ceylon, Australia, New Mexico, Mexico, and England

The fourth volume of a new scholarly edition of D. H. Lawrence's letters, covering
the restless period of his wanderings in the early 1920's from Europe to the Orient and
Australia to Old and New Mexico and back to Europe, before his final return to the
United States

With the publication of the fourth volume of a projected seven, more
than half of the known 5,600 pieces of D. H. Lawrence's correspondence
have appeared in the new Cambridge edition. The quality of the scholarship
and bookmaking here matches the high standards established in the previous three volumes. Volume IV's 848 letters, written between June of 1921
and March of 1924, are presented in an attractive format, with full and
accurate texts (many having previously appeared in incomplete or inaccurate
versions). They are assiduously annotated as to date of composition, identity
of correspondent, unfamiliar allusions, translations of foreign phrases, and
source of text—information of interest primarily to the specialist scholar.
Helpful to the general reader are the detailed chronology of Lawrence's life
and writings during this period, maps of the regions of the world to which
he traveled, sixteen black-and-white photographs of several of the most
important correspondents, a very ample index, and a general introduction
calling attention to the principal themes, places, and personages appearing
in the letters.

The nearly three-year period of Lawrence's life covered in the fourth volume of letters was marked by virtually continual movement. Lawrence and
his wife Frieda, having bitterly departed from England after the conclusion
of World War I, circled the globe in search of a propitious place in which to
live and write. It was a sort of utopian quest for a "new spiritual centre"
which Lawrence called Rananim, where he hoped he might live with a small
circle of friends in something like peace and hope for the future. As early as
1915, Lawrence had begun to associate Rananim with America—more specifically, the still-uncivilized areas of the continent. Like most utopias, however, Lawrence's was in large part defined in reaction against the familiar
world which he had rejected, and which had rejected him. (One of his novels, *The Rainbow*, had been officially banned after its publication in 1915,
and Lawrence, reviled in the popular English press as a pornographer and a
pro-German sympathizer because of his marriage to the cousin of a famous

enemy flying ace, was scarcely able to support himself with his pen during the war.) From Lawrence's viewpoint, postwar England, and by extension all northern Europe in the 1920's, was fatally blighted and doomed. Such things as rampant materialism, labor disputes, political and ideological conflict, and lingering puritanism filled him with apocalyptic despair about the modern world and sent him in search of an alternative. Although increasingly attracted by "unspoiled" America, first he tried the Mediterranean, chiefly Sicily, where he settled for some sixteen months. There Lawrence worked sporadically on such novels as *The Lost Girl* (1920), which he had begun before the war, *Aaron's Rod* (1922), begun back in 1917, and *Mr Noon* (1984), begun in 1920 but never finished. Like all of Lawrence's longer postwar fiction, these works are concerned with quests as much spiritual as geographical, but all three attempt, with uneven success, to incorporate prewar English experiences into that quest, as if Lawrence were trying to clear the decks before the more arduous journey to come. That journey was what he himself later called his "savage pilgrimage," which would take him east from Sicily to Ceylon in February of 1922, thence that spring to Australia, where he would spend the next four months and where he would write *Kangaroo* (1923), before sailing finally to America. Arriving in San Francisco in September, 1922, he settled for a time on a ranch outside Taos, New Mexico, with intermittent journeys to the northern United States, to Mexico, and once even back to England.

This backward, protracted approach to the New World is an index not only of the importance that America had already assumed in Lawrence's imagination but also of the underlying ambiguity that would always characterize his feelings about it. Ostensibly, his quest—expressed, as these letters demonstrate, in both his life and his art—was aimed at discovering a place, a people, and a mode of living that he could affirm. Only a part of Lawrence, however, was able to believe in the possibility of finding an earthly paradise, especially one that could actually be shared with others. Another part of him needed the stimulus of negations as well as ideals. "I love trying things and discovering how I hate them," he wrote to a friend after visiting him in Ceylon. His imagination seemed to depend on an insoluble tension between opposites: hope and despair, thought and impulse, nature and machine, separateness and union with another. During this period, America came to be the prime embodiment of such oppositions in Lawrence's vision as expressed in such works as "St. Mawr" (1925), *Mornings in Mexico* (1927), and above all *The Plumed Serpent* (1926).

Mexico, in particular, assumed an increasingly important role in Lawrence's American dream. As early as November of 1921, sixteen months before his first visit there, Lawrence wrote from Sicily that "the Indian, the Aztec, Old Mexico—all that fascinates me and has fascinated me for years." Although he was deeply impressed with the animistic religion of the Pueblo

Indians that he had seen at first hand in New Mexico and Arizona, he knew as soon as he had spent time in provincial Mexico that this was "really a land of Indians: not merely a pueblo"; even as its socialist government attempted to promote modernization, Mexico was for Lawrence "the Indian *source*: this Aztec and Maya." The old aboriginal gods and their blood-drenched legacy at once attracted and repelled him. In contrast, he despised the European culture that had been transplanted to America—Christianity, democracy, materialism, and the like—which he believed had not truly taken hold of the continent's aboriginal "dark" spirit but had only been applied to the surface like whitewash. In letter after letter, he mocked white America for having concentrated all of its force on the surface of life, where the strongest or most persistent will dominates. "Everything in America goes by *will*," he wrote to his sister-in-law in Germany. "A great negative *will* seems to be turned against all spontaneous life—there seems to be no *feeling* at all." For a writer such as Lawrence, this was ominous enough: "It seems to me, in America, for the inside life, there is just blank nothing. All this outside life—and marvellous country—and it all means so little to one. . . . How can one write about it," he wondered, "save analytically." For Lawrence, a resurgence of the aboriginal must happen in order for life in America to take on inner meaning, and such a resurgence could only be imagined in Mexico, where revolution was a perennial possibility. There alone could he write his "American novel," which he called "Quetzalcoatl" (later retitled *The Plumed Serpent*), and only there could he write to his old friend John Middleton Murry:

> Though England may lead the world again, as you say, she's got to find a way first. She's got to pick up a lost trail. And the end of the lost trail is here in Mexico. Aquí está. Yo lo digo. [Here it is. I say so.]
> The Englishman, per se, is not enough. He has to modify himself to a distant end. He has to balance with something that is not himself. Con esto que aquí está. [With this which is here.]

In less expansive moods Lawrence allowed himself—more overtly in the letters than elsewhere—to express doubts about the attempt to find in alien lands solutions to questions he had raised back in England. From Ceylon he counsels an English expatriate in Sicily that "we make a mistake forsaking England and moving out into the periphery of life. After all, Taormina, Ceylon, Africa, America—as far as *we* go, they are only the negation of what we ourselves stand for and are: and we're rather like Jonahs running away from the place we belong." "Perhaps it is necessary for me to try these places," he wrote to Catherine Carswell. "It only excites the outside of me. The inside it leaves more isolated and stoic than ever. . . . It is all a form of running away from oneself and the great problems: all this wild west and the strange Australia." Although it seemed to be his destiny to wander perpetually, he remained, as he said half-humorously, "English in the teeth of all the world, even in the teeth of England."

If the ambiguous quest for Rananim is the underlying theme of the volume, these letters display many other sides of Lawrence's character and experience as well. About one-quarter of the correspondence is made up of business letters to agents and publishers. It is interesting and instructive to see the often-impulsive, volatile Lawrence taking charge of the business side of his creative endeavors so efficiently and with such assurance. Despite suffering through numerous squabbles between editors and agents on both sides of the Atlantic, he achieved for the first time in his career a modicum of financial security. In 1922, his income in the United States alone was $5,440, or about $34,000 in 1980's purchasing power. He also wrote more introspectively about his ongoing literary projects, and students of Lawrence will find especially valuable insights into *Kangaroo* and *The Boy in the Bush* (1924), on which he collaborated with Australian writer Mary Louisa ("Mollie") Skinner. There are surprisingly few remarks about the work of other contemporary writers; only E. M. Forster, Norman Douglas, Amy Lowell, and Witter Bynner are among his correspondents in this volume. Literary historians will be interested to note Lawrence's slight opinion of James Joyce's *Ulysses* (1922), of which he was able to read "only bits"—and even these only because he knew intuitively that posterity would link his name to the Irishman's as a pioneer, and "I feel I ought to know in what company I creep to immortality." Reading *Ulysses* wearied Lawrence. The novel's mixture of erudition and frank carnality, presented in a stream-of-consciousness style, seemed to Lawrence "so like a schoolmaster with dirt and stuff in his head: sometimes good, though: but too mental." Revealing also are Lawrence's epistolary exchanges with Frederick Carter, an English painter and authority on occult symbolism. Reacting against Carter's esoteric interpretation of astrological symbolism in the Book of Revelation (later published as *The Dragon of the Alchemists*, 1926), Lawrence argued that abstract analytical systems for decoding symbolism are incidental to "what the sign means . . . humanly." In words that apply equally to his own writing, Lawrence insists that "it's life that matters—and the big thing we've lost out of life needs to be recovered, livingly."

Still another group of letters offer insights into Lawrence's personal relationships, especially with women. One of his most important new acquaintances in America was Mabel Dodge Luhan, a well-known patron of the arts in Greenwich Village and Taos. She had invited Lawrence to Taos as early as 1921, and she provided him with living accommodations within reach of her circle of artist friends. Both Lawrence and Frieda soon became wary of Mabel's motives, and Lawrence saw her as the epitome of the antagonistic white "will" which was anathema to the aboriginal "spirit of place" he was seeking. The exchanges between Mabel and Lawrence, presented from her viewpoint in *Lorenzo in Taos* (1932), provide illuminating glimpses into two complex and mercurial sensibilities, of interest equally to contemporary feminists and Laurentian scholars. The letters to Baroness Anna von Richthofen, Lawrence's mother-in-law, are among the most remarkable in the volume. Written in German (helpfully translated in full by the editors), these long missives to "liebe Schwiegermutter" are strikingly frank and diverse in their range of feeling. Lawrence's most evocative descriptions of the places he and Frieda visited tend to come in these letters; surprisingly, some of his most heavily doctrinal reflections are also directed to the baroness, evidently a kind of substitute mother for Lawrence, whose own mother had died in 1910. As for Frieda herself, her presence on the travels precludes, for the most part, a direct presentation in the letters of her relationship with her husband. Still, there is evidence of a serious marital rift in the fall of 1923, when Frieda returned to Europe alone to see her children and her mother while Lawrence returned to Mexico, finding it this time "somehow alien to me." His conviction that "at its best, the central relation between Frieda and me is the best thing in my life, and, as far as I go, the best thing in life" was reinforced by this rare three-month separation. Reunion with Frieda was the only inducement strong enough to interrupt his American sojourn and bring him back to England.

His presence in England afforded an opportunity—his last, as it turned out—for an appeal to his old friends to join him in his American Rananim. The results were disappointing, as only one recruit, Dorothy Brett, accompanied the Lawrences back to the United States. The volume ends with their arrival in New York, "the doom of Europe" behind them, their hope once again renewed. Perhaps after all America, or at least Mexico as it would be transformed imaginatively in *The Plumed Serpent*, would afford a glimpse of "the next great phase" for humanity. Or perhaps not. Perhaps it was all escapist illusion, wish-fulfillment fantasy. The Laurentian apocalypse remained ambiguous to the end. He was able to offer this ironic tribute to Forster: "To me you are the last Englishman," adding with an irony at his own expense, "And I am the one after that." English in the teeth of the world, as he said, even in the teeth of England. These letters unforgettably reveal D. H. Lawrence in all of his contradictions.

Ronald G. Walker

Sources for Further Study

The Christian Science Monitor. October 14, 1987, p. 20.
Los Angeles Times Book Review. December 27, 1987, p. 2.
The Observer. June 21, 1987, p. 24.
The Spectator. CCLVIII, May 23, 1987, p. 51.
The Times Literary Supplement. October 16, 1987, p. 1142.

THE LIFE AND WORK OF BARBARA PYM

Editor: Dale Saiwak (1947-   )
Publisher: University of Iowa Press (Iowa City). 210 pp. $22.50
Type of work: Essays and memoir

Nineteen authors comment on the life and work of an English novelist rediscovered after years of rejection by publishers

Barbara Pym's life was one of quiet happiness and sorrow, of modest success and painful rejection, and of sudden fame when, ironically, she had little time left to enjoy it.

In Dale Salwak's *The Life and Work of Barbara Pym*, the woman and author is considered by nineteen writers, several of whom knew her personally. In part 1, friends recall Pym; the essayists in part 2 analyze and evaluate her novels from several perspectives; the writers in part 3 discuss the rejection of *An Unsuitable Attachment* (1982) and its effect on Pym; the rediscovery and final success of a rejected author; and the connections among Pym's novels and ways in which the novels relate to those who read them. *The Life and Work of Barbara Pym* closes with Gail Godwin briefly celebrating the novelist who "recorded and preserved a corner of English life that was important to her while the sixties raced by on the highroad."

What has been called the Cinderella story of Pym's unusual publishing career has often been told, partly by Pym herself, then in her later years and after her death (in 1980) by a number of other writers. Details of the story are scattered in accounts by several contributors to *Life and Work*.

Pym's first published novel, *Some Tame Gazelle*, was issued by Jonathan Cape in 1950. Cape then published five more Pym novels: *Excellent Women* (1952), *Jane and Prudence* (1953), *Less than Angels* (1955), *A Glass of Blessings* (1958), and *No Fond Return of Love* (1961). Since her novels had been well received by both the critics and the public, Pym expected a ready acceptance of her seventh novel, *An Unsuitable Attachment*; but Cape rejected it in 1963 with the explanation that, as Pym wrote a friend, "they doubted whether they could sell enough copies to make a profit."

Pym discovered that not only did Cape not want her novels; no other publishers did either. She had to endure this rejection until 1977, when a remarkable turn of fortune occurred. In *The Times Literary Supplement* both Lord David Cecil and Philip Larkin cited Pym as one of the "most underrated" novelists of the century.

Quickly, Macmillan accepted two novels that Pym had written during her years of rejection. *Quartet in Autumn* was published in 1977 and *The Sweet Dove Died* in 1978, when it became a best-seller. Cape then reissued the six earlier novels (1977-1979), and E. P. Dutton, in the United States, published *Excellent Women*, *The Sweet Dove Died*, and *Quartet in Autumn*, all in 1978.

Pym, who had a mastectomy in 1971, followed by strokes in 1974 and 1975, was now suffering from terminal cancer. She finished her last novel, *A Few Green Leaves*, not long before she died in 1980. It was published later in the year. *An Unsuitable Attachment*, which Cape had rejected in 1963, was finally published in 1982 by both Macmillan and Dutton. *A Very Private Eye: An Autobiography in Diaries and Letters* appeared in England and America in 1984. Pym's early satirical novel, *Crampton Hodnet*, was published in 1985. Another early novel, *An Academic Question*, came out in 1986, and the list of Pym's finished novels was complete. Several apprentice novels and a number of short stories and other writings remain in manuscript, but an anthology of unpublished Pym writings is being prepared by Hazel Holt, her friend of many years. (Readers who are interested in a more detailed discussion of Pym's manuscripts, personal diaries, and working notebooks, collected at Oxford University's Bodleian Library, will want to consult Janice Rossen's essay "The Pym Papers," one of the most valuable contributions to *The Life and Work of Barbara Pym*.)

Pym was a born writer who penned her first novel at sixteen and wrote several others during her twenties. The revised edition of *Some Tame Gazelle*, originally written shortly after Pym's graduation from Oxford, was not accepted by Cape until she was thirty-six, a rather late age to bring out one's supposed first novel. A less dedicated writer might have been tempted to give up when no publisher would take her seventh, but to Pym writing was a necessary part of living.

In a radio talk in 1978 called "Finding a Voice," she told of her feelings after *An Unsuitable Attachment* had been refused by several publishers. "It was an awful and humiliating sensation to be totally rejected after all those years, and I didn't know what to do about it." Yet, she continued, "I did go on writing, even in the face of discouragement." She not only revised *An Unsuitable Attachment* but she also wrote two additional novels and still kept writing even though she repeatedly failed to find a publisher for any of the books.

Fortunately, Pym had a steady though small income from editorial work at the International African Institute in London. Thus, her failure to sell her novels did not leave her destitute. The work at the institute, which lasted from 1946 until her retirement in 1974, provided not only much material which she adapted to her fiction but also the time to write some of it, as Pym's boss was often absent. She once wrote Larkin: "It ought to be enough for anybody to be the Assistant Editor of *Africa* [the Institute's quarterly magazine], especially when the Editor is away lecturing for 6 months at Harvard, but I find it isn't quite." Holt, Pym's friend and co-worker at the institute, has said that Pym "could no more stop writing than she could stop breathing."

In "The Novelist in the Field: 1946-74," written especially for this volume,

Holt pictures the crowded, dingy quarters in which the two of them worked during most of the years before Pym's retirement. It was such an office atmosphere that Pym had in mind in writing *Quartet in Autumn*. Dr. Grampian, for whom Prudence Bates reads proof and prepares bibliographies (*Jane and Prudence*), is drawn from Professor Daryll Forde, for whom Pym provided the same services. Writing to a friend in 1946 Pym said, "I work for dear Professor Forde, who is brilliant, has great charm but no manners." Some years later, though, she reported that it was "rather nice having Daryll around more . . . and I feel we are two old people cleaving together."

From Pym's association with anthropologists came a number of her most memorable characters. Pym was amused by these writers, many of whom visited the institute to discuss articles to be published in *Africa*. She found their eccentricities amusing. Holt remarks that Pym "speculated about the lives of her authors and invented sagas about them." Yet, says Holt, "Barbara had little interest in anthropology as such and certainly none in Africa—she never expressed a wish to go there." Pym was a novelist, not a scientist.

Muriel Schulz discusses the comic treatment Pym gave to anthropologists themselves and to their views and writing styles. What effects, Pym wondered, might the study of anthropology have on those who studied it? Professor Fairfax, in *Less than Angels*, somewhat resembles the products of the headshrinkers he studies. Rockingham Napier, in *Excellent Women*, questions whether "the study of societies where polygamy is a commonplace encourages immorality?" and he mischievously asks his estranged wife and her Learned Society friend Everard Bone, "Do anthropologists tend to have many wives at the same time?"

Pym's editing of jargon-filled manuscripts and her attendance at meetings of anthropologists led her in several novels to mock the language of the younger generation of professionally trained social scientists. While trying to prepare a collection of seminar papers for a book, Pym wrote a friend, "How nice it would be if the publication of such papers were to be forbidden by law!" In her novels, she could fit such opinions to her fictional purposes, and she indulged in humor which she had to control at the institute.

In Pym's fiction one does not find violence, catastrophes, national or international politics and tensions. Pym's stories are concerned with men and women engaged, as Penelope Lively has written, in a "battle of gender rather than of sex: board comes a long way before bed, children are seldom evident. But love, or the need for love, is everywhere." Pym's characters do not live in a large public world but in a limited one. Their problems are not great ones, nor are they specific to the period in which they live. They are rather, as Lively observes, "the perennial problems of being man or woman, of being old or young, of being vulnerable or impervious, all of which may be tempered by the times but do not . . . have a lot to do with them."

"Where, exactly, is the Pym world?" asks John Bayley. He answers that Pym's characters, like all of us, live in two worlds,

> one of extreme triviality typified by the work situation, social change, irritations, small comforts of eating and drinking, planning clothes, perceiving others. On the other hand we live in a world of romance, aspiration, love-longing, loneliness, despair. . . . In Barbara Pym's novels the two worlds completely coincide without losing their separate identity.

Because Pym writes from her own experience and from her own true feeling, Bayley concludes, "There is really no such thing as a 'Barbara Pym world.' That is the final paradox about her, and the final triumph of her art."

The English historian A. L. Rowse is one of a number of critics who have considered Pym a modern Jane Austen. In "Miss Pym and Miss Austen," he discusses their relation to the society of their times and their rendering of it.

Austen belonged to an upper-class though poor clerical family, and she lived during a time when England had a well-established, structured society in which the aristocracy and country gentry together with middle-class industry and commerce ran the nation. There was, says Rowse, "a proper balance between the elegancies of urban society and the responsibilities of country life."

Pym came from a middle-class family. Her father was a solicitor, her mother the daughter of an ironmonger. During Pym's lifetime, aspects of the old society were disappearing, the aristocracy lost much of its former political power, concrete-and-steel boxes were replacing many of the handsome London buildings destroyed in the war, and country estates were being converted to country clubs or opened to tourists in order to survive the burden of heavy taxation. A rebellious, destructive younger generation showed little respect in "a broken-down, tattered society, with only bits and pieces of a better order showing through."

The new demotic society was a mixture of Asians and Africans living among the native English. The cultured language which Austen knew and used is occasionally stained in Pym's fiction with crude words which would have shocked Austen.

In Austen's novels there are only heterosexual relations, and love is expected to lead to marriage. Pym learned about homosexuality as a student at Oxford, and several homosexuals appear in her novels. Though for some of Pym's women, love leads to marriage, for many it does not, as it did not for Pym herself, who had several affairs which left her saddened in various degrees. Rowse believes that Pym expected too much of men. Austen could have married but did not. Both writers were able to adapt successfully to their status as single women.

There is more comedy and considerably more revelation of men's nature and habits in Pym's novels, apparently as a result of her Oxford experience, her wartime stint with the Women's Royal Naval Service in Italy, her years of work at the institute, and her love affairs or friendships with men throughout most of her adult life.

Both Austen and Pym belonged to the Church of England which, as Rowse says, "in its breadth, imprecision and tolerance—carries and expresses the character of the English people.... Both ... are linked to the central spine of English life and tradition, and give an authentic and faithful depiction of it."

Pym's experiences with love and its joys and disillusionments, her adjustment to her life as a spinster, and her observation of married couples affected her treatment of love and marriage in her novels. Mary Strauss-Noll finds "a curious mixture of romance and cynicism in the attitude of most of Pym's single women." An examination of the novels in which marriage plays an important part leads her to the conclusion that Pym women fare best as widows: They have had their romance but they no longer have the annoyance of putting up with a man's demands and his irritating ways. "They can both have their cake and eat it."

John Halperin, in "Barbara Pym and the War of the Sexes," observes that, "There is a battle going on all right in Pym's novels, but the most interesting thing about it is that no one is winning." Comedy is present in the novels, but they deserve, Halperin believes, "to be read with greater attention paid to their tragic theme: the powerlessness of love, and the pathos, the ultimate failure, of human relations." This is perhaps a gloomier view than Pym herself would have admitted to in her writing.

Readers of Pym's novels have been struck by her repeated use of lines of verse remembered by various characters. Pym's extensive reading of English poetry and her love of it both during her years at Oxford and afterward led her to create men and women who read the poets and recalled their favorite lines. Lotus Snow, in "Literary Allusions in the Novels," illustrates through dozens of quotations Pym's use of verse extending through several centuries of English poetry to the present. Snow also calls attention to Pym's allusions to many novels by various authors, including four of the six published by Jane Austen.

Pym's are not "action" novels, and many readers may share the view spoken by a young woman who was asked why she enjoyed them: "I'm not sure why I read them because, you know, nothing ever really happens in the stories. But when I'm reading *I feel as if I'm there.*" Robert J. Graham, in "The Narrative Sense of Barbara Pym," looks not only at the finished novels but at the many notebook-and-diary entries and the revisions which preceded them, and he answers the young woman. Pym, he says, "knew intuitively what she was doing.... To say that nothing happens in Pym's novels is far from true: Everything happens and much of it is consciously planned, brilliantly evocative and refreshingly authentic."

Editor Salwak and the contributors to *The Life and Work of Barbara Pym* are to be thanked for the volume. Readers unfamiliar with Pym's novels will be stimulated to read them, and Pym devotees will gain an increased understanding and appreciation of what she achieved. Many will rejoice that Pym lived long enough to know that reviewers and literary critics were encouraging an ever-increasing body of readers to discover the comedy, pathos, and charm of style in the work of a once-neglected artist.

Henderson Kincheloe

Sources for Further Study

New Directions for Women. XVI, July, 1987, p. 13.
The Times Literary Supplement. December 25-31, 1987, p. 1420.

THE LIFE IT BRINGS
One Physicist's Beginnings

Author: Jeremy Bernstein (1929-   )
Publisher: Ticknor and Fields (New York). 171 pp. $16.95
Type of work: Autobiographical memoir
Time: From the mid-1930's to 1961
Locale: Rochester, New York; New York City; Cambridge, Massachusetts; Princeton, New Jersey; and Paris, France

A memoir that shows how two vocations—scientist and writer—came together in a single person, with the result that the author is a leading popularizer of science

> *Principal personages:*
> JEREMY BERNSTEIN, a science writer for *The New Yorker* magazine
> PHILIP and
> SOPHIE BERNSTEIN, his parents
> PHILIPP FRANK,
> PERCY BRIDGMAN,
> I. BERNARD COHEN, and
> JULIAN SCHWINGER, his teachers at Harvard University
> MURRAY GELL-MANN, an American physicist
> J. ROBERT OPPENHEIMER, an American physicist
> FREEMAN DYSON, an American mathematician
> T. D. LEE, a Chinese physicist
> C. N. YANG, a Chinese physicist

The title of Jeremy Bernstein's memoir about his early life comes from a letter by the physicist J. Robert Oppenheimer. He wrote to his younger brother, who had just begun to study physics: "I take it . . . that physics has gotten now very much under your skin, physics and the obvious excellences of the life it brings." Bernstein adapts this notion of the special excitement that science can provide—its added life—to his own autobiography. The result is original. The life described in the book does not have the standard frame of earliest memories, places lived, family, marriage, and job, but is subtly different. Bernstein describes his life chronologically, but his contacts with science receive by far the greatest emphasis. This is fitting, because it was science that provided the greatest excitement, the direction, meaning, and even personal contacts in his life. Science was not simply a branch of learning or a discipline. It was life itself.

A second theme of great interest in Bernstein's memoir is his description of his vocation as a writer, specifically a writer about science. There are many different ways of writing about science, some more technical, some more popular. The interpretations of science intended for the general reader are as diverse as those of Carl Sagan, Lewis Thomas, Walter Sullivan (science writer for *The New York Times*), Jacob Bronowski, and Loren Eiseley. Occasionally famous scientists make forays into popularization, as in the *Memoir of a Thinking Radish* (1986) by the British Nobel Prize winner Peter Medawar, or Steven Weinberg's *The First Three Minutes* (1976).

Jeremy Bernstein, who is the science writer for *The New Yorker* magazine, has developed his own particular mode of writing about science, and *The Life It Brings: One Physicist's Beginnings* describes how it came into being. It is different from that of most other writers, and extremely effective.

A general ground rule, consistently followed in his books and articles, is to avoid mathematical formulas. This is not easy, especially when describing recent developments in physics or mathematics; abstractions may be central to a discovery. Bernstein's solution is to describe people whenever feasible, and to let them react, if possible in a colorful or idiosyncratic way, to the abstractions being discussed. "To someone with little knowledge of higher mathematics," Bernstein explains at one point in *The Life It Brings*, "it is hard to explain the distinction between being able to create pure mathematics and being able to understand it. Such a lay person will assume that if you do well in a large number of courses in higher mathematics, you must be a mathematician." True enough. Bernstein modestly writes that he was certain that he himself would never be creative in mathematics. He then proceeds to recount a picturesque encounter with an East Indian graduate student who was a genuine mathematician. He kept strange, nocturnal hours, sleeping by day and going out at night. He is vividly presented:

> My friend moved among abstract ideas as if they were the familiar flowers in a garden. He saw the concepts as vividly and effortlessly as if they were living things. He knew instinctively what statements were true long before he came to proving anything. The proofs, which he could supply if asked, were secondary to the truth.

Bernstein avows that he himself had no such sure intuition, and in this book as well as others he stresses his own lack of aptitude. He was a latecomer to science, constantly obliged to fill the gaps in his knowledge; he was never a prodigy or genius. The ordinary reader, however, is likely to welcome this admission. He, too, has no magical abilities, and he is more likely to trust a writer who inhabits his world and speaks his language. He will let such a writer be his guide.

At one point in Bernstein's career—he was residing at the Institute for Advanced Study at Princeton University—he and a colleague were looking for an integral equation written on a blackboard that described electromagnetic interactions of elementary particles. In Bernstein's words:

> It doesn't matter much what that is except that it was nasty. He had divided the terms into two groups; one was labeled G(x), for "good of x," and the other was labeled H(x), for "horrible of x." We were standing at the blackboard, staring morosely at horrible of x, when Dyson came in with his morning cup of coffee.

Freeman Dyson, a renowned mathematician, agreed to help them, copied down the equation, and disappeared, reappearing twenty minutes later with the solution. The scene is deftly handled, showing Bernstein's characteristic felicities. The personalities are in the forefront, engaged in informal dialogue and banter. Surroundings are sharply observed, as well as concrete, physical objects. The scientists are very human; like anyone else they can become stumped. Bernstein might gently mock them, but he makes fun above all of himself. The rigorous calculating and manipulation of abstractions occurs offstage.

Bernstein is particularly good at describing the personalities of scientists, and he has a sure eye for the telling gesture, the revealing fragment of dialogue or word choice. During his career, he came into direct contact with many of the great scientists of the twentieth century. Murray Gell-Mann, awarded the Nobel Prize in Physics in 1969, attended the same private school in New York City, Columbia Grammar School. Bernstein was an undergraduate and graduate student at Harvard University, where he worked with Philipp Frank, Percy Bridgman, and Julian Schwinger. At Princeton's Institute for Advanced Studies he knew Oppenheimer, Dyson, and Nobel Prize-winners T. D. Lee and C. N. Yang. At Los Alamos, New Mexico, and the Rand Corporation in Santa Monica, California, he worked with many prominent scientists; and when he became science writer for *The New Yorker* he interviewed famous physicists such as Hans Bethe and I. I. Rabi.

This accumulation of personal contacts, together with a thorough understanding of the science involved, has produced an extremely rich fund of anecdotes and illustrative material, often picturesque and with much flavor, that the common reader can easily understand. This abundance of incidental information contributes greatly to the interest of the text. There are stories: about mathematicians from Los Alamos going to Las Vegas to outwit the casinos and about the witty remarks by Oppenheimer. For example, during the heyday of discoveries of subatomic particles, he proposed a prize for *not* finding a particle. Bernstein describes Frank's messy study and the "linear order" created by his wife as opposed to his own "more subtle order"; the French mathematician experimenting with a twenty-five-hour day, and the resulting "secular drift" of his mealtimes; the Hungarian physicist who told a student returning to him after working with another professor, "You are a ship leaving a sinking rat"; a letter from Albert Einstein; and Bernstein's encounters with Adlai Stevenson and André Malraux. The stories are always relevant, serving to illustrate a point. Rarely are they gossip, anecdotes for their own sake.

The secret behind this is that Bernstein, as he confesses at the end of the book, is obsessed by his subject, or drunk on it. He has lived science intensely, passionately, to the extent that it appears to have taken the place of family life. Somewhat solitary, he writes, "I had a great deal of time to think about these experiences, to make them part of some interior mythology." Here he has succeeded, and the anecdotes take their proper place relative to the larger scientific issues which are the core of the book. This is probably the ingredient of his style that is hardest for another science writer to emulate. The "personal mythology" is the fruit of a life lived in science. It is entirely at the level of the ordinary reader, yet it remains science, always fully informed and understood.

A final element in Bernstein's manner of writing about science that distinguishes him from other writers in the field is his modesty. This might appear unimportant at first glance, but it is essential to his outlook. Bernstein is consistently skeptical, commonsensical, and clear. As a result, the reader always has a sense of firm reality under his feet. Science, especially physics, can easily become arcane, a higher magic; for some practitioners it is a secular religion. For Bernstein, it is above all real, the stuff of everyday experience. Clarity and modesty are integrally related. At one point, he writes about the pressure on physicists to publish: "My own response to the pressure was very simple. Since I had always assumed that I had no future in physics, I decided that I might as well enjoy myself and wait to see what, if anything, would happen." Bernstein comments on Oppenheimer's more cryptic remarks: They "were inscrutable because they were inscrutable. Oppie had a way of sprinkling his conversation with obscure—at least obscure to *me*—references to the most esoteric of subjects." On astronomy: "While I was at Harvard I had taken a course in classical astronomy, had found it dull, and had promptly forgotten it." On the speed of developments in contemporary physics: "These were evolving so rapidly that a colleague of mine remarked that he felt 'like a very small dog chasing a very large truck.'" The clarity of Bernstein's writing owes much to this modesty and critical skepticism. Alert and open-minded, he is a perfect blend of insider and outsider.

Bernstein's tone is usually tolerant and bemused, his style careful. As befits a writer for *The New Yorker*, he is an admirer of A. J. Liebling and E. B. White. The reader will not find in Bernstein's books the purple, poetic prose of Eiseley's *The Immense Journey* (1957), or the striking epiphanies of Thomas' *The Medusa and the Snail* (1979). Readers who have more than a nodding acquaintance with science might wish that Bernstein provided more scientific content. For example, his biography of Einstein is a useful, highly readable introduction, but those interested in the substance of Einstein's thought would do well to turn to Abraham Pais' *'Subtle Is the Lord...': The Science and Life of Albert Einstein* (1982).

Each style of scientific writing must be adapted to its particular audience. The rules governing Bernstein's books are clear: They are intended for the nonscientific but literate public. They assume no prior knowledge or mathematical ability. In addition, the reader can feel assured that a subject will not be treated in too complex a manner. Yet, given these ground rules, the reader can expect a lot: a sharp eye for what is striking and colorful, an awareness of the human drama behind science, a sense of humor, charm, and resourceful, literate prose. It is difficult to imagine any reader, from whatever walk of life, feeling intimidated by Bernstein, or putting his book down because of the complexity of his subject. Some readers may want to explore a topic more deeply, and read other, meatier books, but very likely this will be because Bernstein has aroused their curiosity—and his books or articles will have already served their purpose. They are among the finest introductions to scientific topics that are available.

John Carpenter

Sources for Further Study

Booklist. LXXXIII, March 15, 1987, p. 1082.
Chicago Tribune. April 21, 1987, V, p. 3.
Choice. XXIV, July, 1987, p. 1715.
Kirkus Reviews. LV, February 15, 1987, p. 271.
Library Journal. CXII, April 1, 1987, p. 155.
Nature. CCCXXVI, April 30, 1987, p. 914.
The New York Times Book Review. XCII, April 5, 1987, p. 20.
Publishers Weekly. CCXXXI, January 30, 1987, p. 372.
The Washington Post Book World. XVII, March 15, 1987, p. 3.
Wilson Library Bulletin. LXI, May, 1987, p. 71.

THE LIFE OF KENNETH TYNAN

Author: Kathleen Tynan (1937-   )
Publisher: William Morrow and Co. (New York). Illustrated. 597 pp. $22.95
Type of work: Biography
Time: 1927-1980
Locale: London, New York, Los Angeles, and other cities

Kenneth Tynan earned early fame as a drama critic and in later years, as his personal life deteriorated, worked in the theater as a director and literary adviser

> Principal personages:
> KENNETH TYNAN, an Oxford graduate, drama critic, and writer
> ELAINE DUNDY TYNAN, his first wife, a novelist
> KATHLEEN TYNAN, his second wife, a novelist and biographer
> SIR PETER PEACOCK, his father, the mayor of Warrington in the north of England and a businessman
> LETITIA ROSE TYNAN, his mother
> SIR LAURENCE OLIVIER, a noted actor, the director of the British National Theater

Kenneth Tynan was the most famous and influential British drama critic since George Bernard Shaw. In his youth, he was the reviewer for the London *Observer*; he also wrote for magazines, he wrote books about the theater, and for two years he was chief critic for *The New Yorker*. At all times he used his considerable wit and style to contend for a more innovative, open, and sexually frank theater. Later, believing himself restricted by his role as critic, he served for ten years as the chief literary adviser to the British National Theater, headed by Sir Laurence Olivier. In addition, Tynan was the person most responsible for the 1969 staging of *Oh, Calcutta!*, the variety show which introduced unabashed nudity to the stages of New York and London.

The Life of Kenneth Tynan, written by his widow, is thorough and affecting in its study of Tynan's early life. He grew up in Birmingham, apparently unaware until later in life that he was born out of wedlock and that his father, Sir Peter Peacock, had a wife and children with whom he lived part-time in Warrington, where he was the highly respected mayor, a justice of the peace, and a successful businessman. The only child of his parents, Kenneth Tynan was the precocious center of his mother's life; he was sent to a good school, where his early interest in dramatics was encouraged and further developed. In 1945, he entered Oxford University, where he drew immediate attention among the postwar undergraduates for his flamboyant actions and dress. If the young Tynan never felt close to his father, there is no evidence that Sir Peter was ever less than kind to his illegitimate son, and it is clear that he was generous in his financial support; while his father lived, Kenneth Tynan never lacked for anything that money could buy.

By the time he reached Oxford, Tynan had already developed an unusual facility with words, both spoken and written. While in school and at university, he acted in and directed plays, but he seems to have recognized early that the attention he so obviously needed could be attracted most readily by his skill as a debater and his style as a writer. He made certain that in debates he defended the unconventional side and made his points as outrageously as possible. At the same time, he was becoming more and more devoted to the stage, working on university productions, traveling frequently to London to see the latest West End shows, and encouraging road companies to visit Oxford. At the same time, he was sharpening his skills as a theater critic.

After graduation (with less than the first-class honors he had expected), Tynan was active as a provincial theater director and as an actor. (He appeared as the Player King in Alec Guinness' much-maligned production of William Shakespeare's *Hamlet* in 1951.) At the same time, he continued to write magazine articles about the theater, and in 1951 he was given his first job as a critic, for Lord Beaverbrook's *Evening Standard*. In 1952 he replaced a veteran as chief drama critic and reviewer for that paper. Two years later, he took the same position at the London *Observer*, where he was to remain for many years.

The British theater during the early 1950's had become moribund, presenting a diet which was very heavy on Shakespeare and conventional comedies and light on anything experimental. Tynan made frequent visits to the Continent and argued, in his columns, that national theaters on the Continent—especially the French theaters and Bertolt Brecht's East German company—were doing much more exciting and original things. He was sympathetic also toward Samuel Beckett, although less enthusiastic about Beckett's minimalism than he was about Brecht and the Comédie-Française. When something original did happen on the London stage in 1956, Tynan was the most enthusiastic of London critics, lauding the appearance of John Osborne's *Look Back in Anger*, the first salvo fired by the "angry young men."

Kathleen Tynan argues that her husband was a major element in the revival of British theater in the 1950's, with his encouragement of such young actors as Robert Shaw and Peter O'Toole, his enthusiastic support of Osborne, Harold Pinter, and other playwrights, and his sponsorship of Brecht and other Continental dramatists. Yet Tynan seems to have recognized that critics have a limited role in the development of any art form: Originality does not arrive in response to critical demand. Impatient with what he regarded as a passive role, Tynan spent two years as chief drama critic for *The New Yorker*, finding the New York stage more to his liking than its London counterpart was. He also tried his hand at writing screenplays; he wished to direct plays; and he looked for other ways to become more actively involved.

For years, Tynan and others had agitated for the formation of a subsidized national theater for Great Britain. Finally, in 1963, such a theater was formed, with Sir Laurence Olivier as its artistic director and Tynan as his chief adviser in matters of play selection. Much of the second half of *The Life of Kenneth Tynan* concerns this appointment, with its inevitable frustrations. Tynan and Olivier did not always see eye to eye in literary matters or in the selection of directors for their productions. More important, the judgments of the artistic director and his staff were subject to review by a nonprofessional board, which led to bitter quarrels. Finally, Tynan's longstanding hatred of censorship focused on the activities of the Lord Chamberlain, who was empowered to ban any theatrical production on moral grounds; this ancient form of censorship limited the National Theater in its early years and did not end until late in the 1960's.

This biography gives as much attention to Tynan's personal life as to his professional career. After a number of brief affairs as an undergraduate and later in London, in 1951 he married an American woman six years his senior, Elaine Dundy. A fledgling actress, she had gone to England in 1950 hoping to pursue a theatrical career. Within days of their meeting, she and Tynan were engaged. Their marriage lasted, at least in name, until 1963, and produced one daughter, Tracy. Throughout their marriage, the Tynans led a frenetic social life and traveled frequently, despite which Tynan had his most productive years as a critic and Elaine Dundy produced a best-selling novel.

The marriage was not, however, placid. By 1953 Tynan was engaged in what the author calls his "first extramarital fling," and in 1954, he asked the recently divorced wife of American author William Saroyan to marry him, although when she agreed he reneged. Increasingly frequent and bitter public quarrels became a staple ingredient of the marriage. Elaine accused her husband of stifling her own career with his demands on her time and attention. Kenneth, in turn, accused her of denying him the affection and care he needed.

The couple began a pattern of infidelity, separation, and occasional reunion which was to last until Kenneth, in early 1963, began an affair with Kathleen Halton Gates, herself only recently married. In November of that year, Elaine Dundy obtained a divorce. Kathleen, deeply involved in her affair with Tynan, decided to leave her husband, but her divorce did not become final until 1967. In that year, in New York, she and Tynan were married.

The Life of Kenneth Tynan is divided by a chapter entitled "Interlude" in which the author presents some memories of her late husband, as an introduction to the account of their life together. The book does, in fact, break in half at this point. For while Kathleen Tynan describes her husband's later professional activities, the focus of the book shifts from his public life to what eventually became a tormented private life.

The public life was difficult. Tynan was most effective as a writer of short-prose pieces, and in these years he had the satisfaction of completing memorable profiles for *The New Yorker* of such figures as comic actor Mel Brooks, the British actor Nicol Williamson, silent screen star Louise Brooks, and others. As noted above, however, his career with the National Theater, despite numerous critical successes, was frustrating.

Tynan's urge to create and his hatred of censorship did find expression in *Oh, Calcutta!*, for which he was the guiding spirit and to which he contributed some sketches; while the financial success of the show provided him with considerable income, however, it was never taken seriously as a stage production. He began several other projects for stage plays and films which would treat sex forthrightly, but all were abandoned at various stages of development.

On the personal level, Tynan's life became increasingly painful. After nine years with Kathleen, and after five years of marriage and two children, Tynan embarked on an affair with a young actress who shared his interest in exploring sadomasochism. That was a turning point in the marriage. Both Tynan and Kathleen took other lovers; neither could forgive the other for what were regarded as failings in love, but neither could separate. After a while they left their London house and lived in Los Angeles, Puerto Vallarta, or in New York. Until Tynan was debilitated by his longtime battle with emphysema, the couple continued to take extended vacations together in the Greek islands, Tangier, Egypt, Tunis, and especially Spain, which Tynan seems to have loved above all other places. In the final months of his life, Tynan spent much time in hospitals and was heavily dependent upon an oxygen tank which accompanied him wherever he went. He died in a Los Angeles hospital on July 26, 1980, at the age of fifty-three.

Despite its thoroughness and sympathy for its subject, the book has serious difficulties. Kathleen Tynan's limitations as an evaluator are reflected by the occasional remarks which are dropped, without context, into the narrative, such as, "The theater... was drawn up in battle formation. On the one hand Sartre and Brecht, on the other Beckett and Ionesco. Though Ken favored the views of the first group, he recognized the legitimacy of the second." Further, the life of a figure who lives in the theater and has a social life involving leading figures of stage and cinema will inevitably include the mention of famous persons, but Kathleen Tynan's name-dropping, if inevitable, is incessant.

More important, *The Life of Kenneth Tynan* encounters the unavoidable difficulties of a book written by a surviving spouse about a dead husband or wife. Intimate details of no real significance in the subject's life are included because they were important to the author. The description of the deterioration of the Tynans' marriage is subject to suspicions of special pleading: The husband's view of the reasons for the breakdown is necessarily absent.

Finally, others' opinions presented in the book may have been moderated by the fact that those expressing them were doing so to the widow of the man involved. Some of these statements seem forced and artificial.

Nevertheless, Kathleen Tynan has analyzed with admirable honesty the qualities which made her husband engaging, brilliant, and extraordinarily difficult. She shows that his resentment of his father, his anger at his mother for hiding from him the fact of his illegitimate birth, and his eventual guilt for virtually casting his mother aside all contributed to his consuming need to be admired, loved, and served. Kathleen Tynan also shows that her late husband's desire for instant gratification contributed to his inability to create the extended works, theatrical or critical, which would probably have secured for him a more important place in literary history. He was always active, but he moved too fast to write any plays or long books.

Kenneth Tynan was an elegant and pungent stylist who wrote perceptively and memorably about the British and American theater and the people who live in that world. His essays stand the test of time remarkably well, and his profiles of individuals are models of the brief biography. For these reasons, he has a significant place in the literary history of this century. Kathleen Tynan has succeeded in showing what the life of this tormented, brilliant man was like, as well as the forces that made him what he was.

John M. Muste

Sources for Further Study

Library Journal. CXII, October 1, 1987, p. 90.
London Review of Books. IX, December 10, 1987, p. 10.
Los Angeles Times Book Review. November 8, 1987, p. 3.
The New Republic. CXCVII, November 16, 1987, p. 23.
New Statesman. CXIV, December 4, 1987, p. 30.
The New York Review of Books. XCII, December 3, 1987, p. 5.
The New York Times Book Review. XCIII, January 3, 1988, p. 7.
The Observer. September 27, 1987, p. 26.
Publishers Weekly. CCXXXII, September 18, 1987, p. 168.
Time. CXXX, December 7, 1987, p. 85.

LINCOLN'S DREAMS

Author: Connie Willis (1945-   )
Publisher: Bantam Books (New York). 212 pp. $15.95
Type of work: Novel
Time: The 1980's, with dream flashbacks to the 1860's
Locale: Washington, D.C., and Virginia

In this blend of historical and scientific speculation, a researcher helps a young woman unravel the mystery of her haunting dreams about the Civil War period

> *Principal characters:*
> JEFF JOHNSTON, a researcher who provides background for historical novels
> THOMAS BROUN, his employer, a popular historical novelist
> ANNIE, a young woman disturbed by recurrent nightmares
> DR. RICHARD MADISON, her psychiatrist

Although Connie Willis' shorter works have brought her several prestigious awards in science fiction—including the Hugo Award and two Nebula Awards in a single year—they also have much in common with the best mystery writing: mastery of suspense, controlled tension, skill at hiding pertinent clues while leaving red herrings in plain sight. An example is "The Sidon in the Mirror," about an alien being who cannot help "mirroring" and imitating human evil. At the end of the story, the instigator of evil (a murder) is revealed to be not the obvious choice for a villain—an earthman who exudes sadistic menace—but a seemingly innocent young woman who has been blinded by another sadist. The kindhearted alien Mirror, in trying to protect her from further harm, becomes her unwitting tool for revenge.

Willis also demonstrates her flair for the unexpected in "Fire Watch," which earned for her the Hugo Award and one of her Nebula Awards in 1982. In this novella, a twenty-first century history student receives a dismaying practicum assignment: to travel back in time to World War II and defend Saint Paul's Cathedral from German incendiary bombs. He soon comes to care deeply for the Londoners of 1940 and carries out his work with passionate dedication. Returning to graduate school in his own time, however, he is given an examination on World War II statistics—how many bombing attacks, how many persons killed, from what causes? Outraged at the impersonality of these questions, he punches his instructor in the jaw, an act for which he fully expects to be expelled from the university, and possibly jailed. Instead, his instructor sends a handwritten note saying that he has passed the test with honors.

Often, Willis deploys her skills in generic fiction to put a unique twist on messages more commonly found in mainstream writing—the need for compassion toward all living beings, the futility and tragedy of war. For example, her stories of time travel, such as "Fire Watch," suggest that human values are eternal; they are "what is, . . . in us, saved forever."

From there it is only a short step to the premise of *Lincoln's Dreams*: that time itself persists; that the more intensely an individual feels any life experience, the more strongly the response endures beyond the boundaries of that individual's time. *Lincoln's Dreams* is about a young woman who serves as a vehicle for literally keeping the past alive; this role of hers is revealed slowly, as in a mystery plot.

Twenty-three-year-old Annie suffers from vivid, recurrent nightmares full of violent images from the Civil War period—a horse with its legs shot off, a battlefield covered with bodies, a commander groaning, "My fault!" Unable to stop the dreams, she seeks help at the Sleep Institute in Washington, D.C., but her psychiatrist there, Richard Madison, only complicates matters: He tries to push her symptoms into a framework of Freudian thought; he slips powerful drugs into her food without her knowledge; and, as if all this were not enough, he becomes her lover.

Richard's confused, unethical behavior (quickly intuited by Jeff Johnston, who roomed with him in college) is not the only thing that discredits him. Richard also proves unable to explain Annie's situation in a way that fits all the facts. Instead, each day he comes up with a new and more bizarre, quasi-scientific, childhood-trauma theory. The head of the Sleep Institute is equally convinced that Annie's dreams simply manifest the progress of some organic disease.

Jeff, however, suspects that the real truth is of a wholly different order. He earns his livelihood by painstaking research into the milieu of Abraham Lincoln and Robert E. Lee ("I had just spent that whole day trying to find out why General Longstreet was wearing a carpet slipper at Antietam"). Therefore, he soon recognizes the images in Annie's dreams as based on events in the life of General Lee. (The title *Lincoln's Dreams* may be one of Willis' red herrings; Thomas Broun, Jeff's employer, is obsessed with Lincoln, but no one else is.)

Jeff's insight comes early in the story, but the rest of the mystery unravels only gradually: Why are the dreams taking place? When will they end? Who is really having them, Annie or someone else? The more Jeff and Annie understand, the more important it becomes to them that the dreams be allowed to continue. To escape Richard's influence (he is determined to stop the nightmares) and to satisfy Annie's curiosity about the dream images, they hide out near historic battlefields such as Arlington, Virginia, and the adjacent cemeteries. At night, Annie has her devastating dreams; during the day, she and Jeff visit the battlefields that are the scenes of those dreams.

They develop increasingly interesting theories about the dreams. They speculate, for example, that the ancient Egyptians could have been right in regarding dreams as messages from the dead. Later, using a contemporary analogy, Jeff wonders if Annie's dreams might be "a kind of prerecorded

message left by Lee." Whatever their evolving interpretations, Jeff and Annie agree on the purpose of the dreams: to relieve Lee of a tremendous burden of sorrow.

> "What if you had so much guilt and grief that you went on dreaming after you were
> dead? . . . You told me Lee was a good man," Annie said, "and he is, Jeff, but he had to
> send all those boys back into battle. . . . He knew they'd be killed. . . . How could he
> stand it? . . . I think they still haunt him, after all these years, even though he's dead."

Jeff thinks of Lee's dreams as "powerful enough to have blasted their way
across a hundred years to Annie."

Meanwhile, Richard keeps trying to make contact with Jeff through the
latter's telephone-answering machine. Richard's ostensible purpose is to get
Annie back under his professional care, but his messages, each containing a
new theory about sexual guilt, repressed Oedipal attachments, or rebellion
against his authority, sound increasingly strident and implausible. Only near
the end of the story does Richard regain some credibility, by correctly diag-
nosing Annie's angina pectoris and showing genuine concern for her as a patient. Abandoning Freudian interpretations, he now argues that Annie's
nightmares have been premonitory symptoms of her worsening condition.
(Broun has been chasing down a similar theory with respect to Lincoln, who
reportedly dreamed about his own funeral the night before he was assas-
sinated.)

At this point, Annie becomes convinced that she must choose between
self-preservation and duty to Lee. Duty means continuing to have Lee's
dreams, which somehow (it is never fully explained) aggravate her illness.
Jeff, by now hopelessly in love, helps Annie escape Richard once again, but
in so doing he sends her to almost certain death.

Lincoln's Dreams is an intriguing blend of historical detective work and
scientific speculation. In its profound treatment of the love-and-duty theme,
it is also a multilayered love story. The novel does not, however, do equal
justice to the love element on all levels.

The trouble is that the beloved—Annie—is inadequately characterized.
Her past is never explained; her personal mannerisms, if any, are never presented; even her physical description is held to a minimum. She spends most
of her waking hours in a daze or trance, coming to life only when she and
Jeff approach important Civil War battlefields ("I know this place").

Perhaps, by avoiding in-depth portrayal, Willis intended to show Annie as
she would appear to an actual observer: awake to the inner life of her
dreams, but dead to the everyday concerns of other people. In any case, the
reader is given too little of Annie to understand or care about. This is a serious shortcoming in a figure obviously meant by the author to carry so
much philosophical import.

Annie's sketchy characterization leads to an additional problem in the novel: How is the reader to identify with Jeff's love of her? Indeed, that love itself is conveyed only through occasional brief hints, and the range of possibilities in Jeff and Annie's situation is never fully confronted. Despite Richard's recent exploitation of her, Annie does not hesitate to rent a hotel suite with Jeff, a near stranger, and the two spend virtually twenty-four hours a day together. Paradoxically—and unbelievably—Annie never reveals any feelings about Richard's sexual opportunism; yet she shows acute embarrassment upon waking from a sleepwalking episode, witnessed by Jeff, to find that the top button on her nightgown has come undone ("pulled away from the long curve of her throat"). Jeff's unvoiced response to her embarrassment is: "I wanted to shout at her, 'I'm not Richard. I'd never take advantage of you while you were asleep,' . . . but I wasn't sure that was the truth." The reader, however, is all too sure that it is the truth. While it would be cynically presumptuous (and quite out of place in this story) to insist on some physical liaison, most readers probably would prefer to witness more of Jeff's agony—perhaps a vivid conflict of desire versus honor to match Annie's love-and-duty dilemma.

The near-Victorian delicacy of this subject's treatment is linked to the novel's other major problem: an excessively downplayed style. The loves in this story deserve to be told in more dramatic tones—as do the dream interpretations, based as they are on a highly sensational concept. In vain, however, does the reader look for emotional crescendos in the style of *Lincoln's Dreams*. As in her short fiction, so in this novel Willis repeats key phrases for emphasis: "though she was dead. Though she was dead." This device, however, so effective in stories such as "And Come From Miles Around," has little impact in *Lincoln's Dreams*. It is as though Willis had fashioned the novel's style to match Annie's undramatic exterior.

Nevertheless, *Lincoln's Dreams* is a highly imaginative tale founded on a compelling concept. In addressing basic questions such as the nature of dreams, of communication, and of human responsibility, the novel surpasses the confines of the fantasy and science-fiction genre. It may be that the limitations of characterization and style were inevitable, given Willis' approach to the subject. In any case, one hopes for many more full-length works from this important writer.

Thomas Rankin

Sources for Further Study

Booklist. LXXXIII, March 15, 1987, p. 1098.
Kirkus Reviews. LV, April 1, 1987, p. 519.
Library Journal. CXII, April 15, 1987, p. 102.

The New York Times Book Review. XCII, June 7, 1987, p. 18.
Publishers Weekly. CCXXXI, April 3, 1987, p. 67.
Science Fiction Chronicle. VIII, March, 1987, p. 43.
The Washington Post Book World. XVII, May 24, 1987, p. 6.
West Coast Review of Books. XIII, May, 1987, p. 26.

THE LITERARY GUIDE TO THE BIBLE

Editors: Robert Alter (1935-   ) and Frank Kermode (1919-   )
Publisher: The Belknap Press of Harvard University Press (Cambridge, Massachusetts). Illustrated. 678 pp. $29.95
Type of work: Biblical criticism from a literary perspective

This book should be read by anyone seriously interested in the Bible, but it should not be the only guide followed

It is somehow fitting that a work dedicated to a literary understanding of the Bible, that "collection of collections," should be a collection itself. That the collection has forty contributions only makes the harmony more complete (forty being an important symbolic number in the Bible). The scholars are a diverse group, yet with much in common. The vast majority are either literary critics or biblical specialists with a literary bent, yet a medievalist (Bernard McGinn) and an anthropologist (Edmund Leach) are to be found here, too. Many have a Jewish background, and it would be fair to say that even many of those who do not have such a background show an appreciation of the rabbinical tradition of biblical interpretation. It is only natural that this should be so, since the literary approach taken in this volume is much more sympathetic in general to the richness of readings the Bible has produced within postbiblical communities than has been traditional biblical scholarship.

This guide is organized into three sections: Old Testament (Hebrew Bible is the term used within the section), New Testament, and General Essays. Because of the nature of the work, it is not necessary to begin at the beginning, with the exception of the general introduction and the introductions to the Old and New Testament sections. Most readers will find that they want to begin a tome of this size and scope by reading in the book here and there, rather than reading it straight through.

This work is a literary feast of its own, complete with such verbal delicacies as "fabular elegance." Appropriately enough, it has an editorial unity in spite of the great diversity of scholarship represented by the contributors—appropriately, because the editorial tendency is to find the literary/aesthetic unity within the diversity of biblical texts, as well. This tendency serves as a necessary corrective to traditional biblical scholarship's fragmentation of the text, yet at times it becomes tendentious.

The recent crosscurrents between modern literary criticism and biblical criticism on the one hand, and between traditional midrashic methods of interpretation and avant-garde trends in the interpretation of texts in general have made a book such as this one not only possible but inevitable. Many similar approaches and insights to those found in this book had begun to surface within traditional biblical criticism itself in the last few years. This has been largely a result of the rise of redaction criticism, canonical criticism, a renewed interest in the history of interpretation of the biblical texts within believing communities, and the aforementioned influence of developments in the literary field on biblical studies. Even many form critics, the group most often maligned (though not by name) in this volume, have more recently swung away from a concentration on the earliest forms of the text and have been on the forefront of responsible structural analysis of the text as we have it.

Furthermore, much of what is being put forth in this book has been presupposed by biblical scholarship at one time or another, either as a starting point or as one of the many methods one must bring to bear on a text in order to understand both it and its historical contexts fully. Hermann Gunkel, for example, understood the literary (he would have said literary-critical) issues raised in this book well, as did Julius Wellhausen before him (though he took a different point of view with regard to the evidence than do most of these contributors). Martin Noth, Gerhard von Rad, and other more recent biblical critics have continued to note both unity and diversity in the Bible, depending on whether they are talking about the structure or theme of a given text or its lives in the communities which produced and preserved it. Ironically, the legacy of these scholars was nevertheless destined to drive biblical scholarship in a direction which has made the writing of a book such as this one both necessary and timely.

The Old Testament section is both the longest section of the book and the one which hangs together best. Joel Rosenberg's article on Samuel may be one of the better articulations of the editorial tendency. Rosenberg sees Samuel (both books) as a complex unity. He believes the text has been continuously edited until a late date, yet contains very early traditions. Finally, Samuel has been incorporated into the larger story of the Bible as the centerpiece of a "continuous historical account." It is important to note that Rosenberg sees this unified work as a realistic narrative, however, and not as an eyewitness account or compilation of historically verifiable material. One is reminded of the scholar who was once asked whether he believed in the Mosaic authorship of the Pentateuch. He reportedly replied: "I think it is a wonderful mosaic." It would be hard to argue with this kind of sophisticated "unity" from any point of view, and, though they differ in their specific emphasis, the other contributors can be clustered around this kind of general approach.

James Ackerman, for example, seems almost in the mainstream of biblical scholarship when he talks about the redactors of biblical books as the creators of new contexts for old stories. Yet he seems to overinterpret, on the literary side, when he bases his reading on a series of opposing relationships (meat/manna, spirit/word). This kind of reading can only be verified against the backdrop of a more comprehensive analysis. Nothing short of a systematic preference of "word" over "spirit" in this context would overcome the otherwise generally positive attitude of Israelite literature toward spirit as the principle of animation for all life which emanates from God.

The general essays are the most diverse and perhaps for that reason the most entertaining. They also provide an abstract respite from the nearly unrelenting empiricism of the textual analysis in the other two sections.

Gerald Bruns ("Midrash and Allegory") has an intriguingly sophisticated philosophical justification for a literary approach. It is not new—Thomas Kuhn, Michael Polanyī, and Hans Frei have all made similar observations elsewhere—and is presupposed by many other writers in this volume, but Bruns presents it extremely well. In short, he sees much of what has been done in biblical criticism as the result of a Romantic idea of objectivity. A unitary approach, on the other hand, reads the Bible in a manner closer to the way those who passed it on apparently meant it to be read and the way it has in fact been read until the Enlightenment. His critique of the post-Enlightenment conceptual paradigm is well stated. The problem found here permeates the book: We not only cannot go back to prior ways of looking at the world, except imaginatively, but Bruns's critique itself depends upon the very myth or axiom of objectivity to which he is objecting. No other age has been capable of such brutal self-examination.

Edmund Leach's article "Fishing for Men on the Edge of the Wilderness" shows most clearly that the kind of unitary text this book is interested in is not of a religious type, but unity at a literary level, "a unitary work of art." His essay is another critique of biblical criticism's rendering the text a cold, dead, historical artifact, and attempts a recovery of a symbolic reading more consistent with the Bible's actual use throughout history. Yet his brilliant analysis is the ultimate externalization of the text: The Bible "is a corpus of mythology which provides a justification for the religious performances of believers." Religious readers of the Bible and many biblical scholars have at least had this in common: They have sought and found value in the biblical text on what they perceived to be historical—not symbolic or aesthetic—bases.

Gerald Hammond's opinion of English translations of the Bible is one which favors the King James Version (KJV) not only aesthetically, but in terms of communicating faithfully the meaning of the ancient texts themselves. One cannot argue successfully against a version with a history such as the KJV has enjoyed. Nevertheless, Hammond's is a difficult position to maintain, if for no other reason than that language and its use is a moving target. Indeed, nearly every "new" translation of the Bible (including both the Vulgate and the KJV) has been criticized on its first appearance, only to be accepted as the "standard" version, by one group or another, sometime later. Usually it takes only a few generations for the "beauty" (often to be translated "I'm used to the wording") of the traditional version to be abandoned for the intelligibility of a newer one, and even fewer generations for the new, now standard, version to be defended vehemently against even newer competitors as more beautiful and even more meaningful.

In his programmatic introduction to the Old Testament section, Robert Alter makes a comment about the "internally allusive character" of the Hebrew Bible, which he likens to great works of twentieth century literature. He may be accurately describing a literary phenomenon, but he must know that the meaning and intention of the phenomenon itself depend heavily on the disciplines of historiography (largely through archaeology) and anthropology, as poor as these disciplines admittedly are at giving us data about the biblical texts. Put another way, ancient methods of midrash and modern literary allusion very likely have only a superficial congruence, while reflecting radically different modes of thinking about the meaning of speech, texts, events, and their interrelationships both to one another and to other speech, texts, and events.

The inadequacy of interpreting the biblical text from a purely modern literary standpoint can be shown from a relatively simple example. When J. P. Fokkelman says that the "hyperbolic ages" of those mentioned in the genealogical tables of Genesis 5, 10, and 11 "indicate that life is long," he ignores other such tables from ancient Near Eastern literature. These ancient tables indicate by their similar structure—ten personages before and ten after the flood, listed in generally decreasing age until "normal" lifespans are reached—that this was a given formula for connecting primordial and historical time in the literature of the period.

The problem with a focused literary-aesthetic reading of the Bible is the same as with any other single-perspective reading: One cannot possibly take account of the number of necessary, significant elements in the interpretation of a text (any text, but especially an ancient sacred text) by means of a single methodology. What is needed is a holistic methodological perspective from which to adjudicate not so much competing readings as different and perhaps complementary methods. One can see awareness of this at times in this book: David Damrosch ("Leviticus") states that the Bible uses "profoundly literary techniques for ultimately nonliterary ends." What can be understood from this is that (at least these) texts have extratextual significance, which in turn can only be adequately understood by applying other methods along with literary analysis.

Looked at from the beginning, a biblical passage or book can be seen as wonderfully discrete moments of creativity patched together by the glue of time and tradition. Looked at from the end, the same piece of writing can be viewed as an incredibly complex, subtle, yet seemingly simple coherence. In other words, this may not be an either-or situation, but something, at least at certain points, closer to both-and. Jack Sasson has put it simply in his article on Ruth: " . . . one approach rarely excludes the other."

Robert Bascom

Sources for Further Study

America. CLVII, December 5, 1987, p. 431.
Booklist. LXXXIV, September 15, 1987, p. 104.
Chicago Tribune. November 8, 1987, XIV, p. 1.
The Christian Science Monitor. October 21, 1987, p. 19.
Kirkus Reviews. LV, August 1, 1987, p. 1119.
Library Journal. CXII, October 1, 1987, p. 98.
The New Republic. CXCVII, October 26, 1987, p. 28.
The New York Times Book Review. XCII, December 20, 1987, p. 1.
The New Yorker. LXIII, January 11, 1988, p. 94.
Newsweek. January 18, 1988, p. 72.

LITTLE WILSON AND BIG GOD

Author: Anthony Burgess (1917-   )
Publisher: Weidenfield and Nicolson (New York). 460 pp. $22.50
Type of work: Autobiography
Time: 1917-1959
Locale: Great Britain, Gibraltar, and Malaya

Anthony Burgess' autobiography describes his childhood in England, his army years in Gibraltar, and the period he spent teaching in Malaya before discovering, at the age of forty-two, his vocation as a writer

> *Principal personages:*
> JOHN BURGESS WILSON, an author, musician, and writer
> LEWELA "LYNNE" JONES WILSON, his wife

Readers familiar with the works of the prolific Anthony Burgess should not be surprised either to hear that he has written an autobiography or that the work, the first of two projected volumes, is among other things a prolonged and bitter attack on the British establishment and the class system. Since the publication of his first novel in 1953, Burgess has cast an unsentimental eye upon the follies of his countrymen and contemporaries, and there has never been any reason to believe that age would blur his vision or blunt his pen. The author of twenty-nine novels and nearly as many other assorted works of poetry and prose, Burgess has long been established as a social satirist of diverse talents, including the unlikely capacity to write best-selling fiction. *Little Wilson and Big God*, which he announces as his second-to-last book, has the wit, cleverness, and bite of the best of his ingenious works.

The title of the book derives from a scornful comment by an exasperated priest, directed against the adolescent hero (born John Burgess Wilson) when he doubted the Sacrament, and it is a reasonably accurate description of the book's contents: The underlying preoccupation of the autobiography is the author's loss of faith and what is presented as the morbid consequence of this infidelity. A lapsed Catholic, Burgess views his past from the comfortable perspective of his current worldly success, but he is from the beginning perfectly open about the fact that he has never found a point of view to replace the certainties of his youth and that, despite the absurdities of the institutional Church, he would believe in its doctrines if he could. The work is pervaded by a sense of loss and colored by guilt, for the morass of political mismanagement and military ineptitude in which the young hero flounders about after he leaves the church is muddier than the mysteries that drove him away from Catholicism. A secular misanthropist, Burgess is like Saint Augustine before his conversion. *Little Wilson and Big God*, an energetic and comic memoir, owes its underlying shape to the conventions of religious autobiography.

Burgess' story, as described for the reader in this first volume, follows a long downward curve. Born in 1917 to a mother who died of influenza when he was less than a year old, John Burgess Wilson was reared in the provincial city of Manchester, England, by an unloving stepmother and a kind but alcoholic father who bequeathed him little but his musical talent. Burgess depicts a lonely and unprepossessing child. Bookish, without strong family ties, the child was alienated from his classmates by temperament and by choice. His Catholicism, which he took seriously, served to underline his position as an outsider in the Protestant working-class circles that dominated the town.

Young Wilson—he would not become Burgess until well into his fourth decade—was an above-average but not outstanding student who entertained himself with motion pictures, with books—especially the works of Gerard Manley Hopkins and James Joyce, whose religious preoccupations and linguistic intricacies reflected his own interests—and with music, which he taught himself to compose while still in his early teens. Failing repeatedly and perversely to win the scholarships to the Universities of Cambridge or Oxford that might have assured his acceptance into the privileged middle class, Wilson persuaded his family to help finance his education at Manchester University, where he took a degree in English literature. Academic music, his real interest, was closed to him because of his lack of conventional training.

Independence and adulthood brought neither freedom nor relief from the general grimness of a life of near-poverty. He wrote a thesis on Christopher Marlowe in 1943, with bombs falling in the streets around him, became engaged to a passionate Welsh student, and, after the usual unromantic agonies of basic training, was sent to Gibraltar as part of the Army Vocational and Cultural Corps, an educational unit designed to prepare enlisted men for the new society that was to await them when they returned to England to take up the strands of peacetime life. He was low in the military hierarchy, and since he could seldom take his duties seriously it seemed unlikely that he could rise. The task of spouting empty phrases to disgruntled workers who hated the war, the army, the Allies, and the British cause was ludicrous, particularly when he agreed with his audience. Lynne, by now his wife, wrote letters from England recounting her affairs and upbraiding him for his failure to progress. The local girls he took to bed for consolation were on the whole unsatisfactory company. In short, the exhilaration and thrill of army life described in so many wartime memoirs missed him entirely.

Literature would become Wilson's career, but for his first thirty-five years there was little hint of it. His writing was confined to light verse and the occasional obscene acrostic. Music, on the other hand, remained not simply a talent but a necessity, his only relief from impossible and frustrating situations. He had no interest himself in performing, but he composed compulsively for others, writing concerti for ships' orchestras, popular songs in three languages for bar singers, and marches for military bands. In the bohemian circles he frequented with Lynne when he had leave in London and occasionally after the war, he met publishers and poets, but he thought of himself as a musician, and it was only by way of music that he stumbled upon his literary talent: Given an ultimatum by his wife to make one last attempt to make a living at music, he began an opera libretto and found to his great surprise that the sustained exercise of verbal skills was a pleasure and a challenge. The libretto was a failure, but he then very quickly produced one short novel (*A Vision of Battlements*, 1965) based on his Gibraltar experiences, and began a second, *The Worm and the Ring* (1961). The use of myth as a substructure, a technique which had long fascinated him in James Joyce's *Ulysses* and *Finnegans Wake*, at this point provided the necessary bridge for him between the two forms of art. In *A Vision of Battlements*, he used Vergil's *Aeneid*, he explains, and in the second novel, *The Ring of the Nibelungs*, as a kind of ground bass, which allowed him a free hand to experiment with other musical elements in the plot to obtain the complex effects that had always intrigued him in music.

Although the first novel was read with interest by a friendly publisher, it was put aside, and when *Time for a Tiger*, his third novel but first published work of fiction, saw print in 1953, it was not especially successful. The career of a writer in England was as unpromising as that of a composer. There was simply no money in it, no way to live. Teaching adults in rural England, his first civilian job, although it had its temporary pleasures, was clearly another dead end. In desperation, he and Lynne escaped to Malaya to another teaching post, but the heat, the confusion, and the relative isolation there proved even more dispiriting than the dreariness of England. Lynne, lonely and bitter, took refuge in the alcoholism that would finally kill her; Wilson (not yet Burgess on a full-time basis) felt guilty at having destroyed her and was equally miserable. The pressure and the despair, coming upon a man who seemed to possess no beliefs or purposes to sustain him, were devastating. When he collapsed after a second Malayan posting, a brain tumor was discovered. He had, the doctor reportedly said, less than a year to live.

Many literary autobiographies are built around a point of discovery, a revelation of vocation that is equivalent to religious conversion. *Little Wilson and Big God* ends, however, before the fruits of conversion can be gathered. Wilson's continued existence as Anthony Burgess, the writer of the preface in 1986, suggests that a rebirth is in store in the second volume, but the details of the hero's emergence from the hellishness of his early adult life are not hinted at here. The author's Malayan experience may not constitute the "dark night of the soul" dictated by religious convention, but it is hard to see how his moral, physical, and psychological situation could have been much worse than the state described at the end of the book. Alienated from his countrymen, responsible for the sickness of a wife whom he loved, an alcoholic with a sentence of death hanging over him, little John Wilson is left dangling in the middle of his career like one of those sinners depicted hanging above the inferno from the hands of an angry God.

Little Wilson and Big God is intriguing on many levels but, shaped as it is to reflect the dominant interests and convictions of the adult author, it is not a comfortable book to read. The reader may find the young hero's precocity slightly dampening and even self-indulgent: Is it really appropriate to reprint all those youthful poems? Must one admire the fact that the author remembers the lyrics to so many obscure songs, even if their presence does testify to the importance of music in the child's life? In addition, he or she may be put off by the persona Burgess chooses to embody his experiences: The hero has much in common with the central figures of those twenty-nine novels.

The character that emerges from the autobiography is in fact a peculiar one. Burgess describes himself as an angry young man before angry young men became fashionable, but the anger he describes is as much against himself as against the social system. Many of the events he describes would be amusing in a novel, as they often are when he uses them in his fiction, but they have a disturbing effect when they are used to reveal—or conceal—the pathos of an unhappy life. His comments about his wife, for example, who was repeatedly unfaithful to him, are hard to interpret. He claims that he loved Lynne throughout their long marriage, but he describes her as selfish and overbearing, and the apparently comic situations in which they often found themselves clearly lacerated both participants.

Burgess' novels have sometimes been characterized as cold, that is, as essentially detached and formal. A cerebral quality certainly pervades *Little Wilson and Big God*. The reader may sense that the author is analytic, not truly introspective, and that genuine self-revelation is unlikely. Like Vladimir Nabokov, Burgess seems always one step removed from experience, entranced with the challenge of creating effect at the expense of emotive content. Certainly, the epigraph of the book—"Time, in fact, is rather vulgarly dramatic; it is the sentimentalist of the dimensions" (Constant Lambert)—suggests an ironic eye. Given the temperament and the experiences Burgess describes, detachment may have been the price of survival.

It is misleading, however, to complain too much. *Little Wilson and Big God*, with its powerful depiction of an angry working class and a gray and greedy England, is a fine corrective to those readers who romanticize England in general and British Catholicism in particular. Darkened by the shadows of guilt and pain which give definition to the author's experience and make meaningful his title, *Little Wilson and Big God* is a curious and haunting book, an impersonal, personal memoir that occupies a place half-way between melodrama and cruel farce.

Jean W. Ashton

Sources for Further Study

Booklist. LXXXIII, December 15, 1986, p. 603.
The Christian Science Monitor. April 7, 1987, p. 26.
Guardian Weekly. March 22, 1987, p. 18.
Kirkus Reviews. LIV, December 15, 1986, p. 1835.
Library Journal. CXXII, February 15, 1987, p. 148.
The Listener. CXVII, February 26, 1987, p. 20.
London Review of Books. IX, March 19, 1987, p. 22.
The New York Review of Books. XXXIV, May 7, 1987, p. 3.
The New York Times Book Review. XCII, February 22, 1987, p. 9.
The Observer. February 22, 1987, p. 28.
Publishers Weekly. CCXXXI, January 23, 1987, p. 54.
Time. CXXIX, February 16, 1987, p. 70.
The Times Literary Supplement. February 27, 1987, p. 203.
The Wall Street Journal. February 26, 1987, p. 20.

LOOK HOMEWARD
A Life of Thomas Wolfe

Author: David Herbert Donald (1920-   )
Publisher: Little, Brown and Company (Boston). Illustrated. 579 pp. $24.95
Type of work: Literary biography
Time: 1900-1941
Locale: The United States and Western Europe

In a scholarly biography, Donald narrates the life, explains the literary milieu, and clarifies the literary career of an important modern novelist

> *Principal personages:*
> THOMAS WOLFE, an American novelist
> ALINE BERNSTEIN, his intimate friend, a prominent designer for a New York theater company
> MAXWELL E. PERKINS, his editor at Charles Scribner's Sons
> EDWARD C. ASWELL, his editor at Harper and Brothers
> JULIA E. WOLFE, his mother
> W. O. WOLFE, his father

Although he produced several plays, numerous short stories, and other miscellaneous works, Thomas Wolfe (1900-1938) is best remembered for four lengthy autobiographical novels. *Look Homeward, Angel* (1929), based on the author's youth in Asheville, North Carolina, chronicles the life and early education of its hero, Eugene Gant, in a small town. *Of Time and the River* (1935) portrays a restless, questing young hero, also a persona of the author, who attempts to find himself through extensive foreign travels and numerous personal encounters. In *The Web and the Rock* (1939) and *You Can't Go Home Again* (1940), both published posthumously, Wolfe's hero and persona, George Webber, experiences genuine love, disillusionment, frustration in becoming a writer, and optimism for the future.

David Herbert Donald, a distinguished American Civil War historian, has undertaken a challenging subject for biography—challenging because of Wolfe's complicated, conflicted life and the huge amounts of material that a biographer must examine. Yet Donald enjoyed an advantage denied earlier biographers in that he could write with greater candor, those closest to Wolfe now being deceased. The first two-fifths of the text concerns Wolfe's life in Asheville, his education at the University of North Carolina and at Harvard University, and his life in New York until his first novel found a publisher—the first twenty-eight years of his life. The remainder chronicles the final decade of his life—the period of his literary achievement and fame.

In his preface, Donald sets forth what he hopes to achieve in the biography: to narrate a straightforward, biographical account without being unduly judgmental or intrusive, to relate Wolfe to his literary milieu, and to trace his evolution as a writer. All three objectives are accomplished with painstaking care, an abundance of documented detail and analysis, and illuminating insights. For the narrative, he draws heavily on Wolfe's letters, manuscript records, and papers or manuscripts of those who corresponded with him. At times Donald relies upon passages from Wolfe's autobiographical fiction, though he explains that he took care to corroborate fictional passages in other sources.

As for his relationships with other writers, Wolfe felt few lasting or deep influences, and these were likely to occur during rather brief periods of his life. Thus Donald incorporates these accounts in their proper chronological place, clarifying Wolfe's literary indebtedness to James Joyce, Sinclair Lewis, Ernest Hemingway, and F. Scott Fitzgerald, among many others. To clarify the development of Wolfe as a creative writer, Donald explains not only Wolfe's methods of writing but also the reactions of numerous others— teachers, editors, and writers—to his work as it was produced or published. What stands out, what always stands out with Wolfe, is his life as a remarkable individual and his brief and turbulent career as a writer.

As a person, Wolfe has always seemed larger than life, a view that he himself encouraged. At six-and-a-half-feet tall, weighing 250 pounds, he was physically commanding. His appetites for food, drink, and sex were in proportion to his size and his considerable stamina. His intellectual exertions were equally impressive: He claimed that some days he read twelve or fifteen books, and on one occasion he wrote ten thousand words in a day. Eminently likable, with considerable charm, he could usually make a favorable impression, particularly on those who could help him advance his career. He was restless, an inveterate traveler who made numerous trips to Europe and traveled widely in the United States.

Despite his expansive personality and strong physical presence, Wolfe was insecure, moody, highly vulnerable. Sensitive to slights and criticism, subject to phobias and paranoid fantasies, dependent upon alcohol for much of his life, unable to maintain lasting relationships, untidy, unmannerly, negligent of personal hygiene, he lived a restless, troubled existence for his brief thirty-eight years. His parents were a classic mismatch, strong willed but very different. The youngest child in the Wolfe household, he bore the brunt of his parents' antagonism. His mother, Julia, feeling no affection for her husband, looked to him for emotional support, and until he was twelve years old he slept in her bed. Significantly, when he later formed a serious but turbulent love relationship, it was with a woman more than seventeen years his senior. Few readers will disagree with Donald's conclusion that Wolfe was basically a narcissistic personality. Always in need of money, though never seriously deprived, he was willing for others, including his long-suffering, generous mistress Aline Bernstein, to support him. Those who knew him best treated him as a child who never quite grew up. At the University of North Carolina, where his father supported him, he received the money in small amounts upon request, for W. O. Wolfe did not trust him to handle larger sums. At Charles Scribner's Sons, Maxwell E. Perkins set up an account for Wolfe, paid his royalties in small portions, and saw to it that company accountants filed his income-tax returns.

No more able to commit himself to a creed or ideology than to a person, Wolfe developed intellectual interests as his experiences led him. During the ideological ferment of the 1930's, he was first attracted to Fascism, then repelled by it; later attracted to Communism, he was unwilling to attach himself to the movement. The Agrarians, his contemporaries who championed his region, found in him no Southern nostalgia.

Yet, as Donald makes clear, a few intellectual currents influenced his fiction. Always a voracious reader, he especially liked the Greek and Roman classics, a source that invited him to see ordinary human life in mythic terms. At Chapel Hill, he assimilated from his philosophy professor Horace Williams a kind of popularized Hegelianism, a view that disparate forces could be synthesized. Under John Livingston Lowes at Harvard, he first encountered the literary criticism of Samuel Taylor Coleridge, whose view that the imagination could produce a powerfully integrated artistic unity from widely diverse impressions, ideas, and experiences was especially congenial to his nature. He first felt the impact of the psychological theories of Sigmund Freud and Carl Jung after Bernstein introduced him to modern psychoanalysis.

Perhaps the most pervasive influence on Wolfe's fiction was his early interest in drama. At Chapel Hill, where he wrote his first play, and at Harvard as a member of Professor George Baker's celebrated playwriting class, he was ambitious for a career as a dramatist. He possessed a talent for grasping the power of dramatic encounters and an ability to write both description and dialogue. He became familiar with movements in modern drama, notably Expressionism, which advocated the portrayal of inner conflict through manipulation of external reality. Although he was unsuccessful as a dramatist, his efforts brought his talent to the attention of people who would later be of assistance to him.

Turning from drama to the novel, Wolfe sought to produce the epic work of American fiction. An autobiographical work of many volumes, it would depict the culture and history of the nation through the experiences of a single questing individual. He produced millions of words in prose—often vital, charged with metaphor, sparkling in its diction and cadenced with rhythmic grace. He achieved intensities of emotional experience and psychological depths reached by few writers, and the effects of Wolfe's prose at its best are overpowering. Further, his characters were strongly drawn because he copied them from life, often providing only a thin disguise.

Wolfe's first two novels brought him wide acclaim as a serious artist. Although informed critical opinion was somewhat divided, many critics predicted a bright future for him. Others, however, called attention to his artistic weaknesses, which, as Donald points out, were all too apparent. Perhaps because he sought to depict powerful emotional scenes and employed expressionistic techniques, his characters did not develop to any significant degree. A more glaring flaw surfaced early and was never adequately overcome, despite the fact that he himself recognized it: Wolfe lacked a sense of form, of archetectonics. Professor Baker commented after seeing the revised script of Wolfe's play *Welcome to Our City* (1983), "Your gift is not selection, but profusion." Wolfe had written too many words and created too many characters to produce a successful drama. With the novel, he had to rely, reluctantly, on editors who knew how to cut and arrange his prose— hence the fascinating story of his tortuous relationship with his two editors, Perkins and Edward C. Aswell.

After numerous publishers had rejected Wolfe's first novel, *Look Homeward, Angel*, Scribners accepted the work, and Perkins became Wolfe's editor. At the time he was serving as editor for, among others, Fitzgerald and Hemingway. As Wolfe acknowledged, Perkins became much more than an editor—he was father figure, friend, confidant, and "collaborator." The manuscript, which previous editors had judged too long and diffuse to publish, ran to 330,000 words, longer than four average novels of the time. Under Perkins' direction, ninety thousand words were cut. Although some of the reductions were made for reasons of taste, most of the cuts represented an effort to bring about greater unity. The novel was successful when published, though not sufficiently so to provide Wolfe an adequate income.

Between the end of 1929 and December, 1933, when he delivered the manuscript of his second novel to Scribners, Wolfe supported himself with a Guggenheim Fellowship, obtained with Perkins' help, and the sale of his short stories to magazines. In its original form, *Of Time and the River* ran 750,000 words, an indication that Wolfe had not been able to profit from Perkins' skill in organization and compression. After examining the work, Perkins persuaded Wolfe that the huge work should be made into two separate novels, the romantic plot (based upon Wolfe's relationship with Bernstein) to be reserved for later publication. This division and other reductions left 344,000 words. For the remainder of 1934, Wolfe worked, with increasing irritation, under Perkins' direction to reduce the size of his book and to impose a kind of unity on the material. Finally, Perkins made the decision to send the book to the printer. *Of Time and the River* received a generally favorable reception and was commercially successful, though a few respected critics attacked it for its verbosity and loose organization.

Disappointed by the criticism and nursing a host of grievances, real and imaginary, Wolfe resolved to take charge of his own career and leave Scribners. After a period of indecision and searching, he decided to sign with Harper and Brothers where Aswell, a junior editor, had favorably impressed him. With similar regional, educational, and personal backgrounds, the two men took an instant liking to each other. For a generous advance of ten thousand dollars, Wolfe agreed to write for Harpers, signing the contract on the final day of 1937. Before Harpers could publish any book from his pen, indeed before any manuscript could be completed, Wolfe died in September, 1938, of a recurrence of tuberculosis that spread to his brain.

Answell was left to perform the role that Perkins before him had assumed, though without the author's assistance. From the huge bundle of manuscripts Wolfe left behind, Aswell assembled two novels—*The Web and the Rock* and *You Can't Go Home Again*—and a volume of short stories, *The Hills Beyond* (1941). Donald shows that Aswell went further than Perkins as editor, though he followed essentially the same methods. To forestall lawsuits, he changed the names and descriptions of characters. He also provided transitional passages between episodes of the novels, organized the episodes on the basis of a general plan left by Wolfe to form a smooth narrative, and pruned the luxuriance of Wolfe's style. Aswell's editorial alterations have made these final works highly questionable to modern critics. Although Donald shares some of their reservations, he is inclined to doubt that another editor, confronting the same challenges that Aswell faced, could have done better.

During the postwar years, common judgment named as the four great modern American novelists William Faulkner, Ernest Hemingway, John Steinbeck, and Wolfe, in no particular order. Through the winnowing of time, Faulkner has emerged the front-runner, while Wolfe has dropped to a distant fourth. He is now regarded as a writer whose promise remained substantially unfulfilled, though a reassessment is conceivable. Donald has made a significant contribution to our knowledge of Wolfe as an artist, clarifying his strengths without concealing his weaknesses.

Stanley Archer

Sources for Further Study

Booklist. LXXXIII, October 15, 1986, p. 298.
Kirkus Reviews. LIV, November 15, 1986, p. 1697.
Library Journal. CXI, December, 1986, p. 111.
Los Angeles Times Book Review. February 22, 1987, p. 4.
Maclean's. C, March 2, 1987, p. 49.
The New Republic. CXCVI, March 23, 1987, p. 30.
The New York Review of Books. XXXIV, September 24, 1987, p. 34.
The New York Times Book Review. XCII, February 8, 1987, p. 13.
Newsweek. CIX, February 2, 1987, p. 69.
Publishers Weekly. CCXXX, December 19, 1986, p. 38.
Time. CXXIX, March 16, 1987, p. 80.
The Wall Street Journal. February 24, 1987, p. 28.
The Washington Post Book World. XVII, February 1, 1987, p. 3.

LOVE UNKNOWN

Author: A. N. Wilson (1950-   )
Publisher: Viking (New York). 202 pp. $16.95
Type of work: Novel
Time: The 1960's to the 1980's
Locale: England and France

A comic novel about despair, human frailty, love, and saving grace in the contemporary Western world

> *Principal characters:*
> MONICA CUNNINGHAM, a woman whose reserve and self-reliance mask her own desires
> LINDA (BELINDA, or LADY MASON), a woman who mistakes sex for love
> RICHELDIS, the third of this trio of former roommates, a woman who confuses reality with fairy tale and suffers because of her own two-dimensional self and a similarly depthless marriage
> SIMON LONGWORTH, Richeldis' wealthy, handsome, but finally unprincely husband
> BARTLE LONGWORTH, Simon's "dotty" brother
> MADGE CRUDEN, Richeldis' mother, a once-famous London publisher

If *The Whistle Blower* (1987) is the kind of film—a mystery—that only the British can do well, as reviewers have pointed out, then *Love Unknown*, A. N. Wilson's eleventh novel in as many years, is the kind of novel that only the British can do, or, some would say, that only the British would want to do. It is a decidedly dry comedy, its dryness compounded with a liberal dose of references to local products, customs, and places that will please the native reader and puzzle the foreign-born. In considering the rather limited scope, perhaps even the provincialism, of this novel, one is reminded of not only Jane Austen's "little bit . . . of ivory," as she described her fiction, but also of Mark Twain's American impatience with what he regarded as the pettiness and narrowness of her work. "Just because everything is demure on the surface does not mean that underneath there isn't a swirling tempest," warns one of Wilson's characters. She may be right, but not, certainly, about *Love Unknown*, for what swirls beneath the surface is no tempest but is instead the author's careful and at times brilliant undermining of such rhetorical posturing and all that it implies. Working within the long tradition of the English comic novel, Wilson has managed to write a work which is at once a satire and a sad comedy, one in which the traditional form of the comic novel undergoes a subtle but nevertheless significant modification as Austen's bit of ivory comes under the pressure of postmodern process.

The doubleness of *Love Unknown* manifests itself in the very first sentence. "Once upon a time, some twenty years ago, there were three nice young women, who lived together at 73b Oakmoor Road, London N.W.2."

Wilson plays the formulaic opening and the "three nice young women" motif from traditional fairy tales against a Dreiserian realism of setting, and in this way, he introduces the conflict between romance and realism—both as narrative modes and as modes of thought—that will figure so importantly throughout the rest of the novel. The opening sentence suggests as well a certain satirical skepticism on the author's part (or, alternately, on the authorial narrator's) concerning the modern age, one for which a period of only twenty years constitutes a gulf separating present reality from mythic past, an age so trapped in its own present moment and point of view as to be unaware of anything older and perhaps more enduring. Significantly, the novel begins not with the first of its twenty chapters but instead with a thirteen-page "Prehistory," covering the period from the time the three women room together to "the day before the action begins" twenty years later. It is a period about which the memories of the three women are not to be trusted insofar as they have used omission and distortion to turn facts into myths, unconsciously revising reality to fit their versions of past events. Because their memories are faulty and their stories—or histories—not entirely to be trusted, Wilson has a narrator step into his "Prehistory" "to record that happy time on their behalf." This narrative voice—half-solicitous, half-condescending—will subsequently efface himself, surfacing only indirectly in the ordering and editing into a more or less unified account of the various stories that concern the novel's five or six major characters, each story told in the third person but employing a quite different center of consciousness—a technique which keeps the reader off-balance and on his interpretive toes. This is precisely where he or she should be, for *Love Unknown* is very much a novel about the incompleteness of all stories (and all interpretations), including those fictions the characters call their lives.

At first, the three women appear as nearly allegorical figures. Linda, later called Belinda and also Lady Mason, is the Promiscuous Woman, the fool for love who always rushes in where her less oversexed roommates would never think to tread. Monica Cunningham, on the other hand, is intelligent and solitary, a seemingly self-reliant woman who has spent the past fifteen years in Paris, where she has adopted the feminist stance that enables her to continue to live her "spare, uncluttered" existence, as Lady Mason gently describes it. (Monica wonders if her friend really means that her life is "empty"; the reader is inclined to agree, seeing in Monica's desire to master each new foreign language a way to avoid having to deal with real people in any sort of truly human relationship.) Richeldis, the last of the three, is the romantically and then later the conventionally happy one who, in the "Prehistory," has married "the Man of her Dreams" and, as in a fairy tale, "lived happily ever after," which in this novel means until the end of the "Prehistory." Richeldis is a walking cliché, a fairy-tale princess in the Disney mold whose very essence (which is the essence of her *mauvaise foi*, her Sartrean "bad faith") is embodied in her "coo-ing, sweet, even-tempered voice." First a wife and then a mother, Richeldis is so "nothing" herself—so completely self-effacing—that she even omits all first-person-singular pronouns from the letters she writes. For her, there is no "I" at all. That her husband, Simon Longworth, should begin to stray from a marriage to this greeting-card wife is hardly surprising; that he should take up with one of her former roommates, on the other hand, is a bit dismaying (to the reader, that is; Richeldis remains blissfully ignorant of reality), and that this friend should be the severe Monica rather than the endlessly bedded Belinda is a shock to the reader if not to the novel's authorial narrator, who takes everything in stride in proper "stiff upper lip" British fashion. Simon's adultery signals not only the (seeming) end of his and his wife's fairy-tale happiness but also the baselessness of the myth upon which that happiness was founded. The happiness that Monica belatedly demands for herself is equally mistaken in that it is based upon her similarly romantic delusion concerning a prince, Simon, who turns out to be considerably less than charming.

At first the novel seems to be about these three women, but it soon becomes evident that Belinda plays no significant role beyond her allegorical typecasting and as an audience for her friends' unfolding stories and that Richeldis is soon overshadowed by Monica, whose story in turn becomes less interesting than and subordinate to that of Simon, the prince who turns into a frog. Simon comes to center stage but only unwittingly to expose himself, warts and all. Although he has reason enough to be dissatisfied with his marriage to so saccharine a woman as Richeldis, it soon becomes clear that whatever her shortcomings, he is no better a spouse than she. Rather, he is only different in his particular weaknesses, the chief one being a total self-absorption which appears all the more remarkable given his complete inability to act on his own. For Simon, it is everyone else who is wrong, everyone else who is to blame, everyone else who is responsible for whatever threatens to disrupt his pursuit of pleasure and (above all) equanimity. He can cheat his "dotty" brother Bartle out of his fair share of the family wealth and then rationalize his behavior, claiming that Bartle "had neither needed it nor worked for it. Bartle had been too stupid to query the settlement anyway." He can even imagine murdering his wife and rationalizing that act as a way of sparing Richeldis the unhappiness of knowing that he is in love with her best friend. To his credit, Simon does realize that his life, though outwardly successful, has been a failure and that the cause is not his wife but instead the fact that he has lived without love; he understands too that he is not the all-for-love romantic he thought he would be with Monica by his side but is instead a forty-eight-year-old husband, father, and joint director of a sand quarry. It is not Simon's age that is the problem, or his roles as husband or father or administrator. What bars him from love is instead his unstated belief that love is something one either has or else gets—

a possession rather than a quality of mind and soul, the very quality which characterizes virtually every act and thought of his brother, Bartle.

Just as the novel shifts its focus from the women to Simon, so does it shift again from Simon to Bartle, its moral center. An unemployed clergyman whose halitosis was the comic cause of his first wife's leaving him and of his subsequently falling in love with his dental hygienist, Stephanie Moss, Bartle is a ridiculous figure, a walking joke, yet it is no accident that his name echoes that of one of Christ's twelve disciples. Bartle lives with Richeldis' equally if differently dotty mother Madge Cruden; "The main reason for this was that she had asked him. He had nowhere else in the world to live, being what Madge termed a 'hopeless' character." Bartle *is* hopeless; he cannot take care of either his teeth or himself and is so unaware of events that he only finds out about his wife's having divorced him and of her later death when he receives some letters from her lawyers. There is, however, a dark side to all this comic grotesquerie, a side from which the novel's moral center develops. Madge's growing paranoia (her heating system, she believes, has been taken over by hostile forces) and her incontinence are amusing—so humorous that even her own daughter, the story's storybook princess, cannot keep herself from giggling—but Madge's occasional awareness of her own helplessness is not, and neither is Richeldis and Simon's refusal to care for her when she is released from the hospital. That task they assign to Bartle, who accepts it as willingly as he accepts Stephanie as his wife, even though she is pregnant with another man's child. When he is asked to become pastor of a twenty-nine member congregation whose future is as uncertain as Simon's is secure, he accepts that too, building upon this man-made bit of grace the hope of being able to provide for Stephanie and her (now their) child. Oddly and touchingly, the title of this novel seems most to be about its oddest and most touching character, whose surname has nothing to do with his family's considerable financial wealth, which is both literally as well as figuratively "based on sand," but instead reflects upon his great but unassuming love for others. Bartle reaps what he sows—the love that the other characters can only long for. Yet it is their Loves Unknown that most readily attract the reader's inattentive eye: Belinda's succession of partners, for example, or Simon's adulteries, or Monica's affairs with old Professor Allison (the sandy source of her wealth) and later with the sand prince himself, Simon, all of which proves that for them love remains unknown. Were *Love Unknown* a fairy tale, it would end with hero and heroine living happily ever after, but *Love Unknown* is an English comic novel which ends much as it began, with a change of characters but not of situation, putting Bartle in Simon's shoes as if to suggest that the entire novel has formed its own prehistory to Bartle's story, or history, which still remains to be acted out and told. Where Simon bites "off more than he could chew," Bartle, like the British novelist working a bit of ivory, finds virtue in moderation and a measure of salvation in lovingly caring for others (in the novelist's case, the virtue is in attending to the very characters that have been said to have disappeared from fiction in the United States and on the Continent). "My song is Love Unknown,/ My Saviour's Love for Me," goes the hymn that Bartle and Madge sing together, the one "in a flutey sort of tenor," the other "in a deep croak, a cigaretty baritone":

> Love to the loveless shown
> That they might lo-o-vely be.
> O who am I,
> That for my sake
> My Lord should take frail flesh and die?

Bartle may be frail and hapless enough to suffer the same fate as his brother, but he is loving enough to deserve and even get something better, perhaps even salvation.

Robert A. Morace

Sources for Further Study

Booklist. LXXXIII, May 1, 1987, p. 1334.
Contemporary Review. CCL, January, 1987, p. 45.
Library Journal. CXII, May 15, 1987, p. 100.
London Review of Books. VIII, December 4, 1986, p. 24.
Los Angeles Times Book Review. May 3, 1987, p. 3.
The New York Times Book Review. XCII, June 14, 1987, p. 14.
The New Yorker. LXIII, August 31, 1987, p. 98.
Publishers Weekly. CCXXXI, March 15, 1987, p. 72.
Time. CXXIX, June 8, 1987, p. 82.
The Times Literary Supplement. August 29, 1986, p. 932.

MAJOR ANDRÉ

Author: Anthony Bailey (1933-   )
Publisher: Farrar, Straus and Giroux (New York). 200 pp. $15.95
Type of work: Historical novel
Time: 1780
Locale: New York State, in the region along the Hudson River between West Point and New York City

Benedict Arnold's famous conspiracy to surrender the West Point garrison and defect to the British is seen through the eyes of Major John André, Arnold's British contact who was hanged as a spy

> Principal characters:
> MAJOR JOHN ANDRÉ, adjutant general of the British army in New York
> MAJOR GENERAL BENEDICT ARNOLD, commander of the American forces at West Point, New York
> MAJOR BENJAMIN TALLMADGE, the American officer whose suspicions over captured documents lead to André's downfall
> JOSHUA HETT SMITH, a prominent New Yorker and friend of Arnold
> LIEUTENANT JOSHUA KING, an American officer
> COLONEL ALEXANDER HAMILTON, an aide to General George Washington

For more than two hundred years, the gallant British cavalier John André has inspired the literary imagination and piqued the historical curiosity of Americans. André, acting adjutant general of the British army stationed in New York in 1780, is one of those figures who, though of minor importance in the historical events of their time, still capture the emotions of those who come across their intriguing stories.

By the time Winthrop Sargent wrote the first full-length biography in 1861, André was already a kind of cult figure, hero of eight plays and twenty-seven poems. Books devoted to the relationship between André and Benedict Arnold, or to André himself, number more than a score, as British and American scholars and artists try to shed new light on one of the key incidents in America's struggle for independence. The most detailed of these studies, James Flexner's *The Traitor and the Spy* (1953) and R. M. Hatch's *Major John André: A Gallant in Spy's Clothing* (1986), give ample indication of the extent to which this minor figure has been vilified or venerated.

John André, son of an English businessman, was reared in Switzerland and began his adult career in the family business, but soon gave up the countinghouse for the more glamorous life of a soldier. An actor and an artist of some ability, and a man given to furthering his own career, André quickly impressed superiors with his skills as a staff officer. Before he traveled with his regiment to the American Colonies to put down the rebellion there, he had managed to lose his heart to a young coquette named Honora

Sneyd, the ward of Anna Seward, a poetess who was known as the Swan of Lichfield. Marriage was forbidden, however, by Honora's father, so the dejected André, carrying a sketch of his beloved in a locket, crossed the Atlantic in much the same state of mind as the fictional hero of Alfred, Lord Tennyson's *Maud* (1855), who throws himself into a war to ease the pain of a lover's rejection.

Dedication to Honora did not prevent André from flirting with the women he met in America, including young Philadelphia belle Margaret "Peggy" Shippen, whom he met when the British occupied that city. When André went north with General Sir Henry Clinton, Peggy Shippen shifted her affections to one of the Americans who moved swiftly into the abandoned capital of Pennsylvania: General Benedict Arnold.

That irony is not lost on novelist Anthony Bailey, nor are the other details of André's exciting life, which found its close outside New York City, at the end of a hangman's rope. Bailey's *Major André* focuses on the final week of the British officer's life, a week crucial to the outcome of the American Revolution. André was the go-between sent to negotiate with Arnold for the surrender of the American garrison at West Point, an act that, had it been successful, might have thwarted the Americans' chances for throwing off the British yoke.

The details of the plot, the reasons for Arnold's decision to defect to the British and to sell out his countrymen in the bargain, and André's role in arranging for the surrender have been known for some time—in fact, too well-known even from the start, as the plans outlined in Arnold's own handwriting were taken from André when he was captured while returning to British lines after meeting with the general. André had gone ashore from the British ship *Vulture* to meet with Arnold on what was to be neutral territory, but a series of events took him beyond the American lines. After ironing out details for the capture of West Point, André was forced to return by land to British-occupied territory rather than row out to his ship. On the circuitous route he was forced to follow toward New York City, he was captured by American irregulars, taken to a garrison, and interrogated. The suspicious Major Benjamin Tallmadge, fearing the worst about General Arnold, foiled an attempt to return André to Arnold and instead presented the incriminating evidence to General Washington. The rest, as is often said, is history.

Nevertheless, the courage and valor of the British officer, who insisted all along that he was not a spy, captured the admiration of almost everyone who came in contact with him, including many of his captors. Washington himself was pained by the decision he felt compelled to render, based on the evidence unearthed by a board of fourteen general officers who surveyed the captured documents and interviewed André. Despite protestations from André and from the British command, Washington concluded that André was indeed a spy and must hang for his crime.

All these details are captured in Bailey's fast-paced narrative. The novel opens with a brief prologue spoken by Tallmadge, in which the American explains briefly the circumstances of André's capture. This section introduces a series of monologues in which André tells his own story to several different auditors, among whom are Tallmadge, Lieutenant Joshua King, André's servant Peter Laune, and Colonel Alexander Hamilton.

Bailey's decision to handle his story through this unusual variation of the first-person point of view has several advantages. First, it allows readers to hear André in his own language, enhancing the "historical" quality of the text. André relates his tale of intrigue, mistakes, and mishaps swiftly and accurately—as one would expect from a person who was a major participant in the historical event. The factual details of the conspiracy find their way unobtrusively into André's monologues.

Further, having André tell his story to a series of other characters permits Bailey to keep the focus of the narrative on events. The absence of overt psychologizing, and the concurrent portrayal of André as presenting his story as a kind of apologia, may in fact cause the careful reader to notice a similarity between the form of this novel and a popular genre of narrative poetry—the dramatic monologue. Those familiar with such poetry, especially with the monologues of Robert Browning, may sense that more is taking place in this novel than appears on the surface.

That Bailey intends for his readers to recognize parallels between André's narrative and the drama seems evident. The real-life André was himself a dramatist, and Bailey's fictional hero calls attention to that fact on more than one occasion. Further, if there is any consistent pattern of imagery running through André's fictional narrative, it is the image of the drama. The hero makes frequent references to various eighteenth century playwrights to place in perspective events happening around him. Occasionally, he sees himself performing much as an actor would: When he goes ashore to meet Arnold for the first time, he tries "to compose my mind, as before a play, for the part I was taking"; he laments after his capture that this "is not even a play in which I am merely a bad actor, or in which I would at least have the ability to alter some of the lines." The irony of André's situation is made more vivid by his comparisons with the drama. Sadly, he remembers playing Archer in George Farquhar's *The Beaux' Strategem* (1707)—a character who is a gentleman forced to pretend to be a servant—which leads André to note that he was "acting a character who is acting another." Indeed, in his real-life stratagem to pass behind American lines to meet with Arnold, André pretends to be John Anderson and is forced to don the costume of the fictitious businessman, covering his uniform and thereby offering the enemy incontrovertible proof that he is acting as a spy.

Almost assured that his life is soon to end, André muses that, if he could choose a career other than soldiering, he would certainly like to try his hand as a playwright. Later, bantering with Tallmadge about a long piece of doggerel that he had written, André suspects that when the American officer tries to size up his British prisoner, "you find it hard to fit the two characters together, the lighthearted versifier and the ambitious staff officer." Which, indeed, is the real André?" "As far as I am concerned," Bailey's hero tells Tallmadge, "they are compelled to coexist—one could not *be* without the other." André presents himself as an enigma, though one who clearly deserves the sympathy of his captors—and of the reader.

Nevertheless, there lingers in the back of the minds of skeptical readers the thought that perhaps it is all a pose. Is André sincere in his plea that he is simply the victim of a misunderstanding, a soldier abandoned by superiors and caught in a trap not of his own making? Possibly the historical André could make such a claim, but Bailey's hero, speaking as he does in the form of the dramatic monologue and making constant allusions to the art of the drama, is perhaps protesting too much. When one remembers that similar apologies are made by Browning's Duke of Ferrara to excuse the untimely demise of his last duchess, one cannot help but remain faintly disturbed by the histrionics of the debonair but dissembling André.

One cannot be certain that this is what Bailey intends. What is clear, however, is that Bailey wants the reader to empathize with André as a human being facing a death he cannot avoid. Bailey's André is an existential hero, facing death with the realization that his life will have meaning only insofar as he establishes it for himself. To make that point clear, Bailey has his hero observe a caterpillar crawling over a leaf, inching its way forward to the edge, only to turn back when it faces "the great drop that greeted it" at the end of its slow journey. "What was the purpose of that mission? Was it wasted time?" André muses. Though the scene may seem contrived, it serves the same purpose as Ernest Hemingway's famous scene of the ants crawling on the log which Frederick Henry discovers by the fire in *A Farewell to Arms* (1929), or of the turtle making its slow way across the highway in John Steinbeck's *The Grapes of Wrath* (1939): It is a paradigm of the central character's larger struggle.

In dying with dignity, André assures himself a place in the pantheon of heroes of this war in which, in his own view, the best men of the British army have refused to serve. André is no coward; he may not have chosen the role that has been thrust upon him, but he will play the part to the best of his ability, until the curtain falls—or, in his case, until the hangman's noose ends his greatest performance. The performance is, ultimately, heroic; the novel provides exceptional reading pleasure for those who enjoy good acting—and, on the part of author Anthony Bailey, good scripting.

Laurence W. Mazzeno

Sources for Further Study

Booklist. LXXXIII, July, 1987, p. 1649.
Kirkus Reviews. LV, May 1, 1987, p. 656.
Library Journal. CXII, June 15, 1987, p. 82.
Los Angeles Times. July 22, 1987, V, p. 1.
The New York Times. CXXXVI, June 26, 1987, p. C31.
The New York Times Book Review. XCII, July 5, 1987, p. 10.
Publishers Weekly. CCXXXI, May 29, 1987, p. 66.
Time. CXXX, July 27, 1987, p. 65.
The Washington Post Book World. XVII, August 9, 1987, p. 3.